A Game-Theoretic Approach to Political Economy

A Game-Theoretic Approach to Political Economy

Volume 2 of *Game Theory in the Social Sciences*

Martin Shubik

The MIT Press
Cambridge, Massachusetts
London, England

To Julie and Claire. To Marian and to Lloyd with gratitude for the many years of collaboration.

This book was set in Times New Roman by Asco Trade Typesetting Ltd., Hong Kong, and printed and bound by Halliday Lithograph in the United States of America.

AU **Library of Congress Cataloging in Publication Data**

Shubik, Martin.
  A game-theoretic approach to political economy.

  Bibliography: p.
  Includes index.
  1. Game theory.   2. Economics—Mathematical models.
I. Shubik, Martin.   Game theory in the social sciences.
II. Title.
HB144.S58   1985   338.9′001′5193   84–9646
ISBN 0–262–19219–5

Contents

Acknowledgments

This is the second of two volumes that grew out of many years of joint work with Lloyd Shapley. My comments in *Game Theory and the Social Sciences* apply to this volume as well.

A preliminary version of chapters 1 and 2 was prepared as RAND Memorandum RM 904/5 but never published in that form. Chapters 3–6 are based on joint working notes as well as our paper "Price strategy oligopoly with product variation" (*Kyklos*, 1969). Chapters 8–10 are based on joint working notes as well as "The assignment game, I: The core" (*International Journal of Game Theory*, 1971). Chapters 11 and 12 utilize our three papers "On market games" (*Journal of Economic Theory*, 1969), "Pure competition, coalitional power and fair division" (*International Economic Review*, 1969), and "Competitive outcomes in the cores of market games" (*International Journal of Game Theory*, 1976). Chapter 13 utilizes our paper "Quasi-cores in a monetary economy with non-convex preferences" (*Econometrica*, 1966).

Chapters 14–16 are based on my own work and several joint publications with Lloyd Shapley and Pradeep Dubey: Shapley and Shubik, "Trade using one commodity as a means of payment" (*Journal of Political Economy*, 1977), Dubey and Shubik, "The noncooperative equilibria of a closed trading economy with market supply and bidding strategies" (*Journal of Economic Theory*, 1978), "Trade and prices in a closed economy with exogenous uncertainty and different levels of information" (*Econometrica*, 1977), and my paper, "Society, land, love or money" (*Journal of Economic Behavior and Organization*, 1981).

Chapter 17 is heavily based on Shapley and Shubik, "Ownership and the production function" (*Quarterly Journal of Economics*, 1967). Chapter 20 utilizes Shapley and Shubik, "On the core of an economic system with externalities" (*American Economic Review*, 1969), and Shubik, "The 'Bridge Game' economy" (*Journal of Political Economy*, 1971). Chapter 21 utilizes Shubik and van der Heyden, "Logrolling and budget allocation games" (*International Journal of Game Theory*, 1978). I also wish to thank the *Journal of Political Economy* for permission to use our 1977 article, "An example of a trading economy with three competitive equilibria"; David Gale and the *American Mathematical Monthly* for permission to quote from "College admissions and the stability of marriage" by Gale and Shapley (1962); William Vickrey and the *Quarterly Journal of Economics* for permission to paraphase his proof of the Arrow result; and Gerald Thompson, John Kemeny, and Princeton University Press for permission to use a diagram that appeared on page 284 of *Annals of Mathematics Studies* 39 (1957).

Among the many colleagues from whose comments and joint work I have benefited, I am specially indebted to Lloyd Shapley and Pradeep Dubey. I am also grateful to Brian Arthur, Michel Balinski, Mamoru Kaneko, Richard Levitan, William Lucas and several of his students, Elinor and Vincent Ostrom, Martine Quinzii, Sidhartha Sahi, Rheinhard Selten, Heinz Schleicher, Herbert Scarf, Ludo van der Heyden, Schlomo Weber, Robert Weber, Myrna Wooders, and Peyton Young. There are many others whose comments have been valuable. My thanks also go to Bonnie Sue Boyd, Glena Ames, Karen Eisenman, Linda Abelli-Smith, Denise Fennelly, and several others for excellent mathematical typing. Finally I wish to acknowledge the Office of Naval Research and the National Science Foundation under whose generous support much of the research leading to the writing of this book was done.

I Basics

1 Money, Wealth, and Ownership

1.1 Introduction

This volume offers an approach to political economy based on the methods of game theory. A companion volume* has been devoted to the concepts and solutions utilized in this theory. Our concern there was with preferences for events, outcomes, or states of the world, with no particular restriction on the nature of the prospects involved. Here we become more specific, limiting our field of view to outcomes involving economic goods, many of which can be individually owned and traded. Our concern being with political economy, it is useful to delineate the features that distinguish economic problems from other problems of multiperson decision making; for this reason, we shall start off by discussing in this part the special roles played by *money* and *commodities*.

A reference to two well-known treatments of social choice and economic welfare may help to clarify the distinctions we make here regarding commodities and ownership. Kenneth Arrow (1951) in his work on social choice does not limit himself to purely economic considerations. A "prospect" or "social state," as he formulates it, is a general state of the world, which may or may not involve economic variables but which takes no account of individual ownership or consumption as such. In terms of the Bergson–Samuelson analysis (Bergson, 1938; Samuelson, 1948) of welfare economics, however, "prospect" involves explicit economic factors, at least some of which are privately held, as well as noneconomic factors. Although some of the components of a Bergson–Samuelson prospect can be characterized by a point in an allocation or distribution space, one must also append the noneconomic features of the social state, such as the quality of justice or the degree of democracy. In general these cannot be easily quantified. Thus a Bergson–Samuelson prospect may be regarded as consisting of two components (d, s), where d is a point in a distribution space D for economic goods, which might be a Euclidean space, and s is a point in a "social state" space S, which

---

*Martin Shubik, *Game Theory in the Social Sciences: Concepts and Solutions* (Cambridge, MA: The MIT Press, 1982); henceforth *GTSS*.

may have no natural metric structure. Arrow's domain is in effect just the space S (which he assumes to be finite), whereas the purely economic domains we wish to consider in this chapter correspond to the space D.

1.2 Money and Wealth

It is not easy in a brief presentation at this level of abstraction to do justice to the concepts of money, wealth, assets, income, and prices as they arise in microeconomic analysis. Although in our work we shall be actively concerned with only a few aspects of the money phenomenon, it may be helpful, for perspective and to reduce confusion, to sort through these concepts and discuss their role in the construction of economic or game-theoretic models.

The usual textbook definitions of money are functional—the three main functions being to serve as a medium of exchange, as a store of purchasing power, and as a standard of value. Money is also used to resolve problems of trust, credit, human suspicion, and uncertainty. In its physical form it must be easy to recognize, difficult to counterfeit, and easy to handle. Though it must in some sense be durable, it need not be material; the upper limit of durability is reached when it becomes a total abstraction, accepted conventionally and unrelated to any physical substance.

1.2.1 Money in an economic society
Economies with monetary gold or paper or special credit relations bear a relation to moneyless economies similar to that of non-Euclidean geometries to Euclidean geometry. They have different rules or axioms, altering and enlarging the possibilities of the system. The use of a monetary system by a society amounts to the acceptance by its citizens of added conventions or "rules of play" governing their economic behavior. In many respects behavior is freer; in some respects it is more constrained.

We shall comment here on the relation between money and (1) transaction costs, (2) trust, (3) the price system, (4) assets, (5) uncertainty, and (6) financial institutions.[1] In section 1.2.2 we shall turn to monetary features of special relevance to game-theoretic models.

Transaction costs and the "double coincidence of wants"   If there is one person in an economy, there is no trade. If there are two persons, then the first may want certain items more than the second, and other items less. If a trade is worked out, there is a *double coincidence of wants*—each wants and gets a bundle of goods that the other is willing to give up. When there are three or more individuals, there may no longer be double coincidences of wants, even when there are grounds for trilateral trade. For example, A might want the goods of B, B the goods of C, and C the goods of A. But no pair might directly want each other's goods. Thus significant *transaction costs*, over and above the cost of single face-to-face barter, may appear. But if money is available, and if everyone agrees to "want" money and has an adequate bankroll, then there is no need for the double coincidence of wants. A pays B in money, and B uses the money to buy from C, who buys in turn from A. Money frees or "decouples" the market.

There is no doubt that money serves an important economic purpose in lowering transaction costs.[2] This is by no means its only use in an economy, though, or the only peg on which to hang a rational explanation of the "economic value" of money. Transaction costs are costs in the mechanics of exchange, and money tends to mitigate the difficulties they cause in the functioning of the price system. But these cost savings are apt to be minor in comparison with, say, the effects of the enlarged strategic options that the existence of money opens up for the participants in a modern economy.

Money, trust, and laws of contract   Money significantly eases the flow of economic goods and services by greatly reducing the need for trust in one's trading partner. This is especially true when extended periods of time are involved in production or delivery.[3] The existence and enforcement of laws of contract improve the efficiency of trade by substituting trust in the government (i.e., the courts) for higher levels of trust among traders. In particular, such laws enable trading to take place with a far greater degree of anonymity than would be possible otherwise.

When rules enabling a government or its financial representatives to issue currency, and to tax in terms of currency, are included, the game becomes even more complex. We may consider adherence to the laws governing money and finance to be part of a game embedded within a larger game. The economic activities of a society are set within a political and social context. As long as the economic outcome lies within appropriate bounds, the inner game model will be valid. Outside those bounds, political and social reactions to these rules must be considered.

For example, in stable societies, even with an overly liberal use of the printing presses by the government, there are generally accepted laws and customs concerning the use of paper currency.[4] The phenomenon of runaway hyperinflation, as in Germany in the 1920s, may be regarded as arising from a breakdown in the assumption that the laws are rigid rules rather than merely nonbinding conventions of play. These breakdowns are often associated with periods of upheaval and instability, such as occur in the aftermath of war or revolution, when conditions are ripe for the overthrow of established customs. The prime concern of economic analysis, however, is with economies that are sufficiently stable that the laws in general, and the laws concerning money, credit, and contract in particular, are accepted as part of the rules.

Money and the price system   The introduction of money into a barter economy can have a significant effect on the mathematical degree of homogeneity of prices. If we consider a barter economy in which a price system, but not a monetary system, has emerged, then prices are just exchange ratios and are homogeneous of order zero in their effect on trade. Multiplying all prices by the same positive constant changes nothing. But if the same economy uses the dollar, for example, not only as an abstract numerical bookkeeping device but also as a store of value over time—in bonds, savings accounts, formulas for progressive (non-linear) taxation, or in defining the "size" of enterprises for regulatory purposes—then the magnitudes of prices as well as their ratios become significant. The degree of homogeneity returns to zero, however, if we treat the dollar as an additional commodity and permit its price to be other than 1 in terms of some new bookkeeping unit.

Governmental attempts to keep the "purchasing power" of a unit of currency fixed over an extended period of time are tantamount to using the currency as a first approximation to a transferable utility, at least to small traders for most of their economic activities. In such a system both the price ratios between commodities and also the actual numerical values of the prices are deemed significant.

It is important to note that a multiperiod barter economy with all prices presumed known or predictable is not the equivalent of a single-period economy with credit trading and futures markets. The general-equilibrium model of Debreu (1959), for example, which includes trading in time-dated commodities, cannot be regarded as a simple extension of one-period barter, since it entails fundamentally new postulates concerning trade in futures and trust among traders and requires a more explicit modeling of the dynamics of the accounting system (really a rudimentary monetary system) than is necessary in the one-period case.

In a dynamic economy that employs either a fixed issue of paper "fiat" money or a system of futures markets with credit limits expressed in a bookkeeping money, the total quantity of money or credit may act to curb trade that would have taken place in a world with greater trust or unlimited credit (Shubik, 1973; Shapley and Shubik, 1977b). This constraint will also influence the structure of prices. A fully satisfactory theory of the relationship between money and prices must account both for the effects of the money supply and for the mechanisms that exist in the society for changing the money supply.

Money and assets   Historically, a metallic commodity has often been used as a numeraire, with all other prices quoted in terms of ounces of gold or silver. This nonsymmetric treatment of a particular commodity involves certain properties of "moneyness" that are not easy to capture in the usual approaches to general equilibrium. A commodity-money is not just another commodity, nor is it just a formal accounting device of no economic substance. Many societies have used gold as a commodity money, but few, if any, have used ripe tomatoes. The properties of durability, portability, and fungibility, combined with appropriate conditions on intrinsic worth, distribution of holdings, and the size of the overall supply, all appear to be relevant to the selection of a commodity suitable to serve as money. Almost any asset has some monetary properties, and these become more pronounced as the durability, transferability, and general "far-off" usefulness of the item increases (Tobin, 1961). These properties appear to be related to the role that assets can play as hostages or "surety." Fiat money is in a special category, since its monetary properties rest only upon the law and the acceptance of the law. Not being a physical commodity, it is in a sense infinitely durable—a "pure asset"; moreover, it is extremely easy to transport and to transfer.

Without a world government the enforcement agency for a fiat money hardly exists in international trade. Gold appears to be the durable asset that has come the closest to being acceptable to all nations; unfortunately its supply is limited. A better commodity, taking a cue from the Yap islanders, who are said to have used as money the title to large stones that lay underwater off the shore (Einzig, 1948), might be an "international bankers' gold," which by agreement is assumed to be stored only on the planet Pluto, and to increase in amount every year by a few percent. Recent developments toward the use of international drawing rights ("paper gold") suggest a movement in that direction. However, the basic problem with any such currency rests with the enforceability of international law.

Money and uncertainty   Even without resorting to game-theoretic models with their elements of "strategic" uncertainty—that is, uncertainty concerning the willful actions of one's competitors or customers—a case can easily be made for the introduction of monetary or credit systems as a means for coping with the natural uncertainties inherent in the environment. These uncertainties may take many forms: crop failures, variability in production processes, weather conditions, technological advances, and political or other events outside the scope of the model. Money provides a means for distributing risk and for decoupling future time periods from the present.

It is, to be sure, possible to avoid the use of money in the theoretical treatment of a market economy with uncertainty. Arrow (1953) and Debreu (1959) have indicated one way to do this, by means of an elaborate system of markets for *contracts in contingent deliveries*. Their construction is analogous to the reduction of a game from extensive to strategic form. Even leaving aside problems of trust, though, the information overloads this construction entails make the Arrow–Debreu treatment unsatisfactory as a rendition of an actual operating system, for the same reasons that we rarely if ever actually calculate with large, complex games in the strategic form. Radner (1968) has examined some of these difficulties.

A way out is to introduce money into the model and to rely upon futures contracts that are *noncontingent*—for instance, a contract that promises delivery of a ton of wheat next year, regardless of the state of the wheat crop. It may turn out to be prohibitively expensive or even physically impossible to honor the contract when it comes due. Failure to deliver is taken care of, ultimately, by the bankruptcy laws.[5] When we allow noncontingent futures contracts in an uncertain world, we must therefore also specify rules for contract failure and insolvency (Shubik, 1973a).

Thus an enormous simplification in contingency planning and decision making is achieved by the use of money. The price paid is that on occasion a contract will not be honored and the books will not balance. The special rules to take care of such eventualities are by no means arbitrary. It is a fruitful question for the economist to ask: Given a criterion for economic efficiency under uncertainty, what are the optimum bankruptcy laws?

Money and financial institutions   "Money" is a penumbral concept, used to describe devices for coping with many different but overlapping phenomena. Fiat money, gold, land, trading stamps, a steel mill, an insurance policy, a governmental or corporate bond, a common stock certificate, a credit card—all have different intermixes of monetary properties. All also have certain more or less specific institutional overtones. In our most rudimentary applications of the theory of games to economies with money, we shall often ignore these overtones and postulate an ideal, institution-free commodity called, for short, "u-money." This theoretical construct, like many others we are forced to adopt from time to time, is justifiable only as an abstraction and approximation. Whether it is suitable in a given application can only be judged on the basis of an understanding of the real financial institutions involved, and of the modeling problems they might pose were we to try to represent them more explicitly.

A broad array of financial institutions are used to secure the various benefits that a monetary system confers on a modern economy, such as reducing transaction costs, decoupling decision making, providing anonymity among trading partners, tempering the effects of uncertainty and distrust, controlling fluctuations in the macroeconomy, and so on. There are banks and brokerages, insurance companies and loan sharks, credit bureaus and clearing houses, not to mention numerous governmental bodies—each type of institution in its own way influencing the supply, distribution, or usage of money.

Although money itself has certain stabilizing and insurancelike properties in a world with uncertainty, the efficient functioning of a large complex economy at the microeconomic level calls for insurance companies of several different types. Other financial instruments, such as common stocks, provide a means for dealing with indivisibilities and certain ownership risks that are different from the risks handled by insurance companies or by the holding of money or bonds.

Banks, savings and loan associations, credit unions, pawnbrokers, and other lending agencies provide the services appropriate to the efficient treatment of different mixes of risk to the lender. These differences may be due to degrees of knowledge or trust, to inability to forecast the probable outcomes of decisions, to the costs of data gathering and data processing, and to a host of other causes.

When government plays an important role in the provision of public goods and services, further institutions are needed to transmit its decisions through the monetary and financial infrastructure of the economy. These include the treasury, various taxing authorities, and government banks and insurance programs. The government also plays an active regulatory role with respect to most types of private financial institutions and participates in supranational institutions that wrestle with the problems of international finance.

A satisfactory general microeconomic theory, designed to be applicable to a complex mass-market economy, must certainly include a monetary system, together with at least rudimentary models of the key financial institutions, as an integral aspect of its structure.

1.2.2 Money in game-theoretic models
Three different and important properties of money are especially noteworthy in game-theoretic analyses of the economy: (1) money as a strategic decoupling device; (2) monetary control as a criterion for identifying and distinguishing players; and (3) money as a vehicle for side payments.

Strategic decoupling In virtually any type of real economy, competitive or otherwise, Walras's law seldom holds exactly: At most points in time the supply of goods and services will not balance the demand. As goods and services are exchanged for money or credit and vice versa, the loosely coupled, dynamic economic system can be represented by a set of double-entry balanced books, but given the existence of uncertainty, the failure of processes, dishonesty, strategic blunders, and other "imperfections" in the market, trade may never be actually in balance. Monetary and legal mechanisms are invoked to take care of these eventualities. Rules specify the penalties if an individual fails to honor his contract, is unable to pay his debts, or is driven into bankruptcy.

When the economy is modeled as a game in strategic form, the presence of money gives individuals a strategic freedom they would not have otherwise. It suffices to note here the crux of the difficulty: In a no-money, no-credit world, an individual cannot commit himself to buy until he knows what he will be able to sell. Clearing the market is not automatically guaranteed. It may be a theorem that the *solution* of the game will clear the market, but even such a theorem would be vacuous if the rules of the game did not allow for the possibility of imbalance of supply and demand, or other market failure. Without money to absorb such imbalances, the outcome resulting from independent buy and sell decisions by different players in the game model may not even be well defined.[6]

Strategic decoupling is also in evidence when money is used to decentralize the organizational decision process. The executives of a corporation may be more like members of a team (with a single objective) than players in a game (with conflicting objectives), yet it is difficult to imagine any large corporation functioning with any degree of efficiency or profit without the aid of decentralizing procedures or devices such as internal accounting systems, overhead percentages, and departmental budgets. All of these are monetary decouplers, designed to permit suborganizations to operate with some degree of strategic independence.

Strategic decoupling is closely related to dynamic decoupling. As noted previously, money serves as a device for intertemporal as well as interpersonal decoupling, enabling us sometimes to look statically at a situation that is basically dynamic. We might, for example, "close" a model "spatially" by including all relevant members of the economy as players, but to close the model with respect to time will require some static surrogate for those dynamic processes that continue beyond the cut-off point of the model. The storage-of-wealth feature of money often serves this purpose admirably.

Monetary control as a criterion for distinguishing players   Virtually all of the older writings on general equilibrium have been content to postulate only one or two types of economic actor, the consumer or entrepreneur, that is, *Homo oeconomicus*, highly abstracted and deterministically motivated. When there are governmental and financial institutions present, legally able to tax and to take monetary and other fiscal actions not available to the ordinary citizen or corporate entrepreneur, a model of the economy that is game-theoretically closed would have to include several player types not found in the classic barter exchange models or in their modern extensions with unlimited trust, credit, and futures markets. We shall not attempt to investigate in any detail the many possible ways of modeling special financial players. It is evident, however, that money is no longer an inessential veil (if it ever was) when the very rules of the game give the players different strategic scope with respect to money.

Money as a vehicle for side payments   A hypothetical society might, by convention, introduce a fiat money and then operate as though—to a first approximation—this money were freely transferable and comparable between individuals and entered their utility functions as an additive, linear term. We should then have a system operationally equivalent to a system with transferable utility. In such a system many computational, administrative, and other operational aspects of social policy would be much simplified, not to mention the task of the game-theoretical analyst.

We do not assert that this is an actual state of affairs; nor does very much of economic game theory depend crucially on this simplification. We do suggest, however, that as a tactic of empirical exploration, the construction of a Pareto surface based upon coefficients that compare the "worth of money" to different socioeconomic groups might be profitable. One not too farfetched interpretation of the legislative process, for example, is that legislators behave as though such comparisons between groups can be made, while quarreling over the values of the coefficients.

Be that as it may, we shall be making the transferable-utility assumption frequently in our simple models, believing it no worse an oversimplification than the opposite assumption, namely, that no monetary quid pro quo is present at all. By solving an economic game model both with and without "side payments," we may hope to bracket the true situation without undue proliferation of fussy institutional detail.

Identifying money with transferable utility usually entails a sacrifice of realism, certainly, but the analytical benefits may be considerable. Two notable benefits are that it makes possible (1) a separation of a coalition's external problem of how to maximize total gain from its internal problem of how to distribute that gain, and (2) a reduction of the classical competitive-equilibrium problem to a simple concave maximization problem, with all the uniqueness properties that this reduction implies.[7] Such analytical simplifications are not only aids for the theoretician, but are felt beyond the mathematical model. It is at least arguable that they are partly responsible for the money-equals-utility viewpoint that so many real people and real institutions adopt in practical applications such as shopping, bargaining, or matters involving interpersonal welfare comparisons.

1.2.3 The utility of money and wealth

When we discuss the *wealth* of an individual, we usually refer to the amount of money he has on hand or in a bank account, plus any holdings of bonds and other notes of indebtedness, plus ownership claims such as common and preferred stock, evaluated *at market*, plus tangible physical assets, likewise evaluated *at market* or given a value by an independent objective appraiser. Thus, when we say that Mr. Jones's "net worth" is $10,000 or $10 million, we are ascribing a monetary measure to his wealth but we have also implicitly assumed the existence of a society with organized markets that allow nonmonetary holdings to be evaluated in money. In this section we shall explore some of the concepts that underlie the idea of monetary wealth.[8]

The modeling difficulties may be considerable. When we state that an individual is worth X dollars, do we mean that this is the amount of money he would have if he liquidated everything on a "crash" basis in today's market? Are we referring to the amount left after the payment of capital gains or estate taxes and other imposts or transaction costs? Or do we refer to a person's wealth as an "in being" concept—some non-realizable sum of money that represents the expected market value of all of his possessions, based on a hypothetical "orderly" liquidation process and ignoring costs and taxes? Or can the question be reduced to one of personal preferences, in which we let X be the number of dollars, free and clear, that Mr. Jones would accept as equivalent to the entire complex of his worldly possessions, obligations, and prospects? Is there any meaning to a negative total wealth? It is sometimes observed that being sufficiently far in debt, say to the tune of $1 million or more, may bring one many if not all the perquisites of a "positive" millionaire.

In this section we in effect consider a world with only one commodity, representing pure, abstract satisfaction; it might be called "utility pills," "soma" (Huxley, 1932), or even "money." We wish to discuss the possibility of constructing a utility scale to represent a person's desire for this one commodity. In many basic models for studying the utility of money, such as those of Bernoulli or Friedman and Savage, it appears that the "money" involved is some such universal commodity. When later we consider a world with many commodities, we must once more sort out the differences between money as a vague aggregation, like "income" or "buying power," and money as a tangible commodity with special, institutionalized attributes.

In this formulation we do not need a price system to define the wealth of an individual, but we do implicitly assume a kind of ceteris paribus condition on his surroundings. To be poor in Tahiti may be preferable to being rich in New York. "What good is all that money if you do not have your health?" is an interesting question to ask a sick entrepreneur. However, if he has no control over his health, and money cannot help him find a cure, then the question may be extraneous to the analysis of his economic power or well-being.

The Petersburg paradox   One might begin with the assumption that the utility for money is linear:

$$U(x) = ax + b. \tag{1.1}$$

Here x denotes the quantity of "utility pills" and a and b are constants with $a > 0$. Clearly a cardinal utility scale is implied for the individual in question. But if the "monetary-cardinal" utility were simultaneously a "risk-cardinal" utility, then a paradox would arise, as first noted by Nicholas Bernoulli in 1713.[9] He described the following gambling proposition: After paying an entry fee F, the gambler tosses a fair coin until "Heads" first appears; he is then paid 2^T dollars, where T is the number of "Tails" that preceded the first "Head." For example, the sequence TTH wins \$4. The problem is to determine the "fair" fee for this game. More precisely, what is the largest entry fee F that would be acceptable to a rational person whose utility happens to be linear with respect to both money and probability?

In fact, the expected gain in utility, $E\{\Delta U\}$, is easily seen to be infinite, if we consider the series

$$E\{\Delta U\} = -F + \frac{1}{2}(\$1) + \frac{1}{4}(\$2) + \ldots + \frac{1}{2^{T+1}}(\$2^T) + \ldots$$ (1.2)

$$= -F + 50\cent + 50\cent + \ldots + 50\cent + \ldots.$$

Hence any finite fee F ought to be paid—enthusiastically—by our hypothetical gambler. Experience tells us, however, that most rational individuals would not pay more than a few dollars for the opportunity to play this game. Hence, so the popular argument runs, the assumption of a risk-linear utility for money (or for any other commodity, for that matter) is untenable in a theory of rational behavior.

This classic paradox has served as a springboard for so many provocative questions about the nature of money, probability, and utility that people have tended to develop fixed ideas about how to resolve it, and to overlook a very basic flaw in the original argument. We believe that this flaw renders the Petersburg paradox incapable of casting any light on the validity of risk-linear utility functions. The paradox, after all, is not mathematical or logical, but intuitive and empirical; it is based on our feelings and observations on how rational people behave (Menger, 1934). The trouble is that we have no empirical evidence that really applies to situations like (1.2)—that can distinguish between the unbounded game and a corresponding game with a very large bound. The following will make this clear.

Suppose we found someone actually paying a big fee, $F = \$500$, to enter the game described. We would denounce him, quite rightly, as irrational and a fool. But his folly, at least if he justifies the payment by a·computation like (1.2), would lie not in his utility function, but in his gullibility. Should he be lucky in his tosses, his disillusionment would come not when he tries to *enjoy* his millions or trillions, but when he tries to *collect* them. The gambler is presumed to be "sane" and "fairly reasonable," but no sane or even fairly reasonable person is going to believe that the sponsor of the gambling proposition, whoever it is, will actually pay the full prize after an exceptionally long string of "Tails."[10] Under any kind of reasonable assumptions, the true expected value of the game can only be a few dollars; the rest of the $500 might better be spent in purchasing the Brooklyn Bridge from a stranger on a street corner (Shapley, 1972; Samuelson, 1977).

We may seem to be quibbling over contingencies so improbable that any sensible decision maker would treat them as negligible. But the paradox dissolves without them; the sting of the series (1.2) is only in its tail. A numerical example will make this abundantly clear.[11] Suppose the game were run by an honest, bonded gambling house, with resources of, say, $10 million. We may compute $E\{\Delta U\}$ by putting a ceiling of $10 million (about $2^{23.3}$) on the money amounts in (1.2). This gives us $-F + 12$ for the sum of the first 25 terms, and $10^7/2^{24} = 0.5960$ for the total contribution of the terms that follow, with the result that the expected value $E\{\Delta U\}$ is just $-F + \$12.60$. This is not prima facie unreasonable. It does not "strain the imagination" to picture an otherwise sane, rational individual prudently deciding to spend $12, but not $13, on the game in question.

Nonlinear utilities for money   We have just seen that the Petersburg paradox, properly modeled, does not seriously challenge the idea of a linear utility for money. Nor, of course, does it lend any particular support to the idea. Indeed, the main purpose of Bernoulli's "Petersburg" essay was to propose a new functional form for the cardinal utility for money, namely,

$$U(x) = c \log x + d. \tag{1.3}$$

Here x represents the person's total wealth, and c and d are constants with $c > 0$. (Of course, "total wealth" must now be defined in such a way that it is never negative.) A function of this form, being concave, has the property of giving money a *decreasing marginal utility*. Hence a "Bernoullian" individual will always seek to avoid fair gambles. However, his disinclination to gamble will be less pronounced when he is rich than when he is poor, since the function (1.3) becomes more nearly linear (over an interval of a given length) as x increases.

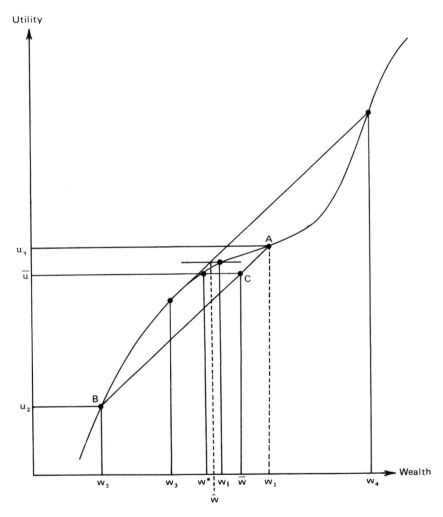

Figure 1.1
Wealth, lotteries, and insurance.

Bernoulli's rationale for logarithmic utility was based in part on intuitive considerations, but more particularly on a mathematical model of marine insurance, which he developed in remarkably modern style; the paper (1738) is well worth reading today. He turns to his uncle's gambling paradox only at the end, pointing out that the use of (1.3) in place of (1.1) would relieve the paradox, since the sum corresponding to (1.2) is then finite. But this relief is only temporary (as he probably realized), since a simple modification in the definition of the gambler's payoff can make the series diverge even for logarithmic utility or, in fact, for any $U(x)$ that is unbounded as $x \to \infty$.[12]

Figure 1.1 depicts another type of utility function for wealth, suggested by Friedman and Savage (1948).[13] This shape, they argue, is consistent with the behavior of an individual who buys both insurance and lottery tickets at the same time. His present situation is typically near a point of inflection. The concavity of the first part of the curve provides an incentive to purchase insurance, while the convexity of the next part makes certain forms of gambling attractive.[14]

To illustrate the reasoning, consider the four points w_1, w_2, w^*, and $\bar{w}$ on the "wealth" scale. Suppose that a person's initial wealth is w_1, which might include items such as a house, valuable paintings, and so forth. In the next period he fears for fire, robbery, or other disasters that could reduce his wealth to w_2. Having sufficiently good statistics (or subjective probabilities), he regards the odds that he will end up at w_2 rather than w_1 as being $1 - \alpha$ to α, where α is some number less than, but perhaps close to, 1. The actuarial or expected money value of his "gamble with Nature" is then given by

$$(1 - \alpha)w_1 + \alpha w_2 = \bar{w}.$$

In the diagram the utilities of the two outcomes w_1 and w_2 are u_1 and u_2, the ordinates of the points A and B, respectively. The utility for the expected value of the gamble is a linear combination of these utilities given by $\bar{u}$, the ordinate of C. Now w^* is a sure outcome that has the same utility as the gamble between w_1 and w_2. If the individual can buy insurance for a premium less than the amount $w_1 - w^*$, it will be worth his while to do so. Moreover, if an insurance company has effectively linear utility, for monetary increments of this order of magnitude, it will be worth their while to sell insurance for any premium greater than $w_1 - \bar{w}$. The concavity of the utility curve ensures that a mutually acceptable premium will exist, say $w_1 - w_I$, giving the individual a "guaranteed" wealth of w_I, whether he is robbed or not, and a utility level u_I.

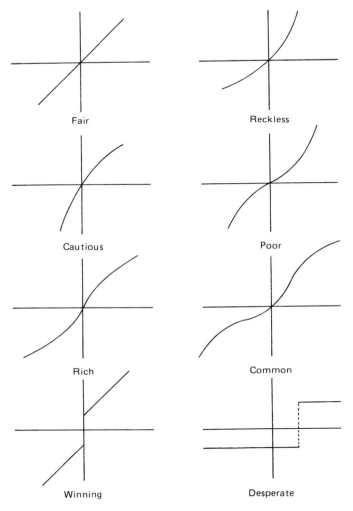

Figure 1.2
Wealth and attitude toward risk.

By similar reasoning we see that the same individual, having bought his insurance, may then be willing to pay $w_I - w_3$ for a lottery ticket with a prize of $w_4 - w_3$, provided the odds of winning give the gamble an expected money value of at least $\hat{w} - w_3$. Since this is less than the ticket price, such a lottery would be profitable to a large, "linear" lottery operator.

Friedman and Savage gave an interpretation of their concave-convex utility function in terms of social class: "On this interpretation, increases in income that raise the relative position of the consumer unit in its own class but do not shift the unit out of its class yield diminishing marginal utility, while increases that shift it into a new class, that give it a new social and economic status, yield increasing marginal utility" (1948, pp. 298–299).

Further is this vein, Markowitz (1952) offered a utility function with three inflection points, suggesting that a person's current wealth will typically be near the middle one. In a more game-theoretical study, Kemeny and Thompson (1957) give an interesting catalogue of utility types in terms of game players and their psychological attitudes toward winning and losing; figure 1.2, reproduced from their paper, will suggest the flavor of their classification. Yaari (1965) presents an interpretation of gambling and insurance in terms of subjective misperceptions of the odds—misperceptions that systematically overstate low probabilities and understate high probabilities. Hakansson (1970) gives a useful summary of this literature and presents a dynamic model to substantiate the shape suggested by Friedman and Savage.

Without going further into the investigation of specific forms for the utility function of an individual (to say nothing of that of a firm or a government), we note the important point that there is no particular empirical or logical reason to assume that the marginal utility for wealth, if nonlinear, is necessarily decreasing. In any case the discussion of the utility of wealth is extremely difficult to disassociate from its social context, from "status quo" effects, and from the dynamics of the individual's evaluative process.

Dynamic considerations   Before leaving this subject we should touch on the relationship between the treatment here and the axiomatic discussion of risk and utility scales in *GTSS*, chapter 4. The axioms presented in appendix A there make virtually no specification of the nature of the economic goods or other factors that describe the alternative prospects, yet most criticisms of the plausibility of these (or similar) axioms are couched in our present context of a one-dimensional commodity, inter-preted as "wealth" and measured in monetary units.

The difficulties sometimes encountered in applying the axioms or in making them seem plausible in this context can usually be traced to carelessness in the preliminary modeling. To illustrate this we turn to a well-known example, due to Allais (1953), that is purported to violate the axioms:

Choice 1: An individual must choose between a prize A of \$500,000 with certainty, and a lottery ticket B with probabilities of

0.1 for winning \$2,500,000,
0.89 for winning \$500,000,
0.01 for winning 0.

Choice 2: The individual must choose between a lottery ticket C with probabilities of

0.11 for winning \$500,000,
0.89 for winning 0,

and a lottery ticket D with probabilities of

0.10 for winning \$2,500,000,
0.90 for winning 0.

Allais argues that many people would prefer A to B but D to C, and that this violates the axiom of strong independence or the "sure-thing principle" (axiom P3 in appendix A.4, *GTSS*). If U is a risk-linear cardinal utility function, then from $A \succ B$ we obtain

$$U(500{,}000) > 0.1\,U(2{,}500{,}000) + 0.89\,U(500{,}000) + 0.01\,U(0),$$

which reduces, if we normalize $U(0) = 0$, to

$$0.11\,U(500{,}000) > 0.1\,U(2{,}500{,}000). \tag{1.4}$$

From $C \prec D$ we obtain, on the contrary,

$$0.11\,U(500{,}000) < 0.1\,U(2{,}500{,}000). \tag{1.5}$$

To account for this paradox we argue that the pair of choices posed by Allais contains a hidden dynamic assumption. Clearly the initial wealth of the individual is important. Thus an individual starting with a fortune of \$1,000,000,000 would very likely choose B over A. But suppose that the individual's wealth prior to being confronted with the choices is

$20,000. We may now examine the difficulty in conceptualizing owner-
ship posed by this example. Choice 1 is likely to be viewed by the subject
not as a simultaneous choice but as a sequential problem. He has been
assured of a rich prize and will be responding, in effect, to the question:
Given that your initial assets are now $520,000, would you be willing to
run a 1 percent risk of losing $500,000 for a 10 percent chance of winning
$2,000,000 more?[15] For the second choice, however, we are asking a
relatively poor individual to choose between two lotteries in which the
chances of winning, though generous, are still so low that he must regard
success as improbable and so judge the alternatives from the standpoint
of a person worth only $20,000.

The point is that a large acquisition of wealth may well be expected to
change one's utility for wealth. Recall, for example, Markowitz's suggestion that a person's utility function may plausibly have a point of inflection
at or near his current wealth level. Allais's first choice situation opens the
door to the dynamic effects of enrichment; his second does not. The
apparent contradiction between (1.4) and (1.5) is resolved by noting that
the U in (1.5) is the "utility-before-enrichment" function, whereas the U
in (1.4) is the "utility-after-enrichment" function (Lesourne, 1975).

1.2.4 Strategic aspects of wealth

One of the major difficulties in constructing models to analyze the utility
of wealth is that one cannot properly isolate the concept of wealth from
the "world of affairs" from which the wealth derives its meaning. In
particular, the clear definition of the strategy space and the specification
of the economic phenomena included in or excluded from the model are
critical.

In financial circles the concept of a *masse de manoeuvre* points to the
role of money in extending the individual's strategy space. Money and
power intermingle at many levels. It is not sufficient to characterize the
individual consumer's utility for money by referring only to insurance
and gambles. This neglects questions of ownership, control, power, and
strategy. One must also be prepared to distinguish (as is seldom done in
the literature in any systematic way) between the attitudes toward money
and risk of individual consumers or wage earners and those of entrepreneurs, corporate managers, or other fiduciary agents. The implicit
utility functions of corporations or other institutions themselves, as
distinct from those of their managers, is yet another subject for study
(McDonald, 1975).

Partially in jest, partially seriously, we suggest that an individual

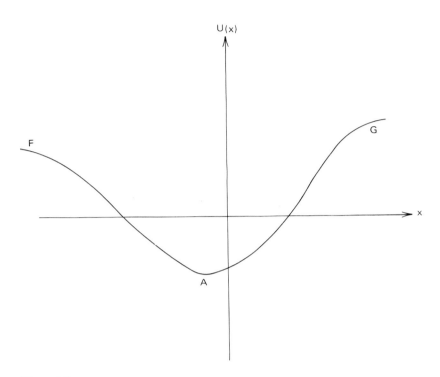

Figure 1.3
The utility of debt.

entrepreneur might, for sound strategic reasons, have the utility function
for money shown in figure 1.3, with a minimum at the point A, corresponding to a net worth of perhaps $-\$30,000$. At the level of several
million dollars, the sign on the amount of money scarcely matters. The
reason is simple. When you owe an amount such as $30,000, there is a
large possibility that your creditors will be willing to take the shirt off
your back. At the points F or G you either have or owe several million
dollars. If you have the assets, you are rich in the ordinary sense, but if
you owe the assets you may also be rich, in the sense that your creditors
may now be your partners whether or not they wish to be. The strategic
power of an individual in enormous debt is considerably greater than that
of someone merely without money!

The modeling problems involved in the investigation of the utility of
money thus fall into three major categories: *dynamic*, *strategic*, and

fiduciary. Dynamics involves such things as the selection of a zero point, the speed and direction of changes in preferences resulting from changes in wealth, and the role of aspiration levels and other sociopsychological factors. Strategic factors enter through questions of liquidity and transferability, and through the relationship between money and economic or political power, though there are also important institutional factors that limit the strategic scope of monetary moves. Finally, in a complex world where most of the major monetary transactions involve fiduciaries operating with the money of others, it is important to know their value scales as well as those of individual wage earners and consumers. The laws concerning fiduciaries and the possibilities of bankruptcy and "negative wealth" further complicate the problem of measuring the worth of money.

Spurious generality is a tempting trap for the theorist investigating political economy. What is the utility of wealth? This is not one question, but many, and none of them is free from context.

EXERCISES

1.1.   *A psychology professor offers to play the "penny" Petersburg Game (1¢ for H; 2¢ for TH; 4¢ for TTH; etc.) with the student who offers him the highest fee. An astute sophomore estimates that the professor would probably honor a $100 payoff but certainly would not be good for $1000 or more. Assuming the sophomore has linear utility, how high should be bid?*

1.2.   *A gambler with the logarithmic utility function (1.3) has an initial wealth of $1000. What is his break-even fee F for the "dollar" game if the house has (a) resources of $1 million or (b) infinite resources? How does the answer depend on the constants c and d?*

1.3.   *Let U(x) be an arbitrary utility function that increases without limit. Define a "Petersburg" payoff rule for which the expected utility increment is infinite.*

1.2.5 A few statistics

This is essentially a book in economic theory, and we shall undertake no detailed empirical work. Nevertheless, to motivate the selection of some structure for the models and to "sweeten the intuition" of the reader, we offer a few pertinent statistics concerning the United States. Unless otherwise noted, they are drawn from the 1980 *Statistical Abstract of the United States*.

In 1979 the total population of the United States was approximately 220.6 million, of which 62.6 million (28.4 percent) were 17 years old or

Table 1.1
Income data, 1979 (billions of $)

1. Gross national product	2368.8
2. Capital consumption	243.0
3. Net national product $(1 - 2)$	2125.9
4. National income	1924.8
5. Personal income	1924.2
6. Tax and nontax payments	299.9
7. Disposable personal income $(5 - 6)$	1624.3
8. Personal outlays	1550.5
9. Personal savings $(7 - 8)$	73.8

Table 1.2
Personal consumption, 1979 ($ per capita)

Personal income	8728
Disposable income	7367
Personal consumption	6848
durables	966
nondurables	2708
services	3174

younger and 24.7 million (11.2 percent) were 65 or older. The population constituted 77.3 million households.

Gross national product was $2,368.8 billion or $10,745 per capita. The estimate of the net stock of fixed, reproducible, tangible wealth was $6,745 billion, with land at around $1,800 billion. Total financial assets were $9,389 billion, with $398 billion in demand deposits and currency.

A brief summary of national income data is presented in table 1.1, and a gross breakdown of personal consumption expenditures is shown in table 1.2.

Figure 1.4 gives the "big game hunter" some basic information at a highly aggregated level as to who the players might be in game models relevant to the study of political economy.

A democratic economy with individual ownership and enterprise relies on open markets, a price system, and the vote. But the properties of these institutions depend upon the number and relative sizes of the actors. The art of modeling entails the judicious description of relevant players. When are there enough players so that they can be approximated by a continuum? What institutions should be considered as single decision units? How are institutional preferences to be described?

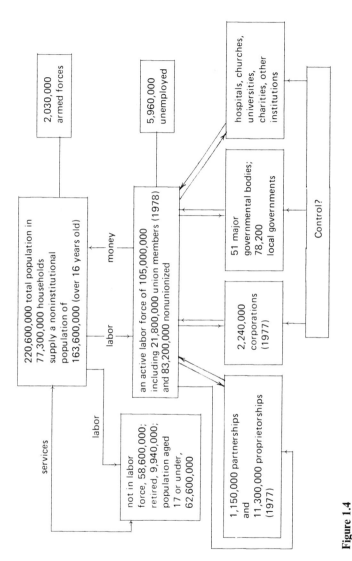

Figure 1.4

Relevant strategic units in potential models of political economy in the United States.

Figure 1.4 suggests several questions concerning the nature of the economic agents. Adults, individuals, households, partnerships, proprietorships, corporations, governmental bodies, and financial and other institutions are all candidates for roles as basic players or decision units in our models of the political economy.

This chapter has discussed wealth and ownership. Much of modern microeconomic theory has no explicit role for money and assets, yet they are important economic strategic facts of life. Money and financial instruments provide strategic decoupling for the activities of agents. They allow dynamic violations of Walras's law, since in disequilibrium the books do not need to balance.

The present participants in an economy have inherited a capital stock from the past and will hand on a capital stock to the future. The financial instruments associated with private capital stock and with government provide the side-payment or quasi-side-payment mechanisms for our society. For some purposes it is reasonable to treat money as transferable, that is, as linearly separable in the utility function. For other purposes the income effect cannot be ignored. But in many of the activities of a modern economy money is both a means of payment and side payment and also a key (but by no means perfect) measure of wealth and welfare.

At an extremely crude level of aggregation, national product is produced by labor and capital. Leaving aside the worth of the population as an asset, we find that our present reproducible capital stock and land are

Table 1.3
Money measures

	Total (billions of $)	Per capita ($)
Currency	106	566
Demand deposits	263	1406
Savings deposits	417	2230
M1-A	370	
M2	1526	
M3	1775	

M1-A = currency plus demand deposits.
M2 = M1-A plus other checkable deposits at banks and thrift institutions plus overnight repurchase orders and Eurodollars, money-market fund shares, and savings and small time deposits at commercial banks and thrifts.
M3 = M2 plus large time deposits and term repurchase orders.

valued at somewhere between $8,500 and $10,000 billion, or around 4 times GNP; thus claims to real assets alone provide a quasi-side-payment mechanism around 4 times GNP and 5–6 times disposable personal income.

There are about 20 different types of financial intermediaries that provide the spectrum of different types of paper (Krooss and Blyn, 1971) used in a modern economy.

Table 1.3 indicates a few orders of magnitude for the amounts and usage of money and near money in 1979. The demand deposit turnover rate in 1979 was estimated at 163 times per year.

Finally, if we consider raw materials, intermediate goods, and distribution and retailing systems, we find that total sales are around 3–5 times the amount of final sales, which were $2,351 billion in 1979.

Notes to chapter 1

1. Another important aspect of money is its role in *international trade*, where several monetary systems separately managed by the respective countries may be in continuous, intricate interaction.

2. Clower (1969, pp. 7–16) gives an excellent discussion of transaction costs and the importance of money in simplifying exchange. See also Foley (1970a), Hahn (1971), and Ostroy and Starr (1974).

3. A self-contained treatment would call at this point for a discussion of the different types of money and of the distinctions between money and credit. It is difficult, and probably unwise, to dissociate the study of money from dynamic models. The laws governing the granting of credit and the enforcing of contracts can be all regarded as extra rules with time components, describing an economic game that is far more complex than a one-period or static economy. See Shubik (1973a, 1975d).

4. The experience of countries such as Chile and Brazil appears to indicate that a chronic "stable" inflation rate of 20–30 percent per annum is not impossible (Harberger, 1963).

5. In a dynamic economy with uncertainty, the contractual aspects of money itself are of interest. Money may be regarded as a generalized form of lottery ticket or insurance policy, in the sense that the individual who accepts it in payment does so in the belief, but not the certainty, that it is a store of wealth and that he will be able to buy something with it in the future. The government stands by to enforce its use in the payment of "all debts public and private." But in the absence of price controls or a currency backed by gold or silver, the government does not promise that the individual can redeem it in goods of fixed economic value.

6. See Shapley and Shubik (1977b). The need for "specialists" on the major stock exchanges illustrates the problem: In effect these are added players who provide

a monetary cushion for day-to-day transactions, subject to a long-run budget constraint.

7. The maximum set of a continuous concave function is in general a closed convex set (possibly empty); if the concavity is strict, then it contains at most one point. (See Rockafeller, 1970, p. 26 ff.)

8. Dictionary references give us some idea of the common usage of the word *wealth*: "All property that has a money or an exchange value; large possessions or resources" (Merriam-Webster). "A great quantity or store of money; valuable possessions, property or other riches. Economic usage: (a) all things that have a value in money, in exchange, or in use. (b) Anything that has utility and is capable of being appropriated or exchanged" (Random House). Synonyms given include: abundance, possessions, assets, goods, property, money, treasure, and fortune.

9. See his letter to Montfort, quoted by Daniel Bernoulli (his nephew) in a celebrated paper on utility twenty-five years after. As that paper appeared in the *Commentarii Academiae Scientarium Imperialis Petropolitanae*, the paradox has come to be known as the "Petersburg" (or "St. Petersburg") paradox.

10. "Any *fairly reasonable* man would sell his chance, with great pleasure, for twenty ducats" (D. Bernoulli, 1738). "If he is *sane*, the gambler will not risk all or even a considerable portion of his wealth" (Menger, 1934). [Italics added.]

Many other authors have chuckled at the absurdity of the huge payoffs required to give the paradox its sting, but only a few permit their hypothetical gamblers the same skepticism. Instead, the hapless subject of the experiment is assumed to be both "rational" and infinitely credulous.

Thus Keynes, in his *Treatise on Probability* (1921), first grants that "we are unwilling to be Paul [i.e., the gambler], partly because we do not believe Peter will pay us if we have good fortune," and then grants that "Peter has undertaken engagements which he cannot fulfill; if the appearance of Heads is deferred even to the 100th toss, he will owe a mass of silver greater in bulk than the sun." But Keynes then continues, "But this is no answer. Peter has promised much, and a belief in his solvency will strain our imaginations; but it is imaginable." With these words he neatly jetisons the image of a rational Paul.

See also Fry (1928), Hirshleifer (1966), Kim (1973), and Brito (1975).

11. Gabriel Cramer (also quoted by D. Bernoulli) was the first to use such a calculation to defend linear utility against the paradox.

12. Karl Menger (1934) was perhaps the first to point this out explicitly. For example, if U is given by (1.3) with $c = 1$, $d = 0$, consider the prize 2^{2^T} dollars instead of 2^T dollars, with T defined as before. Then, if w denotes the player's wealth *after* paying the fee, we have

$$U(w + 2^{2^T}) = \log(w + 2^{2^T}) = 2^T \log 2 + \log(1 + w/2^{2^T}) > 2^T \log 2,$$

and hence

$$\sum_{T=0}^{\infty} \frac{1}{2^{T+1}} U(w + 2^{2^T}) > \sum_{T=0}^{\infty} \frac{1}{2} \log 2 = \infty.$$

(See also exercise 1.3.)

13. Friedman and Savage use the word "income" rather than "wealth," a usage that others have felt to be misleading. See Markowitz (1952), Raiffa (1968), Fleming (1969), and Hakansson (1970).

14. Alchian (1953); see also George Bernard Shaw's (1944) essay with the interesting title "On the vice of gambling and the virtue of insurance."

15. It takes a certain suspension of disbelief to accept the implied restriction in the model, namely, that the individual is not allowed to concoct some means of "laying off" the gamble when the odds are so favorable—that is, hedging or insuring his position, or taking in partners.

2 Commodities, Preferences, and Utility

2.1 Commodities and Preferences

People concerned with the construction and application of economic models must be aware of the many structural distinctions among goods or services and among possible forms of ownership. The abstractness of the theoretical approach, however, usually leads to the adoption of a simplified view. Thus it is often assumed that all goods or services can be measured in well-defined units: silver in ounces of a specific fineness, apples by weight or by number. It is harder to measure the amount of information contained in a message or a patent or the amount of smog received by an individual. Politics and public affairs must also be considered—economics concerns kings as well as cabbages. Foreign policy, police protection, and patriotism all have economic impact, but how do we measure the popularity of a policy or the quantity of patriotism stirred up by a Fourth of July speech?

Similarly, a model of the allocation or distribution of goods requires a concept of ownership. Ownership is the ability to dispose; it involves elements of both possession and control (Shapley and Shubik, 1967b). In the simplest case the good is in the physical possession of a single individual or household, with no social duties, encumbrances, or entailments. This may be a quite unrealistic assumption, since most goods in a modern society are subject at least to taxation, if not to other forms of restriction or regulation. Government-owned property and corporations owned by the general public are two examples of goods that do not have single owners[1] and yet may have well-defined rules of control by individuals, representable by a game model with voting.

In the standard economic models it is usually assumed possible to transfer ownership. Where information or knowledge is involved, this may be difficult. "Know-how" is in some respects like a capital good, but it cannot be bodily transferred. A mathematician may "own" an ability to solve differential equations, and he might change his employer or sell his services, but he cannot sell his talent. He may teach someone else, but in this case he duplicates his "know-how." It is not difficult to think of other types of "possessions" of economic value—leisure, loyalty, credit ratings, insurability, citizenship—that are difficult in principle or practice to transfer to a new owner.

The number of different commodities in a system is another concept that requires care in modeling. In the real world there may be many slightly different commodities of every type, but a manageable, finite-dimensional model must of necessity make approximations and aggregations (for work on infinite-commodity models see Peleg and Yaari, 1970; Majumdar, 1972; Mas-Colell, 1975b). Brand names, for example, may be ignored, or minor variations in quality, grade, or location. The coarseness of aggregation adopted is the modeler's decision and need not reflect real, invariant economic properties of the system. For this reason theoretical results that depend critically on the number of different commodities, or on their grouping into types, should be regarded with great circumspection.

2.1.1 Structure of the commodity space

If there are n clearly defined loci of ownership in the system, accounting for all the goods, then the *distribution space* will factor into a product of n separate *commodity spaces* or *consumption possibility sets*, comprising the bundles of goods that might be owned or consumed by the individual agents. If the model distinguishes m different commodities, and if each can be measured on a scale of real numbers, then the commodity spaces will be subsets of E^m, the Euclidean space of m dimensions. The distribution space will then be a subset of E^{mn}.[2]

Once we have entered the realm of geometrical discourse with these "spaces," the terminology of shape and structure follows naturally, and simple, low-dimensional diagrams become invaluable, if limited, aids to the imagination. It is important to remember, however, that the units in which different goods are measured are not comparable. "You can't add apples and oranges." Hence geometric notions that involve adding or comparing coordinates, such as the notions of distance and angle, can have no intrinsic meaning.[3] Other geometric notions, such as linearity and convexity, as well as topological notions, such as compactness and connectedness, are independent of the scaling of coordinates and will often be significant in the theory.

What might be called the "standard" form is to take the nonnegative orthant of E^m, denoted E^m_+, to be the consumption set for each individual —in other words, let $[0, \infty)$ be the domain of each commodity variable, with every individual eligible to own every commodity. In a descriptive model some commodities may invite special treatment. With credit or "short" sales, for example, negative quantities may be meaningful. Or it may happen that ownership or consumption of certain commodities requires concurrent ownership of other commodities, leading to linear inequalities that cut away part of E_+^m. For example, oil may require storage tanks, but storage tanks need not be filled. There may be natural upper limits, such as the number of hours in a day. Indivisibilities or minimum size requirements may produce gaps, forbidden regions, or even a completely discrete commodity space in the form of a rectangular lattice. Finally, as we have already remarked, the preliminary task of identifying and enumerating the commodities may involve highly arbitrary ad hoc modeling decisions affecting the dimensionality as well as other properties of the commodity space.

In many cases commodity spaces involving such special features as we have been describing may be reduced, by one device or another, to the standard form. For example, "negative wheat" for short sales can be introduced as a separate commodity, if we include a reversible production process that cancels it against real wheat. Or fractional houses or automobiles can be allowed to exist in principle but made so undesirable in practice that no one ever divides a whole house or automobile. Such formal devices may permit a uniform notation and simplify some theoretical investigations, but they are of little value to a descriptive model, where the aim should be to illuminate rather than obscure the characteristics of the real situation. Moreover, these devices generally do not avoid, but merely disguise, any real technical difficulties associated with the special commodities.

Labor and leisure are important special commodities that require careful modeling in studies involving unemployment, education, transportation systems, the "quality of life," and so forth. Clearly they cannot be treated fruitfully in the same way as we treat oranges or apples. They are distinguished (1) by being hard to grade on quality and hence hard to quantify (man-hours are a poor measure since effort and skill as well as time are involved);[4] (2) by their "personal" quality (labor cannot be produced, nor leisure consumed, faster than 24 hours per day per person, and leisure, at least, is nontransferable); (3) by their extreme perishability (a steel plant faced with a strike threat cannot stockpile labor); and (4) by a long tradition of social, psychological, anthropological, and political differentiation from other commodities (Keynes, 1936).

2.1.2 The production possibility set
Production can also be treated geometrically, in much the same terms as consumption. The standard form of the production possibility set is a

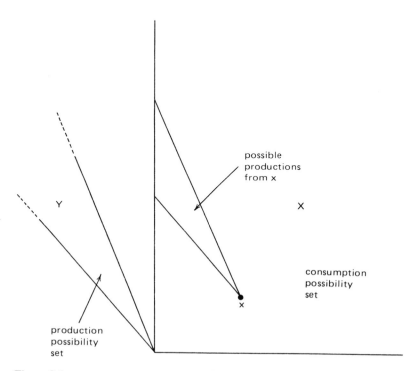

Figure 2.1
Production cones.

convex cone with vertex at the origin and containing no rays pointing into
the positive orthant. That is, each production vector has at least one
negative component, corresponding to an input. A *production move* then
consists in adding a production vector to an existing bundle, subject to the
condition that the resulting sum is still feasible. This is illustrated in
figure 2.1.

Considerations of additivity and divisibility make it natural to assume
that the production possibility set is convex; it is also generally assumed
to be closed. A special case is a single half-line or ray, which can be taken
to represent a single technological process. Often a production possibility
set can be described as the convex hull of a finite collection of rays; such a
polyhedral cone corresponds to a technology that exploits different mixes
of a finite number of processes. If a production set contains a full, infinite
line (e.g., if it is a cone that is not "pointed"), then at least one process

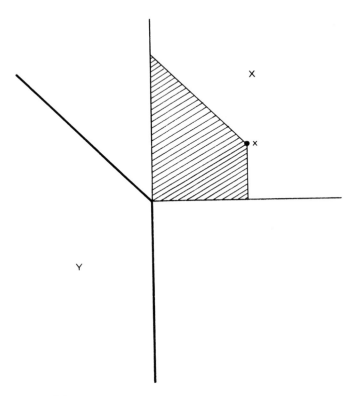

Figure 2.2
Feasible production and free disposal.

must be reversible; for example, six swords make one plowshare and one plowshare makes six swords. But if we include a labor input to each process, for example, we can prevent a complete line from ever occurring and ensure that the cone (or other set) will be pointed. A purely negative production vector represents waste, and by including the entire negative orthant E^m_{-} in the production possibility set, as in figure 2.2, we obtain a modeler's device for depicting *free disposal*, which is an important hypothesis in many classical models.

While closed convex cones may be standard partly because of their mathematical convenience, it is sometimes both more expedient and more realistic to use bounded production possibility sets. A truncated cone, for example, can be used to indicate a rigid capacity constraint, the ultimate example of decreasing returns to scale. Less abrupt examples can be equally well represented using convex, nonconical production sets, which might be either bounded or unbounded. Just as capacity limits (and other instances of decreasing returns to scale) can often be accounted for heuristically by the scarcity of some factor not directly represented in the model (e.g., land or time), so may we often regard a bounded production set as the intersection of a "standard" conical set in a higher dimension with a hyperplane representing the available quantity of the hidden, unimputed factor.

Increasing returns to scale, conversely, require nonconvex production sets, which can bring unpleasant technical and conceptual difficulties. Sometimes the increasing returns can be argued away or "convexified." Thus it may well be that two carpenters can produce five times as much work as one; but then we should hire two carpenters every other day, and none in between, to get the equivalent of one man producing 2.5 times his normal rate. Set-up costs, another source of increasing returns, can sometimes be modeled separately from, but in conjunction with, a convex production possibility set. But some cases of increasing returns, such as oil tanker tonnage or the fencing required per acre of rangeland, stoutly resist such contrivance, and it is fair to say that any well-rounded theory of production should be prepared to accept and cope with nonconvex production sets whenever they arise naturally from the economic or technological facts.

Production possibility sets that are not convex cones—that is, technologies that do not yield unlimited constant returns to scale—lead us back to the question of ownership. This is not merely the question, already troublesome, of how to share profits or losses that come out of the production sector. In a game model the actual strategic capabilities of the players may be in doubt and may require further definition. If capacity is limited, who gets the key to the factory and who gets the short end of the stick? If there are set-up costs, who bears them? If there are increasing returns, who produces at low efficiency to make it possible for others to produce at higher efficiency? Because game theory is concerned with individual decisions as well as decisions by coalitions and subeconomies, these are not idle questions. Merely stating the abstract technological possibilities in the form of a production possibility set does not answer them.

One clear and reasonably flexible way of handling production and ownership is to ascribe to each individual i a *personal production possibility set* Y^i. When two or more individuals are cooperating, they pool their possibilities by simply adding their sets together, thus:

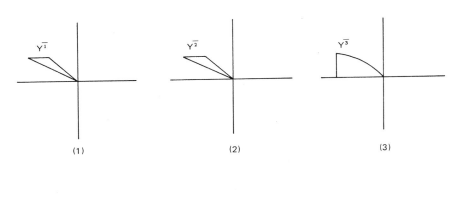

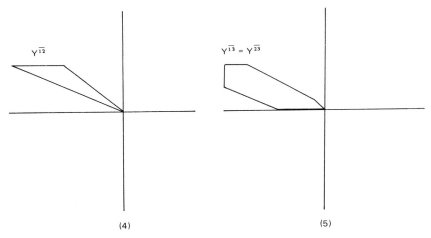

Figure 2.3
Addition of production sets.

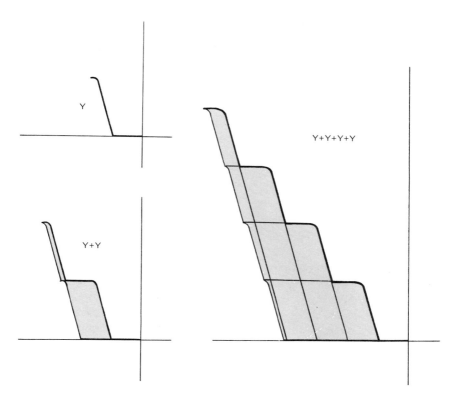

Figure 2.4
Addition of nonconvex production sets.

$$Y^S = \sum_{i \in S} Y^i. \tag{2.1}$$

The addition here is algebraic; that is, Y^S is the set of all sums $\sum_{i \in S} y^i$, where the y^i are selected from the respective Y^i. This is illustrated in figure 2.3. The sets Y^i need not be all alike, since producers will likely have different skills, locations, patents, or capital goods that are not explicitly modeled but that give them distinctive production possibilities.[5] If all Y^i happen to be convex cones, then forming the sum is the same as forming the convex hull. But it is often desirable to use bounded sets such as those in figure 2.3. This is especially true in large economies with many participants, where it might be unreasonable to suppose that individuals or small coalitions could undertake arbitrarily large productive ventures.

On a slightly more technical note, figure 2.4 illustrates the general

principle that large numbers tend to "convexify" a system. Thus, when
we add together a large number of nonconvex sets, the result is "more
nearly" convex, in a certain sense, than the sets we started with. (The
process in figure 2.4 has a set-up cost and a slightly elastic capacity
ceiling.) This principle has been exploited in several places in modern
economic theory, though more often with respect to preferences than to
production.[6] There are two ways of looking at this phenomenon for the
modeler of large systems. The assumption of convexity is not likely to
gain you very much *analytically*, in what you can prove about the system,
but it is also not likely to lose you very much *descriptively*, in your ability
to represent a real situation to a good degree of approximation.

EXERCISE
2.1.   *Consider the possibility of a set X for which $X + X \neq 2X$. Is this
generally true for every nonconvex X?*

2.1.3 Preference assumptions
The last thirty years have seen considerable progress in the treatment of
preference and utility in economic contexts as well as in more abstract
settings (see *GTSS*, chapter 4).[7] We shall now discuss informally the pros
and cons of some of the assumptions that are most commonly made
concerning individual preferences when the domain of alternatives
consists of bundles of economic commodities. Our standpoint will for the
present be static; thus we shall not discuss such subjects as durable versus
nondurable goods, consumption streams, or intertemporal independence
or additivity. Also, assumptions peculiar to numerical utility functions
as opposed to preference relations will be deferred to section 2.3.4.

Independence   "The individual's preferences depend only on his own
ownership or consumption." This means that individuals are not directly
concerned—either positively or negatively—with the economic welfare
of others; in particular, so-called Veblen effects (Veblen, 1899) are ignored,
as well as the possibility of public goods or bads. But the independence
assumption does not exclude the possibility that interpersonal concerns
such as envy, charity, egalitarianism, social efficiency, concern for the
environment, patriotism, or opposition to certain public institutions
might enter the model by way of the "solution concept," that is, might
influence the bargaining or other processes by which a final allocation
is reached. For example, some solution concepts will automatically seek
out a Pareto optimum, even though no individual gives social efficiency
any weight in his own evaluation of the outcome.

The assumption of independence will be important in reducing a market model to what we call a c-game (*GTSS*, chapter 6), which, roughly speaking, is a game without externalities. When this reduction cannot be made, the game-theoretic analysis becomes more difficult, both technically and conceptually.

Desirability and free disposal   "More is better than less." Weak desirability means that no bundle is ever made less desirable by increasing the quantity of any of the component goods. Strong (or strict) desirability means that any such increase makes a bundle actually more desirable. These properties are also called weak and strict monotonicity, respectively.

Underlying this assumption is the idea that ownership confers the right and ability to dispose of goods at no cost. It is easy to think of situations where this would not be a good assumption. Moreover, in some situations where free disposability does make economic sense, it may be better to represent it as a form of production (as in figure 2.2) rather than embed it in the utility functions as a kind of foregone consumption.[8]

Technically the desirability assumption tends to ensure that prices will be positive, or at least nonnegative, since people will have no reason to want to pay to get rid of things. This may be of some importance to the model builder, since negative prices, though perhaps mathematically tractable, may not be compatible with the institutional forms and procedures that accompany price systems in real life.

Nonsatiation   "Every holding can be improved upon." In other words, although a person may find that his desire for a particular commodity or set of commodities is completely satisfied, there will always be some change in his total holdings (presumably an increase somewhere, if we have desirability) that would please him more.

Nonsatiation is another technically important assumption in some price-equilibrium models because it helps prevent prices from becoming indeterminate. It is less important in these game-theoretic models where consumers are not passive price takers but have strategic freedom. However, we often require a stronger property called *local nonsatiation*, which states that near any bundle there is a better bundle. This property, which ensures that there are no "thick" spots on the indifference surfaces, is needed for the existence of strictly concave utility functions.

Nonsatiation may seem heuristically reasonable, since it follows from strong desirability if the consumption set is not bounded. We should remember, though, that economic satisfaction stems basically from a consumption *process*; and if we look at this process more closely, we may find hidden capacity constraints, such as the number of hours in a day, that limit the "amount of satisfaction" an individual can absorb. This could be handled in a model either by replacing the unbounded set E_+^m by a compact consumption set or by retaining E_+^m but abandoning strong desirability. In either case we would likely find points of satiation.

Continuity (or closed preference sets) "There are no sudden jumps in preference." This is most easily visualized if we have a utility function; it states that the function is continuous or can be made continuous. If only a preference relation $\succsim$ is given, then we have the following theorem (Debreu, 1954, 1964; see also Rader, 1963).

THEOREM 2.1. *Let X be a completely ordered subset of a finite-dimensional Euclidean space. If for every x in X the sets $\{y \in X : y \succsim x\}$ and $\{y \in X : x \succsim y\}$ are closed (in X), there exists on X a continuous, real, order-preserving function.*

The assumption that these preference sets are closed in X is equivalent (as Debreu points out) to the more intuitive assumption that if $\{y^{(k)}\}$ is a sequence of points in X having y as a limit, and if every $y^{(k)}$ is preferred (respectively, dispreferred) to x, then y itself is preferred (respectively, dispreferred) to x.

There is a connection between continuity of preferences and perfect divisibility of goods. If we have one or more indivisible commodities and try to represent them in the "standard" commodity space E_+^m by the device of declaring fractional quantities to be worthless (not desirable), then we must give up continuity. On the other hand, if we use a special commodity space X from which the fractional quantities have been deleted, then Debreu's theorem tells us that continuous preferences and utility functions are again possible.

Convexity "The average of a set of bundles is not worse than every one of them." The indifference curves in Figure 2.5a and 2.5d satisfy this assumption, because the preference sets they depict are convex. The assumption fails in 2.5b and 2.5c, however, because in each case the point marked X is dispreferred to both Y and Z.

There is no a priori reason why preference sets should be convex (Farrell, 1959). For example, the two commodities in figure 2.5b might be matched pieces of silverware of two different patterns. A collector might try to obtain a complete set of one or the other. A 100-piece set

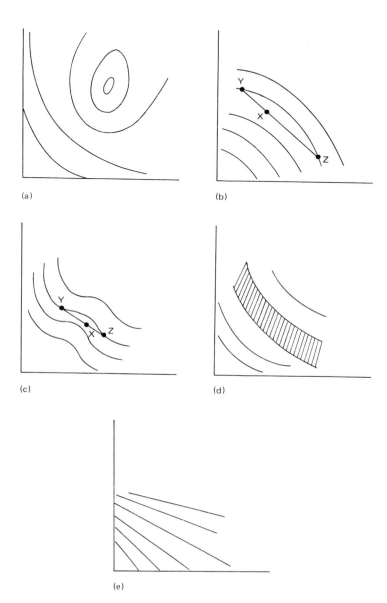

Figure 2.5
Preference contours.

consisting of a mixture of the two patterns would be considerably less desirable than 100 pieces of either pattern alone. A similar, more "economic" example could be contrived using two grades of fuel, or laborers drawn from different linguistic stocks. There are implicit production processes in these examples; and, as in the case of production with increasing returns, it is often possible to argue away or "convexify" the raw data. For example, if a continuing market for the goods is assumed to exist, then an individual should not be disturbed at holding a "bad" mixture of goods, for he can expect to trade up to something better in the future, regardless of what the prices might be.[9] An "induced" preference map could then be constructed, which would be the "convexification" of the original (Shapley and Shubik, 1966).

Another road to convexity follows the argument of large numbers, as in the discussion accompanying figure 2.4 above. Briefly restated, in a large model with many "small" consumers it may not matter very much to the overall solution if we use the actual, nonconvex preferences or replace them by their convexifications. When we describe the final allocation, however, instead of a whole class of consumers getting a bundle such as X in figure 2.5c, perhaps two-thirds of them would get Y and one-third Z. In short, a hypothetical average consumer will often be convex even when the true individuals are not.

2.1.4 Utility functions
It was once thought that the use of indifference curves (or the equivalent modern preference-relational formulation) freed economic theory from the need to consider utility functions. Even Samuelson (1948) noted: "With this skepticism has come the recognition that a cardinal measure of utility is in any case unnecessary; that only an *ordinal* preference ... is required for the analysis of consumer's behavior." This comment may hold true for a restricted set of consumer decisions made under certainty in a perfectly functioning market system. However, for a broad range of economic problems, such as decision making under uncertainty, including uncertainty voluntarily introduced by the decision makers, bargaining, oligopoly, and welfare theory, it does not hold true.

Indifference curves provide a contour map of an individual's preferences and also provide information about the order, but not about the intensity, of those preferences. This is illustrated in figure 2.6. Here the axes labeled X and Y delineate the commodity space; the axis labeled Z is the individual's utility scale. A utility function is a mapping from the commodity space into the utility space; it attaches "heights" in the Z dimension to contour lines in the XY plane.

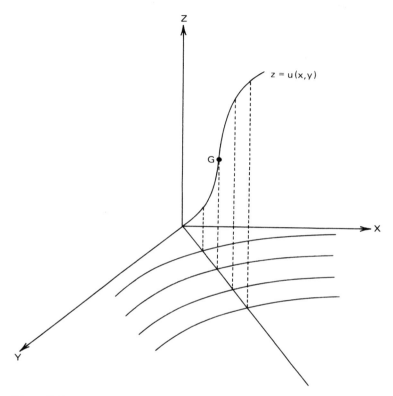

Figure 2.6
Preference and utility.

If we are interested only in the preference ordering of the consumer, then no particular significance need be attached to the utility function used to portray this information. Any order-preserving transformation of the utility scale will provide another function that can serve equally well. But when our interests extend to concepts that require cardinal utility (such as concavity or differentiability), marginal utilities, the utility of wealth, or multiperson game situations, then the particular function chosen may matter a great deal. For example, we can see from figure 2.6 that hypotheses concerning increasing and decreasing marginal utility may be equally consistent with the shape of indifference curves in the commodity space; we have drawn a utility function with an inflection to show this.

The assumptions discussed in the previous sections for preference relations all have their counterparts in the context of utility functions. The meaning of independence is unchanged. Desirability translates into monotonicity, weak or strict. Nonsatiation means not that the utility function is necessarily unbounded, but only that it does not attain its maximum value. The connection between closed preference sets and continuous utility functions has already been discussed. Finally, convexity of the preference sets translates into quasiconcavity of the utility function.

The added structure of a utility scale and a utility function sets the stage for strengthened forms of several of these assumptions. Thus nonsatiation can be strengthened to saying that utilities are unbounded; note, however, that this is not an ordinal concept, since order-preserving transformations of the reals exist that map unbounded sets onto bounded sets (for example, the arc tangent) and vice versa.[10] Similarly continuity can be strengthened to uniform continuity, differentiability, or even twice-differentiability.[11] Finally, the quasiconcavity condition is very often strengthened to an assumption of concavity;[12] this has the effect (if utility is taken to be risk-linear) of removing any incentive to gamble with the commodities in question. (Thus a risk-neutral individual situated at the point G on the nonconcave utility function indicated in figure 2.6 would be very happy to play "double or nothing.") There may be no a priori reason why utility functions should be concave over bundles of economic goods, unless perhaps the idea of diminishing marginal utility with increasing quantity can be elevated to a sort of psychological axiom. But whenever concavity fails in a real application, we should expect markets for such items as lottery tickets and insurance policies to spring up. Theoreticians unwilling to allow such markets in their models would be well advised to assume concave cardinal utility functions for their economic agents (Shubik, 1975c).

Since many solution concepts and applications are ordinal in their nature, while many analytical techniques are much simplified when concave utility functions are available, it is of interest to ask whether quasiconcave functions can always be made actually concave by order-preserving transformations. The answer is, in general, in the negative. A simple example in two dimensions is provided by a family of indifference curves consisting of nonparallel straight lines, as in figure 2.5d. No concave function exists whose level sets agree with these lines, even in a small neighborhood.[13] Thus even to assume that the preference relation *could* be represented by a concave utility function is more restrictive than merely assuming convex preference sets. However, the added restriction is slight, since the excluded cases are in a certain sense degenerate, and it has been shown that for most purposes any family of convex preference sets can be approximated by families arising from concave utility functions (Mas-Colell, 1977b).[14]

2.1.5 A few numbers and an interpretation

What do consumers buy? Who are the consumers? What technical properties of goods and services shape their preferences and shape markets?

The ultimate consumer can be considered to be the individual, the household, or the family. Although children under 16 years of age may not work, they do buy. The sizes of these groups in 1979 were as follows:

Total population	220,600,000
Population over 16	166,300,000
Households	77,300,000
Families	57,500,000

Depending upon the question to be answered, the representation of consumer preference, the number and nature of the arguments in any representation of the consumer's preferences or utility function, and the number of commodities postulated to exist in the economy will vary. A few crude statistics will, however, indicate some bounds on specification. The U.S. Government *Standard Industrial Classification Manual* breaks down all goods and services produced in the United States into 99 major groups and lists a four-digit code for each. There is also a seven-digit code used in some commercial publications such as *Predicasts*, where a listing of items manufactured covers more than 22 pages at around 400 items per page, or around 9000 items with a seven-digit code. This classification does not include size, quality, brand, age, or location—all of which could be used to proliferate a classification. For example, it has been estimated that a major supermarket may carry 30,000 line items.

Most items for sale are not final consumer goods or services but are factors in their production. When we turn to consumer goods, certain conventional divisions in the categorization of types and numbers of goods and services appear. Setting aside public goods and services, a common split is into consumer durables and other items. Consumer durables may be subdivided into houses, automobiles, furniture, and other durables. An indication of the level of aggregation of goods and services for conventional household planning is given by a Shaeffer–Eaton categorization of a household budget book. The 25 items listed are as follows: meats, groceries–vegetable, dairy products, school expenses, church–charity, laundry–tailor, drugs–medical care, beauty care, household help, enter-

Table 2.1
Expenditures on an intermediate budget ($)

Food	5044
Housing	4594
Transportation	1851
Clothing and personal care	1668
Medical care	1176
Other family consumption	1021
Gifts, contributions, other	877
Social security	1256
Income taxes	3031
Total	20517

tainment, beverages, cigarettes–tobacco, carfare–parking, household purchases, wearing apparel, gifts, telephone, gas, electricity, heat, rent or mortgage, insurance, taxes, auto expense, vacations.

An upper bound on reasonable levels of detail for consumer expenditures is given by the listing in the Bureau of Labor Statistics consumer expenditure survey, which is used primarily for revising the consumer price index, but also for econometric work on consumer models, market research, and family budget planning. More than 1700 separate codes were developed to differentiate purchases by class, and 1651 items in 24 groups were recorded in a description for a diary sample of 27,000 households.

The expenditures for a family of four on an intermediate budget in 1979 are indicated in table 2.1.

In 1978 there were 77,167,000 occupied housing units and 76,473,000 reported households in the United States. Of the white population, 68.1 percent owned their residence; for others, ownership was 43.8. Around 5 percent owned a second home.

Of the total of 84,618,000 housing units, 55,523,000 were one-family houses. Over 90 percent of the housing units had electricity, and among these over 99 percent had refrigerators, television, radios, and vacuum cleaners, 77.3 percent had washing machines, and 55.5 percent had room air conditioners.

In 1977 84.1 percent of households had automobiles; 47.5 percent had one car, 28.8 percent had two, and 7.8 percent had three or more. The total number of cars in use in 1977 was 99.9 million.

In terms of our analysis, these statistics suggest the following approach. It is reasonable, and is indeed current applied economic practice, to include financial assets in the utility function, since money and other financial instruments provide a considerable part of the mechanisms of trade in a modern economy. Furthermore, especially in short-term analysis, financial instruments are a means for linking in the past and the future without requiring explicit models of process.

The way household budgets are thought about and studied suggests that the utility function be given a structure of the form

$$\phi(I_1, I_2, \ldots, I_5, f_1(x_{1,1}, x_{1,2}, \ldots, x_{1,k_1}), f_2(x_{2,1}, x_{2,2}, \ldots x_{2,k_2}), \ldots,$$
$$f_{25}(x_{25,1}, x_{25,2}, \ldots, x_{25,k_{25}}), g_1, g_2, m),$$

where there are four or five indivisible consumer durables consisting of housing, automobiles, major appliances, furniture, and minor appliances. Food, clothes, household supplies, and other more or less continuous consumer purchases should (as suggested in *GTSS*, chapter 4) be represented by 20–25 aggregate functions within the utility function indicating the hierarchy of classification in consumer perception and behavior. The data lend some credence to the proposition that almost all individuals tend to saturate on two houses, two or three automobiles, and two or three of most major appliances. The three financial instruments are equities, debt instruments, and money.

Although a detailed discussion of financial instruments will not be given here, it should be noted that the size of the consumer good indivisibilities of houses, automobiles, major appliances, and furniture is manifested not merely in the physical properties of the items but in the need for special credit facilities to finance mortgages and consumer debt. Furthermore, rental arrangements and time sharing of vacation homes provide examples of institutional arrangements designed to modify the influence of indivisibility on the consumer.

2.2 Transferability of Goods, Money, and Utility

Economics is fundamentally concerned with the creation, distribution, and consumption of things of value. One of the places where game theory contributes to economics is in the study of distribution. The manner in which a game-theoretic model copes with transfers of ownership is therefore of prime importance.

In the most completely structured models, all transfers of money or goods are explicitly provided for in the rules and can occur only at designated points in the play of the game. The model builder can stipulate details such as taxes, transportation costs or delays, restrictions as to time or place, and information conditions as he sees fit.

Such detailed specifications may be appropriate or even indispensable when we analyze particular market forms. But it often turns out that game solutions (especially those of the cooperative variety) are not very sensitive to details of process, provided there are "enough" opportunities for transfer of the goods or monies in question. When this is the case, many specific rules of the game can be replaced by a general, sweeping provision that certain goods, money, or even utility are "freely transferable" among consenting players.

The effects of postulating free transferability are threefold. First, of course, there is a loss of realism, since transfers in real life are never absolutely free. This may be no worse than the effects of the other idealizations that are inevitably present in any model. Whether the loss of realism is tolerable in a given case depends in large part on the kind of conclusions one hopes to draw from the analysis.

Second, there is a great simplification of the formal details of the model. For example, the act of purchasing something (from a willing vendor) need not be represented as a move in the game if both money and the good being purchased are assumed transferable. In fact, the simplification is so great that many situations that would be intractable to mathematical analysis if one attempted an accurate representation of the real transfer processes, are easily handled with the aid of transferability assumptions.

Third, there is an increase in the generality of the model, in that the same formulation now covers a wider class of economic phenomena by obliterating the differentiating features. There is, of course, a corresponding loss of discrimination in the results of any analysis performed on the model; and our willingness to pay this price so frequently in this book bespeaks the early state of development of economic game theory.

2.2.1 Transferable utility and u-money
In models where a transferable money has been postulated, we often go a step further and combine the individual assumption of a money-based cardinal utility with the interpersonal assumption of free transferability. The result is tantamount to making utility itself transferable. Transferable utility can be axiomatized mathematically without formal reference to money.[15] It is difficult, though, to imagine any practical realization of these axioms without the aid of money, and a highly idealized money at that. We have coined a term, "u-money," for use in formal or other closely reasoned contexts as a way of guarding against stray connotations of the ordinary word.[16] The question whether transferable utility is a

justifiable assumption in a given model then becomes a question of whether the properties of the monetary apparatus in the real situation approximate the ideal properties ascribed to u-money.

We shall enumerate the properties of u-money, since this hypothesis has widespread structural implications for the model, affecting the outcome space, preference relations, and strategic possibilities.

First, it must be possible to break up the description of any outcome P into a "material" situation, $\mu(P)$, and a distribution of u-money, $\xi(P)$. The latter is a vector whose ith component $\xi^i(P)$ represents the level of u-money of the ith individual in the model. The outcome is completely determined when we know these two components. Thus we have, symbolically,

T1: $P = f(\mu(P), \xi(P))$.

Second, an individual's utility for an outcome must be independent of the u-money levels of others and must depend on his own level in a directly additive way. Thus

T2: $u^i(P) = g^i(\mu(P)) + \xi^i(P)$.

Third, if S is any set of individuals, and if π is an arbitrary "side-payment" vector for S such that $\sum_{i \in S} \pi_i = 0$ and $\pi_j = 0$ for all $j \notin S$, then to every outcome P feasible for S there must correspond an outcome Q, equally feasible for S, such that

T3: $\mu(Q) = \mu(P)$ and $\xi(Q) = \xi(P) + \pi$.

These conditions touch in various ways on the role of money as a decoupler—between the model and the outside world, between different individuals, and even between parts of the strategic decision problem in that they permit a coalition to separate the problem of maximizing total return from the problem of distributing it.

2.2.2 Bounds on transfers

The transferability assumption T3, as stated, implies that arbitrarily large transfers of u-money are feasible. Taken at face value, this appears to destroy any hope of a useful approximation of real money by u-money.[17] The situation is saved only when we can demonstrate that the solutions in a game with transferable utility do not actually depend on the possibility of arbitrarily large transfers, so that bounds *could have been* introduced (e.g., by giving each player only a finite supply of u-money) without affecting the analysis in any essential way.

Such bounds would not only clutter the model but in most cases would also fail to add realism. Indeed, when one's ready cash is exhausted, one turns to other liquid assets or to credit. Unless we are specifically studying a bankruptcy problem, the solution should not depend on an individual's floor for u-money. If it does, the model is almost certainly wrong since the other ideal properties of u-money will have been seriously violated long before the floor is reached. A person or firm scraping the bottom of the money and credit barrel will assuredly display an income effect, for example, in violation of T2.

The basic question, then, is whether the approximation of real money to u-money holds good *over a sufficiently large range*. If the answer is definitely negative, as it often is, then transferable utility should not be used.

Another moral can be drawn from the above discussion, applicable even to models without transferable utility: It is seldom proper to treat money as just another commodity in trade. If formal or notational considerations make it expedient to do so, then care should be taken to provide enough money in the initial holdings so that the nonnegativity condition (which, to be sure, is not always realistic even for commodity holdings) will not introduce an unnatural discontinuity.

2.2.3 A comment on methodology
It has been a prevailing fashion in economics to formulate the elementary, tutorial models of exchange and production on a barter basis. Though perhaps removed from everyday experience, such models are nevertheless easy to think about and work with, and they have an air of abstract generality that is appropriate to the fundamental questions they treat. Money is indeed a sophisticated phenomenon, with many nonelementary ramifications. Build a theory of barter economics first, we are urged, and let money appear, if at all, only in the form of a commodity in exchange.

Underlying this approach, if not wholly responsible for it, is the idea that money is a complication. In game-theoretic models, however, which involve an extra level of complications, the inclusion of money paradoxically tends to make things easier. The expediency of the "barter-first" approach is therefore called into question. Money, the decoupler, smooths away many of the difficulties that arise in dealing simultaneously with several independently motivated sources of strategic decision. Both the models and their solutions are simpler to formulate, analyze, and interpret if some form of money is present, and especially so if the money is u-money.

Our view is not merely that transferable utility should be invoked whenever possible as a technical aid, but that it is methodologically respectable to do so. A monetary decoupler is a very basic feature of human economic behavior. In situations where we, as modelers, are already willing to assume that both goods and information are freely exchangeable, it would be difficult in life and hence unrealistic in a model to forbid participants to adopt some kind of comparator and carrier of value.

Thus it is not at all inappropriate, in certain classes of models, to provide for some form of money from the outset. The idealization of u-money, which leads directly to transferable utility, is at least a convenient point of departure. Later elaborations can delve into the important but less than vital questions of transfer restrictions, income effects, credit costs, foreign exchange, and so on. To exclude money dogmatically from elementary models or to include it as just another commodity, whether technically expedient or not, is to shut one's eyes to the unique and remarkable roles it plays in the real marketplace.

2.3 A Caveat on Utility Functions

In a famous World War I cartoon Old Bill is standing up to his waist in the mud in a shell hole. Another soldier is peeping in with considerable doubt on his face. Old Bill suggests that if his visitor can find "a better 'ole," he should go to it. Thus it is with utility functions (and even complete preference orderings) as a basis for the construction of an elaborate microeconomic theory. Our psychological assumptions are flimsy in the extreme.

For the most part, we make the assumption of the existence of utility functions because we believe that, despite its problems, it can lead us to useful insights, and at the moment we do not know of a better 'ole to go to that would do better at furthering our understanding of economic equilibrium and, in some instances, process.

Even though we are making conservative assumptions, we should at least note several of the major difficulties that they entail. Three important items that pose a challenge to utility theory are (1) risk perception, (2) fiduciary behavior, and (3) desire for variety.

In both economics and psychology it has been observed that human decision making does not match the Bayesian view. Furthermore we have no satisfactory theory for the generation of initial prior probabilities. It is becoming increasingly clear to many economists that concepts which at first glance appear to be easily described by a one-dimensional set are not treated that way by most individuals. We do not perceive cold as negative heat, nor sickness as negative health, nor losses as negative profits. There are qualities (possibly involving the instinct for survival) that differentiate the members of these pairs. For example, the emphasis laid by businessmen on "downside analysis" does not appear to fit easily with utility theory.

Arrow (1982), drawing somewhat on the work of Tversky and Kahneman (1981), has suggested that the empirically observed deviations from economic prediction "are consonant with evidence from very different sources collected by psychologists." A useful bibliography together with definitions in the growing field of judgment is provided by Anderson et al. (1981). Yet, despite the disquiet and the experimental evidence, no better alternative theory yet exists.

Much of the development of game theory has heavily utilized measurable utility; and von Neumann and Morgenstern even preferred to adopt an objective probability viewpoint, thus explicitly avoiding questions of cognition, perception, and the formation of probability estimates. Kadane and Larkey (1982) challenge this viewpoint and suggest the adoption of a Bayesian game-against-Nature approach. But this plea (as Harsanyi has noted) would weaken the clear mathematical characterizations of the normative solution concepts of game theory without providing an adequate alternative in the form of a reasonably verifiable behavioral theory.

Leaving aside the problems with probabilities, it appears to me that not only is much of economic activity performed by individuals acting on the behalf of others, but that a simplistic economic-agency view of the relationship is not adequate. Love, honor, trust, and faith are not easily characterized by the economic model of agency. Although economics may have much to teach sociology, it is possible that on such topics as the indoctrination of family loyalty, sociology may have something to teach economics.

The third topic is presented somewhat gloomily in the work of Scitovsky entitled *The Joyless Economy* (1976), which raises several fundamental questions concerning boredom, the pursuit of novelty, comfort, pleasure, wealth, and happiness.

All of these points tie in with the concerns of those developing behavioral theories of economics. The fact that no satisfactory alternative theory exists to cover any of these three points does not mean that they are not important. We must keep them in mind lest we begin to believe more than has been established by extending our theorizing from a fragile base.

Notes to chapter 2

1. Unless the government or the corporation is regarded as a "player" in its own right; see the discussion in *GTSS*, chapter 2.

2. The dimension may be less than *mn* for two reasons: (1) Some of the commodities may be "personal" in nature, in the sense that they can be owned or consumed only by particular individuals. (2) The system may be "conservative," in the sense that some or all commodities cannot be produced or destroyed, but only traded; the resulting constant-sum conditions will reduce the dimension of the rest of the set of possible distributions accordingly.

3. The established custom of calling such spaces "Euclidean" is therefore historically incorrect; "Cartesian" might be better.

4. Yet if time is not the measure, labor and leisure are no longer direct complements, and they must then be modeled as separate goods.

5. A generalization is to postulate a production set $Y(S)$ for every set of individuals S and to impose in place of (2.1) either *superadditivity*,

$$Y(R \cup T) \supseteq Y(R) + Y(T) \quad \text{whenever} \quad R \cap T = \varnothing,$$

or more generally (if the $Y(S)$ are convex) the condition of *total balance*,

$$Y(S) \supseteq \sum_{R \subset S} f_R Y(R)$$

for all sets of coefficients $f_R \geq 0$ that are nonnegative and satisfy $\sum_{R \ni i} = 1$ for every i in S. (See section 6.6, *GTSS*.) This generalization allows one to model complementarities among producers (see Boehm, 1974b).

6. See, for example, Shapley and Shubik (1966), Aumann (1966), Starr (1969), and Arrow and Hahn (1971, chapter 7). See also the Shapley–Folkman lemma, a fundamental theorem embodying this principle.

7. The modern foundations for a theory of consumer choice were laid by Hicks in his *Value and Capital* (1939), following Slutsky (1915) and Edgeworth (1881); see also Hicks and Allen (1934) and Samuelson (1948). The work of Debreu (1959) using set theory may be said to have initiated the mathematically more elegant and general "modern" approach.

8. These dual representations of free disposal exemplify a more general relationship that exists between production and consumption. A model with production possibilities Y^i and utility functions u^i is equivalent, for many purposes, to one without production and with utility functions $\tilde{u}^i$ given by the "Rader transformation"

$$\tilde{u}^i(x) = \max_{y \in Y^i} u^i(x + y).$$

For this transformation to work, however, the original X^i must be enlarged to $\tilde{X}^i = X^i - Y^i$, so in general we lose the "standard form" for the consumption sets. In the case of pure free disposal, $Y^i = E^m_-$, this does not happen, since $E^m_+ - E^m_- = E^m_+$, so the effect of the Rader transformation in this special case is just to replace u^i by its "monotonic cover," the smallest monotonic function that majorizes it. See Rader (1972), pp. 258–261, or Billera and Bixby (1974).

9. Thus, in figure 2.5b, no matter what "price line" we draw through the point X, it will include a point at least as good as Y.

10. A paradox arises if we try to permit unbounded utilities when the prospect space includes that of being allowed to choose from a given set S of commodity bundles, where S may be infinite. Evidently the utility of such a prospect ought to be the supremum (least upper bound) of the utilities of the bundles offered in S. If this supremum is not attained, then the opportunity to choose from S is paradoxically more valuable than any one of the choices in S. In particular, the utilities of the bundles cannot be unbounded if the utility function is to be real-valued.

In a way, the above opportunity-to-choose prospect is a nonprobabilistic analog to the Bernoulli lottery (see section 1.2.3), which is also worth more than any one of its possible outcomes if the utility for monetary gain is assumed to be unbounded.

11. Differentiability is often required in work with the "value" solution (see Aumann and Shapley, 1974, or the "diffeomorphic" approach of Smale, 1981). Twice-differentiability is required, for example, in the definition of a "regular" economy (see Debreu, 1970, 1976a). The difficulties in justifying or even explaining such assumptions in practice are obvious. But it is sometimes possible to argue that departures from differentiability are "improbable" or "pathological" occurrences, in some sense, or that nondifferentiable systems are adequately approximated by differentiable ones.

12. A real-valued function u defined on a convex subset X of a linear space is *quasiconcave* if for all x and y in X we have $u(z) \geq \min[u(x), u(y)]$ for every z on the line between x any y. It is *concave* if we always have $u(z) \geq au(x) + (1 - a)u(y)$, where a is the linear distance between z and y divided by the linear distance between x and y.

13. See de Finetti (1949). While the example is simple to describe, it is not expected that the conclusion will be obvious to most readers.

14. When a concave-function representation does exist, it is possible to construct a "minimal" or "least-concave" representation in a natural way (see Debreu, 1976b).

15. This was in essence the approach adopted by von Neumann and Morgenstern (1944: see esp. pp. 8, 604). In their examples and applications, however, they invariably use money as the vehicle for "side payments."

Rader (1966) has introduced a concept of "quasitransferable preferences" that can be applied to ordinal preference structures. In brief, preferences are said to be quasitransferable if whenever two outcomes P and Q are feasible for a group of individuals, with everyone weakly preferring P to Q and at least one person strongly preferring P to Q, there exists an outcome P' feasible for the group such that everyone strongly prefers P' to Q.

16. The term "util" or "utile" (a unit of utility) has been employed for roughly the same purpose. We prefer to measure u-money in common units such as dollars or, if the distinction is vital, in "u-dollars."

17. For example, in a real application we would expect (1) that major redistributions of money will also affect the material properties of the system; (2) that income effects, quite apart from any nonlinearity of the money–utility relationship, will render T2 invalid when large amounts of money are involved; and (3) that actually carrying out large transfers will involve significant transfer costs.

II Oligopoly

3 On Market Models

"People of the same trade seldom meet together, even for merriment and diversion, but the conversation ends in a conspiracy against the public, or in some contrivance to raise prices. It is impossible indeed to prevent such meetings, by any law which either could be executed or would be consistent with liberty and justice. But though the law cannot hinder people of the same trade from sometimes assembling together, it ought to do nothing to facilitate such assemblies; much less to render them necessary."
Adam Smith, *The Wealth of Nations*

3.1 Approaches to the Study of Oligopoly

There are two divergent reasons for constructing and studying models of oligopolistic markets. The first, springing primarily from theoretical considerations, centers on the attempt to reconcile theories of oligopolistic behavior with microeconomic theories of the functioning of a closed economy. The general-equilibrium theory of the price system appears to be inconsistent with existing theories of oligopoly in that it is virtually "institution-free": No explanation is given for the sizes of industries in terms of the numbers of firms, or even for the existence of firms; rather, all entrepreneurs are potentially in every market simultaneously.

The need to reconcile the study of oligopoly with the study of the economy as a whole is of particular importance for examining the welfare implications of oligopolistic market structures. Can we construct measures for the cost or gain to society as a whole caused by the existence of oligopolistic industries, as contrasted with other forms of industrial organization? How efficient is an oligopolistic market? What is meant by oligopolistic power? How few is too few? Although oligopoly theory and general-equilibrium theory may be separately useful for particular purposes, an understanding of why they are inconsistent with each other may also raise valuable questions and lead to improved models.

The second reason for studying oligopoly models is to make predictions about, or give advice to, specific firms in specific industries. This requires a considerable amount of specialized knowledge and ad hoc modeling. A model for any specific market must be hand-tailored. In general the study of individual firms and markets requires institutional materials and must reflect dynamic features. Often the major part of a study of a specific market consists in identifying the important strategic variables in that market. In one it may be price, in another quality and promptness of delivery; in still another financing conditions and rebates may be critical in the analysis. There is no a priori method for deciding what factors will be of prime importance.

Our study of oligopoly will be limited to the first reason described. The tools of game theory are particularly useful for this purpose. Moreover, a primarily static analysis can still yield many worthwhile results.

Thus we shall not investigate specific markets; nor shall we indulge in "reaction functions" and quasidynamic descriptions of the actions and reactions of duopolists or oligopolists in abstract markets whose structural particulars are not described (Friedman, 1977a). There is no substitute for "knowing your business" in the study of oligopolistic markets. Several generations of graduate students have studied "leader-follower" analyses (Stackelberg, 1952), "kinked-oligopoly-curve" arguments (Sweezy, 1939), and a host of models that have in common a meagre basis of extremely casual empiricism, combined with a high degree of arbitrariness in modeling. These models cannot be properly called dynamic because, with few exceptions, the theoretical writings in oligopoly have presented only the "big picture." This has meant ignoring inconvenient details such as bankruptcy possibilities, cash-flow conditions, or production-line flexibility that give oligopolistic markets structure. Yet it is this structure that enables the applied economist with a feeling for the technology and institutions to carry out an effective industry study.

The field of oligopoly is large, and the scope of our analysis will be limited with respect to the more immediate questions to be answered. In particular, although we believe that game-theoretic methods are extremely useful, we do not pretend that they are the only methods that should be employed. Careful empirical studies are needed; behavioral theories promise to be fruitful; and computer simulations of firms and industries offer a promising new way to study dynamics (Cohen, 1960; Nelson and Winter, 1982).

Game theory can be applied to the dynamic problems in oligopoly. The extensive form of a game is of considerable use in describing the details of moves and the information conditions in an industry. A class of "games of economic survival" has been investigated (Shubik and Thompson, 1959; Shubik, 1959b). Several business or oligopoly games based on game-theoretic modeling have been both played and analyzed mathematically (Hoggatt, 1959; Shubik with Levitan, 1980). But in spite of the temptation to build dynamic models, and in spite of the importance of many questions concerning the functioning of particular oligopolistic industries, we shall divide difficulties and limit our scope by adhering to a basically static, abstract analysis.

3.1.1 Historical sketch

The problems of industrial control and the implications of oligopolistic competition are of considerable social importance, but they are extremely difficult and pose many logical and empirical challenges. Ingenuity is required to construct models that are relevant, consistent, and complete, and there are major problems in obtaining adequate information. Perhaps it is the combination of these analytical difficulties with the clamor for answers to "burning questions" that has caused the present strong dissatisfaction with the state of oligopoly theory.

The perceived needs and the available tools have led to the development of two distinctive approaches to the study of oligopolistic competition. These can be characterized as the *mathematical* and the *institutional* approaches. The history of mathematical analysis of oligopolistic competition dates from the work of Cournot (1897), and there is also a considerable literature generated by institutional economists, lawyers, and administrators interested in formulating and implementing public policy (Packer, 1963; Posner, 1972, 1976).

It is our belief that both the mathematical and the institutional approaches to oligopoly are natural and necessary. An adequate general theory would combine the degree of abstraction stressed in the mathematical approaches with the concrete recognition of institutional facts and details emphasized by those more directly concerned with the control of industry.

Since the 1930s several developments have tended to lessen the dichotomy between there approaches. The work of Chamberlin (1948a), Zeuthen (1930), Stackelberg (1952), and other economists began to bridge the gap between the more formal mathematical models and a richer description of the environment. This was especially true of Chamberlin, who emphasized the role of product differentiation and introduced several new and highly relevant variables into the formal models. Since then there has been a considerable expansion of work that is less formal than that of Cournot, Edgeworth, or von Neumann and Morgenstern and yet is more inclined toward theorizing and analysis than toward the institutional approach (Fellner, 1949; Brems, 1951; Bain, 1956; Baumol, 1959; Krelle, 1961; and many others).

In the last 25 years the growth of operations research, management science, and the behavioral sciences in general, together with the advent of the computer as a means for studying large systems, has resulted in the emergence of a fourth approach to the study of the firm and markets. This approach can be broadly described as the behavioral or management-science theory of the firm.[1]

Economists in particular and behavioral scientists in general are often somewhat careless in their use of the word "theory." Very often a few unproved conjectures are labeled a theory. At this time there is no one behavioral theory of the firm, but there have been starts made along a large number of potentially fruitful avenues toward such a theory (e.g., Nelson and Winter, 1982).

3.1.2 Game theory and the study of oligopoly

Modeling and mathematical analysis provide the basis for mathematical economics. In this and subsequent chapters, using the tools of game theory developed in *GTSS*, we suggest a unifying framework that links the work of Cournot, Bertrand, Edgeworth, Hotelling, Chamberlin, and many others together by means of noncooperative solution concepts, and the work of Edgeworth, Bowley, Zeuthen, Chamberlin, and others by means of cooperative solution concepts. Most of the previous results are obtained, although in some instances, such as Chamberlin's large-group equilibrium or the handling of oligopolistic demand, we find that the previous analysis was incomplete or inconsistent.

If game theory could only provide a unification and consistency check for previous work it would be of some interest but of limited lasting value. In the following chapters a number of new results are indicated. In particular the role of capacity and the effect of inventories are considered, the question "How many is many?" is examined, and an approach to embedding a model of an oligopolistic market in a closed economy is suggested.

3.2 General Modeling Assumptions

Most discussions of oligopoly, and much of microeconomics, deal with "open" models in which most of the economy is regarded merely as part of the environment. For instance, consumers may be treated as an aggregate mechanism rather than as individuals with active roles in a market. In analyzing the behavior of oligopolists, people interested in social policy are often more concerned with the welfare of the consumers than with that of the owners of firms; hence pejorative words such as "collusive" are used to describe actions that, in closed economies, might be described as "cooperative."

3.2.1 Collusion vs. competition
An underlying problem in the control of oligopoly is that actions that are jointly optimal from the viewpoint of the competing firms may be regarded by society as a whole as highly undesirable. It is possible to define a Pareto-optimal surface for a group of firms in competition. This has precisely the same welfare connotations *for the firms* as it does more generally for society in a theory of social welfare.

Theories of oligopolistic competition have been applied to open models and, in general, lead to solutions that are not Pareto-optimal to the participants under consideration. In this sense it becomes meaningful to distinguish between *cooperative* and *noncooperative* theories as, respectively, those that always consider solutions that are Pareto-optimal to the players involved, and those that generally (if not always) have solutions that are not Pareto-optimal.

In the open models to be considered in this part we shall find this difference clearly illustrated for various theories of market behavior: on one side the von Neumann–Morgenstern and other concepts of cooperative solution; on the other side the Cournot, Chamberlin, and Nash theories of noncooperative behavior, as well as the Walras theory of competitive equilibrium.

If the open models are embedded in larger, closed systems, then this method of distinction between cooperative and noncooperative solutions becomes harder to maintain. Divisions of proceeds that were not Pareto-optimal in the open game may become so when viewed from the vantage point of a closed society. The consumers may gain when the producers fail to attain their collusive optimum.

3.2.2 The consumers
In most societies there is a pronounced asymmetry between the roles of consumers and producers. Such differences are fundamental and must be made explicit in any game-theoretic treatment of markets. In this part only the producers are dealt with as independent strategic entities.

The open model will be contrasted later with the closed model; hence in part III consumers will be treated as full-fledged players rather than as strategic dummies.

For present purposes we assume that consumers are individuals (or family groups) who have well-defined sets of preferences, who do not bargain, but who adjust their purchases according to the prices that confront them. We limit ourselves to a static theory. It is assumed that the individual consumer is small in relation to the size of most markets with which he deals. For this reason the consumer's individual or aggregate strategic role will not be considered; it is replaced by a price-taking mechanism.

3.2.3 The commodity
Our initial models will deal with a single commodity, although later we shall consider the effect of product differentiation. The markets modeled are open, small slices of the economy, for example retail markets for sugar, lettuce, hairpins, cigarettes, beer, consumer durables, or other mass consumption and production items. We set up our demand schedule in terms of price and quantity; however, we must note that whenever one descends from the abstract to the concrete in discussing consumer markets, it is difficult to find commodities for which competition does not depend heavily upon other variables, such as advertising or other taste-changing devices. If we were directly concerned with detailed policy problems in the control or the running of oligopolistic firms, it would be necessary to investigate the specific strategic worth of advertising, distribution, or product variation as weapons. Here our major concern is to investigate the implications of different theories of behavior, given only a broad sketch of the strategic abilities of the individuals involved.

Consideration of the indivisibility of goods will be suppressed in this part but will figure prominently in one of the analyses of part III.

3.2.4 The demand function
To simplify our work we shall generally assume that the demand curve (or curves, when we consider product differentiation) is linear, as would arise from quadratic utility functions with additive linear money terms. Although this is undoubtedly a very special case, for estimating market structure it is a reasonable sort of approximation with which to start. Furthermore, given quadratic functions, it will often be possible to calculate explicit solutions for our models, even in the case of multi-product markets (e.g., Shubik with Levitan, 1980). We shall try to point

out places where the actual nature of our results, as opposed to their accessibility to computation, depends too critically on these special assumptions.

The models in the following chapters are neoclassical, inasmuch as we ignore income effects on the consumers and thus use a "Marshallian" money. Where the consumer is also large and possibly a producer, as in the case of an oligopsonist, or where his decision is of sufficient importance to himself, such as in the buying of a house, the income effect cannot always be ignored.

As Hicks (1939, pp. 36–37) has noted, the asymmetry in supply and demand is manifested as a difference in the importance of the income effect. A change in the price of a chocolate bar by one or two cents has almost no income effect on the final customer (with the possible exception of buyers for large institutions such as hospitals); however, a small change in the price of either the final product or a major factor of production has a considerable income effect on the producer of the item.

3.2.5 The producers

In this part our concern is with the relation between producers and the mass of consumers. Thus we are not concerned with problems of the supply side of the firm at this time; we regard firms as attempting to maximize their incomes given supply conditions. This neglects substitution problems in factor markets and allows us to avoid having to discuss immediately the owners or managers of the firm and their private preferences.

Firms are assumed to be large relative to consumers. We consider their strategic role. They may form coalitions, bargain with each other, make threats, limit their production, and so forth. There are, of course, many industries to which these assumptions do not apply. For example, there are many hundreds of thousands of small service areas in which the individual firms are scarcely bigger than the consumers, and in which features such as the interplay among the owners' own labor, their managerial role, and their income are dominant.

Almost all commodities pass through one or more levels of a distribution system as well as through several levels of manufacture. At this time we do not distinguish between manufacturers and distributors or brokers, although we note that their "production" conditions may be decisively different. (An important role of the distributor is to produce information, and of the broker is to act as fiduciary or third party, especially in situations where there are major asymmetries between the power and size of the ultimate buyers and sellers.)

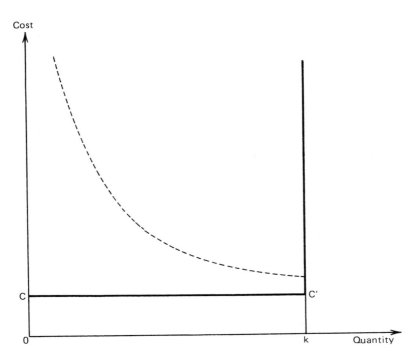

Figure 3.1
Linear average costs with capacity limitation.

Firms in most modern societies tend to be multiproduct and in many cases multiplant (see Baumol, Panzer, and Willig, 1982). To understand the behavior of a specific firm in a specific market it is undoubtedly important to take both of these factors into account. For most of our analysis (and especially for comparison with other work), however, the assumption of a single product greatly simplifies the task and, we believe, gives qualitatively the same results as would models including multi-product, multiplant firms.

3.2.6 The cost function

For ease of computation we assume that each firm has constant average costs, subject to a capacity limitation. Few important features of economic analysis are lost by using this simplified model.[2] The cost conditions are displayed in figure 3.1; the line CC' shows the average cost of production, and the vertical at k marks the capacity limit. This may be compared with the U-shaped average cost curve that is given in most textbooks. With the addition of a fixed overhead (or an entry or set-up cost), the firm's average total cost curve becomes more nearly U-shaped, as illustrated by the dashed curve in figure 3.1. In practice, the distinction between fixed and variable costs is somewhat arbitrary, depending upon accounting conventions and selection of the time period. We shall return to the discussion of fixed costs in chapter 7, when conditions for entry and exit are discussed.

We should note, however, that our assumptions on costs and demand do rule out the possibility of multiple intersections between the supply and demand curves. In particular, inferior goods and certain forms of operation under excess capacity have been ruled out. We return to these matters in chapter 5.

3.2.7 Threats and strategic variables

In chapters 4 and 5 the strategic variable under the control of each firm is assumed to be its level of production. The frequent complaint that this is too unrealistic may or may not be justified, depending upon the analysis proposed. Firms under pure competition, for example, have by assumption no control over price. For firms accepting a cooperative or collusive solution, however, the details of the strategies are unimportant except in their effect upon the threat possibilities and the power of coalitions.

At this point we must note that the game-theoretic treatment of threats is unsatisfactory in two important respects: in matters of dynamics and in what we might call the coding problem. In most situations involving negotiation, the timing of moves, offers, and threats is critical. Changes in relative bargaining power over time, and expectations of future change, cannot be ignored. For example, it is important to be able to calculate the cost of a strike and to estimate how long each side can withstand the attrition. Although we can include these features formally by discussing games in strategic form, we do so at a considerable cost, since we are then forced into a rigid oversimplification of the bargaining and negotiation process, especially as regards sociopsychological and communication problems.

Game-theoretic models are based on the assumption that all rules are given and all commitments are honored. There is no easy way to introduce a category of verbal "commitments" that are less than binding. Thus the coding problem, involving the linking of words and deeds, is virtually ignored. In the study of problems such as labor-management negotiations, international bargaining, and cartel formation, where timing, sociopsychological factors, verbal interplay, and posturing are important, game theory and most other mathematical approaches as well appear to have only limited usefulness. (On bargaining and negotiation see Raiffa, 1982.)

As a first approximation, however, the failure of game-theoretic models to account for these difficulties does not appear to be fatal. Indeed, if we consider the various solution concepts merely as normative suggestions, the models are often entirely adequate.

Given that we are willing to live with a level of simplification that rules out the essential factors of many important problems, what further costs do we incur by sharply limiting the choice of strategic economic variables? Three basic types of single-time-period strategic models are of interest: We can take as the strategic variable the quantity offered to the market, the price, or price and quantity simultaneously.

Our emphasis on quantity in chapters 4 and 5 may seem less realistic than permitting the firms to select both a rate of production and a price; but a one-period model with price-only strategies would deny firms the flexibility of adjusting inventories in response to market conditions. Industries differ in their need for such flexibility. In situations involving special tooling or long production times (as in agriculture) the production decision may be inflexible whereas all firms can adjust prices instantaneously. In the case of a mail-order firm that sells trinkets, though, it may take only a few days to obtain more stock, but it may not be reasonable to change prices until a new catalog is issued.

3.3 A Few Statistics on Firms and Markets

In 1977 there were 74,000,000 households constituting the major portion of U.S. consumers. Consumers accounted for $1.210 trillion of personal consumption expenditures; $33 billion was spent on private domestic investment, and $456 billion was spent by governments. Table 3.1 indicates the numbers of corporations, partnerships, and proprietorships servicing the economy.

Business receipts add up to $4.399 trillion. This volume of business must be compared with $1.878 trillion in final sales, giving a ratio of 2.4 to 1.

Figure 3.2 shows the manufacturing–wholesale–retail–final customer chain for 1977, with the ratios of one group to the next noted.

Table 3.2 provides the data for figure 3.3, which illustrates the concentration of corporate assets. Using the four-firm concentration rates

Table 3.1
Corporations, partnerships, and proprietorships (1977)

Industry	Number (thousands)			Business Receipts (billions of $)		
	Pr	Active Pa	Active Co	Pr	Active Pa	Active Co
Total	11346	1153	2241	393.9	117.6	2827.5
Agriculture, forestry, fishing	3177	121	67	74.6	13.5	31.3
Mining	71	22	19	4.6	5.9	95.4
Construction	994	69	216	42.8	14.2	174.8
Manufacturing	224	28	230	10.0	8.8	1571.8
Transportation, public utilities	385	17	84	13.9	3.8	318.9
Wholesale and retail trade	2264	193	674	160.5	48.6	1253.2
wholesale	307	29	239	33.5	16.6	617.7
retail	1862	164	433	123.6	32.0	634.1
Finance, insurance, real estate	895	476	434	19.3	43.9	407.5
Services	3302	227	514	67.8	37.8	171.3

Co: corporations. Pr: proprietorships. Pa: partnerships.

Manufacturers

224,000 proprietorships
28,000 partnerships
230,000 corporations

482,800

1:1.19

Wholesalers

307,000 proprietorships
29,000 partnerships
239,000 corporations

575,000

1:4.28

Retailers

1,862,000 proprietorships
164,000 partnerships
433,000 corporations

2,459,000

1:30.09
or
1:87.86

74,000,000 households
or
216,058,000 individuals

Figure 3.2
The manufacturing–wholesale–retail chain.

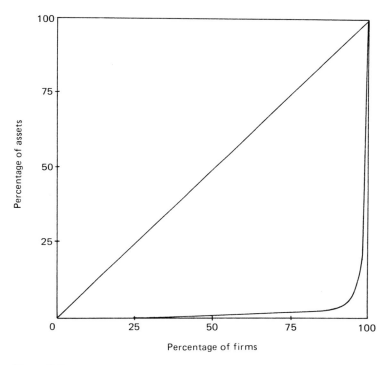

Figure 3.3
Concentration of corporate assets.

Table 3.2
Distribution of corporate assets

Assets ($)	Percentage of corporations	Percentage of assets
$< 10^5$	56.9	0.8
10^5-10^6	35.4	4.7
10^6-10^7	6.4	7.0
$10^7-2.5 \times 10^7$	0.6	4.1
$2.5-5 \times 10^7$	0.3	4.4
$5-10 \times 10^7$	0.2	5.1
$1-2.5 \times 10^8$	0.1	7.3
$> 2.5 \times 10^8$	0.1	66.6

from the 1972 census of manufactures, we find that in around 43 percent of all manufacturing industries the first four firms had above 40 percent of sales, and 4.9 percent were in the range 80–100 percent.

In 1979 the top 500 manufacturing firms had assets of $1.0347 trillion and 16,195,000 employees; the second 500 had assets of $78.8 billion and 1,785,000 employees.

In terms of the models and analysis in chapters 3–7 and some of the cooperative analysis, these few figures, the *Statistical Abstract of the United States*, the *Fortune* 500 listing, and recent texts on industrial organization such as Scherer (1980) or Williamson (1975) suggest that some level of oligopoly is more the rule than the exception in U.S. industry. Cooperative rather than noncooperative theory may therefore be a better fit for larger interfirm sales. Smaller firms can, at least for some purposes, be approximated by an ocean or a continuum, but this is emphatically not the case for the larger firms. The representation of individual consumers in aggregate by an ocean is far more defensible than is such a representation for firms.

How good an approximation is the profit-maximizing firm and the utility-maximizing consumer? It clearly depends upon the questions being asked. If we are studying large defense system procurement or the expansion plans of General Electric, the model of the simple profit maximizer is inadequate. Assets, accounting conventions, internal bureaucratic structure, and the nature of risk assessment must all be considered. If, however, we are asking whether noncooperative oligopoly theory can be made logically consistent with general equilibrium theory (as we do in chapter 7), then as a first cut the extreme simplifications appear to be reasonable.

The statistics in table 3.1 give a crude indication of the sizes of economic units. Obviously the aggregation and averaging destroy much of the information. To offset this table 3.3 gives a few selected figures for specific organizations.

These figures support two observations. First, most economic and politicoeconomic activity involves organizations or institutions with more members than one individual's span-of-control, so that most economic decision making takes place within a bureaucratic structure. Second, the ratio of employees to institutions leads us to expect that the degree and quality of competition on the two sides of the labor market will be considerably different (table 3.4).

Even at this crude level of aggregation, the ratios are more or less consistent with our intuition. Government establishments are large,

On Market Models

73

Table 3.3
Government, unions, and AT&T, 1970

Institution	Civilian employees or members
Federal government	2,763,000
State and local governments	10,944,000
California	1,108,000[a]
New York	952,000[b]
Teamsters Union	1,924,000[c]
United Auto Workers	1,074,000[c]
AT&T	855,000

[a]State: 248,000; local: 860,000.
[b]State: 216,000; local: 736,000.
[c]1978 figures.

Table 3.4
Institutions and employees

	Employees (thousands)		Number of institutions (1979)	Average number of employees per institution
	1960	1979		
Total (excluding agriculture)	54,189	89,482	—	
Government	8,353	15,612	78,000	200.0
Manufacturing	16,796	20,972	482,000	43.5
Wholesale and retail	11,391	20,137	3,034,000	6.6
Services	7,378	17,043	1,835,000	9.3
Transportation, public utilities	4,004	5,154	—	
Construction	2,926	4,644	1,200,000	3.9
Mining	712	1,014	31,000	32.7
Agriculture (hired)	1,885	1,273	2,333,000	1.6
Agriculture (family)	5,172	2,501		
Finance, insurance, real estate	2,629	4,963	—	

—: Too diverse an aggregate.

mining and manufacturing are larger than retailing and services, and there are still a great number of firms and construction establishments with minimal payrolls.

Finally, although the numbers of firms and families give some indication of the sizes of the markets, they do not indicate how the markets are segmented by transportation and other transaction costs. A quick indication of the segmentation is given by the division of the United States into the following population groupings:

Standard Metropolitan Statistical Areas	281
Towns (> 100,000 population)	171
Counties	3138
Populated places (> 100)	61238

Notes to chapter 3

1. See, e.g., the work of March and Simon (1958), Cyert and March (1963), Bonini (1963), and Clarkson (1962), and also the work on financial models of the firm by Marris (1964, 1979).

2. See Bishop (1952). A treatment of duopoly models involving nonlinear costs can be found in Shubik (1959b). Neither of these works, however, investigates the implications of the cooperative game-theoretic approach.

4 Duopoly

4.1 Special Models and General Results

We now proceed to an exhaustive exploration of a particular class of market models that are "one-sided" in the sense of being viewed throughout only from the supply side. Here the consumers are not "players," and their welfare is considered only indirectly, via a postulated demand schedule for the good in trade. We shall begin with the case of duopoly. This will enable us to discuss in preliminary fashion many features of the general case while the notation is still simple and while graphical and geometrical arguments are still easy to use. A number of specific, simplifying assumptions will also be made, as discussed in the preceding chapter. We shall, however, try to account for the effects of any loss of generality, and in cases where the difference between the specific example and the general case appears to be important we shall prove more general results or otherwise indicate the nature of the differences.

4.2 The Basic Duopoly Model and Its Presolutions

For the consumers we postulate a linear, aggregate demand function, of the form

$$p = a - bq, \tag{4.1}$$

as shown in figure 4.1. Here p denotes price, q quantity, and a and b are positive constants. This is the function that would result, for example, if we were to assume that the aggregate utility, measured in dollars, from the possession of q units of the good is given by the quadratic[1]

$$u = aq - \tfrac{1}{2}bq^2, \qquad \text{where } 0 \le q \le a/b. \tag{4.2}$$

The consumers are not, however, considered to be players (but see section 4.4).

The players, 1 and 2, are producers; each has a linear cost function,

$$C_i(q_i) = c_i q_i \qquad (i = 1, 2),$$

and also a capacity limit k_i, so that his strategic choice in the game is the selection of a production level q_i from the interval

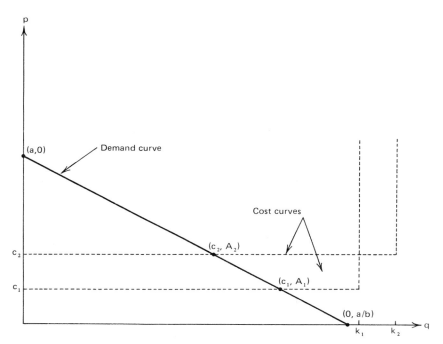

Figure 4.1
Duopoly: costs and demand.

$0 \le q_i \le k_i \qquad (i = 1, 2).$

We shall start by assuming that the limits k_i are too large to have any effect (as in figure 4.1).

The revenue to player i is $pq_i = (a - bq)q_i$, where $q = q_1 + q_2$. Hence his profit is

$$P_i = (a - c_i - bq)q_i \qquad (i = 1, 2), \tag{4.3}$$

which we take to be his *payoff function*. Let us write A_i for $(a - c_i)/b$, a useful constant that will turn up frequently in the analysis to follow. Thus we have $P_i = bq_i(A_i - q)$. We can interpret A_i as the quantity required to drive the price down to c_i, and hence as a measure of the market demand seen by player i.

4.2.1 The Pareto set
The relation between *strategy* pairs (q_1, q_2) and *payoff* pairs (P_1, P_2) is

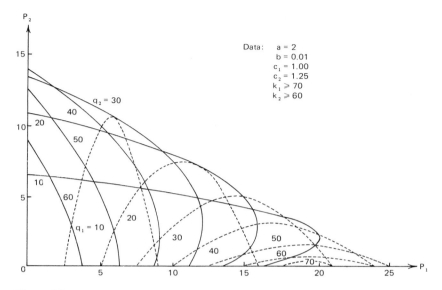

Figure 4.2
Duopoly: relation between production (q_1, q_2) and profit (P_1, P_2).

shown in figure 4.2. The two families of parabolas represent constant-production lines for player 1 (dashed) and player 2 (solid), respectively. The envelope of these curves is the Pareto surface of the model. It can be found by equating the Jacobian of the transformation (4.3) to zero,

$$\begin{vmatrix} \dfrac{\partial P_1}{\partial q_1} & \dfrac{\partial P_1}{\partial q_2} \\[2ex] \dfrac{\partial P_2}{\partial q_1} & \dfrac{\partial P_2}{\partial q_2} \end{vmatrix} = 0, \tag{4.4}$$

which yields

$$2q^2 - \tfrac{3}{2}(A_1 + A_2)q + \tfrac{1}{2}(A_1 - A_2)(q_1 - q_2) + A_1 A_2 = 0. \tag{4.5}$$

If the costs are unequal, with say $c_1 < c_2$, then the graph of (4.5) has the appearance of figures 4.3a, b, or c. If $c_1 = c_2$, then (4.5) simplifies to

$$(2q - A)(q - A) = 0, \tag{4.6}$$

where $A = A_1 = A_2$, and a configuration like figure 4.3d results.

Transferring these data to the payoff space and using (4.3), we find that only the portions of these graphs marked *EFG* give rise to Pareto

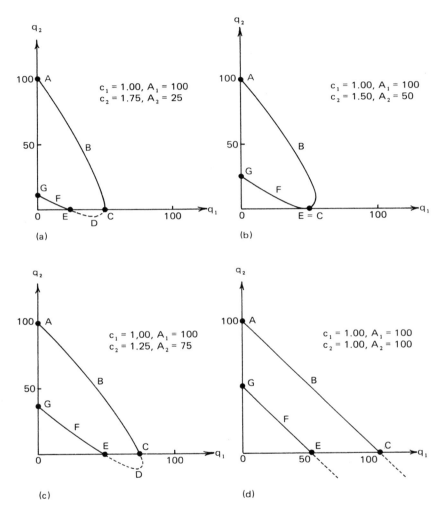

Figure 4.3
Optimal production schedules.

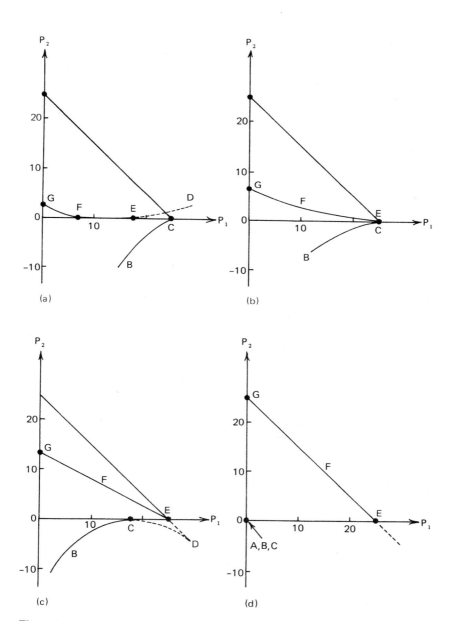

Figure 4.4
Pareto sets (cores) and threat curves.

optima. These are shown in the payoff graphs of figure 4.4, similarly labeled *EFG*. The dashed portions of these graphs refer to negative values of q_2 and are shown only for reference purposes. The other portions have an interpretation in terms of optimal threats, to be discussed in section 4.3.1.

If the costs are widely different, as in figure 4.4a, the Pareto set turns out to be disconnected, with the isolated point *C* preferred by the first producer to the point *E*. His "monopolistic" price is actually below the other producer's average cost in this case.

4.2.2 The characteristic function and the core

In the game without side payments, the characteristic function is set-valued. Since there are only two players, though, and hence no coalitions of intermediate size to consider, it does little more than describe the space of imputations. Specifically, $V(\overline{12})$ gives us the Pareto set, as just described, while $V(\overline{1})$ and $V(\overline{2})$ give us the individually rational lower bounds for each player: $P_1 = 0$, $P_2 = 0$. These bounds stem from the observation that each producer can prevent a loss by simply not producing anything (there are no fixed costs in this model), but he cannot guarantee himself a profit, since the price could be driven down below his average costs through overproduction by the other producer. Note that this argument depends on the assumption that the capacities of the producers are effectively unlimited.

As in any two-person game, the core is the entire space of imputations and also the unique stable-set solution. It happens in this case that the space of imputations is precisely the Pareto set, since the latter contains no individually irrational points. Even if one player were willing to take a loss, this would not help the other player. Thus the core of the game is precisely the Pareto set. Note that this conclusion also depends on unlimited capacities.

The core is not a convex surface unless $c_1 = c_2$. In other words, both players could generally do better than a given "undominated" point in the core, *in expected value*, by a coordinated mixed strategy. One of them, selected at random with the appropriate probability, would shut down his plant while the other would supply the market as a monopolist. The potential gains through this strategem appear to be quite small in the present model, and we shall ignore them for now, so as to give our treatment the broadest possible contact with the standard non-game-theoretic treatments. If the discrepancy were more pronounced, we would be hard put to justify the exclusion of mixed strategies from our analysis.[2]

The qualitative effect of the admission of mixed strategies can be

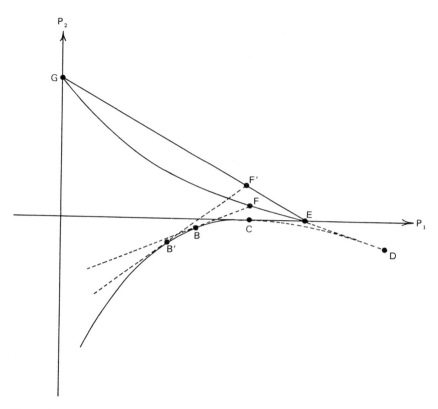

Figure 4.5
Convexification by the use of mixed strategies.

gauged from an inspection of figure 4.5, which is based on the data of figures 4.3c and 4.4c. The Pareto surface changes from GFE to $GF'E$.

4.2.3 Side payments: Joint maximization

If firms can combine their revenues, and side payments between them are permitted, then in a cooperative solution they will seek to maximize the *sum* of their profits. But from (4.3) we have

$$P_1 + P_2 = q(a - bq) - c_1 q_1 - c_2 q_2, \tag{4.7}$$

and it is evident that (in the absence of capacity restrictions) this will be maximized by setting the higher-cost production equal to zero and optimizing with respect to the other. Let $c_m = \min(c_1, c_2)$. Then, by differentiating, we find that

$$a - 2bq - c_m = 0,$$

and the maximizing q is $(a - c_m)/2b = A_m/2$, where $A_m = \max(A_1, A_2)$. Hence we obtain the following characteristic function:

$$v(\overline{1}) = v(\overline{2}) = 0, \qquad v(\overline{12}) = bA_m^2/4. \tag{4.8}$$

The Pareto set is a straight line, with slope -1, touching the Pareto set of the no-side-payment case, as represented by the diagonal lines in figure 4.4. The core is the portion of this line lying in the first quadrant. It depends only on the costs of the more efficient producer (player 1), who in effect pays the other producer to stay out of the market and then reaps the fruits of monopoly.

If there is a great disparity in costs, as in figure 4.4a, the presence or absence of side-payment possibilities would make a considerable difference to the producers. In any case, side payments eliminate any incentive to use mixed strategies.

In the case of equal costs (figure 4.4d), there is no need to distinguish between a side-payment and a no-side-payment theory, or to consider mixed strategies, because all imputations can be obtained by adjusting production rates.

4.2.4 Capacity limits
Thus far we have ignored the production ceilings, k_1 and k_2, assuming them too high to be operative in the market under consideration. If this is not the case, the existence of capacity limits can affect the characteristic function in two ways. (1) A moderately low capacity for one producer can cause certain Pareto-optimal outcomes to be no longer individually rational for the other producer. The imputation space and the core, but not the Pareto set, will thus be reduced in size. (2) A very low capacity, for either or both producers, will make some or all of the previously optimal production schedules infeasible and shift the Pareto set inward from its unlimited-production position. These two effects are illustrated in figure 4.6 for the case of equal average costs.

(1) Suppose $k_2 < A_1$, which is the quantity required to drive the market price down to c_1. Then the first producer can always unilaterally assure himself a positive profit. In fact, if his own capacity is not too severely limited, he can set $q_1 = (A_1 - k_2)/2$ and obtain a profit of $b(A_1 - k_2)^2/4$ at worst (at $q_2 = k_2$). If his capacity is too small for the strategy, that is, if $k_1 < (A_1 - k_2)/2$, he can set $q_1 = k_1$ and obtain a

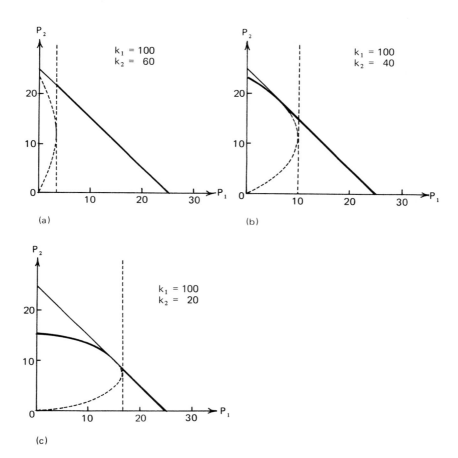

Figure 4.6
Effect of capacity limits on the Pareto set and the core. Here $a = 2$, $b = 0.01$,
$c_1 = c_2 = 1.00$, $A_1 = A_2 = 100$.

profit of $bk_1(A_1 - k_1 - k_2)$ at worst. The imputation space, and hence the core, is smaller than it would be for $k_2 \geq A_1$. (Compare figure 4.6a with figure 4.4d.)

(2) Suppose $k_2 < A_2/2$, which is the most the second producer is ever called upon to produce in a Pareto-optimal production schedule. Then (4.5) no longer applies for values of q_1 close to zero; it is replaced by the linear equation $q_2 = k_2$. The Pareto sets of figure 4.4 are thereby adjusted in the vicinity of the point G; the curve becomes a parabola, concave to the left. This is illustrated for the equal-costs case in figures 4.6b and 4.6c.

Note that the adjustment in the Pareto set described in (2) does not involve profit levels for the first producer that are above his adjusted minimum as described in (1). Thus the shape of the core is not affected. In other words, the restricted capacity of the second producer may weaken his ability both to hinder the other (through overproduction) and to cooperate in a peaceful division of the market. Each of these effects can be significant—for example, if the first producer has very high costs— but the first, if present, renders the second irrelevant.

If side payments are allowed, the Pareto set is not changed by capacity limitations unless the lower-cost producer's production is limited to less than his monopolistic production rate, $k_i < A_i/2$, or, if costs are equal, unless $k_1 + k_2 < A/2$. But the contraction of the imputation space and the core, described under (1) above, occurs whether or not there are side payments.

4.2.5 An economic interpretation
In general the Pareto-set and imputation-space presolutions portray the arena for economic warfare and the size of potential gain through co-operation or collusion. The differences between the side-payment and the no-side-payment models show that the presence of side payments helps collusion. Furthermore it improves the "blackmail" possibilities for an inefficient producer.

Even though the solutions are basically static, they depend considerably upon the capacity limits of the firms. This represents a link to dynamic analysis. Furthermore, in even a casual consideration of economic warfare it is evident that costs and capacity help to delineate the "firepower" of a firm. Even a static theory of oligopoly needs to encompass the roles of capacity limitations and overheads. As a start, with this simple model and these preliminary solution concepts, capacity plays a critical role. The natural extension is to take entry and exit into account.

4.3 The Basic Duopoly Model: Three Solutions

The core of a two-person game is nothing but the imputation space, which delineates a broad range of collusive outcomes that are available to the oligopolists. We would prefer a solution concept that selected a single outcome, and we shall consider three such concepts in this section: the value, the noncooperative equilibrium, and the competitive equilibrium or efficient point.

4.3.1 The value
Since the value is a cooperative solution, we may consider its application here as the use of a fair-division process by a cartel in order to determine a division of the profits obtained from cooperation. The model is clearly not a c-game, in which threats play no part. One can damage one's competitor by overproducing so as to drive down the market price. But in so doing one runs the risk of a loss, since the other may also choose to produce on a large scale. (We are assuming that the production decisions are made simultaneously and are irrevocable.) Accordingly it is appropriate to evaluate the threat potentials by means of the Nash two-person cooperative theory.

When we equated the Jacobian of the payoff function to zero in (4.4) in the course of finding the Pareto set, we were actually determining all strategy pairs (q_1, q_2) with the following property: If a small change in q_1 causes the fortunes of the players to change in a certain ratio, then a small change in q_2 causes them to change in the same ratio. This is, of course, a property of the Pareto surface, since if the ratios were different, a joint change of strategy could be found that would produce a joint improvement in payoff. Equal exchange ratios are also a property of the optimal threats, except that here there is a distinction in sign. In the threat case a small change of strategy causes both payoffs to rise or fall together. On the Pareto surface one rises while the other falls.

The "threat curves" in figure 4.4, then, comprise the points at which the damage-exchange ratio is positive and does not depend on which player's strategy is varied. The ratio is equal to the slope of the threat curve itself.

To determine the value of the game, we must find a point B on the threat curve (see figure 4.4) and a point F on the Pareto curve, such that the slope of the line joining the two points is equal to the slope of the threat curve at B and the negative of the slope of the Pareto curve at F. The first point is the "conflict payoff," which would result if the optimal threats were carried out; the second is the value of the game. (The corresponding strategy pairs are labeled B and F in figure 4.3.) Since the algebraic details of the calculation are not attractive, we shall be content with this geometrical description of the solution.

We should remark that a strict application of Nash's theory, in the case of unequal costs, would yield a somewhat different result (F' instead of F in figure 4.5), since he requires the Pareto surface to be convex. Indeed, without such convexity the uniqueness of the solution is not assured in general. It appears, however, that in our present model the nonconvexity is so slight that we always get a unique solution anyway, without recourse to convexification—that is, without bringing mixed strategies into consideration.

In the case of equal costs this distinction disappears; also, the threat curve becomes trivial. There are many pairs of threat strategies that yield equal damage ratios (the line ABC in figure 4.3d), but they all yield the same payoff, namely, zero to both players. The optimal threat for each player, represented by the point B, is nevertheless unique; it involves production of an amount $A/2$, so that the market is exactly saturated and profits are zero.[3] At the Nash point F, each player produces $A/4$, and the value of the game is $bA^2/8$ to each player.

With side payments available (or with equal costs) the threat point is determined by each firm maximizing its "damage-exchange rate." Each is willing to sacrifice a dollar of profit as long as it does at least a dollar of damage to its opponent. The selection of optimal threats can, on occasion, be regarded as a solution in itself. It amounts to each trying to maximize the difference in their payoffs or

$$\operatorname{maxmin}(P_1 - P_2), \tag{4.9}$$

as discussed in $GTSS$, chapter 7.

The value is a cooperative solution that is highly sensitive to the threat structure of an industry. Leaving aside personality quirks or bargaining ability, it reflects the inherent economic power of the firms in a society and an industry where bargaining and collusion are permitted.

4.3.2 The noncooperative equilibrium
If each duopolist acts independently, neither offering to cooperate nor attempting to induce (e.g., by threats) the other to cooperate, then a case can be made for applying the so-called noncooperative or equilibrium-point solution concept.[4] This is an equilibrium situation in which each player knows the strategy of the other player yet has no incentive to change his own strategy.

In general, such equilibria may not exist unless mixed strategies are introduced; and when they do exist, they are often not unique. In our present model, however, as in many comparable discussions in the literature of economics, there does exist a unique, unmixed equilibrium point, that is, a unique pair $(q_1^{\#}, q_2^{\#})$ such that

$P_1(q_1, q_2^{\#})$ is maximized at $q_1 = q_1^{\#}$,

$P_2(q_1^{\#}, q_2)$ is maximized at $q_2 = q_2^{\#}$.

Its nature is sufficiently illustrated by the equal-cost case, where we have

$$q_1^{\#} = q_2^{\#} = \frac{a - c}{3b} = \frac{A}{3}. \tag{4.10}$$

In effect, each producer takes exactly half of the market that is left after the other's production has been absorbed. The profits realized are

$$P_1^{\#} = P_2^{\#} = \frac{(a - c)^2}{9b} = \frac{bA^2}{9}, \tag{4.11}$$

giving a payoff point somewhat below the Pareto set. (Recall that the value solution in this case is $P_1 = P_2 = bA^2/8$.)

The solution is similar in nature in the cases of restricted capacity or unequal costs. We shall defer the details until we consider the n-person case in the next chapter.

The noncooperative equilibrium can be illustrated geometrically (figure 4.7). It is the intersection of two equal-quantity curves ("isoquants"), the point where the curves are orthogonal, with horizontal and vertical tangents, respectively.

One attractive feature of the noncooperative-equilibrium solution as applied to oligopoly theory, or to experimental games for that matter, is that it can be associated with conditions of relatively low information and communication. For example, in an experimental game we might provide players only with information concerning moves made during the previous period (table 4.1). Furthermore they may be forbidden to communicate. In such a situation one might wish to investigate the hypothesis that each player tries to maximize his payoff on the assumption that the other repeats his previous action. This gives rise to two difference equations of the form

$P_1(q_1, q_{2,t-1})$ is maximized at $q_{1,t}$,

$P_2(q_{1,t-1}, q_2)$ is maximized at $q_{2,t}$. $\qquad$ (4.12)

If each starts with the assumption that the initial production of the other

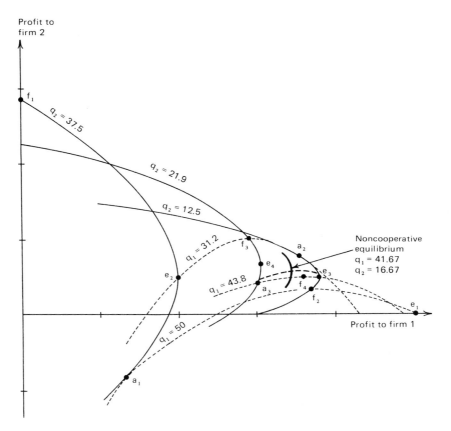

Figure 4.7
Convergence to the noncooperative equilibrium.

Table 4.1
Convergence to the noncooperative equilibrium

	Period						
	1	2	3	4	5	6	Limit
1's expected profit	25.00	9.77	19.14	15.26	17.80	16.82	
2's expected profit	14.06	1.56	4.79	2.44	3.23	2.69	
1's quantity	50.00	31.20	43.80	39.10	42.20	41.00	41.67
2's quantity	37.50	12.50	21.90	16.60	18.00	16.40	16.67
Actual price	1.125	1.562	1.344	1.453	1.398	1.426	1.4167
1's actual profit	6.25	17.58	15.04	17.70	16.81	17.46	17.361
2's actual profit	−4.69	3.91	2.05	3.17	2.67	2.88	2.778

is zero, then their expected and actual trajectories are as shown in figure 4.7. Points e_t are those expected by player 1, f_t those expected by player 2, and a_t the actual outcomes. This is an instance of what Stackelberg (1952) called a "leader–leader" relationship. Here this particular process happens to converge to the noncooperative equilibrium. All that is required is that both players never learn from experience. This particular dynamic formulation does have the advantage that it is simple and can at least be checked experimentally. Although many oligopoly experiments have been run, however, there appears to be little evidence to support this time path.

The selection of processes such as the one above is connected with the problem of finding iterative processes that lead to equilibrium points. No generally convergent processes of "learning" or "fictitious play" are known (Shapley, 1964a), but there are mathematical programming methods, not imitative of "rational" behavior, that find equilibria at least when the strategy spaces are finite (Lemke and Howson, 1964; Wilson, 1969b). We believe that the economic modeling problem of providing a useful dynamic description of an adjustment process requires far more institutional detail, behavioral knowledge, and experimentation than is currently available.

Wald (1951) has explored the conditions for the existence and uniqueness of the Cournot equilibrium under more general conditions than we shall attempt to cover.

It must be noted that capacity limitations affect this solution only when capacity is very low ($k_i < A/3$). When there is more than enough capacity for both firms to satisfy production at the level $A/3$, then an increase in capacity has no effect on the solution. This is an indication of the unimportance of threats in this solution. When entry is considered, though, the situation changes (see chapter 6).

4.3.3 The competitive equilibrium

Another solution concept—the competitive equilibrium or, more accurately when entry is not considered, the efficient point—bears mention here, although it is not strictly game-theoretic in nature. In it we assume that a market price is proposed by some outside administrator, or by some hitherto unspecified bargaining procedure or mechanism within the market. The producers then choose their q_i so as to maximize profits, on the assumption that the stated price will hold. In general this will create an imbalance between supply and demand. However, there will exist an equilibrium price, p^*, and corresponding optimal productions, q_1^* and q_2^*, that will just fill the demand at that price and clear the market.

Because of the special form of our present cost functions, this theory leads to a trivial result unless the capacity limits are operative. Indeed, if there is plenty of capacity, we have simply

$$p^* = \min(c_1, c_2). \tag{4.13}$$

The higher-cost producer (if costs are unequal) produces nothing; the other produces $q^* = (a - p^*)/b$, just clearing the market. The profits to both are zero. If costs are equal, any productions q_1^* and q_2^* totaling q^* will serve.[5]

If there is not enough low-cost capacity to saturate the market, then the equilibrium price will be higher, and one or both producers will show a profit.

For a numerical example, let the total cost curves be as shown in figure 4.8, and let the demand curve be given by $a = 2$, $b = 0.01$, that is,

$$p = 2 - 0.01q.$$

Then the efficiency price is $p^* = \$1.25$, the production schedule is $(q_1^*, q_2^*) = (60, 15)$, and the net profits are \$15 and 0, respectively.[6] If the demand were still larger relative to the capacity, say

$$p = 2.4 - 0.01q,$$

then $p^* = \$1.40$, and both players produce at capacity, earning profits of \$24 and \$6, respectively.[7] The profits per unit are the linear-programming "shadow" prices for additional capacity (Dantzig, 1963),

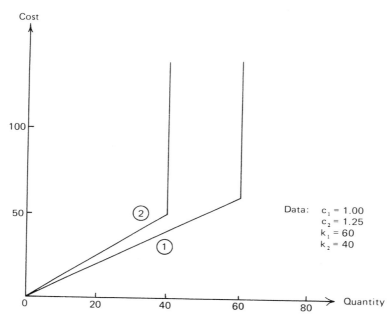

Figure 4.8
Cost functions.

which would be obtained if we regarded the firms as a single technological process and solved for efficient production levels in an open market.

Observe that in most cases the competitive-equilibrium solution is definitely suboptimal from the point of view of the duopolists, singly or together. Zero profits are not uncommon, and even in the last example described above they can do much better by limiting production. For example, if both cut their production in half, the price would go up to $1.90, and profits of $27 and $13 would result.

4.4 Closing the Model

The last two solutions discussed have been described as "competitive" or "noncooperative," to distinguish them from solutions in which the players necessarily achieve a Pareto-optimal distribution of wealth. In many situations it is quite impossible for players to achieve such a distribution without communication, and it becomes a metaphysical question to decide from observation of behavior and a description of the environment whether "collusion," "cooperation," or "competition" has taken place. The operational meaning of these words, in terms of market behavior and economic information, is not at all clear.

The way to unravel this difficulty, to the extent that it is not simply semantic, appears to be through a detailed consideration of the communications structure, the organization of the market, and the effectiveness of available mechanisms for achieving given results by means of suboptimization or decentralization. In any discussion of nonoptimality due to market imperfections, however, we must not lose sight of the fact that "optimality" is a relative concept, dependent upon the identity of the group of people whose utilities are considered important. Accordingly, even in the intentionally one-sided analysis of this chapter, we must refer occasionally to the closed model in which consumer utilities (if not consumer strategies) are represented, in order to keep our perspective.

For the immediate purpose it does no harm to aggregate consumers into a single "player," using the monetary utility function (4.2) as a basis for the linear demand curve. The aggregate payoff to the consumer, after subtracting his expenditures, is then

$$P_c = aq - \tfrac{1}{2}bq^2 - pq,$$

which reduces, by (4.1), to

$$P_c = \tfrac{1}{2}bq^2. \tag{4.14}$$

This payoff is a function only of the production strategies, since strategically the consumer is a dummy.

Our use of a consumer utility function in which money has constant marginal utility is an approximation that admittedly limits the scope of the remarks in this section. It does, however, permit us to express our analysis in terms of the *consumer surplus*, which is a well-defined and useful concept only when there is no income effect (i.e., when there is a constant marginal utility for money).

Marshall (1922) defined consumer surplus as the difference between the amount of money paid by the consumer and the amount he would pay rather than forego his purchase. In our present case this is just the amount P_c. In general, with a demand function $p = \phi(q)$, it is

$$\int_0^q \phi(x)\,dx - q\phi(q),$$

as illustrated in figure 4.9a.

Duopoly

93

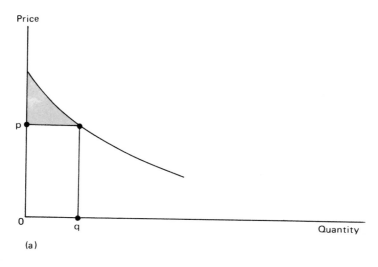

(a)

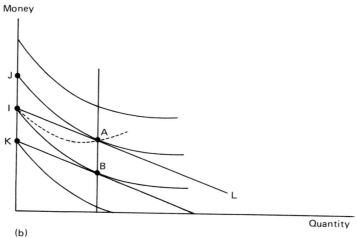

(b)

Figure 4.9
Illustrating consumer surplus and the income effect.

To see why this concept is unsatisfactory when there is an income effect, we may observe that the consumer surplus is intended as a monetary measure of what is essentially a utility difference. To illustrate, suppose that the indifference curves between money and the commodity have the appearance of figure 4.9b. The initial, no-purchase position is at I, with a utility u_1. If the consumer makes an optimal purchase at the price indicated by the slope of the line IL, he will arrive at the position A, with a utility u_2. (The dashed curve through I and A indicates his optimal purchases at other prices.) Clearly $u_2 > u_1$, but how can we ascribe a monetary value to the difference?

Two approaches might be tried. We might suppose that the consumer is in the market and ask how much it would cost to compensate him for being expelled. Clearly we must raise his income from I to J, which lies on the u_2 curve. Alternatively we might suppose that he is out of the market and ask how much he would be willing to pay to be permitted to enter. The answer is that he would lower his income down to the point K, which lies on the tangent to the u_1 curve. Unfortunately we have no assurance that $KI = IJ$, in general. But if money has a constant marginal utility, then the indifference curves will be parallel, in the sense that one can be obtained from the other by a rigid, vertical translation, and then necessarily $KI = IJ$.

In our present seller-oriented approach to oligopolistic competition in a single market, ignoring income effects on the consumer side therefore gives us, at small cost, a convenient way of measuring through the consumer surplus the degree of oligopolistic exploitation.

4.4.1 The Pareto set
The Pareto set must now be viewed in three dimensions, using (4.14). Figure 4.10 shows its appearance in the equal-cost case, with and without effective capacity limits. The set of all possible outcomes is a curved convex surface swept out by a family of parallel line segments corresponding to the different total production levels. The Pareto set is the heavily outlined portion of this surface. Note that it may include an individually irrational region of negative profit to both producers, as at the top of figure 4.10a.

Capacity limits are illustrated in figure 4.10b; they not only cut back the top of the Pareto set, wiping out the "irrational" region, but also distort its lower boundary. Along the one-dimensional "tail of the kite," the second firm is at capacity, $q_2 = 20$, while the first produces an amount between 0 and 30.

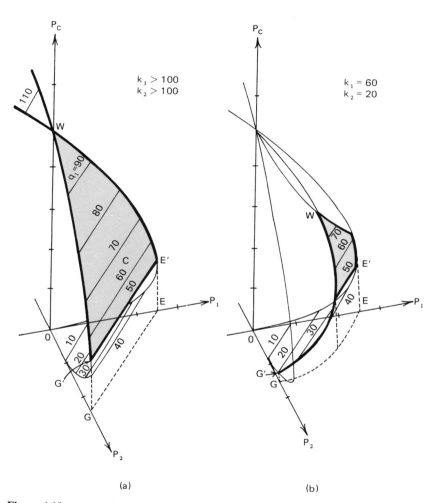

(a)   (b)

Figure 4.10
Pareto sets in the closed model (equal costs).

As usual, the equal costs have masked some additional features. In figure 4.11, which is based on the data of figure 4.4b, we see that the equal-production lines are no longer parallel to one another, so that the ruled surface they sweep out is neither convex nor concave at any point. Convexification by means of mixed strategies therefore becomes, as before, a significant possibility that, as before, we shall nevertheless proceed to disregard.

More strikingly, the inequality in costs creates a new one-dimensional section of the Pareto surface ($E'YW$ in the figure) that could scarcely have been anticipated from the equal-cost diagrams. Points on this curve correspond to prices between the two firms' average costs. Rather than let the less efficient firm produce at a loss (leading to an outcome such as X in figure 4.11, which lies behind the $P_2 = 0$ plane), all three players would prefer a higher production at a lower price, supplied entirely by the more efficient firm (as at Y).

The relation of the closed model to the previous, open model may be seen by projecting the various diagrams down onto the $P_c = 0$ plane, that is, by ignoring the utility of the consumer. Figures 4.10a, 4.10b, and 4.11 then reduce to figures 4.4d, 4.6c, and 4.4b, respectively. The Pareto set in each case is the curve GE, the image of $G'E'$ in the three-dimensional representation. We see, therefore, that the open-model Pareto set consists of that subset of the closed-model Pareto set that is "worst" from the point of view of the consumers.

In sum, merely by taking the consumer's utility into account we can enlarge the Pareto "solution" in their favor, without giving them any strategic options or otherwise changing the economics of the situation. This gives a good example of the relativity of the optimality concept.

4.4.2 The noncooperative equilibrium

The letter C in figure 4.10a marks the noncooperative-equilibrium point, with productions $(33\frac{1}{3}, 33\frac{1}{3})$; for unequal capacities the point is at $(40, 20)$. Both of these are on the Pareto-optimal surface in three dimensions. This must be true if the cost conditions of the duopolists are identical. It may fail when their costs differ, although in the case illustrated in figure 4.11 the noncooperative equilibrium has production strategies $(50, 0)$, yielding the Pareto point E'.

The location of the noncooperative equilibrium with respect to the Pareto-optimal surface in a closed model is of considerable importance to economic policy. An attack can be leveled against an oligopolistic market from the viewpoint of either distribution or efficiency. In the

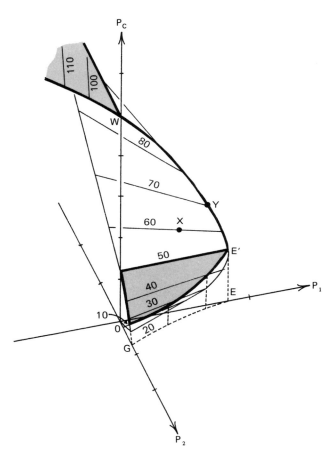

Figure 4.11
Unequal costs.

first case one might argue that according to some social criterion the firms are earning "too much." In the second instance, if the noncooperative equilibrium is not Pareto-optimal for society as a whole, we can argue that controls or a change in market organization would put the whole economy in a position to gain (Debreu, 1951).

Two important properties of noncooperative equilibria are their *uniqueness* and their *efficiency*. The one-shot Cournot models considered here have unique equilibria. Rosen (1965) discussed general conditions for the uniqueness of pure-strategy noncooperative equilibria for concave games. Uniqueness is in fact the exception rather than the rule. The presence of a unique equilibrium may enhance the possibilities for finding dynamic processes that converge to an equilibrium (see Goodman, 1980), but other difficulties (such as the characterization of threat strategies, communication, and information) appear when we attempt to study dynamics.

The efficiency of noncooperative equilibria when there are few players is clearly of considerable policy concern. Dubey (1980) and Dubey and Rogawski (1982) have shown under completely general conditions that noncooperative equilibria are generically inefficient; that is, almost always we can expect that the outcomes from a noncooperative equilibrium will yield payoffs that are not Pareto-optimal. This result provides an added incentive for the construction of a welfare measure of oligopoly loss.

4.4.3 The efficient point
The strategic helplessness of the consumers is shown by the fact that most solutions do not change in their favor when we close the model. In particular, the efficient point (W in the figures) could hardly be expected to move, since it is already the most favorable imputation in the game for the consumers.[8] In figure 4.10b the firms produce at full capacity, making a profit. In figure 4.11 the inefficient firm is priced out of the market while the other produces and sells at cost.

By projecting W onto the $P_c = 0$ plane we see once again that the efficient point is definitely not optimal in the open model. With consumer utility included, however, it becomes optimal.

4.4.4 The core
The core, too, is the same in the open and closed models, since, under our strategic assumptions, coalitions involving the (aggregated) consumer player do not offer any advantage. The closed representation does, however, help us to contrast the core with the efficient-point solution. When

there is plenty of capacity, as in figures 4.10a and 4.11, the competitive solution W and the core $G'E'$ occupy opposite extremes in the space of imputations. The competitive equilibrium is best for the consumer; and the core is best for the producer.

With effective capacity constraints, the contrast is still more striking. The efficient point, which was never an imputation in the two-person (open) game, is now not even an imputation in the three-person (closed) game, since it is not individually rational. In effect, the efficient point does not allow either firm to profit from the limited capacity of the other firm. The core, meanwhile, shrinks to a proper subset of the set $G'E'$ in the presence of capacity constraint, as shown in figure 4.10b, expressing the fact that when one firm cannot saturate the market, the other can unilaterally guarantee itself a positive profit. This was previously illustrated in figure 4.6 (figure 4.6b is the projection of figure 4.10b).

4.4.5 The value
The value, too, is unchanged, since a strategic dummy can be assigned zero weight in the utility comparison induced by a no-side-payment game (see *GTSS*, chapter 7).

A cautionary note is necessary, since the device of treating all the consumers as a single player is inappropriate for a solution concept that relies so heavily on "external symmetry," that is, on putting all players on an equal footing. The proper game model here is to represent the consumer side as an infinite continuum, each individual member of which is negligible to the market as a whole in his purchases and consumption. If this model were constructed and its value solution determined, however, the result would be the same, precisely because the consumers, separately or en masse, are still strategically helpless.[9]

4.4.6 The closed model with side payments
It might be instructive, finally, to examine the effect of closing the side-payment version of the duopoly model. This is not equivalent to applying side-payment theory to the three-person model with a strategic dummy, which we have just been treating, since the consumer player (or players) would then become active bargaining participants, willing and able to pay for benefits received.

The correct extension, instead, would be to introduce restricted side payments only, that is, payments between the duopolists. If we did so, we would obtain comparisons with the open-model solutions in sections 4.2 and 4.3 quite analogous to the comparisons we have already discussed for the no-side-payment case.

Notes to chapter 4

1. Compare Allen and Bowley (1935), Chipman (1965, p. 692), or Diewert (1969).

2. The possibility of one firm producing nothing is related to entry and exit conditions.

3. In this case the threat point coincides with the competitive equilibrium. This is always true in symmetric market games, but not so without symmetry. (See Shubik, 1959b.)

4. In this case, with production as the independent variable, this leads to the Cournot solution.

5. The use of constant average costs and an open model have led to a first indication of one of the paradoxical results of microeconomic theory under partial-equilibrium competitive conditions. If one firm is more efficient than the others and has the capacity, then the "industry" will end up with only that firm active. If several firms have the same constant average costs, then the theory does not predict how the market is to be split between them.

   A standard way around the paradox is to argue that after some point the firms will exhibit decreasing returns to scale, which can be attributed to overcrowding, difficulties in administration, and so forth. Unless one wishes to abandon the assumption that any production function is at least homogeneous of the first degree, the decreasing-returns-to-scale model of a firm cannot be defended. The difficulties concerning entry, size of the firm, and numbers in an industry disappear when one works with closed models of the economy. These comments will be amplified further in chapter 7.

6. Remarkably, this outcome is not individually rational in the game version of the model. Player 2, by producing $q_2 = 7.5$, can assure himself a profit of \$0.56 if the market prices are not administered.

7. This is still not individually rational, since player 2 can assure \$7.56 in the game version.

8. It must be stressed here that as long as we do not consider entry, it is more proper to speak of the solution in which all firms take the price as given and adjust their production accordingly as "the efficient-point solution" rather than as the competitive equilibrium. The first instance is usually associated with a unified economy; when entry is considered, the model of the market with price as given is a decentralized one.

9. In principle the core should also be treated in this way in the closed model, since if coalitions involving the consumer side had any effectiveness whatsoever, we would want to consider coalitions involving all possible fractions of the whole. Since they do not, we are spared this complication.

5 Generalization to *n* Firms

5.1 The Concept of an Industry

In keeping with the approach outlined at the beginning of chapter 4, we shall carry out an intensive analysis of a rather special model, indicating where possible the more general validity of our results. Even working with simple models, we can often make explicit some of the problems that are easy to gloss over in verbal treatments or in facile attempts at mathematical generality.

In particular, if we are to talk sensibly about the effects of the number of competing firms and of their relative sizes, we must come to grips with the notion of an industry. Obviously the working definition of an industry should depend on the purposes for which it is to be used. In line with our immediate concern with size and number of firms we take a simple view: An industry is merely a group of firms selling the same product to the same set of customers. Product differentiation is suppressed, as well as the possibility of discriminating among customers and the possibility of firms entering or leaving the industry. These factors will be considered in later chapters; but for the present purpose the key property is the strategic interdependence of the firms, and we can model this clearly and adequately without going beyond the case of identical products.

Indeed we are able to satisfy many of our objectives within the still narrower confines of an equal-cost model. Among the technical simplifications obtained by concentrating on this model, an important one is the erasing of most of the distinctions between the side-payment and no-side-payment theories, since with equal costs the effect of a u-money can for the most part be achieved through coordinated production decisions.

We shall repeatedly have occasion to construct series of similar game models of different sizes, in order to examine the transitional and limiting properties of economic systems as the number of participants is increased. The simplest way to do this is to take a given model and expand it homogeneously. We thereby retain a valid basis for comparison between different sizes, which is especially important when we pass to the limit.

Such an expansion is of course merely a didactic device—a manipulation of models—and is not intended to represent a real economic process in which new firms enter a growing industry.

A formal equivalence often exists between homogeneous expansion in this sense and the process of fragmentation or disaggregation of the economic agents in a model of fixed absolute size. The latter may be easier to think about, though, especially when we touch the limiting case itself. Thus, in the infinite-player models that we shall occasionally consider, it will be easier to work with infinitely small players than with infinitely large quantities of goods.

As we increase the number of producers in the present one-sided analysis, we maintain homogeneity not by explicitly increasing the number of consumers (whom we are not counting anyway), but rather by expanding the aggregated consumer demand.

5.2 The Model

Generalizing the demand structure of chapter 4 to the case of n firms, we shall assume that the monetary measure of the total benefit consumers derive from q units of the commodity is

$$u = aq - bq^2/n \qquad (5.1)$$

(cf. equation 4.2). The price p that will induce consumers to purchase q units is therefore

$$p = a - 2bq/n, \qquad (5.2)$$

generalizing (4.1). Thus the absolute size of a one-nth part of the market remains constant as a function of n. As a result, solution elements pertaining to individual firms do not require rescaling when n is changed, although elements pertaining to the industry as a whole must be divided by n before valid comparisons can be made.

As before, there will be cost parameters c_i and capacity parameters k_i that will characterize the different firms. In subsequent chapters parameters pertaining to overhead and entry will be introduced; until then, the profit of a firm is merely the direct generalization of (4.3):

$$P_i = q_i \left(a - c_i - \frac{2bq}{n} \right) = bq_i \left(A_i - \frac{2q}{n} \right) \quad (i = 1, 2, \ldots, n). \qquad (5.3)$$

Here q (as always) is the sum of the productions q_i, and A_i is our old friend $(a - c_i)/b$.[1]

The n-person game to be solved, then, has strategies q_i, constrained by $0 \le q_i \le k_i$, and payoffs P_i given by (5.3).

As already noted, the equal-average-cost case $c_i \equiv c$ will suffice for most of our investigation. In this case (5.3) reduces to

$$P_i = bq_i \left(A - \frac{2q}{n} \right) \quad (i = 1, 2, \ldots, n), \tag{5.4}$$

which we shall use until further notice.

5.2.1 The Pareto set and the imputation space
Until we come to the solution concepts in which coalitions play a role, this model behaves almost exactly like its duopoly counterpart treated in chapter 4, and we can move quickly through the preliminary analysis. The Pareto set, if there is plenty of capacity, is given by the linear equation

$$\sum q_i = \frac{nA}{4}$$

in the strategy space, which transforms to

$$\sum P_i = \frac{nbA^2}{8} \tag{5.5}$$

in the payoff space. With side payments the Pareto set is the entire hyperplane (5.5); without side payments it is the simplex carved out of that hyperplane by the n inequalities $P_i \ge 0$, since if even one firm were producing at a loss, all firms would benefit by having it shut down.

Since the individually rational limits are also $P_i \ge 0$ $(i = 1, 2, \ldots, n)$, the imputation space with plenty of capacity is the same simplex; this holds true whether or not side payments are allowed.

If capacity is limited, (5.5) continues to apply only so long as the total capacity of the industry is at least $nA/4$, the amount required for monopolistic production at average cost c. In general we have

$$\sum P_i = \begin{cases} \dfrac{nbA^2}{8} & \text{if } K \ge \dfrac{nA}{4}, \\[2ex] \dfrac{2bK}{n}\left(\dfrac{nA}{2} - K \right) & \text{if } K \le \dfrac{nA}{4}, \end{cases} \tag{5.6}$$

where K denotes the total capacity $\sum k_i$.

The imputation simplex in the side-payment case, however, is affected as soon as K gets down to approximately $nA/2$, since individual firms will then be protected against a total saturation of the market by the others. The individually rational limits are, in general,

$$P_i \geq 0 \qquad\qquad\qquad \text{if } K - k_i \geq \frac{nA}{2},$$

$$P_i \geq \frac{b}{2n}\left(\frac{nA}{2} - (K - k_i)\right)^2 \quad \text{if } K - k_i \leq \frac{nA}{2} \leq K + k_i, \qquad (5.7)$$

$$P_i \geq \frac{2bk_i}{n}\left(\frac{nA}{2} - K\right) \qquad \text{if } K + k_i \leq \frac{nA}{2}.$$

This is quite analogous to what we observed in section 4.2.4.

Without side payments the imputation space is no longer a simplex, unless each producer happens to be big enough to produce $nA/4$ by himself—an unlikely state of affairs if n is large. If $K > nA/4$, then some adjustment of individual production rates is possible without diminishing the total profit, but the utility transfers thereby made possible will not in general extend all the way into the "corners" of the side-payment imputation simplex. Hence the no-side-payment imputation space may be a simplex with its "corners turned down." If several players are near their individually rational minimum, then the others may not have the capacity to raise total production to the monopolistic level. This effect did not appear with $n = 2$ (compare figure 5.7); it appears in a small way for $n = 3$ and becomes increasing prominent for larger n.[2]

EXERCISE
5.1. *Determine the side-payment and no-side-payment imputation spaces for $n = 3$, $nA/2 = 10$, $b = 1$, and $k_1 = k_2 = k_3 = k$, letting k range from 0 to 5.*

5.2.2 The efficient point
As in the case of duopoly, the efficient point yields zero profits if there is unlimited capacity. This solution requires a total production of $nA/2$, double the monopolistic rate. If the combined capacities come to less than $nA/2$, then everyone produces at capacity and enjoys a positive profit.

The price at the efficient point is

$$p_{\text{eff}} = \max\left(c, a - \frac{2bK}{n}\right) = c + \max\left[0, \frac{2b}{n}\left(\frac{nA}{2} - K\right)\right], \qquad (5.8)$$

and hence the payoffs are

$$P_i = \max\left[0, \frac{2bk_i}{n}\left(\frac{nA}{2} - K\right)\right] \quad (i = 1, 2, \ldots, n).$$

Comparing this with (5.7) we see that the efficient point is either just barely individually rational or, in the case $|K - nA/2| < k_i$, actually irrational. This confirms what we found in chapter 4. Note, however, that the extent of the "irrational" case is relatively small when *n* is large.

5.3 The Noncooperative Solution

The noncooperative solution gives us the first interesting results that depend on the size of the industry, in contrast to the rather barren generalizations so far noted.

To find the equilibrium point we set $\partial P_i/\partial q_i = 0$ in (5.4) and obtain

$$q + q_i = \frac{nA}{2} \quad (i = 1, 2, \ldots, n). \tag{5.9}$$

These are necessary conditions for a pure-strategy equilibrium $(q_1^\#, q_2^\#, \ldots, q_n^\#)$ in the interior of the strategy space. Summing on *i* yields

$$(n + 1)q = \frac{n^2 A}{2},$$

and substituting for *q* in (5.9) and solving for q_i yields

$$q_i^\# = \frac{nA}{2(n + 1)} \quad (i = 1, 2, \ldots, n). \tag{5.10}$$

This proves to be the unique equilibrium point, provided only that there is enough capacity to sustain it, that is, provided that $k_i \geq q_i^\#$ for all *i*. The noncooperative price is

$$p^\# = c + \frac{bA}{(n + 1)}, \tag{5.11}$$

and the associated payoffs are

$$P_i^\# = \frac{nbA^2}{2(n + 1)^2} \quad (i = 1, 2, \ldots, n),$$

generalizing what we found in chapter 4.

As *n* grows, this solution becomes worse and worse for the oligopolists, converging in the limit to the efficient-point solution:

$$q_i^{\#} \to \frac{A}{2}, \qquad p^{\#} \to c, \qquad P_i^{\#} \to 0.$$

For the passive, price-taking consumers, of course, the solution becomes better and better as n increases. Figure 5.1 illustrates this. Thus oligopolistic production blends imperceptibly into efficient production. This is the first of many such results we shall have occasion to describe. The rate of convergence, of the order of $1/n$, is typical. To be sure, the total profit to the producers remains positive, converging to the amount $bA^2/2$, but it is divided among more and more competitors as n increases (see table 5.1).

5.3.1 Limited capacity
If not all producers can attain the production level stipulated in (5.10), the noncooperative solution changes in a natural way. Those who cannot attain $nA/2(n + 1)$ produce at capacity; the others produce more if they can.

In fact, for the general solution we have

$$q_i^{\#} = \min(k_i, q_0) \quad (i = 1, 2, \ldots, n), \tag{5.12}$$

where

$$q_0 = \frac{nA}{2} - \sum_{i=1}^{n} q_i^{\#}. \tag{5.13}$$

The price that results is

$$p^{\#} = c + \frac{2bq_0}{n},$$

and the profits are

$$P_i^{\#} = \frac{2bq_0 q_i^{\#}}{n} \quad (i = 1, 2, \ldots, n). \tag{5.14}$$

Here q_0 represents the amount by which total production is held below the efficient rate and also (because of our linear demand function) the production rate adopted by all firms that have sufficient capacity (see figure 5.2). Equations (5.12) and (5.13) uniquely determine q_0, and it can be shown that q_0 is at least as large as the unlimited capacity rate $nA/2(n + 1)$ of (5.10).

EXERCISE
5.2.   *Show that in the limited-capacity case q_0 satisfies*

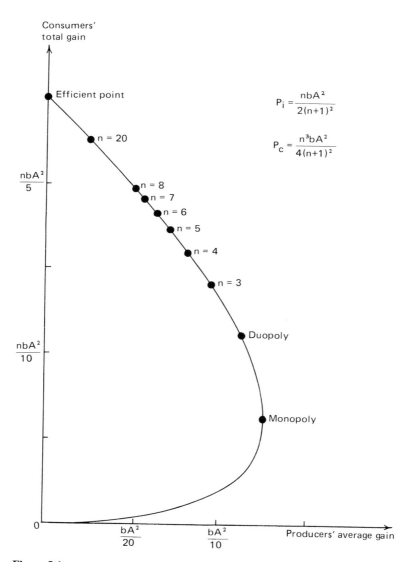

Figure 5.1
Convergence of the noncooperative equilibrium to the efficient point.

Table 5.1
Convergence of the noncooperative equilibrium

n	Symmetrical joint maximization	Noncooperative equilibrium	Efficient point
1	12.5	12.50	0
2	12.5	11.11	0
3	12.5	9.38	0
4	12.5	8.00	0
5	12.5	6.94	0
10	12.5	4.13	0

Individual payoffs ($bA^2 = 100$), plenty of capacity.

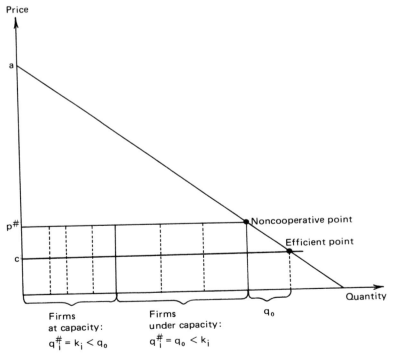

Figure 5.2
The noncooperative equilibrium with unequal capacities.

$$q_* \le q_0 \le q_* + \sum_{i=1}^{n} \max(0, q_* - k_i),$$

where $q_* = nA/2(n+1)$ is the equilibrium-point production without capacity constraints.

5.3.2 Convergence

The convergence question is more complex than in the case of unlimited capacities, since the symmetry of the players is lost. Indeed the structure of the industry may be such that an oligopolistic advantage can be maintained even in the presence of arbitrarily many firms. We shall give an example of this and then describe conditions under which convergence to the efficient point is assured.

The example is very simple. Let one firm have effectively unlimited capacity, say $k_i = nA/2$. Let the other $n - 1$ firms have identical capacities of $k_i = A/3$. (Any other capacity between 0 and $A/2$ would do as well.) Solving (5.12) and (5.13), we obtain

$$q_0 = \frac{(n+2)A}{12},$$

whence

$$p^{\#} = c + \frac{(n+2)bA}{6n} \to c + \frac{bA}{6} \text{ as } n \to \infty.$$

The price thus stays distinctly above c even though the industry has capacity to supply the whole market efficiently. What is happening, of course, is that a substantial fraction of the necessary capacity is in the hands of one producer who, as n increases, comes to act more and more like a monopolist.

THEOREM 5.1.   *Let $\{k_i\}$ be an infinite sequence such that*

$$k_n/n \to 0 \quad as \quad n \to \infty. \tag{5.15}$$

Let $p^{\#}(n)$ denote the noncooperative price of the equal-cost n-firm market with capacities $k_1, k_2, \ldots, k_n$; and let $p_{\text{eff}}(n)$ denote the efficient-point price of the same market. Then

$$p^{\#}(n) - p_{\text{eff}}(n) \to 0 \quad as \quad n \to \infty. \tag{5.16}$$

Proof. For each n there are two possibilities:

(a) $q_i^{\#} = k_i$ for all i;
(b) $q_0 < k_{\max}(n) = \max_{1 \le i \le n} k_i$.

When (a) occurs, we have $p^{\#}(n) = p_{\text{eff}}(n)$, since all firms are producing at capacity. If there are only finitely many occurrences of (b), then (5.16) follows immediately. If (b) occurs for an infinite set $\mathcal{N}_b$ of values of n, we observe that

$$p^{\#}(n) = c + \frac{2bq_0}{n} < c + \frac{2bk_{\max}(n)}{n}.$$

It is a simple exercise to show from (5.15) that $k_{\max}(n)/n \to 0$. Hence $p^{\#}(n) \to c$ for n in $\mathcal{N}_b$. But since $p^{\#} \geq p_{\text{eff}} \geq c$ always, we have $p^{\#}(n) - p_{\text{eff}}(n) \to 0$ for n in $\mathcal{N}_b$. Hence (5.16) follows. ∎

The condition (5.16) ensures that all firms are ultimately small compared to the total market demand, which is proportional to n in our model. Other conditions could be used instead, for example, one that allowed firms to have large capacities but required that there be many such firms, so that the situation encountered in the example at the beginning of this section would not occur.

EXERCISES

5.3. *Show that $p^{\#}(n)$ does not converge to $p_{\text{eff}}(n)$ if*

$$k_n = \begin{cases} 5An & \text{for n a power of 10,} \\ A/20 & \text{otherwise.} \end{cases}$$

(Here the capacities are fixed, finite numbers, unlike the example of non-convergence in the text.)

5.4. *Show that the theorem remains valid if (5.15) is replaced by the condition that $k_n \to \infty$.*

5.3.3 A more general model

The preceding results on convergence are more general than our basic linear model might indicate, and it is worth a digression to establish this fact, before we turn to the cooperative solutions.

Consider a market composed of n firms with total cost functions $C_i(q_i)$ that are continuous, nondecreasing, and *convex* on the interval $0 \leq q_i \leq k_i$, with $C_i(0) = 0$. Let the demand be given by a function $\Phi(q)$ that is continuous, strictly decreasing, and *concave* on the interval $0 \leq q \leq \hat{q}$, with $\Phi(\hat{q}) = 0$.

These conditions imply no fixed costs and nondecreasing marginal costs. Thus the average costs can only rise, and the U-shaped case is ruled out (see figure 5.3). As for the demand the concavity of Φ ensures that

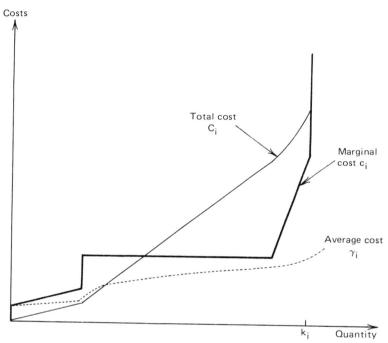

Costs

Total cost
C_i

Marginal
cost c_i

Average cost
γ_i

k_i Quantity

Figure 5.3
Illustrating the relations among cost curves.

that while a price cut always expands the demand (thus ruling out the phenomenon of inferior goods), the amount of expansion will vary inversely with the price. The greatest effect on demand, for a given price cut, comes at the top of the price scale.

Because the convexity and concavity conditions do not exclude linearity, our basic model is still with us. In fact, since we do not actually need the full force of these conditions in what follows, the basic linear model is not even the borderline case it might appear to be.

The payoff function is

$$P_i(q_1, q_2, \ldots, q_n) = q_i \Phi(q) - C_i(q_i) \quad (i = 1, 2, \ldots, n), \tag{5.17}$$

where $q = \sum q_i$ as usual. We note that under our assumptions each P_i is a strictly concave in a q_i and concave in q. This may be seen most readily by twice differentiating (5.17) formally, as though the necessary derivatives all existed, and then recognizing that the result is negative and will remain negative even if finite differences are substituted for the derivatives.

Despite the possibility of nonexistent derivatives, it will be convenient to introduce the marginal costs $c_i(q_i)$, using multivalued functions if necessary. Accordingly we take $c_i(q_i)$ to be the slope of all nondecreasing linear functions that support the convex function C_i at q_i.[3] By this device we can accommodate in the model discontinuous marginal costs, which can arise quite naturally when there are several production methods of differing efficiencies. By "filling in" the discontinuities (including any gaps at the ends), we obtain for the graph of c_i a continuous curve in the plane, running monotonically from zero at $q_i = 0$ to infinity at $q_i = k_i$. (See figure 5.3.)

The inverses c_i^{-1} are functions of a similar kind—monotonic nondecreasing with continuous graphs, multivalued where c_i was constant and constant where c_i was multivalued. With the aid of these inverses we can describe the *efficient-point solution* in a concise way: p_{eff} is the unique solution of the equation

$$p = \Phi\left(\sum_{i=1}^{n} c_i^{-1}(p) \right). \tag{5.18}$$

(Note that the right-hand side of this equation, which is in general multivalued, has a continuously decreasing graph, which crosses the strictly increasing graph of the left-hand side at exactly one point.) The efficient total production $q_{\text{eff}} = \sum c_i^{-1}(p_{\text{eff}}) = \Phi^{-1}(p_{\text{eff}})$ is also unique, though the individual shares $q_{i,\text{eff}} = c_i^{-1}(p_{\text{eff}})$ need not be.

In order to find the noncooperative equilibrium point, it is convenient also to introduce a *marginal demand function*, $\phi(q)$. This is the derivative of Φ where it exists, and, as with the c_i, it will be assumed to take on all values between the right- and left-hand derivatives when the slope of Φ changes discontinuously. Thus the graph of ϕ starts at the origin, becomes negative at once, and finally drops off to $-\infty$ at $q = \hat{q}$.

A necessary and sufficient condition for an equilibrium point can now be obtained by "differentiating" (5.17) and equating the result to zero, thus:

$$q_i\phi(q) + \Phi(q) - c_i(q_i) = 0 \quad (i = 1, 2, \ldots, n). \tag{5.19}$$

Remember that ϕ and the c_i may be multivalued. Thus, at any equilibrium point the n equations (5.19) must hold for some set of values of the multivalued functions. (The values for $\phi(q)$ need not agree in different equations.) The necessity of these conditions is easy to see; the sufficiency follows from the fact, already noted, that the payoff functions are concave.

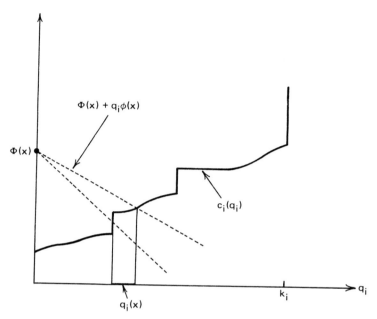

Figure 5.4
Illustrating the solutions of $c_i(q_i) = \Phi(x) + q_i\phi(x)$.

THEOREM 5.2. *Assuming convex total costs and concave demand, as specified above, a noncooperative equilibrium point exists. It may not be unique, but the total production $q^* = \sum q_i^*$ is unique, as is the price $p^* = \Phi(q^*)$. If Φ is differentiable at q^*, then the q_i^* are also unique.*

The idea of the proof is to use an artificial production target x to determine demand conditions $\Phi(x)$ and $\phi(x)$, which in turn elicit production decisions $q_i(x)$ from the individual firms. As x varies upward from 0, the sum of the $q_i(x)$ goes down, until the unique point of coincidence $x^* = \sum q_i(x^*)$ is encountered.

Now for the proof itself. Consider the equation

$$c_i(q_i) = \Phi(x) + q_i\phi(x), \tag{5.20}$$

where q_i is the variable and x is, for the moment, any number in the interval $0 \leq x \leq \hat{q}$. We assert that (5.20) has a solution, $q_i(x)$, that is either unique or a closed interval. Moreover, we assert that $q_i(x)$, regarded as a (possibly multivalued) function of x, is nonincreasing and has a continuous graph.

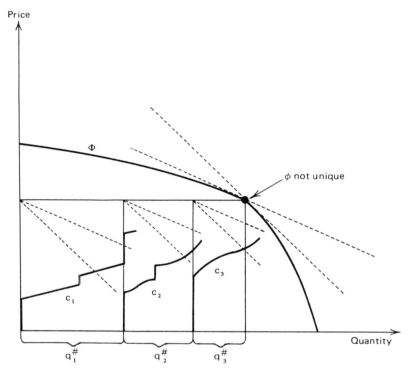

Figure 5.5
An example of a nonunique equilibrium point.

These assertions can be immediately verified from figure 5.4.[4] The strictly descending straight lines (dashed) always intersect the graph of $c_i(q_i)$ in a single point. But because $\phi(x)$ may be multivalued, there may be a "fan" of lines, giving rise to the possibility of a closed interval of solutions (as shown). If x increases, then $\Phi(x)$ decreases and $\phi(x)$ decreases or remains constant, so the new line (or fan of lines) will lie distinctly beneath the old; hence the value of $q_i(x)$ does not increase.

Now consider the following equation in x:

$$x = \sum_{i=1}^{n} q_i(x). \tag{5.21}$$

This bears a strong resemblance to (5.18): On the left-hand side we have a single-valued function that increases continuously from 0, while on the right-hand side we have a function that, like its separate terms, is nonnegative, does not increase, and has a connected graph. We conclude that there is a unique x^* satisfying (5.21). Moreover, if Φ is differentiable at x^*, $\phi(x^*)$ is single-valued, and we avoid the "fan" situation. All the $q_i(x^*)$ are then unique.

If we now identify x^* with q^*, $\Phi(x)$ with p^*, and $q_i(x^*)$ with q_i^* for $i = 1, 2, \ldots, n$, we see that all of the statements in the theorem have been established.

The nonuniqueness possibility is illustrated in figure 5.5. The individual market shares q_i^* can be varied, provided that their sum q^* remains fixed and the marginal costs $c_i(q_i^*)$ have values in the intervals permitted by the multivalued slope of Φ at q^*. We emphasize that the nonuniqueness does not extend to the individual players; each one's equilibrium-point strategy is determined when the strategies of the others are given. What is more, each equilibrium is stable, in the sense that each player selects the unique maximum of a strictly concave objective function.

EXERCISES

5.5.   *Show that for our conditions on C_i to be satisfied it is necessary but not sufficient that the average cost function $\gamma_i = C_i/q_i$ be nondecreasing, and it is sufficient but not necessary that γ_i be nondecreasing and convex.*

5.6.   *Show that the convexity of C_i can be weakened to the condition that $c_i(q_i) - \phi(0)q_i$ be nondecreasing. Can the term $\phi(0)q_i$ be replaced here by $\phi(q_i)q_i$? By $\Phi(q_i)$?*

5.7.   *Show that the concavity of Φ can be weakened to the condition that Φ/ϕ be an increasing and $\Phi + q\phi$ a decreasing function of q (both are negative; see figure 5.6). Find an example of a nonconcave demand function that satisfies these conditions.*

5.3.4 Convergence in the general model

To investigate convergence we shall replicate the model homogeneously. Let there now be n *types* of firms, each type having a cost function C_i as above, and let there be r firms of each type. In our analysis n will be fixed and r variable. In order for the demand to keep pace with the growth of r, we take the demand function in the rth model to be

$$\Phi_r(q) = \Phi(q/r),\tag{5.22}$$

where Φ is as above. Obviously each Φ_r inherits the properties postulated for Φ, and we have

$$\phi_r(q) = \phi(q/r)/r.\tag{5.23}$$

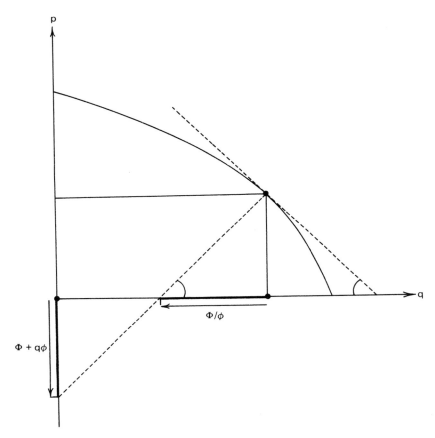

Figure 5.6
Illustrating the conditions of exercise 5.7.

If q_{ij} denotes the production of the jth player of type i, the payoff function can be written

$$P_{ij}(q_{11}, q_{12}, \ldots, q_{1r}, q_{21}, q_{22}, \ldots, q_{2r}, \ldots, q_{n1}, q_{n2}, \ldots, q_{nr})$$
$$= q_{ij}\Phi_r(q) - C_i(q_{ij}),$$

where q here denotes the sum of all the q_{ij}.

The efficient-point solution is essentially independent of r, since the equation corresponding to (5.18) is

$$p = \Phi_r\left(\sum_{j=1}^{r} \sum_{i=1}^{n} c_i^{-1}(p)\right), \tag{5.24}$$

which reduces with the aid of (5.22) to (5.18) itself. Thus the efficient price is just p_{eff} of the previous section, and the same individual production rates will serve, though the total production is of course multiplied by r.

Applying the theorem of section 5.3.3 for a fixed r, we see that the noncooperative equilibrium point exists and satisfies the nr equations

$$q_{ij}\phi_r(q) + \Phi_r(q) - c_i(q_{ij}) = 0 \qquad (i = 1, 2, \ldots, n; j = 1, 2, \ldots, r) \tag{5.25}$$

(compare (5.19)); moreover the total production $q^*(r)$ and the noncooperative price $p^*(r) = \Phi_r(q^*(r))$ are unique even if the individual strategies $q_{ij}(r)$ are not. We are now ready to pass to the limit.[5]

THEOREM 5.3. *Under conditions of convex total costs and concave demand, as stated at the beginning of section 5.3.3,*

$$p^*(r) \to p_{\text{eff}} \quad as \quad r \to \infty$$

for the r-times replicated model.

Proof. We first observe that $p^*(r) \geq p_{\text{eff}}$ for all r. The convergence will be established by showing that for any price p' that is greater than p_{eff} we eventually have $p^*(r) < p'$.

Let $q_{i,\text{eff}}$ $(i = 1, 2, \ldots, n)$ be efficient individual productions for the unreplicated model, with sum equal to $q_{\text{eff}} = \Phi^{-1}(p_{\text{eff}})$. Defining $q' = \Phi^{-1}(p')$, we have $q' < q_{\text{eff}}$. Choose r so large that the inequality

$$(p' - p_{\text{eff}})r > |\phi(q')|q_{i,\text{eff}} \tag{5.26}$$

holds for all i and for all values of the (possibly multivalued) term $\phi(q')$; the latter cannot be infinite because $q' < q_{\text{eff}} \leq \hat{q}$. If we define $x = q'r$, then $\phi_r(x) = \phi(q')/r$, and we have for each i

$$|\phi_r(x)|q_{i,\text{eff}} < p' - p_{\text{eff}}.$$

Since $\Phi_r(x) = \Phi(q') = p'$ and $\phi_r(x) \leq 0$, we can rewrite this as

$p_{\mathrm{eff}} < \Phi_r(x) + q_{i,\mathrm{eff}}\,\phi_r(x)$.

Compare this with equation (5.20) (with subscripts r added). Since p_{eff} is by definition a value of $c_i(q_{i,\mathrm{eff}})$, we see that the solution of that equation must be a number (or set of numbers) greater than or equal to $q_{i,\mathrm{eff}}$. Call that solution $q_{ij}(x)$. Summing over all nr players, we find

$$\sum_{i=1}^{n}\sum_{j=1}^{r} q_{ij}(x) \geq r \sum_{i=1}^{n} q_{i,\mathrm{eff}} = r q_{\mathrm{eff}} > r q' = x.$$

Thus x is too small to satisfy the analog of (5.21), the equation we solve to obtain the total equilibrium production $x^{\#} = q^{\#}(r)$. Hence $q^{\#}(r) > x = q'r$, and we have

$$p^{\#}(r) = \Phi_r(q^{\#}(r)) < \Phi_r(q'r) = \Phi(q') = p',$$

as was to be shown. ∎

Although we have not shown it rigorously, the form of the condition (5.26) on the choice of r suggests that the rate of convergence of $p^{\#}(r)$ to p_{eff} is of order $1/r$.

EXERCISE
5.8. *Using methods similar to those in the proof of the theorem, show that the sequence $p^{\#}(r)$ decreases monotonically to its limit. Under what conditions is the limit attained for a finite r?*

The result presented above is a slight generalization of Cournot's (1897) famous result. Wald (1951) has shown that other possibilities exist for nonuniqueness of the noncooperative equilibrium in the Cournot model; and as can be seen from the examples in *GTSS*, chapters 8–10, the noncooperative equilibrium is, in general, a far less satisfactory solution than it might at first appear to be. Nevertheless from Cournot to the present time a great amount of economic theorizing about oligopoly has been based upon an implicit or explicit assumption that the multiplicity of noncooperative equilibria is not very important in market models and that "as the number of competitors becomes large" the competitive equilibrium is approached.

5.4 Cooperative Solutions

In the cooperative game unlimited capacity implies a "pure deterrence" situation in which every producer has the power to ruin the market for everyone. This is both uninteresting and economically implausible. For our basic investigative model we shall therefore assume, in the equal-cost case, that the total capacity of all firms is just enough to supply the whole market at cost.

The appearance of the deterrence model here is primarily due to inadequate modeling of the rules of capacity, investment, overheads, and entry. Following our policy of dividing difficulties, we defer comment on those important features until chapter 7.

For convenience of notation we shall use N to denote the set of all n firms and express capacity as a set function; thus $k(S) = \sum_S k_i$, where S is any subset of N. The assumption of limited capacity then takes the form

$$k(N) = \frac{n(a-c)}{2b} = \frac{nA}{2}. \tag{5.27}$$

5.4.1 The characteristic function

In the eyes of a coalition S, the worst that can happen is for the opposing coalition to "flood the market" with its full capacity $k(N - S)$. The best defense for S is to produce $q_S = k(S)/2$, which satisfies half the remaining demand and assures a profit of at least $2bq_S^2/n$. Hence the characteristic function is

$$v(S) = \frac{b}{2n} k(S)^2 \quad \text{for all } S \subseteq N. \tag{5.28}$$

The important thing to observe about this function is that it is convex, a coalition's worth being directly proportional to the square of its capacity. This means that in this game cooperation "snowballs": The larger a coalition grows, the more attractive it looks to those still outside. Coalition formation yields "increasing returns to scale."

This characteristic function must be used with great care, however, for we do not on the face of it have a c-game. Flooding the market may be a good threat for $N - S$ against S, but it is not simultaneously a good defense for $N - S$ against the corresponding threat from S, since it would yield zero profit. In other words, carrying out the threat strategy is costly, and (5.28) takes no account of this. Before we can legitimately apply the characteristic function, we must be sure that it adequately represents the game for the purpose at hand, despite its insensitivity to threat costs.

At any rate, (5.28) does give us the data for the imputation space. The imputations are just those payoff vectors $(\alpha_1, \alpha_2, \ldots, \alpha_n)$ that satisfy $\sum_N \alpha_i = v(N)$ and $\alpha_i \geq v(i)$, where

$$v(N) = \frac{b}{2n}k(N)^2 = \frac{bnA^2}{8},$$ (5.29)

using (5.27), and

$$v(\bar{i}) = \frac{b}{2n}k_i^2 \quad \text{for all } i \in N.$$ (5.30)

Note that the game is not in normalized form. The total capacity is tight enough so that even an individual producer can assure himself a profit.

EXERCISE
5.9. *Determine the characteristic function if the total capacity is only $nA/4$. Determine it also for total capacity $(nA/2) + K$, for all K satisfying $|K| \le \min_i k_i$. Verify that these characteristic functions are also convex.*

5.4.2 The core, stable set, and bargaining set
For the core at least, the characteristic function is adequate. The presence of costly threats does indeed weaken the interpretation of the core as a solution of the game, but it does not change the way in which the core is defined. An imputation α is in the core if there is no coalition that can assuredly do better by itself, which means

$$\sum_S \alpha_i \ge v(S) \quad \text{for all } S \subseteq N.$$

The first thing to note is that the core is not empty. Consider, for example, the payoff vector v that divides the total profit according to capacity, so that

$$v_i = \frac{k_i}{k(N)}\frac{bnA^2}{8} = \frac{bA}{4}k_i.$$ (5.31)

The significance of this particular imputation will be discussed presently. For the moment we merely observe that for any coalition S,

$$\sum_S v_i = \frac{bA}{4}k(S) = \frac{b}{2n}k(N)k(S) \ge \frac{b}{2n}k(S)^2 = v(S),$$

Actually, since the game is convex, we can derive a detailed description of the core, as well as of several other solution concepts. For one thing the core is complete, in that every coalition plays a role in determining its boundaries. In fact, for each S there are imputations (near but outside the core) that are blocked only by S. Since this remark is valid for singletons as well as for larger coalitions, completeness entails a very large core, touching all of the facets of the imputation simplex.

Another property of the core is its external stability. That is, the non-core imputations are all dominated by elements of the core. This implies that the core is the unique stable-set solution of the game. The core is also the full bargaining set of the game and contains both the kernel and the nucleolus.

A further idea of the size and shape of the core may be obtained from the construction for the extreme points. Take the players in each of the $n!$ possible arrangements and award to each player the amount he adds to the worth of the coalition consisting of his predecessors. For example, in the symmetric case where the players have identical capacities $k_i \equiv A/2$, the extreme points of the core are all the permutations of the vector

$$\frac{bA^2}{8n}(1, 3, 5, \ldots, 2n - 1).$$

The core is thus a large, roughly spherical, multifaceted polyhedron. In fact, if we inscribe a sphere in the imputation simplex, touching all the facets, then this sphere will be completely within the core. The radius of the sphere can be shown to be $\sqrt{1 - (1/n)}bA^2/8$; thus the core does not converge to a point as $n \to \infty$.

In the nonsymmetric case the core may not be quite so "spherical," but it will remain large since it will still touch every face of the imputation simplex. Figure 5.7 illustrates the case $k_i = i$ for $n = 4$. In general an individual producer with capacity k_i can receive in the core anything from his minimum,

$$v(\bar{i}) = \frac{bk_i^2}{2n},$$

up to the amount he would bring in if he were last to join the grand coalition,

$$v(N) - v(N - \bar{i}) = \frac{bAk_i}{2} - \frac{bk_i^2}{2n}.$$

His "spread" in the core is therefore

$$\frac{bAk_i}{2} - \frac{bk_i^2}{n} = \frac{b}{n}k_ik(N - \bar{i}).$$

As $n \to \infty$, this converges to the positive amount $bAk_i/2$.

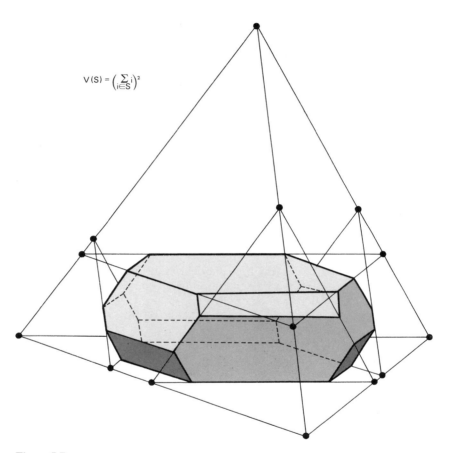

$$V(S) = \left(\sum_{i \in S} i\right)^2$$

Figure 5.7
Core of a typical four-product market with unequal capacities.

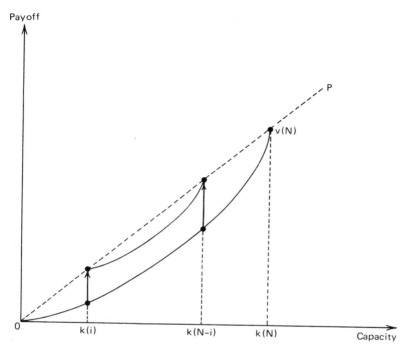

Figure 5.8
A convex measure game.

5.4.3 The nucleolus and the kernel

An indication of how far the core is shifted off-center in the nonsymmetric case can be obtained by computing the nucleolus, which is a sort of "center" of the core. This proves to be quite easy in the present case.[6] Represent (5.28) graphically as a *convex measure game*, as in figure 5.8. When we apply the nucleolus construction, we see that each point on the graph corresponding to a coalition S will rise until both $v(S)$ and $v(N - S)$ simultaneously touch the "line of sight" OP, whereupon they must stop or else wipe out the core. (The quadratic form of (5.28) is important here.) When the core is reduced to a single point, that point—the nucleolus v— must be directly proportional to the vector of capacities $(k_1, k_2, \ldots, k_n)$. In fact,

$$v_i = \frac{v(N)}{k(N)} k_i = \frac{bA}{4} k_i. \tag{5.32}$$

Thus, large and indeterminate as it is, the core solution does tend to favor the producers according to their relative capacities.

Because this model is a convex measure game, it follows immediately that the kernel coincides with the nucleolus.

5.4.4 Economic interpretation

What is the economic meaning and the level of generality of our study of the core and other solutions of this particular model? We might say that the resultant set of imputations describes limits on the outcomes to be expected from cartel negotiations. As the number of firms increases, the core does *not* shrink to a point. Thus, ceteris paribus, the presence of added firms does not qualitatively change the possibilities for collusion. This would occur only if we added considerations of communication and bargaining costs and the possibility of entry.

The reader may be aware that when a closed model of the economy is considered, it has been proved that the core converges (Edgeworth, 1881; Shubik, 1959a; Debreu and Scarf, 1963). The difference in the results is due to feedback differences in the two models and also to differences in the roles of the players.

The behavior of the core is highly sensitive to capacity limitations. The more excess capacity there is, the larger the core becomes, up to the point where any firm can supply the market by itself, in which case all imputations are in the core.

Once more we see capacity playing a critical role along with costs. When we consider the one-point cooperative solutions, this still holds, as was shown for the nucleolus.

5.4.5 The value

In *GTSS*, chapter 7, we noted that the value solution associated with any convex characteristic function lies at the center of gravity of the vertices of the core. As an example, we solved the case of a quadratic measure game and found that the value was proportional to the measure.[7] Thus the value and the nucleolus of (5.28) coincide, and we have another check on the general location of the core.[8]

In the case of nonsymmetric capacity limitations, the value of the game is not difficult to compute if we base it on the characteristic function above. When player i joins a coalition S, he increases its worth by an amount

$$\frac{b}{2n}([k(S) + k_i]^2 - [k(S)]^2) = \frac{b}{2n}[2k_i k(S) + k_i^2].$$

To average this increment over all coalitions of size s (excluding player i) we first replace $k(S)$ by $(s/(n-1))[k(N) - k_i]$ and then average over all values of s from 0 to $n - 1$, obtaining

$$\phi_i^v = \frac{1}{n}\sum_{s=0}^{n-1}\frac{b}{2n}\left(\frac{2sk_i[k(N) - k_i]}{n-1} + k_i^2\right)$$

$$= \frac{bk_i[k(N) - k_i]}{n^2(n-1)}\frac{n(n-1)}{2} + \frac{bk_i^2}{2n}$$

$$= \frac{b}{2n}k_i k(N)$$

$$= \frac{a-c}{4}k_i.$$

In other words, the values calculated in this way are directly proportional to the capacity.

This value determination is not legitimate, however, if we are interested in the value as a solution, not merely as a core descriptor. The reason, as we have already emphasized, is that we are not dealing with a c-game. A more reasonable or realistic value computation must therefore be based on the "modified" characteristic function $h(S)$ ($GTSS$, chapter 7), rather than the function $v(S)$ of (5.28). This we can obtain by solving the two-person cooperative game between S and $N - S$. First we note that

$$h(S) + h(N - S) = v(N) = \frac{b}{2n}k(N)^2, \tag{5.33}$$

by the joint optimality principle. It remains to solve the zero-sum "difference" game, with payoffs $P_S - P_{N-S}$. This game proves to have a saddlepoint in pure strategies, given by

$$q_T = \min[k(T), k(N)/2], \quad \text{where } T = S \text{ or } N - S.$$

This is the "optimal threat" for any coalition against its complement: Produce $k(N)/2$ if you can, otherwise produce at capacity. The value at the saddlepoint is

$$-\frac{b}{2n}[k(S) - k(N - S)]^2 \quad \text{if } k(S) \leq k(N - S),$$

$$\frac{b}{2n}[k(S) - k(N - S)]^2 \quad \text{if } k(S) \geq k(N - S); \tag{5.34}$$

setting $h(S) - h(N - S)$ equal to this value and applying (5.33) yields

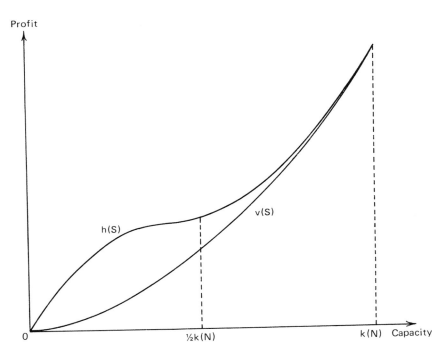

Figure 5.9
Characteristic functions.

$$h(S) = \begin{cases} \dfrac{b}{2n}[k(S)^2 + k(N-S)^2] & \text{if } k(S) \geq k(N)/2, \\[2mm] \dfrac{b}{2n}[2k(S)k(N-S)] & \text{if } k(S) \leq k(N)/2. \end{cases}$$

(This could be written in several other ways because of the identity $k(S) + k(N-S) = k(N)$.) The relation between this two-piece quadratic and the original v is depicted in figure 5.9.

The case distinction at $k(N)/2$ makes it difficult to write down the values ϕ_i explicitly. It is possible, though, to obtain quite good bounds on the value if the producers are approximately equal in size. In fact, let σ denote the standard deviation of the numbers $k_1, k_2, \ldots, k_n$. Then

$$\frac{bk_i k(N-\bar{\imath})}{2(n-1)} \leq \phi_i^h \leq \frac{b[k_i k(N-\bar{\imath}) + n\sigma^2]}{2(n-1)} \qquad (5.35)$$

if n is even, and

$$\frac{(n + 1)bk_i k(N - \bar{\imath})}{2n^2} \le \phi_i^h \le \frac{(n + 1)b[k_i k(N - \bar{\imath}) + n\sigma^2]}{2n^2} + \frac{b[k(N)]^2}{2n^3}$$

(5.36)

if n is odd. (We omit the derivation, which is not difficult.) These bounds are illustrated in the next section.

The value based on this revised characteristic function differs from the nucleolus. As a qualitative observation, it can be shown that for producers of below-average capacity the value is more favorable than the nucleolus, whereas for the largest-capacity producers the situation is reversed.

If we let n increase indefinitely and let σ tend to zero, all of these bounds converge to $bAk_i/4$; the distinction between the nucleolus and the value thus vanishes in the limit.

5.4.6 Summary of solutions and an example

For a numerical example, take $n = 4$, $a = \$4$, $c = \$1$, and $b = 0.0006$. Then $A = \$5000$, so that a total capacity of $k(N) = 10,000$ units will just saturate the market at cost price. Let the individual capacities be

$$k_1 = 1000, \quad k_2 = 2000, \quad k_3 = 3000, \quad k_4 = 4000.$$

The two characteristic functions (original and modified) are as follows:

$k(S)$	$v(S)$	$h(S)$	$k(S)$	$v(S)$	$h(S)$
1000	\$ 75	\$1350	6000	\$2700	\$3900
2000	300	2400	7000	3675	4350
3000	675	3150	8000	4800	5100
4000	1200	3600	9000	6075	6150
5000	1875	3750	10000	7500	7500

The core is illustrated in figure 5.7. The numerical ranges of payoffs in the core are given in table 5.2. The nucleolus exactly bisects this range for each player, and it is also the center of gravity of the 24 vertices of the core.

The value is not hard to compute exactly in a game of this size. Not surprisingly, the bounds from (5.35) are not very sharp: $\sigma = 500\sqrt{5} \approx 1118$.

Large capacity is rewarded in the value calculation, but the reward is not necessarily proportional to capacity. The economic merit of the

Table 5.2
Ranges of payoffs in the core

Player	Core payoffs ($)	
	Low	High
1	75	1425
2	300	2700
3	675	3825
4	1200	4800

solution is that it offers a reasonable way for taking threats into account and then arriving at a "fair-division" split for the members of the cartel.

If different costs as well as capacities were introduced, the calculation would become far more complex, with considerable interaction between cost and capacity advantages.

In the noncooperative equilibrium we find that the two smaller players produce to capacity while the two larger players restrict production to 2333 units apiece, thereby keeping the price at \$1.70, about midway between the monopolistic price of \$2.50 and the competitive price of \$1.

Adding the producers' total profits to the consumers' aggregate utility increment $aq - bq^2/n - pq = bq^2/n$ (see (5.1) and (5.2)) reveals that the total economic value under the cooperative solutions is \$11,250; under the noncooperative solution, \$14,183; and under the competitive or "efficient" solution, \$15,000.

In the cooperative game we have examined, side payments have been restricted to producers only. Consumers are price takers who cannot make lump-sum transfers to the producers. If they could, the Pareto-optimal surface would be *ESF* in figure 5.10 rather than *EMN*. In this instance the monopoly point of the game without full side payments, *M*, is not Pareto-optimal in the game with unrestricted side payments.

In modeling a real market it appears reasonable to impose such limits on transferability, separating the roles of consumers and producers. A more compelling case can be made for comparing the worth of \$1 to two companies such as Ford or General Motors than to an individual consumer and Ford.

Once more it must be stressed that if production costs are the same and capacities are sufficient, then side payments can be achieved among firms through their production policies even when direct monetary side payments are forbidden by law.

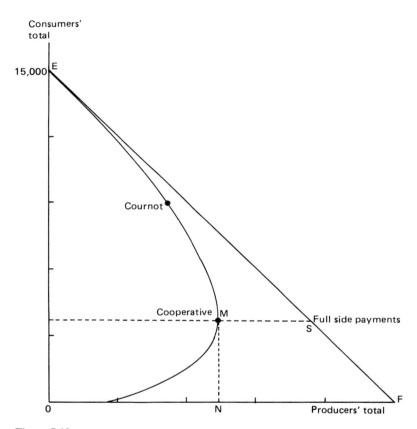

Figure 5.10
Partial and full side payments.

5.5 A Dominant Firm

In keeping with our concern for numbers and sizes of competitors we now consider a single large firm controlling a fixed fraction f of the capacity of the industry, together with a large number of small firms. As previously, we shall assume that the total capacity is exactly enough to supply the market at the "efficient" price $p = c$. Thus if "1" is the dominant firm,

$$k_1 = \frac{fnA}{2},$$
(5.37)

$$k_i = \frac{1-f}{n-1} \frac{nA}{2} \quad (i = 2, 3, \ldots, n).$$
(5.38)

Note that as n increases the model does not expand in a completely homogeneous manner in the sense described at the beginning of section 5.1. We are in effect fragmenting the small firms but not the large firm.

5.5.1 The noncooperative equilibrium
The noncooperative equilibrium is easily found. If we assume that the large firm is at least twice the size of any of the small firms, we have $f \geq 2/(n+1)$, which entails $k_i \leq nA/2(n+1)$ for $i \neq 1$. Applying the method of section 5.3, we find the equilibrium-point strategies:

$$q_1^\# = q_0 = \frac{k_1}{2} = \frac{fnA}{4},$$

$$q_i^\# = k_i = \frac{1-f}{n-1} \frac{nA}{2} \quad (i = 2, 3, \ldots, n).$$

Note that the total quantity produced is proportional to n, so that the market price,

$$p^\# = \frac{fbA}{2} + c,$$

is independent of n. It does not matter how many small firms there are; what sustains the "oligopolistic" price is the shortage caused by the underproduction of the large firm:

$$P_1^\# = \frac{f^2 nbA^2}{8},$$

$$P_i^\# = \frac{2f(1-f)}{n-1} \frac{nbA^2}{8} \quad (i = 2, 3, \ldots, n).$$

The associated payoffs are only f^2 of the profit that a monopolist would command, namely $v(N) = nbA^2/8$. The small firms divide another $2f - 2f^2$, leaving $(1 - f)^2$ unclaimed. For example, if $f = 0.2$ and $n = 33$, the noncooperative profits are $0.04 + 0.01 + \ldots + 0.01$, or only 36 percent of the potential collusive profit.

It is also interesting that the first firm gets no more than its individual minimum, $v(\overline{1})$, while the others do much better due to their "parasitic" position in the market structure.[9]

As the number of small firms increases and their sizes diminish, they become virtually pure competitors. But it is precisely the fact that the small firms are not sufficiently organized or "do not have enough sense" to limit their production that ruins the market for the large firm.

In this instance we might wish to talk of the dominant firm as the market leader inasmuch as the small firms can be regarded as adjusting passively to its behavior.

5.5.2 Cooperative solutions
From section 5.4.6 we know that this is a convex game and hence that the core, bargaining set, and stable sets all coincide. Thus the cooperative solutions can be characterized by a description of the core, the nucleolus (which coincides with the value of the game in characteristic-function form), and the value of the game, with the threat power of the firms reflected in the use of the h-function.

Figure 5.11 illustrates the core and other solutions for $n = 3$, $f = 3/4$, and $k_2 = k_3 = 1/8$; it holds in substantially the same form as the number of small firms grows.

The feasible set of payoffs is the simplex ABC. The individually rational set of payoffs is $A'B'C'$. The nucleolus at N, the center of gravity of the core, is located in proportion to capacities. The range of the core for the dominant firm is from f^2 to $(2f - f^2)$.

We conclude that market domination by additional capacity alone is advantageous to the large firm, but only in direct proportion to capacity at the nucleolus, and it could be even less in the core, going down to a payoff proportional to f^2.

5.5.3 Concluding remarks
While the noncooperative equilibrium appears in many ways to be a natural solution for the study of oligopolistic competition, cooperative solutions provide a basis for displaying the potential for collusion and the worth of cartelization. The von Neumann–Morgenstern characteristic

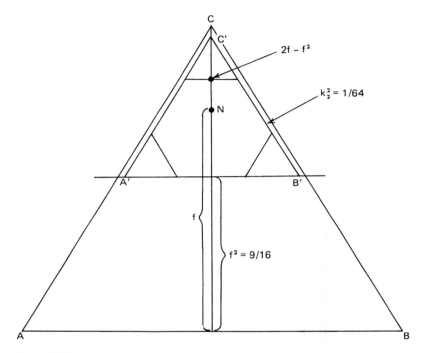

Figure 5.11
Cooperative solutions with a dominant firm.

function fails to reflect the threat possibilities available in oligopolistic markets; but short of going to a fully dynamic theory, an approximate measure of threats can be obtained by using the Harsanyi modification to the characteristic function.

Antitrust laws forbidding direct monetary side payments and certain forms of explicit direct communication and enforceable contracts do not prevent collusion or cooperative behavior in general; they merely make its manifestation somewhat more complicated than it would be otherwise.

In application the search for cooperative solutions requires a study of all combinations among *n* firms. For most important instances of oligopolistic competition or cartelization, however, *n* is between 3 and 10. Thus the number of nonempty coalitions is between 7 and 1023. Moreover the special features of the actual problems at hand will often cut down the combinatoric calculations considerably.

Notes to chapter 5

1. Note that the quantity required to drive the price down to c_i is not A_i, as previously, but $nA_i/2$. Since n is now a potential variable, we do not wish to hide it by using an abbreviation for $n(a - c)/2b$.

2. It may be that the points involved in this effect—the imputations of the side-payment model that cannot be achieved without side payments—are so extreme that they always give some player more than his incremental worth to *any* coalition and hence (see Milnor, 1952, or chapter 11 of Luce and Raiffa, 1957) have no influence on the principal cooperative solutions.

3. A convex function always has left- and right-hand derivatives, with the former less than or equal to the latter. Where they are equal, c_i is that number; where they are unequal, c_i takes on all values in the closed interval between them.

4. Our reliance on graphical arguments points up the essentially topological nature of this and the following theorem.

5. Note that although our functions are more general than those of theorem 5.1, our method of passing to the limit (by replication) is more special.

6. In *GTSS*, chapter 11, it was shown that the nucleolus in a game with a core is obtained by shrinking the core, simultaneously increasing all the numbers $v(S)$ at the same rate except for those that cannot be increased without wiping out the core. When none can be increased further, the single point that remains is the nucleolus.

7. The proportionality depends on "zero" being the point of no profit for each producer, rather than the point of minimum profit $v(i)$. Thus, if the game had been normalized, the values would have been proportional to $k_i(k(N) - k_i)$ instead. This means that in the distribution of the excess profits, over and above the sum of the individual producers' enforceable minima, the smaller players do somewhat better than their proportion of the total capacity, and the larger players somewhat worse. For example, with capacities in the ratio $1:2:3:4$, the normalized values are in the ratio $9:16:21:24$. This remark applies equally to the nucleolus.

8. These two kinds of "center" do not generally coincide for convex measure games.

9. We have $P_i^\#/v(\bar{i}) = 2f(n - 1)/(1 - f)$, which is at least 4 and increases with n.

6 Monopolistic Competition

6.1 The Price Game

In the classical writings on duopoly it has been observed that it is possible to formulate duopoly models in which the firms use either quantity or price as their strategy. The use of *quantity* as a strategic variable, as in the preceding two chapters, leads to the well-known Cournot (1897) model. Both Bertrand (1883) and Edgeworth (1925) investigated *price* models, in which the sellers were assumed to be selling an undifferentiated product, but they obtained different results (see also Mayberry, Nash, and Shubik, 1953). The difference can be ascribed to their assumptions concerning capacity restrictions (or, equivalently, rising marginal costs).

The principal difficulty in dealing with price-strategy models comes in describing the demand conditions that prevail when unequal prices are quoted. This is especially striking when the products are totally undifferentiated, since all will rush to buy from the firm with lower prices, creating discontinuities in consumer behavior. Even with some differentiation among the products, however, contingent demand curves can have kinks and bends that make them hard to analyze (Shubik, 1959b, chapter 5; Shubik with Levitan, 1980).

Chamberlin (1933) suggested in his theory of monopolistic competition that one should treat each competitor as a monopolist, in the sense of providing a slightly differentiated product or service, even though all competitors may purportedly be selling the same good. Hotelling (1929) suggested location as a means for distinguishing firms otherwise selling the same product.

We stress throughout this work that developing a theory requires a mixture of modeling and analysis. When viewed in these terms, the work of Chamberlin represented a considerable step forward in modeling the economic environment, but as analysis it fell far short of the clarity of Cournot and Edgeworth. The mechanism behind the Chamberlinian "large-group equilibrium" is nothing other than that of a noncooperative equilibrium, treated verbally and not adequately worked out.

Shubik (1959b) and Shubik with Levitan (1980) have compared the works of Cournot, Bertrand, and Edgeworth and have integrated them within the framework of game theory. Chamberlin has also been considered, but full justice cannot be done to his work unless entry is taken into account.

Although we shall start with a brief recapitulation of some of the classical oligopoly models, the prime purpose of this and the next chapter is to raise questions and point out problems in the extension of formal oligopoly models. What are good questions in oligopoly theory? Why are they interesting? What do we require to answer them?

Economics is not logical analysis alone. Mathematics is useful for organizing and understanding facts, but it is not a substitute for them. Models of the behavior of few firms based upon few facts tend to produce few interesting results. Yet a good parsimoniously designed model, even if it yields an unsatisfactory, unrealistic solution, may point the way to better and richer models. It is with this in mind that we sketch a fairly simple set of models before asking what questions are worth considering.

6.1.1 Undifferentiated products: Bertrand and Edgeworth

In his critique of Cournot, Bertrand (1883) suggested that price rather than quantity be taken as the independent variable. He argued that if this were done, and if the producers were selling identical goods, the price would go immediately to the competitive equilibrium. The argument is simple: Since the products are absolutely identical, all customers will prefer to buy from the firm offering the lowest price. Hence, if supplies are unlimited, no price above cost can be sustained as an equilibrium, because there will always be an incentive to earn larger profits by slightly undercutting the competition and seizing the entire market, rather than sharing it. Ironically the quest for larger profits leads (in the case of equal costs) to zero profits for both firms.

Edgeworth (1925) extended the analysis of the duopoly price-strategy model by considering firms with steeply rising average costs (or, equivalently, limited capacities). He noted that if a firm did not or was unable to produce for the whole market, consumers might buy from the higher-priced as well as the lower-priced firm. He further argued that instead of settling down to the competitive level, the price in such a market would be indeterminate and would tend to fluctuate over a range. This range has been described as the "Edgeworth cycle."

What determines the demand left for the higher-priced firm if the lower-priced firm fails to satisfy all customers? At what capacity level does the Bertrand solution change over to the Edgeworth solution? How is the situation affected by the presence of more competitors? What is the range of the Edgeworth cycle? To answer these questions adequately, we must investigate the conditions of demand in a market in which the sellers are naming different prices.

6.1.2 The structure of oligopolistic demand

In chapters 4 and 5, when we discussed competition among firms that use quantity as their strategic variable, we determined market price by relating it to the sum of all quantities offered: $p = f(\sum_{i=1}^{n} q_i)$. This determination is simple and highly aggregative, and it hides a considerable amount of the detailed structure of the market. Price is selected so that the market always clears. There is no problem with unsatisfied demand and no need to know anything about individual demand. This is not true when price enters the model as a strategic variable.

A simple consideration of consumer behavior under conditions of short supply is sufficient to indicate that even a single, price-taking individual might then elect to buy the same commodity from more than one source at different prices. This is illustrated in figure 6.1, which shows a set of indifference curves between money and a single commodity. The point M marks the individual's initial endowment; he has none of the commodity, and the ordinate of M is his initial money supply. Suppose that several firms offer to supply him at different prices, the lowest being represented by the slope of the line MST. If the lowest-priced firm had sufficient capacity (or stock in inventory), the consumer would purchase an amount equal to the abscissa of the point S, where MST is tangent to an indifference curve. Suppose, however, that the capacity of this firm is only the amount indicated by the abscissa of K; the consumer is not yet satisfied, and he will now look to a higher-priced supplier. The next best price is indicated by the slope of the line KRV. Assuming that this supplier has enough capacity, the consumer will buy from him until the point R is reached; otherwise he will turn to yet another supplier.

In general the stocks of a supplier tend to be larger than the needs of any single customer, so that the effects of capacity constraints fall more on groups of customers than upon individuals. If a supplier cannot satisfy all of his customers, which ones will he supply, and what will be the demand characteristics of the unsatisfied group? This important applied problem in marketing has no single answer. It depends upon a host of specific economic and sociological factors, such as the spatial distribution of the customers, their knowledge of the market, their habits, and their social class.

The development of an adequate theory of oligopolistic demand has

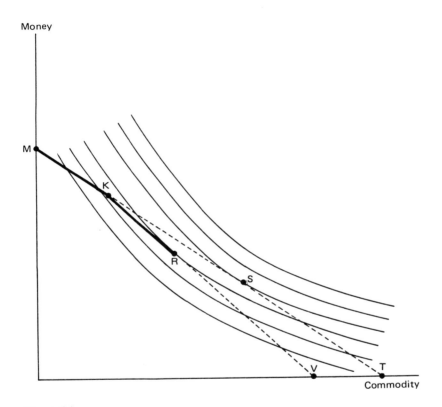

Figure 6.1
Buying at two prices.

long been recognized as a central problem in the understanding of
oligopolistic markets. Even if we restrict ourselves to pure price and
quantity models of competition, leaving out all problems of location,
information, advertising, and other facts of life, the portrayal of consumer
demand poses deep difficulties. A general rationing problem must be
solved; and as prices are varied, the resulting patterns of demand can
easily be such as to destroy all hope of finding an equilibrium in an
oligopolistic market.

The difficulties with the structure of demand and the existence of
equilibria were already recognized by Edgeworth (1925). Shubik (1959b),
Levitan (1966), and Shubik with Levitan (1980) developed a relatively
simple theory of *contingent demand* in which they showed that demand

functions contingent upon the prices and supplies of other producers' goods could easily assume many shapes and be neither concave nor convex. This feature could result in the destruction of any (pure-strategy) noncooperative equilibrium (as shown by Edgeworth, 1925).

There is an important relationship and contrast between the work on contingent demand and that on kinked oligopoly demand. The former, given k firms, with each firm i characterized by price p_i and supply q_i, studies the structure of contingent demand functions,

$$d_i = f_i(p_i | p_1^*, p_2^*, \ldots, p_{i-1}^*, p_{i+1}^*, \ldots, p_k^*; q_1^*, q_2^*, \ldots, q_{i-1}^*, q_{i+1}^*, \ldots, q_k^*),$$
(6.1)

in which the prices and supplies of all firms other than i are fixed and the demand d_i is considered as a function of p_i. The assumption behind the kinked oligopoly demand analysis is that the prices and supplies of firms other than i can be treated as functions of firm i's behavior. The purpose of the analysis is to present a simple compact description of dynamics based upon behavioral conjectures of the other competing firms' reactions. Reid (1981) gives a useful overview of this work. In my view it is a useful conceptual device for the corporate strategic analyst who wants to form a "quick and dirty" view of how market reactions might influence the demand for his product. As employed in oligopoly theory, though, it lacks both the institutional detail of a good industry study and the precision and logical rigor one expects of modern mathematical economics or applied operations research.

The description and analysis of oligopolistic demand poses many problems. In particular it can scarcely be operationalized without an understanding of marketing and spatial competition, yet to date there has been little linkage between the study of marketing and formal oligopoly theory.

The contingent-demand construction was suggested explicitly to show that introducing the possibility of trading at more than one price together with capacity constraints imposes logical requirements on the shapes of oligopolistic demand curves. In fact, as shown in Shubik (1959b), marketing questions such as who is served first must be answered before the demand can be fully specified. Furthermore an attempt was made to sort out statics from dynamics. In my view neither the kinked oligopoly demand nor the contingent-demand construction is of much use in studying oligopolistic competition unless supplemented by an appropriate ad hoc study of marketing realities.

6.2 Product Differentiation

The Cournot, Bertrand, and Edgeworth analyses all assumed a single undifferentiated product. A simple quadratic utility function,

$$U = aq - \frac{bq^2}{n} \quad \text{with } 0 \le q \le \frac{na}{2n}, \tag{6.2}$$

was employed. We modify this to illustrate product differentiation. This will enable us to obtain the shapes of contingent demand functions directly by solving the resultant constrained optimization problem when limited quantities of differentiated goods are being offered at different prices. Despite its relative simplicity, the model will be rich enough to illustrate some interesting features of oligopolistic demand and to serve as a basis for the study of noncooperative behavior as the number of competitors is increased and the level of differentiation is changed.

The aggregate utility function is

$$U = aq - \frac{bq^2}{n} - \varepsilon \left[\left(\frac{\sum q_i^2}{n} \right) - \frac{q^2}{n^2} \right] - \sum p_i q_i, \quad \text{where } q = \sum q_i. \tag{6.3}$$

Here ε may be interpreted as a parameter that controls the degree of product differentiation. If it is zero, the products are perfect substitutes, and we are back at (6.2) (with $n = 2$). When $\varepsilon = nb$, the utility function becomes separable, and the products are independent of one another, being neither substitutes nor complements. For $0 < \varepsilon < nb$ the (aggregate) consumer is seen to put a premium on diversity, seeking equal holdings of the different firms' products if all other things are equal. Undoubtedly we should consider more general and more realistic forms for the utility function, but this form enables us to examine the structure of a market with symmetrically differentiated goods in detail without being overwhelmed with complications.

Equation (6.3) contains the parameter n in several terms, in preparation for an investigation of limiting behavior in markets with increasing numbers of firms. Before limiting behavior can be examined adequately, though, we must consider several different interpretations of the limiting levels of substitutability. For the present discussion of contingent demand we limit ourselves to $n = 2$. Here

$$U = aq - \frac{bq^2}{2} - \frac{\varepsilon}{4}(q_1 - q_2)^2 - p_1 q_1 - p_2 q_2. \tag{6.4}$$

Using (6.4) and the condition for consumer optimization, we may solve for consumer demand in terms of prices:

$$\frac{\partial U}{\partial q_1} = a - bq - \frac{\varepsilon}{2}(q_1 - q_2) - p_1 = 0, \tag{6.5}$$

$$\frac{\partial U}{\partial q_2} = a - bq - \frac{\varepsilon}{2}(q_2 - q_1) - p_2 = 0. \tag{6.6}$$

By addition and subtraction of these equations we obtain

$$2a - 2bq = p_1 + p_2,$$

$$-\varepsilon(q_1 - q_2) = p_1 - p_2,$$

which yield

$$q_1 = \frac{2a - (1 + 2b/\varepsilon)p_1 - (1 - 2b/\varepsilon)p_2}{4b}, \tag{6.7}$$

and similarly for q_2. These solutions hold only if

$$\varepsilon \geq \frac{2b(p_1 - p_2)}{2a - p_1 - p_2}, \tag{6.8}$$

which is obtained directly from (6.7) by setting $q_1 \geq 0$. If $p_1 > p_2$ and

$$0 \leq \varepsilon \leq \frac{2b(p_1 - p_2)}{2a - p_1 - p_2}, \tag{6.9}$$

then $q_1 = 0$, and from (6.4) we obtain

$$q_2 = \frac{a - p_2}{b + \varepsilon/2}; \tag{6.10}$$

thus we have a continuous contingent demand with the two "kinks" shown by $AKDFG$ in figure 6.2. The labels are for the case in which p_1 is fixed and p_2 varies.

Because the goods are not perfect substitutes, the low-priced firm will never obtain "all of the market" in the sense of the amount ON that would be sold if both charged the low price. The gap GN is a measure of the lack of substitutability. The line AN is an "apples and oranges" addition of the amounts sold by both when they charge the same price. The line AE gives the amount sold by one firm on the assumption that the other is charging the same price. The equations for the three line segments AK, DF, and FG that make up the contingent demand are given. At the point F the second firm has completely priced the first out of the market.

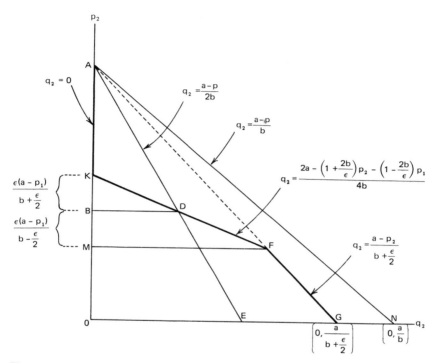

Figure 6.2
Demand with product differentiation.

It has been shown by Levitan (Levitan, 1966; Shubik with Levitan, 1980) that the calculation of the structure of contingent demand in an oligopolistic market is equivalent to a problem of rationing in a general-equilibrium market. The existence of these curves is evident; the difficulty comes in calculating their shapes. Levitan (1966) provides an appropriate algorithm for certain classes of demand. This algorithm has been employed in an oligopoly market game (Shubik with Levitan, 1980).

Under more general conditions the contingent demand can take on many shapes. In particular, capacity limitations will cause extra kinks.

6.2.1 The noncooperative price duopoly without capacity constraints

When the firms have equal costs and capacity constraints are not tight, we can solve for the noncooperative equilibrium in the market by observing that a symmetric equilibrium will exist. This enables us to write down payoff or revenue functions involving demands as given in (6.7). Thus

$$P_i = (p_i - c)\frac{2a - (1 + 2b/\varepsilon)p_i - (1 - 2b/\varepsilon)p_j}{4b} \quad (i = 1, 2; j = 2, 1) \quad (6.11)$$

can be written and solved analytically, yielding

$$p_i = \frac{2a + c(1 + 2b/\varepsilon)}{3 + 2b/\varepsilon}. \tag{6.12}$$

A straightforward check that this is an equilibrium point is obtained by setting the price of one firm to (6.12) and checking for the other's maximum using all three segments of his contingent demand.

When $\varepsilon = 2b$, the point G in figure 6.2 is moved to E, and (6.12) simplifies to

$$p_i = \frac{a + c}{2};$$

each may then charge his monopoly price.

The solution given by (6.11) when $\varepsilon \neq 0$ is not the efficient-point solution for this duopolistic market. If the economy were being run for the benefit of the consumer, the condition that price equals cost would still prevail. As differentiation is removed ($\varepsilon \to 0$), though, even with only two competitors the noncooperative equilibrium (without capacity constraints) approaches the efficient solution, as indicated by the Bertrand model.

6.2.2 Noncooperative oligopoly

We can use much the same methods as in chapter 5 to study oligopolistic competition with differentiated products. The models discussed here have been worked out in detail elsewhere (Shubik with Levitan, 1980), so that we shall note only the market structure and the results. Using (6.3) as the utility function we can derive for the symmetric noncooperative equilibrium

$$p_i = \frac{n(n - 1)bc + \varepsilon(na + c)}{n(n - 1)b + \varepsilon(n + 1)}. \tag{6.13}$$

As $\varepsilon \to 0$, $p \to c$ as we have already noted in the case of duopoly. Here, however, we have a further convergence result. As $n \to \infty$, we also observe that $p \to c$. In other words, as the number of competitors increases, even though they are selling differentiated products, the noncooperative equilibrium approaches the efficient-point solution at which price equals costs. (For a treatment of nonsymmetric oligopoly with differentiated products see Shubik with Levitan (1980).)

The results will be qualitatively the same for firms with increasing marginal costs provided that they are not so steep as to have an effect similar to that of capacity restriction.

As the number of firms is increased, a new problem arises in the modeling of a market. Should the term ε be regarded as remaining constant, or should it change with increasing n? Keeping ε constant implies that the degree of substitutability between the product of any one firm and the products of its competitors increases in proportion to n. If we wished to model a market in which the amount of autonomy or differentiation between any given firm and the rest of the market remained constant, then ε would have to be replaced by εn. We can see from (6.13) that when ε is replaced by εn and $n \to \infty$, price does not approach the efficient-point solution (Shubik, 1970; Schwödiauer, 1970); in fact,

$$p(n \to \infty) = \frac{c + \varepsilon a/b}{1 + \varepsilon/b}. \qquad (6.14)$$

This distinction was not made by Chamberlin.

The problem here is essentially an empirical one (although the concept of "closeness" of products calls for techniques capable of encompassing a continuum of products; see Bewley, 1972). For most products a more reasonable model may be for the products of the first few additional competitors to maintain their individuality and "distance" from each other. After five or six competitors, substitutes start to crowd in.

The Cournot or quantity-strategy model can also be calculated for this instance, and we find

$$p_i = \frac{nb(a + nc) + \varepsilon a(n - 1)}{n(n + 1)b + \varepsilon(n - 1)}. \qquad (6.15)$$

For $\varepsilon = 0$ this coincides with (5.11).

The price-strategy game noted above has been studied for capacity constraints, and closed-form solutions have been obtained. Although formally we can consider the degree of product differentiation to be under the strategic control of the firms, the study of product variation strategies leads into conceptual and empirical difficulties concerning both the description of innovation and the demand for untried products.

This game has also been analyzed in a nonsymmetric version with a vector of weights used to indicate differences in the attractiveness of the firms products. The game exists in a computerized version and has been utilized for both experimental and teaching purposes.

6.2.3 Noncooperative solutions
Noncooperative solutions are by definition ones that do not employ side payments in the sense of the theory of cooperative games. This does not exclude the possibility that money payments between firms might be regarded as formal moves within the model of a market. Even at this level the game theorist is in a position to point out that there is no simple way to distinguish between situations in which "legitimate" bills are being paid and those in which bribes or other socially undesirable payments are being made. If two firms in competition also buy goods or services from each other, the possibilities for virtually any form of communication and side payment increase with the complexity of the trading relationship. No simplistic blanket ruling will be sufficient to achieve the social purpose of restricting the forms of communication or side payment. For this reason, even were we given a clearly stated social purpose, the application of social control to a specific set of firms is a hand-tailoring job. Detailed empirical, legal, and game-theoretic study is called for.

At an extremely crude and aggregate level of analysis, we can examine two simple propositions:

1. Banning direct monetary side payments among firms tends to increase the level of competition at no cost to the efficiency of a market.

2. Restricting direct communication between competitors tends to increase the level of competition at no cost to the efficiency of a market.

When firms do not buy from each other and limit their moves to price, production, advertising, or product differentiation, the noncooperative-equilibrium solution does not involve side payments in any sense, so that for this solution to the models we have studied so far the first question is not relevant.

The (essentially) static oligopoly models of Cournot, Chamberlin, and others provide no clear picture of the types of permissible communication. The mathematical models in normal or strategic form imply independent selection of strategies without communication. However, any attempt to make sense of the literature on the "kinked oligopoly demand curve" or of Chamberlin's (1933, chapter 5) small-group equilibrium forces us to specify the means of signaling and transmitting threats or contingency plans among competitors so that each can form an expectation of the others' reactions to a move such as price cutting. This requires an analysis of dynamics.

In general it appears that a restriction on direct communication makes it more difficult for firms to coordinate moves or to signal threats. Thus the possibility of "quasicooperative outcomes," which can be enforced noncooperatively by threats, is weakened.

Restricting the flow of communication may decrease the efficiency of a market by making it far easier for firms to commit blunders. When there are only few firms, a lessening of communication can also increase the possibility for socially undesirable economic warfare.

6.3 Entry and Exit: Open Models

6.3.1 A preliminary to dynamics

We have suggested that a microeconomic dynamics is required for an adequate study of oligopolistic behavior and industrial organization. Yet the analysis presented in this volume deals essentially with statics, simply because there are many difficulties to be overcome before a dynamics can be developed with any confidence. Prior to the study of process, a description of the carriers of process must be given; and the carriers of process, even at the most abstract level, are institutions. The institutions appear when the modeling is performed using either the strategic or the extensive form of a game.

The first steps toward the development of an economic dynamics are clearly present in Marshall's use of comparative statics in the study of firm and industry behavior in a partial-equilibrium setting. We shall argue here that before dealing with dynamics we can formalize the type of comparative statics employed in partial-equilibrium analysis in a manner that makes the models logically consistent with general-equilibrium theory. This will provide new results of relevance to the study of oligopolistic competition without requiring institutional detail or a noninstitutional dynamics.

Before we attempt to model entry, merger, or exit using statics, we must discuss the specific difficulties encountered in modeling a firm or an industry. Possibly the key element is *indivisibility*, which is manifested in many ways. Indivisibility in industry is frequently associated with durability, costliness, and complexity. A nuclear power plant whose construction takes ten years, an automobile plant, a refinery—in all these examples the "indivisibility" is a complex intermix of organization, technology, costs, durability, and the attendant inflexibility that accompanies expensive, long-lived manufacturing establishments in a changing environment.

Indivisibility, size, and durability call forth new institutions. In particular, the immense capital requirements necessitate the corporate form, joint ownership, and fiduciary management. In many ways a corporation is a complicated form of local public good with all the attendent economic problems.

Both economics and accounting recognize the behavioral, sociopsychological fact that organizations are more than their assets. Indeed the intangibles may be more important than the tangibles. Knowledge, organization, management, esprit de corps, imagination, morale, intelligence, discipline, loyalty, perceptivity, and ethical imperatives are ingredients that differentiate the living institution from an inventory of tangible assets. Unfortunately they are all "off-balance-sheet" items. A safe way to treat them in accordance with Generally Accepted Accounting Principles is to value them at zero. A slightly less draconian way used by the microeconomist is to tuck all these factors into the familiar U-shaped average-cost function.

Because of the dynamics of competition and the fact that most production involves the employment of durable assets in even more durable enterprises, studies of the performance of specific industries must consider technological and institutional detail, including organizational and asset structure.

Available transaction technologies, tax laws, and the accepted ownership devices for large collections of assets have called forth money, markets, accounting procedures, and financial instruments. The presence of risk and the need for finance imply that an economic dynamics of the firm, if it is to be adequate for the most interesting questions concerning oligopolistic behavior, must include cash flows, financial constraints, bankruptcy, and insolvency conditions.

Learning, set-up and liquidation costs, invention, and innovation are also frequently central to the study of oligopolistic behavior.

The analytically distinct factors required by an adequate dynamic theory of oligopoly behavior are thus as follows:

1. Ownership and management.

2. Organization and information.

3. Production technologies, indivisibility, increasing returns to scale.

4. Transaction technologies, markets, transportation.

5. The treatment of risk.

6. Innovation, invention, learning, set-up, and liquidation.

7. Financial factors, cash flows, bankruptcy.

Any model of oligopolistic competition, if it is to be well defined and analyzable, also requires the specification of:

8. Initial and ending conditions.

9. The solution concept to be applied.

In the remainder of this section our concern is narrowed to the treatment of the entry and exit of firms in the context of open or partial equilibrium.

6.3.2 Entry in oligopoly theory

Chamberlin, whose *Theory of Monopolistic Competition* revived oligopoly theory several decades ago, devoted some thought to the problem of entry in oligopoly. Though he posed new questions in other areas of oligopoly theory, his view on entry came largely from the traditional framework emanating from perfect competition. His view can be summarized as follows: "Insofar as profits are higher than the general competitive level in the field as a whole or in any portion of it, new competitors will, *if possible*, invade the field and reduce them."

Basing his analysis of long-run oligopolistic adjustments to equilibrium on this principle, Chamberlin concluded that even though prices may exhibit monopolistic effects under oligopoly, entry will drive profits to competitive levels. Long-run equilibrium will be attained at the so-called tangency point where the industry demand curve is tangent to the long-run average-cost curve. An implication of the tangency condition is that under monopolistic competition firms will tend to operate with excess capacity. Chamberlin's conclusion was controversial, but it provided a starting point for further discussions of the role of entry in oligopoly theory.

Chamberlin's view, though not really distinct from the traditional perfect-competition views on entry, contained important parenthetical remarks on the subject. He suggested that not only would potential entrants be different, but also that the effects of their entry into competition would be asymmetric. He observed:

Again, if high average profits lead new competitors to invade the general field, the markets of different established producers cannot be wrested from them with equal facility. Some will be forced to yield ground, but not enough to reduce their profits below the minimum necessary to keep them in business. Others may be cut to the minimum, and still others may be forced to drop out because only a small demand exists or can be created for their particular variety of product. Others, protected by a strong prejudice in favor of theirs, may be virtually unaffected by an invasion of the general field—their monopoly profits are beyond the reach of competition. (Chamberlin, 1933, p. 82)

An important note is that Chamberlin's book provides both a large-group and a small-group theory. The former is close to competitive equilibrium in spirit, while the latter explicitly takes interaction into account and is closer to a noncooperative-equilibrium analysis.

Triffin (1940, chapter 3) also saw entry (and exit) of firms as relevant to oligopoly theory, especially when competition is viewed in a general-equilibrium framework. Unfortunately neither the general-equilibrium nor the noncooperative-equilibrium analysis was at that time sufficiently developed for Triffin to do much more than sketch an approach.

Schumpeter argued persuasively that the kind of competition that counted most in a capitalist economy, as far as economic progress goes, is "the competition from the new commodity, the new source of supply, the new type of organization . . . competition which commands a decisive cost and quality advantage and which strikes not at the margins of profits and the outputs of the existing firms but at their foundation and very lives" (Schumpeter, 1950, p. 84). He termed this kind of generalized competition from the new and its effects "creative destruction." He therefore saw the entry of new firms, like other forms of competition from the new, as deadly competition that had to be featured more prominently in economic theory. Indeed, to him, competition from the new was more important than already existing competition, which was what dominated most of economic theory.

The excess-supply controversy raised by Chamberlin's *Theory of Monopolistic Competition* provided further impetus to the development of entry theory. Harrod (1952, pp. 139–174), among others, reexamined the arguments leading to the Chamberlin's conclusion that monopolistic competition tends to give rise to excess capacity, especially when there is relative freedom of entry. He observed that the Chamberlinian firm would not be exhibiting very much farsightedness if it set its price at a level that ultimately attracted new firms into the industry, shifting the marginal revenue curve to the tangency point, which gives rise to excess capacity. He suggested, instead, that the rational firm would set prices to discourage entry and would even forego some potential short-term profits in order to control as large a market share as possible. Unfortunately Harrod's treatment of entry under imperfect competition, carefully scrutinized, does not make clear the difference between Chamberlin's analysis of large and small groups. In a small group facing a threat of entry, rational firms would need to weigh some short-term benefits against other costs arising from the erosion of market position; this is less likely in a large group. (Paradoxically, when explicit threats are considered, the Nash noncooperative-equilibrium analysis suggests outcomes that appear to be quasicooperative but can be enforced noncooperatively.)

Edwards (1955) pointed out that new entrants need "connections" in the market. Resources such as financing, raw materials, marketing outlets, and technical know-how are critical to successful market penetration. Paul (1954), Hahn (1955), and others pointed out that discouraging entry was not necessarily the most rational strategy for established firms. Some such firms would prefer to charge the short-run profit-maximizing price and let entrants establish themselves as they pleased. Others would just use rules of thumb such as full-cost pricing, perhaps worrying about entry but not about excess capacity.

Hicks (1954), in his consideration of the excess-capacity controversy, modeled established firms as seeking an advantageous tradeoff between short-run profit maximization and long-run erosion of market share. He concluded that the optimum prices of established firms, as well as their scales of operation, are best determined by optimizing a weighted sum of short- and long-run profits. The weights should depend on factors such as the relative sizes of their profits and their discount rates. This argument suggested that the straightforward entry-prevention strategy of Harrod was not necessarily optimal, even if practical arguments could be made in its favor.

A major step forward was taken by Bain (1956), who sought to identify, theoretically and empirically, how entry, evaluated in terms of the advantages that established firms have over potential entrants, can influence performance within an industry. These advantages originate from diverse sources. Bain presented a well-documented and well-argued analysis of how economies of scale, capital requirements, absolute cost differences, and profit differentiation within an industry can contribute toward imperfections in competition. These structural advantages favoring established firms can weaken the pressure of potential competition, an important regulator of long-run industry performance, permitting such firms to increase their profits and control in the industry more than they would if barriers did not exist.

Bain (1956, p. 5) viewed the entry of a new firm into an industry as involving a combination of two events: (1) the establishment of an independent legal entity, new to the industry as a producer, and (2) the introduction by that firm of new physical production capacity.

Sylos-Labini (1962), in a nonmathematical analysis bolstered by two numerical examples, concluded not only that were there several equilibrium prices and industrial structures but also that the equilibrium attained depends on the initial structure of the industry, the types of firms involved (potential entrants as well as established firms that participate in the adjustment to equilibrium), and the absolute market size in the industry.

In his review of Bain and Sylos-Labini, Modigliani (1959) showed within a traditional microeconomic framework how the limit price can be endogenously determined from the cost and demand curves facing the entrants, under various conditions of entry. This was an important contribution to the theory since it had previously been generally assumed that the limit price was determined exogenously.

Shubik (1959b), using an analogy with a concept of Admiral Mahan, suggested the "firm-in-being" as a means of including potential entrants as players whether they enter or not.

Williamson (1963) argued that limit-price theory was too deterministic. Due to uncertainties in oligopolistic interaction the application of a limit-pricing strategy cannot absolutely prevent entry. Realistically it generates a probability that the market will be penetrated. That is, the probability of market penetration, in terms of both number of entrants and times of entry, is increased when the actual price exceeds the limit price. Stigler (1966, pp. 216–229) also suggested that established firms would find it worthwhile to control the rate of entry. These extensions of limit-price theory have provided a basis for mathematical optimization models of pricing under the threat of entry that take dynamics and uncertainty into consideration. Pashigian (1968), Kamien and Schwartz (1971), Gaskins (1971), and Lippman (1980) have made contributions in this direction. These models conclude that, under threat of entry in a dynamic and uncertain environment, the optimum price lies between the entry-prevention price and the short-run profit-maximizing price. Moreover, the optimum price depends on the level of uncertainty in each time period, the effects of entry on market shares, the discount rate, and other cost data.

Friedman (1977a, b) focused on multiperiod markets, introducing the concept of a "weak noncooperative equilibrium." His firms control three moves in each period, one involving the choice of an exit probability and the others the choice of price and investment. A weak equilibrium point is one at which changes in all three categories are not considered simultaneously. To determine these equilibria one seeks strategies over time that are stable for changes in survival or exit probabilities and also for changes in price and investment (but not necessarily for changes in all together). Friedman developed the conditions under which they exist.

A further development in the analysis of oligopoly in a dynamic quasicooperative context was made by Selten (1973), who started from a symmetric Cournot model supplemented by specific institutional assumptions about the possibilities of cooperation. Selten (1974) and Kreps and Wilson (1982a) have considered sequential entry, predation, and reputation in an attempt to model strategically the way in which a reputation for toughness is built up or destroyed by actions taken against earlier entrants or potential entrants in a sequence.

An important advance weaving together the observations of Schumpeter and the behavioral theory of the firm has been made by Nelson and Winter (1982). Their approach is highly complementary to the dynamic game-theoretic approaches; indeed any attempt to specify long-term strategies leads us quickly to realize that the complexity and size of the available set of strategies is so overwhelming that extra conditions must be imposed before any fruitful analysis can take place. But the most promising clues for limiting or simplifying strategies are triggered by words such as search, satisficing, decentralized decision making, innovation, flexibility, viability, and organizational slack.

6.3.3 A simple model of entry

In this section we shall model some of the salient factors of entry in as simple a manner as possible in a static setting. We can divide firms into two categories: those already in the market and "firms-in-being" (see Shubik, 1959b). As a crude first approximation we shall summarize the many different barriers to entry in a single number that we shall call the entry cost D. We consider as a special case two firms already in a single-product market and a third contemplating entry (see Nti and Shubik, 1981b).

The variable cost of the firms are assumed to be linear, and their products are sold in a market where price is a linear function of total output. The established firms have no fixed costs, but the potential entrant faces a differential fixed-cost disadvantage arising from the set-up and other costs associated with activating the production and marketing of the product. The firms are assumed to be symmetric.

Let the variable cost of firm i be

$$c_i(q_i) = cq_i, \tag{6.16}$$

where q_i is the firm's nonnegative output; let the relation $\phi(\cdot)$ determining price be

$$p = \phi(q) = \frac{a - q}{b}, \tag{6.17}$$

where b is a positive parameter related to the slope of the demand curve and $p = 0$ if the total output q exceeds the market size a; and let $D \geq 0$ be the entry cost.

The decision variable of an established firm will simply be how much of the good it should offer for sale. The potential entrant, on the other hand, must select a probability of entry together with a corresponding output level. All decisions are made simultaneously and noncooperatively, and we shall limit ourselves to a one-shot, single-stage game. The game may therefore be considered to be in normal form with all the relevant information, strategies, and payoffs included in the specified entry and production strategies and profits. We wish to identify and interpret the noncooperative-equilibrium solutions for the model.

Using a result of Nti and Shubik (1981a), we search for equilibrium solutions involving no randomization in outputs. If the potential entrant, labeled 0, uses an entry-production strategy (δ, q_0) while the established firms, 1 and 2, produce q_1 and q_2 respectively, then the expected profits are

$$\Pi_0 = \frac{\delta}{b}\left[q_0\left(a - \sum_{i=0}^{2} q_i\right) - cbq_0 - Db \right], \tag{6.18a}$$

$$\Pi_1 = \frac{1 - \delta}{b}\left[q_1\left(a - \sum_{i=1}^{2} q_i\right) - cbq_1 \right] + \frac{\delta}{b}\left[q_1\left(a - \sum_{i=0}^{2} q_i\right) - cbq_1 \right], \tag{6.18b}$$

$$\Pi_2 = \frac{1 - \delta}{b}\left[q_2\left(a - \sum_{i=1}^{2} q_i\right) - cbq_2 \right] + \frac{\delta}{b}\left[q_2\left(a - \sum_{i=0}^{2} q_i\right) - cbq_2 \right]. \tag{6.18c}$$

Suppose $\delta = 0$ is part of an equilibrium solution to (6.18). Then the expected profits of firms 1 and 2 are maximized if the partial derivatives of (6.18b) and (6.18c) with respect to q_1 and q_2, respectively, are zero. (The second-order conditions for maxima hold trivially in this and subsequent optimizations.) So we have

$$q_1 = \frac{a - bc - q_2}{2}, \qquad q_2 = \frac{a - bc - q_1}{2}. \tag{6.19}$$

But $\delta = 0$ can be part of an equilibrium solution only if the potential entrant cannot possibly make a positive profit. The maximum profit attainable by the potential entrant if it enters will be negative if

$$q_1 + q_2 > a - bc - \sqrt{4Db}. \tag{6.20}$$

This constraint ensures that the potential entrant actually stays out of competition.

The unique solution to (6.19) is

$$q_1 = q_2 = \tfrac{1}{3}(a - bc) = q_{\text{duopoly}},$$

which satisfies the constraint (6.20) if

$$D > \frac{(a - bc)^2}{36b}.$$

Thus the traditional Cournot duopoly solution emerges if the entry cost exceeds $(a - bc)^2/36b$, which is related to the total profit in the market.

If $\delta = 1$ is part of an equilibrium solution, then taking partial derivatives of Π_0, Π_1, and Π_2 with respect to q_0, q_1, and q_2, respectively, and setting the resulting expressions to zero yields

$$q_0 = \tfrac{1}{2}(a - bc - q_1 - q_2),$$
$$q_1 = \tfrac{1}{2}(a - bc - q_0 - q_2), \tag{6.21}$$
$$q_2 = \tfrac{1}{2}(a - bc - q_0 - q_1).$$

But $\delta = 1$ will actually be part of an equilibrium solution only if the potential entrant will make a nonnegative profit if it enters into competition. We thus have a nonnegative profit incentive constraint,

$$q_1 + q_2 \leq a - bc - \sqrt{4Db}. \tag{6.22}$$

The unique solution to (6.21) is

$$q_0 = q_1 = q_2 = \tfrac{1}{4}(a - bc) = q_{\text{triopoly}}.$$

Substituting for q_1 and q_2 in (6.22), we obtain a bound on the entry costs for which the three-firm solution will hold. That is, the traditional Cournot triopoly solution emerges if

$$D < \frac{(a - bc)^2}{16b}.$$

Let $D_1 = (a - bc)^2/36b$ and $D_2 = (a - bc)^2/16b$. The regions of low and high entry costs are demarcated by D_1 and D_2, respectively. If entry costs are lower than D_1, the three-firm Cournot solution is obtained; and if entry costs exceed D_2, the Cournot duopoly solution is the equilibrium solution.

For entry costs between D_1 and D_2, an interesting phenomenon emerges in the analysis: Both the Cournot duopoly and triopoly solutions can be enforced by means of threats. There is a *cowardly duopolists solution* in which the potential entrant makes known its intention to start producing at the triopoly output level and the established firms, believing that entry is a foregone conclusion, accommodate the newcomer. And there is also a *cowardly entrant solution* in which the established firms make known their intentions to maintain a duopoly output and the potential entrant, believing that the established firms will fight entry, decides to stay out of competition.

A fascinating feature of the cowardly entrant solution is that the force of potential competition still works to prevent the established duopolists from *jointly* maximizing their profits. For the duopolists to jointly maximize their profits and simultaneously exclude the potential entrant from competition, their outputs q_1 and q_2 would have to satisfy both

$$q_1 + q_2 = \tfrac{1}{2}(a - bc)$$

and the nonpositive profit-incentive condition (6.20). But such a solution cannot hold when $D < (a - bc)^2/36b$.

There is another equilibrium solution in the intermediate range of entry costs that does not involve threats: All the firms fight it out. The potential entrant randomizes its entry decision at a positive probability δ, introducing uncertainty into the industry. This solution must satisfy

$$-2q_0 + a - q_1 - q_2 - bc = 0,$$
$$-2q_1 + a - \delta q_0 - q_2 - bc = 0,$$
$$-2q_2 + a - \delta q_0 - q_1 - bc = 0,$$
$$q_0(a - q_1 - q_2 - q_0 - bc) - Db = 0,$$

and is therefore unique:

$$q_1 = q_2 = \tfrac{1}{2}(a - bc - \sqrt{Db}),$$
$$q_0 = \sqrt{Db}, \qquad \delta = \frac{6\sqrt{Db} - (a - bc)}{\sqrt{4Db}}.$$

Thus if entry is randomized when entry costs lie in the intermediate range, the outputs of the established firms lie between the traditional Cournot duopoly and triopoly levels, and the potential entrant produces less than the Cournot triopoly level if it enters. The asymmetry between the potential entrant and the established firms is revealed in the distribution of outputs, with the established duopolists holding a larger market share even if entry occurs. If entry does not occur, however, the established firms would accumulate inventories that would let future potential entrants know that they cannot hope to enter as bona fide triopolists.

The prime purpose of this investigation is to consider the qualitative aspects of a simple model with entry. The price-variation or Bertrand–Edgeworth model has been calculated elsewhere (Nti and Shubik, 1981b); it shows qualitatively the same features except that capacity considerations are explicitly important. In both models, however, a critical feature emerges. Even with simultaneous moves and as much symmetry as possible, the equilibrium points for the market model with entry are *not* unique in the range of economic interest (i.e., in the range where entry costs are not totally prohibitive).

The three types of equilibrium encountered each have a plausible but essentially dynamic story attached to them. If the duopolists think that the entrant will enter regardless, there is a formally defined equilibrium with entry. If the entrant is convinced he will be blocked, there is an equilibrium without entry. And there is a "fighting zone." The essential characteristics of the entry problem are set-up or entry costs, capacities, information, and flexibility. What do the incumbents know about the identity, speed, and staying power of the entrants? What do the potential entrants know about the willingness to fight of the existing firms?

The above results are general, and a formal proof is provided by Nti and Shubik (1981a).

In any study of entry, production, finance, management, and marketing details must all be considered in estimating both the costs and the timing of entry. Conveying threats and building reputations depend explicitly upon the dynamics of multimove competition. Unless we invoke a special structure or radically limit the types of strategies firms can employ, threats can be used to establish almost any outcome in a multistage game as an equilibrium. Thus the abstract theory has little resolving power.

This suggests that useful commentary on oligopolistic dynamic requires a considerable knowledge of industrial structure. In particular, if in as simple a model as the one calculated in this section several equilibria with different prices are feasible, general arguments in support of limit pricing as a barrier to entry are certain to be inadequate without specific institutional detail or special behavioral insights to bolster the arguments.

6.3.4 Entry and competition

The approaches described above have been concerned specifically with the dynamics or statics of entry into markets with oligopolistic competition. There is another question that merits a rigorous answer. As the number of firms becomes large, with the size of each relative to the market as a whole being small, does the noncooperative analysis of entry provide an adequate approximation of our idea of a competitive market?

The partial-equilibrium story for firms and industries was sketched by Marshall. The large-group equilibrium with entry for oligopoly was sketched by Chamberlin. Both gave intuitively reasonable verbal descriptions of process backed with diagrams. Neither offered any precision or specifically addressed set-up costs and indivisibilities.

Possibly the earliest detailed discussion of a firm's cost function with indivisibilities and U-shaped average costs was that of Joseph (1933). She considered a fixed unit plant cost and a variable cost factor $\phi(q)$ for the production of q units of output from one unit of plant. For purposes of illustration she used

$$\phi(q) = aq^2 + bq. \tag{6.23}$$

Let p_1 be the cost to maintain a unit of fixed plant, and p_2 the unit cost of the variable input. Then the unit cost of output when n units of fixed plant are used is

$$c_n = \frac{np_1}{q} + \frac{np_2}{q}\phi\left(\frac{q}{n}\right) = \frac{np_1}{q} + p_2\left(\frac{aq}{n} + b\right). \tag{6.24}$$

Figure 6.3 shows how average costs vary when more and more fixed-capacity units are employed. The actual minimum average cost for any output is given by a scalloped curve $ABCDEFG$, which, when two or more units of the integral input are used, varies between c_* and c^* and, as output increases, approaches c_* as $1/n$ (c^* is the highest average cost paid prior to the introduction of a new plant).

Intuitively this simple observation should provide a basis for a rigorous analysis of equilibrium conditions for entry that will enable the theorist

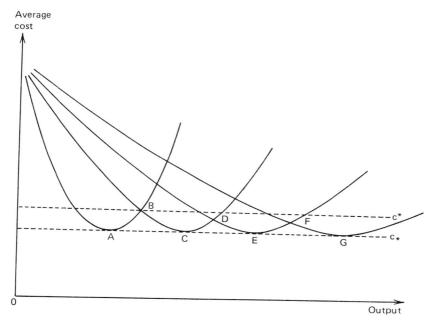

Figure 6.3
Multiplant average costs.

to achieve two goals. First, it suggests an approach to establishing consistency between models of oligopoly with entry and the model of the competitive price system. Second, it provides a means of introducing the number of active firms and even the number of plants as an endogenous part of the analysis.

Set-up costs, other entry costs, and indivisibilities destroy the concavity of profit functions or the convexity of preference contours. These are common conditions used in the existence proof for competitive equilibria, but they are not necessary. As the overall size of the market grows relative to the size of any firm, we may hope that set-up costs or other indivisibilities become progressively less important with respect to the market as a whole. Thus we may consider ε-equilibria as approximate equilibria, with the approximation becoming better as the size of the market grows relative to that of the competitors. Or we may obtain direct proofs of existence without using concavity.

Novshek (1980a) has proved the existence of a noncooperative equilibrium with entry that approaches the competitive equilibrium. He takes

$$c(q) = \begin{cases} 0 & \text{if } q = 0, \\ c_0 + v(q) & \text{if } q > 0 \text{ and } c_0 \geq 0, \end{cases} \tag{6.25}$$

where $v \geq 0$, $v' > 0$, $v'' \geq 0$, average cost is minimized at $q = 1$ for $p = f(q)$ twice differentiable, $f' < 0$ for $f > 0$, and there exists a competitive output q^* such that $f(q^*) = c(1)$ (the minimum average cost).

In his proof Novshek considers a sequence of games containing progressively smaller identical firms. A firm of size α has costs $c_\alpha(q) = \alpha c(q/\alpha)$. Thus for a countable but infinite supply of firms a game (α, c, f) can be defined. A noncooperative equilibrium with free entry consists of an integer n describing the number of active firms and a set of production levels $(q_1, q_2, \ldots, q_n)$ that comprise an n-firm Cournot equilibrium with no incentive for additional entry. In order to carry through the comparison between the competitive and noncooperative equilibria, Novshek used the condition $f(q^*) = c(1)$, which guarantees the existence of a competitive equilibrium for all games (α, c, f) without our having to worry about the integral nature of the number of firms. An intuitively more natural approach might be to dispense with this condition and consider ε-competitive equilibria, ε-noncooperative equilibria, and possibly also ε-cores.

6.4 What Are the Questions?

Why study oligopoly theory? What interesting and useful questions does it pose? What are the techniques and methods available for deriving answers? What questions can be answered? By whom? For whom?

Several basically different motivations lead to the study of competition among the few. To start with, there are questions that revolve around the efficiency of competition and the social control of industry:

• What is meant by economic competition? Is economic efficiency inversely related to the number of competitors in a market when they are few? How many is "many" in a market? Is "bigness" an economic, legal, political, or social concern?

• Do barriers to entry exist? How should they be measured? What are the economic consequences of the separation of ownership from management?

• What sort of industrial organization promotes technological change, innovation, and the efficient introduction of new products? How does production technology influence competition (including indivisibilities, set-up costs, joint production, and producer externalities)?

● How important to our analysis of industry and competition are marketing, distribution, advertising, and finance?

● What lessons, if any, does economics have for the development of corporate strategic planning and marketing?

● Does a strategic microanalysis of competition cast any light on the macroeconomic problems of employment, production, and investment?

● Are the various theories of oligopoly logically consistent with general equilibrium theory? Is this even an interesting question? If so, why?

● What are the roles of money and finance in oligopolistic competition?

● Should society control the availability of information in a competitive economy? If so, how should this be done? How important are search processes? What can or should be done about ignorance and uncertainty?

The study of competition among the few, unlike the study of Walrasian equilibria, requires many approaches rather than one. We have offered a brief listing of some of the more pertinent approaches together with observations and disclaimers on what has been left out or included. In particular, depending somewhat upon the questions being posed, the study of competition among the few can involve (1) formal oligopoly theory, (2) industrial organization, (3) marketing, (4) organization theory, (5) theories of innovation, (6) local public goods and externalities, (7) information theory, (8) finance, (9) general-equilibrium theory, and (10) certain aspects of accounting and law.

The focus of the present work has been primarily upon the role of numbers in competition or cooperation, with the economic information restricted basically to products, prices, and quantities. No attempt has been made to take into account features such as innovation that are frequently of considerable importance in the study of actual competition.

In the context of competition involving price, products, and quantities it is my belief that formal game-theoretic models have something useful to say about "How many is 'many'?" (see Shubik with Levitan, 1980). In a limited way the formal models provide extra insights into problems of entry, though for specific understanding detailed knowledge of industrial organization is generally required.

Game-theoretic oligopoly theory, like its verbal predecessors, has only limited value without specific ad hoc models to describe the phenomena being studied. Unfortunately the very precision and elegance of a mathematical model can pose dangers that are not encountered in a verbal argument. The appearance of abstraction in a mathematical model can lead to false assumptions about its generality (or lack of generality).

The elegance of a thin book such as Debreu's *Theory of Value* can be extremely misleading and the wrong model to follow when we investigate a topic in which institutional and technical detail count. Part of the attraction of recent developments in consumer, production, and general-equilibrium theory is that they have been noninstitutional or at least preinstitutional.

Oligopoly theory has to be process- and mechanism-oriented. It is intrinsically institutional. One of the purposes of this volume is to reconcile mathematical oligopoly theory with general-equilibrium theory, not because this will somehow give the appearance of mathematical elegance to oligopoly theory, but rather because it will allow us to take the next step in building institutions into the general-equilibrium framework.

Nor is our object to further the study of equilibrium analysis per se, but rather to use the strategic form to set up the preliminary apparatus needed for an eventual study of dynamics. A careful specification of the rules of the game necessitates an abstract description of the institutions; they are the carriers of process and are implicit in the rules.

I assert that in the process of embedding the noncooperative oligopoly game in a closed system it is natural to "invent" money. Thus the task of reconciling mathematical oligopoly models with general-equilibrium analysis leads to the development of a microeconomic theory of money and financial institutions.

It is my firm belief that noncooperative-equilibrium theory is more general and more basic than general-equilibrium theory. The two are consistent with each other, but the noncooperative theory goes considerably further. Not only can a Cournot or Bertrand–Edgeworth basis be supplied for the properties of Walrasian equilibria, but the oligopoly models provide insight into behavior among both the few and the many. Furthermore, the models can be easily modified to extend the analysis to situations with nonsystematic information and with economic weapons other than quantity and price.

Mathematical oligopoly theory has concentrated primarily on formal models with price or quantity or price, quantity, and location as the strategic variables. From Cournot onward, with considerable impetus given by the methodology of game theory and Nash's generalization of the noncooperative equilibrium, a series of increasingly carefully formulated models for strategic analysis has been presented. Extensions of the original, relatively simple models have been made to include entry, exit, and some rudimentary attempts at multistage analysis and the exploration of information conditions. Unfortunately the proliferation of plausible but not explicitly institutional dynamic models is so great that the development of a dynamic theory of any great generality without the introduction of more economic structure is in my opinion unpromising. Details such as the nature of time lags in capacity construction, liquidation, entry, and the setting up of distribution systems provide useful structure.

Modern industrial organization studies as typified by the text of Scherer (1980) and the works of Williamson (1975) and Spence (1977) indicate a direction in which formal models are hand-tailored and the basic considerations of oligopoly theory are examined in an institutional context. A new industrial organization and a mathematical institutional economics are being developed.

The importance of marketing as a scholarly discipline does not yet seem to have been fully appreciated in the development of a strategic theory of competition. Even a glance at an elementary business school text such as that of Kotler (1980) reveals a broad array of strategic weapons far beyond price and quantity. Distribution and retailing systems, advertising, product variation, and service as well as product innovation are all recognized explicitly. The modern behavioral theory of the firm (see Nelson and Winter, 1982) contains a blend of industrial organization, marketing, organization theory, and innovation theory that is much needed if economic advice is to be applied to industrial control and development policy.

The corporation with employees and stockholders has many of the features of a local public good, and deep problems are posed both in the logic of group control and optimization and in the social psychology of industrial organization (for surveys see Williamson, 1981; Marris and Mueller, 1980).

Along with the consideration of multistage models of competition has come an interest in information conditions. The models tend to be abstract, based upon games in extensive form or repeated games of indefinite length (see *GTSS*, chapter 3). The development is typified by the works of Harsanyi (1967, 1968a,b), Selten (1975), Radner (1968), Kreps and Wilson (1982b), Dubey and Shubik (1977a,b, 1981), and Milgrom and Weber (1982). None of these works, however, has been able to provide an adequate picture of the sale of information and the role of experts and advisers in economic life.

A satisfactory theory of multiperiod oligopolistic behavior will contain a considerable component of finance. Assets, their durability, the time it takes to construct them, and the possibilities of bankruptcy and insolvency form an important part of the structure of corporate markets. A preliminary attempt to capture some of these features has been made in the development of games of economic survival and models involving bankruptcy (Shubik, 1959b; Shubik and Thompson, 1959; Miyasawa, 1962; Shubik and Sobel, 1980; Hellwig, 1977, 1981).

In applications of economic analysis to policy questions in the control of industry or in the direction of an oligopolistic firm, accounting methods and the legal environment provide much of the structure needed to define the rules of the game. Accounting and legal conventions in general impose considerable constraints on the way in which much basic microeconomic information is prepared. Accounting conventions interacting with tax laws produce strategic opportunities for competitors that tend to be ignored in the development of broad theory; in the study of actual competition, however, they may be of considerable importance.

Modern oligopoly theory began with Cournot. Strategic mathematical oligopoly theory has evolved through the work of Bertrand (1883), Edgeworth (1925), Hotelling (1929), Wald (1951), von Neumann and Morgenstern (1944), Nash (1953), Shubik (1959b), Selten (1973), Telser (1972, 1978), and many others (for a review see Friedman, 1982).

The less mathematical development—marked, however, by a larger discussion of the economic modeling—includes Chamberlin (1933), Zeuthen (1930), Stackelberg (1952), Fellner (1949), and Bain (1956). Chamberlin, for instance, represented a mathematical step backward from the clarity and precision of Cournot, but a considerable step forward in modeling and economic insight concerning competition among the few.

A more behavioral and institutional approach is given by Schumpeter (1934), Sylos-Labini (1962), Marris (1964, 1979), Cyert and March (1963), and Nelson and Winter (1982), among others.

In the past ten years, under the joint impetus of game theory and the concern with entry, there has appeared a considerable literature on dynamic mathematical models. Many references to this literature have already been noted in section 6.3.2 and are not repeated here. The thrust of the work is toward understanding limit pricing, entry, prediction, toughness, reputation, and the physical and behavioral blocks to competition.

Even more recently there has been a concern with reconciling general-equilibrium theory and oligopoly theory. In particular the Cournot and Bertrand–Edgeworth models of duopoly have been treated in the context of a closed economy. The main purpose of this work has been to establish logical consistency between apparently diverse bodies of literature. In my opinion, however, not enough stress has been laid upon the important role that markets and money play in achieving this reconciliation. It will be suggested in part IV that when these features are recognized, the way is opened to the development of a theory of money and financial institutions that is consistent with general-equilibrium theory. The natural way to embed oligopolistic competitions into a closed economy is to invent money and markets.

There is also a growing literature on experimental economies that is primarily concerned with oligopolistic markets. This includes Chamberlin (1948), Hoggatt (1959), Siegal and Fouraker (1960), Friedman (1967), Shubik, Wolf, and Eisenberg (1972), Sherman (1972), Smith (1962, 1979), Sauermann (1967, 1970, 1972, 1974, 1976, 1977, 1978), and many others. A review of some of this literature is given in Shubik (1975a,b). To some extent this work has been motivated by an interest in whether the solution concepts suggested by the various theories of oligopolistic behavior are of any predictive value in the laboratory.

The growth in theory and in experimental economics has been paralleled in the last ten years by a modern theory of industrial organization. An adequate survey of this considerable body of literature is not within the scope of this volume. This development merits notice, though, because the field of industrial organization bridges theory and practice and is helping to reconcile institutional studies with oligopoly theory.

7 Oligopoly and General Equilibrium

7.1 On Closing the Market Model

Chapters 3–6 have been devoted to models of oligopolistic competition in which consumers are not considered as strategic players and feedback from the economy as a whole is excluded. These simplifications are reasonable as a first-order approximation for exploring the manifestations of oligopolistic power. For example, using the solution concepts of joint maximization, the noncooperative equilibrium, and the competitive equilibrium, we can construct suggestive and useful measures of oligopolistic structure by comparing profits at the three solution points. Profit levels above the noncooperative equilibrium can be regarded as evidence of implicit or explicit collusive behavior (for the construction of a collusion index see Shubik with Levitan, 1980).

In several examples we have forged a direct relationship between noncooperative and cooperative analyses by starting with a market described in strategic form and then deriving the coalitional or cooperative form, the characteristic function, or the h-function. These techniques in modeling and in the application of game theory are of far broader applicability than one might suspect from our examples, in which price and production have been the only strategic variables considered.

The technique of starting with a strategic description of the game and then deriving a cooperative form is a useful way to check collusive and threat possibilities in any set of firms, regardless of the strategic variables. The institutional features in the strategic description, whether product variation, innovative finance, organizational flexibility, or other factors, are all mapped into an abstract, noninstitutional (but static) representation of power, profit, and collusive possibilities.

Much work on oligopoly theory has been either not sufficiently institutional and process-oriented or not formulated at a sufficiently abstract level.

Understanding the process and strategic possibilities available in any oligopolistic market does indeed require detailed ad hoc knowledge of the basic economic weapons available in the market. Yet it is possible to map the myriad of detail into a form that captures the essence of the potentials of power, profit, threat, and the possibilities for economic warfare or cooperation.

To reconcile the open models of oligopolistic competition with the general-equilibrium models, the economist must consider the role of entry into competition and how to account for consumers as strategic (even if weak) players. These two problems are considered in this chapter.

All models of oligopolistic competition are in fact peculiarly institutional. The slice of the economy being modeled is described as a game in strategic form with the customers as strategic dummies. The use of money is assumed, and the firms are run by profit-maximizing entrepreneurs. In contrast, the models of bilateral monopoly and general equilibrium have essentially one economic actor: the consumer-trader. In the Arrow–Debreu formulation of general equilibrium (Arrow and Debreu, 1954; Debreu, 1959) the firms are essentially mechanistic noninstitutional fictions with no strategic role to play.

We argued in *GTSS* that in the full development of a strategic theory of political economy we may need as many as five differentiated players: the citizen (as consumer, laborer, or voter), the industrialist or businessman, the financier, the politician, and the administrator or bureaucrat. For the full reconciliation of oligopoly theory and general equilibrium we need to model the strategic roles of at least the consumer and firms. This we shall finally be able to achieve in part IV, but, prior to attempting this, in part III we shall present an essentially noninstitutional, cooperative theory of games that is naturally consistent with general-equilibrium theory.

In this chapter we take the *n*-person strategic model of competition analyzed in chapter 5 and "close the model" in two different ways, one utilizing the special institutional aspects of the game in strategic form and the other ignoring them.

7.1.1 The demand side of the market
There remains the possibility that the consumers are neither mechanisms nor strategic dummies but are strategically involved as players. We stress again that when we model large segments of an economy over time, we are confronted with a problem that no longer involves only economic considerations. The public acts for the most part as a price-taker in the short term but can easily react in a strategically important way through long-term political and social mechanisms. At this point, however, our attention turns to the consumer as a strategic player.

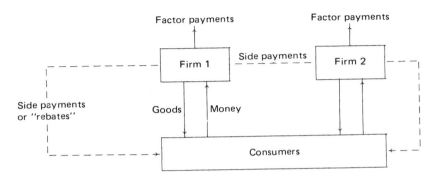

Figure 7.1
A closed market with u-money.

7.1.2 The supply side of the market

The models in previous chapters treated supply aspects of the market in terms of costs. We did not ask how the firms obtained their factors of production. The models were open on the factor supply side in the sense that no feedback adjustment was made to account for how movements in the factor markets affect consumers.

For simplicity and for purposes of comparison we maintain this separation in sections 7.2 and 7.3. As a first-order approximation we argue that the major aspects of welfare investigations can be covered by considering the consumers and firms as active players in the final product market. Thus the model is still not completely closed (see figure 7.1).

We also need to specify who runs the firms and what becomes of their profits. In the first two models we make the simplest of assumptions (which leaves the models open in yet another way), namely that the firms are run by owners who wish to maximize their profits.

7.2 A Two-Sided Closed Market: Noncooperative Solutions

We start with a game-theoretically closed two-sided market that can be compared to the duopoly model of chapter 4. As before, each producer has a production function $C_i(q_i) = c_i q_i$ and a capacity limitation k_i. The firms begin with money as their only factor of production, which they convert into a final product they can sell. Instead of representing the consumers by a linear demand function, however, we now assume m consumers with utility functions quadratic in the product and linear in a money.

Before we can fully specify the models we must settle several details concerning markets, price, profit, utility maximization, and the possibility of side payments. We might postulate an utterly free market in which different customers buy at different prices from any firm, but it would be more in spirit with the law in some countries to require that firms charge every customer the same price for the same product. The same market price to all might be circumvented in some situations by side payments or rebates to customers.

If we give the customers complete strategic freedom to work out any deal, then the distinction between price and quantity as the independent variable "in the market" disappears when we analyze the cooperative game including both customers and firms. The resultant game becomes a c-game, and the threat structure is thereby considerably simplified.

We wish to contrast three theories: (1) general-equilibrium theory; (2) cooperative game theory (primarily core and value solutions); and (3) noncooperative theory (primarily the Cournot–Nash models rather than the Edgeworth or Bertrand variations). All three take as their starting point basic economic information concerning consumers, firms, initial endowments, and preferences. They differ in the further assumptions they make. We shall contrast the assumptions for six models associated with the three approaches. One model is noted for the general equilibrium, two for the noncooperative equilibrium, and three for coalitional or cooperative analysis. They will be illustrated for the one-product linear demand and constant-cost model of chapter 3; but the modeling and analysis can be directly generalized.

All approaches start with the following assumptions. There is a set M of producers and a set N of consumers. Each producer i is characterized by a product transformation,

$$y_i = cx_i, \quad c > 0, \tag{7.1}$$

defined for $0 \leq x_i \leq k$ ($i \in M$). Each producer has a capacity limit k. The production process transmutes c units of money into 1 unit of the consumer good. The initial endowment of each firm is its "working capital" B (where $B/c \geq k$).

Each consumer j is characterized by a utility function

$$\phi_j(z_j, w_j) = az_j - \frac{b}{2}z_j^2 + \lambda w_j, \quad a, b, \lambda > 0, \tag{7.2}$$

defined for $0 \leq z_j \leq a/b$ ($j \in N$), where z_j is j's final holding of the consumer good and w_j is his holding of money. The initial endowment of each consumer is A units of money.

The producers are assumed to have utility only for money. Profits can be defined as the change from producers' initial money holdings,

$$\Pi_i = g_i - cx_i, \tag{7.3}$$

where g_i is the amount of money received by firm i and cx_i is the amount spent in producing x_i. Note that up to this point nothing has been said about price; g_i is just a money income, with no specification of how it is earned.

7.2.1 The general-equilibrium model
A competitive equilibrium exists if a price can be found that clears all markets given that producers maximize their profit and consumers maximize their utility. We start by postulating the existence of prices that producers and consumers take as given. We then prove that prices that clear markets and lead to efficient trade and production to exist.

Model 1 (competitive equilibrium) Let the marginal utility of money, λ, be 1, for convenience. Let u_j be the amount of money bid by consumer j. A competitive equilibrium exists if we can find, for a given p, a u_j that maximizes

$$\frac{au_j}{p} - \frac{b}{2}\left(\frac{u_j}{p}\right)^2 + (A - u_j) \quad \text{for } 0 \le u_j \le a/b \tag{7.4}$$

and a q_i that maximizes

$$(p - c)q_i \quad \text{for } 0 \le q_i \le k, \tag{7.5}$$

such that $\sum_{i \in M} q_i = \sum_{j \in N} x_j$, where $x_j = u_j/p$.
  It is easy to check that there is a competitive equilibrium,

$$p = a - \frac{mk}{n}b \quad \text{for } 0 \le k \le \frac{n}{m}\left(\frac{a - c}{b}\right), \tag{7.6}$$

where capacity is low enough to keep p above c. For a larger capacity $p = c$, profits are zero, and the division of production is indeterminate.
  For purposes of comparison among the models, consider the ratio n/m as fixed and take $k = (n/m)[(a - c)/b]$. This gives firms precisely the capacity to supply the market at $p = c$.

7.2.2 Markets in strategic form
In order to define a game representing production and exchange fully in strategic form we must describe the strategies of the players as well as their payoffs. A natural model is the one suggested in chapter 4 with

consumers treated as strategic dummies and firms regarded as active players.

Model 2 (Cournot) Assuming that firm i uses a production strategy, offering for sale an amount q_i with $0 \leq q_i \leq k$, we can postulate a price-formation mechanism that clears the market up to saturation:

$$p = \begin{cases} a - \dfrac{b}{n} \sum_{i \in M} q_i & \text{for } 0 \leq \sum q_i \leq \dfrac{na}{b}, \\ 0 & \text{for } \sum q_i > \dfrac{na}{b}. \end{cases} \qquad (7.7)$$

Competition among m firms can then be described by having each trying to maximize

$$\Pi_i = q_i \left(a - \frac{b}{n} \sum_{i \in M} q_i - c \right). \qquad (7.8)$$

This yields an interior noncooperative equilibrium of the form

$$q_i = \frac{n}{m+1} \frac{a-c}{b} \quad \text{for} \quad \frac{n}{m+1} \frac{a-c}{b} \leq k \qquad (7.9)$$

or a boundary equilibrium $q_i = k$ otherwise. For the interior solution profit and price are

$$\Pi_i = \frac{n}{b} \left(\frac{a-c}{m+1} \right)^2 \quad \text{and} \quad p = \frac{a+mc}{m+1}. \qquad (7.10)$$

This is in essence the Cournot model as presented in chapters 4 and 5 with the minor modification that the number of consumers appears as an explicit parameter.

Model 3 (strategic market game) In this model we regard all $n + m$ players, both firms and consumers, as strategic players. A strategy by a consumer j is to select a level of expenditure u_j; a strategy by a firm i is to offer an amount q_i for sale. Price is determined as

$$p = \sum_{j \in N} u_j \Big/ \sum_{i \in M} q_i; \qquad (7.11)$$

and a little straightforward manipulation gives

$$u_i = p \left[\frac{a(n-1) - np}{b(n-1)} \right] \quad \text{and} \quad q_i = \frac{n}{m} \left[\frac{a(n-1) - np}{b(n-1)} \right]. \qquad (7.12)$$

Table 7.1
Comparison of noncooperative and competitive equilibria

	Competitive equilibrium	Cournot	Strategic market game
p	c	$\dfrac{a + mc}{m + 1}$	$\dfrac{cm}{m - 1}$
q_i	$\dfrac{n}{m}\left[\dfrac{a - c}{b}\right]$	$\dfrac{n}{m + 1}\dfrac{a - c}{b}$	$\dfrac{n}{m}\left[\dfrac{a(n - 1) - np}{b(n - 1)}\right]$
u_j	$\left[\dfrac{a - c}{b}\right]c$	$\dfrac{m}{m + 1}p\left[\dfrac{a - c}{b}\right]$	$p\left[\dfrac{a(n - 1) - np}{b(n - 1)}\right]$

7.2.3 A comparison of three models
The three noncooperative solutions are summarized in table 7.1. We note that for a constant ratio n/m, as $n \to \infty$ both noncooperative solutions converge to the competitive equilibrium.

Is the price more or less in the Cournot market than in the strategic market game? This depends upon whether

$$\frac{a + mc}{m + 1} \gtreqless \frac{cm}{m - 1}, \quad \text{or} \quad a \gtreqless \frac{2cm}{m - 1}. \tag{7.13}$$

Paradoxically, when costs are relatively low, $c < [(m - 1)/m](a/2)$, the strategic market game equilibrium yields a price higher than the Cournot equilibrium. Thus consumers would be better off if they relinquished their strategic freedom.

7.3 A Two-Sided Closed Market: Cooperative Solutions

7.3.1 The Edgeworth cooperative game
Utilizing the basic economic data of section 7.2 we may define a game in coalitional form without first defining a strategic form or even postulating the existence of price.

Model 4 (Edgeworth game)   Fixing capacity at

$$k = \frac{n}{m}\left(\frac{a - c}{b}\right)$$

for all firms, we consider a market with a set M of firms and N of consumers. We assume that any subset $S \subset M$ of firms can deal with any

Table 7.2
The core of the Edgeworth game

	Consumers		
Firms	1	2	∞
1	(0, 1/2) to (1/2, 0)	(1/4, 1/4) to (3/4, 0)	(1, 0)
2	(0, 1/2)	(0, 1/2) to (1/4, 1/4)	(1, 0)
∞	(0, 1/2)	(0, 1/2)	(0, 1/2)

subset $T \subset N$ of consumers and that a coalition $S \cup T$ can work out any deal in any way it pleases.

This is a c-game; once the coalition $S \cup T$ has formed, the joint gain of its members is totally independent of the actions of nonmembers. There are no externalities caused by interconnections among players who are required to trade through organized markets.

The characteristic function can be defined as follows:

$$v(S) = sB, \qquad v(T) = tA,$$

$$v(S \cup T) = \begin{cases} t\dfrac{(a-c)^2}{2b} + sB + tA & \text{for } \dfrac{m}{n}t \le s, \\[3mm] s\dfrac{n}{m}\dfrac{(a-c)^2}{b}\left[1 - \dfrac{1}{2}\dfrac{ns}{mt}\right] + sB + tA & \text{for } \dfrac{m}{n}t > s. \end{cases}$$

To show the essential structure of this game we can normalize one-person coalition values to zero and set $a = b = 1$ and $c = 0$. Since players of each type are symmetric, only numbers, not the specific sets of each type, matter. When $n = m$, we can then write the characteristic function in profile form as

$$f(s, t) = \begin{cases} t/2 & \text{for } t \le s \ (k = 1), \\ s - s^2/2t & \text{for } t > s. \end{cases} \tag{7.14}$$

Tables 7.2 and 7.3 show the core and value for one, two, or many strategic players on each side of the market. In both tables the first entry is the payoff to a firm at a type-symmetric solution point and the second is the payoff to a consumer. Because capacity is pegged at $k = 1$, the games with two firms and one consumer have excess capacity whereas those with two consumers and one firm have too little. The other cases similarly have too little, too much, or just the right amount of capacity.

As the overall size of the game grows, so does the payoff. Hence the

Table 7.3
The value of the Edgeworth game

	Consumers		
Firms	1	2	∞
1	(1/4, 1/4)	(5/12, 2/12)	(1, 0)
2	(1/12, 1/3)	(5/24, 7/24)	(1, 0)
∞	(0, 1/2)	(0, 1/2)	(0, 1/2)

imputations change size. For the games with profiles $(1, 1)$, $(1, 2)$, $(2, 1)$, and $(2, 2)$, the imputations add to $1/2$, $3/4$, $1/2$, and 1, respectively. Note that the value is not necessarily in the core, but for $n = m \rightarrow \infty$ they both coincide with the competitive equilibrium, which gives the imputation $(0, 1/2)$.

It is an easy exercise to check that the two noncooperative markets do not in general yield Pareto-optimal solutions.

7.3.2 Cooperative solutions based on strategic market games
In section 5.4.1 we developed the characteristic function and the Harsanyi function for the nonsymmetric market model in which only the firms are regarded as strategic players. The point we want to make here concerns modeling and not mathematics. The two models in strategic form suggested in section 7.2.2 were based on the same basic economic information but with somewhat different assumptions about market structure and the strategic roles of firms and consumers. Either model can serve as a basis from which a game in coalitional form can be constructed. However, because in both models trade is assumed to take place through a market mechanism in which prices are formed, an externality has been created, and the resultant game is not a c-game (Shubik, 1971c). Phrasing this another way, in the characteristic function described in section 7.3.1, once two subsets of players S and T have decided to trade together, they can ignore all remaining players; if they are required to trade through a market mechanism, this is not so.

It is reasonably natural to imagine a coalition among firms who are selling to passive consumers represented by a market mechanism. Thus the cooperative game of section 5.4.1 is defined only on coalitions of firms. But if all firms in M can sell to the market, what actions do we attribute to the coalition $\bar{S}$ when the coalition S has formed (with $S \cup$

$\overline{S} = M$)? A pessimistic way to evaluate what S can achieve is to limit its payoff to what it can guarantee, as follows.

Model 5   The characteristic function of the Cournot market is

$$v(S) = \max_{i \in S} \min_{j \in \overline{S}} \sum_{i \in S} \Pi_i, \tag{7.15}$$

where Π_i is the payoff to firm i as a function of the strategies of all strategic players. The assumption is that regardless of cost or hurt to itself $\overline{S}$ tries to damage S as much as possible by actions such as flooding the market. This calculation together with a description and illustration of the generally large core was carried out in sections 5.4.1 and 5.4.2.

This model may seem far too pessimistic. A more reasonable description of the worth of coalitions might be obtained by taking into consideration the cost of threats to the threatener. This was done in section 5.4.5 utilizing a method suggested by Harsanyi to calculate a modified characteristic function.

Model 6 (Harsanyi characteristic function of the Cournot market)   Denoting the Harsanyi function by $h(S)$, we determine its value for any S by solving two linear equations:

$$h(S) + h(\overline{S}) = \max_{S} \max_{\overline{S}} \sum_{i \in M} \Pi_i,$$

$$h(S) - h(\overline{S}) = \max_{S} \max_{\overline{S}} \left(\sum_{i \in S} \Pi_i - \sum_{j \in \overline{S}} \Pi_j \right). \tag{7.16}$$

We could use this (in general not superadditive) function to determine the core, but, as indicated in section 5.4.5, the calculation is biased toward the value.

Model 7 (Harsanyi function of a strategic market game)   If we begin with model 3, then in order to calculate the Harsanyi function we must consider mixed coalitions of firms and consumers who must trade through the market but can now engage in coordinated restrictions or increases in production and consumer boycotts or increases in demand.

7.3.3 Oligopoly and market structure
Do the details of market structure matter to the economist investigating the efficiency of a price system when there are individual firms and consumers with no externalities beyond the interlinkage imposed by the

existence of a trading technology itself? The answer is emphatically yes and no. Yes, when there are few buyers or sellers. No, when there are many buyers and sellers. Dubey, Mas-Colell, and Shubik (1980, pp. 340–341) have suggested an axiomatization of the idea of a market. They suggest five properties:

1. Convexity: Traders have available a convex set of strategies.

2. Anonymity: From the point of view of the market, only the message sent by the agent matters.

3. Continuity of outcomes with respect to strategies. (We note that the Bertrand and double-auction markets do not satisfy this condition.)

4. Aggregation: The trading possibilities of any player are influenced only by the mean of the messages of the other players (and not, say, by the variance).

5. Nondegeneracy: Individual players must have a substantial influence on their trading possibilities in the market.

When these properties are satisfied, then for an economy with a continuum of active players there will be many ways to construct strategic market games that will yield an equivalence between the noncooperative and the competitive equilibria. But this depends explicitly on the assumption of many small players. The preponderant industrial form is oligopoly; and when there is competition among the few, the specific market structure influences all of the solutions.

The price-formation mechanism is in general a weak externality that can be obliterated by numbers. Moreover, as suggested by tables 7.2–7.4, when the numbers are large, different solutions reflecting different intentions predict the same outcomes.

Measure-theoretic methods have been used to characterize behavior in an economy characterized by large or "atomic players" confronting an ocean of small agents. Most of this work has involved exchange economies only, employing core theory. An exception is the investigation of Okuno, Postlewaite, and Roberts (1980); considering an exchange economy with two commodities as a strategic market game with atoms and a continuum of traders, they show the expected inefficient features of the noncooperative equilibrium and consider conditions leading to incentives to merge.

The first nonsymmetric models embedding a Cournot-style model in a general-equilibrium context were proposed by Shapley and Shubik (1967a) and, more generally, by Gabszewicz and Vial (1972). The first symmetric model of a strategic market game was provided by Shubik

(1973). Shubik (1979) also constructed a symmetric two-sided auction market that extended the Bertrand–Edgeworth approach to competition in a closed exchange economy. This has been further formalized and analyzed by Dubey and Shubik (1980b) and by Dubey (1982). A related Bertrand model has been considered by L. K. Simon (1981). The striking result from these models is that if there are two active traders on each side of the market for each commodity, the noncooperative equilibria are competitive equilibria immediately. This contrasts with the gradual approach of the noncooperative to the competitive equilibria in Cournot models under replication.

The conclusion to be drawn from the price-game analysis is not that with price and quantity as strategic variables, competition begins at two. Rather, it is that if communication and cooperation are ruled out, it is possible for competition to start at two. The striking Bertrand-like result that holds for two is nevertheless based on a single-period model. When two large institutions are around for a long time, possibilities for communication and accommodation appear. It is unlikely that two competitors are always enough for competition.

In the development of economic theory it is not sufficient to prove existence or limit theorems. We must ask if the models are good and relevant to the questions being asked. We also need to know why the questions themselves are interesting. Can one embed the Cournot oligopoly model in a closed economic model either nonsymmetrically or symmetrically and obtain limit behavior (or continuum) results linking the noncooperative with the competitive equilibria? Both parts of this question are of interest to the economic theorist. The modeling required to answer them must at least provide for logical consistency, but it may do more. It may focus our attention on different economic phenomena of importance.

It is my assertion that the natural embedding of a symmetric model of the Cournot (and other) noncooperative games into a general-equilibrium context requires the explicit introduction of a price-formation mechanism, money, and credit. The class of strategic market games is more than a means to reconcile noncooperative oligopoly theory with general-equilibrium theory for large numbers. It opens up the study of oligopolistic elements in a closed economy.

The study of oligopolistic behavior required dynamics, for the most part. But microeconomic dynamics calls for a specification of structure that is not present in general-equilibrium theory. Koopmans has observed that general-equilibrium theory is preinstitutional. Noncooperative game theory provides the next step toward an economic dynamics. It provides rules of the game that can be viewed abstractly as institutional structure. In particular (as noted in chapter 1) money plays a natural role as a strategic decoupling device in closed oligopoly models. At equilibrium the books balance and money disappears. But under disequilibrium the use of money (and other financial instruments) provides the extra degree of freedom needed for simultaneous actions by the competitors.

Game-theoretic modeling methods pertaining to the strategic form require that all states of the system both in and out of equilibrium be specified by the rules. An easy way to describe the system in disequilibrium without postulating the feasibility of all bilateral trades is to invent money and a market for each good.

7.4 Entry and Exit: Closed Models

7.4.1 A closed model with active and inactive firms

Novshek and Sonnenschein (1978) developed the first rigorous model of a closed economy with entry. Their work is a direct extension of that of Novshek on entry in an open economy with small firms.

They start by defining a Walrasian private-ownership economy with nonconvex production functions. They then derive a sequence of economies $\mathscr{E}(\alpha)$ by replicating the consumers $1/\alpha$ times and contrast this sequence with an economy $\hat{\mathscr{E}}$ with a continuum of infinitesimally small firms in which each industry has a cone-shaped production set. As $\alpha \to 0$, the $\mathscr{E}(\alpha)$ approach $\hat{\mathscr{E}}$.

A Cournot or quantity-strategy game is defined for the α sequence and compared with the $\mathscr{E}(\alpha)$. It is assumed that price varies smoothly with the quantity actions of the firms. Prices are expressed relative to the first commodity, $p_1 = 1$, and firms maximize profits in terms of this commodity. The consumers are regarded as price-takers. It is assumed that there exist a finite set of firm types and a countable infinity of firms of each type. Each firm has an efficient scale of production bounded away from zero. It is further necessary to assume that demand is downward-sloping to the right in all markets.

The existence of noncooperative equilibria is established utilizing a minimal form of mixed strategy (there is a probability only on the choice that a firm is in or out of the market). It is shown that the Walrasian equilibria of $\mathscr{E}$ can be obtained as a limit of noncooperative equilibria as $\alpha \to 0$ and that every limit of the noncooperative equilibria as $\alpha \to 0$ is a Walrasian equilibrium.

Mas-Colell (1981) adopted a somewhat different set of assumptions. He assumed that constant returns to scale do not hold in the aggregate, and he established that if (p^*, y^*) are the prices and productions at a nondegenerate Walrasian equilibrium of a limit economy and if the Walrasian supply is single-valued in a neighborhood of p^* (no constant returns to scale in the aggregate), then for every sequence of approximating economies there is a sequence of noncooperative equilibria (possibly involving mixed strategies) that converges to (p^*, q^*).

Mas-Colell's result does not use the downward-sloping demand condition, which in the context of general equilibrium is quite restrictive. He showed that at an equilibrium only a vanishingly small fraction of the firms use mixed strategies.

The proof of the results noted above are beyond the mathematical scope of this book. But the essence of the economic problem and why it is of interest can be appreciated without the proof. The noncooperative equilibrium is a far more general solution concept than the Walrasian equilibrium. A noncooperative equilibrium may exist in games for which a competitive equilibrium cannot even be defined.

An alternative interpretation of the Walrasian model is as a game with a continuum of nonatomic economic agents. We can examine a sequence of strategic market games with players whose overall size becomes diminishingly small with respect to the economy as a whole. Do the noncooperative equilibria of these finite-player games approach the continuum model? The answer in general is yes. This suggests not only that the noncooperative equilibrium is reasonably consistent with the competitive equilibrium, but that it can be used to yield results where the competitive-equilibrium model is not adequate—for example, in closed economies with an intermix of mass markets and oligopolistic sectors.

More important, however, is the proposition that the presence of small set-up costs and small, efficient scale (see Novshek and Sonnenschein, 1978) is compatible with the existence of Walrasian equilibria and also allows an endogenous determination of the number of active firms.

One unfortunate modeling feature of the work of Novshek and Sonnenschein (1978) on Cournot and Walrasian equilibria is that they assume the availability of "a countable infinity of firms of a variety of basic types." There must always be a "shadow supply" of firms out of the economy. I conjecture that much the same results can be obtained by giving all players a set of "off-balance-sheet" assets such as managerial skills that can be used only above a threshold level and are of limited capacity. In a closed economy everyone must be somewhere; thus there can be no net entry or exit, and the act of entry or exit can be seen only by comparative statics. Given a society in which all individuals have resources and special skills, there will be butchers, bakers, and candlestick makers at equilibrium. A change in resources or preferences will move some butchers or bakers elsewhere. Thus an analysis using comparative statics will show local exit and entry, even though globally the same people are still there.

7.4.2 A note on entry, exit, and merger

Most work on general equilibrium and much of that on oligopoly theory utilizing the Cournot–Nash equilibria has been static rather than dynamic. Yet it is clear that the analysis of entry, exit, or merger calls at least for comparative statics. To reconcile the Cournot–Nash and Walrasian equilibria one must build closed strategic market games. The problems of nonconvexity caused by set-up costs, indivisibilities, and other factors are related to but different from the problems of entry, exit, and merger. With the former, the nonconvexity itself is the key factor. With the latter, capital, time, information, and flexibility are central. The papers of Novshek (1980a, b), Novshek and Sonnenschein (1978), and Shubik and Wooders (1984b), for example, provide reasonably adequate models of set-up costs but do not catch the fundamental nonsymmetry between a firm in existence and a firm-in-being or potential entrant.

Accounting conventions make an important distinction that most equilibrium models ignore under the implicit or explicit claim that distinctions between capital and current accounts are abitrary. Yet in general, entry and exit costs are capital-account items, and set-up costs and overheads are current-account items. The distinction between accounts, which is undoubtedly somewhat arbitrary may nevertheless provide a good way to model an economy that is closed in space and agents but open in time. In particular, capital stock needs to be represented in some aggregated form.

An adequate study of entry, exit, and merger requires specification of the game in extensive or at the least in strategic form. An extensive description of threats, timing, signaling, and explicit negotiation is, however, beyond the scope of general-equilibrium modeling. In the extensive form we can more or less manage an entry move or set-up expenditure, purchase of materials, production, and sales; but it is hard to remain general and yet fully specify a complex game in extensive form.

An easier way to finesse institutional detail while maintaining set-up or entry distinctions is to go directly to a coalitional form without specifying individual strategies. This is the approach adopted by Shubik and Wooders (1984a, b) utilizing the ε-core. The entry, exit, and merger of firms can be regarded as implicit in the coalition-production conditions at a level sufficient to illustrate properties of the ε-core and to construct examples in which the utilization of production sets by various coalitions can be interpreted as the endogenous formation of firms. Yet one must guard against making easy analogies in which the bridging of the gap between verbal description and mathematics requires great flights of imagination. Both the cooperative-game approach and the work utilizing games in strategic form have taken only a rudimentary step in reconciling game-theoretic models of closed economies with the Walrasian system.

7.4.3 Some problems in modeling the corporation

Under replication the small, individually owned, off-balance-sheet items become better and better integrated into the price system. What emerges is a reasonable model of an economy with small owner-run firms. Basic difficulties remain, however, if we wish to model the large manager-run corporation in which the off-balance-sheet items are not merely individual talents ignored by accountants but overall organizational skills and items such as "good will" that have long defied clear specification, let alone quantification.

Even leaving aside the problems in modeling entry and exit, we encounter considerable difficulties in trying to incorporate large stockholder-owned firms in a closed economy into noncooperative-game models. Dubey and Shubik (1978b), for example, formulated and analyzed an economy with production and exchange as a three-stage game in extensive form: In the first set of moves resources were exchanged; this was followed by production and then a final round of exchange. But in such multistage games, unless all players are presumed to be insignificantly small, there are major problems involving information and a proliferation of equilibrium points.

Even with an adequate internal model of the corporation, we must assume that large corporations will in general be owned by more than one individual. Such ownership will often be manifested in the holding of voting shares. Several new problems must now be dealt with:

1. Under what conditions should an individual owner maximize profits rather than utility?

2. What corporate goal should a group of managers have?

3. What rules or laws are required to make voting stock powers consistent with the existence of a price system?

4. At what minimum level of model complexity does the trading of shares take on economic significance?

5. At what minimum level of complexity do mergers take on economic significance?

Dubey and Shubik (1980a) established some intuitively obvious conditions under which an individual manager will attempt to maximize the profits of his firm rather than his own utility. The firm must have no market power, either in final product or factor markets, and there must be laws against self-serving practices such as selling to oneself at less than the market price.

When the firm is run by a group of managers (often with manager-selected outside directors), what that group tries to optimize can hardly be specified without developing a theory of bureaucratic behavior. Baumol (1959), Shubik (1961), Marris (1964, 1979), Williamson (1975), and others have explored goals for upper management and have suggested that declared profit and expected profit are only two of many possibilities. There is little doubt that factors such as size of sales, size of the organization, job security, and personal advancement are important; but they bear different weights depending on time and place. There is at present no satisfactory theory of corporate managerial behavior.

In the Arrow–Debreu model of an economy with a price system, shares appear as an accounting device to allocate the payment of profits. There is never any essential reason to trade them. Yet we see trading take place in both "thick" and "thin" markets. Although noncontrol stockholders rarely, if ever, vote on the production choices of the firm, on occasion there are proxy fights for control, and then the strategic importance of the stockholder's vote emerges.

There is a growing literature on the stockholder-owned firm in partial-equilibrium economics and finance (see, e.g., Diamond, 1967; Ekern and Wilson, 1974; Leland, 1974; Grossman and Hart, 1979), but the available models are incompatible with closed strategic market games, and there are several other weaknesses that have yet to be overcome. There is no tractable, plausible formal model of an exchange and production economy with voting shareholders. The effort to create such a model is in and of itself a useful exercise in mathematical institutional economics.

7.4.4 A few statistics
What are the magnitudes involved in the phenomena being modeled? The description of firms in competition in chapter 3 will serve as back-

Table 7.4
Corporate failures

	Mining and manufacturing	Wholesale	Retail	Construction	Commercial service
Liability under $100,000	476	450	2368	867	697
Liability over $100,000	643	437	1038	596	344
Total	1122	887	3406	1463	1041

Table 7.5
Corporate population, entry, and exit

Year	Active corporations	New incorporations	Failures	Exits
1975	2,023,600	326,300	11,400	?
1976	2,082,200	375,000	9,600	279,100
1977	2,241,900	436,200	7,900	225,700

ground for some statistics on entry, exit, and merger.

In 1977 there were 11,346,000 proprietorships, 1,153,000 partnerships, and 2,241,900 active corporations in the United States. There were 436,200 new incorporations and 7900 failures (*Statistical Abstract of the United States*, 1980, table 972, p. 576).

The failures are categorized in table 7.4. These figures are consistent with "eyeball empiricism." Mining, manufacturing, and wholesaling tend to have larger economic units than retailing, construction, and services. The failures constitute a fraction of a percent and, for many developments of the theory of competition, can be ignored. An adequate theory must, however, take bankruptcy and reorganization into consideration (Shubik and Wilson, 1977; Dubey and Shubik, 1979).

Most exit is not by failure but by voluntary liquidation or merger. To see this, consider the number of corporations, new incorporations, and failures shown in table 7.5. The estimates of exits are rough; they do not include, for example, mergers, which in 1977 were at 1182, of which 581 involved companies with assets of $100 million or more.

Theoretically the life of a corporation is infinite. In fact, in the United States corporations have a far shorter expected life than humans, but

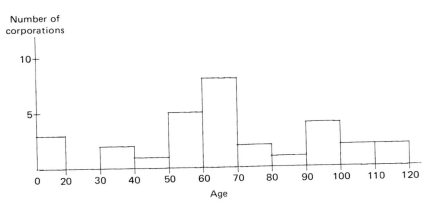

Figure 7.2
Ages of the thirty largest industrial corporations.

with a much larger spread. In particular, it appears that the probability of survival through the first few years of existence is far less than that of a human, but thereafter (controlling for size) it is approximately constant. There appears to be a positive relationship between size and the probability of survival.

In 1981 there were 30 industrial corporations listed in the *Fortune* 500 with sales above $10 billion. Figure 7.2 shows the ages (starting from the date of last incorporation reported in Moody's) of these giants. The operational ages are underestimated since, for example, the three under twenty are International Telephone and Telegraph (1968), Sun Oil Company (1971), and U.S. Steel (1965). Dupont, which was founded in 1802, is listed as dating from its 1915 incorporation.

Perusal of Moody's banking statistics reveals over 40 banks more than 120 years old. The Swedish firm of Stora Kopparbergs Bergslags AB, which had sales of $955.6 million in 1977, has records dating back to 1288 but was probably operating a century earlier. This appears to be the oldest still-operating corporation.

A study by Payne (1978) of Scottish limited companies formed between 1856 (the year of the Joint Stock Companies Act) and 1895 found that 311 of 2936 were still extant in 1970. The average lifetime of the ones that had died by 1970, listed for each cohort from 1856 to 1895, varies from a low of 11.3 years (1856) to a high of 47.4 years (1859), with an overall average of 16.4 years. The mortality rates for English companies reported by Shannon (1932) are higher.

These few remarks suggest that the "biology" of the corporation is considerably different from that of the human. At the same time it should be clear that the corporation is a vital legal and economic entity whose existence poses both theoretical and applied problems in the study of the control and transmission of human assets.

The analysis of entry in section 7.4.1 focused on the question of whether noncooperative oligopoly theory could be made consistent with Walrasian theory. The answer was yes if the minimum-optimal-scale (MOS) plant output is small enough. I prefer to rephrase the question as: Can we show that the Walrasian theory is a special case of more general noncooperative-equilibrium theory? Given that it appears to be, we might ask what MOS looks like in U.S. industry. Scherer (1980, chapter 4) summarizes and comments on the estimates of Pratten and Weiss on MOS and the percentage increment in costs for operation at 50 percent of MOS for 23 industries.

If we were to use as a rule of thumb that the noncooperative model converges to the competitive model approximately as $1/n$ (see Shubik with Levitan, 1980), then our criterion for an approximately structurally competitive market might require somewhere between 10 and 50 firms of around the same size. This suggests that an MOS above 10 percent of demand is certainly oligopolistic; less than 2 percent may lead to a structure of essentially pure competition, and in between would be a gray zone. The data noted above indicate that a substantial fraction of U.S. manufacturing can best be described as oligopolistic.

Another factor in questioning the domain of application of general-equilibrium theory concerns the goals and motivation of the firm. The meaning of ownership, a central problem in law and anthropology, is glossed over in most economic theory. Even without delving deeply into the motivations of management, the model of the firm run by a profit-maximizing owner-entrepreneur does not match the facts.

As noted by Berle and Means (1932), corporate ruling groups are often not the major owners of a corporation but groups in a position to control the election of a majority of the board of directors. This pioneering work was updated by Larner (1966), who found that managerial control of corporate boards was increasing (see table 7.6).

7.5 Some Methodological Problems in Modeling Oligopolistic Competition

We have alluded to several basic methodological problems concerning the use of the strategic and coalitional forms of game theory to represent

Table 7.6
Control of the 200 largest nonfinancial corporations in 1963

	Total	Industrial	Public utilities	Transport	Control (%)	Assets (%)	Assets (billions of $)
Privately owned	0	0	0	0	0	0	0
Controlled by majority stockholders	5	3	1	1	2.5	1	3.3
Dominant minority	18	18	0	0	9	11	28.2
Legal device (pyramid, voting trust)	8	5	0	3	4	3	8.8
Management control	169	91	58	20	84.5	85	224.4
Total	200	117	59	24	100	100	264.7

oligopolistic structure and to define solutions. This section deals with the following problems:

1. A distinction must be made between perfect equilibrium points and other equilibria; the former may not exist whereas the latter are abundant.

2. The nonuniqueness of equilibria in multistage models raises several basic questions concerning the scope, limitation, and interpretation of the application of noncooperative theory to the analysis of multistage models of oligopoly.

3. The Edgeworth characteristic function is a misleading and inadequate model for the study of cooperative oligopolistic behavior when numbers are small.

7.5.1 Perfect and other equilibria

With price as the strategic variable, one can easily construct simple models of duopoly that have no pure-strategy perfect equilibrium points if customers are not regarded as strategic players. The simplest such model is based on Bertrand: Suppose that two sellers have one unit each of a homogeneous good. Their customers are a continuum of small buyers whose overall demand is $q = 3 - p$, where p is a single offering price. This can be represented in a fully closed model as follows. Let the endowment of buyer i be given by the densities $(0, m_i)$, where the first entry refers to the good and the second to a money, and his preferences by a utility function $\phi_i = 3q_i - (q_i^2/2) + m_i - pq_i$. The sellers have endowments $(1, 0)$ each, and each has a utility function $\pi_j = (1 - q_j) + w_j$, where $1 - q_j$ is the value of leftover inventory and w_j is the amount of money earned by seller j.

Each seller's strategy is to name a price at which he will sell his supply. The sellers announce their prices to all customers simultaneously. Each customer then selects an amount to buy from one or both sellers. A customer's strategy can be regarded as a function specifying what mix he will buy for any given set of prices.

It is easy to show that the competitive equilibrium is $p = 1, q_1 = q_2 = 1$. But this price level and distribution of resources cannot be maintained as a *perfect equilibrium* (see *GTSS*, chapter 9). Suppose that the strategy employed by all customers is: *Buy from the cheapest seller first, split orders if they charge the same, and buy from the higher-priced seller if I still have demand at that price.* The amounts bought by customers at any pair of prices can be calculated from basic consumer choice theory and a marketing convention on the order of service. If firm 1 charges $p_1 = 1$ and offers

$q_1 = 1$, only half the demand at that price is satisfied. If the other firm then raises its price, it can profitably and monopolistically discriminate against the remaining demand. This destroys the equilibrium.

Edgeworth (1925) and many others studying the partial-equilibrium model have noted the absence of an equilibrium in pure strategies, but the literature makes no distinction between perfect and other equilibria. Roberts and Sonnenschein (1977) present an example (using a Cournot mechanism) in an unnecessarily general mathematized form to make the point that the Bertrand–Edgeworth example applies to closed as well as to open economic models. The same point has been made above simply by reinterpreting the Bertrand–Edgeworth models as closed.

The fact that a system has no perfect equilibrium does not imply that it has no equilibria at all. Dubey and Shubik (1981) have demonstrated that in a set of games without exogenous uncertainty, the equilibrium points in a game with low information remain equilibrium points in any game obtained by refining that information. In particular, if we remodel the Roberts–Sonnenschein game as a game with simultaneous moves and hence with a single information set for each player, with the firms bidding quantities of goods and the consumers quantities of money, then the game has a pure-strategy noncooperative equilibrium that remains an equilibrium (but not perfect) in the game where the firms move first and the consumers' strategies are functions.

The choice in modeling between having buyers move simultaneously with sellers to form a price and having sellers set a price that buyers must accept, although they can adjust their purchases, is more delicate than is generally recognized in the literature. Even the most casual economic observation suggests that, at least for a large part of retail trade in the United States, firms name prices and consumers then buy. Stock markets, sealed bids, and auctions offer somewhat different price-formation mechanisms. Nevertheless, it remains important to all models to make clear the distinction between simultaneous- and sequential-move mechanisms.

As soon as sequential moves are allowed, strategies can become complex functions, and equilibria then tend to proliferate. One way to cut back the number of equilibria is to introduce special requirements. The perfect equilibrium has the extremely strong property that the strategies employed are in equilibrium in every subgame as well as in the game as a whole. The Bertrand–Edgeworth examples of duopoly in which customers are not players but are represented by a demand function have neither perfect nor other pure-strategy equilibria. However, if we replace the duopolists in the models of Bertrand (1883), Edgeworth (1925), or Shubik

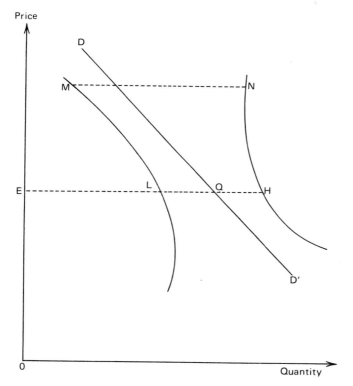

Figure 7.3
Uncertain demand.

(1959b, chapter 5) by a continuum of sellers, it can be shown that a perfect equilibrium point does exist.

For an open model and a somewhat special example Shubik (1959b, chapter 5) showed the convergence of the mixed-strategy perfect equilibrium under replication to the competitive equilibrium. The work of Mas-Colell (1981) noted in section 7.4.1 provides proof of the approach of mixed-strategy perfect equilibria to a Walrasian equilibrium under general conditions.

Paradoxically a realistic complication of a strategic market model can bring in a perfect equilibrium for a finite number of firms when it would not otherwise exist. We assume that the firms are uncertain about consumer demand at any given set of prices. The presence of this exogenous uncertainty may wipe out the firms' need to employ mixed strategies at a perfect equilibrium. Levitan and Shubik (1971b) gave an example of this phenomenon. Figure 7.3 is suggestive of how marketing departments perceive the demand they face. The estimate of demand may be linear, as indicated by DD', but the linear approximation works best for the small range around Q, the expected sales at the expected equilibrium price E (often based on price history). When the firm considers prices far away from previous market prices, the range of the variance increases—for example, from LH to MN.

7.5.2 On nonuniqueness

When there are few competitors and entry and exit are considered, threats are plausible, the probability of the existence of pure-strategy equilibria is high, and the probability of uniqueness is extremely low. The proliferation of noncooperative equilibria suggests that applying the noncooperative-equilibrium theory by itself to a relatively crude representation of an oligopolistic market is not particularly useful. One may require a different theory, such as the quasicooperative cartel theory of Selten (1973), or, more likely, more institutional detail concerning specific market structure. The demonstration of the consistency of noncooperative theory with Walrasian theory under the appropriate conditions is gratifying, but it answers the first of a series of important questions, not the last.

Cooperative Models of Closed Economic Systems

8 Two-Sided Markets: The Assignment Game

8.1 Introduction

In chapters 3–6 the analysis was based primarily on models of an open segment of the economy described as a game in strategic form. In chapter 7, although the strategic form was stressed, an attempt was made to close the model. For some purposes, such as an investigation of the core, a description of the game in cooperative form is required. In part II the game in cooperative form, when needed, was derived from the game in strategic form.

In part III we adopt a different approach. We shall work primarily with models of the economy as games in cooperative form with no attempt to describe the underlying games in strategic form. This approach contrasts with that in part II as Cournot's (1838) treatment of duopoly and oligopoly contrasts with Edgeworth's (1881) treatment of bilateral monopoly and bargaining. The strategic form is oriented toward process and institutions. The cooperative form minimizes institutional description and process analysis.

For our first intensive investigation of a two-sided market we turn to the "assignment game," a model formulated and studied by Shapley and Shubik (1971). The play in this game hinges almost entirely on the effort to find optimal matchings of individual producers to individual consumers. The number of players of each type is not restricted; we can, within the same framework, run the gamut from monopoly (or monopsony) to markets with very large numbers of players on both sides. The mathematical analysis will be carried a good deal further than will be possible for most of the models in this book, and the reader will thus have a good opportunity to observe the interplay of several of the solution theories introduced in *GTSS*, in an application where none of them is trivial.

The economic assumptions underlying this model are admittedly restrictive—this is the price paid for mathematical tractability—but they are not totally unrealistic. They will focus attention on what is perhaps the most basic element of competitive economics—the interaction between separately maximizing individuals—to the exclusion of many important but secondary phenomena. Let us list the main assumptions:

1. Money and utility are equivalent.
2. Side payments are permitted.
3. The objects of trade are indivisible.
4. Supply and demand functions are inflexible.

For comment on the first assumption we refer to the extended discussion in chapters 1 and 2, merely adding the observation that in the open marketplace, where there are many individuals buying and selling for money (often as fiduciaries and trustees), the total monetarization of utility comes closest to practical realization. Here, if anywhere, the assumption is defensible.

The second assumption is largely one of convenience in modeling and analysis. By permitting free transfer of money among all participants we avoid the necessity of providing in a special way for the ordinary payments from a customer to his supplier. It is perhaps worth noting that the avoidance of payments to third parties (side payments), in markets where such payments are in fact avoided, is often a matter more of custom or ethics than of fixed rules. Indeed, in analyzing the present games where side payments are possible, we shall discover certain stable sets—that is, certain standards of behavior—in which third-party payments are excluded. The game permits them; the solution forbids them.

The third assumption is unusual, since it is more often the opposite hypothesis (fungibility and perfect divisibility) that is imposed in the name of simplicity or mathematical tractability. Indivisibility is usually a problem, not an asset. Our present assumption leads us into combinatorial mathematics and away from the differential calculus. There is no dearth of economic applications under this assumption; an example is Böhm-Bawerk's classic horse market, which is the archetype of the assignment game with indivisible goods. Our formulation is significantly more general, however, since it permits product differentiation among the items in trade, as well as differences in the values that the traders place on each item. The market in private homes offers a good practical illustration of the general assignment game (see section 8.2.1), and we shall refer to it often for heuristic orientation.

Indivisibility plays an important role in many economic affairs. It is the basis for arguments in support of increasing returns to scale. It is far more than an incidental friction or minor invariable in economic life. Thus a formal treatment of it is perhaps even more merited than the analysis in this chapter indicates.

Inflexibility, the fourth assumption, in a way includes the third. For the indivisible commodity we shall assume that each producer has a supply of exactly one item, and each consumer a need for exactly one item. For a perfectly divisible good we could have achieved much the same effect by assuming step-type supply and demand functions. This latter point of view will be useful later, in discussing generalizations of the original model.

8.2 The Assignment Game

We shall now formulate the assignment game in detail, motivating it in terms of a market in private homes. Another interpretation, less specific and hence more versatile, will be outlined in section 8.2.3.

8.2.1 A real-estate market

Let there be m homeowners in the market, and n prospective purchasers. We shall refer to them simply as *sellers* and *buyers*, respectively. The ith seller values his house at c_i dollars, while the jth buyer values the same house at h_{ij} dollars. These are true utility valuations, not estimates of market price. They might be thought of as arising from the existence of a further supply of housing outside of the model. If $h_{ij} > c_i$, then a price favorable to both parties exists. We do not, however, assume that this inequality holds in all cases, or indeed in any case at all.

The possible moves in the game include the transfer of any house from its owner to any buyer and the transfer of money from any player to any other. As we have pointed out before, we do not need to spell out the detailed scheduling of contracts, bids, offers, or payments, although such tactical features would be quite conspicuous in any account of the rules of the game in extensive form. All that we require can be summed up in one simple observation: If i sells his house to j at a price p_i, and if both avoid dealing with third parties, then i's profit or gain is exactly

$$p_i - c_i \tag{8.1}$$

and j's profit is exactly

$$h_{ij} - p_i. \tag{8.2}$$

We have no way at present of ascertaining p_i, but we can postpone the

question. Since prices are not formally distinguished from other side payments, they will drop out of our initial calculations, only to reappear rather
unexpectedly when the solution of the game begins to take shape.

8.2.2 The characteristic function

The characteristic function can now be determined, at least in principle.
Let M denote the set of all sellers and N the set of all buyers. It is obvious
that

$$v(S) = 0 \quad \text{if} \quad |S| = 1, \tag{8.3}$$

since no player, without help from another, can affect a profitable transaction. More generally, we see that M and N are both "flat":

$$v(S) = 0 \quad \text{if} \quad S \subseteq M \quad \text{or} \quad S \subseteq N. \tag{8.4}$$

In other words, only a "mixed" coalition can assure the making of a
profit.

The simplest mixed coalition consists of just two players, one of each
type. For this case we have

$$v(\overline{ij}) = \max(0, h_{ij} - c_i) \quad \text{if} \quad i \in M \quad \text{and} \quad j \in N. \tag{8.5}$$

For brevity we denote this number by a_{ij}. Note that it does not depend on
the price, since that is merely an internal transfer as far as the coalition is
concerned.

A moment's reflection reveals that these mixed pairs are the only vital
coalitions in the game. The best that a larger coalition can do is to split up
into a number of separate trading pairs. The mn numbers a_{ij} determine v
completely. Specifically v is the smallest superadditive function on $M \cup N$
satisfying (8.3) and (8.5).

In order to compute v for larger mixed coalitions, we must pick a set of
transactions that will maximize the coalition's total gain. Put symbolically,
we have

$$v(S) = \max(a_{i_1 j_1} + a_{i_2 j_2} + \ldots + a_{i_k j_k}), \tag{8.6}$$

with the maximum to be taken over all arrangements of $2k$ distinct players
$i_1, i_2, \ldots, i_k$ in $S \cap M$ and $j_1, j_2, \ldots, j_k$ in $S \cap N$, where $k \leq \min(|S \cap M|,$
$|S \cap N|)$. The evaluation of an expression such as (8.6) is commonly called
the "assignment problem"; accordingly we shall refer to games of this
form as *assignment games*.[1]

For relatively small coalitions S (say, less than 10 players) the maximum
in (8.6) can usually be discovered by inspection, as in the following two

examples:

$S \cap N$		
0	2	0
2	0	2
0	2	0

$S \cap M$ (for the left matrix)

$S \cap N$		
5	8	2
7	9	6
2	3	0

$S \cap M$ (for the right matrix)

In the first there are four equally valuable assignments, each worth 4. In the second there is just one, worth 16. For larger matrices several systematic methods are available for finding the optimal assignment (see, e.g., Dantzig, 1963, chapter 15).

For the most part we shall be interested in evaluating (8.6) only for the coalition of all the players: $S = M \cup N$. The number $v(M \cup N)$ is obviously very important, since it determines the Pareto set. The other large coalitions, being nonvital, have little effect on the solutions.

8.2.3 A partnership game

The characteristic function (8.6) is completely symmetric between buyers and sellers, although the original market model was not. Our second assignment game, in sidestepping most of the preliminaries that went into the real-estate version, has the conceptual advantage of being symmetrical from the start (Gale and Shapley, 1962).

We imagine an economic milieu in which two types of agents, say "producers" M and "consumers" N, are constrained for one reason or another to conduct their business under exclusive bilateral contracts. Thus, after an initial period of jockeying for position, a number of "partnerships" are formed, and all transfers of goods must occur within them. (Money transfers are not restricted.) In this model we do not care particularly about the nature of the goods involved; we need merely state that to every possible partnership (i, j) there is associated a nonnegative number a_{ij} denoting the (monetary) value of the potential profit of that partnership. If we regard the system as a cooperative game, it is apparent that the characteristic function is given by (8.6).

A contract between players i and j must of course specify how the profit a_{ij} is to be divided between them (or distributed to third parties via side payments). A prudent "economic" man playing this game would be loath to enter a partnership for a stated share of the proceeds until he had satisfied himself that more favorable terms could not be obtained elsewhere. We can imagine each player setting a price on his participation, with no contracts signed until all prices on both sides are in harmony. One may well ask, Does a set of stable "harmonious" prices really exist? Mathematically this question can be put as follows: Do there exist numbers $p_i > 0$ such that

$p_i + p_j = a_{ij}$ if i and j are ultimately partners,

$p_i + p_j \geq a_{ij}$ if they are not?

The answer is in the affirmative, as we shall presently demonstrate. This fact is of central importance throughout the analysis of the assignment game.

8.2.4 Complementarity
Before studying the solutions of the assignment game, we digress briefly to emphasize a significant property of the characteristic function.

The superadditivity property is obvious, by definition, since combining two coalitions only enlarges the set of possible assignments. Less obvious is the way in which the marginal value of an individual player responds to changes in the make-up of the coalition to which he belongs. Intuitively we would expect a player's marginal value to a coalition to be great when there is an excess of players of the opposite type, and small when there is a surplus of players of the same type. In other words, similar players should be substitutes and dissimilar players should be complements. The following theorem gives expression to this intuitive idea.

Some special notation will be useful: Let S^p denote the coalition consisting of S and the added player p. (We shall use this notation only when p is not already a member of S.) The *marginal value* of player p to the coalition S is defined as

$$m_p(S) = v(S^p) - v(S).$$

The following result can then be established (Shapley, 1962):

THEOREM 8.1.   *If p and q are players of opposite type, one in M and one in N, then*

$$m_p(S^q) \geq m_p(S)$$

for all $S \not\ni p, q$. If they are players of the same type, the inequality is reversed.

This theorem is simply a statement about the sign of the "second difference" $v(S^{pq}) - v(S^p) - v(S^q) + v(S)$. When this quantity is positive, the players are complementary inputs to the process of coalition formation; when it is negative, they are substitutes.

8.3 The Core

8.3.1 Linear-programming form of the model
It will be useful at this point to recast the assignment program (8.6) into linear-programming (LP) terminology.

Consider just the assignment problem for the coalition of all players—that is, the determination of $v(M \cup N)$. Introduce the mn nonnegative variables x_{ij}, $i \in M, j \in N$, and impose on them the $m + n$ conditions

$$\sum_{i \in M} x_{ij} \leq 1, \qquad \sum_{j \in N} x_{ij} \leq 1. \qquad (8.7)$$

(We may interpret x_{ij} in the real-estate game as the fraction of the ith house sold to player j, or in the partnership game as the probability that a partnership $\{i, j\}$ will form.) The LP problem is then to maximize the following *objective function*:

$$z = \sum_{i \in M} \sum_{j \in N} a_{ij} x_{ij}. \qquad (8.8)$$

It can be shown that $z_{\max}$ is attained at a lattice point, with all $x_{ij} = 0$ or 1 (see Dantzig, 1963, p. 318). Thus the fractions artificially introduced disappear in the solution, and the (continuous) LP problem is equivalent to the (discrete) assignment problem we started with. Hence $z_{\max} = v(M \cup N)$.

Every LP problem can be transposed into a dual form, which is another problem of the same type; the solutions of the two problems are intimately bound up in each other (see Dantzig, 1963, p. 129). In the present case the dual has $m + n$ nonnegative variables $u_1, u_2, \ldots, u_m, v_1, v_2, \ldots v_n$, subject to the mn inequality conditions:

$$u_i + v_j \geq a_{ij}. \qquad (8.9)$$

The *dual objective* is to minimize the sum

$$w = \sum_{i \in M} u_i + \sum_{j \in N} v_j. \qquad (8.10)$$

A fundamental theorem states that

$$w_{\min} = z_{\max}.$$

What meaning does the dual problem have in the context of our market game? Let (u^*, v^*) be a pair of nonnegative vectors that minimize

w, subject to (8.9). Then we have

$$\sum_{i \in M} u_i^* + \sum_{j \in N} v_j^* = w_{\min} = z_{\max} = v(M \cup N). \tag{8.11}$$

This tells us that (u^*, v^*) is an imputation of the game. Moreover (8.9) tells us that for every pair $i, j,$

$$u_i^* + v_j^* \geq a_{ij} = v(\{i, j\}).$$

It follows that (u^*, v^*) is undominated by any vital coalition. Therefore (u^*, v^*) is in the core. This proves the existence of a core.

Conversely, any imputation in the core satisfies the conditions for a solution to the dual LP problem. Hence we have:

THEOREM 8.2.   *The core of the assignment game is precisely the set of solutions of the LP dual of the assignment problem.*

8.3.2 Prices
Our venture into the field of linear programming has proved most fruitful. We have already garnered (1) a proof of the existence of the core, (2) a characterization of all the points in the core, and (3) an assurance of effective computational procedures for both the characteristic function and the core.[2]

The reader schooled in linear programming will now expect an attempt to relate the dual solutions to a pricing mechanism. In fact, the relation is very simple. In order to achieve the payoff u_i^* promised by a given core vector (u^*, v^*), the owner of the ith house must sell it at a price

$$p_i^* = c_i + u_i^*. \tag{8.12}$$

If all the sellers attach such prices to their homes, then the typical buyer j will be confronted by a choice among the m possible net gains

$$h_{ij} - p_i^*, \quad i \in M. \tag{8.13}$$

If these values are all negative, he will stay out of the market and end the game with a profit of zero; otherwise he will seek to maximize (8.13). This is equivalent to maximizing

$$a_{ij} - u_i^*, \tag{8.14}$$

in view of (8.12) and (8.5). We know by (8.9) that none of these quantities exceeds v_j^*. On the other hand, the minimization of the dual objective form (8.10) ensures that at least one of them is equal to v_j^*. To sum up, player j's maximum profit is precisely v_j^*, and he is led to it by direct comparative shopping.

Might several shoppers find that the same house is their "best buy"? In the most common case, where there is a unique optimal assignment and where the chosen vector (u^*, v^*) lies in the interior of the core, the answer is no. The price schedule (8.12) then leads the players unambiguously to a nonconflicting allocation of goods that maximizes the welfare of the group as a whole and obtains for each individual the specified amount u_i^* and v_j^*.

In exceptional "degenerate" cases there may be ties in the buyers' preferences, and care must be taken to resolve the ties without assigning the same house to more than one buyer. That is always possible can be demonstrated by a simple perturbation argument. With prices based on vectors outside the core, on the other hand, it is never possible to make such an assignment, if the buyers are optimizing and the total welfare is maximized.

8.3.3 Structure of the core

The core of the assignment game only rarely consists of just a single imputation.[3] Consequently the price structure just described is seldom unique. In this section we shall account for the multiplicity of solutions and discuss what it means in the market context.

In general, if numbers a_{ij} are chosen at random, the optimal assignment is unique. This implies that a dual solution (u^*, v^*) exists in which the strict inequality $u_i^* + v_j^* > a_{ij}$ holds for all pairs (i, j) that are not part of the optimal assignment. (Any interior point of the core will serve.) Let (i', j') be in the optimal assignment. Then a small amount can be transferred from $u_{i}^{*\prime}$ to $v_{j}^{*\prime}$ without spoiling the dual solution. It follows that there are at least $\min(m, n)$ "degrees of freedom" in the core. On the other hand, the dimensionality of the core is never greater than $\min(m, n)$ because if the u-components of a core vector are given, then the v-components are completely determined, and vice versa.

A picture of the core is beginning to take shape. It is a closed, convex, polyhedral set whose dimension is typically equal to $\min(m, n)$ but is sometimes less due to degeneracies (special arithmetical relations among the a_{ij}).[4] The dimension of the imputation space, in which the core is embedded, is $m + n - 1$, which is considerably larger than $\min(m, n)$.

We next show that the core tends to be elongated, with the long axis oriented in the direction of marketwide price trends. There is a "high-price" corner at the vertex where every seller gets his highest profit and every buyer his lowest profit. At the opposite, "low-price" corner the reverse is true. The distance between these two extremities is greater than or equal to that separating any other pair of points in the core.

Thus, to a great extent the fortunes of all players of the same type rise and fall together.[5]

We shall encounter this phenomenon repeatedly in market games, in their stable sets as well as their cores. The heuristic principle can be stated as follows: Intergroup allocations are relatively indeterminate in a cooperative solution; intragroup allocations are relatively precise.

THEOREM 8.3.   *Over all imputations in the core, let u_i^* and u_{*i} denote the highest and lowest payoffs, respectively, to player $i \in M$, and similarly v_j^* and v_{*j} to player $j \in N$. Then the payoff vectors (u_*, v^*) and (u^*, v_*) are themselves in the core of the game. Moreover, no pair of imputations in the core are further apart than these two.*

The heart of the proof is in the following lemma, which says in effect that the greatest lower (or least upper) bound of any two points in the core is also in the core.

LEMMA.   *Let (u', v') and (u'', v'') be any two imputations in the core. Define*

$$\underline{u}_i = \min(u_i', u_i''), \qquad \underline{v}_j = \min(v_j', v_j''),$$
$$\bar{u}_i = \max(u_i', u_i''), \qquad \bar{v}_j = \max(v_j', v_j'').$$

Then the vectors $(\underline{u}, \bar{v})$ and $(\bar{u}, \underline{v})$ are imputations and are in the core.

Proof. For any i and j we have

$$\begin{aligned}
\underline{u}_i + \bar{v}_j &= \min(u_i' + \bar{v}_j, u_i'' + \bar{v}_j) \\
&\geq \min(u_i' + v_j', u_i'' + v_j'') \\
&\geq a_{ij},
\end{aligned}$$

using (8.9). Hence $(\underline{u}, \bar{v})$ is undominated. It remains to show that it is an imputation. It is obviously nonnegative; we must therefore show only that its components add up to $v(M \cup N)$. For convenience, label the players so that the pairs $(1,1), (2,2), \ldots, (k,k)$, where $k \leq \min(m, n)$, describe an optimal assignment. Then

$$\begin{aligned}
\underline{u}_i &= \min(u_i', u_i'') = \min(a_{ii} - v_i', a_{ii} - v_i'') \\
&= a_{ii} - \max(v_i', v_i'') = a_{ii} - \bar{v}_i
\end{aligned}$$

for $i \leq k$. Also, for $i, j > k$ (if any) we have $\underline{u}_i = \bar{v}_j = 0$. Hence

$$\sum_{i \in M} \underline{u}_i + \sum_{j \in N} \bar{v}_j = \sum_{i=1}^{k} a_{ii} = v(M \cup N).$$

This completes the proof of the lemma. ∎

To prove the theorem, simply take a finite collection of core vectors that includes all the extreme values going into the definitions of u^*, u_*, v^*, and v_* and apply the lemma repeatedly to construct additional core vectors until (u^*, v_*) and (u_*, v^*) are reached. For the last statement of the theorem, note that any two points (u', v'), (u'', v'') in the core necessarily satisfy the inequalities:

$$|u_i' - u_i''| \le u_i^* - u_{*i} \quad \text{for all } i \in M,$$
$$|v_j' - v_j''| \le v_j^* - v_{*j} \quad \text{for all } j \in N.$$

Thus the stated result holds not only for Euclidean distance but for any distance function that depends only upon the absolute values of the coordinate differences.

8.3.4 A simple example

Let there be three sellers $M = \{1, 2, 3\}$ and three buyers $N = \{1', 2', 3'\}$ as follows:

Houses	Sellers' basis	Buyers' valuation		
(i)	(c_i)	h_{i1}	h_{i2}	h_{i3}
1	$18,000	$23,000	$26,000	$20,000
2	15,000	22,000	24,000	21,000
3	19,000	21,000	22,000	17,000

These data lead at once to the following (a_{ij}) matrix, already considered in section 8.2.2:

$$
\begin{array}{ccccc}
 & & N & & \\
 & 1' & 2' & 3' & \\
1 & 5 & \textcircled{8} & 2 & 4 \\
M \quad 2 & 7 & 9 & \textcircled{6} & 5.5 \quad u(\text{units of } \$1000) \\
3 & \textcircled{2} & 3 & 0 & 0 \\
 & 2 & 4 & 0.5 & \\
 & & v & &
\end{array}
$$

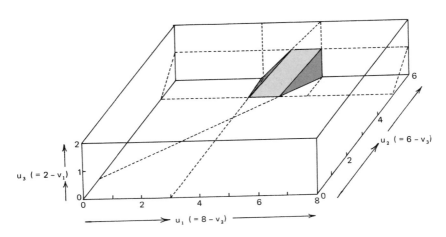

Figure 8.1
The geometry of the core.

The unique optimal assignment is shown circled, the total gain being $16,000. One of the core vectors (u, v) is also shown. The reader can verify that the matrix $(u_i + v_j)$ majorizes (a_{ij}), with equality only on the circled entries. The prices corresponding to this core vector are $22,000, $20,500, and $19,000, respectively. Given these prices, the first buyer clearly prefers the third house, since his gain there is $2000 as opposed to $1000 at house 1 and $1500 at house 2. Similarly, the second buyer prefers the $4000 gain at house 1 to the gains of $3500 and $3000 at houses 2 and 3. Finally, house 2 is the only one the third buyer would even consider at the stated prices.

The nonuniqueness of this solution is evident, since none of the buyers' comparisons were closer than $500, and only one seller (the third) is at, or even close to, his cost. Thus any one price could be raised by $500, or either of the first two prices lowered by $500, without moving outside of the core. Or all three prices could be increased together, in a marketwide price movement, until the "weakest" buyer (the third) is driven out.

The geometry of the core is shown in figure 8.1. Since optimality demands the unique set of assignments $(12', 23', 31')$, we have depicted just the rectangular 3-dimensional region in the (5-dimensional) imputation space where the equations $u_1 + v_{2'} = 8$, $u_2 + v_{3'} = 6$, $u_3 + v_{1'} = 2$ are satisfied. (The imputations outside this region cannot be attained without the aid of "third-party" side payments.) The core is a five-sided poly-

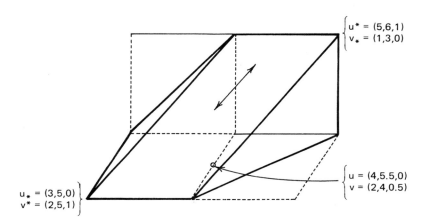

$$\begin{cases} u^* = (5,6,1) \\ v_* = (1,3,0) \end{cases}$$

$$\begin{cases} u = (4,5.5,0) \\ v = (2,4,0.5) \end{cases}$$

$$\left. \begin{matrix} u_* = (3,5,0) \\ v^* = (2,5,1) \end{matrix} \right\}$$

Figure 8.2
The core.

hedron situated within this region, touching the boundaries $u_3 = 0$ and $v_{3'} = 0$. The solution point discussed above happens to lie in the bottom face, as shown by the open dot in figure 8.2. The two-headed arrow indicates the direction of marketwide price changes. The low-price corner (u_*, v^*) is at the lower left; the high-price corner (u^*, v_*) at the upper right. The (Euclidean) distance between them is $\sqrt{6}$ times \$1000, or \$2449; the distance measured in terms of the total effect on the sellers as a class is \$4000.

An alternative to calculating the extreme points of the core by computing all basic solutions to the dual of the assignment problem has been given by Thompson (1978). He shows that the original game may be recast as a transportation problem and the core calculated by solving all basic solutions to the dual of the transportation problem.

8.4 A Stable-Set Solution

Like most other large games, our present market model turns out to have a great multiplicity of stable-set solutions (see *GTSS*, chapter 7). We shall not attempt here to explore the extent of this multiplicity or to speculate on its meaning, but shall concentrate instead on the construction of a single solution, with a natural interpretation, that is derived from the cores of a class of subgames and can therefore be computed by solving— that is, optimally assigning—certain of the (a_{ij}) submatrices. This construction does not depend on any particular assumptions concerning the a_{ij}. In a later section we shall take a special, highly symmetric case (all a_{ij} equal) and attempt to describe the full set of stable-set solutions.

All stable sets include the core C, and we saw earlier how the payoff vectors in the core could be achieved without any side payments other than the direct payments from the buyers of the houses to their respective former owners. The set of all imputations that can be so achieved will be called the *principal section* (B) of the imputation space A. The solution V that we shall construct is the only one that is entirely contained in B, that is, the only one that does not require third-party payments in some form. According to the standard of behavior that V represents, such payments are unethical, and it is interesting that there should be just one standard of behavior of this kind that is stable.

8.4.1 Compatible subgames
For convenience, we assume that the players have been so numbered that the optimal pairings lie along the main diagonal of the matrix, giving us

$$\sum_{i=1}^{\min(m,n)} a_{ii} = v(I). \tag{8.15}$$

(If there is more than one optimal assignment, we must choose a fixed one at this point and stick with it.) Two auxiliary set functions will also be useful:

$a_M(S) = \sum a_{ii}$ summed over $i \le \min(m,n)$ such that $O_i \in S \cap M$,
$a_N(S) = \sum a_{ii}$ summed over $i \le \min(m,n)$ such that $P_i \in S \cap N$.

Let Q be a fixed set of players. We shall define a subgame in which only the members of Q appear as nondummy players. Let us write Q' for $I - Q$. The characteristic function of the subgame is

$$v_Q(S) = v(S \cap Q) + a_M(S \cap Q) + a_N(S \cap Q). \tag{8.16}$$

Thus the excluded players are awarded what they would get if they made their best possible deals under the given optimal assignment and are then disqualified from entering into any transactions.

A study of (8.16) reveals that $v_Q(I) \ge v(I)$ always holds, since the "diagonal" assignment applied to the OA matrix of the subgame ensures that $v_Q(I)$ is at least $\sum a_{ii}$. Two effects contribute to the possibility of inequality. First, the members of Q may be able to improve on the diagonal assignment, since Q will in general include some of the partners of the excluded players; second, the excluded set Q' may include some matched pairs $\{O_i, P_i\}$ with $a_{ii} > 0$, and the resulting double payments to the dummies will boost $v_Q(I)$ above $v(I)$. A subgame in which neither of these effects appears, so that $v_Q(I) = v(I)$, will be called *compatible*, and the class of sets Q giving rise to compatible subgames will be denoted $\mathcal{Q}$.

We note that $\mathcal{Q}$ is not empty, since $I \in \mathcal{Q}$. We also note that any players O_i or P_i with $a_{ii} = 0$ or $i > \min(m, n)$—the "no-trade" players—can be excluded without causing incompatibility. These exclusions will in general enlarge the core C. Now consider any player who participates nontrivially in the given OA but receives a zero gain at some point in the core of one of the compatible subgames. We can then exclude his partner in the OA from the game without increasing $v_Q(I)$. The cores of the new and old subgames will of necessity have the given point in common, but neither core will in general include the other. Since such "zero" players can always be found (on both sides in a square OA problem and on the "long" side of a rectangular OA problem), we are assured of a whole chain of compatible subgames in which the players of one type are eliminated one by one, in some order, and a similar chain in which players of the other type are excluded.[6]

8.4.2 A numerical example
Consider the following OA matrix:

	P_1	P_2	P_3	P_4
O_1	(4)	0	5	0
O_2	0	(4)	0	1
O_3	1	0	(3)	0
O_4	0	5	0	(3)

Its value of 14 is achieved only by the "diagonal" assignment. To determine $\mathcal{Q}$, we might first try excluding player O_1, giving him a fixed payment of 4. Since the resulting 3×4 OA matrix has value 10, we see that the subgame is indeed compatible. If we next try to exclude O_2 instead of O_1, we find that a value of 12 can be achieved by the other seven players, making $v_Q(I) = 16$. This subgame is therefore not compatible. A complete tabulation of the compatible subgames is given below, expressed in terms of the excluded sets Q':

M only	N only	Mixed
O_1	P_2	$O_1 P_2$
O_4	P_3	$O_4 P_3$
$O_1 O_3$	$P_1 P_3$	$O_1 O_3 P_2$
$O_1 O_4$	$P_2 P_4$	$O_2 O_4 P_3$
$O_2 O_4$	$P_2 P_4$	$O_4 P_1 P_3$
$O_1 O_2 O_4$	$P_1 P_2 P_3$	$O_1 P_2 P_4$
$O_1 O_3 O_4$	$P_2 P_3 P_4$	

The original game, $Q' = 0$, and certain inessential games with $|Q'| = 4$ are also compatible.

8.4.3 Mathematical description of the solution V

The *principal section* B is defined to be the set of all imputations (u, v) satisfying

$$u_i + v_i = a_{ii}, \quad 1 \le i \le \min(m, n). \tag{8.17}$$

All core vectors have this property; hence $C \subset B$. Since the "diagonal" assignment is optimal in all compatible subgames, we also have $C_Q \subset B$ for all $Q \in \mathcal{Q}$.

Because of (8.17) the points of B can be identified by their "u" coordinates alone. Since each u_i varies independently between 0 and a_{ii}, we see that B is a rectangular parallelepiped, of dimension $\min(m, n)$, unless some of the a_{ii} are zero. Of special interest are the two diametrically opposite "corners," $(a_{..}, 0)$ and $(0, a_{..})$, at which all the players of one type receive zero gain.

The set V can now be defined; it is the union of the cores of all the compatible subgames:

$$V = \bigcup_{Q \in \mathcal{Q}} C_Q. \tag{8.18}$$

In view of the preceding remarks, we have

$$A \supset B \supset V \supset C. \tag{8.19}$$

Before sketching the proof of stability we shall state two simple but useful properties of the set V. The first is little more than a transcription of the definitions; the second is a consequence of the "chain" construction described at the end of section 8.4.1.

LEMMA 1. *A vector in the principal section B is an element of V if and only if for every pair i, j at least one of the following holds:*
(i) $u_i + v_j \geq a_{ij}$,
(ii) $u_i = a_{ii}$, or
(iii) $v_j = a_{jj}$.

LEMMA 2. *V contains the two corners $(a_{..}, 0)$, $(0, a_{..})$ of the principal section B, together with a continuous monotonic curve connecting them and passing through any preassigned point $(\bar{u}, \bar{v})$ of the core. Specifically, all vectors of the form $(u(\tau), v(\tau))$ with*

$$u_i(\tau) = \mathrm{med}(0, \bar{u}_i + \tau, a_{ii}),$$
$$v_j(\tau) = \mathrm{med}(0, \bar{v}_j - \tau, a_{jj}),$$

where "med" denotes the median, are in V.

8.4.4 Proof that V is stable

We shall first show that V is internally stable. Suppose that $(x, y) \succ (u, v) \in V$, with $\{O_i, P_j\}$ the effective coalition. Then $u_i + v_j < x_i + y_j \leq a_{ij}$. By lemma 1, this entails either $u_i = a_{ii}$ or $v_j = a_{jj}$. Hence either $x_i > a_{ii}$ or $y_j < a_{jj}$. Hence (x, y) is not in V, and V is internally stable.[7]

We shall next show that V dominates all imputations outside the principal section B. Suppose $(x, y) \notin B$. Then $x_i + y_i \neq a_{ii}$ for some i. In fact, $x_i + y_i < a_{ii}$ for some i since the sum of all coordinates is equal to the sum of the a_{ii}. By lemma 2 we can find $(u, v) \in V$ with $x_i < u_i < a_{ii} - y_i$. Then $v_i = a_{ii} - u_i > y_i$. Hence $(u, v) \succ (x, y)$ via $\{O_i, P_i\}$, and we have shown that V dominates $A - B$. The final step is to show that V dominates $B - V$.

8.4.5 Solutions in the symmetric case

There is one special case of the OA game that has been investigated extensively from the viewpoint of stable-set solution theory. The results are given in detail elsewhere, and we shall just summarize them here. The special case consists in taking all of the a_{ij} equal to 1. This makes the market completely symmetric among the buyers and among the sellers, and eliminates the effects of product differentiation. We should therefore expect a "narrow" core (see section 8.3.3). It also eliminates the effects of product indivisibility. An important version of this case is discussed in chapter 9. This same game is also a highly symmetric version of the *divisible*-product game, about which we shall have more to say in chapter 10.

The characteristic function has the following simple form:

$$v(S) = \min(|S \cap M|, |S \cap N|),$$

where $|S \cap M|$ as usual denotes the number of elements in the set $S \cap M$. We do not assume that the numbers of buyers and sellers are equal; hence $v(I) = \min(m, n)$.

Since all assignments are optimal, there is not much to be gained in looking at the associated OA problem. The core is easily determined:

$$C = \{(1, 1, \ldots, 1; 0, 0, \ldots, 0)\} \qquad \text{if } m < n,$$
$$C = \{(t, t, \ldots, t; 1 - t, 1 - t, \ldots, 1 - t): 0 \leq t \leq 1\} \quad \text{if } m = n,$$
$$C = \{(0, 0, \ldots, 0; 1, 1, \ldots, 1)\} \qquad \text{if } m > n.$$

In other words, there is a one-point core completely favoring the scarce type of player if the market is unbalanced, and a line-segment core traversing the imputation space if it is balanced. The latter runs the full gamut from "cutthroat prices" to "all-the-traffic-will-bear."

Looking just at the cores, we would conclude that the market is highly sensitive to the balance between supply and demand. This is not surprising in view of the abrupt inflexibility of the demand and supply curves; there is literally no "give" in the situation. On the other hand, we are modeling the market as a cooperative game, and it would seem plausible that with a little collusion among themselves the players of the more numerous type ought to be able to do something to overcome the handicap of their excess numbers.[8] Although the cores may be adequately descriptive solutions for a highly competitive sort of market, they are too crude to reflect properly the cooperative possibilities. The stable-set solutions, as we shall see, do better in this regard.

The balanced case   The case $m = n$ is quickly disposed of. If (u, v) is any imputation not in the core, then $\min_i u_i + \min_j v_j$ is necessarily less than 1. Hence there will be an imputation in the core that dominates (u, v): The most disgruntled buyer and the most disgruntled seller will be able to make a better deal. Thus the core dominates its complement and is therefore the unique stable-set solution of the game. An illustration for $m = n = 2$ is given in figure 8.3.

This result may be summed up in the following statement: If there

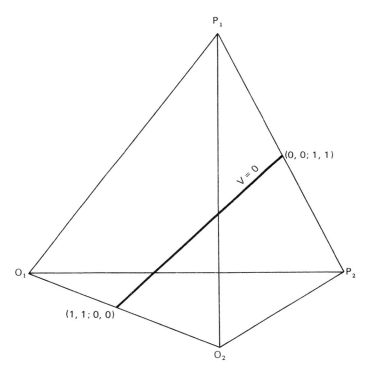

P_1

$(0, 0; 1, 1)$

$V = 0$

O_1

P_2

$(1, 1; 0, 0)$

O_2

Figure 8.3
The unique stable set for $m = n = 2$.

are as many buyers as sellers, and if the participants of each type are indistinguishable, then all transactions must take place at the same price; the price, however, is unrestricted except for the condition that no profits are negative.

Monopoly and monopsony   The most extreme imbalance occurs in the case of monopoly or monopsony: $\min(m, n) = 1$. We may as well assume that $m = 1$, $n > 1$. The core here is the single point $(1; 0, 0, \ldots, 0)$. We note that since $v(I) = 1$ the market reduces to a *simple game* (see *GTSS*, chapter 6), in which the winning coalitions are precisely those containing the monopolist O_1.

The stable-set solutions are not hard to describe. Given n functions $f_j(t)$ on the unit interval $0 \le t \le 1$ which are continuous, nonnegative,

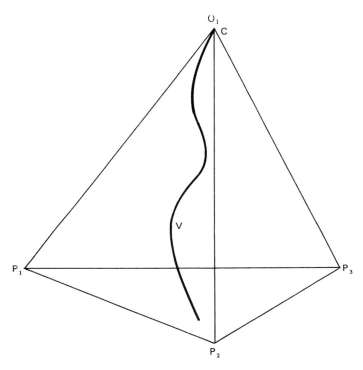

Figure 8.4
A stable set with a monopolist.

and nonincreasing, and which satisfy

$$\sum_{j=1}^{n} f_j(t) = 1 - t,$$

the set of imputations of the form

$$(t; f_1(t), f_2(t), \ldots, f_n(t)), \quad 0 \le t \le 1,$$

constitutes a stable set. Moreover, every stable set is of this form. In other words, the stable sets are the monotonic arcs that connect the core with arbitrary points on the opposite face of the imputation simplex (figure 8.4). We have encountered similar monotonic arcs before (*GTSS*, chapter 6) and shall again. In the literature they are sometimes called "bargaining curves."

A description of one of these solutions in terms of our real-estate model might go somewhat as follows: The shopper who finally buys the lone house that is up for sale—we can not tell from the solution which one this is since all shoppers desire the house equally—shares his gain with the other shoppers by making side payments. He is repaying them, perhaps, for active help in negotiating with the monopolist or passive help in just staying out of the way. The amounts of payment are conventional, that is, they are determined sociologically by the "standard of behavior," but they may depend on the price at which the transaction finally takes place. The price, however, is not conventional but quite arbitrary; it is determined by direct bargaining between the seller and buyer. No standard of behavior not of this kind is stable.

There is a rather neat division of indeterminacy here. Cooperative forces create and maintain the "bargaining curve"; competitive forces fix the price. We must know both in order to discover the outcome.

The arbitrariness of the functions f_j, and the corresponding plethora of possible solutions, is not in itself a bad thing. It merely confirms the undoubted fact that a great variety of collusive arrangements are possible and workable, and the simplicity of the underlying game model does not sharply limit the complexity of the "sociologies" that can be superposed on it.

Nevertheless, some standards of behavior are more easily described and perhaps more "natural" than others. In particular, if we apply the methods of section 9.1 to this example, we obtain a special class of solutions, namely the n straight-line segments joining the core $(1; 0, 0, \ldots, 0)$ with each of the imputations $(0; 1, 0, \ldots, 0)$, $(0; 0, 1, 0, \ldots, 0)$, $\ldots$, $(0; 0, 0, \ldots, 0, 1)$. Geometrically these are edges of the simplex A.[9] Heuristically they represent standards of behavior in which a particular customer does business with the monopolist, to the exclusion of the others.[10]

The general unbalanced case   A complete characterization of the solutions for $m \neq n$, $\min(m, n) = 1$, is not yet available, but a good deal is known about them. They are always monotonic arcs similar to those just described, spanning the imputation simplex from the $u = 0$ face to the $v = 0$ face; what is unknown is the precise set of restrictions on their routes. Since the heuristic considerations in this case closely parallel those of the previous subsection, we shall content ourselves here with just the technical description.

Let two families of functions be given this time, $\{f_i(t)\}$ and $\{g_j(t)\}$, defined on $0 \leq t \leq 1$, and let them be continuous, nonnegative, and respectively nondecreasing and nonincreasing. Let them satisfy the further conditions

$$\sum_{i=1}^{m} f_i(t) = t \min(m, n), \qquad \sum_{j=1}^{n} g_j(t) = (1 - t)\min(m, n).$$

The solutions will then be monotonic arcs of the form

$$\{(f_1(t), f_2(t), \ldots, f_m(t); g_1(t), g_2(t), \ldots, g_m(t)): 0 \le t \le 1\}. \qquad (8.20)$$

However, not all such monotonic arcs will be solutions.

Since $f_i(0) = 0$ for all i and $g_j(1) = 0$ for all j, these arcs always span the imputation simplex A. Let us define two special subsets of A:

$$E = \{(u, v): u_i + v_j \le 1 \text{ for all } i, j\},$$
$$F = \{(u, v): \max_i u_i + \min_j v_j \le 1 \quad and \quad \min_i u_i + \max_j v_j \le 1\}.$$

Evidently F contains E, and both contain the core C. The principal sections B, relative to the various possible optimal assignments, are all in F but not in E. In general, E is convex and F is not.

We can now give a formal statement of the known results for the general symmetric OA game.

THEOREM 8.4.
(i) *Every stable set is a monotonic arc of the form* (8.20), *containing the core C and spanning the imputation simplex A.*
(ii) *Every monotonic arc spanning A that is entirely within E is a stable set.*
(iii) *The intersection of all stable sets is precisely C.*
(iv) *The union of all stable sets contains E and is contained in F.*

All that remains in doubt, after this theorem, is the status of monotonic spanning arcs that enter the region *F-E*. Examples worked out for the five-person game $m = 2$, $n = 3$ show that some such sets are stable, some are not (Shapley, 1959b).

Theorem 8.4 is valid for the special cases discussed in the preceding two subsections. In the balanced case, $m = n$, it turns out that $E = C$, giving us the unique solution already described. In the monopoly case it turns out that $E = F = A$, so that the "doubtful" region *F-E* is non-existent and the full set of solutions as given in the theorem matches the description in section 8.4.2.

A corollary of the theorem is that no player ever receives a gain of more than 1 in any stable-set solution. Another corollary is that there is only one solution that exhibits the full symmetry of the game, namely, the straight-line set consisting of all imputations of the form

$(s, s, \ldots, s; t, t, \ldots, t)$,   where $ms + nt = \min(m, n)$.

(Note that the underlying symmetry of the game implies a corresponding symmetry of the *set* of solutions but not of each individual solution.) This solution could be rationalized in terms of "collective bargaining" between a Buyers' Association and a Sellers' Association, with the profits of each being divided equally among the members. It could also be rationalized in terms of a model in which contacts between buyers and sellers occur randomly and sales are effected at a uniform market price. Here the payoff vector components would have to represent the expected values of the ultimate monetary profits.

In the unbalanced case there will also be a number of partially symmetric solutions in which the extra players of the more numerous type are completely excluded but all other players are treated symmetrically. If $e = |m - n|$ is the measure of the imbalance of the game, then there will be $\min_e(m, n)$ such symmetric discriminatory solutions. An example would be

$$V = \{(t, t, \ldots, t; 1 - t, 1 - t, \ldots, 1 - t, 0, 0, \ldots, 0): 0 \le t \le 1\},$$

where we have assumed $m < n$. These solutions are of course the ones that can be achieved without any side payments to third parties (section 8.4); they are in fact the cores of the subgames obtained by actually dropping the extra players. There are no other solutions that exclude as many as e players from a share of the profits. In other words, if the standard of behavior permits no side payments to the nontrading players, then the price must be uniform throughout the market, with no third-party payments among the trading players.

8.4.6 Other solutions
Among the better-known solutions there remain the value, the bargaining set, the kernel, the nucleolus, and an alternative formulation of the market as a game in strategic form to be solved for noncooperative equilibria. In chapter 9, limiting ourselves to the simple case of the Böhm-Bawerk market, we consider the value, the nucleolus, and the noncooperative solution as well as the core and stable set.

8.5 Related Games and Indivisibilities

8.5.1 The marriage and college-admissions problems
Closely related to the assignment game is the *marriage problem* (Gale and Shapley, 1962). Consider a set M of men and a set N of women Each

man has a preference ordering (without ties) on all of the women as potential mates, and vice versa. In contrast with the housing market there is no money (although in fact dowries have often been used). The problem is one of pure matching.

Gale and Shapley construct a simple and straightforward algorithm for finding an optimal stable assignment. An assignment is stable if among the final couples there is no man and no woman who could both be made better off by marrying each other.

Suppose men α, β, γ and women A, B, C have the following rankings:

	A	B	C
α	1, 3	2, 2	3, 1
β	3, 1	1, 3	2, 2
γ	2, 2	3, 1	1, 3

Here the first number is the man's ranking of the woman and the second is the woman's ranking of the man. Thus α ranks A, B, and C in that order. In total there are 6 assignments of which 3 are stable. They include giving each man his first choice, each woman her first choice, or everyone their second choice.

A stable assignment is called M-optimal (N-optimal) if every member of set M (N) is at least as well off under it as under any other stable assignment. Gale and Shapley show that there will be an optimal assignment for the men if they do the proposing or for the women if they propose. They do not discuss the marriage problem (or the related college-admissions problem) as a cooperative game, but give an actual procedure for assignment:[11]

To start, let each boy propose to his favorite girl. Each girl who received more than one proposal rejects all but her favorite from among those who have proposed to her. However, she does not accept him yet, but keeps him on a string to allow for the possibility that someone better may come along later.

We are now ready for the second stage. Those boys who were rejected now propose to their second choices. Each girl receiving proposals chooses her favorite from the group consisting of the new proposers and the boy on her string, if any. She rejects all the rest and again keeps the favorite in suspense.

We proceed in the same manner. Those who are rejected at the second stage propose to their next choices, and the girls again reject all but the best proposal they have had so far.

Eventually (in fact, in at most $n^2 - 2n + 2$ stages) every girl will have received a proposal, for as long as any girl has not been proposed to there will be rejections and new proposals, but since no boy can propose to the same girl more than once, every girl is sure to get a proposal in due time. As soon as the last girl gets her proposal the "courtship" is declared over, and each girl is now required to accept the boy on her string.

We assert that this set of marriages is stable. Namely, suppose John and Mary are not married to each other but John prefers Mary to his own wife. Then John must have proposed to Mary at some stage and subsequently been rejected in favor of someone that Mary liked better. It is now clear that Mary must prefer her husband to John and there is no instability.

The proof of stability in the marriage game is clearly equivalent to establishing the existence of a point in the core. The vital coalitions consist only of couples.

Crawford and Knoer (1981) generalize the Gale–Shapley algorithm in application to a job-matching game; Kaneko (1982) offers a further generalization.

The college-admissions problem differs from the marriage problem in two respects. First, from the viewpoint of the colleges, although their desires will eventually saturate, they will want considerably more than one student each. If we wish to further the analogy, mass polyandry or polygamy is called for. The second difference involves the existence of tuition and scholarships. If money is regarded as a separable linear utility, then we face a problem mathematically similar to the housing market except that the sellers (colleges) are offering many apartments in an apartment house although the buyers (students) still want only one unit each. Kaneko (1976) generalized the Shapley–Shubik assignment game for many units for sale and a separable u-money.

As in the case of the housing market, Kaneko was able to prove that the core always exists by showing that this integer problem can be regarded as a linear program with integer solutions that yield prices and competitive equilibria. His second result, however, is strikingly different. In the assignment game with each seller trading only one unit, the core and the competitive equilibria coincide. Here, if there are not at least two sellers in competition, then it is easy to construct examples in which the core contains more than the competitive equilibrium. For example, consider one seller with two identical apartments and two buyers one of whom values an apartment considerably more than the other. The core will contain points at which the seller sells to the two buyers at different prices.

8.5.2 The central assignment game
Kaneko (1982) has offered an abstract generalization that covers both the Shapley–Shubik assignment game and the marriage problem. The essential feature in common between the assignment game and the marriage problem is that only pairs of players, one from each of two types, form the vital coalitions. Rather than build up a characteristic function from the intrinsic properties of the individual utility functions and the nature of the transactions, Kaneko placed conditions directly upon the characteristic function. He then showed that the central assignment game has a nonempty core.

It is straightforward to generalize to a many-type assignment game, and Kaneko and Wooders (1982) have considered such a generalization. Even for a world with three sexes instead of two, though, they have a counterexample showing that a core may not exist. (A remark attributed to an unnamed game theorist—much in the style of the new home economics—is that the reason why God chose two sexes is that he wanted to preserve the core property of the appropriate assignment game.)

8.5.3 The core and indivisibilities
The assignment games examined have been shown to have cores. But it is possible that indivisibility alone is sufficient to destroy the core property. Two simple examples with and without side payments illustrate this (Shubik, 1971a; Shapley and Scarf, 1974).

We assume that there are n people in an economy with one unit of one producer good, "time," and each with a utility function or a value for the possible consumer good, the possibility of playing a game of Bridge.

For simplicity we assume that Bridge requires four players, each with one unit of time. The production function for Bridge games can be described as

$$x = [t/4];$$

that is, the output is the largest integer in the number $t/4$.

For further simplicity we assume that the utility function for each individual is $U_i(x_i) = x_i$, where x_i is the amount of Bridge playing he obtains. In this trivial case x will be 0 or 1, since each individual has time for only one game.

An interesting distinction between the side-payment and no-side-payment games occurs in this example. If we assume side payments, then we can specify the characteristic function as

$$v(S) = 4[s/4] \text{ for all } s, \text{ where } s = |S| \text{ and } S \subset N;$$

$v(S)$ may be read as "the value that can be obtained by a set of players S." Since the game is symmetric, we save ourselves a small amount of notation and use only s, the number of players in the set S, since all sets of the same size have the same total value even though they may have different players.

If we do not wish to allow for transferable utilities, we must use the "characterizing function" for each member of the coalition. The characterizing function for the five-person game is

$$V(\overline{i}) = 0 \qquad \text{for } i = 1, 2, \ldots, 5,$$
$$V(\overline{ij}) = (0, 0) \qquad \text{for all pairs } i, j,$$
$$V(\overline{ijk}) = (0, 0, 0) \qquad \text{for all triads } i, j, k,$$
$$V(\overline{ijkl}) = (1, 1, 1, 1) \quad \text{for all tetrads } i, j, k, l,$$
$$V(\overline{12345}) = (1, 1, 1, 1, 0), (1, 1, 1, 0, 1), (1, 1, 0, 1, 1), (1, 0, 1, 1, 1), \text{ or}$$
$$(0, 1, 1, 1, 1).$$

Although the side-payment game may not have a core, the no-side-payment game always has a core. It is easy to observe that if we treat the Bridge-game problem as an economy, a price system only exists when the number of players is divisible by four (or trivially when the number of players is less than four).

The side-payment core exists only for $n = 1, 2, 3, 4, 8, 12, \ldots, 4k$ (k an integer). For $n = 1, 2, 3$ the core is trivial; no group can obtain anything. For $n = 4$ the core is every imputation in the game with side payments. For the no-side-payment game the core is all imputations for all of these games, but there is no price system unless n is divisible by 4.

In this model the economy suffers from the effects of the indivisibility or the integral aspects of Bridge. As the numbers increase, the price system and the core appear and disappear periodically.[12]

Does it seem reasonable to have the price system disappear when the economy has 1,000,001 people instead of 1,000,000? A way to avoid this undesirable situation is to introduce a lottery ticket for Bridge. We assume that for any n each individual sells his time in exchange for a lottery ticket that carries a probability of $(4/n)[n/4]$ that he plays in a Bridge game and $1 - (4/n)[n/4]$ that he is left out. As the number of players increases, the probability of getting into a Bridge game comes arbitrarily close to 1.

The interpretation of the "lottery ticket" in this case is quite natural. If we leave out special social structure, then everyone has the same chance to find a game. Although the indivisibility may still cause an annoyance, and one, two, or three people may fail to play, the odds against playing become insignificantly small as the numbers increase. The price of the lottery ticket becomes approximately the same as in the guaranteed game.

As long as the number of types of indivisible factors of production and their capacities are both finite, the core will still appear and disappear in a periodic manner as the population mix of the different owners of resources is or fails to be in the correct ratio. As the size of the economy grows, there will still remain the possibility of a mismatch of resources; relative to the whole economy, though, the amount of the mismatch approaches zero.

The implication of this example is that, when indivisibilities are small relative to an economy as a whole, they do not matter very much, and lottery tickets can be formally introduced to preserve the price system; otherwise the lottery aspect will come about by a relatively minor amount of queuing or by social convention to correct for minor aberrations from the price system. In many instances, though, the indivisibilities in society are large relative to the economy as a whole; hence the approximation and limit argument will not apply.

Shapley and Scarf (1974) considered n traders in a market in which each owns a single indivisible good, each has a preference rank ordering on all goods, and each wants no more than one unit. They established the existence of the core and of competitive prices but showed that the core can also contain noncompetitive points. They also showed in the counterexample we shall now discuss that the result with indivisibilities does not extend to instances in which individuals want more than one item.

Let three traders have symmetric holdings in a tract of nine houses, as shown in figure 8.5. (Thus trader 1 owns houses 1, 1', and 1''.) For reasons inscrutable, each trader wants to acquire three houses in a row, including exactly one of his original set. Moreover, each prefers the long row that meets this condition to the short row.

We shall show that this example of a slightly more general trading

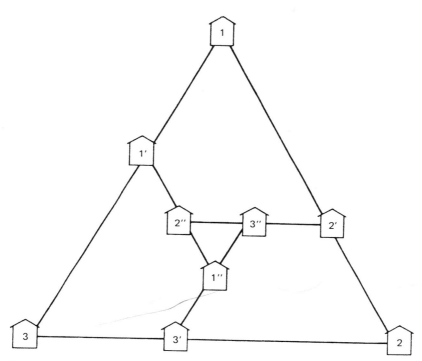

Figure 8.5
The three-house market.

game (in that the goods are to some extent complementary) is not balanced, and indeed has no core, thereby dispelling the idea that the core might prove a general remedy for market failure due to indivisibility.

The configuration of the tract is such that any two traders can make a profitable exchange. For example, a swap of 1′ and 1″ for 2 and 2′ gives trader 1 his long row and trader 2 his short row. Let us assign numerical values 2, 1, and 0 to the possession of the long row, the short row without the long row, and neither row, respectively. Then the two-person coalitions have single "corners":

$V(\{1,2\})$: $(2,1,-)$,
$V(\{1,3\})$: $(1,-,2)$,
$V(\{2,3\})$: $(-,2,1)$.

The three-person coalition cannot improve upon these pairwise exchanges; its characteristic function is thus generated by three "corners":

$V(\{1,2,3\})$: $(2,1,0)$, $(1,0,2)$, $(0,2,1)$.

The three singletons can achieve only 0.

This game is clearly not balanced, since the point $(1,1,1)$ is in $V(\{1,2\})$ $\cap V(\{1,3\}) \cap V(\{2,3\})$ but not $V(\{1,2,3\})$. Moreover, the game has no core, since each of the generators of $V(\{1,2,3\})$ is interior to one of the $V(\{i,j\})$. In other words, the set $V(\{1,2,3\})$ is completely "covered up" by the union of the $V(\{i,j\})$.

8.5.4 Nonseparable money

A natural generalization in a different direction is to consider trading of indivisible commodities when one continuously divisible commodity is used by traders as a money but does not enter the utility function as a linearly separable term. Still maintaining the condition that no individual wants more than one indivisible good, Kaneko (1982) extends the analysis to the assignment market without transferable utility and shows the existence of a core and competitive equilibrium. There is a set M of m sellers, each with one item for sale, and a set N of n buyers. Let e_i^i be the initial unit endowment of indivisible item e_i hold by seller i. Let w^i ($i = 1$, 2, $\ldots$, $n + m$) be the initial holding of money. Each player $i \in M \cup N$ has preferences defined over the set of all pairs consisting of an indivisible good and an amount of money; the preferences are assumed to give rise to a weak ordering, which is monotonic with respect to money and has the property that, for any two pairs, if (e_j^i, w^i) is preferred to (e_k^i, w^i), there exists some amount Δ^i such that (e_j^i, w^i) is indifferent to $(e_k^i, w^i + \Delta^i)$. He also extends the results for the existence of a core and a price system to a generalized assignment market with sellers offering more than one unit and buyers desiring only one unit, with a money as described above.

Quinzii (1982a) offers a further generalization and unification in the form of a model with a commodity money in which all agents neither own nor want more than one unit of an indivisible good. Her generalization comes in providing an overall model that covers both the "exchange models" illustrated by Shapley and Shubik (1972–74), Shapley and Scarf (1974), and Kaneko (1976, 1982) and the pairing problem of Gale and Shapley (1962). No assumption of complete symmetry or asymmetry is made about the players. For the pairing models new restrictions appear. In essence we need to take into account the fact that if A is married to B, then B is to A. This restriction can destroy the conditions for balance. She also establishes that if money enters into the preferences of the agents and is also in an appropriate way "sufficient," then the core and competitive equilibria coincide.[13] Furthermore the "pairing models" have a different behavior with respect to decentralization; she provides an example with money but no competitive equilibrium.

8.5.5 Roommates

It appears that the guaranteed existence of the core with indivisibilities requires that the only vital coalitions be of size two. But that alone is not sufficient. There can be cycles among the two-person coalitions that destroy the core. Consider three individuals of the same sex who must inhabit two rooms, two in one room and one alone. Suppose that their preferences are as follows:

		Roommate		
		A	B	C
	A	3	2	1
Preference of	B	1	3	2
	C	2	1	3

Here (A, A) is interpreted as A's preference for rooming alone and (A, B) is A's preference for rooming with B. It is easy to check that there is a dominance cycle with two-person coalitions. The pairing from two types or sexes rules out the cycles.

8.5.6 Cooperative or strategic assignment games

A key feature of the analysis of the house market as a game in coalitional form was that the actual process of trade, that is, the strategic form of the game, was assumed away. Implicitly this means that for the purposes of the analysis at hand, search, communication, and bargaining costs are assumed to be negligible. We do not describe how buyers find sellers or any of the other mechanics of trade.

If we wish to model the house market as a game to be solved for a noncooperative equilibrium, we need to specify a trading mechanism, and there are many ways to do so. Demange (1982) has specified a game in strategic form for the Shapley–Shubik house market and has shown that there is one and only one Vickery–Groves mechanism that leads buyers to disclose their value for various objects when declaring strategies that lead to a strong noncooperative equilibrium. She constructs a mechanism that favors buyers whenever sellers have no information on the buyers. Each seller is assumed to announce a reservation price justified by a maxmin view of trade. The Vickery–Groves mechanism she suggests is a generalization of the Vickery auction, in which the highest bidder is awarded the object for sale but pays the price of the second-highest bidder.

A general problem that has not yet received sufficient attention is the relationship between markets and auctions. Although some goods sold at auction (tulip bulbs, fish, or furs) can be approximated as being continuous, they are in fact sold in standard bundles after being graded and sorted. Indivisibility and variety appear to be characteristic of auctions; speed of trading also appears to be of importance, as does the relevance of various levels of uncertainty. A useful survey of auctions and competitive bidding has been given by Milgrom and Weber (1982), but the link between assignment models and noncooperative games is only beginning to be explored.

Houses are frequently sold sequentially in open auction in Australia. In the United States the house market is run by brokers, and many of the problems encountered appear to involve poor evaluation, inadequate search strategies, and lack of information.

Both sealed simultaneous bids and open sequential bidding provide a large class of noncooperative games. It is worth considering what sorts of plausible strategic game mechanisms would have strong noncooperative equilibria, that is, equilibria that are also in the core of the associated cooperative game.

A noncooperative game has been suggested for the housing market. We might also ask if there is a noncooperative game for the marriage market. Herodotus (see Rawlinson, 1910) suggested one used by the Illyrians:

Of their customs, whereof I shall now proceed to give an account, the following (which I understand belongs to them in common with the Illyrian tribe of the Eneti) is the wisest in my judgment. Once a year in each village the maidens of age to marry were collected all together into one place; while the men stood round them in a circle. Then a herald called up the damsels one by one, and offered them for sale. He began with the most beautiful. When she was sold for no small sum of money, he offered for sale the one who came next to her in beauty. All of them were sold to be wives. The richest of the Babylonians who wished to wed bid against each other for the loveliest maidens, while the humbler wife-seekers, who were indifferent about beauty, took the more homely damsels with marriage-portions. For the custom was that when the herald had gone through the whole number of the beautiful damsels, he should then call up the ugliest—a cripple, if there chanced to be one—and offer her to the men, asking who would agree to take her with the smallest marriage-portion. And the man who offered to take the smallest sum had her assigned to him. The marriage-portions were furnished by the money paid for the beautiful damsels, and thus the fairer maidens portioned out the uglier. No one was allowed to give his daughter in marriage to the man of his choice, nor might any one carry away the damsel whom he had purchased without finding bail really and truly to make her his wife; if, however, it turned out that they did not agree, the money might be paid back. All who liked might come even from distant villages and bid for the women. This was the best of all their customs, but it has now fallen into disuse.

Needless to add, this auction process would have given a different result if the men had been auctioned!

8.6 A Comment on Indivisibilities

It has been suggested that consumer indivisibilities can be more or less usefully categorized into five or so classes including houses, automobiles, major consumer durables, furniture, and other. The objects involved are usually not merely (or even always) large but also expensive and durable. Financing problems have called forth specialized financial institutions to facilitate trade.

Most individuals and families desire no more than two or three residences, automobiles, and other major durables. But the desire for more than one unit can rule out the existence of a core in the associated assignment game. Fortunately, the size of any consumer durable is in general small in comparison with the economy as a whole; hence one should be able to establish an appropriate approximate result for large economies. This has been considered by Mas-Colell (1977a).

When we turn to indivisibilities in production, it no longer appears to be as realistic to expect that they are small enough to be negligible. The assets of the top 500 corporations and the costs associated with items such as ships, power plants, pipelines, or dams bring in an intermix of problems involving indivisibilities, oligopolistic competition, and joint ownership. At best we may hope for approximations to cover industries with small firms and small set-up costs where one can argue with a certain amount of justification that the size of the durables and the financial requirements, although large to an individual, are insignificant to the economy as a whole.

Notes to chapter 8

1. Equation (8.6) can be taken as the general definition of $v(S)$ since (if properly interpreted) it includes (8.3)–(8.5) as special cases.

2. It should be noted that the core can be found without solving the multitude of assignment problems arising from the submatrices of $(a_{ij}: i \in M, j \in N)$. In this sense the core in a large assignment game is easier to compute than the characteristic function itself. The reason is that only a relatively small number of coalitions are essential.

3. The left-hand example at the end of section 8.2.2 is such a game. Its core consists of the single vector $(0, 2, 0; 0, 2, 0)$.

4. If the original data of the real-estate version of the game are chosen at random, then the value 0 will be favored over other values in the assignment matrix, and nonunique solutions may occur with positive probability. But this merely reflects indeterminacy in the choice of inactive buyer–seller pairs among players who are actually priced out of the market. The u_i or v_j for such players are identically zero in the core, and the dimension of the core is reduced accordingly.

5. Let us try to make this intuitively plausible. For simplicity assume $m = n$. Suppose that we have a core vector at which all players make a positive profit. Then a small positive constant can be subtracted from all of the sales prices without upsetting the stability of the solution. Each partnership makes the same profit as before, and no individual is forced to take a loss. This price-cutting can be continued until some seller is priced out of the market—his profit goes to zero. The process can of course be reversed, raising all prices by equal amounts until one of the buyers is driven out. Thus there is a natural "degree of freedom" within the core that corresponds to marketwide price movement.

If $m \neq n$, the same discussion applies, except that it may not be possible to drive any of the players of the less numerous type down to zero.

6. Note that we cannot automatically square off an arbitrary subgame by eliminating the no-trade players, since such players will in general correspond to nonzero a_{ii}. This explains why we may find no subgames outside of the two chains alluded to in the text. The two-sided compatible exclusions appearing in the following example are in fact quite unusual.

7. We have actually proved something stronger: that V is undominated by B. Anti-

cipating our proof of external stability, we can therefore state that $V = B - \text{dom } B$, that is, V is the "core" of the principal section.

8. We are thinking of something like a buyers' strike to force the price down, or a voluntary limitation of production to keep the price up. Such maneuvers are of course not Pareto-optimal in the present case, but simply as threats held in reserve they might be expected to have an influence on the course of negotiations.

9. These are the solutions associated with the minimal winning coalitions of the game, as described in *GTSS*, chapter 7.

10. The multiplicity of solutions of this type arises from the multiplicity of optimal assignments and hence of the principal section B (see section 9.1.5).

11. Dubins and Freedman (1981) have considered the Gale–Shapley algorithm as the basis for a noncooperative truth-revelation game in college admissions. The students all inform the colleges of their preferences, but there is an option to lie. The authors prove that this game with preference specification as the strategy of the individual has a truth-revealing noncooperative equilibrium. It may not hurt a student to lie given that all others are telling the truth, but it does not help him. If coalitions of liars are permitted, some could gain.

12. This unsatisfactory state of affairs is not encountered with the value of a game to a player (Shapley and Shubik, 1969). For the n-person game the value of the ith player is $\Phi_i = (4/n)[n/4]$, which fluctuates between 1 and $1 - 3/n$ for $n = 4k + 3$ and $k \geq 1$.

13. Even if the economy has a continuum of small agents, the assumption of an appropriate distribution of a divisible money is necessary for equivalence of the competitive equilibrium and the core. Khan and Yamazaki (1981) provide a counter-example.

9 The Böhm-Bawerk Market

9.1 A Classic Example

This chapter explores a specific example in depth. The example will provide qualitative as well as quantitative insights into the resolution power of various solutions. Moreover, we shall use it to highlight the contrast in economic analysis between "lumpy" exchange and exchange involving smoothly divisible commodities; we shall treat indivisibilities here and then proceed to the continuous case in chapter 10.

9.1.1 The horse market

Discussions of price theory in classical economics are often enlivened by allusions to "Böhm-Bawerk's horses," the central figures in a microcosmic market detailed by that author in his *Positive Theory of Capital*. Since this imaginary but numerically specific market model translates directly into an 18-person cooperative game, it makes an inviting target for the "big-game hunter" anxious to try out his techniques. (Eighteen may be a small number in economics, but it is a large number in game theory!) Apart from the test of skill, there is the prospect of an instructive confrontation between the different types of game solutions—cores, stable sets, values, etc.—and the classical solution as put forward by Böhm-Bawerk.

The basic data of the market are shown in table 9.1. Eight individuals each have one horse for sale. Ten other individuals each wish to buy one horse. The horses themselves are all alike, but the traders have different "subjective valuations," ranging between $10 and $30, of what it is worth to own a horse (Böhm-Bawerk, 1923, p. 203; we have arbitrarily replaced pounds with dollars). No restrictions are placed on communication or on transfers of money or of horses. The game problem, informally stated, is to decide how the inherent profitability of the market, arising from the differences in subjective valuation, is to be distributed among the players.

9.1.2 The characteristic function

The reader will recognize that the present example represents a simplification of the general assignment game in one important respect: the absence of product differentiation. The matrix of inputs (h_{ij}) has been replaced by

Table 9.1
The worth of a horse

Sellers		Buyers	
A_1 values a horse at	$10	B_1 values a horse at	$30
A_2	$11	B_2	$28
A_3	$15	B_3	$26
A_4	$17	B_4	$24
A_5	$20	B_5	$22
A_6	$21.50	B_6	$21
A_7	$25	B_7	$20
A_8	$26	B_8	$18
		B_9	$17
		B_{10}	$15

a vector (h_j). The assignment matrix (a_{ij}), defined by

$$a_{ij} = \max(0, h_j - c_i), \tag{9.1}$$

therefore has the special property that in each 2×2 submatrix

a	b
c	d

with nonzero entries, the sums $a + d$ and $b + c$ are equal. In short, it only matters who buys and who sells, not how they pair up. Hence the actual assignment problem is trivial, and the characteristic function for the game can be written down explicitly.

In fact, let S be an arbitrary coalition with members denoted by $A_{i_1}, A_{i_2}, \ldots, A_{i_l}, B_{j_1}, B_{j_2}, \ldots, B_{j_m}$, where the sellers A_i are arranged in order of increasing c_i and the buyers B_j in order of decreasing valuations h_j. Then we have

$$v(S) = a_{i_1 j_1} + a_{i_2 k_2} + \ldots + a_{i_k j_k}, \tag{9.2}$$

where $k = \min(l, m)$. In other words, for computational purposes we can assume that the "strongest" buyer in any coalition buys from the "strongest" seller in that coalition, and so on down the line, until either the players of one type are exhausted or a pair is reached that cannot trade at a profit.

Applying this to the data in table 9.1, we find that

$$v(M \cup N) = 20 + 17 + 11 + 7 + 2 + 0 + 0 + 0 = 57. \tag{9.3}$$

This amount is the total profit inherent in the market. It is achieved whenever the first five buyers acquire the horses of the first five sellers.

9.2 The Core

The core, too, is easy to determine, since the absence of product differentiation leads to a uniform market price. To see this let (u, v) be a typical imputation in the core. If the net amount of money received by an active seller i—$u_i + c_i$—should happen to be less than the net amount of money paid by an active buyer j—$h_j - v_j$—then domination would automatically occur:

$$u_i + v_j < h_j - c_i = a_{ij}.$$

Hence the active sellers must take in at least as much as the active buyers pay out. Since the inactive traders cannot be forced to pay anything, it follows that all transactions in an undominated imputation must take place at the same price.

Thus the core C can be described by a single parameter p such that if $(u, v) \in C$, then

$$u_i = \max(0, p - c_i), \quad i \in M,$$
$$v_j = \max(0, h_j - p), \quad j \in N.$$

The range over which p varies is limited by the requirement that $\sum u_i + \sum v_j = v(M \cup N)$, which can only be satisfied if equal numbers of players of each type are active, so that they have $u_i = p - c_i$ or $v_j = h_j - p$. Geometrically the core is a straight line segment.

In the numerical example, a price in the interval $\$21 \le p \le \$21.50$ permits exactly five players of each type to trade at a profit. If the price were to exceed the upper limit, the sixth seller would put up his horse for sale, and an imbalance would be created that would tend to drive the price down again. Similarly a price less than $\$21$ would find six (or more) buyers competing for five (at most) horses. The core is therefore the segment with endpoints

$$(11.5, 10.5, 6.5, 4.5, 1.5, 0, 0, 0; 8.5, 6.5, 4.5, 2.5, 1.5, 0, 0, 0, 0, 0);$$
$$(11, 10, 6, 4, 1, 0, 0, 0; 9, 7, 5, 3, 1, 0, 0, 0, 0, 0).$$

These are of course the extremal imputations (u^*, v_*) and (u_*, v^*) described in section 8.3.3.

9.2.1 Relation to the general assignment game

The one-dimensional "stick" core we have found in the Böhm-Bawerk model represents the most extreme form of the elongation described in theorem 8.3; this is a consequence of the lack of differentiation among the objects of trade.[1] If a small random perturbation were applied to the model, giving the buyers slightly different subjective valuations of the different horses up for sale, then the dimension might jump from 1 to 5, but the core would remain very slender since it is a continuous function of the parameters. If the buyers should become more dissimilar in their utility functions, the core would grow fatter. The ultimate in this direction would be the game in which each buyer has only one horse that he can accept at any price. Since the bargaining for each horse is then independent of the rest, the game would decompose into smaller games, and the core would take the form of a rectangular parallelepiped (i.e., a product of intervals).

9.2.2 Discussion

The core that we have determined for this game is precisely the classical solution given by Böhm-Bawerk. A uniform market price is established at a level that, though not precisely determined, is constrained within fairly narrow limits. If the consumers and suppliers in the market are sufficiently numerous, and if the tastes of the former and the costs of the latter are sufficiently variegated, then something close to a determinate outcome can be predicted. It is the classical balance of supply and demand.

9.2.3 Bargaining and threat potentials

From the game-theoretic viewpoint, certain weaknesses in this solution soon become apparent. For one thing, the weak players in the game receive no consideration, although they are by no means dummies. To be sure, they are powerless to interfere with the imputations in the core, which by definition are unblockable. In fact, there is not a vital coalition among them. Nevertheless, consider the role of the weak buyer B_6 in our numerical example. It is his valuation (\$21) that establishes the price floor of the classical solution. Were he to "go home," the floor would drop to \$20, and the sellers as a group would very likely suffer. By his very presence—his willingness to pay any amount up to \$21 for a horse—he performs a valuable service to some of the players (and a disservice to others). What is it worth?

A similar role exists for the weak seller A_6, who in our example sets the price ceiling of \$21.50. In lesser measure, the other weak players also have some bargaining power. The seventh buyer, for example, might argue that his participation in the bidding tends to limit the sixth buyer's threat value; if he should refrain, then the latter might be able to command a larger "bribe" for remaining on the scene and making the bids that force the price up into the Böhm-Bawerk range.

The marginal strong players A_5 and B_5 also help to determine the price level, and since their expected profits are in any case rather small, their threats to behave "irrationally" could also carry some weight. In our example, the departure of the fifth buyer would cause the price range in the core to drop from \$21–21.50 to \$20–\$21. (See table 9.1.) Would the other four buyers be willing to pay, say, fifty cents each to bring this about? (If they were, then Pareto optimality, in the guise of a counteroffer by the sellers, might induce him to return to the market, to his further profit.)

To complete the picture, we should note that the top players of each type are in an extremely poor bargaining position. They are vulnerable to all the threats we have been describing, and they have no very credible counterthreats: They have too much to lose. A man who is desperately in need of a horse is obviously at a disadvantage in haggling over the price, if his need is known. His situation practically invites collusion among the horse merchants. But the core gives no hint of this.

We are not arguing against the classical solution as such, but rather that it simply may not be possible to realize the bargaining potentials of the Böhm-Bawerk market within a given institutional form. Sanctions against collusion or compensation, or physical barriers to communication, may be stronger than the "corruptive" forces described. (Even then it would be useful to have a theory that predicted the strength and direction of these forces, if only to allow design of more effective barriers.) As we have emphasized before, the solution concept to apply in a given game situation depends greatly on the institutional context in which the abstract model was found. (It also depends, of course, on the type of answers—e.g., predictive or normative—that we wish the theory to provide.) A corollary is that if we want a full understanding of an abstract model out of context, we must explore a variety of solution concepts.

9.2.4 Other solution concepts

The reason for turning to the stable-set solutions, after discussing the shortcomings of the classical (core) solution, can be summed up by the dictum: The core is undominated but does not dominate. Stability, without artificial constraining barriers, requires a wider span of possible outcomes than is permitted by the core alone.

To illustrate, consider the imputation that might arise after a completely successful buyers' strike: the sellers are all required to offer their wares at cost. The result is zero profit to all sellers, and some distribution of $v(M \cup N)$ to the strong buyers. This is an extreme outcome, and it is certainly not stable. The number one seller, for instance, can always find a buyer who will allow him a positive profit while showing a net gain himself. However, there is no imputation *in the core* that dominates this extreme imputation. Although the active buyers are paying unequal prices, they are paying less than the lowest core price. Hence there is no effective coalition that would support a shift to one in the core.

In the next section we shall obtain some of the stable sets of the Böhm-Bawerk game. We shall find that each one contains, in addition to the core and many other imputations, an extreme "buyer's market" imputation of the kind just discussed, as well as a similar "seller's market" imputation in which all buyers make zero profit. It has been shown that this phenomenon occurs in all stable-set solutions (B. Peleg, private communication).

In section 9.4 we shall return to the Böhm-Bawerk game and investigate its value solution. We shall discover that the value is not in the core, and that it recognizes explicitly and quantitatively many of the bargaining-position effects discussed above, especially the courtship of the marginal players, both weak and strong, and the price discrimination against the strongest players.

9.3 A Class of Stable-Set Solutions

The stable-set analysis of the Böhm-Bawerk game offers a good introduction to the more complex considerations that arise in the general assignment game. We cannot give a complete catalogue of stable sets, even in the numerical example that we have been using for illustration. There is a class of solutions, however, that can be described easily and systematically and admits a direct interpretation on economic grounds. These solutions involve just the "strong" players (the top five of each type in our numerical example) and entail no third-party payments whatever.

9.3.1 Construction of a solution

Let there be given an arbitrary arrangement of the strong players into buyer–seller pairs. Thus, in our numerical example we might have the pairs in table 9.2. We shall call these *active pairs*. Assume (for the sake of describing the solution) that the market functions in the following conventional way. An "official price" p_0 is announced—this can be any

Table 9.2
Active pairs

Sellers	Buyers
A_1 ($10)	B_1 ($30)
A_2 ($11)	B_2 ($28)
A_3 ($15)	B_3 ($26)
A_4 ($17)	B_4 ($24)
A_5 ($20)	B_5 ($22)

number whatsoever. The active pairs that can trade at that price do so. The active pairs that cannot trade at that price (without loss) trade instead at the nearest feasible price to it, thus giving a profit of zero to the player who would have taken a loss at the official price. Hence the sales price for any active pair is the median of the two valuations and the official price.

For example, $p_0 = \$27$ applied to the partition of table 9.2 would lead to the following series of transactions:

A_1 sells to B_3 at $26,

A_2 sells to B_5 at $22,

A_3 sells to B_1 at $27,

A_4 sells to B_2 at $27,

A_5 sells to B_4 at $24.

The associated imputation (profit vector) would be

Sellers: $(16, 11, 12, 10, 4, 0, 0, 0)$,

Buyers: $(3, 1, 0, 0, 0, 0, 0, 0, 0, 0)$.

(The high price means that most of the profit goes to the sellers.)

Now let p_0 sweep through all possible values, from the valuation of the strongest player ($10) to that of the strongest seller ($30). It is a theorem that *the resulting set of imputations is stable.* The proof will be given presently.

Since the original partition was arbitrary, the method gives us $5! = 120$ different stable-set solutions. We note that they all contain the core, as they must; when p_0 is in the Böhm-Bawerk interval, a uniform price prevails and the arbitrary pairing-off is irrelevant. But outside the core, the pairings determine which sellers have to undersell to subsidize the weaker buyers in a "seller's market" (p_0 high), and which buyers must cover the losses of the weaker sellers in a "buyer's market" (p_0 low).

9.3.2 Geometrical form of the solution

Let us examine briefly the geometrical structure of these stable sets. It is clear that they are polygonal (composed of a chain of straight line segments). One end of the chain is at an imputation giving zero profit to all buyers; the other is at one giving zero profit to all sellers. (These correspond to $p_0 = \$30$ and $p_0 = \$10$, respectively.) Somewhere in the middle lies the core. The vertices of the solution (points at which the direction changes) mark the places where some player's profit drops to zero. In other words, failure to change direction at these points (when moving from the core) would take us out of the imputation space. Thus the stable set may be visualized as an indefinite linear extension of the core, the external portions projected back onto the boundary of the imputation simplex. The direction of the projection is determined by the arbitrary designation of the "active" pairs.

The foregoing is simply a geometrical restatement of our previous description of the solution as the accommodation of an "official" price to the realities of the individual valuations.

In figure 9.1 a stable-set solution is depicted for the case of just two strong players of each type. We assume that the active pairs are A_1, B_1 and A_2, B_2. The shaded rectangular cross section is the set of imputations attainable by transactions within the active pairs, with no third-party payments. The heavy line is the stable set. The dashed line is the linear extension of the core. The core itself may be less than the entire middle segment, because of possible dominations by coalitions involving the unspecified weak players.

9.3.3 Proof of stability

The proof of stability is relatively simple, and we shall be able to do it mainly with words. Internal stability follows from the monotonic character of the set V. No buyer–seller pair (active or not) can *both* profit from a change in "official" price. Hence no vital coalition prefers any one imputation in V over any other, and internal stability is ensured.

External stability is established in two stages. Consider first an imputation y in which all active coalitions receive their values (e.g., one in the shaded region in figure 9.1). If y is not in V, then it cannot be generated by the official price mechanism. It follows from the continuity of V that there will be a p_0 that will cause one active coalition to trade at a price higher

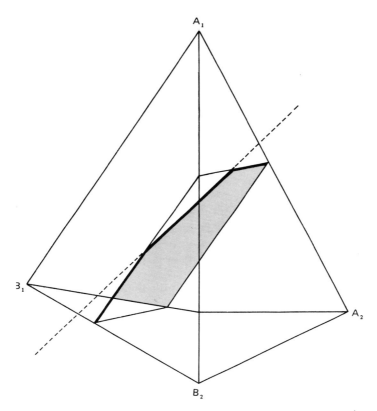

Figure 9.1
Stable set with coalitions $\overline{A_1 B_1}$ and $\overline{A_2 B_2}$ active.

than at y while another active coalition trades at a price lower than at y. Denote by $z(p_0)$ the V-imputation generated by p_0. Now the buyer member of the first coalition, and the seller member of the second, will both prefer $z(p_0)$ to y; moreover, as a coalition they can enforce their shares of $z(p_0)$ simply by trading with each other at the price p_0, which is a rational price for both of them because their profits at $z(p_0)$ are positive. Hence y is dominated by V.

Consider finally an imputation in which not all active coalitions receive their values (in the figure, a point off the rectangular cross section). Then some active coalition receives less than its value v. But in the set V their payoffs run the gamut from $(0, v)$ to $(v, 0)$, continuously, and their joint profit is identically v. Hence at some V-imputation they both do better and can enforce it. This completes the proof of external stability, and hence of stability.

9.3.4 The principal section

The set of imputations in which all active coalitions receive their values plays an essential role in the theory of general assignment games as well as in the Böhm-Bawerk games now being discussed. In the general case the set will again contain the core plus at least one stable-set solution. This is the *principal section* introduced in section 8.4.3. In some assignment games it is unique; in the present game, with no product differentiation, it is not. Since it comprises outcomes that can be reached through private transactions within the separate active coalitions, a principal section will remain part of the imputation space even if we change the model by imposing a restriction on side payments.

Note in the solution V that domination of points outside the principal section is accomplished by the active coalitions, while domination of points inside the principal section requires the intervention of inactive coalitions. The latter are nevertheless composed solely of strong players; the weak players are entirely discriminated against in V.

9.3.5 Interpretation of the solution V

What are the behavioristic implications of the solution V? Will unequal prices (the identifying characteristic of V-imputations outside the core) occur in practice? The theory ventures no prediction on this point, in the absence of further contextual information. The standard of behavior of V can be reduced to three maxims:

1. Neither give nor receive money except for goods in exchange.

2. Be loyal to your designated partner.

3. Accommodate to the general market price, as closely as possible.

These constraints might arise in a fairly mechanical way out of the specific institutional form of the market (but they must not be absolutely binding!), or they may have an ethical or sociological basis. What we have proved is that they describe a system that is stable, and that this stability would be destroyed, in one way or another, if some of them were relaxed or if further constraints were imposed. Unequal prices create a tension within the system—a temptation to "unethical" (or extrainstitutional) behavior; the system counters by providing preferred, "ethical" reactions to any and all such "unethical" proposals. Will the original price schedule thus be reaffirmed, or will it be replaced by one of the reactions? This question cannot be answered in the abstract. Since the "reactions" generally reflect a more nearly uniform price schedule, we have here a force that, in some applications at least, would tend to drive the outcome toward the core. In such cases the core would be the outcome set, and the stable-set solution a sort of reference set. The classical solution would prevail in the outcome, maintained and "policed" by the existence of a stable social superstructure that manifests itself in the solution V. In other contexts, however, one might plausibly rationalize V as an outcome set in its own right.

9.3.6 Other stable sets
The stable sets described here by no means exhaust the possibilities. Without going into excessive detail, we will mention two other types:

(1) The strong players may be paired off differently, depending on whether the official price is above or below the Böhm-Bawerk range. In effect, two solutions of the original type can be "grafted" together at the core, and the resulting set will be stable. It will not ordinarily lie within a single principal section (see figure 9.2), since the set of active coalitions depends on the official price. Nevertheless no third-party payments are required. Of the above maxims, only the second is modified. The weak players are still totally excluded.

(2) In another class of stable sets, when the official price is above the Böhm-Bawerk range, some or all of the excess paid by the buyers may be diverted to certain of the weak sellers—namely those whose costs are sufficiently low to permit them to enter the market at the official price. (Thus, in the notation of section 9.3.1, seller A_3 might transfer up to $2 of the $27 he receives from B_1 to the weak seller A_7, whose cost is $25, ostensibly to keep him from bidding the price down.) Similar considera-

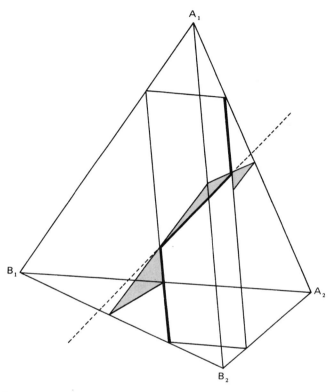

Figure 9.2
Another stable set of the game in figure 9.1.

tions may be given to the weak buyers when the official price is below the Böhm-Bawerk range.

Thus the threat potentials of the weak players described in section 9.2.3 are actually realized under certain stable "standards of behavior." This effect was first noted by von Neumann and Morgenstern (1947, pp. 572–573) and is illustrated in figure 9.3 for the case of two sellers and one buyer. The principal section is the edge A_1–B_1. The portion of the solution in the small triangle is a more or less arbitrary curve running from apex to base.

9.4 The Value Solution

Clearly the horse market in which groups of traders can form coalitions is adequately represented by its characteristic function (see *GTSS*, chapter

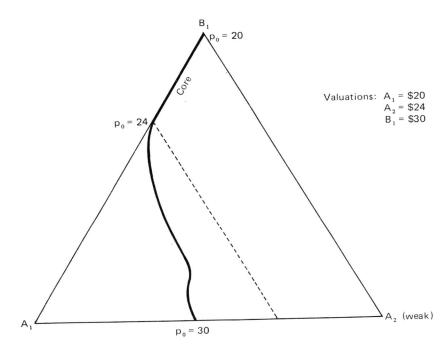

B₁

$p_0 = 20$

Core

$p_0 = 24$

Valuations: A₁ = \$20
A₂ = \$24
B₁ = \$30

A₁

$p_0 = 30$

A₂ (weak)

Figure 9.3
A market with two sellers and one buyer.

7). The value solution can thus be applied directly to this market (Shapley, 1953).

Given the characteristic function, the value of a particular player X may be defined as his average contribution to the worth of a typical coalition $\mathscr{C}$:

$$\phi_X = E\{v(\mathscr{C} \cup \{X\}) - v(\mathscr{C})\}, \quad X \notin \mathscr{C}. \tag{9.4}$$

The appropriate weights to use in forming this average turn out to depend on the size of $\mathscr{C}$, with the result that each value of $c = |\mathscr{C}|$ (from 0 to 17 in this case) occurs with equal total weight in the sum.[2]

A random process that generates these weights in the form of probabilities is easily described: Mix up the players, line them up in a row, and take $\mathscr{C}$ to be the set of players to the left of player X. This process is independent of the particular player X; it can be used to find the values of all players simultaneously.

Table 9.3
Data from 1225 Monte Carlo trials

Player	Total gain[a]	Average gain	Variance[b]	Estimated P.E.[c]	Adjusted P.E.[d]
A_1	9627.00	7.859	18.653	± 0.083	± 0.084
A_2	7527.50	6.145$^-$	12.200	0.067	0.074
A_3	5439.00	4.440	10.207	0.062	0.063
A_4	3713.50	3.031	8.110	0.055	0.052
A_5	1817.00	1.483	5.445	0.045	0.037
A_6	1036.00	0.846	5.554	0.046	0.028
A_7	697.00	0.569	1.233	0.021	0.023
A_8	396.00	0.323	0.600	0.015	0.017
A_9	201.00	0.164	1.048	0.020	0.012
A_{10}	75.00	0.061[e]	0.788[e]	0.017[e]	0.008[e]
B_1	12333.50	10.068	19.560	0.085	0.095
B_2	11399.00	9.305$^+$	19.090	0.084	0.091
B_3	7055.00	5.759	11.125	0.064	0.072
B_4	4949.00	4.040	11.016	0.064	0.060
B_5	2161.50	1.764	4.181	0.039	0.040
B_6	1025.00	0.837	3.804	0.038	0.027
B_7	251.00	0.205$^-$	0.520	0.014	0.014
B_8	122.00	0.100[e]	0.158[e]	0.008[e]	0.010[e]

a. The average gain $\bar{g}$ is an unbiased estimate of the value.
b. The variance estimate V was obtained from a subsample of 100 trials.
c. Probable Error $= 0.6745\sqrt{V/1225}$.
d. Adjusted Probable Error $= 0.03\sqrt{\bar{g}}$; the coefficient 0.03 was determined empirically.
e. Compare the true values given in the text.

In terms of the market model, we can imagine the traders arriving at the marketplace one by one, in a random order, with each new arrival getting credit for the increase in total profit (if any) that his presence makes possible. A player's value is then equal to his expected gain under this scheme, assuming that all orders of arrival are equally likely.

An exact calculation of these expectations appears to be very difficult because of the large number of possible coalitions. For this reason we had a Monte Carlo program written that closely parallels the above verbal description, and we ran off some 1225 "horse fairs." The resulting gains for different players are shown in table 9.3.

To get an idea of how far the averages might be from the true values, the variances of a subsample of 100 trials were computed and converted into estimates of probable error. Since these estimates are themselves unreliable individually, we "smoothed" them (last column of table 9.3) on the basis of a first-order assumption that the variances should be proportional to the average gains.

An independent check on the results is available for the cases in which the error term is most serious, namely the two "weakest" players A_{10} and B_8. Since these players usually contribute nothing to a coalition, their exact expectations can be computed rather easily. The details for A_{10} follow:

Partition the 18! possible orderings into six classes according to the relative placement of A_{10}, B_1, and B_2; each class has probability 1/6. In order for A_{10} to score at all, he must be either the second or the third of these three. In the case $(\dots B_1 \dots A_{10} \dots B_2 \dots)$ a gain of \$5 will be recorded for him, but only if none of A_1–A_9 precedes him (reading from left to right). Counting cases, we see that this event has probability 1/22, since only $10 \cdot 9!$ of the $220 \cdot 9!$ ways of inserting A_1–A_9 are favorable. This case thus contributes (5/22)/6 to the expectation. Similarly the case $(\dots B_2 \dots A_{10} \dots B_1 \dots)$ contributes (4/22)/6. In the remaining two cases, where A_{10} comes after both B_1 and B_2, a gain of \$5 is recorded if none of A_1–A_9 precedes A_{10}, and \$4 if precisely one does. The respective probabilities are 1/220 and 3/220, and the contribution from these cases is therefore (5/220 + 4/220)/3. Adding up these results we obtain

$$\phi_{A_{10}} = 31/330 = 0.09393\dots,$$

in contrast to the Monte Carlo estimate of 0.061 ± 0.017.

A similar computation gives

$$\phi_{B_8} = 17/180 = 0.09444\dots,$$

in place of our estimate 0.100 ± 0.008. B_8 scores somewhat more often than A_{10} since he has fewer rivals, but his gains when he does score are somewhat smaller; these two effects very nearly cancel, as it happens.

It is not difficult to obtain the exact variances for these two cases as well. They are $0.4124\dots$ and $0.291\dots$, respectively, indicating true probable errors of $\pm 0.0124\dots$ and $\pm 0.0104\dots$ for the average of 1225 trials.

9.4.1 A comparison of results
The analysis of Böhm-Bawerk predicts the establishment of a uniform market price at some undetermined level between \$21 and \$21.50. The

Table 9.4
Estimated value and effective price

Player	Estimated value ($)	Effective price ($)	Side payments ($) @ $21.01	@ $21.25
A_1 ($30)	7.86 ± 0.08	22.14	−1.13	−0.89
A_2 ($28)	6.14 ± 0.07	21.86	−0.85	−0.61
A_3 ($26)	4.44 ± 0.06	21.56	−0.55	−0.31
A_4 ($24)	3.03 ± 0.05	20.97	+0.04	+0.28
A_5 ($22)	1.48 ± 0.04	20.52	+0.49	+0.73
A_6 ($21)	0.85 ± 0.03	—	+0.85	+0.85
A_7 ($20)	0.57 ± 0.02	—	+0.57	+0.57
A_8 ($18)	0.32 ± 0.02	—	+0.32	+0.32
A_9 ($17)	0.16 ± 0.01	—	+0.16	+0.16
A_{10} ($15)	0.09	—	+0.09	+0.09
All buyers	24.94	21.01	−0.01	+1.19
B_1 ($10)	10.07 ± 0.09	20.07	−0.94	−1.18
B_2 ($11)	9.31 ± 0.09	20.31	−0.70	−0.94
B_3 ($15)	5.76 ± 0.07	20.76	−0.25	−0.49
B_4 ($17)	4.04 ± 0.06	21.04	+0.03	+0.21
B_5 ($20)	1.76 ± 0.04	21.76	+0.75	+0.51
B_6 ($21.50)	0.84 ± 0.03	—	+0.84	+0.84
B_7 ($25)	0.20 ± 0.01	—	+0.20	+0.20
B_8 ($26)	0.09	—	+0.09	+0.09
All sellers	32.07	21.01	+0.02	−1.18

limits arise from the need to balance supply and demand by keeping players A_6 and B_6 out of contention. The "weak" players, from A_6 and B_6 on down, receive no consideration of any kind from the "strong" players A_1–A_5, B_1–B_5. In contrast, the value solution, if it is regarded as descriptive of the outcome of a single play of the game, reveals both non-uniformity of pricing and profit-sharing with the weak players. Both effects are relatively small but clearly discernible despite the uncertainty represented by the error term. (See table 9.4 and figure 9.4.)

The effective prices for the ten strong players cover a range from approximately $20 to approximately $22, considerably wider than Böhm-Bawerk's limits from a uniform price. The average buyer pays $21.41; the average seller gets $20.59. The difference goes into the side payments to the weak players. The total profit of all sellers combined is $32.07, which

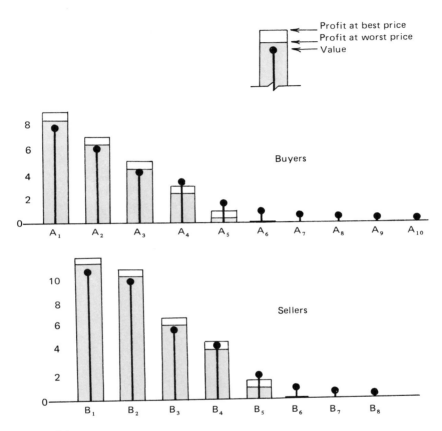

Figure 9.4
Values compared with core profits.

corresponds to what they would get if there were a uniform price of $21.01 and no side payments. Although this figure (if accurate) is just within the Böhm-Bawerk interval, there is no particular reason to believe that this would remain true if the parameters of the problem were changed.

By assuming a fixed price, we can treat the price irregularities of the value solution as though they arose from side payments among the strong players (last columns of table 9.4). These payments, taken with the amounts received by the weak players, form a strikingly regular pattern, reaching a peak for the players whose variations are closest to the assumed price. In other words, the less "incentive" a player has to trade (if he is strong) or to refrain from trading (if he is weak), the more consideration he receives in the solution. A theoretical explanation is given in section 9.4.2. The heuristic explanation presumably lies in the fact that the borderline players can somewhat credibly threaten to upset the optimum trading arrangement by entering or leaving the market, as the case may be. In contrast, extreme players such as A_1 and B_8 would incur heavy personal losses from such actions, and their threats are correspondingly less believable. The value solution gives us a quantitative measure of what these "threat" possibilities are worth on the average.

The two sorts of side payments, for strong and weak players, are not strictly comparable, since the former depend on an arbitrary fixed price. Of the two prices used in table 9.4, the first, $21.01, is the one that makes the side payments within each group, buyers and sellers, balance separately. The second, $21.25, was singled out because it gives a good fit when the buyers and sellers are plotted on the same "incentive" scale (figure 9.5).

9.4.2 Some inequalities on the values

In this section we give a general proof of the inequality relations

$$\phi_{A_i} \le \phi_{A_j} \le \phi_{A_i} + a_j - a_i \quad \text{if } a_i < a_j,$$
$$\phi_{B_i} \le \phi_{B_j} \le \phi_{B_i} + b_i - b_j \quad \text{if } b_i > b_j, \tag{9.5}$$

which serve to establish the monotone decreasing character of the side payments as a function of "incentive" (see figure 9.2). It will suffice to consider the first line of (9.5).

Let $\mathscr{C}$ be a coalition not containing either A_i or A_j, and let x_j be the gain that results from the inclusion of A_j:

$$x_j = v(\mathscr{C} \cup \{A_j\}) - v(\mathscr{C}).$$

The inclusion of A_i instead will in general yield a smaller gain, since the

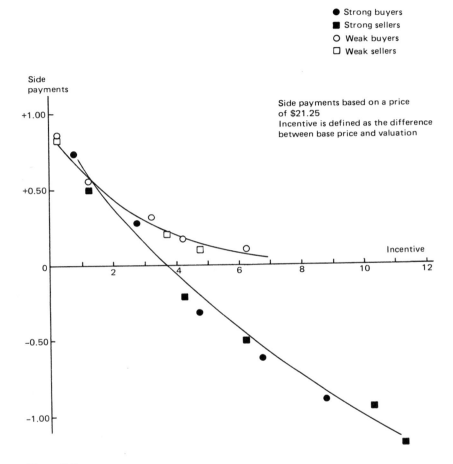

Figure 9.5
Relation between side payments and incentives.

latter's personal evaluation is less by $a_j - a_i$. In fact, it is not difficult to verify from (9.4) that

$$x_i \le x_j \quad \text{and} \quad x_i \ge x_j - a_j + a_i, \tag{9.6}$$

where $x_i = v(\mathscr{C} \cup \{A_i\}) - v(\mathscr{C})$.

Similarly, let $\mathscr{D}$ be a coalition containing both A_i and A_j, and compare the *losses* y_i, y_j that are suffered as a result of the removal of A_i and A_j, respectively:

$$y_i = v(\mathscr{D}) - v(\mathscr{D} - \{A_i\}), \quad y_j = v(\mathscr{D}) - v(\mathscr{D} - \{A_j\}).$$

Again it is easily verified that

$$y_i \le y_j \quad \text{and} \quad y_i \ge y_j - a_j + a_i. \tag{9.7}$$

Now consider an arbitrary pair of orderings of all the players that are identical except for the transposition of A_i and A_j:

$$\overset{\mathscr{C}}{\overbrace{\underset{\underset{\mathscr{D}}{\underbrace{\dots A_j \dots A_i \dots \,.}}}{\dots A_i \dots A_j \dots ,}}}$$

Taking $\mathscr{C}$ and $\mathscr{D}$ as shown, we see that the gains of A_i and A_j in the first ordering are

$$g_i = x_i, \quad g_j = y_j,$$

while in the second they are

$$g_i = y_i, \quad g_j = x_j.$$

The average gains from the two orderings satisfy

$$\bar{g}_i \le \bar{g}_j \le \bar{g}_i + a_j - a_i,$$

by (9.6) and (9.7).

Since the values ϕ can be expressed as averages in turn of the average gains $\bar{g}$ from $n!/2$ such pairs of orderings, the conclusion is evident.

9.4.3 A variant of the original game

In the classical theory the two strongest "weak" players play a significant role: They set upper and lower bounds on the price interval within which the trading takes place, although they do not participate in the trading themselves. If B_6 were not present, the upper limit would rise to $22, the

Table 9.5
Data from 400 Monte Carlo trials with players A_6 and B_6 omitted

Player	Total gain	Average gain[a]	Adjusted P.E.[b]
A_1	3199	7.9975	± 0.148
A_2	2472	6.1800	0.131
A_3	1715	4.2875	0.109
A_4	1268	3.1700	0.093
A_5	646	1.6150	0.067
A_7	288	0.7200	0.045^-
A_8	137	0.3425	0.031
A_9	90	0.225	0.024^-
A_{10}	45	0.1125^c	0.018^d
B_1	4153	10.3825	0.169
B_2	3888	9.7200	0.164
B_3	2367	5.9175	0.128
B_4	1621	4.0525	0.106
B_5	764	1.9100	0.073
B_7	103	0.2575	0.027
B_8	44	0.1100^c	0.017^d

a. The average gain is an unbiased estimate of the value.
b. The adjusted probable error is based on the empirical formula used in table 9.3; no separate variance estimates were made.
c. The exact values, by direct computation, are $0.11616 \ldots$ for A_{10} and $0.12301 \ldots$ for B_8.
d. The true probable errors are 0.02401 and 0.02062 for A_{10} and A_8, respectively.

price at which A_5 would be forced out of the market. If A_6 were not present, the lower limit would drop to \$20, determined (as it happens) by the valuations of both A_7 and B_5. (See table 9.1.) The Böhm-Bawerk interval with both A_6 and B_6 absent is thus four times as wide as the old one and is unsymmetrically situated with respect to it. It occurred to us that the values of the reduced 16-person game, in conjunction with the results already obtained, might yield further useful insights.

The results of 400 Monte Carlo trials for the 16-person game are shown in table 9.5. We did not make fresh estimates of the probable errors; they can be expected to be larger than those in table 9.3 by a factor of about $\sqrt{1225/400} = 1.75$ for players with comparable values, and we have used this factor in deriving the numbers in the last column of table 9.5.

Figures 9.6 and 9.7 correspond to figures 9.4 and 9.5, respectively, though with a different base price is used in figure 9.7. The comparison is

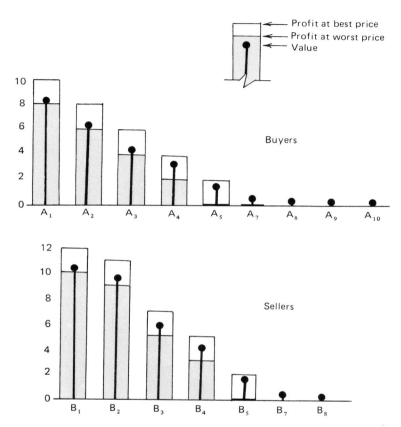

Figure 9.6
Values compared with core profits; players A_6 and B_6 omitted.

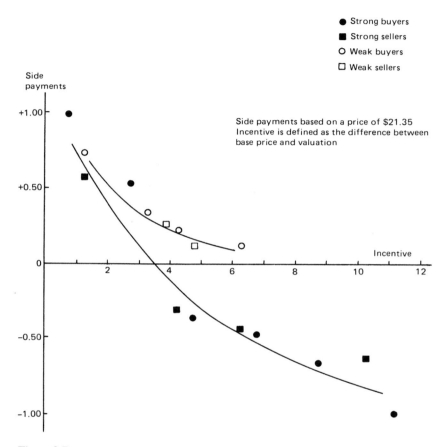

Figure 9.7
Relation between side payments and incentives in the reduced game.

most interesting with regard to what does not happen. There are no sharp shifts in value. There is no tendency apparent for the new distribution to adjust itself to the new Böhm-Bawerk interval ($20, $22); in fact the change, if any, seems to be in the opposite direction, toward higher prices. The side payments of $0.85 and $0.84 formerly received by A_6 and B_6 seem to have been redistributed fairly smoothly among the remaining players; at least the visible irregularities cannot be given much significance in face of the indicated probable errors.

9.5 Other Solutions

9.5.1 The nucleolus
The nucleolus n for the Böhm-Bawerk market is trivial to calculate. We move in the "walls" of the core at equal speed (see *GTSS*, chapter 11), stopping whenever the core would be obliterated by further movement. In this case, since the core is one-dimensional, we move in the ends; thus the nucleolus is the midpoint of the core, or the imputation (11.25, 10.25, 6.25, 4.25, 1.25, 0, 0, 0; 8.75, 6.75, 4.75, 2.75, 1.75, 0, 0, 0, 0, 0). This is equivalent to a price of $n = 21.25.

9.5.2 The competitive equilibrium
The competitive-equilibrium solution for the horse market is a price p such that each individual maximizes his utility subject to his budget constraint. It is straightforward to check that any price in the range $21 \le p \le 21.50 is a competitive equilibrium. In particular the set of competitive equilibria produce imputations that exactly cover the core.

We might consider increasing the number of traders in the horse market to study what happens to the range of prices that are competitive equilibria. Instead of 18 traders we might replicate the market k times and consider $18k$ traders, with k of each of the 18 trader types. Nothing changes; the increase in the number of competitors does not narrow the range of the core or the competitive-equilibrium prices.

A narrowing of the price range requires not merely more competitors but competitors with different tastes, so that the "distance" between the closest marginal pair narrows. If tastes remain the same, there is no narrowing of the level of indeterminacy in price.

9.5.3 The noncooperative equilibrium
In section 8.5.1 we noted that there are many ways in which we could formulate trading in a market as a game in strategic form. We offer one specific version here.

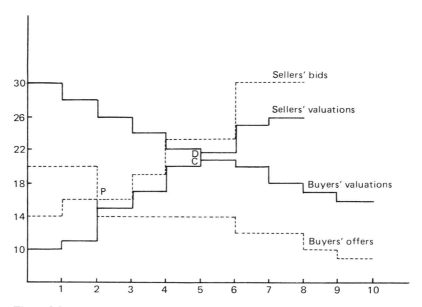

Figure 9.8
Bids, offers, and values.

Assume that a brokerage mechanism accepts bids and offers from all traders. It charges no commissions. When all bids and offers are received, the broker solves the simple optimal assignment problem and selects a price as follows.

A strategy of seller i is to name the lowest price x_i at which he will sell his horse. A strategy of buyer j is to name the highest price y_j that he is willing to pay for any horse. The market mechanism does not know the preferences of the traders. It merely accepts and aggregates bids and offers.

The brokerage mechanism draws the cumulative bid and offer curves, as indicated by the dashed lines in figure 9.8. The solid lines represent the actual values of a horse to the buyers and sellers. The market price is determined by the intersection of the bid and offer curves. The price $p = \$16$ is indicated at the point P where two horses are sold. Given the actual values, optimal trade would be five horses, and the price range indicated by DC is $\$21 \leq p \leq \$21.50$.

Several detailed rules are required before the market mechanism is fully defined. It is at this point that a certain arbitrariness in the institutional design appears. This is illustrated immediately when there is an excess of either supply or demand at the intersection of bids with offers. A convention for rationing must be specified. In the case of figure 9.8, at the price $p = \$16$ the demand is for two horses but the supply is three. The convention adopted is that the final sales are selected from the marginal sellers chosen randomly. Thus at $16 two sellers are willing to supply the last horse, and the market randomly selects one of them.

It is assumed that all sellers offering below the market price and all bidders bidding above the market price execute their transactions at market prices.

If the intersection of bids and offers has a vertical section, such as DC, and if buyers and sellers bid and offer at their actual valuations, then the market picks a price midway between the marginal bid and offer (in this case the midpoint of DC).

It can be seen that all the competitive equilibria for which $\$21 \leq p \leq \$21.50$ and sales are five horses can be obtained as outcomes from noncooperative equilibria. Let the five bidders who value a horse most highly all bid in the range $21–$21.50, and let the rest bid less. The five most eager sellers offer their horses at the same price, and the rest offer theirs at a higher price.

EXERCISES

9.1.   *Show that there are noncooperative equilibria other than the ones noted above that give outcomes identical with the competitive equilibria.*

9.2.   *Show that there is no noncooperative equilibrium with active trade with a price outside the range* $\$21 \leq p \leq \$21.50$.

Given this mechanism, the market need never know the actual valuations of the traders. A trader has no incentives, if selling, to offer at less than valuation or, if buying, to bid more than the horse is worth. Related games in strategic form with continuous goods and formal proofs of the nature of the noncooperative equilibria are given elsewhere (Shubik, 1981a; Dubey, 1982; Dubey and Shubik, 1980b).

These equilibria are strong in that they are Pareto-optimal. Not only are simple traders unable to improve, but neither can any group in the market. The mechanism involved is a double-auction market. Schotter (1974) considers variations of auction mechanisms. If the horses are auctioned sequentially, as can be seen by a glance at figure 9.8, depending on our assumptions concerning individuals' knowledge of each others' preferences and the sequence in which the horses are auctioned, it is easy to construct models in which many of the trade prices fall outside the cooperative game core. These models are closely related to the models of trade by stock-market specialists in a double-auction market.

Notes to chapter 9

1. A technical explanation can be found in the large number of optimal assignments that are possible. Multiplicity in the primal solutions of a linear-programming problem is commonly accompanied by reduced dimensionality of the dual solutions.

2. The coefficients are given by $c!(n-1-c)!/n!$ (see *GTSS*, chapter 7, or Shapiro and Shapley, 1960).

10 Two-Sided Markets: The Edgeworth Game

" 'Is it peace or war?' asks the lover of 'Maud,' of economic competition, and answers hastily: It is both, pax *or* pact *between contractors during contract,* war, *when some of the contractors* without the consent of others recontract."

Francis Ysidro Edgeworth (1881), p. 17

10.1 Introduction

In this and the next three chapters we investigate the close relationships that link the traditional approach to the economics of exchange and production with certain results from the theory of multiperson games. In order to divide difficulties, we concentrate first on a simple "Edgeworth" model having just two types of players, each supplying a commodity that is consumed by both. A reasonably exhaustive treatment then becomes possible. These limitations are removed in the more general models of chapters 11–13.

In contrast with the two-sided markets of the preceding two chapters, the commodities are now assumed to be homogeneous and infinitely divisible. Our concern is no longer with questions of product differentiation, or optimal buyer-to-seller matching, but with the nature of individual preferences, with the effects of different numbers of participants, and with the role of monetary mechanisms in the marketplace.

We develop parallel models with and without transferable utility. The former correspond to markets with two goods in trade plus a freely transferable u-money that is in plentiful supply and is linearly related to the individual utilities. The other models—without transferable utility—may be interpreted either as pure barter situations with two consumable goods or, if we prefer, as markets in which one commodity is being exchanged for some *numéraire* or store of value which might be in short supply or exhibit income effects.

Because of the absence of production and the fixed number of traders, the supplies of any commodity are inelastic. In this sense we are dealing with "Austrian" models of exchange, of which the Böhm-Bawerk horse market discussed in chapter 9 is a simple example.

The feature upon which we continue to lay the most stress in our models is the interrelationship between several different concepts of solution, which embody various properties that might be deemed desirable in an economy. Let us review them again briefly, beginning with three "pre-solution" concepts that we frequently have occasion to use:

● The *Pareto set* comprises all outcomes that are socially optimal, in the sense that any other outcome would be worse for at least one individual.

● The *imputation space* consists of those Pareto-optimal outcomes that are individually rational, in that no individual gets less than he can obtain unilaterally.

● The *characteristic function* lists the Pareto sets for all subsets of the participants, as well as for the market as a whole.

● The *core* comprises those outcomes that are coalitionally stable, in the sense that any other outcome can be blocked by some subset of the participants.

● A *stable set* (von Neumann–Morgenstern solution) represents a more subtle social equilibrium, consisting of a set of "conventional" outcomes that dominate all other outcomes, but not each other.

● The *value* is a single outcome, representing an ethical norm or "fair division," which is obtained by averaging the characteristic function in a certain manner.

● A *competitive solution* is an equilibrium state in which each individual separately maximizes his own welfare, without negotiation, in the presence of known "competitive" prices. This is an essentially non-game-theoretic concept connected to concepts of administrative decentralization.

● A *noncooperative equilibrium*, in contrast, has each individual proceeding on the assumption of fixed strategic behavior by the other individuals. This is the usual viewpoint in classical oligopoly theory; depending on how the strategic "rules of the game" are written, it can lead to the solutions associated with the names of Cournot or Bertrand, or to the so-called Edgeworth cycle (see chapter 6 or Shubik, 1959b, chapter 5). As indicated in part II, modeling the strategic form requires specifications of details that are not relevant to the other solutions.

These solution concepts are, of course, not unrelated. As will be shown, all competitive outcomes are in the core. We already know that the core is part of every stable set. All stable sets, and the value as well, are contained in the imputation space, which is a subset of the Pareto set. But the value is not necessarily in the core, nor in any stable set. There can be a great many stable sets, each containing a great many outcomes. The competitive and noncooperative solutions may be unique, but this is not always true; the latter is frequently not Pareto-optimal.

One of our goals in this part is to show how, under appropriate circumstances in large markets, various of these solutions prescribe the same outcome. This will produce powerful arguments in support of certain forms of limiting behavior.

10.2 Consumer Preferences

At this point we touch briefly on some topics in the theory of individual choice in order to clarify our assumptions on consumer behavior and to lay a basis for later generalizations.

A *consumption set* consists of the possible bundles of goods that might comprise an individual's total holding at the end of the trading period, available to him for consumption or other disposition outside the compass of the model. Usually it is convenient to use the same consumption set for all individuals.

In the restricted, two-commodity models of this chapter, the common consumption set, sometimes called the *commodity space*, is identified either with the set of nonnegative pairs (x, y) (the closed positive quadrant) or, in the transferable-utility case, with the set of triples (x, y, ξ) with $x \geq 0$, $y \geq 0$. Here ξ represents "money" or "credit," which of course is not an ultimate item of consumption. Rather, it serves to decouple the particular market from outside sources of true consumables. The fact that arbitrarily large positive and negative values of ξ are permitted is nothing more than a technical convenience; in every case we could instead define a bounded commodity space that would be equivalent for all purposes of the model.

An individual is supposed to have a numerical utility function, defined and continuous on his consumption set. His utility is supposed to be independent of other people's consumptions or utilities. For certain solution concepts ordinal utility is sufficient, which will allow us to employ arbitrary continuous order-preserving transformations; for others a cardinal utility is necessary (see the Bargainers Paradox in *GTSS*, chapter 5), and only linear order-preserving transformations will be admitted. Quasiconcavity—convexity of the sets of bundles preferred or indifferent to any given bundle—will always be assumed. Not all quasiconcave functions are concave, or can even be made so by continuous order-preserving transformations, but we generally assume concave or concavifiable functions, even for the ordinal solutions, in order to avoid the conceptual burden of explaining how and why mixed strategies are forbidden to the traders.[1]

We assume utility functions to be monotonic in each variable—sometimes strictly monotonic. Since the latter implies no saturation in any commodity, it goes beyond the mere assumption of free disposal processes.

Differentiability of the utility functions will often be convenient, but it is not an entirely innocent assumption. For example, piecewise-linear (polyhedral) utility functions are equally natural in many contexts, yet they have qualitatively different uniqueness and convergence properties with respect to some solution concepts.

10.2.1 Price–consumption curves: The income effect

In figure 10.1 the point R is meant to represent an intial holding of, say, an egg producer in search of ham for breakfast; he holds plenty of the y good (eggs) but none of the x good (ham). The straight lines out of R are typical *price rays*, representing possible final holdings given the opportunity to spend eggs to buy ham at various prices. The points M_i are the utility-maximizing points on their respective rays. If we vary the exchange ratio, the locus of the points M_i is the *price–consumption curve* (Hicks, 1939, p. 30ff.). This is one way of representing consumer demand.

Normally we might expect the consumption of an item to increase as its price drops. This is shown by the left-to-right progression of the points M_1, M_2, M_3 in figure 10.1a, indicating an increasing consumption of ham as it becomes progressively cheaper relative to eggs. But in figure 10.1b the progression of the M_i is from right to left, showing that a fall in price can also lead to a decrease in consumption. This happens when one good is "inferior" to the other. The conditions for this are discussed below.

More generally, we may view y as a composite of all others commodities in a complete consumer economy. Then the ordinate of R represents the individual total purchasing power (Hicks, 1939, p. 33; Samuelson, 1948, p. 143). By partial-equilibrium analysis we can construct a demand schedule for the individual as the price of x changes, ceteris paribus. Assuming that the necessary derivatives exist, we obtain by straightforward calculus the following version of Slutsky's equation (Hicks, 1939, p. 309; Samuelson, 1948, p. 102):

$$\frac{\partial x}{\partial p} = -x\frac{\partial x}{\partial b} + \frac{u_y}{u_{xx} - 2pu_{xy} + p^2 u_{yy}}, \tag{10.1}$$

where p is the price ratio between the x good and the y good and $b = \overline{OR}$

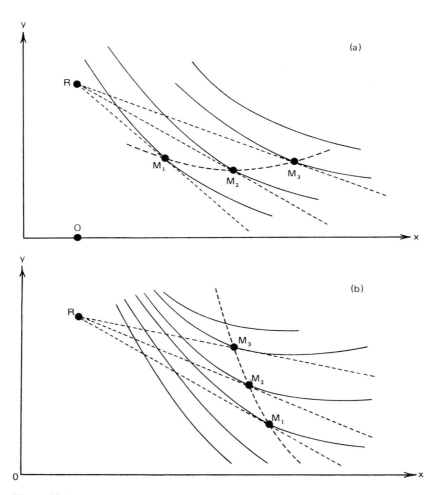

Figure 10.1
Price–consumption curves. (a) Increasing consumption with decreasing price.
(b) Decreasing consumption with decreasing price.

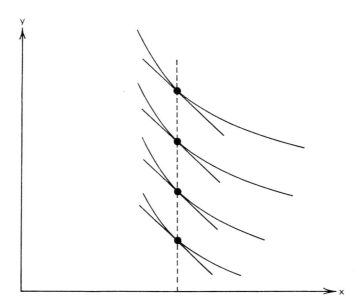

Figure 10.2
Illustrating the absence of an income effect.

is the purchasing power. The result of a change in price is the sum of an *income effect* (the term $-x\,\partial x/\partial b$) and a *substitution effect* (the last term, which, despite appearances, does not depend on the particular utility function u). The latter term is necessarily negative,[2] but the income effect can go either way, and if it is sufficiently positive, as in figure 10.1b, it can outweigh the substitution effect.

An important special case occurs when the income effect is absent, that is, when $\partial x/\partial b = 0$ in (10.1). Then the slope of the indifference curve through any point (x, y) is independent of y, and hence the indifference curves are "parallel." More precisely, they are all vertical translations of any one of them and can be represented in the form

$$y = f_\alpha(x) \equiv f_{\alpha_0}(x) + c(\alpha),$$

where α is an index used to label the curves, α_0 is any fixed index, and $c(\alpha)$ is the appropriate translation constant (figure 10.2).

This representation implies the existence of a utility function having a very special form, namely,

$$U(x, y) = u(x) + y. \tag{10.2}$$

To see this, define $u(x) = -f_{\alpha_0}(x)$. Then an arbitrary contour $U(x, y) = c$ has the equation

$$y = f_{\alpha_0}(x) + c.$$

In this way a "monetary" utility scale can be found, determined up to an additive constant, in which the y good serves as *numéraire*. The function $c(\alpha)$ maps the original, arbitrary labels α onto this scale.

If y is interpreted as money, then (10.2) asserts that the marginal utility for money is constant. Whether this is an acceptable approximation to reality will depend largely upon the range of variations in money holdings contemplated for the individuals in the model.

We remark that the foregoing holds, essentially without change, if x is a vector representing holdings of several goods. Thus, in this chapter, our two-commodity models with side payments could be based on three-commodity utility functions of the form

$$U(x, y, \xi) \equiv u(x, y) + \xi. \tag{10.3}$$

In fact, we shall make direct use only of the two-commodity function $u(x, y)$. The third commodity corresponds to the u-money discussed in chapter 1.

10.2.2 Interpersonal conditions

Whereas in a general theory an individual's utility is based on preferences among different states of the world, including future prospects, in this chapter we assume that nothing but an individual's own holdings are relevant to his evaluations of outcomes. In the two-commodity models we shall consider, the payoff to each trader will be equal to his utility for the quantities of the two goods he holds at the conclusion of trading, plus or minus the amount of his net side payment, if any. The holdings of the other players may affect his play but not his score.

In no-side-payment game theory individuals' utility scales are quite independent. The only occasion for interpersonal comparisons occurs in the "value" solution, but here one derives the utility exchange ratios from the facts of the game. No extrinsic comparability is assumed, and the exchange ratios obtained have no validity outside the model.

With side payments, or u-money, a comparison of utilities is indeed implied, but only by way of the money mechanism. Fundamentally the individual utilities are still independent. If $10 is taken from A and given to B, then A loses "$10 worth of A-satisfaction" and B gains "$10 worth of B-satisfaction." These phrases have meaning because of the independence property expressed by (10.3). The units of measurement could well be different for different individuals; it is only for the sake of convenience that we reduce all scales (by linear transformations) to "u-dollar" units.

It should be noted that (10.3) is not an interpersonal condition; it is assumed separately for each individual. Here, again, we see money in its role of decoupler.

Once more we stress that our present models make the strong (and often unrealistic) assumption of independence of individual welfare. There is no value attached to good will or to being happy (or envious) when other traders prosper. In the modeling of many strictly economic markets this is probably a reasonable assumption; in bargaining situations involving sociological and political considerations it may not be.

10.2.3 Symmetry between producers and consumers

Hicks (1939, pp. 36–37) examines conditions under which an individual comes to the market not only as a buyer but also as a seller. It is evident from the text that the asymmetry of treatment between buyers and sellers is essentially an asymmetry between consumption and production. In this chapter, since we do not deal with production, the distinction is not yet relevant. Our models may be thought of as consisting simply of "traders" on both sides of the market. Symmetric models of this kind might arise in a primitive barter economy, after the harvest has been gathered, or in situations where there is a short-term inflexibility of the production rate.

10.3 Bilateral Monopoly

We open our discussion with the case of a market in which there are just two traders, dealing in two infinitely divisible commodities. Since neither commodity can have any monetary connotations, we do not use the terms "buyer" and "seller," but refer to the traders simply as player 1 and player 2. Player 1 begins the game with the bundle $(a, 0)$, $a > 0$, that is, with a units of the first commodity and none of the second. Player 2 enters the market with the bundle $(0, b)$, $b > 0$.

The preference systems of the players are described by means of utility functions,

$$u^i(x, y) \quad (i = 1, 2).$$

For the moment these will be regarded merely as ordinal measures of utility. We assume that they are continuous and strictly increasing in both x and y, and that their level sets (contours),

$u^i(x, y) = $ constant,

are convex curves. We sometimes assume that the utility functions, and hence their contours, are continuously differentiable.

10.3.1 The Edgeworth box

By an *allocation* we mean a pair of commodity bundles, one to each player. The following diagrammatic system for representing allocations will be used throughout this chapter. Let the point $X = (x, y)$ denote the allocation in which the *second* trader gets the bundle (x, y). The totals being constant, player 1 necessarily gets $(a - x, b - y)$. Since all holdings are nonnegative, the possible allocations X describe a rectangle like the one shown in figure 10.3. The game opens at R. By exchanging goods, the players can move out toward the center of the "box." Generally speaking, player 1 would like to push the final position as far down and to the left as he can, away from O^1; player 2 would rather move it up and to the right, away from O^2.

In this representation, which in effect superimposes the two consumption sets, the utility functions will be denoted by Ψ^1 and Ψ^2, respectively, defined by

$$\Psi^1(X) = u^1(a - x, b - y), \qquad \Psi^2(X) = u^2(x, y).$$

The family of curves $\Psi^2 = $ constant appear as convex in the diagram; the family $\Psi^1 = $ constant appear as concave. The heavy curve RB^2 represents a limit below which player 2 will not go, since he would be better off not trading at all; similarly RB^1 for player 1. The region enclosed by these curves represents the set of individually rational final allocations. It is possible, of course, for this region to be empty or, rather, to consist of the single point R. In that case there would be no profitable trades, and the game would be inessential.

The points at which the two sets of indifference curves are tangent to one another represent maximal allocations, in the sense that from such a position no trade is possible that benefits both traders. In figure 10.3 these fall along the arc D^1D^2. Assuming differentiability, the equation of this curve can be written

$$\Psi^1_x/\Psi^1_y = \Psi^2_x/\Psi^2_y. \tag{10.4}$$

Other maximal points are usually found along the perimeter of the box, as at O^1D^1 and O^2D^2 in the figure. Together with the locus of common tangents, they constitute the *Pareto set* of the model. The portion C^1C^2 that lies between the two indifference curves through R—that is, the

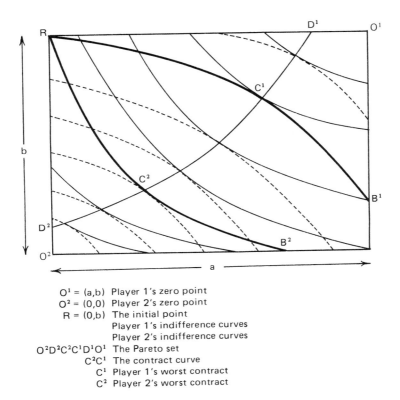

Figure 10.3
The Edgeworth box.

individually rational portion—we call, after Edgeworth, the *contract set*
or *contract curve*.

Although not shown in figure 10.3, the contract curve may well contain
boundary maxima as well as common-tangent maxima (figures 10.7 and
10.9 below provide examples). The contract set always exists in some
form or another, even without differentiability or convexity. (For an
unusual-looking contract set arising from nonconvex preferences see
chapter 12.) Even under our present assumptions of differentiability and
convexity, the "curve" may exhibit transverse appendages, or even spread
out to cover an area, but only if the indifference curves are not strictly
convex. One can prove, however, that the contract set is always closed
and simply connected.

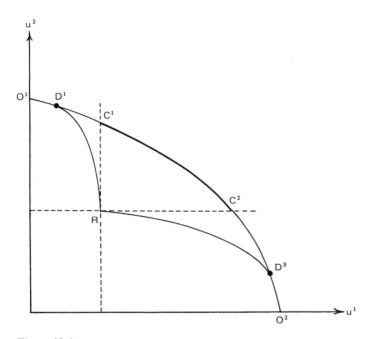

Figure 10.4
The contract curve in utility space.

10.3.2 Solutions without transferable utility

Edgeworth proposed the contract curve as the solution to the bilateral bargaining problem, writing that "It is in the interest of both parties that there should be *some settlement*, [namely] one of the contracts represented by the contract-curve between the limits [C^1 and C^2]. But *which* of these contracts is arbitrary" (Edgeworth, 1881, p. 29). His reasons (half a century before any systematic theory of games existed) were the same as those that underlie the core concept. This will become quite clear when his treatment of markets with more than two traders is considered in section 10.5.

The imputation space and the core   In order to analyze the bilateral monopoly model as a game, we must transfer our attention to the utility space. The functions Ψ^1 and Ψ^2 are used to map the Edgeworth box onto the set of feasible payoffs (figure 10.4). The image of the contract set under this mapping is exactly the set of imputations, and we have (since this is a two-person game):

THEOREM 10.1. *The core of a bilateral monopoly is the image, in the utility space, of the contract set.*

To interpret this result in the commodity space, we merely observe that all allocations off the Pareto set can be blocked by the two-person coalition, while all allocations outside the individually rational zone can be blocked by the one-person coalitions. The surviving, unblockable allocations are those in the contract set.[3]

The core in this case is also the unique stable set of the game. Thus, at the two-person level Edgeworth's solution matches two of our game-theoretic solution concepts. This relationship is quite trivial, but we mention it here in preparation for chapter 12, where the number of traders on each side of the market will be expanded and coalitions of intermediate size will enter the picture.

Prices and the competitive equilibrium If the two goods are always exchanged in a definite ratio, then the possible outcomes are points on a straight line emanating from R, with the fixed exchange ratio reflected in the slope of the line. One way of restricting the trading to such a line would be to announce an arbitrary price for each commodity, in terms of some hypothetical money-of-account, and to insist (i) that transfers of goods only take place at these prices, and (ii) that each player's accounts be in balance at the end of the trading period.

As a game, this constrained market is of little interest since there is no game-theoretic motivation for the price-fixing agency. Given prices, each player would typically fix on an outcome most to his liking, and the battleground would reduce to the interval between those two outcomes. For example, in figure 10.5a, if trading is restricted to the line RS, player 1 would most prefer the point M^1, and player 2 the point M^2. In the utility space (figure 10.5b), the line RS becomes a curve, which may or may not cross itself but which at least must be monotonic, as shown, between M^1 and M^2.

What is interesting and economically significant about this fixed-price model is that there is always at least one price ray RS for which the constrained game is inessential—for which M^1 and M^2 coincide. The resulting outcome, which we denote W (for "Walras"), necessarily lies on the contract curve. We call it a *competitive allocation*, and the prices that give rise to it *competitive prices*.[4] In the differentiable case the price ray is tangent to both sets of indifference curves at the competitive allocation, and the defining condition is

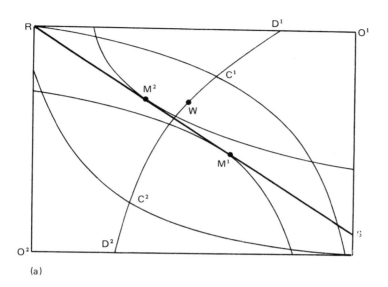

(a)

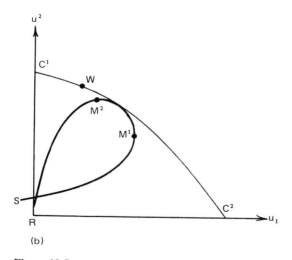

(b)

Figure 10.5
The fixed-price game.

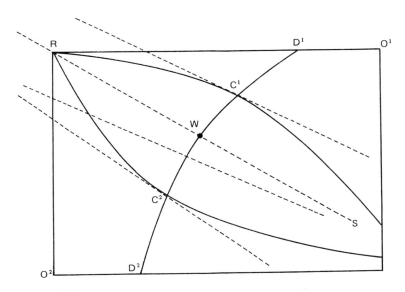

Figure 10.6
Existence of the competitive equilibrium.

$$\frac{\Psi_x^1}{\Psi_y^1} = \frac{y - b}{x} = \frac{\Psi_x^2}{\Psi_y^1}. \tag{10.5}$$

Note that (10.5) includes (10.4), the defining condition for the Pareto set.

A visual "proof" of the existence of a solution to (10.5) is illustrated in figure 10.6, in which the indifference-curve tangents are indicated for points along the contract curve. The tangent at C^1 surely passes *above* R, because the arc RC^1 is convex. Similarly the tangent at C^2 passes *below* R. With continuity, there must be at least one intermediate tangent, RWS, that passes exactly through R.

Actually, as is well known, the existence of competitive allocation depends only upon the convexity of the indifference curves, regardless of continuity or differentiability considerations.

Uniqueness The point W is unique in figure 10.6, as it happens. For other sorts of indifference curves, even without visible peculiarities, there may be many competitive allocations, each with a different set of equilibrium prices. All that we need do to obtain an example, in fact, is to make two of the tangents in a diagram such as figure 10.6 meet at some point *within* the Edgeworth box in such a way that the initial point lies within the angle made by the two tangents. A specific numerical example with three competitive allocations will be given in section 10.3.3.

Another kind of nonuniqueness can occur when there are flat spots on the indifference curves. The contract "curve" might then intersect at crucial price ray in an interval, rather than at a single point, and a whole set of competitive allocations might arise from a single equilibrium price ratio. These allocations would be essentially equivalent, however, in that they would all map onto the same imputation in the utility space.

The value In this section we consider the "fair division" of goods from the game-theoretic point of view. Since there are just two players, and since the only effective threat on either side is to refuse to trade, we have a *pure bargaining problem*, and the value of the game may be obtained by the product-maximization method of Zeuthen (1930), Nash (1950), and Harsanyi (1956). First, however, we must complete the specification of the model in one respect.

So far only ordinal preferences have been invoked. Game theory provides no way of evaluating a purely ordinal model. (See "The Bargainers" in *GTSS*, section 4.3.2.) We must therefore assume that our utility functions $u^i(x, y)$ not only *rank* the alternative bundles of goods for each traders but give valid comparisons of *utility differences* at different points on his scale. Thus each u^i must now be assumed to be determined up to a linear order-preserving transformation. Previously they were determined only up to continuous order-preserving transformations.

The need for more than ordinal utilities can be ascribed to the fact that the value solution at least implicitly involves a process of negotiation in which utility differences (intensities of preferences) as well as utility levels are significant.[5] It is sometimes asserted that cardinal utilities have no operational meaning in economics, but advocates of that view are generally wedded to a single solution concept, namely the competitive equilibrium (e.g., Samuelson, 1948, pp. 91, 173). They do not consider such game-theoretic processes as threats and bargaining that tend to relate intensities at different parts of the scale or between the scales of different persons; nor do they face the problem of widening the preference field to include probabilistic combinations of prospects. Either one of these extensions of the "operational" economic horizon is enough to drive us from ordinal to cardinal utilities.

To avoid the distraction of having to consider or justify the exclusion of mixed strategies in the game model, we now assume that the functions

$u^i(x, y)$ are concave as well as monotonic. This implies, but is not implied by, the previously assumed convexity of the indifference curves. It also implies that the set of feasible payoffs, even without resort to mixed strategies, has a "northeast" frontier that is concave to the origin.

The determination of the value is based on the *disagreement point R* with utility coordinates $\Psi^1(R) = u^1(a, 0)$, $\Psi^2(R) = u^2(0, b)$. Let $V = (x^*, y^*)$ be any allocation that maximizes the product

$$[\Psi^1(V) - \Psi^1(R)] \cdot [\Psi^2(V) - \Psi^2(R)].$$

Then the value of the game is given by

$$\phi_1 = \Psi^1(V) = u^1(a - x^*, b - y^*),$$
$$\phi_2 = \Psi^2(V) = u^2(x^*, y^*).$$

This fair-division allocation V necessarily lies on the contract curve. It is generally unique, the only exception occurring when the indifference curves on which it lies have flat spots and are tangent along an interval. Thus the value *imputation* ϕ is always unique.

Note that the geometric location of V cannot be read off from the Edgeworth box directly, since it depends on the utility functions themselves, not just on their contours. In fact, a nonlinear order- and concavity-preserving transformation of the utilities could be found that would move V to any other place on the contract curve, except possibly an endpoint. (Compare *GTSS*, section 4.3.2.)

In the differentiable case, ϕ is easily seen to be defined by the equations

$$\frac{\Psi^1_x}{\Psi^2_x} = \frac{\Psi^1(V) - \Psi^1(R)}{\Psi^2(V) - \Psi^2(R)} = \frac{\Psi^1_y}{\Psi^2_y}. \tag{10.6}$$

These of course include the equation for the contract curve. (Compare equations (10.1) and (10.2) above.)

The ratio in (10.6) represents the *intrinsic utility-comparison factor* of the game. This is the rate of exchange between the two players' utility units that would have to prevail in order for the transferable-utility value of the game to be achievable without actual transfers of utility.

10.3.3 Numerical examples
The following concrete example is used throughout the chapter. We have tried to keep the data as simple as possible, short of trivializing the problem, so that readers can check the calculations.

PASTRAMI ON RYE. *A butcher, at closing time, has four pounds of leftover cold cuts, which he proposes to share with his friend the baker, who has five loaves of unsold bread. Their preferences can be described by saying that they seek to maximize the functions*

$$u^1(x, y) = (10 + x)^2(2 + y) \quad (the\ butcher's),$$
$$u^2(x, y) = (2 + x)(3 + y) \qquad (the\ baker's),$$

(10.7)

respectively, where x refers to pounds of meat and y to loaves of bread.[6]

The Edgeworth box for this example is depicted in figure 10.7.

Analysis of the box diagram   We have at once

$$\Psi^1(x, y) = (14 - x)^2(5 - y),$$
$$\Psi^2(x, y) = (2 + x)(3 + y).$$

(10.8)

The locus of common tangents is a hyperbola,

$$xy - 17x + 18y + 14 = 0.$$

(10.9)

The contract curve, unlike those previously illustrated, includes a portion of the boundary of the box (D^1C^1 in figure 10.7).

The competitive solution is unique in this case. The equation of the equilibrium price ray, RW, turns out to be

$$16x + 17y = 85.$$

(10.10)

For example, meat at 16¢/lb and bread at 17¢/loaf would be "competitively" priced. To achieve the competitive allocation, W, the butcher must trade 3.25 pounds of meat for 3.06 loaves of bread. (See table 10.1.)

Figure 10.7 also shows the two *price–consumption curves* (see section 10.3.1) for this example, which we here call "response curves." If a fixed price is announced, then the respective optimal trades for the two players will lie on the indicated curves at the points where they intersect the price ray in question. (See also figure 10.5a.) The response curves intersect at the competitive allocation, which is unique in this case. If we assume that one player has the power to name the price, then under optimal play a "monopolistic" solution results, defined by the point of tangency of the price namer's utility curves with the other's response curve (R^1 or R^2 in the figure). This noncooperative solution, which is not Pareto-optimal, will be discussed and illustrated later in the chapter.

The value   The functions u^i in (10.7) are not concave as they stand, and the set of feasible payoffs that they generate is not convex on its "northeast" frontier (figure 10.8a). To avoid the need for mixed strategies, we assume that the true cardinal utilities are the concave functions $\hat{u}^1$, $\hat{u}^2$

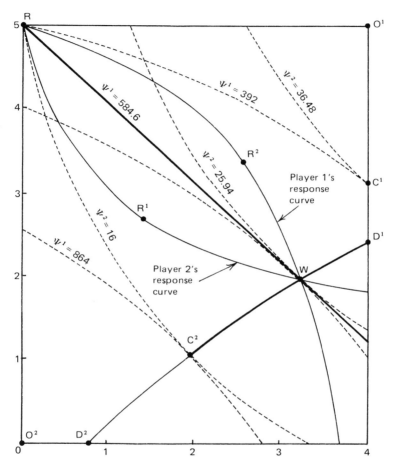

Figure 10.7
The Edgeworth box for Pastrami on Rye.

The Edgeworth Game

Table 10.1
Solution data for Pastrámi on Rye

Point	Coordinates (x, y)	Utilities				Description (from baker's standpoint)
		u^1	u^2	$\hat{u}^1$	$\hat{u}^2$	
R	(0.00, 5.00)	392.0	16.00	7.319	4.000	Initial point
O^1	(4.00, 5.00)	200.0	48.00	5.848	6.928	Absolute maximum
C^1	(4.00, 3.08)	392.0	36.48	7.319	6.040	Best "rational" contract
D^1	(4.00, 2.46)	454.60	25.94	7.689	5.720	Worst contract (buying all butcher's goods)
W	(3.25, 1.94)	584.60	25.94	8.362	5.093	Competitive solution
V	(3.18, 1.89)	507.8	25.35	8.424	5.035	Value solution
C^2	(2.00, 1.00)	864.0	16.00	9.524	4.000	Worst "rational" contract
D^2	(0.82, 0.00)	1,215.4	8.47	10.671	2.910	Best contract (selling all his goods)
U	(0.60, 0.00)	1,256.6	7.80	10.791	2.794	Joint maximum ("utilitarian point")
O^2	(0.00, 0.00)	1,372.0	6.00	11.112	2.449	Absolute minimum
R^1	(1.41, 2.66)	687.9	19.30	8.828	4.393	Optimum as price taker
R^2	(2.56, 3.38)	473.7	29.09	7.795	5.393	Optimum as price namer

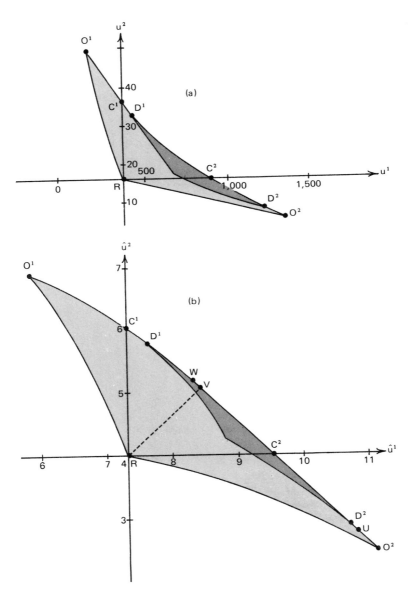

Figure 10.8
Utility spaces for Pastrami on Rye. (a) The (u^1, u^2) space. (b) The $(\hat{u}^1, \hat{u}^2)$ space.

defined by:

$$\hat{u}^1 = \sqrt[3]{u^1}, \qquad \hat{u}^2 = \sqrt{u^2}. \tag{10.11}$$

These order-preserving transformations do not affect the previous calculations. Their effect on the payoff space can be seen in figure 10.8b:
The Pareto set $O^1 C^1 C^2 O^2$ now curves in the right direction.

The value of the game occurs geometrically at the point V in figure 10.8b,
at which the tangent to the Pareto set has the same absolute slope as the
line RV. The numerical values are included in table 10.1. We see that the
value solution is slightly less favorable to the baker than the competitive
solution W. As pointed out earlier, however, a different transformation
(10.11) could change this.

The intrinsic utility-comparison ratio (the slope of the line RV) proves
to be 1.08 "butcher-utils" per "baker-util."

An example with three competitive solutions

THE TOURISTS. *Ivan has 40 rubles in his pocket and wants some dollars.
John has $50 to spare and would be happy to exchange some for rubles.
Their utility functions (x = rubles, y = dollars) are*

$$u^1(x, y) = x + 100(1 - e^{-y/10}) \quad (Ivan, in rubles),$$
$$u^2(x, y) = y + 110(1 - e^{-x/10}) \quad (John, in dollars). \tag{10.12}$$

The utility functions are easily seen to be concave. The locus $D^1 D^2$
of common tangents is the straight line

$$y = x + 50 - 10 \log 110 = x + 2.995.$$

The contract curve runs along this line and a short piece $C^1 D^1$ of the
boundary of the box, as shown in figure 10.9.

The conditions for a competitive allocation reduce to a transcendental
equation:

$$x(1 + 11e^{-x/10}) = 10 \log 110,$$

which has *three* roots in the region of interest. These lead to the three
competitive solutions W, W', W'' shown in figure 10.9 and in table 10.2.
Their relation to the two response curves is also shown in figure 10.9.

If we take a contract point between W and W', the line of common
tangency passes above R; if we take one between W' and W'', it passes
below R. (Compare figure 10.6.) This means that the equilibrium prices
associated with W' are dynamically unstable, in the sense that raising
the price of either good would create a positive excess demand for that

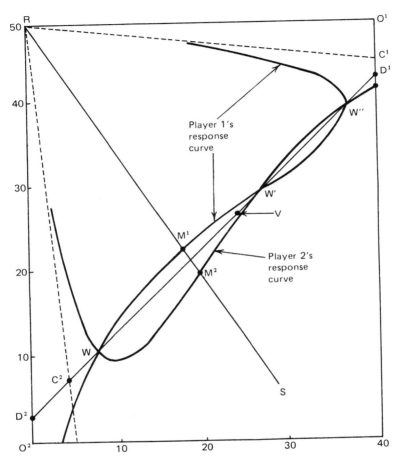

Figure 10.9
Three competitive equilibria.

The Edgeworth Game

275

Table 10.2
Numerical data for The Tourists

	Allocation (to John)	Exchange ratio (R: $)	Payoffs		
			Ivan (R)	John ($)	
R	0.00R + $50.00	—	40.00	50.00	Initial point
C^1	40.00R + $44.89	—	40.00	154.89 }	Endpoints of
C^2	4.83R + $ 7.83	—	133.69	50.00 }	core
W	7.74R + $10.74	5.07:1	130.29	70.01 }	Competitive
W'	26.83R + $29.82	0.75:1	99.87	132.30 }	solutions
W''	36.78R + $39.77	0.28:1	67.26	146.99 }	
V	23.00R + $25.99	—	107.94	124.96	Value solution

good (see, e.g., Samuelson, 1948, p. 260ff.; Scarf, 1960; Negishi, 1962). This in turn (in a suitable dynamic model) would tend to drive that price up still further. The other two solutions, W and W'', are dynamically stable in this sense (Shapley and Shubik, 1977b; see also Gale, 1963).

The value The functions (10.9) being concave as they stand, the value of this game can be computed without further assumptions. The reader can verify that conditions (10.3) reduce to the equation

$$11(110 - x)e^{-x/10} - x = 120 - 10 \log 110,$$

whose unique root gives us the point V, situated between W and W'. The implicit utility-comparison ratio is 0.906 "Ivan" util to 1 "John" util. This is not the same as the commodity-exchange ratio at the point V (0.956 ruble to the dollar).

10.4 Bilateral Monopoly with Money

The introduction of unrestricted side payments into our model is very much like the introduction of a third commodity that traders can use for measuring, storing, and transferring value. There are two important points to bear in mind, however. First, this u-money is not subject to the usual nonnegativity conditions. Second, it enters into the utility functions in a very special way.

As to the first point—the absence of a lower bound—when we apply an Edgeworth-type model to a real exchange situation in which money of some kind plays a part, we may discover that the assumption of unrestricted side payments is more realistic than the money-is-just-another-commodity point of view. Both assumptions are of course over-simplified idealizations, but it should be observed that in a real market-place there is generally no sharp lower limit to an individual's liquid assets. Rather, as one goes further into debt, there may be a gradual increase either in the direct cost of borrowing or in the strategic dis-advantage of having to obtain credit. In other words, the special linear relationship between money and utility—if it exists at all—will break down long before any "floor" is reached.

Nevertheless, it will sometimes be useful to exploit the technical near-equivalence between the side-payment game and the corresponding no-side-payment game in which each trader has plenty of the added com-modity. The connection between the two models is given by the identity

$$U^i(x, y, \xi) \equiv u^i(x, y) + \xi \quad (i = 1, 2), \tag{10.13}$$

which we have already discussed in section 10.2.2 and in chapters 1 and 2. Technically speaking, however, transferable utility ordinarily makes things easier; and when there is a choice between equivalent models, we generally prefer to work with the one with side payments.

10.4.1 The generalized box diagram
The geometrical convenience of the Edgeworth diagram suffers somewhat in the transition to side payments, but it is not entirely lost. Had we merely added a third commodity, the box would become three-dimensional—a rectangular parallelepiped. There would be two families of indifference surfaces, presenting their convex sides to diametrically opposite corners. With strict convexity, each surface of one family would be tangent at one point to a surface of the other family, and the points of tangency would in general describe a curve traversing the box. The contract set would include at least part of that curve, together with, perhaps, a one-dimensional extension along the sides or edges of the box. Instead of price rays, we would have to consider "price planes" passing through the initial point. All this is in direct analogy to the two-commodity case already described.

With u-money for the third commodity, most of the foregoing de-scription still applies, but two faces of the parallelepiped must be removed, making the "box" an infinite rectangular cylinder (figure 10.10). We hasten to point out the individually rational zone is nevertheless finite in extent, since neither trader can rationally pay out in money more than his maximum utility gain for goods, namely $u^i(a, b) - \Psi^i(R)$. This

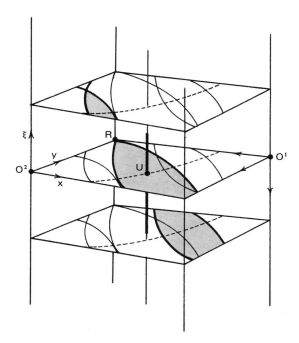

Figure 10.10
The Edgeworth box with side payments.

zone is convex and roughly lenticular in shape; its cross sections are the shaded areas in figure 10.10.

One effect of (10.13) is to make the utility contour maps on all the cross sections "carbon copies" of each other, though the utility *values* are displaced across these maps as we change levels. Another effect is to cause the Pareto set to be a straight line parallel to the ξ-axis (or a convex bundle of such lines). For it is clear that any allocation of goods and money that maximizes the sum $U^1 + U^2$ will also maximize $u^1 + u^2$, and the latter is independent of ξ. This allocation (unique in the case of strict convexity) was called "utilitarian" by Edgeworth; it will be designated U in our diagrams.

The Pareto set has nothing to do with individual rationality and extends indefinitely from U in both directions. The contract set, indicated by the heavy vertical line in figure 10.10, is the bounded portion of the Pareto set that lies within the individually rational zone. Note that the contract set need not contain U itself, although it does here. In other words, the jointly optimal distribution of goods may require a side payment before it becomes acceptable to both of the traders as individuals.

10.4.2 The game-theoretic solutions

We still have a two-person game, and so the contract curve, the imputation space, the core, and the unique stable set all coincide. A numerical characteristic function now exists:[7]

$$v(\overline{1}) = \Psi^1(R), \qquad v(\overline{2}) = \Psi^2(R), \qquad v(\overline{12}) = \Psi^1(U) + \Psi^2(U). \quad (10.14)$$

Figure 10.11 shows two typical configurations in the utility space. In part a, U is an imputation; in b, it is not.

The value of the game is simply the midpoint of the core:

$$\phi_i = \Psi^i(R) + \tfrac{1}{2}[\Psi^1(U) - \Psi^1(R) + \Psi^2(U) - \Psi^2(R)] \quad (i = 1, 2).$$

Achievement of this payoff requires a net u-money transfer from 1 to 2 of

$$\tfrac{1}{2}[\Psi^1(U) - \Psi^1(R) - \Psi^2(U) + \Psi^2(R)].$$

If this number is positive—that is, if player 1 pays—then his utility unit must have been intrinsically the *less* valuable in the no-side-payment game. The player with the more valuable unit always gains the most when side payments are introduced. The other player—the one with a trading deficit—may even find his value decreased, despite the overall improvement in the game. Indeed, if the no-side-payment imputation space includes U, his value is necessarily decreased when side payments are added.

Pastrami on Rye is qualitatively like figure 10.11b. But a glance at figure 10.8 shows that the no-side-payment game already has an imputation space that is almost straight and almost at a 45° angle with the coordinate axes. Hence, adding side payments should not make much difference to the game or to its solutions. This is borne out by a comparison of tables 10.1 and 10.3.

10.4.3 The competitive equilibrium

We can define the competitive equilibrium for markets with transferable utility by treating u-money as just another commodity and then using (10.13) to establish a fixed relationship between u-money and the competitive money-of-account. The net effect, however, can be described without reference to an enlarged market or to a money-of-account. We simply remove the individual budget constraints and replace them with linear rewards (penalties) for trading surpluses (deficits). Thus, given

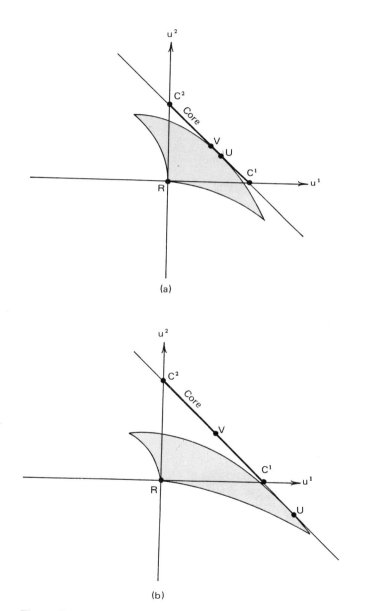

Figure 10.11
The utility space for the side-payment game.

Table 10.3
Solution data for the side-payment game[a]

	Allocation (player 2)	Payment ($) (1 → 2)	Final payoff ($) 1	2	
R	0.000, 5.000	—	7.319	4.000	Initial point
U	0.601, 0.000	—	10.791	2.794	Joint maximum
C¹	0.601, 0.000	3.472	7.319 (0)	6.266 (+0.226)	Endpoints of core
C²	0.601, 0.000	1.206	9.585 (+0.061)	4.000 (0)	
V	0.601, 0.000	2.339	8.452 (+0.028)	5.133 (+0.098)	Value solution
W	0.601, 0.000	2.246	8.545 (+0.183)	5.040 (−0.053)	Competitive solution (prices: $0.537, $0.514)

a. Numbers in parentheses show the change from the no-side-payment case (table 10.1).

prices π_1, π_2 for the two goods, player 2 seeks to maximize

$$u^2(x,y) + \pi_2(b-y) - \pi_1 x, \tag{10.15}$$

subject only to the conditions $x \geq 0$, $y \geq 0$. Player 1, similarly, seeks to maximize

$$u^1(x,y) + \pi_1(a-x) - \pi_2 y, \tag{10.16}$$

subject to the same constraints. At equilibrium prices the two maximizing bundles must add up to (a,b), clearing the market.

Note that the separate prices and not just their ratio have meaning. In effect, we are pegging the price of u-money at 1.

A competitive solution in the side-payment theory is described by a set of prices, an allocation of goods, and a side payment. Existence presents no problem. In fact, indirect topological arguments are no longer needed; the solution or solutions can be obtained constructively, as follows: First, we argue that the competitive *allocation* must be a utilitarian point, U, since otherwise the competitive payoff would not be Pareto-optimal. That is, the allocation X must maximize $\Psi^1(X) + \Psi^2(X)$. Second, the equilibrium *prices* must then be such that (10.15) and (10.16) are maximized at U. Finally, the *side payment* for each player must be equal to what it costs, at those prices, for him to buy and sell his way from the initial allocation, R, to U.

Geometrically (see again figure 10.10), we may imagine a "price plane" passing through U, tangent to both indifference surfaces at that point. The normal to that plane will be proportional to the vector $(\pi_1, \pi_2, 1)$. The point at which the plane meets the ξ-vertical through R will represent (by its height above R) player 2's net trading deficit—the amount of u-money he must transfer to player 1.

In the differentiable case we have

$$\Psi_x^2 = \pi_1 = -\Psi_x^1,$$
$$\Psi_y^2 = \pi_2 = -\Psi_y^1, \qquad \qquad (10.17)$$
$$r^2 = \pi_2(b - y) - \pi_1 x = -r^1,$$

where r^i denotes the net u-money payment to player i. This set of equations should be compared with the no-side-payment equations (10.5).[8]

Compared to the no-side-payment case, the present competitive equilibrium is much more nearly a single-valued solution concept. However, nonuniqueness can still creep in, as shown in figure 10.12. The following propositions should be fairly evident from the geometry of the figures.

THEOREM 10.2. *The competitive allocations U form a nonempty convex set. If at least one of u^1 and u^2 is strictly concave, then the competitive allocation is unique.*

THEOREM 10.3. *If at least one of u^1 and u^2 has differentiable contours at some competitive allocation, then the associated competitive price vector is unique.*

THEOREM 10.4. *If, at every competitive allocation, at least one of u^1 and u^2 has differentiable contours, then both the competitive price vector and the final payoff are unique.*

Note that if a contour of $u^i(x, y)$ runs into a boundary—such as the line $x = 0$—at a nonzero angle, then the contour is not considered differentiable at that point. Thus nonuniqueness of the competitive solution is possible even if both u^1 and u^2 are strictly concave, differentiable functions. But this only occurs when the joint maximum U occurs at a corner of the box, as illustrated in figure 10.13.

In Pastrami on Rye (table 10.3) U falls on the baker's boundary, but the differentiability of the butcher's utility function at that point is enough to preserve uniqueness. The situation is qualitatively like figure 10.13b.

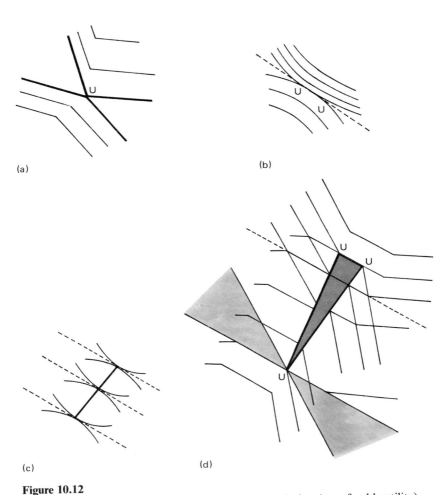

Figure 10.12
Possibilities for nonuniqueness of the competitive solution (transferable utility).
(a) Allocation unique, contours not differentiable, prices and final utility not
unique. (b) Allocation not unique, prices unique, utility transfer not unique, final
utility unique (contours not strictly convex). (c) Allocation not unique, contours
differentiable, prices unique, utility transfer not unique, final utility unique
(utility functions not strictly concave). (d) Allocation not unique, contours not
differentiable and not strictly convex, prices unique (and the same) for all
allocations but one, utility transfers and final utility not unique.

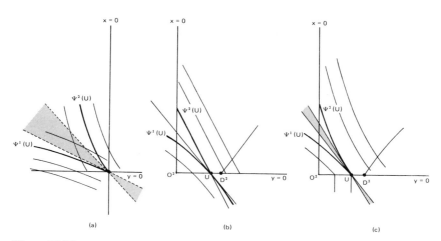

Figure 10.13
Boundary solutions.

Had we modified the butcher's preferences to give him no increase in utility for holding more than five loaves of bread, the situation would resemble figure 10.13c instead. The price for bread could then fluctuate from the $0.514 given in table 10.3 down to $0.466 without destroying the equilibrium. The price of a pound of meat, however, would remain fixed at $0.537. The net payment from butcher to baker could therefore be as low as $2.005, leading to a final imputation of ($8.786, $4.799).

The point is that bread can be made cheaper, to the benefit of the butcher, if he has no incentive to buy more than five loaves. Paradoxically, the butcher may be able to change the competitive solution in his favor merely by diminishing his desire for goods that he can never obtain anyway, since they are not available in the market. This example shows how what happens outside the "box" can affect the competitive solution.

10.4.4 Summary and critique of solutions

Bilateral monopoly, for all its economic structure, is basically just a two-person pure bargaining game. As such, game theory teaches us to expect an indeterminate outcome in the absence of sociological preconditions.

The purely economic model supplies no such preconditions, and only two of our solutions point to anything more definite than the whole space of imputations: the competitive equilibrium (possibly nonunique) and the value. Either solution could serve as an agreement point for the two parties—a "formula" or "working arrangement" for reconciling their divergent interests. But without such an understanding between the parties (which would be an example of a sociological precondition), neither solution has any real normative force. As a predictor, a case could be made for the value, using the Zeuthen–Harsanyi bargaining model (see *GTSS*, chapter 7). But the price-oriented competitive solution seems almost irrelevant to the problem in such a "thin" market.

In fairness we should remark that the competitive equilibrium has never been seriously intended as a "solution" to monopolistic or monopsonistic markets. As we shall discover, it grows in importance with the size of the market.

Thus our multisolutional analysis of bilateral monopoly with and without money has garnered several solutions that merely reflect the indeterminacy of open two-sided bargaining, as well as two solutions that are sharper but of uncertain applicability.[9] The effort that we have expended to this point is justified not by these meager results but by the foundation they provide for the analysis of larger markets.

Notes to chapter 10

1. An example of a nonconcavifiable quasiconcave function is one that exhibits a fanlike array of straight, nonparallel contours in the neighborhood of a point; no concave function has this property (see section 2.3.3).

Most classical formulations tacitly exclude probabilistic exchanges (even of the "I'll match you for the odd coconut" variety) between traders. But to say that this exclusion of self-generated risk is a rational consequence of individual preferences, not a fiat of the model, leads almost inevitably to concave utilities—indeed, to concave cardinal utilities (see Shubik, 1975c).

2. If the denominator vanishes, as at a flat spot on the indifference curve, then there may be a discontinuity in x as a function of p, but not necessarily. This can easily be shown graphically.

3. Properly speaking the core is a set of payoff vectors, not a set of allocations. Some writers (Debreu and Scarf, 1963; Aumann, 1964) have not observed this distinction, finding it convenient to use the word "core" for the set of unblockable allocations, that is, the contract curve itself or its multitrader analogues. This usage is harmless enough in models without transferable utility and without production, but it leads to confusion when either of these elements is added.

4. Ironically the term "competitive" has been attached by tradition to the solution concept that has the least to do with game theory. The "competitors" compete only indirectly, by optimizing independently within the price structure, without interaction or intercommunication of any kind.

5. This is made explicit in "Zeuthen's Principle," which can serve as a basis for the value solution. See Harsanyi (1956, 1965).

6. Homogeneous functions such as $u^i = x^m y^n$ would be even easier to work with but would obscure a number of details, since the three allocations C^i, D^i, and O^i would then coincide.

7. Normalization of the game to $\Psi^1(R) = \Psi^2(R) = 0$ would shorten this and the following expressions.

8. To obtain (10.5) from (10.17) we must impose the constraint $r^1 = r^2 = 0$ (eliminating side payments), while at the same time introducing undetermined proportionality factors in the first two equations (eliminating extrinsic comparability of utility).

9. It has been suggested that the price system could serve as a decentralizing device in a socialist or otherwise jointly owned economic system. Thus, for example, a firm might wish to employ a "shadow pricing" system for internal management.

11 Market Games

11.1 Introduction

In the last three chapters we have examined the properties of some two-sided game models of economic exchange. We have noted that the concept of a competitive equilibrium is intimately related to the formation of prices by the interaction of many individuals trading in a market. In chapter 12 we focus our attention on the many-person problem. Here we shall consider in depth the relationship between exchange economies in general and their representations as games in coalitional or cooperative form; this chapter is therefore somewhat more technical than the others.[1]

We are led to a surprisingly simple mathematical criterion that identifies precisely which games can arise from economic models of exchange (with money). In fact, this criterion identifies a very fundamental class of games, called "totally balanced," whose further study seems merited quite apart from any consideration of solution abnormalities. Our derivation of the basic properties of these games and their solutions makes a substantial application of the recently developed theory of *balanced sets* (Bondareva, 1963; Shapley, 1967; Charnes and Kortanek, 1967; Scarf, 1967) as well as of the older work of Gillies (1953, 1959) on *domination-equivalence*.

In this section we confine our attention to the classical theory with side payments; this corresponds in the economic interpretation to the assumption that an ideal money, free from income effects or transfer costs, is available. We further restrict ourselves to exchange economies without explicit production or consumption processes, in which the commodities are finite in number and perfectly divisible and transferable and the traders, also finite in number, are motivated only by their own final holdings of goods and money, their utility functions being continuous, concave, and additive in the money term. For some purposes these structures do not matter. But for our larger purpose—that of initiating a systematic study of market games as distinct from games in general—some relaxation may be desirable, particularly with regard to money.

11.2 Games and Cores

For this chapter we define a *game* to be an ordered pair $(N; v)$, where N is a finite set (the players) and v is a function from the subsets (coalitions) of N to the set of real numbers satisfying $v(0) = 0$; v is called the *characteristic function*. A *payoff vector* for $(N; v)$ is a point α in the $|N|$-dimensional vector space E^N whose coordinates α^i are indexed by the elements of N. If $\alpha \in E^N$ and $S \subseteq N$, we write $\alpha(S)$ as an abbreviation for $\sum_{i \in S} \alpha^i$.

The *core* of $(N; v)$ is the set of all payoff vectors α, if any, such that

$$\alpha(S) \geq v(S) \quad \text{for all } S \subseteq N \tag{11.1}$$

and

$$\alpha(N) = v(N). \tag{11.2}$$

If no such α exists, we say that $(N; v)$ *has no core*. (In this usage the core may be nonexistent, but it is never empty.)

11.2.1 Balanced sets of coalitions

A *balanced set* $\mathcal{B}$ is a collection of subsets S of N with the property that there exist positive numbers γ_S, $S \in \mathcal{B}$, called *weights*, such that for each $i \in N$,

$$\sum_{\substack{S \in \mathcal{B} \\ S \ni i}} \gamma_S = 1. \tag{11.3}$$

If all $\gamma_S = 1$, we have a partition of N; thus balanced sets may be regarded as generalized partitions. For example, if $N = \overline{1234}$, then $\{\overline{12}, \overline{13}, \overline{14}, \overline{234}\}$ is a balanced set, by virtue of the weights $1/3$, $1/3$, $1/3$, $2/3$.

A game $(N; v)$ is called *balanced* if

$$\sum_{S \in \mathcal{B}} \gamma_S v(S) \leq v(N) \tag{11.4}$$

holds for every balanced set $\mathcal{B}$ of weights $\{\gamma_S\}$.[2]

THEOREM 11.1. *A game has a core if and only if it is balanced.*

This is proved elsewhere. In Scarf's (1967) generalization to games without transferable utility, all balanced games have cores but some games with cores are not balanced. If our present results can be generalized in this direction, we conjecture that it will be the balance property, rather than the core property, that plays the central role.

11.2.2 Totally balanced games

A *subgame* of $(N;v)$ is a game $(R;v)$ with $0 \subset R \subset N$. Here v is the same function, but implicitly restricted to the domain consisting of the subsets of R. A game will be said to be *totally balanced* if all of its subgames are balanced. In other words, all subgames of a totally balanced game have cores.

Not all balanced games are totally balanced. For example, let $N = \overline{1234}$, and define $v(S) = 0, 0, 1, 2$ for $|S| = 0, 1, 3, 4$, respectively, and for $|S| = 2$,

$$v(\overline{12}) = v(\overline{13}) = v(\overline{23}) = 1,$$
$$v(\overline{14}) = v(\overline{24}) = v(\overline{34}) = 0.$$

This game has a core, including the vector $(1/2, 1/2, 1/2, 1/2)$ among others. But it is not totally balanced, since the subgame $(\overline{123};v)$ has no core.

11.3 Markets and Market Games

A *market* is a special mathematical model, denoted (T, G, A, U). Here T is a finite set (the traders); G is the nonnegative orthant of a finite-dimensional vector space (the commodity space); $A = \{a^i : i \in T\}$ is an indexed collection of points in G (the initial endowments); and $U = \{u^i : i \in T\}$ is an indexed collection of continuous, concave functions from G to the reals (the utility functions). When we wish to indicate that $u^i = u$ for all $i \in T$ (the special case of "equal tastes"), we shall sometimes denote the market by the more specific symbol $(T, G, A, \{u\})$.

If S is any subset of T, an indexed collection $X^S = \{x^i : i \in S\} \subset G$ such that $\sum_S x^i = \sum_S a^i$ will be called a *feasible S-allocation* of the market (T, G, A, U).

A market (T, G, A, U) can be used to generate a game $(N;v)$ in a natural way. We set $N = T$ and define v by

$$v(S) = \max_{x^S} \sum_{i \in S} u^i(x^i) \quad \text{for all } S \subseteq N, \tag{11.5}$$

where the maximum runs over all feasible S-allocations. Any game that can be generated in this way from some market is called a *market game*.[3]

In the equal-tastes case, $u^i = u$, we have

$$v(S) = |S| u \left(\sum_S a^i / |S| \right) \quad \text{for all } S \subseteq N; \tag{11.6}$$

this is a simple consequence of concavity. In the still more special case where u is homogeneous of degree 1, we have simply

$$v(S) = u\left(\sum_S a^i\right) \quad \text{for all } S \subseteq N. \tag{11.7}$$

11.3.1 Some elementary properties

The following two theorems are of a routine nature; they show that the property of being a market game is invariant under "strategic equivalence," and that the set of all market games on N forms a convex cone in the $(2^{|N|} - 1)$-dimensional space of all games on N.

THEOREM 11.2.   *If $(N;v)$ is a market game, if $\lambda \geq 0$, and if c is an additive set function on N, then $(N; \lambda v + c)$ is a market game.*

Proof. We merely take any market that generates $(N;v)$ and replace each utility function $u^i(x)$ by $\lambda u^i(x) + c(\{i\})$. ∎

THEOREM 11.3.   *If $(N;v')$ and $(N;v'')$ are market games, then $(N, v' + v'')$ is a market game.*

Proof. Let (N, G', A', U') and (N, G'', A'', U'') be markets that generate $(N;v')$ and $(N;v'')$, respectively. We shall superimpose these markets, keeping the two sets of commodities distinct. Specifically, let G be the set of all ordered pairs (x', x'') of points from G' and G'', respectively; let A be the set of pairs (a'^i, a''^i) of correspondingly indexed elements of A' and A''; and let U be the set of sums

$$u^i(x', x'') = u'^i(x') + u''^i(x'')$$

of correspondingly indexed elements of U' and U''. One can then verify without difficulty that the elements of U are continuous and concave on the domain G (which is a nonnegative orthant in its own right), so that (N, G, A, U) is a market. Finally, one can verify without difficulty that (N, G, A, U) generates the game $(N; v' + v'')$. ∎

11.3.2 The core theorem

THEOREM 11.4.   *Every market game has a core.*

This theorem is well-known and has been generalized well beyond the limited class of markets we are now considering. Nevertheless we shall give two proofs, both short, for the sake of the insights they provide. In the first we determine a competitive equilibrium for the generating market (a simple matter when there is transferable utility) and then show that the competitive payoff vector lies in the core. In the second we show directly that the game is balanced and then apply theorem 11.1.

Proof 1. Let $(N;v)$ be a market game, and let (N, G, A, U) be a market that generates it. Let $B = \{b^i : i \in N\}$ be a feasible N-allocation that achieves the value $v(N)$ in (11.5) for $S = N$. The maximization in (11.5) ensures the existence of a vector p (competitive prices—but possibly negative!) such that for each $i \in N$ the expression

$$u^i(x^i) - p \cdot (x^i - a^i) \quad \text{for } x^i \in G \tag{11.8}$$

is maximized at $x^i = b^i$. Define the payoff vector β by $\beta^i = u^i(b^i) - p \cdot (b^i - a^i)$; we assert that β is in the core. Indeed, let S be any nonempty subset of N, and let Y^S be a feasible S-allocation that achieves the maximum in (11.5), so that $v(S) = \sum_S u^i(y^i)$. Since b^i maximizes (11.8), we have

$$\beta^i \geq u^i(y^i) - p \cdot (y^i - a^i).$$

Summing over $i \in S$, we obtain

$$\beta(S) \geq \sum_S u^i(y^i) - p \cdot 0 = v(S),$$

as required by (11.1). Moreover, if $S = N$, we may take $Y^S = B$ and obtain $\beta(N) = v(N)$, as required by (11.2). ∎

Proof 2. Let (N, G, A, U) be a generating market for $(N;v)$; and for each $S \subseteq N$ let $Y^S = \{y_S^i : i \in S\}$ be a maximizing S-allocation in (11.5). Let $\mathscr{B}$ be balanced, with weights $\{\gamma_S : S \in \mathscr{B}\}$. Then

$$\sum_{S \in \mathscr{B}} \gamma_S v(S) = \sum_{S \in \mathscr{B}} \sum_{i \in S} \gamma_S u^i(y_S^i) = \sum_{i \in N} \sum_{\substack{S \in \mathscr{B} \\ S \ni i}} \gamma_S u^i(y_S^i).$$

Now define

$$z^i = \sum_{\substack{S \in \mathscr{B} \\ S \ni i}} \gamma_S y_S^i \in G, \quad \text{for all } i \in N.$$

Note that z^i is a center of gravity of the points y_S^i, by virtue of (11.3). Hence, by concavity,

$$\sum_{S \in \mathscr{B}} \gamma_S v(S) \leq \sum_{i \in N} u^i(z^i). \tag{11.9}$$

But $Z = \{z^i : i \in N\}$ is a feasible N-allocation, since

$$\sum_{i \in N} z^i = \sum_{S \in \mathscr{B}} \sum_{i \in S} \gamma_S y_S^i = \sum_{S \in \mathscr{B}} \gamma_S \sum_{i \in S} a^i = \sum_{i \in N} a^i.$$

Hence the right side of (11.9) is less than or equal to $v(N)$, and we conclude from (11.4) that the game is balanced and from theorem 11.1 that it has a core. ∎

Corollary. *Every market game is totally balanced.*

Proof. If $(N; v)$ is generated by the market (N, G, A, U) and if $O \subset R \subseteq N$, then we may define a market (R, G, A', U'), where A' and U' are derived from A and U by simply omitting all a^i and u^i for i not in R. This market clearly generates the game $(R; v)$. Hence $(R; v)$ is balanced. ∎

Our next objective is to prove the converse of this corollary, namely that every totally balanced game is a market game.

11.4 Direct Markets

A special class of markets, called *direct markets*, will play an important role in the sequel. These have the form $(T, E_+^T, I^T, \{u\})$, where u is homogeneous of degree 1 as well as concave and continuous. Here E_+^T denotes the nonnegative orthant of the vector space E^T with coordinates indexed by the members of T, and I^T denotes the collection of unit vectors of E^T (in effect, the identity matrix on T).

Thus, in a direct market each trader starts with one unit of a personal commodity (time, labor, participation, "self"). When this is brought together with other personal commodities, we can imagine that some desirable state of affairs is created, having a total value to the traders that is independent (because of homogeneity and equal tastes) of how they distribute the benefits.

Let e^S denote the vector in E^N in which $e_i^S = 1$ or 0 according as $i \in S$ or $i \notin S$; geometrically these vectors represent the vertices of the unit cube in E_+^N. Then the characteristic function of the market game generated by a direct market can be put into a very simple form:

$$v(S) = u(e^S) \quad \text{for all } S \subseteq N \tag{11.10}$$

(compare (11.7)). Note that only finitely many commodity bundles are involved in this expression.

11.4.1 The direct market generated by a game

Thus far we have used markets to generate games. We now go the reverse route, associating with any game (not necessarily a market game) a certain "market of coalitions."[4] Specifically, we shall say that the game $(N; v)$ "generates" the direct market $(N, E_+^N, I^N, \{u\})$, with u given by

$$u(x) = \max_{\{\gamma_S\}} \sum_{S \subseteq N} \gamma_S v(S) \quad \text{for all } x \in E_+^N, \tag{11.11}$$

maximized over all sets of nonnegative γ_S satisfying

$$\sum_{S \ni i} \gamma_S = x_i \quad \text{for all } i \in N. \tag{11.12}$$

To explain this market, we may imagine that each coalition S has an activity $\mathscr{A}_S$ that can earn $v(S)$ dollars if all the members of S participate fully. More generally, it earns $\gamma_S v(S)$ dollars if each member of S devotes the fraction γ_S of "himself" to $\mathscr{A}_S$. The maximization in (11.11) is then nothing but an optimal assignment of activity levels γ_S to the various $\mathscr{A}_S$, subject to the condition (11.12) that each player i distribute exactly the amount x_i of "himself" among his activities, including of course the "solo" activity $\mathscr{A}_{\{i\}}$.

The utility function defined by (11.11) is obviously homogeneous of degree 1, as required for a direct market. But before we can claim to have defined a market, let alone a direct market, we must also establish that (11.11) is continuous and concave. Continuity gives no trouble. To show concavity, it suffices (with homogeneity) to prove that

$$u(x) + u(y) \le u(x + y) \quad \text{for all } x, y \in E_+^N.$$

This is not difficult. By definition, there exist sets of nonnegative co-efficients $\{\gamma_S\}$ and $\{\delta_S\}$ such that

$$u(x) = \sum_{S \subseteq N} \gamma_S v(S), \qquad u(y) = \sum_{S \subseteq N} \delta_S v(S),$$

and

$$\sum_{S \ni i} \gamma_S = x_i, \qquad \sum_{S \ni i} \delta_S = y_i \qquad \text{for all } i \in N.$$

Hence $\{\gamma_S + \delta_S\}$ is admissible for $x + y$, and (11.11) yields

$$u(x + y) \ge \sum (\gamma_S + \delta_S) v(S) = u(x) + u(y),$$

as required.

11.4.2 The cover of a game
We shall now use the direct market generated by a game $(N; v)$ to generate in turn a new game $(N; \bar{v})$; schematically,

arbitrary game → direct market → market game.

We shall call $(N; \bar{v})$ the *cover* of $(N; v)$.

Combining (11.10) with (11.11) and (11.12), we obtain the following relation between v and $\bar{v}$:

$$\bar{v}(R) = \max_{\{\gamma_s\}} \sum_{S \subseteq R} \gamma_s v(S) \quad \text{for all } R \subseteq N, \tag{11.13}$$

maximized over $\gamma_S \geq 0$ such that

$$\sum_{\substack{S \subseteq R \\ S \ni i}} \gamma_S = 1 \quad \text{for all } i \in R. \tag{11.14}$$

Note that we could have taken (11.13) and (11.14) as the definition of a cover, thereby bypassing the intermediate market. Indeed, the cover of a game proves to be a useful mathematical concept quite apart from the present economic application.

We see immediately that

$$\bar{v}(R) \geq v(R) \quad \text{for all } R \subseteq N, \tag{11.15}$$

since one of the admissible choices for $\{\gamma_S\}$ in (11.13) is to take $\gamma_R = 1$ and all other $\gamma_S = 0$. Moreover, the equality cannot always hold in (11.15) since $\bar{v}$ comes from a market game while v was arbitrary. Thus the mapping $v \to \bar{v}$ takes an arbitrary characteristic function and, by perhaps increasing some values, turns it into the characteristic function of a market game.

LEMMA 11.1. *If $(N; v)$ has a core, then $\bar{v}(N) = v(N)$, and conversely.*

Proof. Let α be in the core of $(N; v)$. Then

$$\bar{v}(N) = \max_{\{\gamma_s\}} \sum_{S \subseteq N} \gamma_s v(S)$$

$$\leq \max_{\{\gamma_s\}} \sum_{S \subseteq N} \gamma_s \alpha(S) = \max_{\{\gamma_s\}} \sum_{i \in N} \alpha^i \sum_{S \ni i} \gamma_s$$

$$= \max_{\{\gamma_s\}} \sum_{i \in N} \alpha^i = \alpha(N)$$

$$= v(N),$$

the successive lines being justified by (11.13), (11.1), (11.4), and (11.2). In view of (11.15), we therefore have $\bar{v}(N) = v(N)$.

Conversely, if $(N; v)$ has no core, then (11.4) fails for some balanced set $\mathscr{B}$ with weights $\{\gamma_S\}$. Defining $\gamma_S = 0$ for $S \notin \mathscr{B}$, we see that (11.14) holds (for $R = N$). Then (11.13) and the denial of (11.4) give us

$$\bar{v}(N) \geq \sum_{S \subseteq N} \gamma_s v(S) = \sum_{S \in \mathscr{B}} \gamma_s v(S) > v(N).$$

Hence $\bar{v}(N) \neq v(N)$. ∎

LEMMA 11.2. *A totally balanced game is equal to its cover.*

Proof. Let $(N;\bar{v})$ be the cover of $(N;v)$, and let $0 \subset R \subseteq N$. Then it is clear from the definitions that the cover of $(R;v)$ is $(R;\bar{v})$. But if $(N;v)$ is totally balanced, then $(R;v)$ has a core and $\bar{v}(R) = v(R)$ by lemma 11.1. Hence $\bar{v} = v$. ∎

THEOREM 11.5. *A game is a market game if and only if it is totally balanced.*

Proof. We proved earlier (corollary to theorem 11.4) that market games are totally balanced. We have just now shown that totally balanced games are equal to their covers, which are market games. ∎

11.4.3 Equivalence of markets

There is one more result of some heuristic interest that we can extract from the present discussion, before entering the realm of solution theory. This time we follow the scheme:

arbitrary market → market game → direct market.

Let us call two markets *game-theoretically equivalent* if they generate the same market game. Then the two markets in the above scheme are equivalent in this way, since the cover of the game in the middle is just the market game of the market on the right, and these two games are equal by lemma 11.2. This proves:

THEOREM 11.6. *Every market is game-theoretically equivalent to a direct market.*

11.5 Solutions

An *imputation* for a game $(N;v)$ is a payoff vector α that satisfies

$$\alpha(N) = v(N) \tag{11.16}$$

and

$$\alpha^i \geq v(\{i\}) \quad \text{for all } i \in N. \tag{11.17}$$

A comparison with (11.1) and (11.2) shows that the imputation set is certainly not empty if the game has a core.[5]

Classical solution theory (see also *GTSS*, chapter 6) rests on a relation of "domination" between imputations. If α and β are imputations for $(N;v)$, then α is said to *dominate* β (written $\alpha \succ \beta$) if there is some nonempty subset S of N such that

$$\alpha^i > \beta^i \quad \text{for all } i \in S \tag{11.18}$$

and

$$\alpha(S) \le v(S). \tag{11.19}$$

A *solution* of $(N; v)$ is defined to be any set of imputations, mutually undominating, that collectively dominate all other imputations. Our only concern with this definition, technically, is to observe that it depends only on the concepts of imputation and domination; any further information conveyed by the characteristic function is disregarded.

The core is also closely dependent on these concepts. In fact the core, when it exists, is precisely the set of undominated imputations. The converse is not universally true—there are some games that have undominated imputations but no core.[6] We can rule this out, however, by imposing the very weak condition

$$v(S) + \sum_{N-S} v(\bar{i}) \le v(N) \quad \text{for all } S \subseteq N, \tag{11.20}$$

which is satisfied by all games likely to be met in practice.[7]

11.5.1 Domination-equivalence

Two games will be called d-equivalent (domination-equivalent) if they have the same imputation sets and the same domination relations on them. It follows that d-equivalent games have precisely the same solutions or lack of solutions. If they have cores, they have the same cores; moreover, within the class of games satisfying (11.20), the property of being balanced is preserved under d-equivalence. However, the property of being totally balanced is not so preserved, as the following lemma reveals.

LEMMA 11.3.   *Every balanced game is d-equivalent to its cover.*

Proof. Let $(N; v)$ be balanced. By lemma 11.1, $\bar{v}(N) = v(N)$, and by (11.13), $\bar{v}(\{i\}) = v(\{i\})$; hence the two games have the same imputations. Denote the respective domination relations by $\succ$ and $\succ'$. By (11.15) and (11.19), we see at once that the latter is, if anything, stronger than the former; that is, $\alpha \succ \beta$ implies $\alpha \succ' \beta$. It remains to prove the converse.

Assume, *per contra*, that α and β are imputations satisfying $\alpha \succ' \beta$ but not $\alpha \succ \beta$. Then for some nonempty subset R of N we have

$$\alpha^i > \beta^i \quad \text{for all } i \in R,$$

and

$$\alpha(R) \le \bar{v}(R). \tag{11.21}$$

To avoid $\alpha \succ \beta$ we must have

$$\alpha(S) > v(S) \tag{11.22}$$

for all S, $0 \subset S \subseteq R$. Referring to the definition of $\bar{v}$, we see that there are nonnegative weights γ_S, $S \subseteq R$, such that

$$\bar{v}(R) = \sum_{S \subseteq R} \gamma_S v(S)$$

and

$$\sum_{\substack{S \subset R \\ S \ni i}} \gamma_S = i \quad \text{for all } i \in R.$$

Hence, using (11.22),

$$\bar{v}(R) < \sum_{S \subseteq R} \gamma_S \alpha(S) = \alpha(R).$$

The strict inequality here contradicts (11.21). ∎

By a "solution" of a market we shall mean a solution of the associated market game.

THEOREM 11.7. *If $(N;v)$ is any balanced game whatever, then there is a market that has precisely the same solutions as $(N;v)$.*

Proof. The main work has been done in lemma 11.3. Indeed, let $(N, E_+^T, I^T, \{u\})$ be the direct market generated by $(N;v)$. Then the solutions of this market are the solutions of $(N;\bar{v})$, which by the lemma is d-equivalent to $(N;v)$ and hence has the same solutions. ∎

11.5.2 A technical remark

The notion of d-equivalence is essentially due to Gillies (1953, 1959), though he worked with a broader definition of imputation, not tied to the characteristic function by (11.16). He defined a *vital coalition* as one that achieves some domination that no other coalition can achieve, and showed that two games are d-equivalent (in the present sense) if and only if they have (i) the same imputation sets, (ii) the same vital coalitions, and (iii) the same v-values on their vital coalitions.

A necessary but not sufficient condition for a coalition to be vital is that it cannot be partitioned into proper subsets, the sum of whose v-values equals or exceeds its own v-value. Sufficiency would require the generalized partitioning provided by balanced sets.

Given a game $(N;v)$, we can define its *least superadditive majorant*

$(N; \tilde{v})$ by

$$\tilde{v}(S) = \max_h \sum v(S_h),$$ (11.23)

the maximization running over all partitions $\{S_h\}$ of S. (Compare (11.13), (11.14).) It can be shown that $\tilde{v}(N) = v(N)$ if and only if $(N; v)$ has a core (see lemma 11.1), in which case the two games are d-equivalent. Thus every game with a core is d-equivalent to a superadditive game.

As Gillies observed, though, d-equivalence can also hold nontrivially among superadditive games. That is, it may be possible to push the v-value of some nonvital coalition *higher* than the value demanded by superadditivity, without making the coalition vital.[8] We are using the full power of this observation, since the cover $\bar{v}$ can be thought of as the greatest d-equivalent majorant of v. Thus $v \leq \tilde{v} \leq \bar{v}$, and all three may be different.

11.6 Examples

Lucas's 10-person game with no solution has players $N = \overline{1234567890}$ and the following characteristic function:

$$v(\overline{12}) = v(\overline{34}) = v(\overline{56}) = v(\overline{78}) = v(\overline{90}) = 1,$$
$$v(\overline{137}) = v(\overline{139}) = v(\overline{157}) = v(\overline{159}) = v(\overline{357}) = v(\overline{359}) = 2,$$
$$v(\overline{1479}) = v(\overline{2579}) = v(\overline{3679}) = 2,$$
$$v(\overline{1379}) = v(\overline{1579}) = v(\overline{3579}) = 3,$$ (11.24)
$$v(\overline{13579}) = 4,$$
$$v(N) = 5,$$
$$v(S) = 0 \quad \text{for all others } S \subset N.$$

The game has a core, containing among others the imputation that gives each "odd" player 1 (Lucas, 1967a,b; see also *GTSS*, chapter 6).[9] It is not superadditive (for example, $v(\overline{12}) + v(\overline{34}) > v(\overline{1234})$); but it is d-equivalent to its least superadditive majorant $(N; \tilde{v})$, which can be calculated using (11.23). Moreover, one can verify that the latter is totally balanced, so that $\tilde{v} = \bar{v}$. Thus $(N, \tilde{v})$, defined by (11.23) and (11.24), is a market game with no solution.

The corresponding market with no solution, provided by theorem 11.7, has ten traders and ten commodities, plus money. The traders have identical continuous concave homogeneous utilities $u(x)$, which may be calculated by applying (11.11)–(11.24). Note that positive weights γ's

Table 11.1
A ten-person production game

Inputs										Output
x_1	x_2	x_3	x_4	x_5	x_6	x_7	x_8	x_9	x_{10}	x_{11}
1	1									1
		1	1							1
				1	1					1
						1	1			1
								1	1	1
1		1				1				2
1		1						1		2
1				1		1				2
1				1				1		2
		1		1		1				2
		1		1				1		2
1			1			1		1		2
	1			1		1		1		2
		1			1	1		1		2
1	1					1		1		3
1				1		1		1		3
		1		1		1		1		3
1	1			1		1		1		4

need be considered only for the 18 vital coalitions and the 10 singletons.[10] Of course, this is not the only utility function that works, since only a finite set of its values are actually used.

11.6.1 A production model

Perhaps the most straightforward economic realization of Lucas's game takes the form of a production economy. The production possibilities are generated by 18 specific processes, which produce the same consumer good (at constant returns to scale) out of various combinations of the raw materials (table 11.1). Each entrepreneur starts with one unit of the correspondingly indexed raw material. The utility is simply the consumer good, $u(x) = x_{11}$; hence it is not necessary to postulate a separate money.

This type of construction is perfectly general; a production model can be set up in a similar fashion for any other game in characteristic-function form, one activity being required for each vital coalition. The market game generated by such a model will be the cover of the original game and will have the same core and solutions, provided that the original game was balanced.

11.6.2 Other examples

Lucas (1967a,b, 1968) gave several examples of games in which the solution is unique but does not coincide with the core. He also described a symmetric 8-person game, very similar to the above 10-person game, that has an infinity of solutions but none that treats the symmetric players symmetrically (Lucas, 1968). Shapley (1968) described a 20-person game, of the same general type, every one of whose many solutions consists of the core, which is a straight line, plus an infinity of mutually disjoint closed sets that intersect the core in a dense point-set of the first category. A common feature of all these "pathological" examples is the existence of a core; hence, by theorem 11.7, they are d-equivalent to market games that have the same solution behavior.

We close with another pathological example, of an older vintage (Shapley, 1959a), which because of its simple form leads to a direct market with utilities that we can write down explicitly. The game has n players, with $n \geq 4$, and its characteristic function is

$$v(N - \{1\}) = v(N - \{2\}) = v(N - \{3\}) = v(N) = 1,$$
$$v(S) = 0 \quad \text{for all other } S \subset N.$$

(11.25)

Thus, to win anything requires the participation of a majority of $\overline{123}$ plus all the "veto" players $4, 5, \ldots, n$. The core is the set of all imputations α that satisfy $\alpha_1 = \alpha_2 = \alpha_3 = 0$. It is easily verified that the game is totally balanced: $v = \bar{v}$. There are many solutions, but the remarkable feature of the game is a certain subclass of solutions, determined as follows.

Let B_e denote the set of imputations α that satisfy $\alpha_1 = 0$, $\alpha_2 = \alpha_3 = e > 0$. Thus B_e is an $(n - 3)$-dimensional closed convex subset of the imputation space. In (11.14) it was shown that one may extend any closed subset of B_e to a solution of the game by adding only imputations that are at least $e/2$ distant from B_e.[11] The arbitrary starting set remains a distinct, isolated portion of the full solution. For example, if $n = 4$ (the simplest case), an arbitrary closed set of points on a certain line can be used.

To determine the direct market of this game, we apply (11.11)–(11.15) and obtain the utility function

$$u(x) = \max_{\{\gamma^i\}} (\gamma^1 + \gamma^2 + \gamma^3),$$

maximized subject to

$$\gamma^1 \geq 0, \quad \gamma^2 \geq 0, \quad \gamma^3 \geq 0,$$
$$\gamma^2 + \gamma^3 \leq x_1, \quad \gamma^1 + \gamma^3 \leq x_2, \quad \gamma^1 + \gamma^2 \leq x_3,$$
$$\gamma^1 + \gamma^2 + \gamma^3 \leq x_i \quad (i = 4, 5, \ldots, n),$$

where γ^i abbreviates $\gamma_{N-\{i\}}$. This reduces to the closed form

$$u(x) = \min\left(x_1 + x_2, x_1 + x_3, x_2 + x_3, \frac{x_1 + x_2 + x_3}{2}, x_4, \ldots, x_n\right).$$
$$(11.26)$$

We see that u is the envelope-from-below of $n + 1$ very simple linear functions.

Thus, an n-trader, n-commodity market whose solutions contain arbitrary components, as described above, is obtained by giving the ith trader one unit of the ith commodity $(i = 1, 2, \ldots, n)$ and assigning to all traders the utility function (11.26).

The pathological results involving stable sets warn us to treat the application of stable-set solutions with caution. There is nothing obviously pathological about the Lucas 10-person game viewed as a market game with complementarities in production.

11.7 Competitive Equilibria and Direct Markets

The so-called competitive solution is not a game-theoretical concept but is based on the notion of an imposed schedule of prices which, if accepted by all the members of the economy, will balance supply and demand in each commodity, "clearing the market" to everyone's satisfaction. In our present setting we must remember that money (or "transferable utility") is implicitly one of the commodities in exchange, so that the ith trader's complete utility function has the form

$$U^i(x^i, \xi^i) = u^i(x^i) + \xi^i. \tag{11.27}$$

Here ξ^i denotes i's final money balance. If we wish to follow the classical definition of competition, we must keep this new commodity explicitly in view. A typical price schedule can then be written as

$$(\pi, 1) = (\pi_1, \pi_2, \ldots, \pi_m, 1), \tag{11.28}$$

where we have set the price of money at 1, as a convenient normalization. These prices serve to evaluate everything, including money, in terms of some new accounting unit.

Acting competitively in the face of (11.28), the ith trader will seek to maximize (11.27) subject to the "budget" constraint

$$\pi \cdot x^i + \xi^i = \pi \cdot a^i + \xi^i_0, \tag{11.29}$$

which equates the inflow and outflow of the accounting unit. Here ξ^i_0 denotes i's initial money balance. On the assumption of freely transferable utility, ξ^i is an unrestricted variable, so we may solve (11.11) and eliminate ξ^i from (11.27). Trader i's goal can now be restated as an attempt to maximize

$$u^i(x^i) + \xi^i_0 + \pi \cdot (a^i - x^i), \tag{11.30}$$

where x^i is now chosen unrestrictedly from E^M_+. For the price schedule $(\pi, 1)$ to be in competitive equilibrium, there must exist a set of maximizing choices by the different traders that fit together or form a feasible N-allocation, since only then can the market be cleared to everyone's satisfaction.

By this roundabout path we have arrived at the desired definition.[12] A competitive solution in our model is an ordered pair (π, z^N), where π is an arbitrary M-vector of prices[13] and z^N is a feasible N-allocation, such that

$$u^i(z^i) - \pi \cdot z^i = \max_{x^i \in E^M_+} \left[u^i(x^i) - \pi \cdot x^i \right] \quad \text{for all } i \in N. \tag{11.31}$$

In other words, each trader maximizes his "trading profit." Note that we have omitted the terms ξ^i_0 and $\pi \cdot a^i$ appearing in (11.30), since they are irrelevant to the maximization problem.

Moving to the payoff space, we shall call a vector α *competitive* if it arises from a competitive solution (π, z^N), as follows:

$$\alpha^i = u^i(z^i) - \pi \cdot (z^i - a^i) \quad \text{for all } i \in N. \tag{11.32}$$

It is not hard to establish that the competitive allocations are just the ones that maximize total utility, $\sum_{i \in N} u^i(x^i)$. It follows that the set of all competitive payoff vectors of a market is nonempty, compact, and convex. Moreover, it has already been shown that this set is a subset of the core. Hence each competitive payoff vector is a core vector. The reverse is not generally true; indeed, the competitive solution is often unique whereas the core is typically a set of $|N| - 1$ dimensions.[14] The following theorem shows, however, that in a direct market the set of competitive vectors and the core coincide.

THEOREM 11.8. *Every payoff vector in the core of a game is competitive in the direct market of that game.*

Our notation for theorems 11.8 and 11.9 will be somewhat different from that of previous sections. Outcomes of the game will be expressed as N-tuples of utility, $\alpha = \{\alpha^i : i \in N\}$, measured in some common monetary unit and called *payoff vectors*. A payoff vector α will be said to be *feasible* if $\sum_{i \in N} \alpha^i \le v(N)$; *efficient* if $\sum_{i \in N} \alpha^i = v(N)$; *individually rational* if $\alpha^i \ge v(\{i\})$ for each $i \in N$; and *coalitionally rational* if $\sum_{i \in S} \alpha^i \ge v(S)$ for each $S \subseteq N$. The set of feasible, coalitionally rational payoff vectors will be said to comprise the *core* of the game; thus α is the core if and only if

$$\alpha \cdot e^S \ge v(S) \quad \text{for all } S \subset N, \tag{11.33}$$
$$\alpha \cdot e^N = v(N),$$

where e^S is an N-vector with $e_i^S = 1$ if $i \in S$ and $e_i^S = 0$ if $i \in N - S$. Geometrically the core is a compact convex polyhedron, possibly empty.

A market consists of a finite set N of "traders"; a finite set M of "commodities"; an $|M|$-dimensional Euclidean orthant E_+^M of "bundles"; and, for each $i \in N$, an initial bundle $a^i \in E_+^M$ and a continuous concave utility function u^i from E_+^M to the reals.

A market generates a game in the natural way noted in section 11.4. To define the direct market for any game v, we first put the commodities M into one-to-one correspondence with the players N. The initial allocation is then given by $a^i = e^{\{i\}}$, $i \in N$. The traders all have "equal tastes," that is, identical utility functions, $u^i \equiv u$, given by

$$u(x) = \max \sum_{S \subseteq N} \gamma_S v(S), \tag{11.34}$$

the maximum running over all $\{\gamma_S \ge 0 : S \subseteq N\}$ satisfying[15]

$$\sum_{S \subseteq N} \gamma_S e^S = x. \tag{11.35}$$

From (11.6) and (11.7) and the definition of "balance" one can verify that the utility function of the direct market of a totally balanced game satisfies

$$u(e^R) = v(R) \quad \text{for all } R \subseteq N. \tag{11.36}$$

Proof. Let α be in the core of v.[16] The idea will be to show that α itself can be used as a competitive price vector for the direct market of the game. By (11.36) and (11.33) we have

$$u(e^N) = v(N) = \alpha \cdot e^N. \tag{11.37}$$

In other words, the "value" of the total supply of goods e^N is the same in utility terms as it is when computed using α as a price vector.

Next, take an arbitrary bundle $x \in E_+^M$, and let $\{\gamma_S : S \subseteq N\}$ be any set of nonnegative coefficients satisfying (11.37). Then, by (11.33) and (11.35),

$$\sum_{S \subseteq N} \gamma_S v(S) \le \sum_{S \subseteq N} \gamma_S(\alpha \cdot e^S) = \alpha \cdot \sum_{S \subseteq N} \gamma_S e^S = \alpha \cdot x.$$

Hence, by (11.34),

$$u(x) \le \alpha \cdot x. \tag{11.38}$$

We can now show that α is a competitive payoff vector. Define prices by $\pi_i = \alpha^i$ for $i \in N$. At these prices a trader trying to choose x^i to maximize his "trading profit" $u(x^i) - \pi \cdot x^i$, as in (11.31), will find that he cannot make it positive, because of (11.16), but that he can make it zero by choosing x^i to be the bundle e^N, because of (11.15).[17] By the homogeneity of u, any fraction f^i of that bundle also yields a trading profit of zero. Thus we can construct a competitive solution (π, z^N) by taking $z^i = f^i e^N$, where the f^i are any nonnegative numbers that sum to 1. Moreover, (π, z^N) yields the desired payoff vector α, since we have, from (11.32),

$$u(z^i) - \pi \cdot z^i + \pi \cdot a^i = 0 + \pi_i = \alpha^i \quad \text{for } i \in N. \; \blacksquare$$

Theorem 11.8 tells us that every point in the core of a market game is competitive for at least one of the associated markets, namely the direct market. The next theorem refines this result by showing that for each core point there are associated markets for which only that point is competitive.

THEOREM 11.9. *Among the markets that generate a given totally balanced game, there is at least one that has any given core point as its unique competitive payoff vector.*

Proof. Let v be totally balanced, let d be a real number, and define the set function v_d by

$$v_d(S) = v(S) \quad \text{for all } S \subset N,$$
$$v_d(N) = v(N) + d. \tag{11.39}$$

The game v_d is obviously totally balanced if $d \ge 0$. Let u_d denote the utility function for the direct market of v_d (see (11.6), (11.7)). By (11.8) we have

$$u_d(e^S) = v_d(S) \quad \text{for all } S \subseteq N. \tag{11.40}$$

Let α be an arbitrary core point of v, and define the function $u_{d,\alpha}$ by

$$u_{d,\alpha}(x) = \min(u_d(x), \alpha \cdot x). \tag{11.41}$$

This is continuous and concave; thus it can serve as the utility function of a market with equal tastes, using the same commodity space and initial bundles as the direct market of v. We shall show that for any positive value of d this market has the properties claimed in the statement of the theorem, namely (a) that its market game is v and (b) that its unique competitive payoff vector is α.

(a) Since we have equal tastes and homogeneity of degree 1, the market game w generated by $u_{d,\alpha}$ is given by

$$w(S) = u_{d,\alpha}\left(\sum_{i \in S} a^i\right) = u_{d,\alpha}(e^S) \tag{11.42}$$

(compare with (11.7)). By (11.41) and (11.40), this means that

$$w(S) = \min(v_d(S), \alpha \cdot e^S).$$

By (11.39) and (11.33), we see that this minimum is equal to $v(S)$ both when $S \neq N$ and when $S = N$. Hence $w = v$ as claimed.

(b) As noted previously, the competitive solution maximizes total utility. Each competitive price vector will therefore be the gradient of a linear support to $u_{d,\alpha}(x)$ at $x = e^N$, since $u_{d,\alpha}$ is homogeneous of degree 1 and concave. But when d is positive, $u_{d,\alpha}(x)$ coincides with the linear function $\alpha \cdot x$ in at least a small neighborhood of $x = e^N$, by (11.41), because u_d is continuous and

$$u_d(e^N) = v_d(N) > v(N) = \alpha \cdot e^N.$$

Hence $\alpha \cdot x$ is the only support at $x = e^N$, and the unique competitive prices are $\pi_i = \alpha^i$ for $i \in N$. As we saw in the proof of theorem 11.8, these yield the payoff vector α. This completes the proof of theorem 11.9. ∎

By a simple extension of this proof, a market can be constructed having any given closed convex subset of the core as the set of competitive payoff vectors. Indeed, it is only necessary to define

$$u_{d,A}(x) = \min_{\alpha \in A} u_{d,\alpha}(x),$$

where A is the desired convex set, and proceed as above. (We omit the details.) When A equals the core, the market obtained in this way is independent of the parameter d and in fact reduces to the direct market; this more general construction thus unifies theorems 11.8 and 11.9.

The relationship between the core and the competitive equilibrium can be viewed in terms of the information that is lost in passing from a market to the game that it generates. In the first place, all details concerning the commodities and their distribution among the traders are suppressed, since the analysis of the market game takes place in the utility or payoff space, not the allocation space. In the second place, the game actually takes cognizance of only a finite number of the possible outcomes of the market process, namely the best result for each coalition. Most of the detailed preference information contained in the utility functions is ignored, as may be seen clearly in equations (11.36) and (11.42), where the utilities are evaluated only at the vertices of a cube.

This loss of information suggests that the core is a blunt solution concept and accounts for the many-to-one correspondence between markets and their market games. It is not surprising that we were able to find plenty of markets (even without looking beyond the special type of market in which the commodities are identified with the traders) having just the competitive outcomes that we needed for our proofs.[18]

11.8 No-Side-Payment Market Games

The side-payment or u-money assumption is clearly a considerable restriction when we consider market games. It obliterates the income effect, which is important in many situations.

When we map from an exchange economy to a game without side payments, the space of games we obtain is far richer than those with side payments (the analog of the function v being set-valued), but there is a great loss of information and a similar many–one relationship between markets and games. It turns out, however, that the locus of competitive payoffs is not the entire core of the game, but only a certain "inner core." This inner core can also be characterized game-theoretically, without explicit reference to any economic model; this is done in appendix A.

Billera and Bixby (1974) were able to prove that for no-side-payment games every market game is totally balanced. It is still an open question whether all totally ordinally balanced no-side-payment games are market games.

There is now a substantial literature at a technical level beyond this book on the complexity of the attainable set of utility outcomes in a no-side-payment game, where complexity is defined as the least number of commodities needed to produce the feasible set of utility outcomes. Weber (1980) gives a useful summary of the work of Billera (1974),

Billera and Bixby (1973, 1974, 1976), Billera and Weber (1979), Weber (1977, 1978), and several others.

How interesting as a characterization of complexity is the number of commodities? This is not clear to me. From the viewpoint of economic application, the number of steps required to compute a point in the core, or a competitive equilibrium of the original economy, appears to be of more interest as a measure of complexity. Intuitively one might feel that of two exchange economies with the same number of traders that give rise to the same game but have different numbers of competitive equilibria, the one with more equilibria is more complex.

Notes to chapter 11

1. This chapter is based extensively on two papers by Shapley and Shubik (1969a, 1976).

2. These conditions are heavily redundant; it suffices to assert (11.4) for the *minimal* balanced sets $\mathscr{B}$ (which, moreover, have unique weights). In the case of a super-additive game, only the minimal balanced sets that contain no disjoint elements are needed (see Shapley, 1967).

3. For examples see Shapley (1952, 1959b, 1964b), Shapley and Shubik (1966, 1969a), Shubik (1959a). The abstract definition of "market game" proposed in Shapley (1952) is not equivalent to the present one, however.

4. The essence of this model was suggested by D. Cantor and M. Maschler (private correspondence, 1962).

5. Some approaches to solution theory omit (11.17), relying on the solution concept itself to impose whatever "individual rationality" the situation may demand (Gillies, 1959; Shapley, 1952). This modification in the definition of solution would make little difference to our present discussion, except for eliminating the fussy condition (11.20). In particular, theorem 11.7 and all of section 11.6 would remain correct as written.

6. We are indebted to E. Kohlberg for this observation.

7. Thus (11.20) is implied by either superadditivity or balancedness, but is weaker than both. For a game in normalized form, with $v(\bar{\imath}) = 0$, it merely states that no coalition is worth more than N.

8. For example, at the end of section 11.2, $v(\overline{123})$ may be increased from 1 to 3/2 without making $\overline{123}$ vital.

9. The full core is a five-dimensional polyhedron with vertices e^S: $S = \overline{13579}, \overline{23579}, \overline{14579}, \overline{13679}, \overline{13589}$, and $\overline{13570}$.

10. The singleton weights are needed as slack variables, because we used "=" in (11.24) instead of "≤."

11. The metric used here is $p(\alpha, \beta) = \max_i |\alpha_i - \beta_i|$. Our present claim entails a slight change in the construction given in Shapley (1959a), which merely keeps the rest of the solution away from the arbitrary subset of B_e, rather than from B_e itself.

12. We could, of course, have stated and justified the following definition directly, keeping the transferable utility hidden beneath the notational surface. We wished, however, to establish a firm connection with the standard definition of competitive equilibrium and to clear up the "mystery" of the missing budget constraint in (11.31).

13. We have not been assuming that utilities are nondecreasing, and so we do not assume here that prices are nonnegative. This approach also entails using "$=$" rather than "$\leq$" in the budget condition (11.29). Note also that our prices π_j are not just ratios but have meaningful magnitudes.

14. A sufficient condition for uniqueness of the competitive payoff is that the functions u^i all be differentiable and that at least one competitive allocation be strictly positive. A sufficient condition for the core to be full-dimensional is that all the inequalities (11.2), except the trivial case where $\gamma_N = 1$, be satisfied strictly.

15. At least one such set of weights exists. For example, take $\gamma\{i\} = x_i$ for $i \in N$, with $\gamma_S = 0$ for all other coalitions S.

16. If v is not balanced, the core is empty, so that the theorem is vacuously true. If v is balanced but not totally balanced, the core coincides with that of the cover of v (see lemma 11.3), and hence we can assume v to be totally balanced.

17. Indeed, if he could make it positive, he could make it arbitrarily large, and no maximum would exist. But this is a special consequence of homogeneity; in general, with just concave utilities, a positive trading profit is quite possible at the competitive equilibrium.

18. The Shapley–Shubik direct market was a representation of a market game by an exchange economy with one good for each trader. S. Hart (1982) has shown that an n-person side payment market game can be represented by an economy with only $n - 1$ commodities.

12 Markets with Many Traders

12.1 Two-Sided Markets with Many Traders: The Core

We now extend the model of chapter 10 to the case of many traders on each side of the market. Since we are not yet seeking wide generality in our formulation, we do not hesitate to make simplifying assumptions whenever they help to make the essential lines of the development shorter and more graphic.

Specifically we assume that although there are many traders, there are only two *types* of trader, each equally numerous in the market. Traders $1, 2, \ldots, n$ each start with the bundle $(a, 0)$, while traders $n + 1, n + 2, \ldots, 2n$ each start with the bundle $(0, b)$. We also assume that the first n traders have identical tastes, expressed by a continuous, monotonic, concave utility function $u^1(x, y)$; similarly $u^2(x, y)$ for the remaining n traders. We refer to this kind of market as a *replicated bilateral monopoly*. We first treat the no-side-payment (barter) case.

The high (and certainly unrealistic) degree of symmetry in this model admittedly obliterates many interesting features of multiperson trading games. But it enables us to focus all the more strongly on our present objective, which is to study the behavior of the different kinds of solution as a function of n, especially as n becomes large, and to draw some elementary conclusions concerning the relationships between monopolistic (or oligopolistic) markets at one extreme, and pure competition at the other.

12.1.1 Edgeworth's analysis

One effect of all this symmetry is to enable us to retain the Edgeworth box as a diagrammatic tool. Specifically, the box serves to represent all the *symmetric allocations*—the ones that allocate the bundle $(a - x, b - y)$ to all players of type 1 and (x, y) to all players of type 2. Of course, we cannot completely disregard the allocations that are not symmetric, but we shall find that the symmetric ones play the decisive role.

With a little more trouble, the nonsymmetric allocations can also be depicted (figure 12.1). If we plot each trader's holding as a separate point, we obtain $2n$ points of the form $(a - x^i, b - y^i)$ or (x^{n+i}, y^{n+i}) for the ith player of type 1 or 2, respectively. Let $(\bar{x}^t, \bar{y}^t)$ denote the average holding of

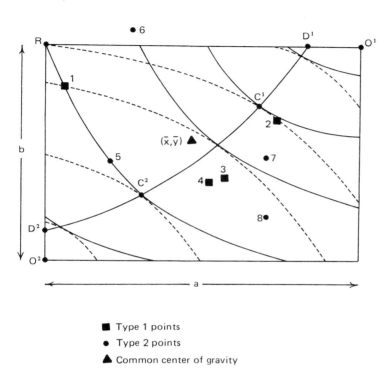

■ Type 1 points
● Type 2 points
▲ Common center of gravity

Figure 12.1
An asymmetric allocation ($n = 4$).

the players of type t. Then the center of gravity of the first n points is just $(a - \bar{x}^1, b - \bar{y}^1)$, and that of the last n is $(\bar{x}^2, \bar{y}^2)$. The supply conditions

$$\sum_{i=1}^{2n} x^i = na, \qquad \sum_{i=1}^{2n} y^i = nb \tag{12.1}$$

then require that these two centers of gravity coincide. Note that the box boundaries are no longer inviolate; a type 2 point, for example, can lie above the RO^1 line. The centers of gravity, however, must lie within the box.

12.1.2 Recontracting and the core
In the $2n$-person model the Pareto set is ordinarily a set of allocations of dimension $2n - 1$. Of these, the symmetric allocations comprise only a one-dimensional subset, corresponding exactly to the Pareto allocations

in the two-person model. Similarly the set of individually rational, symmetric, Pareto allocations is just a copy of the contract curve of the bilateral monopoly model.

A case can be made for discarding the nonsymmetric allocations—or most of them—as follows. With respect to a given allocation, let i and j be players (of type 1 and type 2, respectively) who are below average in the sense that

$$\begin{aligned}
u^1(x^i, y^i) &< u^1(\bar{x}^1, \bar{y}^1), \\
u^2(x^j, y^j) &< u^2(\bar{x}^2, \bar{y}^2).
\end{aligned} \tag{12.2}$$

It is clear that these players, by themselves, could reach a mutually more advantageous distribution of goods. For example, the distribution $(\bar{x}^1, \bar{y}^1), (\bar{x}^2, \bar{y}^2)$ would serve. Even if one inequality in (12.2) were replaced by equality, a joint improvement would be possible. One below-average trader of either type is enough to ensure the existence of a profitable "recontract."

In a nonsymmetric allocation there is almost always at least one below-average trader. The only exception occurs when players of the same type hold different bundles along the same linear segment in an indifference curve, so that averaging yields no improvement. But even in that case the allocation must be symmetric in the utility space.

THEOREM 12.1. *Let X be an allocation that has unequal utility for two traders of the same type. Then X can be "blocked" (recontracted at a profit) by some two-person coalition comprising one trader of each type.*

Note that this "blocking" is merely an extension of the processes whereby (1) the coalition of the whole "blocks" allocations that are not Pareto-optimal, and (2) the one-trader coalitions "block" allocations that are not individually rational. Since Edgeworth proposed to apply the recontracting principle systematically to all possible submarkets, in order to narrow the set of allocations that ultimately qualify for his "contract set," and since recontracting is nothing more than a specific instance of the general game-theoretic process of domination, Edgeworth's solution corresponds exactly to the core. Making use of the preceding theorem, we therefore have the following generalization of theorem 10.1.

THEOREM 12.2. *The core of a replicated bilateral monopoly is the image, in the utility space, of the (recontracted) contract set. It consists entirely of symmetric imputations.*

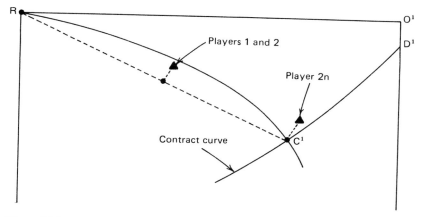

Figure 12.2
The coalition $(1, 2, 2n)$ blocks C^1.

12.1.3 The shrinking core

Thus far, invoking just coalitions of size 1, 2, and $2n$, we have demonstrated that the core of the $2n$-person game is no larger than the core of the corresponding two-person game.[1] We have not shown that it is any smaller; nor, for that matter, have we shown that it is not empty. Before discussing these questions in general, we can give a quick demonstration that some shrinking, at least, is to be expected.

It will suffice to consider the symmetric allocation C^1 (figure 12.2). Here the type 1 players are all getting their individually rational minimum, which we might as well take to be 0. Suppose $n \geq 2$, and consider the three-person coalition $\{1, 2, 2n\}$. First, we observe that they could attain payoff levels equal to what they get in C^1 by recontracting as follows:

Player	Initial	Final	Payoff
1	$(a, 0)$	$(a, 0)$	0
2	$(a, 0)$	$(a - x, b - y)$	0
$2n$	$(0, b)$	(x, y)	$u^2(C^1)$

where x and y are the coordinates of the point C^1. Second, suppose we observe that each player of type 1 takes the bundle $(a - x/2, b/2 - y/2)$. If this indeed gives them a positive payoff,[2] then a small transfer of goods to player $2n$ will yield a "recontract" that is preferred by all three players to C^1. Hence C^1 is not in the core.

The blocking effectiveness of the different coalitions can be expressed and compared in terms of the sets of allocations or payoff vectors they can block. In the payoff space these are, of course, just the interiors of the characteristic sets $V(S)$ of the various coalitions. When we narrow our attention to the symmetric allocations or symmetric payoff vectors, however, these blockable sets no longer depend on the specific coalitions S, but only on their compositions in terms of player types. Indeed, all that is relevant is the *type-composition ratio* of the coalition—the relative number of players of types 1 and 2. Thus, in the example just discussed the symmetric allocation C^1 can equally well be blocked by any coalition consisting of two type 1 traders and one type 2 trader, or by any coalition consisting of four of type 1 and two of type 2, or 400 and 200 for that matter if n is large enough.

Figure 12.3 shows schematically and qualitatively the relationships among these regions of effectiveness in the symmetric payoff space; a similar diagram could be constructed in the Edgeworth box. Thus the curve labeled 1/2 represents the upper boundary of the set of symmetric payoff vectors that belong to $V(S)$, where S can be any coalition containing exactly twice as many type 2 players as type 1 players. We have tried to include enough different cases to indicate the underlying continuous dependence of the blockable set on the type-composition ratio. At one extreme (labeled 1/0) we have the individual rationality condition for type 1; at the halfway point (1/1) we have the condition of Pareto optimality; at the other extreme (0/1) we have type 2 individual rationality. For fixed n, of course, the set of available ratios is discrete, but as n increases they become arbitrarily dense.

THEOREM 12.3. *If p, q, r, s are positive integers, with*

$$\frac{p}{q} < \frac{r}{s} < 1 \quad or \quad \frac{p}{q} > \frac{r}{s} > 1,$$

then any symmetric allocation blockable by a coalition of type composition (p,q) is also blockable by any coalition of type composition (r,s).

Proof. Suppose that $p/q < r/s < 1$. Let X be a symmetric allocation, and let Y denote a suballocation ($p + q$ bundles), feasible for a coalition of p type 1 players and q type 2 players, that is preferred to X by each of them. Define $a = s - r$ and $b = qr - ps$, where a and b are positive integers. We shall construct a suballocation Z of $a(p + q) + 2b$ bundles, feasible for a hypothetical coalition S having $ap + b$ members of the first type, $aq + b$ of the second. (It doesn't matter if these numbers are larger than n.) We

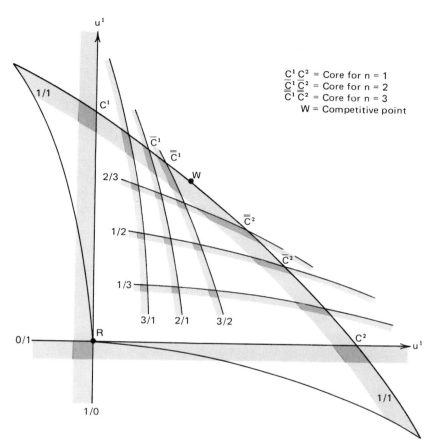

Figure 12.3
Shrinking of the core in the replicated Edgeworth game. The label a/b indicates
the boundary of a region dominated by coalitions in which the ratio of type 1 to
type 2 players is a/b.

start by replicating Y a times; then we adjoin bundles of each type from X. This suballocation is clearly feasible for S. A small transfer from one of the first group of bundles (those derived from Y) to each of the others (the "X bundles") will now provide a nearby, feasible suballocation that is strictly preferred to X by everyone in S. Finally, we obtain Z by averaging the holdings of all players of each type; because of convexity, this averaging among identical traders can only increase utility, without of course destroying feasibility. Thus Z represents a subcontract that could be used to block X, if a coalition like S could be assembled.

But what is the type composition of S? The players of the first type in it number

$$ap + b = (s - r)p + qr - ps = (q - p)r.$$

Those of the second type number

$$aq + b = (s - r)q + qr - ps = (q - p)s.$$

Thus Z is just an (r, s) coalition replicated $q - p$ times. Since Z is symmetric within S (as a result of the averaging step), we can apply the Z bundles to any (r, s) coalition and be assured of feasibility as well as preferability to X. Hence X is blockable as required. The argument for $p/q > r/s > 1$ is similar. ∎

If we call a coalition whose composition ratio is the same as that of the market as a whole *balanced*, then theorem 11.3 can be summed up in the statement that the more nearly balanced a coalition, the more effective it is in blocking allocations that are subject to recontract. However, a perfectly balanced coalition (ratio 1/1) is ineffective against Pareto-optimal allocations; the slightly off-balance coalitions are more powerful in this respect. This principle also holds in connection with more complex markets.

Referring again to figure 12.3, we can begin to visualize the behavior of the core of the game as a function of n. As n increases, ratios closer to 1/1 (on both sides) become available. The core begins at $n = 1$ as the entire imputation space $C^1 C^2$, but it is progressively whittled down to $\bar{C}^1 \bar{C}^2$, $\bar{\bar{C}}^1 \bar{\bar{C}}^2$, etc., as players are added—more precisely as more and more copies of the original bilateral monopoly are added to the market. Since the blocking ability of a coalition does not depend on the value of n, the core can only shrink as n is allowed to increase.[3] Under suitable smoothness conditions there will be a positive shrinkage with every increase in n, although examples with polygonal indifference curves are easily conjured up in which the shrinking stops.[4]

12.1.4 Convergence of the core to the competitive solution

Since replication causes a uniform, homogeneous expansion of the market, the competitive solution remains essentially independent of n. Specifically: (1) *competitive prices* for bilateral monopoly remain in the replicated market, and conversely; (2) a *competitive allocation* for bilateral monopoly defines a symmetric competitive allocation for the replicated market, and conversely (but there may also be nonsymmetric competitive allocations in the larger market); and (3) the *competitive imputations* in the $2n$-person case are all symmetric and correspond exactly to the competitive imputations in the two-person case. Note that the possibilities for nonuniqueness (see sections 10.3.2, 10.4.3) are in no way diminished in the expanded model.

THEOREM 12.4. *Every competitive imputation is in the core.*

Proof. This important theorem reappears in increasingly more general settings. Intuitively, it asserts that the competitive solution, though derived from strictly decentralized premises, is nevertheless immune to collusive manipulation. The proof is quite simple. Suppose X is a competitive allocation, based on prices π_1, π_2 for the two goods, and suppose that S is a prospective blocking coalition. By the π-value of a bundle (x, y) we shall mean the quantity $\pi_1 x + \pi_2 y$. If S is to block X, then a recontract must be found that gives each member of S a bundle with greater π-value than his initial bundle $(a, 0)$ or $(0, b)$, since at X he has attained the maximum utility possible at his given allocation. But the π-value of the coalition's holdings is fixed, regardless of how they redistribute goods among themselves. Hence no blocking can occur. ∎

Since a competitive imputation always exists, we have as a corollary that the core of the replicated market game is not empty.

The final and most remarkable result of this section concerns the behavior of the core as $n \to \infty$. We have already shown that the core can only diminish in size and that it always includes the competitive imputation or imputations. We shall now show that in the limit it includes nothing else.

THEOREM 12.5. *The core of an n-times replicated bilateral monopoly converges, as $n \to \infty$, to the set of competitive imputations.*

Proof. We already know that the core consists only of symmetric imputations and that every symmetric imputation can be achieved by a symmetric Pareto-optimal allocation, such as that represented by X in figure 12.4. Suppose that X is not competitive; our task is to show that it can be blocked, provided n is large enough. Since X is not competitive, the price

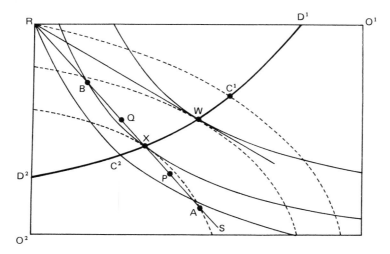

Figure 12.4
Illustrating the blocking of a noncompetitive allocation.

ray RXS will not be tangent to the indifference curves through X, and two intervals XA and XB are defined, as shown in the figure. A bundle that lies on the line between X and A will be preferred by a type 1 player to the bundle he gets at X, and similarly one between X and B for a type 2 player.[5]

Now we must consider what happens when an unbalanced submarket— a coalition of type composition (p, q) with $p \neq q$—carries out exchanges according to a fixed ratio between the goods, such as represented by the price ray RXS. We need only watch the average holding of each type of trader. As trading progresses, each average bundle will move out from the initial position R along the price ray in question. Since the market is unbalanced, the two averages will not coincide (compare figure 12.1). Rather, the points will move out at a rate inversely proportional to the number of individual bundles making up the respective averages. Thus, in figure 12.4 the distances RP and RQ must be in the ratio of q to p.

The construction of a blocking coalition for X is now clear. We must select points P and Q from the intervals XA and XB, respectively, in such a way that ratio RQ/RP is a rational number, say p/q with p and q both integers. Then, assuming that n is at least $\max(p, q)$, we select a coalition S having p type 1 members and q type 2 members. Finally, we construct a suballocation for S by allotting the bundle indicated by p to the type 1 members and the bundle indicated by Q to the type 2 members. This suballocation is feasible for S and is universally preferred by S to the given allocation X. Hence X is blocked, and it remains blocked for all larger n. ∎

When X is very near a competitive allocation, the intervals XA and XB are typically very short, and the points P and Q must consequently be chosen very close to each other. This illustrates once again that the most effective blockers are ones that are nearly, but not quite, balanced.

One consequence of theorem 12.5 is that when there are several competitive equilibria, as in the second numerical example of section 10.3.3, the core must split into two or more pieces at some value of n and must remain disconnected for all larger n.

12.1.5 The side-payment game

The first connection between the competitive solution and the core was made in the analysis of the two-sided market game with a u-money (Shubik, 1955a, 1959a). The mathematical convenience of introducing a money of constant marginal utility enables one to define the characteristic function by a simple joint maximization. Edgeworth (1881, p. 53) had already noted the possibility of interpersonal comparison of utility and termed the point of joint maximization the *utilitarian point*.

We present here a simple proof of the convergence of the core to the competitive equilibrium in the side-payment game (Shapley and Shubik, 1969b). We consider two types of traders distinguished only by their initial commodity bundles, $(a, 0)$ or $(0, b)$. Let there be km traders of the first type and kn of the second (here k is to be regarded as variable, m and n as fixed). The relative composition (μ, ν) of the market will thus remain fixed at $\mu = m/(m + n)$, $\nu = 1 - \mu = n/(m + n)$.

All traders are assumed to have the same concave, twice-differentiable utility function of the separable form $u(x, y) + \xi$, where ξ is the net change from the initial money level. The characteristic function of the game, which will depend only on the numbers s and t of traders of each type in a coalition, will be written $v(s, t)$. Because of equal tastes, the total utility for any coalition is maximized by an equal sharing of goods, and we have at once

$$v(s, t) = (s + t)u(\sigma a, \tau b), \tag{12.3}$$

where (σ, τ) is the relative composition of the coalition, that is, $\sigma = s/(s + t)$, $\tau = 1 - \sigma = t/(s + t)$. Note that v is homogeneous of the first degree: $v(\lambda s, \lambda t) = \lambda v(s, t)$. This holds regardless of the homogeneity of u.

Pareto optimality can be achieved by allocating $(\mu a, vb)$ to everyone, followed by an arbitrary money transfer. To support this allocation the competitive prices must be

$$\pi_x = \frac{\partial u(\mu a, vb)}{\partial x} \quad \text{(first good)},$$

$$\pi_y = \frac{\partial u(\mu a, vb)}{\partial y} \quad \text{(second good)}.$$

The competitive payoffs are then given by

$$
\begin{aligned}
w_1 &= u(\mu a, vb) + \mu a \pi_x - vb\pi_y \quad \text{(first type)}, \\
w_2 &= u(\mu a, vb) + vb\pi_y - \mu a \pi_x \quad \text{(second type)}.
\end{aligned}
\tag{12.4}
$$

In these expressions the first term is the utility of the final holding, the second the payment received for selling off part of the initial holding, and the third the money spent on buying the other good.

There may be competitive allocations other than $(\mu a, vb)$, since u need not be strictly concave. But the competitive imputation w is unique, as are the prices.[6] Note also that w_1 and w_2 are independent of k. As we change the size of the market, the competitive solution remains fixed.

Next we examine the behavior of the core. Expanding u in (12.3) in a Taylor series about $u(\mu a, vb)$, we have

$$v(s, t) = (s + t)[u(\mu a, vb) + (\sigma - \mu)a\pi_x + (\tau - v)b\pi_y + O((\sigma - \mu)^2)].$$

Using (12.4) and the relation $\sigma - \mu = v - \tau = \sigma v - \tau\mu$, we find

$$v(s, t) = sw_1 + tw_2 + (s + t)O((\sigma - \mu)^2). \tag{12.5}$$

Moreover, by concavity, the remainder term is either zero or negative. Hence $v(s, t) \le sw_1 + tw_2$, and the competitive imputation satisfies every coalition and is an element of the core.

Now let α be any Pareto-optimal imputation—one with total payoff $v(km, kn)$. If α is not symmetric, so that it gives unequal payoffs to some pair of traders of the same type, and if $k > 1$, then the m worst-treated traders of the first type and the n worst-treated traders of the second type must together get less than $v(m, n)$. Hence they can block α. It follows that if $k > 1$, the core is confined to the one-dimensional set P of symmetric Pareto-optimal imputations. We can parametrize this set by distance from w, thus: $P = \{\alpha(c): -\infty < c < \infty\}$, where

$$
\begin{aligned}
\alpha_1(c) &= w_1 + c/\mu \quad \text{(first type)}, \\
\alpha_2(c) &= w_2 - c/v \quad \text{(second type)}.
\end{aligned}
$$

As we have seen, $\alpha(0) = w$ is in the core. We shall not determine the exact upper and lower bounds for c in the core, which depend somewhat irregularly on m, n, and k. But the convergence of these bounds to zero, and hence the convergence of the core to the competitive solution, can be shown quite easily.[7]

In fact, let Q be a coalition having $km + kn - 1$ members, lacking only one trader of the first type. Then $\alpha(c)$ awards Q the amount

$v(km, kn) - w_1 - c/\mu.$

If we use (12.5) to estimate the characteristic function of Q, we obtain

$v(km - 1, kn) = v(km, kn) - w_1 + O(1/k).$

Thus, if c is positive and k is sufficiently large, then Q can block $\alpha(c)$. Similarly, if c is negative and k is large enough, then a coalition lacking just one trader of the second type can block $\alpha(c)$. In the limit, only the competitive imputation $\alpha(0)$ remains unblocked.

12.2 Two-Sided Markets with Many Traders: The Value

12.2.1 Some heuristic remarks
Fair division in a socioeconomic situation requires the application of yet another solution concept from the theory of games: the value. This solution seeks to evaluate each player's position in the game a priori, taking into account both his own strategic opportunities and his bargaining position with respect to gains attainable through collaboration. A detailed discussion of the many variations suggested and the problems involved in the construction of a fair-division solution is given in *GTSS*, chapter 8. The remarks here, however, will be reasonably self-contained.

The value can be defined most easily when a common measure of utility exists, together with a vehicle, such as money or credit, that permits utility to be transferred freely among the players. A value can still be defined in the absence of such transferability, but intrinsic rates of utility comparison between the players must then be derived from the strategic and bargaining possibilities of the game itself, and multiple solutions are possible.

Intuitively speaking, the value solution seeks to impute the proceeds of total cooperation among the participants in a way that takes fair account of each person's contribution to each possible cooperative venture. In calculating the value of an economic game, one must determine the marginal worth of an individual to every subset of other individuals and form an average.[8] Thus an ability to measure the economic "worth" of a set of individuals is presupposed. If a money (in the sense of the preceding paragraph) is available, then utilities can be measured on a common scale, and the worth of a coalition can be defined as the maximum combined wealth that the coalition can achieve for its members by its own efforts. These worths, determined for every possible subset of players, comprise the characteristic function from which the value of the game can be computed by the formula

$$\phi_i = \sum_{S \ni i} \frac{(s-1)!(n-s)!}{n!} [v(S) - v(S - \{i\})], \qquad (12.6)$$

where s and n denote the number of elements in S and N, respectively. An equivalent definition, often easier to work with, is

$$\phi_i = \frac{1}{n!} \sum_{w \in \Omega} [v(Pw,i \cup \{i\}) - v(Pw,i)], \qquad (12.7)$$

where Ω is the set of all orderings of N and Pw,i is the set of predecessors of player i in the ordering w.

Historically the formula for the value was first derived from postulates of symmetry, Pareto optimality, additivity, and—most crucially—the value's sole dependence on the kind of information conveyed in the characteristic function (Shapley, 1953). Harsanyi (1959), working constructively from a model of the bargaining process, and later Selten (1960, 1964), working deductively from postulates on the move and payoff structure of the game, arrived at a value definition that applies the same mathematical formula to a modified characteristic function.[9] In the present economic models without externalities, this modification proves to be irrelevant; the classical characteristic function yields the Harsanyi–Selten value and is simpler to work with.

In general, the value can lie outside the core. That is, there may be coalitions that could seize by their own efforts more than they are allotted in the value. Indeed, the value exists even when the core is empty.

When no "money" is available, evaluation of the game must proceed indirectly. We assume that utility is transferable and then try to arrange matters so that the value imputation does not, in the end, require any net transfer of utility. This seems at first too much to arrange, but we do have some freedom to maneuver. Since the individual utility scales are not a priori related to each other, or to a common monetary unit, we are free to adjust them separately before making utility transferable. (Equivalently we could leave the individual units alone but permit transfer only at prescribed rates of exchange, as in an international money market.) This freedom to rescale (or to prescribe rates of exchange) proves to be just enough to ensure the existence of a value that is feasible, in the sense that it can be achieved with no net transfer of utility. Thus the value solution, in the "no-transfer" theory, can be defined as the set of all feasible "transfer" values.

The plausibility of the no-side-payment definition rests on a form of the "independence of irrelevant alternatives" principle, namely, the assertion that if the solution with transfers permitted can be achieved without transfers, then it must remain a solution when transfers are forbidden. Of course, one might object that the possibility of transfers can influence the outcome even in cases where the ultimate net transfer is nil.

An alternative view of the value definition depends on the observation that adopting a particular outcome of an n-person game not only implies that an interpersonal comparison of utilities has taken place, but implies it in two distinct ways. The first way relates the given outcome to other possible outcomes on the Pareto surface, basing the comparison on the existence of trade-offs that were available but did not occur. The second way relates the given outcome to the initial positions (and strategic potentials) of the contestants, using it to infer something about the relative intensities of their desires. The first method infers the individuals' weights in the measuring of social welfare; the second, their weights in the sharing of social profit. Our present value concept embodies a principle of equivalence between these two methods of interpersonal comparison; the values of the game are just those outcomes for which the two sets of derived weights coincide.

Under this definition a value of the game thus represents a kind of equilibrium. It is as though the players introduced a money-of-account as an aid to rational bargaining, but with the prices of different individuals' "units" chosen so that when the books are closed all accounts are miraculously in balance. The game itself is called upon to provide an intrinsic, "equitable" comparison among the personal utility units. As previously noted, the comparison factors are not always unique.

The money-of-account analogy suggests a close affinity between the value of the game and the competitive equilibrium. They are not the same, however, as can be seen from the fact that the former makes essential use of cardinal utility whereas the latter does not. A nonlinear, order-preserving transformation of the utilities will generally change the value but not the competitive equilibrium or, for that matter, the core.

12.2.2 Convergence of the side-payment value

For any trader the value represents his expected marginal worth to a coalition chosen at random. We can express this, for a trader of the first type, as follows:

$$\phi_1(k) = E\{D_1(s, t)\}, \tag{12.8}$$

where E is an averaging operator and D_1 is the finite difference

$$D_1(s, t) = v(s + 1, t) - v(s, t).$$

The precise form of E could be stated, but it is not relevant here. Indeed, any method of averaging the increments D_1 that will sustain the "almost all" statements in the next paragraph will suffice. The convergence theorem is therefore valid for a whole class of values that might be defined.

Now let equation (12.3) be regarded as defining a function $v(s, t)$ for all positive real numbers s and t. Like u it is twice differentiable. Using homogeneity, a simple Taylor expansion, and (12.3), we have

$$
\begin{aligned}
D_1(s, t) &= (s + t)\left[v\left(\sigma + \frac{1}{s + t}, \tau \right) - v(\sigma, \tau) \right] \\
&= \frac{\partial v(\sigma, \tau)}{\partial \sigma} + O\left(\frac{1}{s + t} \right) \\
&= \frac{\partial v(s, t)}{\partial s} + O\left(\frac{1}{s + t} \right) \\
&= \frac{\partial}{\partial s}[(s + t)u(\sigma a, \tau b)] + O\left(\frac{1}{s + t} \right) \\
&= u(\sigma a, \tau b) + \tau a \frac{\partial u(\sigma a, \tau b)}{\partial x} - \tau b \frac{\partial u(\sigma a, \tau b)}{\partial y} + O\left(\frac{1}{s + t} \right).
\end{aligned}
$$

The last line closely resembles the formula for ω_1 in (12.4). Indeed, if $s + t$ is large and (σ, τ) is close to (μ, ν), then $D_1(s, t)$ will approach the competitive payoff ω_1, as required. But if k is large enough, then "almost all" coalitions will be large, and "almost all" coalitions will have compositions approximating (μ, ν). This latter statement will be recognized as a form of the law of large numbers. The precise statement is as follows: Given any $\varepsilon > 0$, a number k_ε can be chosen so large that for any $k \geq k_\varepsilon$ a randomly chosen coalition will, with probability at least $1 - \varepsilon$, have size $s + t$ large enough and composition (σ, τ) near enough to (μ, ν) to ensure that $|D_1(s, t) - \omega_1| \leq \varepsilon$. Hence we may write

$$\phi_1(k) = (1 - \varepsilon)(\omega_1 + \delta(k)) + \varepsilon C_1(k) \quad \text{for all } k \geq k_\varepsilon, \tag{12.9}$$

where $|\delta(k)| \leq \varepsilon$ and $C_1(k)$ is the appropriately weighted average of the $D_1(s, t)$ for the "exceptional" coalitions too far from (μ, ν).

Let us consider the implications of (12.9). If $C_1(k)$ were known to be bounded, we could conclude that $\phi(k) \to \omega_1$, and we would be done. A lower bound for $C_1(k)$, namely $v(1, 0)$, follows at once from the definition of D_1 and the superadditivity of the characteristic function. An upper bound for $C_1(k)$ cannot be deduced so directly, however, unless restrictions are imposed on the behavior of $u(x, y)$ near the boundaries of the positive quadrant. But there is a trick that takes us around this difficulty. We observe that both the value and the competitive imputation are Pareto-optimal; hence

$$m\phi_1(k) + n\phi_2(k) = m\omega_1 + n\omega_2 \quad \text{for all } k. \tag{12.10}$$

The lower bound on $C_1(k)$ tells us that $\liminf \phi_1(k) \geq \omega_1$, that is, no limit point (finite or infinite) of the sequence $\{\phi_1(k)\}$ is less than ω_1. Hence, by (12.10) we have $\limsup \phi_2(k) \leq \omega_2$. To complete the proof we merely return to (12.8) and repeat the whole argument with types 1 and 2 interchanged, obtaining $\limsup \phi_1(k) \leq \omega_1$ and $\liminf \phi_2(k) \geq \omega_2$. In this way we finally establish the convergence of the value imputation $\phi(k)$ to the competitive imputation ω.

To sum up the essential idea of the proof: The partial derivatives of the characteristic function $v(s, t)$ show that the marginal value of a player to a large, nearly balanced coalition is substantially equal to his competitive payoff. However, if the economy is big enough, almost all coalitions are large and nearly balanced.

12.2.3 A symmetric market game
Our first model is chosen for the contrast it provides between the value and the other solutions under discussion. We find that the value gives an intuitively more satisfactory measure of the "equities" of the situation while avoiding the violent discontinuity exhibited by both the competitive equilibrium and the core. Also, exploiting that discontinuity, we obtain a simple example of convergence to different limits, by the value and the other solutions, when the set of traders is expanded linearly but not homogeneously.

The model can be formulated in terms of gloves. Each player starts with one glove, and the players may trade gloves, or buy or sell them for money, without restriction. At the end of the game an assembled pair is worth \$1 to whoever holds it. For example, there might be an outside market that would pay that price.

The characteristic function of the game, which states the dollar potential of each coalition S, is given by the equation

$$v(S) = \min(|S \cap R|, |S \cap L|). \tag{12.11}$$

Here R and L are the original sets of owners of right- and left-handed gloves, respectively, and $|X|$ is the number of elements of the set X.

Equation (12.11) expresses a rudimentary form of complementarity between economic units of different types. Traders on the same side of the market stand in the position of perfect substitutes; traders on opposite sides are perfect complements. A further discussion of this characteristic function is given by Shapley (1959b).

The competitive equilibrium and the core   Let $r = |R|$ and $l = |L|$, and suppose first that $r < l$. Then the equilibrium price of left-handed gloves in a competitive market is zero, and the members of R can acquire complete pairs at no cost. The unique competitive imputation in dollars is therefore

$$\begin{aligned} \omega_i &= 1 \quad \text{for } i \in R, \\ \omega_j &= 0 \quad \text{for } j \in L. \end{aligned} \tag{12.12}$$

The case $r > l$ is just the opposite. In the transition case, $r = l$, the equilibrium prices are not unique; we know only that the sum of the two prices must be \$1. A continuum of competitive imputations results, as follows:

$$\begin{aligned} \omega_i(p) &= p \quad \text{for } i \in R, \\ \omega_j(p) &= 1 - p \quad \text{for } j \in L, \\ 0 &\leq p \leq 1. \end{aligned} \tag{12.13}$$

The core of the game necessarily contains all competitive imputations. In this case it happens to contain no other imputations. Indeed, in any noncompetitive imputation the least-favored member of R and the least-favored member of L get less than \$1 combined and can therefore form a blocking coalition. Thus the core is also given by (12.12) (or its opposite) or by (12.13).

The value   To calculate the value we shall make use of a "random-order" version of the definition in which an imputation is built up one player at a time by awarding to each player the increment that he brings to the coalition consisting of his predecessors. The value of the game is equal to the average of these imputations, over all possible orderings of players.

Let $\phi_{\text{right}}(r, l)$ denote the sum of the values to the r members of R. If we consider separately those orderings that end with a member of R (probability $r/(r + l)$) and those that end with a member of L (probability $l/(r + l)$), we obtain the following difference equation:

$$\phi_{\text{right}}(r, l) = \frac{r}{r + l}[\phi_{\text{right}}(r - 1, l) + v(R \cup L) - v(R' \cup L)]$$
$$+ \frac{l}{r + l}[\phi_{\text{right}}(r, l - 1)], \tag{12.14}$$

where R' is any set satisfying $R' \subset R$, $|R'| = r - 1$. If we assume that $r > l$, thus eliminating the v terms in (12.14), then the relevant boundary conditions are

$$\phi_{\text{right}}(r, 0) = 0 \quad \text{and} \quad \phi_{\text{right}}(r, r) = \frac{r}{2} \quad \text{for all } r,$$

and the solution of the difference equation for $r \geq l$ is

$$\phi_{\text{right}}(r, l) = \frac{r}{2} - \frac{r - l}{2} \sum_{k=0}^{l} \frac{r! \, l!}{(r + k)!(l - k)!}.$$

(The reader may verify this by direct substitution in (12.14).) This amount is divided equally among the members of R. With the aid of Pareto optimality,

$$\phi_{\text{right}} + \phi_{\text{left}} = v(R \cup L) = l,$$

the values to members of L are easily determined. The complete value imputation for $r \geq l$ is

$$\phi_i = \frac{1}{2} - \frac{r - l}{2r} \sum_{k=0}^{l} \frac{r! \, l!}{(r + k)!(l - k)!} \quad \text{for } i \in R,$$
$$\phi_j = \frac{1}{2} + \frac{r - l}{2l} \sum_{k=1}^{l} \frac{r! \, l!}{(r + k)!(l - k)!} \quad \text{for } j \in L. \tag{12.15}$$

The case $r \leq l$ is symmetrical. Table 12.1 gives an idea of how these equations behave for small numbers of traders.

The value solution definitely favors the "short" side of the market, individually and collectively. For example, if $l < r$, the members of L, with less than half the population, get more than half the total profit,

Table 12.1
Value to a member of R

r	l							
	0	1	2	3	4	5	6	7	8
1	0	0.500	0.667	0.750	0.800	0.833	0.857	0.875	0.889
2	0	0.167	0.500	0.650	0.733	0.786	0.822	0.847	0.867
3	0	0.083	0.233	0.500	0.638	0.720	0.774	0.811	0.838
4	0	0.050	0.133	0.272	0.500	0.629	0.710	0.764	0.802
5	0	0.033	0.086	0.168	0.297	0.500	0.622	0.701	0.755
6	0	0.024	0.060	0.113	0.194	0.315	0.500	0.616	0.693
7	0	0.018	0.044	0.081	0.135	0.214	0.330	0.500	0.610
8	0	0.014	0.033	0.061	0.099	0.153	0.230	0.341	0.500

which is $v(R \cup L) = l$. On the other hand, the "long" side of the market is not totally defeated, as in the other solutions discussed. The value of the game is less abruptly sensitive to the balance between supply and demand than the competitive equilibrium and the core, since it gives some credit for the bargaining position of the group in oversupply.[10] It is not strange that the competitive solution, with its decentralized outlook, fails to recognize collusive bargaining power, but it is a little surprising that the core—a cooperative-game concept—misses it as well.

Asymptotic behavior   Figure 12.5 shows the effect of altering the ratio of trader types, holding the size of the market fixed. In the lower graph, with ten times as many traders, the slope of the curve in the vicinity of the transition case is noticeably steeper. In the limit the curve approaches the step shape associated with the core and competitive solutions.

The effect of increasing the size of the market while holding the ratio of trader types fixed is illustrated in table 12.2 for the ratio $2:1$. We see that owning a right glove is worth $16\frac{2}{3}¢$ when there are three traders, but less than $6¢$ if there are 30 traders and less than $1¢$ if there are 300. The general asymptotic formulas for a fixed ratio $a:b$, with $a > b$, are

$$\phi_i(ak, bk) = \frac{b}{(a-b)^2 k} - \frac{3b(a+b)}{(a-b)^4 k^2} + O(k^{-3}) \quad \text{for } i \in R,$$

$$\phi_j(ak, bk) = 1 - \frac{a}{(a-b)^2 k} - \frac{3a(a+b)}{(a-b)^4 k^2} + O(k^{-3}) \quad \text{for } j \in L.$$

(We omit the derivation.) The rate of convergence of the value to the

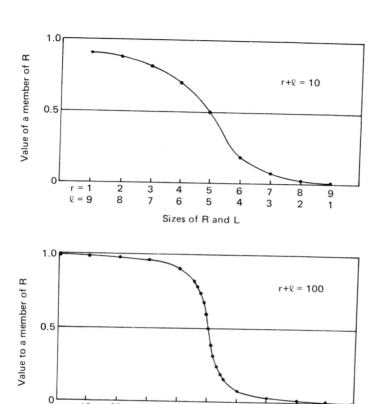

Figure 12.5
Value as a function of composition.

Table 12.2
Value solutions for trader types in ratio $2:1$

r	l	ϕ_i	ϕ_j	ϕ_{right}	ϕ_{left}
2	1	0.1667	0.6667	0.333	0.667
4	2	0.1333	0.7333	0.533	1.467
6	3	0.1131	0.7738	0.679	2.321
8	4	0.0990	0.8020	0.792	3.208
10	5	0.0884	0.8232	0.884	4.116
20	10	0.0589	0.8822	1.178	8.822
200	100	0.0092	0.9816	1.842	98.158
as $r = 2l \to \infty$		$\dfrac{1}{l} - \dfrac{9}{l^2}$	$1 - \dfrac{2}{l} + \dfrac{18}{l^2}$	$2 - \dfrac{18}{l}$	$l - 2 + \dfrac{18}{l}$

competitive imputation is of order $1/k$. The same rate has been observed in other examples and may be presumed to be typical for homogeneously expanding markets.

Another asymptotic result is available. If we let the market expand with the difference $d = r - l$ held constant, we obtain the following estimates:[11]

$$\phi_i(r, r-d) = \frac{1}{2} - \frac{d}{2}\sqrt{\frac{\pi}{r}} + O(r^{-1}) \quad \text{for } i \in R,$$

$$\phi_j(r, r+d) = \frac{1}{2} - \frac{d}{2}\sqrt{\frac{\pi}{r}} + O(r^{-1}) \quad \text{for } j \in L.$$

In other words, if traders are added in equal numbers on both sides of the market, the distinction between "long" and "short" disappears in the limit, and all get equal shares of the profit. This provides an example (if $d \neq 0$) of a linearly, nonhomogeneously expanding market in which the value and the competitive imputation do not tend to the same limit.

Concluding remarks Still another solution concept—the von Neumann–Morgenstern stable sets—has been applied to the symmetric market game (12.11) by Shapley (1959b). He found that in the transition case, $r = l$, the unique stable set is the core itself, that is, the straight line of imputations defined by (12.13). In the other cases, $r > l$ and $r < l$, there are infinitely many stable sets, each one a continuous curve of imputations emanating from the one-point core and possessing certain monotonicity properties. Thus a "pricelike" parameter can always be identified, but most of the stable sets will involve some kind of price discrimination in the form of unequal treatment of traders of the same type.

A nonsymmetric generalization of the present example is Böhm-Bawerk's horse market. In chapter 9 it was shown that traders who are priced out of the market receive consideration in the value of the game but not in the core or competitive equilibrium; the stable sets are again continuous, monotonic curves. We could have avoided the use of money in this example if we had made the commodities continuously divisible and given the traders identical (cardinal) utility functions:

$$u^i(x, y) = \min(x, y) \quad \text{for all } i \in N. \tag{12.16}$$

Money would then be superfluous, since the relevant utility transfers could be accomplished (on a constant-sum basis) by transferring bundles containing equal amounts of the two commodities.

A final remark: The discontinuous behavior of the competitive equilibrium and the core in this example makes them less favorable candidates as models of economic reality for this market than the value, the bargaining set, or the formation of syndicates. We return to this point in section 12.3.

12.2.4 A market without transferable utility

To illustrate the application of the theory of games without transferable utility, we present a simple two-sided Edgeworth market in which both the core and the value can be determined explicitly, but in which there is not so much symmetry that the solutions are uninteresting. In addition to providing working experience with the new value concept, the example will illustrate several theoretical points.

Let there be n traders on each side of the market and two goods in trade, but no money or credit. The initial holdings are $(1, 0)$ for type 1 and $(0, 1)$ for type 2. The (cardinal) utility functions are

$$\begin{aligned} u_1(x, y) &= \sqrt{xy} && \text{(type 1),} \\ u_2(x, y) &= \sqrt{x^2 + y^2 + 23xy} && \text{(type 2).} \end{aligned} \tag{12.17}$$

The number 23 is only a convenience; all that really matters is that these functions are concave, homogeneous of degree 1, and symmetric in the two goods.

Figure 12.6 is the Edgeworth box for this market. The origin represents the allocation that gives $(0, 0)$ to type 2, and hence $(1, 1)$ to type 1. The opposite corner C' is the "origin" for type 1, and R is the initial no-trade

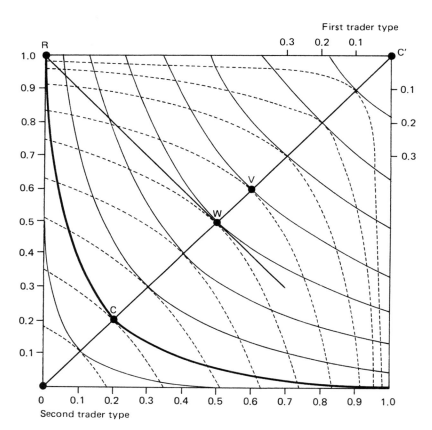

Figure 12.6
The Edgeworth box.

point. The segment CC' is Edgeworth's contract curve for the case of two traders or $n = 1$. (The point V, the value allocation for $n = 1$, will be determined later.) The unique competitive allocation w, which gives all traders $(1/2, 1/2)$, is represented by the point W; this is independent of n.

The core Although we have already discussed the convergences of the no-side-payment core in section 12.1, we present an explicit example here to contrast the core and value. For $n = 1$ the core comprises the whole contract curve CC'. More precisely, the core is the image of CC' in the utility space under the mapping (12.13), as shown in figure 12.7.

For $n > 1$ we first observe that all imputations in the core must be symmetric, since any nonsymmetric imputation can be profitably blocked by a two-man coalition consisting of one least-favored trader of each type. We may therefore transfer our attention from the $2n$-dimensional space of all imputations to the two-dimensional subspace of symmetric imputations.

Because of the homogeneity of (12.17), the Pareto-optimal symmetric imputations lie along the straight line OC' in figure 12.7, whose equation is

$$5u_1 + u_2 = 5. \tag{12.18}$$

The core for each n is a subset of this line. It remains to discover which points on the line can be blocked. As in the model of section 12.2.3, the most efficient blockers are coalitions that have almost, but not quite, the same relative composition as the market as a whole.

To verify this, let $r(S)$ denote the ratio of first types to second types in an arbitrary coalition S, and let $(1 - t, 5t)$, $0 \le t \le 1$, be an arbitrary point on OC' representing the symmetric imputation α_t. Then a routine calculation reveals that for S to block α_t it is necessary and sufficient that $r(S)$ lie strictly between 1 and a certain critical ratio

$$r_t = \frac{t(t^2 - 0.04)}{(1 - t)(t - t^2 - 0.04)}.$$

Note that $r_{1/2} = 1$; the competitive imputation $\alpha_{1/2}$ cannot be blocked since there is no number strictly between 1 and 1. However, any other α_t will be blocked by some coalition if n is sufficiently large.

For each n the coalitions of size $2n - 1$ provide the best type-composition ratios available, namely $(n - 1)/n$ and $n/(n - 1)$. Setting r_t equal to these numbers in turn, and solving for t, gives us the endpoints of the

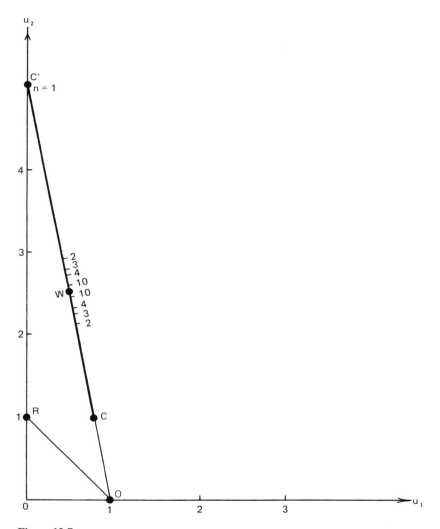

Figure 12.7
The utility space (symmetric payoffs only), showing the shrinking of the core to
the competitive payoff. We have used the same letters to denote allocation points
in the (x, y) space and the corresponding payoff points (imputations) in the (u_1, u_2)
space.

Table 12.3
Endpoints of the core

n	C		C'	
1	0.800	1.000	0.000	5.000
2	0.577	2.116	0.421	2.897
3	0.546	2.272	0.453	2.733
4	0.533	2.337	0.467	2.665
5	0.525	2.374	0.474	2.628
10	0.512	2.440	0.488	2.560
as $n \to \infty$	$\dfrac{1}{2} + \dfrac{21}{184n}$	$\dfrac{5}{2} - \dfrac{105}{184n}$	$\dfrac{1}{2} - \dfrac{21}{184n}$	$\dfrac{5}{2} + \dfrac{105}{184n}$

core. We have done this numerically for several values of n, as shown in table 12.3 and figure 12.7. Asymptotically the length of the core varies inversely with the size of the market.

The value   We now turn to the value. Our technique, as explained in section 12.2.1, will be to introduce a set of weights $\{\lambda_i\}$, nonnegative and not all zero, on which we can base hypothetical exchanges of utility among the traders. Thus, if α is a payoff vector attainable in the market, we assume that $\alpha + \beta$ is also attainable for any β such that $\sum \lambda_i \beta_i = 0$. Given the weights, we are in a position to calculate the λ-transfer value of the game. This value is in general infeasible, that is, not attainable by commodity transfers alone. We must try to find weights that yield a feasible λ-transfer value; this will be, by definition, a value of the original market without transferable utility.

We shall first dispose of the possibility of a nonsymmetric solution—one that gives different payoffs to traders of the same type. This would require unequal weights, since the value formula itself is symmetric. Suppose that $\lambda_j < \lambda_k$, where j and k are traders of the same type, and consider how the λ-transfer value might be attained. Regardless of utility transfers, the allocation of goods must maximize the weighted sum of utilities. Any goods of positive utility that j could transfer to k would increase this sum because of the following comparison:

$$\lambda_k u(x^j + x^k, y^j + y^k) \geq \lambda_k [u(x^j, y^j) + u(x^k, y^k)]$$
$$\geq \lambda_j u(x^j, y^j) + \lambda_k u(x^k, y^k), \tag{12.19}$$

with strict inequality on the second line if $u(x^j, y^j) > 0$. Hence j's share of the goods allocation must be worthless. But his payoff in the λ-transfer value is easily seen to be positive, even if $\lambda_j = 0$. It follows that the λ-transfer value can be attained only with the aid of a utility transfer, making it infeasible for the original game. We conclude that only equal weights need be considered for traders of the same type.

With symmetry established, the λ-transfer characteristic function can be written in the form $v^\lambda(s, t)$, where the pair of integers (s, t) is the type composition of the coalition in question. A simple fact about this function will be useful.

LEMMA 12.1.   *If $st \neq 0$, then $v^\lambda(s, t) = v^\lambda(t, s)$.*

Proof. The inequality (12.19), which depends on the concavity and homogeneity of (12.17), shows that any coalition can attain its maximum λ-weighted total utility while concentrating all its goods in the hands of at most two traders, one of each type. For a coalition of composition (s, t), with neither s nor t equal to 0, there will be an optimal allocation that might give (x, y) to one trader of type 1, $(s - x, t - y)$ to one trader of type 2, and nothing to the rest. This allocation is worth $A = v^\lambda(s, t)$ to the coalition. Now consider a second coalition of composition (t, s). A possible allocation is (y, x) to one trader of type 1, $(t - y, s - x)$ to one trader of type 2, and nothing to the rest. Since the utility functions are symmetric in the commodities, this must be worth the same amount, A, to the second coalition. Hence $v^\lambda(t, s) \geq A = v^\lambda(s, t)$. Repeating the argument, we conclude that $v^\lambda(t, s) = v^\lambda(s, t)$. ∎

Let us now consider the value formula in its "orderings" version. The λ-transfer value ϕ_i^λ to a typical trader of type 1 can be expressed as a linear function of all the $v^\lambda(s, t)$, where s and t are integers ranging from 0 to n. Consider how the coefficient of a particular $v^\lambda(s, t)$ is formed. There will be positive contributions from coalitions containing i and negative contributions from coalitions not containing i. For the positive part we must count the number of orderings that put i in position $s + t$ and put exactly $s - 1$ other type 1 traders in positions preceding $s + t$. This number is

$$\binom{n - 1}{s - 1}\binom{n}{t}(s + t - 1)!(2n - s - t)!,$$

or zero if $s = 0$. Similarly, for the negative part we must have i in position $s + t + 1$, and exactly s other type 1 traders in positions preceding $s + t + 1$. The number of orderings that do this is

$$\binom{n-1}{s}\binom{n}{t}(s+t)!(2n-s-t-1)!,$$

or zero if $s = n$. The desired coefficient of $v^\lambda(s, t)$ is the difference of these two numbers divided by the total number of orderings, which is $(2n)!$. This reduces to

$$\binom{n}{s}\binom{n}{t}\frac{(s+t-1)!(2n-s-t-1)!(s-t)}{(2n)!} \tag{12.20}$$

or

$$-\frac{1}{2n} \quad \text{if } s = t = 0$$

or

$$\frac{1}{2n} \quad \text{if } s = t = n.$$

Since the coefficient (12.20) is antisymmetric in s and t, the lemma permits us to cancel the bulk of the terms in the value formula. This cancellation makes the whole calculation manageable. We are left with

$$\phi_i^\lambda = \frac{1}{2n}v^\lambda(n, n) + \sum_{s=1}^{n}\binom{n}{s}\frac{(s-1)!(2n-s-1)!s}{(2n)!}v^\lambda(s, 0)$$

$$- \sum_{t=1}^{n}\binom{n}{t}\frac{(t-1)!(2n-t-1)!t}{(2n)!}v^\lambda(0, t) - \frac{1}{2n}v^\lambda(0, 0).$$

Homogeneity of v^λ reduces this to

$$\phi_i^\lambda = \frac{1}{2}v^\lambda(1, 1) + \sum_{s=1}^{n}\binom{n}{s}\frac{s!(2n-s-1)!s}{(2n)!}[v^\lambda(1, 0) - v^\lambda(0, 1)].$$

This, in turn, can be reduced to the very simple expression

$$\phi_i^\lambda = \frac{1}{2}v^\lambda(1, 1) + \frac{1}{n+1}[v^\lambda(1, 0) - v^\lambda(0, 1)].$$

A symmetrical argument yields

$$\phi_j^\lambda = \frac{1}{2}v^\lambda(1, 1) - \frac{1}{n+1}[v^\lambda(1, 0) - v^\lambda(0, 1)],$$

where j is a typical trader of type 2.

Thus far only the concavity, symmetry, and first-degree homogeneity of the utility functions have played a role. We now refer to the particular functions (12.17) and make the simple determinations

$$v^\lambda(1,0) = 0,$$
$$v^\lambda(0,1) = \lambda_j,$$
$$v^\lambda(1,1) = \max(\lambda_i, 5\lambda_j).$$

Inserting these values, we obtain

$$\phi_i^\lambda = \frac{1}{2}\max(\lambda_i, 5\lambda_j) - \frac{1}{n+1}\lambda_j \quad \text{(type 1)},$$

$$\phi_j^\lambda = \frac{1}{2}\max(\lambda_i, 5\lambda_j) + \frac{1}{n+1}\lambda_j \quad \text{(type 2)}. \tag{12.21}$$

This is the λ-transfer value. The question is: For what choices of λ_i and λ_j is it feasible?

Clearly only the ratio between λ_i and λ_j is significant. The situation is illustrated in figure 12.8 for the case $n = 1$. In general, let α be any feasible, symmetric imputation. Then $5\alpha_i + \alpha_j \leq 5$ (cf. (12.18)). But if α is to be a value of the game, we must have $\lambda_i\alpha_i = \phi_i^\lambda$ and $\lambda_j\alpha_j = \phi_j^\lambda$ for some choice of λ_i and λ_j. Hence the following inequality must be satisfied:

$$5\lambda_j\phi_i^\lambda + \lambda_i\phi_j^\lambda \leq 5\lambda_i\lambda_j, \tag{12.22}$$

with λ_i and λ_j nonnegative and not both zero. If we substitute (12.21) into (12.22), we find that $\lambda_i \leq 5\lambda_j$ implies

$$\left(\frac{5}{2} - \frac{1}{n+1}\right)(\lambda_i - 5\lambda_j) \geq 0,$$

while $\lambda_i \geq 5\lambda_j$ implies

$$\left(\frac{5}{2}\lambda_i + \frac{1}{n+1}\lambda_j\right)(\lambda_i - 5\lambda_j) \leq 0.$$

It follows that the only solution is $\lambda_i = 5\lambda_j$; and this conclusion is independent of n. Hence the value of the game is unique and is given by

$$\phi_i = \frac{1}{2} - \frac{1}{5(n+1)} \quad \text{(type 1)},$$

$$\phi_j = \frac{5}{2} + \frac{1}{n+1} \quad \text{(type 2)}.$$

Table 12.4 is intended for comparison with table 12.2. In figure 12.9 all

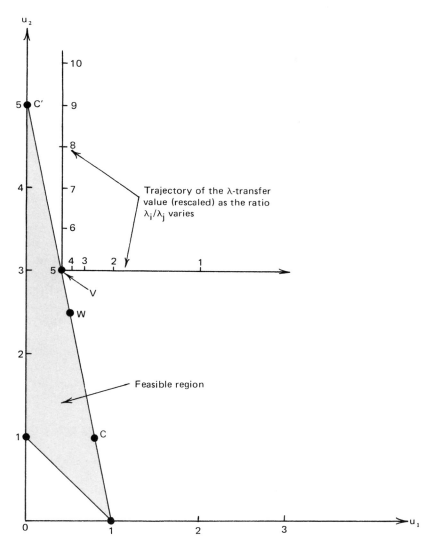

Figure 12.8
Feasibility of the λ-transfer value ($n = 1$).

Table 12.4
The value

n	V	
1	0.400	3.000
2	0.433	2.833
3	0.450	2.750
4	0.460	2.700
5	0.467	2.667
10	0.482	2.591
as $n \to \infty$	$\dfrac{1}{2} - \dfrac{1}{5n}$	$\dfrac{5}{2} + \dfrac{1}{n}$

three solutions are shown together as functions of market size. We see that the value is always more favorable to traders of type 2 than the competitive solution, and that it begins inside the core but moves outside at $n = 3$ because of its somewhat slower rate of convergence. These comparisons should not be interpreted too broadly, however, since as indicated in section 12.2.1, the no-transfer value is essentially a cardinal concept, while the other solutions are not. If we tamper with our example, applying nonlinear transformations to the traders' utilities, we can alter all such qualitative features. Indeed, for any fixed n, a pair of differentiable order- and concavity-preserving transformations can be found for (12.17) that place the value point V at any designated spot in the interior of the contract curve CC' without affecting the other solutions.

12.3 Two-Sided Markets with Many Traders: The Bargaining Set, Kernel, and Nucleolus

12.3.1 Definitions
The bargaining set, kernel, nucleolus, and several of their variants are discussed in *GTSS*, chapter 11, but for convenience we define them again here. We begin with the *excess* of a coalition S at an imputation a:

$$e(S, a) = v(S) - \sum_S a_i. \tag{12.23}$$

The excess is the difference between the amount being offered to the members of a coalition S and the amount that they could get by themselves.

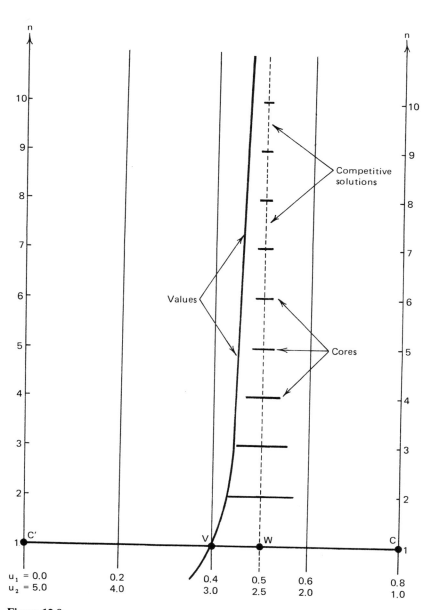

Figure 12.9
Convergence of solutions.

A simple three-person example illustrates this. Let each trader i have a utility function of the form $U_i = \sqrt{x_i y_i} + m_i$, where x_i and y_i are the amounts of two goods held by i and m_i is his store of u-money. Initial endowments are $(2,0,0)$, $(2,0,0)$, and $(0,2,0)$. Note that $x_i \geq 0$ and $y_i \geq 0$ but m_i can be positive or negative. The characteristic function is

$$v(\overline{0}) = 0, \qquad v(\overline{1}) = v(\overline{2}) = v(\overline{3}) = 0,$$
$$v(\overline{12}) = 0, \qquad v(\overline{13}) = v(\overline{23}) = 2,$$
$$v(\overline{123}) = 2\sqrt{2} \approx 2.83.$$

Suppose that there is a suggestion to split the wealth according to the imputation $a = (0.8, 1, 1)$. The excesses are

$$e(\overline{0}, a) = 0, \qquad e(\overline{1}, a) = -0.8, \qquad e(\overline{2}, a) = e(\overline{3}, a) = -1,$$
$$e(\overline{12}, a) = 0 - 1.8 = -1.8, \qquad e(\overline{13}, a) = 2 - 1.8 = 0.2,$$
$$e(\overline{23}, a) = 2 - 2 = 0,$$
$$e(\overline{123}, a) = 0,$$

An excess can be positive, negative, or zero. If it is positive, the coalition involved could obtain more by independent action than it is being offered. If it is negative, the coalition is being offered more than it could obtain by independent action.

The *nucleolus* is the imputation at which the maximum excess obtained by any coalition is minimized (see Schmeidler, 1969).

The *kernel* is the set of imputations a such that for any two traders i and j

$$\max_{\substack{i \in S \\ j \notin S}} e(S, a) = \max_{\substack{j \in T \\ i \notin T}} e(T, a). \tag{12.24}$$

In words: The maximum excess that can be obtained by a coalition S that has trader i as a member but excludes trader j equals the maximum excess that can be obtained by any coalition T that has trader j as a member but excludes trader i.

Intuitively the left side of (12.24) provides a measure of the "pressure" that trader i can bring to bear on j through his appeal to potential allies. The right side shows the pressure of j on i. An imputation in the kernel can be regarded as an equilibrium outcome of bilateral bargaining among all pairs of players. For our three-person example (figure 12.10), the kernel consists of the single point $(0.4, 0.4, 2.0)$. The maximum excess that any coalition obtains at this point is -0.4. In terms of bilateral bargaining,

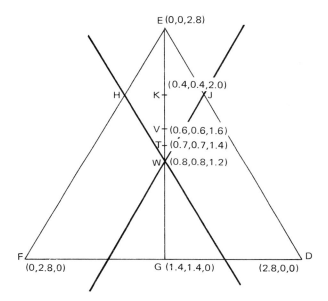

Figure 12.10
A three-person market.

each pair of traders has been willing to "split the difference" in the sense that they evenly trade off claims as represented by the excess. (The kernel is not necessarily a single point. In a market game the kernel will have some points in the core but can extend beyond it. For an example of a non-converging kernel in a replicated market game see *GTSS*, chapter 11.)

Figure 12.10 also shows the core, competitive equilibrium, and value for the three-person market. The diamond-shaped area *EHWJ* is the core. No coalition of traders can effectively rule out any imputation in this area. The point *T* is the competitive-equilibrium imputation brought about by a price system of $(1, 2)$. The kernel is at the point *K*, which is also within the core but does not include the competitive equilibrium.

The value solution, which stresses fair division and is obtained by averaging the individual's marginal contribution to all coalitions, is shown here by the point *V*.

The kernel suggests a principle of bargaining. In a sense the measurement of equal excesses implies the willingness of the bargainers to think in terms of splitting differences and compromising. The so-called bargaining set concentrates more on the straight bargaining strength of one individual against the others.

A *bargaining point* is an imputation with the property that for any trader i, any "objection" that might be raised by i can be met by a "counterobjection." An *objection* of i exists if i can find a coalition S that contains him as a member and a new imputation b such that every member of S can obtain more than they were being offered in the original imputation. Suppose that the original imputation is $a = (a_1, a_2, \ldots, a_n)$, and that there is another imputation b; then an objection can be expressed as

$$b_k > a_k \quad \text{for all } k \in S,$$
$$\sum_S b_k = v(S). \tag{12.25}$$

A *counterobjection* exists if there is another coalition T, which may have some members in common with S but excludes i, such that the members of T by independent action could guarantee themselves at least as much as they were being offered in imputations a or b. Call this third imputation g; then the counterobjection can be expressed as

$$g_k \geq b_k \quad \text{for } k \in S, T,$$
$$g_k > a_k \quad \text{for } k \in T, k \notin S, \tag{12.26}$$
$$\sum_T g_k = v(T).$$

This solution concept was suggested by observing players in an experimental game. It exists in the literature in several variants whose details will not be considered here.

A bargaining point has stability against the attempt of any individual to argue that any other is being overrewarded. If i complains that he is being underrewarded, there is always a group in a position to counter his complaint with one of their own. This stability refers to a single imputation or distribution of wealth. A specific game may have many bargaining points. The set of all bargaining points is called the *bargaining set*.

The core is always contained within a bargaining set. Any point in the core is stable in the sense that no individual i has an objection. Since no objection is possible, no counterobjection is needed to enforce stability. The kernel is also within the bargaining set, as can be seen by observing that the excess available to a counterobjecting coalition at any point in the kernel will be equal to the excess available to the coalition used in the objection.

In the game illustrated in figure 12.10 the bargaining set coincides with the core.

12.3.2 Convergence of the bargaining set

We have noted that the kernel lies within the bargaining set. Hence, if we could demonstrate that in a replicated market game the bargaining set approached a limit, we would also have shown that the kernel approached the same limit. For this reason we turn immediately to the behavior of the bargaining set in a replicated market game.

In sketching our proof that the bargaining set approaches the competitive equilibrium when there are many players in a market, we shall consider a game that looks special but can be shown to be more general than it appears to be. This is the direct market introduced in chapter 11.

Suppose that there are n types of traders in an economy, each having one unit of a (different) commodity to trade or contribute to a coalition. There is a single final product, which we might call "manna" or wealth, produced from all n commodities in the society. There is a production function $y = \phi(x_1, x_2, \ldots, x_n)$ that is homogeneous of degree 1 and continuously differentiable (i.e., in the appropriate sense, y is smooth).

We assume that each individual's welfare depends directly and linearly on the amount of the final product, y_i, that he obtains. Viewed this way, economic activity focuses on production, with each individual contributing his unit of resource to the process.

In the original market we can assume r_i individuals of type i ($i = 1$, $2, \ldots, k$). The kth replication of this market will have kr_i individuals of type i. Without loss of generality we assume that there is initially one individual of each type.

It is easy to develop a characteristic function for this market game. In production any individual is as good as any other of the same type. Thus all coalitions with the same composition of types will have equal productivity. If we define the *profile* of a coalition S by $s = (s_1, s_2, \ldots, s_n)$, then

$$v(S) = \phi(s_1, s_2, \ldots, s_n); \qquad (12.27)$$

each individual in S contributes his unit of resource to the production. We must note, however, that the production function $\phi(x)$ is continuous, whereas the characteristic function $v(S)$ is defined only for a set of integral points that could be portrayed as the lattice points on a grid. These are shown in figure 12.11 for the special case in which there are two types of individuals and the production function is given by $y = \sqrt[3]{x_1 x_2^2}$. A series of isoproduct contours is included. For a direct market game with four players of each type there are 16 coalitions with distinct profiles, and the amounts that these coalitions can obtain are shown by the 16 lattice points marked.

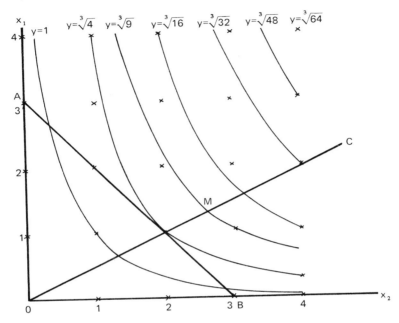

Figure 12.11
Coalition productivity with a production function $y = \sqrt[3]{x_1 x_2^2}$.

Not all coalitions are equally efficient. In particular, coalitions in which individuals of the second type are twice as numerous as individuals of the first type are the most efficient for any fixed number of individuals (this is, of course, immediately reflected in the competitive-equilibrium price ratio of 1:2). The line AB shows what can be obtained if the quantities of the two resources must sum to three. The three-person coalitions will be able to obtain the amounts indicated by the four lattice points $(3,0)$, $(2,1)$, $(1,2)$, and $(0,3)$. In this instance the coalition $(1,2)$ is the most efficient combination for any resource restriction along the line AB. If we look at the restriction that the quantities of the resources sum to four, the most efficient combination is at M, which is not integral. An optimal coalition for achieving the output denoted by M would have to consist of fractional parts of individuals, precisely 4/3 and 8/3 (in the ratio 1:2).

For market games a relationship between the kernel and the core can be established that holds for one or more replications:

THEOREM 12.1. *For a replicated market game the core is always contained within the kernel.*

Proof. Consider two traders i and j of the same type and an imputation in the core. The excess of any coalition at an imputation located within the core is less than or equal to zero. Either trader can, however, form a coalition excluding the other which is a diminished image of the whole economy and hence can achieve a maximum excess of zero. Hence every point of the core is within the kernel. ∎

This result is not true without at least one replication. This in shown in figure 12.10, where the kernel is a single point within a large core.

THEOREM 12.2.   *For any $\varepsilon > 0$ the bargaining set β of the kth replicated game $k\Gamma$ is contained in the strong ε-core for all sufficiently large k.*

The formal proof of this theorem is given in appendix B. Here we shall give a sketch that lends itself to a straightforward economic interpretation. The trader i who leads the formulation of an objection "for shorter hours and better pay" for his group S will always be in a position to bring off a successful objection that cannot be countered if all individuals are not being paid at a rate equal to their marginal productivity.

For the economy as a whole, because the production function is homogeneous of order 1, we know that payments to all individuals at competitive prices will exactly exhaust product. If there are k individuals of each type, each with a unit of his good, then

$$k \sum_{i=1}^{n} p_i = \phi(k, k, \ldots, k) = k\phi(1, 1, \ldots, 1), \tag{12.28}$$

where the $p_i = \partial\phi/\partial s_i$ are the prices. Thus in the kth iteration of the original game the imputation arising from the competitive equilibrium can be expressed as:

$$\overbrace{(p_1, p_1, \ldots, p_1}^{k}, p_2, p_2, \ldots, p_2, \ldots, p_n, p_n, \ldots, p_n).$$

Any other imputation can be expressed as an nk-dimensional vector $(a_1, a_2, \ldots, a_{nk})$, where each entry can be interpreted as the price paid for the product of that individual.

Suppose that an imputation $(a_1, a_2, \ldots, a_{nk})$ other than the competitive equilibrium has been suggested. To show that this imputation is not in the bargaining set we must construct an objection against which there is no counterobjection. This is done by finding the coalition $S \cup \{i\}$ with maximum excess for the imputation a and showing that the excess can be distributed among the members in such a way that no other group excluding i can do as well.

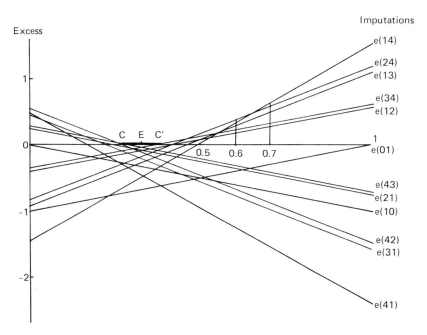

Figure 12.12
An "excess"ive illustration.

Figure 12.12 illustrates how this can be done. It shows how the argument is developed for symmetric imputations (imputations in which every in-individual of the same type receives the same amount). The calculations are based on the example in figure 12.11 of a market with two types of traders and four traders of each type. The sum of the amounts that a group consisting of a typical player of each type can obtain must equal one; hence we can represent the symmetric imputations along the abscissa in the range $(0, 1)$. The point a on the imputation line signifies that a trader of type 1 obtains a and a trader of type 2 obtains $1 - a$.

The ordinate is used to represent the excess obtained by any coalition at every imputation a. The excess for a specific coalition can be shown to vary in a linear manner as the imputation is changed. The excess achieved by a coalition with the profile $(1, 2)$ is now

$$e(12, a) = v(1, 2) - a - 2(1 - a) = \sqrt[3]{4} - 2 + a = -0.41 + a. \qquad (12.29)$$

This is denoted by the line $e(12)$. The excesses for each profile are noted.

Completely balanced coalitions, which are miniatures of the economy as a whole and in this case consist of $(1, 1)$, $(2, 2)$, and $(3, 3)$, always have an excess of zero:

$$e(kk, a) = v(k, k) - ka - k(1 - a) = k - ka - k + ka = 0. \qquad (12.30)$$

The core of this market is represented by the line CC', and the competitive equilibrium is at the point E.

Suppose that the imputation $(0.6, 0.4)$ is proposed. The coalition that has the maximum excess over this can be seen to be of profile $(2, 4)$. For the imputation $(0.7, 0.3)$ the best profile is $(1, 4)$.

The set of all of the straight lines representing the excess obtainable at different imputations by the various coalitions can be bounded by an envelope curve. This curve can be regarded as describing the excess an "ideal" coalition containing fractional traders could obtain. This is equivalent to using the production function rather than the characteristic function for calculating the excesses. In this case the excess is both continuous and differentiable. The envelope is going to be of considerable use when we wish to determine the composition of the coalition with the greatest excess with regard to a specific imputation.

The numbers a and $1 - a$ may be regarded as the going wage rates for a unit of labor or input from individuals of types 1 and 2 at a specific imputation. The ideal coalition with maximum excess $(a, a, \ldots, 1 - a, 1 - a, \ldots)$ can be found immediately by the following rule:

maximize $\sqrt[3]{x_1 x_2^2} - ax_1 - (1 - a)x_2$, where $x_1 \leq 4$ and $x_2 \leq 4$. (12.31)

This is similar to the familiar profit-maximizing condition for a firm in a competitive market.

In the construction of an objection, as we can see from the maximization, it is in the interest of the leader of the objection to use the largest of the coalitions with maximum excess. (This is like a firm with constant returns to scale expanding continuously until some resources are finally exhausted.)

Given the ideal coalition for the construction of an objection, we select one of the actual coalitions available at the lattice points nearest to that coalition. The key aspect of the proof now follows. The leader of the objection gathers his group together. He offers them all their (ideal) marginal productivity to the coalition *plus* a small bonus. The bonus is determined by the difference between the amounts being offered at the imputation a minus their marginal productivity. This latter amount is a measure of each person's extra worth to the coalition. As long as the leader retains a small fraction of the bonus, he is better off than at the imputation against which he is leading a challenge; he can use the remainder of the bonus to pay the others more.

Specifically the leader will use his extra resources to pay a bonus to all members of his group after they are paid their ideal marginal productivity. The difference between types who are fully used and types who are not fully used is that the former are still in demand and bring a greater net productivity to the coalition than the latter, at the wages at imputation a.

Consider the imputation $(0.6, 0.4)$ in figure 12.12. From (12.31) we obtain

$$\frac{1}{3}\left(\frac{x_2}{x_1}\right)^{2/3} = 0.6 \quad \text{and} \quad \frac{2}{3}\left(\frac{x_1}{x_2}\right)^{1/3} \geq 0.4, \text{ where } x_2 = 0.4, \tag{12.32}$$

from which we deduce that the ideal coalition consists of 1.656 traders of the first type and 4 of the second. The excess is $2.98 - 0.6(1.656) - 0.4(4) = 0.39$. Suppose that a trader of the second type leads an objection. He cannot use an ideal coalition with fractional players, so he uses the coalition $(2, 4)$, which has an excess of 0.38. The ideal marginal productivity for the coalition $(1.656, 4)$ is 0.6 and $\frac{2}{3}(0.745) = 0.497$. The leader of the objection (say the first trader of the second type) may propose to pay his group

$$(0.6 + \varepsilon/6, 0.6 + \varepsilon/6, 0.4 + \varepsilon/6, 0.497 + \varepsilon/6, 0.497 + \varepsilon/6, 0.497 + \varepsilon/6),$$

where $\varepsilon = 3.18 - 2(0.6) - 4(0.1) - 3(0.497) = 0.09$. When the market has been replicated sufficiently, the ratios in the integral coalitions become sufficiently close to any ideal coalition.

It remains to establish that there can be no counterobjection to an objection with this structure. Any individual not in the objecting group can lead the counterobjection. He can include in his group anyone except the leader of the objection. He must pay anyone not in the objecting group at least as much as they were offered in the original imputation. If he uses anyone in the objecting group, he must pay them at least as much as the leader of the objection offered them. Even if he personally were as badly underpaid originally as the leader of the objection, however, he cannot form a coalition with more excess than the objectors. Hence his wage bill will more than exhaust total product.

These observations hold for symmetric imputations. It can be shown that essentially the same reasoning holds for nonsymmetric imputations; the objector will raise the payments in his group until they slightly exceed the marginal productivity of its members in the largest coalition with the most efficient profile. That profile is used by the original objector specifically to prevent any counterobjector from forming an equally cheap, equally efficient coalition.

In the example it is easy to check that the counterobjector must be one of the two players of the first type not used in the objection, and no effective counterobjection to the objection to $(0.6, 0.4)$ exists.

12.3.3 An interpretation

The bargaining set catches the essence of political bargaining, and to some extent the adversary process, in the context of a larger society. The active proponent of change (the leader of the objection) lines up his forces calling for change. This challenge to the status quo invokes a response, and others come forward in opposition to form the adversary group.

The conditions under which a price system will emerge in this process are quite general, in the sense that as long as the usual conditions for the existence of a competitive equilibrium are satisfied and there are sufficient individuals in the economy, we can vary the specific definition of the bargaining set to allow for more than one leader of the objection or counterobjection and to permit some limitations on or variations of coalition formation without stopping the emergence of the price system.

The coalitions called for are similar to those temporary political coalitions that come into being to block a specific rezoning proposal or new local tax, in which the really active opponents and proponents are few in number and the goal is relatively simple.

The kernel reflects bilateral bargaining power more than an adversary process embedded in a broader context. The focus is on equitable interaction between specific individuals, and in particular it stresses "equal work for equal pay." If we were to consider organizations such as labor unions as individual players, then in general the economic model would not have sufficient players for any theorem depending upon large numbers to be particularly relevant; hence the convergence of the kernel is of less economic interest than that of the bargaining set. The kernel, however, does provide a good portrayal of bilateral struggle among large unions in which each pair examines the wage structure in terms of a pairwise comparison of "fairness."

12.3.4 An experimental game

As part of a series of simple experiments, the game whose characteristic function is described below has been used to solicit opinions from various audiences concerning how they feel the gains from cooperation should be shared (Shubik, 1975, 1978a, 1979a):

$$v(\overline{0}) = 0,$$
$$v(\overline{1}) = v(\overline{2}) = v(\overline{3}) = 0,$$
$$v(\overline{12}) = 0, \qquad v(\overline{13}) = v(\overline{23}) = 4,$$
$$v(\overline{123}) = 4.$$

It is easy to see that there is a core, nucleolus, kernel, and bargaining set at $(0, 0, 4)$ and a value at $(2/3, 2/3, 8/3)$. There is also a von Neumann–Morgenstern stable set consisting of the line from $(0, 0, 4)$ to $(2, 2, 0)$. This is a market game, and all markets that it represents have competitive equilibria with payoffs at $(0, 0, 4)$. A point of the form $(a, a, 4 - 2a)$ with $a > 0$ was the predominant selection.

Where the core appears to be glaringly nonsymmetric, it is not selected. Maschler (1976) suggests the same; he gives an instance in which the bargaining set appears to be more plausible.

12.4 General Exchange Economies

12.4.1 Convergence of the core
The discussion of the "shrinking" of the core in section 12.1 was restricted to a two-sided market. Debreu and Scarf (1963) have provided a clear general proof of the convergence of the core under replication to the competitive equilibria. They stated that "an entirely straightforward extension of our results on the core to an economy in which production is possible can be given." Unfortunately, as argued in chapter 13, there are several serious problems in the modeling of production, and a satisfying extension is by no means straightforward.

12.4.2 Other considerations
The method of replication utilized by Edgeworth, Shubik, and Debreu and Scarf is intuitively straightforward and captures the concept of many "butchers, bakers, and candlestick makers." But even Edgeworth was not satisfied with perfect replication; he felt that some small variation should be allowed for.

Furthermore, if our concern happens to be with the relationship between game-theoretic solutions and the competitive equilibrium for economies with large numbers of small traders, a measure-theoretic approach in which the individual trader is of measure zero has much to recommend it as a mathematical portrayal of individual powerlessness combined with group influence in the mass market. Aumann (1966) pioneered this approach, and for market games with a continuum of traders he established an equivalence theorem showing that the core points and the imputations selected by the competitive price system coincide. Anderson (1978), Mas-Colell (1979), and others have extended this work, taking into account the size of the blocking coalitions needed and obtaining bounds on the degree of noncompetitiveness of an economy. Hildenbrand (1982) provides an excellent survey of the many investigations of core properties including conditions on types of traders, differentiability and smoothness, and nonconvexity of preference sets.

Utilizing the basic work on values of nonatomic games by Aumann and Shapley (1974), Aumann (1975) proved that with sufficient smoothness an equivalence result can be established between the no-side-payment values and the competitive equilibria. Mas-Colell (1977c) provided an asymptotic version of Aumann's result. S. Hart (1977) considered both side-payment and no-side-payment market games without assuming differentiability. He established that in a perfectly competitive market every value allocation is competitive. Dubey and Neyman (1984) proved the coincidence of the core, the value, and the competitive equilibrium as a single result.

What should hold particular interest for the nonspecialized economic theorist is that these results begin to provide an extensive conceptual sensitivity analysis for the attractiveness of the price system in a large economy under many conditions, including different solution concepts such as the core, the value, and the noncooperative equilibrium.

12.4.3 On the rate of convergence of the core
The core is a cooperative game concept, and in the form presented in this chapter the models of exchange hardly form the basis for an insightful investigation of oligopolistic behavior. Nevertheless, "How many is many?" is such an important question for the study of competition and collusion that it is worth considering how fast the core shrinks.

Shapley (1975) provided an example of a slowly converging core for markets with differentiable, strictly concave utility functions. He considered the glove market, but instead of a nondifferentiable corner (implying complete complementarity between left- and right-hand gloves), he allowed the contours to be differentiable but controlled the steepness of the curvature, which enabled him to construct an arbitrarily slow speed of convergence.

Debreu (1975) established that for regular economies only a set of initial allocations of measure zero will yield cores that converge more slowly than $1/k$, where k is the replication number (see also Grodal, 1975). Aumann (1977) showed that the condition of genericity in Debreu's theorem (i.e., almost always rather than always) cannot be removed for any level of differentiability.

I conjecture that an analogous result holds for strategic market games in which quantities are the strategic variables, even though experience with Bertrand–Edgeworth models indicates immediate convergence upon one replication. Thus, at best, competition is fully present for $n = 2$, but "almost always" is approached as $1/n$. It is my belief that these insights have policy significance. It is virtually always desirable in markets or even in other institutions to have at least two groups competing—and most of the benefits from competition are obtained somewhere between 2 and 20 almost always.

Notes to chapter 12

1. Some care is required in comparing sizes of sets that lie in spaces of different dimensions. In the present case we are implicitly making use of the "natural" mapping: $(x, y) \leftrightarrow (x, x, \ldots, x, y, y, \ldots, y)$ between points in the two-person payoff space and symmetric points in the $2n$-person payoff space. However, this mapping does not preserve (Euclidean) distance. Thus the distance from $(0, 1)$ to $(1, 0)$ is $\sqrt{2n}$. Unless we state otherwise, the size comparisons implied by our use of words such as "shrink" and "converge" refer to the image sets in the two-person payoff space.

2. If the contour from R to C^1 is a straight line, no improvement is possible. In this case C^1 is actually a competitive allocation and is not blockable by any coalition.

3. But see note 2.

4. The glove market of section 11.2.3 has a nonshrinking core. More generally, one can construct a market in which there are no vital coalitions of size greater than k. Then the core will remain fixed for $n \geq k - 1$. The horse market in chapter 9 also has a nonshrinking core.

5. If the utility contours are not differentiable, one of the intervals (but never both!) may collapse to the single point X. But then we can find a nearby price ray that properly crosses both contours and use it instead. One of the intervals may also be unbounded; this creates no difficulty.

6. Differentiability is important here. For example, the utility function in section

12.2.3 is not differentiable at $x = y$, and the nonuniqueness of the competitive prices and imputations for the case $r = 1$ is the direct result.

7. Although we have discussed the idea of the replication of an economy before, as a reminder we define it as follows: Let k identical economies be regarded as a single economy with kn traders of n different types. The competitive price vector of the enlarged market is just π, while the competitive imputation is just the kn-dimensional vector $(w, w, \ldots, w)$ (k times). The characteristic function of the enlarged market is homogeneous of the first degree, in the sense that $v(hS) = hv(S)$, where hS denotes a coalition having exactly h times as many traders of each type as S.

8. We illustrate with a three-person example. We assume that pairs 12, 13, and 23 can divide 50¢, 50¢, and 80¢, respectively, failing a general agreement to divide $1. Player 1 is in the weakest position. His marginal worth to the coalition $\overline{123}$ is just 20¢; to $\overline{12}$ and $\overline{13}$ he is worth 50¢; and to the "coalition" 1, consisting of himself alone, he contributes nothing. Averaging these numbers (giving equal weight to each size of coalition, not to each coalition) we find player 1's value to be $23\frac{1}{3}$¢. A similar calculation gives $38\frac{1}{3}$¢ to player 2 and the same to player 3. This imputation happens to be outside the core, since the coalition $\overline{23}$ can be better alone.

9. Use of the classical characteristic function implies in effect that a coalition always expects the worst as far as the actions of outside players are concerned. In the present economic context this "worst" is simply a boycott, involving no special costs to the outside players. In other contexts the most damaging threats might be so costly to make that they should be discounted in determining the worth of a coalition. It is therefore advisable, in a general value theory based on a characteristic function, to recast the definition in terms of "optimum threats" in the sense of Nash (1953).

10. For example, if $r = l + 1$, the members of R, faced with total defeat under pure competition, might select two of their number to withdraw from the market, thus turning the tables on L. This behavior would not be Pareto-optimal, since only $l - 1$ pairs of gloves could be formed, but the threat is credible enough and might well raise the price for right-handed gloves.

The reader will recognize this as a standard price-support tactic in situations where collusion is possible. Of course, the value of the game does not directly consider such details of process, but it recognizes and measures the coalition potentials that make such maneuvers effective.

11. The method of derivation, in brief, is to multiply the summands in (12.5) by $(r + l)!/r!l!$ to obtain truncated sums of binomial coefficients that can be estimated with the aid of Stirling's formula.

13 Extensions of Market Games

13.1 Introduction

In this chapter we consider a number of modeling questions concerning the representation of economic systems by market games. The market game and the exchange (or exchange and production) economy on which it is based are models at a high level of abstraction. They suppress institutional detail and even abstract away information that is present in studies of exchange economies.

In an exchange economy with m commodities and n traders the analysis exemplified by applications of the Edgeworth box is based on a description of the economy in $m \times (n-1)$ dimensions. The game-theoretic approaches, in contrast, are based on an analysis of the combinatorics of cooperation in a space of n dimensions, where the details concerning preference or indifference to specific bundles of commodities have been minimized. Figures 12.3 and 12.4 provide examples of the mapping from the distribution space to the payoff space.

Putting the matter as simply as possible, if individuals have preferences defined over all endowments that can be represented by a utility scale, then the game theorist who wants to investigate the core, value, or any other solution needs to know only the feasible set of trading outcomes in the payoff space, in particular the shapes of the 2^n sets of feasible outcomes to all coalitions. There are, however, many different exchange economies, some with more commodities than others, that give rise to the same market game.

The above remarks hold for economies with production as well as exchange. When production is considered, however, the economist faces new difficulties in modeling the economy as a market game. In the mathematical analysis of a price system with production and exchange, it is well known that when the production sets are cones, no profits are recorded by the firms; hence ownership of the production technology is irrelevant to the analysis of the model. When the production sets are convex but not cones, profits appear and must be distributed. This is easy to do in the context of the general-equilibrium model of the economy with a price system. All individuals are simply assigned shares in all firms. The profit assigned to a firm is the difference between the market values of its outputs and its inputs. Each firm pays out its profits to stockholders in proportion to the amount of shares held. This nonstrategic approach to the economy solves by assumption three problems that are not solved in the game-theoretic formulation of production and exchange: the existence of a price system, the definition of profits to a firm, and the control aspects of owning voting shares.

A cooperative-game model with convex production sets must either represent firms as players or define production technologies usable under specified conditions. In some sense production becomes a local public good. The model must also be explicit about the nature of ownership shares. If they are modeled explicitly, then is there any significance to the vote? We shall return to this point in section 13.3.

The handling of the nonconvexity of preference or production sets will be important for attempts to extend core theory to situations with more general preferences, set-up or entry costs, or local public goods. The possiblity of using quasicores and ε-cores is discussed in sections 13.2 and 13.4.

The general-equilibrium analysis introduces an array of futures markets trading in contingent goods in order to take care of exogenous uncertainty. The application of cooperative-game models to replicated economies with uncertainty requires a specification of the treatment of risk as numbers increase. This is considered in section 13.5.

A natural extension of core theory within the confines of market games would be to the investigation of oligopolistic competition. This is considered in section 13.6 but there are considerable conceptual and modeling difficulties involved. In particular, we must restrict ourselves to statics, even though most of the interesting questions concerning oligopoly involve dynamics: The study of oligopolistic competition is most naturally done in the context of explicit market structures.

The triumph of general-equilibrium theory was to present a model along with results at a preinstitutional level. Unfortunately, when some or all players are large in relation to the economy, the market structure can make a difference. If this is the case, then even for core theory one should first construct a strategic market game (see chapter 15), then define a cooperative game on the basis of this strategic form. The cooperative game will not be the same as the market game constructed directly from information concerning preferences, endowments, and production technology with no market structure given. Results of core theory based on market games can be misleading and paradoxical when compared with our intuitive view of oligopoly because relevant details have been thrown away by our failure to model strategic structure.

13.2 Quasicores and Nonconvex Preferences

The discussion in the last three chapters was in terms of individual traders with convex preference sets. Without convexity neither a competitive equilibrium nor a core may exist. However, the general tenor of the results here is that nonconvexity in preference sets is economically unimportant when the number of participating individuals is large.

More specifically, we show under quite general conditions that even if the true core cannot be assured, because of nonconvexity, nevertheless certain quasicores will always appear when the number of traders in the market is large enough. These quasicores are characterized by the requirement that recontracting traders must show a definite positive profit before being permitted to block a proposed final allocation. A distinction must be made ("strong" vs. "weak" ε-cores) depending on whether the ε-threshold is applied to the whole set of recontracting traders or to each one individually. The conditions for existence are somewhat different in the two cases.

The ε-cores, in a double limit process involving both ε and the number of traders, shrink down in Edgeworthian style onto the competitive allocations of an economy obtained by "concavification" of the original utility functions (Shubik and Wooders, 1982). In the original market these allocations, though feasible, need not be Pareto-optimal. The associated prices, on the other hand, may lead under individual optimization only to infeasible allocations—that is, to mismatched supply and demand. The prices will at least be in *pseudoequilibrium*, however, in the sense that if the excess demand for any good is positive, then another scheme of individual optimizations can be found that makes it negative, and vice versa. (Nonuniqueness of optimum demand schedules is to be expected when preferences are nonconvex.)

Recently attention has been focused on the economic implications of nonconvex preferences. Unfortunately convexity is too often assumed in economics merely because tools for handling the opposite assumption have been lacking. Not the least important feature of the approach adopted here lies in the contribution to the mathematical technology of nonconcave utility functions. We have already mentioned the device of concavification; we shall also introduce a condition of "spannability" that helps restore some of the regularity lost when concavity is abandoned, and that seems potentially useful beyond the immediate context of cores and competitive equilibria.

The mathematical results we shall present are to a certain extent illustrative, rather than comprehensive, since they rest on two fairly drastic assumptions in an otherwise very general setting. This is partly a matter of technical expedience. It is often good policy, especially in the social sciences, to work with simplified models in order to gain insight and discover techniques for tackling more complex situations. But we should emphasize that our present assumptions appear to have no direct bearing on the main subject of this investigation, namely, the effects of nonconvex preferences on the existence of cores.

First, as in previous chapters, we shall assume that in addition to the actual commodities in exchange there is available a "money" that can be separated out of individual utility functions in the following way:

$$u^i(x_1^i, x_2^i, \ldots, x_m^i, \xi^i) \equiv U^i(x_1^i, x_2^i, \ldots, x_m^i) + \lambda_i \xi^i. \tag{13.1}$$

Here x_j^i is the amount of the jth commodity held by the ith individual, ξ^i is his "money" level, and λ_i is a constant. We assume that (13.1) holds to a sufficient degree of approximation for a range of values of ξ^i sufficiently wide to encompass the action of the model. Like the actual commodities, "money" is assumed to be perfectly divisible and freely transferable; unlike them, it is not constrained by an a priori lower bound.

It is worth reemphasizing that this idealized money, though sometimes called "transferable utility," does not entail interpersonal comparisons of utility at the psychological level. Money serves merely to decouple individual tastes. If a dollar is taken from millionaire X, then his utility is diminished by one dollar's worth of X-utils; if it is given to begger Y, then the latter's utility is increased by one dollar's worth of Y-utils. There is no psychological comparison of "degrees of happiness." The key phrase "one dollar's worth" has meaning because of (13.1), which is assumed to hold separately for each individual.

The second assumption is that all individuals in the exchange economy have equal tastes. Formally this means that their utility functions u^i are interrelated by order-preserving transformations f_{ij}:

$$u^i(x_1, x_2, \ldots, x_m, \xi) \equiv f_{ij}(u^j(x_1, x_2, \ldots, x_m, \xi)) \quad \text{for all } i, j. \tag{13.2}$$

Since we are free to recalibrate the individual utility scales, we can express all preferences by means of a single function u. This kind of assumption is often made in economic modeling.

It will become clear that "equal tastes" do not symmetrize the model to the point of triviality. For one thing, the initial endowments of the traders may be different. Moreover, the solutions that one gets with nonconvex preferences are often nonsymmetric even when the initial holdings are identical; that is, the "economics" of the situation can drive identical traders to behave differently.

The advantage of assuming (13.2) is that it will allow us to write down explicitly certain optimizing allocations, beginning at (13.17) below. This simplifies the mathematical arguments in several places, but similar proofs of similar theorems have been carried out without this aid (Starr, 1969; Hildenbrand, 1974; Anderson, 1978).

The combined effect of our assumptions is to permit us to postulate a single utility function for goods and money of the form

$$u(x_1, x_2, \ldots, x_m, \xi) \equiv U(x_1, x_2, \ldots, x_m) + \xi, \tag{13.3}$$

applicable to all traders in the economy.

13.2.1 An example
The following example is intended to give some idea of the role played by money and equal tastes in a market with nonconvex preferences. The model is highly symmetric, having n identical traders and two identical goods, but the competitive and core solutions, when they exist, will require nonsymmetric behavior on the part of the traders.

The nonconcavity in the preference sets (see figure 13.1) comes from preferred ratios in the consumption process. For a numerical utility function we take

$$U(x) = \max[\min(2x_1, x_2), \min(x_1, 2x_2)]. \tag{13.4}$$

The traders are assumed to start with one unit of each good apiece.

For example, the goods might be gin and tonic. Each trader is indifferent as between weak drinks (1:2) and strong drinks (2:1), but he will not take both and will reject intermediate (or more extreme) concoctions.

In looking for a competitive equilibrium we first observe that unequal prices will never work, whether or not there is money available, since the traders would all want to buy the cheaper good and sell the other. With equal prices, however, a competitive allocation can sometimes be reached. In fact, if n is even, each person can trade 1/3 unit of one good for an equal amount of the other and end up with an efficient bundle—either

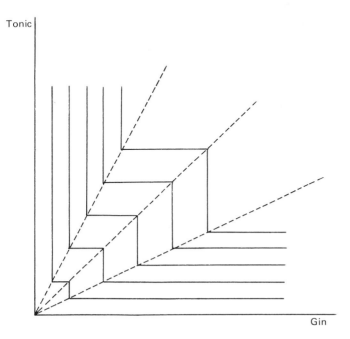

Figure 13.1
Gin and tonic.

(4/3, 2/3) or (2/3, 4/3). The result is worth 4/3 to everyone. (Of course, it may require cooperative action or a determined hostess to decide who is to get which drink!)

If n is odd, there is no series of exchanges (at equal prices) that gives everyone an efficient ratio, and without money there can be no competitive equilibrium. Rather, we have the pseudoequilibrium situation noted above, in which the excess demand for either commodity can be construed as either positive or negative but not zero.

Introducing money changes the picture somewhat. In the even case the competitive prices and final utility levels remain as before, but the allocative possibilities are opened up. Because of the first-degree homogeneity of (13.4) we can let some of the traders liquidate their holdings for cash, provided others spend an equal amount to increase their consumption and all stick to efficient ratios. In the odd case this same option works to circumvent the previous difficulty in matching supply and demand, and it is easy to find feasible competitive allocations. For example, one person might sell out completely, leaving an even number of traders to divide the goods efficiently. The final payoff, as in the even case, will be exactly 4/3 to each trader. Thus money can overcome the "ill" effects of nonconvexity.

The homogeneity of (13.4) is crucial to this result. Had we assumed diminishing returns to scale, money would no longer "save" the odd case. To show this we modify the utility function to be the square root of the function is (13.4). Then the equilibrium price for each good is (as it turns out) precisely $\sqrt{1/12}$. What is important is not the number but the fact that each trader has only two ways to optimize, neither involving any net money transfer. In short, money would be irrelevant, and there would be no competitive solution.

What of the cores? Returning to the original function (13.4) and assuming $n = 2$, one can easily determine the Edgeworth contract curve for the no-money case. It proves to be a rather spectacular "curve": four triangular regions arranged in a ring. The core, its image in the utility space, is the bent line QPR in figure 13.2. It includes the competitive payoff P and is included in the set of Pareto-optimal payoffs SPT. The introduction of money is not easily shown in the commodity space because of the added dimension, but in the utility space the effect is simply to move the Pareto set out to the straight line with slope -1 passing through the point P, of which the segment $Q'PR'$ constitutes the core.

For $n > 2$ the recontracting principle takes over with a vengeance; the shrinking is immediate and total. The cores actually contain no points other than the competitive payoffs. That is, when n is odd and side payments are not permitted, there is no core at all; in all other cases the core is a single point. This drastic curtailment of the core is rather atypical and may be ascribed to the simple polyhedral form chosen for the indifference map.

These assertions about cores are not meant to be obvious. The proofs, given in appendix C, may be of interest to the reader wishing experience with the techniques of core analysis.

Speaking informally and intuitively, a coreless game ought to be more competitive and harder to stabilize than one with a core. Indeed, in any game an observed outcome falling outside the core would seem to admit just two interpretations: it is a *transient event* in some dynamic process, or it is evidence of a *social structure* among the players that inhibits some coalitions from developing their full potential. On the other hand, an observed outcome in the core tells us nothing about the organization of society. The core is sociologically neutral.

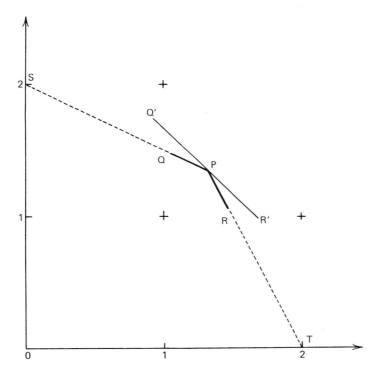

Figure 13.2
The utility space. The Pareto-optimal set is SPT, the competitive payoff P, the core QPR (with side payments the core is $Q'R'$).

13.2.2 Quasicores

The mathematical results presented here depend on the device of enlarging the core by a small amount. Two related concepts are needed. If ε is a small positive number, we define the *strong ε-core* as the set of payoff vectors α satisfying

$$\sum_s \alpha_i \geq v(S) - \varepsilon \quad \text{for all } S \subset N, \tag{13.5}$$

where s denotes the number of elements of S. We define the *weak ε-core* as the set of payoff vectors satisfying

$$\sum_s \alpha_i \geq v(S) - s\varepsilon \quad \text{for all } S \subset N. \tag{13.6}$$

It is easy to verify the following chain of set-inclusions:

weak ε-core $\supset$ strong ε-core $\supset$ weak $\frac{\varepsilon}{n}$-core $\supset \cdots \supset$ core,

where n is the number of players in the game.

These quasicores are not merely technical devices, looking toward an eventual convergence theorem. They provide a way, for example, of taking into account the costs of coalition formation. Under the weak definition the costs would depend on the size of the coalition; in the strong case there would be a fixed charge. Alternatively we might regard the organizational costs as negligible, or as already included in $v(s)$, but view the ε or $s\varepsilon$ as a threshold below which the blocking maneuver—the actual exercise of "group rationality"—is not considered worth the trouble.

13.2.3 The market model

Let there be m different commodities and t_0 different types of traders, distinguished by the stocks of goods they hold at the beginning of the trading session. The initial endowment of a player of type t will be denoted by a vector

$$a^t = (a_1^t, a_2^t, \ldots, a_m^t).$$

If S is a set of players and s_t denotes the number of players in S of type t, then the aggregate initial endowment of S may be written as follows:

$$a(s) = \sum_{t=1}^{t_0} s_t a^t,$$

where s, called the *profile* of S, is an abbreviation for the integer vector $(s_1, s_2, \ldots, s_{t_0})$. The total supply of goods in the game is then $a(n)$, where n is the profile of the set N of all players.

At the conclusion of trading, the players hold bundles x^i $(i \in N)$, which must account for the total quantities initially present in the market. Thus we have

$$x^i \in E_+^m \quad \text{and} \quad \sum_N x^i = a(n), \tag{13.7}$$

where E_+^m denotes the closed positive orthant of Euclidean m-space. Subject to these constraints, all final allocations are assumed possible. (In particular, the outcome is not assumed to be symmetric between players of the same type.) In addition, there can be direct transfers of money among the players. Thus, if U is the common utility measure for goods from (13.3), the possible final payoffs will take the form

$\alpha_i = U(x^i) - \pi_i \quad$ for all $i \in N$,

subject to (13.7) and $\sum_N \pi_i = 0$.

By symmetry, the characteristic function depends only on the profiles of the coalitions. Since internal money transfers will cancel, we have

$$v_U(s) = \sup_{y^\nu} \sum_{\nu=1}^{s} U(y^\nu), \quad \text{with all } y^\nu \in E_+^m \text{ and } \sum y^\nu = a(s). \tag{13.8}$$

Players outside the coalition do not affect this value, since they can neither force others nor be forced into dealings with coalition members.[1]

To ensure that the "sup" in (13.8) is finite, we shall assume from the outset that U is bounded above on compact subsets of E_+^m or, equivalently, that there is a continuous function K such that $U(x) \leq K(x)$ for all $x \in E_+^m$. (Compare condition (13.10) below.)

Let $\Gamma_U(n)$ designate the game we have just defined. The subscript U will serve to distinguish it from an auxiliary game to be introduced in section 13.2.4.

An allocation $\{x^{*i}\}$ satisfying (13.7) is called *competitive* if there exists a price vector $p = (p_1, p_2, \ldots, p_m)$ such that, for each individual $i \in N$, the bundle x^{*i} maximizes the expression

$$U(x^i) - p \cdot (x^i - a^i). \tag{13.9}$$

The numbers p_j are called *equilibrium prices*. Observe that there are no "budget" conditions $p \cdot (x^i - a^i) = 0$, since our money enters directly into the complete utility function (13.3). Had we approached this definition via a budgeted money-of-account, taking our present "valuable" money to be the $(m + 1)$st commodity, then the usual definition would give us equilibrium prices $p'_1, p'_2, \ldots, p'_{m+1}$, related to those above by $p_j = p'_j / p'_{m+1}$. Thus the actual numbers p_j are significant, not just their ratios, as is evident from the form of (13.9).

Let α_i^* denote the maximum of (13.9) for a given equilibrium price vector p^*. Then it is a simple matter to show that the vector α^*, which we shall refer to as a *competitive imputation*, is in the core of the game $\Gamma_U(n)$. Indeed we have at once

$$\sum_N \alpha_i^* = \sum_N U(x^{*i}) \leq v_U(n),$$

verifying the feasibility requirement. To verify the core inequalities we fix $S \subset N$ and $\varepsilon > 0$ and, using (13.8), find bundles $y^i \in E_+^m$ such that

$$\sum_s U(y^i) \geq v_U(s) - \varepsilon \quad \text{and} \quad \sum_s y^i = a(s).$$

Since α^* maximizes, we have

$$\alpha_i^* \geq U(y^i) - p^* \cdot (y^i - a^i) \quad \text{for each } i \in S.$$

Summing, we obtain

$$\sum_s \alpha_i^* \geq \sum_s U(y^i) \geq v_U(\mathfrak{d}) - \varepsilon.$$

Since this is valid for arbitrarily small ε, it follows that $\sum_s \alpha_i \geq v(S)$ for all $S \subset N$, which completes the proof of the following theorem.

THEOREM 13.1.   *Every competitive imputation is in the core.*

We remark that this result does not depend on equal tastes, since in the proof just given each $U(\cdot)$ could be replaced by $U^i(\cdot)$. It should also be emphasized that nothing has been said about the existence of a competitive solution.

13.2.4 Concavification of the utility function
For the theorem on weak ε-cores we shall impose almost no conditions on the function U. It need not be concave, continuous, or monotonic, and it may be either bounded or unbounded. We shall require, however, that its asymptotic growth be no more than linear, and that it be bounded from below on all compact subsets of E_+^m. To this end we assume the existence of a linear function L_0 and a continuous function K_0 such that the inequalities

$$K_0(x) \leq U(x) \leq L_0(x), \tag{13.10}$$

hold for all x in the commodity space E_+^m.

Let us now define a function C on E_+^m as follows:

$$C(x) = \sup \sum_{h=1}^{m+1} \lambda_h U(y^h),$$

$$\text{where} \quad \lambda_h \geq 0, \quad \sum \lambda_h = 1, \quad y^h \in E_+^m, \quad \sum \lambda_h y^h = x. \tag{13.11}$$

The finiteness of this "sup" is ensured by (13.10), indeed we have $C(x) \leq L_0(x)$. The function C is concave, it majorizes U, and it is the least such function.[2] It is continuous at every interior point x of E_+^m and possesses a linear support there, that is, a linear function L such that $L \geq C$ and $L(x) = C(x)$. If the "sup" in (13.11) is actually achieved for all x, we say that U is *spannable*.

We intend to use C as an artificial utility function in defining a *concave majorant game* $\Gamma_C(\mathfrak{n})$, identical in every other respect to the game $\Gamma_U(\mathfrak{n})$

previously defined. The characteristic function v_C has a simple explicit form. Since players have identical, concave utilities (hence convex preferences), a coalition achieves maximum profit by dividing its total endowment equally among its members, and we have

$$v_C(\jmath) = sC\left(\frac{a(\jmath)}{s}\right).$$
(13.12)

We see that $v_C(\jmath)$, like $a(\jmath)$, is homogeneous of degree one:

$$v_C(k\jmath) = kv_C(\jmath) \quad (k = 0, 1, 2, \ldots),$$
(13.13)

indicating constant returns to scale to a uniformly expanding coalition in the artificial game $\Gamma_C(n)$. For the true game $\Gamma_U(n)$, on the other hand, we do not have homogeneity in general, but only the inequality

$$v_U(k\jmath) \geq kv_U(\jmath) \quad (k = 0, 1, 2, \ldots),$$
(13.14)

a consequence of superadditivity. Our results on the existence of ε-cores will hinge on showing that $v_U(\jmath)$ is nevertheless "almost" homogeneous, in a sense made specific in the lemmas accompanying theorems 13.2 and 13.4.

13.2.5 Existence of the weak ε-core
We consider exchange economies based on utility functions U satisfying (13.10).

THEOREM 13.2. *For every profile $n = (n_1, n_2, \ldots, n_{t_0})$ and for every $\varepsilon > 0$, there exists a constant k_0 such that all games $\Gamma_U(kn)$ with $k \geq k_0$ possess weak ε-cores.*

LEMMA ON WEAK ε-HOMOGENEITY OF v_U. *For every profile $\jmath$ and for every $\varepsilon > 0$, there exists a constant $k_0(\jmath, \varepsilon)$ such that*

$$v_C(\jmath) - \varepsilon \leq \frac{1}{k}v_U(k\jmath) \leq v_C(\jmath)$$
(13.15)

holds for all $k \geq k_0$.

Proof. Fix $\jmath$ and ε, and let $x^* = a(\jmath)/s$. Then, by (13.12), $v_C(\jmath) = sC(x^*)$. Using (13.11), find a convex representation $x^* = \sum \lambda_h y^h$ such that

$$C(x^*) \leq \sum_{h=1}^{m+1} \lambda_h U(y^h) + \frac{\varepsilon}{2s}.$$
(13.16)

Let l_h denote the greatest integer in $ks\lambda_h$ $(h = 1, 2, \ldots, m + 1)$. Then

$$\sum l_h y^h \le ks \sum \lambda_h y^h = ksx^* = a(k\mathfrak{s}). \tag{13.17}$$

Thus, in a coalition with profile $k\mathfrak{s}$ it is possible to assign the bundle y^1 to the first l_1 players, y^2 to the next l_2 players, and so on. If "$<$" holds in (13.17), there will be goods left over after this allotment, but there will also be at least one player left over. Allotting the excess goods equally among the extra players gives them each an allocation y^* that lies within the convex hull of $\{y^h\}$. Since there are at most m extra players, we can write down an upper bound for the amount that such an allotment of excess might cause to be deducted from the total coalition utility:

$$B = m \cdot \left| \min_{y^*} K_0(y^*) \right|, \quad \text{where } y^* \in \text{convex hull of } \{y^h\}.$$

This is the only use we shall make of the function K_0 introduced in (13.10). The important fact about this bound is that it is independent of k.

We have thus described a feasible allocation whose value to the coalition is at least $\sum l_h U(y^h) - B$. Thus

$$v_U(k\mathfrak{s}) \ge \sum l_h U(y^h) - B.$$

Applying (13.16) and the definitions of λ_h and x^*, we obtain

$$v_U(k\mathfrak{s}) \ge ks \sum \lambda_h U(y^h) + \sum (l_h - ks\lambda_h) U(y^h) - B$$

$$\ge ksC(x^*) - \frac{k\varepsilon}{2} + \sum (l_h - ks\lambda_h) U(y^h) - B$$

$$\ge kv_C(\mathfrak{s}) - \frac{k\varepsilon}{2} - \sum |U(y^h)| - B$$

$$= kv_C(\mathfrak{s}) - \frac{k\varepsilon}{2} - \frac{k_0\varepsilon}{2},$$

where

$$k_0 = \frac{2}{\varepsilon} \left(\sum |U(y^h)| + B \right) \ge 0.$$

Then $k \ge k_0$ implies that

$$v_U(k\mathfrak{s}) \ge kv_C(\mathfrak{s}) - k\varepsilon,$$

giving us one side of (13.15). The other side is a consequence of (13.13) and the general inequality $v_U \leq v_C$. This completes the proof of the lemma. ∎

Proof of theorem 13.2. Let α be the payoff vector associated with a competitive allocation of the concave game $\Gamma_C(n)$. For example, let $x^* = a(n)/n$ and take

$$\alpha_i = C(x^*) - p^* \cdot (x^* - a^i) \quad \text{for all } i \in N,$$

where p^* is the gradient of any linear support function $L^* \geq C$ with $L^*(x^*) = C(x^*)$.[3] By theorem 13.1 α is in the core of $\Gamma_C(n)$. Moreover, for every k the k-fold replication of α is the payoff vector of a competitive allocation of the larger game $\Gamma_C(kn)$ and lies in its core. Denote this k-fold replication (a vector with kn components) by $\alpha^{(k)}$. We shall now construct a nearby imputation $\beta^{(k)}$ of the game $\Gamma_U(kn)$.

Denote the difference $v_C(kn) - v_U(kn)$ by g; clearly $g \geq 0$. Choose an arbitrary n-vector γ whose components sum to g/k and satisfy

$$0 \leq \gamma_i \leq \alpha_i - v_U(i),$$

where i denotes the profile of the one-player set $\{i\}$. This is possible because of the two inequalities

$$g/k \leq v_C(n) - v_U(n) \leq \sum_i (\alpha_i - v_U(i)),$$

$$0 \leq v_C(i) - v_U(i) \leq \alpha_i - v_U(i).$$

The first follows from (13.13), (13.14), $\sum_N \alpha_i \geq v(N)$ applied to $\Gamma_C(n)$, and the superadditivity of v_U; the second is a consequence of $\alpha_i \geq v(\{i\})$ for all $i \in N$ applied to $\Gamma_C(n)$. Let $\gamma^{(k)}$ be the k-fold replication of γ, and define

$$\beta^{(k)} = \alpha^{(k)} - \gamma^{(k)}. \tag{13.18}$$

This is the desired imputation of $\Gamma_U(kn)$. We wish to show that it lies in the weak ε-core, in the sense of (13.6), whenever k is greater than the constant $k_0(n, \varepsilon)$ provided by the lemma.

Consider, therefore, an arbitrary subset S of the set of all kn players. Note first that

$$\sum_S \alpha_i^{(k)} \geq v_C(s) \geq v_U(s), \tag{13.19}$$

since $\alpha^{(k)}$ is in the core of $\Gamma_C(kn)$ and $C \geq U$. We also have

$$\sum_S \gamma_i^{(k)} \leq s\frac{g}{k} = sv_C(n) - \frac{s}{k}v_U(kn) \leq s\varepsilon, \tag{13.20}$$

since each $\gamma_i \geq g/k$ and $k \geq k_0(n, \varepsilon)$. Combining the last three equations now gives the desired result:

$$\sum_S \beta_i^{(k)} \geq v_U(\jmath) - s\varepsilon. \tag{13.21}$$

This completes the proof of theorem 13.2. ∎

Examples demonstrating the nonemptiness of weak ε-cores in a variety of economic models have been given by Wooders (1984) and Shubik and Wooders (1984a, b).

We note that $\gamma \to 0$ as $\varepsilon \to 0$, so that the weak ε-cores can be said in a certain sense to possess at least one limit point, namely, the imputation α replicated an infinite number of times. Let us state this more precisely. Given any competitive payoff α of the concave game $\Gamma_C(n)$ and any $\delta > 0$, then for all sufficiently small $\varepsilon > 0$ and for all $k \geq k_0(n, \varepsilon)$ there is an n-vector, at a distance less than δ from α, whose k-fold replication is in the weak ε-core of $\Gamma_U(kn)$.

In analogy with results of Debreu and Scarf (1963), the above does not hold when α is not a competitive payoff of $\Gamma_C(n)$. This means that the weak ε-cores converge (in the above sense) to exactly the set of competitive payoffs of the concavified game (see Shubik and Wooders, 1982).

13.2.6 Spannability
The extremely weak condition (13.10) so far imposed on the utility function will need to be reinforced before a result analogous to theorem 13.2 can be derived for strong ε-cores; we shall require "spannability" and a certain amount of differentiability for U. Our primary purpose, of course, is the study of the effects of nonconcavity, not the wholesale abandonment of regularity assumptions of all kinds. Our policy of keeping the hypotheses as general as possible, however, serves to clarify precisely what our results do and do not depend upon.

We shall postulate, then, that U is *radially differentiable* and *spannable*. The first assumption means that U is differentiable along all rays in E_+^m emanating from the origin (although we shall in fact need the existence of radial derivatives only at points where U and C are equal). This is considerably weaker (if $m > 1$) than assuming the existence of first partial derivatives $\partial U/\partial x_i$. (Figure 13.1 provides an example.) We do not demand that the radial derivatives be continuous or, indeed, that U itself be continuous.

The second assumption means that there exists a concave function $C \geq U$ such that for each $x \in E_+^m$ there are $m + 1$ (or fewer) points $y^h \in E_+^m$

and weights $\lambda_h \geq 0$ such that

$$\sum \lambda_h = 1, \qquad \sum \lambda_h y^h = x, \qquad \sum \lambda_h U(y^h) = C(x).$$

This clearly implies that U is bounded above by a linear function, as previously assumed on the right-hand side of (13.10). The matching assumption that U is bounded below by a continuous function, as on the left-hand side of (13.10), is not implied and will not be needed.

The notion of spannability appears to be quite fundamental to any investigation of the relaxation of convexity conditions. Hence a short digression is in order to linking this notion to other analytic conditions.

We call U *sublinear* if for every function L with positive coefficients, the difference $U - L$ has a finite upper bound. For example, logarithmic (Bernoullian) utility is sublinear, as is any bounded utility function.

THEOREM 13.3.   *If U is continuous, sublinear, and strictly increasing, then U is spannable.*

Proof. Define C as in (13.11), take x^* interior to E_+^m, and let L be a linear support to C at x^*. Then L is strictly increasing in each x_j, and so is $L/2$. By sublinearity, we can find a function L' parallel to $L/2$ such that $L' \geq U + c$, where c is a preassigned positive constant. Let R denote the region of E_+^m in which $L \leq L'$. Clearly R is compact and contains x^*. We now wish to consider convex representations of x^* that "almost" achieve the value $C(x^*)$, in the sense of the "sup" in (13.11). In order to distinguish between vertices lying within R and those outside, the representations will be written in the following way:

$$x^* = \alpha y + \bar{\alpha} z = \alpha \sum \lambda_h y^h + \bar{\alpha} \sum \mu_k z^k, \qquad y^h \in R, \quad z^k \notin R. \qquad (13.22)$$

Here $\bar{\alpha}$ denotes $1 - \alpha$ and is understood to be 0 if there are no points of the second type in the representation, that is, if z is not well-defined. (Note that y is always well-defined; this follows from the fact that x is outside the convex set $E_+^m - R$.) Given $\varepsilon > 0$, by (13.11) we can find a representation satisfying

$$\alpha \sum \lambda_h U(y^h) + \bar{\alpha} \sum \mu_k U(z^k) \geq C(x^*) - \varepsilon.$$

Hence

$$\alpha L(y) + \bar{\alpha} L'(z) - \bar{\alpha} c \geq L(x^*) - \varepsilon,$$

or, from (13.22) and the linearity of L, $\varepsilon \geq \bar{\alpha}[L(z) - L'(z) + c]$. Since

$$[L(z) - L'(z) + c] \geq c > 0 \quad \text{for } z \in E_+^m - R,$$

we see that $\bar{\alpha} \to 0$ as $\varepsilon \to 0$. But since L' and $L/2$ are parallel, the expression in brackets is of the form $L'(z) + c'$, with a new constant c'. Thus, even though $\|z\|$ may be unbounded, we nevertheless have $\bar{\alpha}\|z\| \to 0$ and $\bar{a}L'(z) \to 0$ as $\varepsilon \to 0$. Hence $y = (1/\alpha)(z^* - \bar{\alpha}z) \to x^*$ as $\varepsilon \to 0$, and

$$\sum \lambda_h U(y^h) \geq \frac{1}{\alpha}[C(x^*) - \varepsilon - \bar{\alpha}\sum \mu_k U(z^k)]$$

$$\geq \frac{1}{\alpha}[C(x^*) - \varepsilon - \bar{\alpha}L'(z)] \to C(x^*).$$

Since the y^h are restricted to the compact region R and since U is assumed to be continuous, there exists a limiting representation $x^* = \sum \lambda_h y^h$ with $\sum \lambda_h U(y^h) = C(x^*)$. Hence C is spanned by U at the arbitrary interior point x^*.

If x^* is not interior to E_+^m, this argument is not directly valid, since a linear support L may not exist. But we can then reduce the dimension of the problem without affecting either the definition of $C(x^*)$ or the hypotheses of continuity, sublinearity, and strict monotonicity, In the reduced problem x^* will be interior. ∎

This theorem is not sharp. For example, it is apparent from the proof that "strictly increasing" is hardly necessary; a certain very weak *insatiability condition* would suffice instead, as follows: For each $x \in E_+^m$ and each $j = 1, 2, \ldots, m$, there is a $y \in E_+^m$ differing from x only in the jth component such that $y_j > x_j$ and $U(y) > U(x)$.

Another extension results from the observation that if U is spannable and L is linear, then $U + L$ is spannable, despite the fact that adding L can destroy both sublinearity and monotonicity (or insatiability).

We now consider a simple example, with just one commodity and one type of player, to show how crucial spannability and differentiability will be to the existence of strong ε-cores in the limit. Let $U(x) = [x/2]$, the greatest integer less than or equal to $x/2$, and let all the initial endowments be one unit. Here $C(x) = x/2$, and U is spannable but not (radially) differentiable. (See figure 13.3.) For a coalition with s members we have

$$v_U(\mathfrak{s}) = [s/2] \quad \text{and} \quad v_C(\mathfrak{s}) = s/2.$$

If the game happens to have an odd number of players, $n = 2r + 1$, then in any Pareto-optimal payoff vector the most-favored player receives at least r/n units. The $2r$ least-favored players therefore receive at most $r - r/n$. This must be compared with the amount r that they can obtain

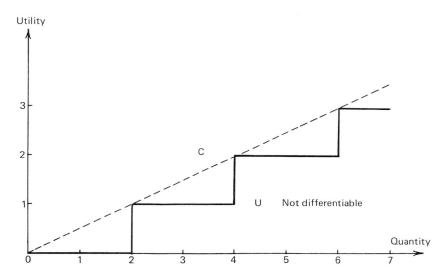

Figure 13.3
A spannable but not differentiable function.

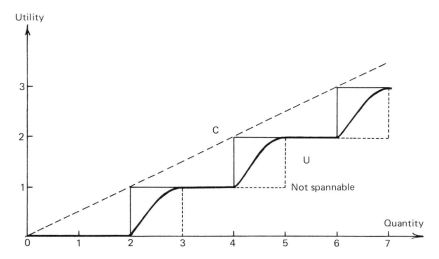

Figure 13.4
A differentiable but not spannable function.

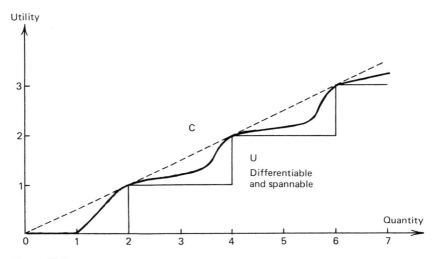

Figure 13.5
A differentiable and spannable function.

in coalition. The difference, r/n, converges not to 0 but to $1/2$ as $r \to \infty$. Hence strong ε-cores do not exist for large, odd n and small ε.

Now let us change U to spoil spannability, but at the same time make U differentiable. (See figure 13.4; the precise form of the curved parts of U within the small squares is immaterial.) One can then verify that

$$v_U(s) = U(s) = \left[\frac{s-1}{2}\right] \qquad (s = 1, 2, \ldots).$$

In other words, a coalition can do no better than allot all its goods to one player.[4] If there happen to be an even number of players in this game, $n = 2r$, then the least-favored set of $n - 1$ players will always get $(r - 1) - (r - 1)/n$ or less, compared with the amount $r - 1$ they can obtain in coalition. Again, the difference goes to $1/2$ as $r \to \infty$, and strong ε-cores do not exist for large, even n and small ε.

Finally, let us restore spannability, as in figure 13.5, taking care to make U differentiable at the points of contact with C. A coalition with $n = 2r + 1$ members will now be able to make an allotment consisting of $2 + 1/r$ units to r of its members and nothing to the other $r + 1$ members, and thereby receive a total utility of $r(1 + 1/2r - O(1/r^2))$. Thus we have $v_U(n) = n/2 - O(1/n)$. This is also valid for even n, trivially. For any n, then, the imputation that gives equal shares to all will assign to each s-player set an amount $(s/n)v_U(n) = s/2 - O(1/n)$. This must be compared with the amount, at most $s/2$, that they can obtain in coalition: In this case the difference does go to zero, and we have strong ε-cores in the limit as $n \to \infty$ for arbitrarily small ε.

13.2.6 Existence of the strong ε-core

We now consider exchange economies based on a utility function U that is radially differentiable and spannable.

THEOREM 13.4.   *For every profile n and for every $\varepsilon > 0$, there is a constant k_0 such that every game $\Gamma_U(kn)$ with $k \geq k_0$ has a strong ε-core.*

LEMMA ON STRONG ε-HOMOGENEITY OF v_U.   *For every profile δ and for every $\varepsilon > 0$, there exists a constant k_0 such that*

$$v_C(\delta) - \frac{\varepsilon}{k} \leq \frac{1}{k} v_U(k\delta) \leq k_C(\delta) \tag{13.23}$$

holds for all $k \geq k_0$. (Compare (13.15).)

Proof. Fix δ and ε and let $x^* = a(\delta)/s$. Then

$$v_C(\delta) = sC(x^*). \tag{13.24}$$

Using the spannability of U, we can find a convex representation $x^* = \sum \lambda_h y^h$ such that $C(x^*) = \sum \lambda_h U(y^h)$. Given k we wish to "move" the points y^h slightly to make the coefficients λ_h integral multiples of $1/ks$. The technical details of this maneuver have been relegated to note 5 at the end of this chapter; the result is a new convex representation $x^* = \sum \mu_h z^h$ for each k, with the property that for each h, $ks\mu_h$ is an integer, and

$$ks|U(z^h) - L^*(z^h)| \to 0 \quad \text{as } k \to \infty, \tag{13.25}$$

where L^* is any linear function supporting C at x^*. (This result makes essential use of the radial differentiability of U.)

The new representation is a feasible allocation of any coalition with profile $k\delta$; thus $v_U(k\delta) \geq \sum ks\mu_h U(z^h)$. Using (13.25), we have for sufficiently large k,

$$v_U(k\delta) \geq ks \sum \mu_h L^*(z^h) - \varepsilon.$$

The right-hand side is equal to $ksL^*(x^*) - \varepsilon$ by linearity. This in turn is equal to $ksC(x^*) - \varepsilon$. Applying (13.24) gives the desired result:

$$v_U(k\delta) \geq kv_C(\delta) - \varepsilon.$$

The other inequality in (13.23) is immediate by (13.13). ∎

The proof of theorem 13.4 itself proceeds exactly like that of theorem 13.2 but uses the more powerful lemma just established. Note that to ensure that the constructed imputation $\beta^{(k)}$ is in the strong ε-core, we must use ε/n for ε in applying the lemma. The last line of the proof (compare (13.21)) will then read as follows:

$$\sum_s \beta_i^{(k)} \geq v_U(\partial) - \frac{s\varepsilon}{kn} \geq v_U(\partial) - \varepsilon.$$

The remarks at the end of section 13.2.5, concerning the limiting behavior of weak ε-cores, apply equally to the present case.

13.3 Production and Market Games

13.3.1 The core with production and exchange
Unfortunately the easy and intuitively satisfactory way of modeling an exchange economy as a game in coalitional form does not carry over to economies with production and exchange. Except for the case of strictly constant returns to scale, we are simply unable to avoid the institutional implications of the existence of the firm. With constant returns to scale, production sets are cones; all profits are allocated to measurable factors, and there is no surplus that must be assigned as a return to some mysterious, unspecified, untraded factor that we can call management, the firm, or the organization.

Because there are no positive profits in an economy with constant returns to scale, shares in the productive plant can be assigned arbitrarily without an effect on the economic imputation of wealth. When production sets are convex but not cones, profits must be assigned. But unless we assume the individual ownership of the implicitly hidden facts of production, the firm with stockholders becomes a special (and fortunately rather simple) type of local public good (see chapter 19).

General-equilibrium theory, which is both nonstrategic and static, could finesse the problems of institutional or corporate indivisibility and control by including a nonvoting class of shares reflecting the proportions for the division of profits. Because the basic question being asked in general-equilibrium theory concerns the existence of an efficient price system satisfying supply and demand and budget constraints including dividends, the simultaneous solution of the system implies not only that the individual takes prices as given, but that he also knows precisely what dividends to expect and can spend them immediately without any difficulties involving cash flow.

Although modeling in the cooperative form limits the institutional detail to a minimum, these models are not completely institution-free. To specify the set of outcomes attainable by a group of individuals who together own less than 100 percent of the shares of a firm, we must specify the production or control possibilities of the group.

General-equilibrium theory at best has the number of firms in an economy given exogenously. In contrast, the neoclassical partial-equilibrium theory of the firm and industry has considerably more institutional content, assuming the use of money and the existence of set-up costs, overheads, and capacity constraints. These assumptions yield production sets that are in general not convex and also make it possible to sketch an endogenous theory of firm size and of the number of firms in competition.

Restricting ourselves to examining production and exchange using the cooperative form of a game, we find three types of difficulties: (1) the description of joint production conditions; (2) set-up costs; and (3) voting and the control of the firm. The first two will be dealt with here; the third is discussed briefly in section 13.3.3 and considered again in chapter 20.

An easy but limited way to treat production is to make the production correspondence that describes the technology available to each coalition additive (Hildenbrand, 1968). This amounts to preserving the c-game property. Coalition formation yields no gains in production. In a subsequent paper Hildenbrand (1970) defined a coalition production economy in such a way as to guarantee the balancedness of the overall game.

Boehm (1974a) assumed additivity of production sets over replications of economies. Boehm (1974b), Sondermann (1974), Champsaur (1974), and Ichiishi (1977) made sufficient assumptions to guarantee balancedness of the derived game. Surveys of the different approaches are given by Hildenbrand (1982), Oddou (1982), and Shubik and Wooders (1984b). Oddou (1982) established that equivalence between the competitive equilibria and the core for games with a continuum of traders requires that "the production correspondence exhibits constant returns to scale with respect to coalitions." But this is essentially the assumption that preserves the c-game or preinstitutional aspect of the game.

Firms are institutions; production sets are not. They relate to each other technologically as a kitchen does to a recipe. Implicit in the way most recipes are written is the property of constant returns to scale. Explicit in the way kitchens are run are set-up costs, capacity constraints, and eventually decreasing returns to scale. The modeling problem in applying core theory to production is not to avoid abstraction but rather to catch the essence of an economic institution at a high level of abstraction. Many of the difficulties involved are illustrated in Williamson's (1975) discussion of markets and hierarchies. These involve the presence of capital in terms of both specialized organization and physical assets. These can be abstractly characterized by set-up costs and capacities.

Before turning to nonconvex production sets we might ask how interesting the coincidence of the core and the competitive equilibrium is for an economy with exchange and production. It is my contention that the economic interest lies more in the nature of the difficulties encountered in attempting to define the mathematical model than in the theorem itself. To force the model onto a Procrustean mathematical bed in order to prove a theorem is to lose the main values of mathematical economics, which come in providing a way to check the consistency and completeness of economic models and to draw implications from complete and consistent models.

13.3.2 Nonconvex production sets

A criticism leveled against the Shapley–Shubik treatment of quasicores is that it is constrained to games with side payments. A similar idea involving "flattening out holes" in convex sets and showing that if they are not too big they should not matter too much, yields approximate results for exchange economies with nonconvex preferences or for no-side-payment games arising from such economies. If we take care in our modeling, it should also be possible to consider production. Starr (1969) considered exchange economies with nonconvex preferences. Broome (1972), Dierker (1971), Henry (1972), and Mas-Colell (1977a) have all considered exchange economies with indivisibilities. Quinzii (1982) has considered core existence with increasing returns.

Shubik and Wooders (1984a, b), based on the work of Wooders (1984) and Shapley and Shubik (1966), consider sufficient conditions for the existence of nonempty cores in a sequence of replicated games. These results can be applied to a general model of a coalition production economy with few restrictions on the production sets.

To develop a replication model of a coalition production economy we take as given a basic correspondence Y mapping subsets of agents into production possibility sets. For each coalition S of agents we take the set of all partitions of S into nonempty subsets as the set of allowable coalition structures of S; that is, the aggregate production possibility set for S is

$$\bar{Y}[S] = \bigcup_{P \in \mathscr{P}(S)} \sum_{S' \in P} Y[S'],$$

where $\mathscr{P}(S)$ is the set of all partitions of S into nonempty subsets. The class of allowable coalition structures can be shown to be generalizable. For our theorems the important and essential feature of allowable coalition structures is the superadditivity of $\bar{Y}$, so that for disjoint subsets S and S', $\bar{Y}[S] + \bar{Y}[S'] \subset \bar{Y}[S \cup S']$. A natural set of allowable coalition structures that ensures the superadditivity of $\bar{Y}$ is the set of partitions. No balancedness assumptions are made. There may also be set-up costs, nonconvexities, and indivisibilities. One of the few restrictions made is that there be some convex cone Y^* satisfying the usual properties of a production set, with each set $Y[S]$ contained in Y^*.

Two results will show the nonemptiness of approximate cores of the economy for all sufficiently large replications. One is a theorem concerning the non-emptiness of the weak asymptotic core of sequences of super-additive replicated games. The other is that, given $\varepsilon > 0$, for all sufficiently large replications of the economy there are allocations that are, in per-capita terms, approximately feasible and cannot be "ε-improved upon" by any coalition of agents. Informally, for the first theorem we relax the feasibility condition and for the second the condition that an ε-core allocation cannot be ε-improved upon by any coalition of agents.

Two simple examples will illustrate our model as applied to set-up costs and capacity limits.

Model 1 (set-up costs with decreasing returns to scale)   Consider a set A of n individuals each with a utility function of the form

$$U^i = \min[x^i, y^i] \qquad (13.26)$$

and initial endowments $(2, 0)$ for each agent. Any coalition S containing s members has available s production functions of the form

$$y = \max[0, (a\sqrt{-z} - 1)], \qquad (13.27)$$

where z is the (negative) input of the first good. The production function has a set-up cost of one unit of input. Furthermore, as shown in figure 13.6, the symmetric optimization can be represented on a diagram showing the preferences of a representative individual. The curved lines represent the production possibility frontiers.

Given the simplicity of the utility functions, at a symmetric equilibrium we require $x^i = y^i$. Thus inputs will be $n(2 - x^i)$, and if s "plants" or production functions are used,

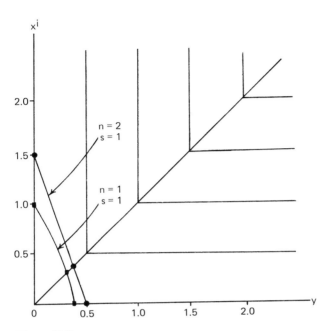

Figure 13.6
Preferences and production with set-up costs.

$$nx = as\sqrt{\frac{2n}{s} - \frac{nx}{s}} - s \tag{13.28}$$

(the superscript i is implicit) or

$$nx + s = a\sqrt{sn(2 - x)}, \tag{13.29}$$

giving

$$x = \frac{-s(2 + a^2) + a\sqrt{4s^2 + s^2a^2 + 8sn}}{2n}. \tag{13.30}$$

The n individuals acting together must select an optimal number of plants to operate. Utilizing (13.30) we optimize over integral values of s. In table 13.1 per-capita payoffs are illustrated for $a = 1$. In this case the optimum has 40 percent of the firms (production functions) active. Thus for $n = 5k$ the optimal number of firms is k, where $k = 1, 2, \ldots$. The characteristic function for any game with $n \le s$ can be constructed from this table.

Table 13.1
Per-capita payoffs

	n					
s	1	2	3	4	5	10
1	0.3028	0.3956	0.3975	0.3853	0.3708	0.3110
2	—	0.3028	0.3744	0.3956	0.4000	0.3708
3	—	—	0.3028	0.3593	0.3845	0.3941
4	—	—	—	0.3028	0.3492	0.4000
5	—	—	—	—	0.3028	0.3956
6	—	—	—	—	—	0.3845

For $a > 1$ the optimal coalition size grows smaller. Fewer active plants per capita are needed.

Returning to $a = 1$, games with $n = 1, 2, 3$, and $0 \mod 5$ have cores. All others have ε-cores for sufficiently large positive ε; furthermore, ε can be allowed to become arbitrarily small as $n \to \infty$.

Model 2 (set-up costs, constant returns to scale, and capacity) Figure 13.7a shows the production function utilized in model 1. The presence of decreasing returns to scale plus a set-up cost produces a U-shaped average-cost curve and leads automatically to the definition of a minimum efficient size for the firm. If constant returns are assumed, apart from the set-up cost, then without an exogenously introduced capacity the firm would have unlimited (though diminishing) increasing returns to scale as it spreads its overhead over larger production (figure 13.7b). Figure 13.8 shows this for the production function given by

$$y = \max[0, -az - 1]$$

with no capacity constraint. It is drawn for $a = 1$, with individual resources of $(2,0)$. The three production conditions illustrated—AC_1P_1, AC_2P_2, and AP_∞—show the utilization of one firm by 1, 2, and then a continuum of agents. The well-known problem of pricing with increasing returns is illustrated. If price is set at $p = 1$, only variable costs are covered, excluding set-up costs. In the continuum case the set-up costs are spread so thin that they are zero per capita, and $p = 1$ covers full costs as indicated by AP_∞.

For the unrestricted capacity the characteristic function can be written as

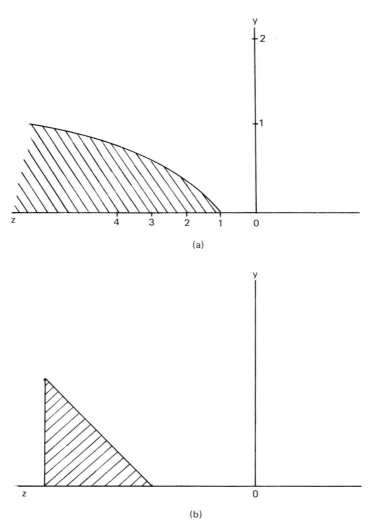

Figure 13.7
U-shaped average costs.

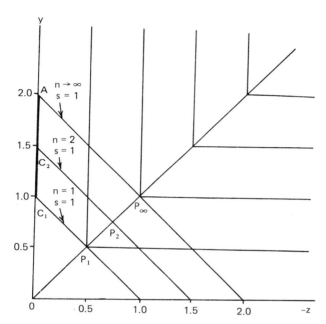

Figure 13.8
Set-up costs and increasing returns to scale.

$$f(0) = 0,$$
$$f(s) = \frac{s}{a+1}\left(2a - \frac{1}{s}\right) \qquad (s = 1, 2, \ldots, n).$$

(13.31)

(Since only numbers, not identity, count here, we use $f(s)$ rather than $v(S)$ or $V(S)$.) This is totally balanced; cores exist for games of any size.

If a capacity constraint is imposed, this is not true. We illustrate this with $a = 1$ and a capacity constraint on each individual firm of $k = 3/2$; then

$$f(0) = 0,$$
$$f(s) = \frac{3}{4}(s - 1) + \frac{1}{2} \qquad (s \text{ odd}),$$

(13.32)

$$f(s) = \frac{3s}{4} \qquad (s \text{ even}).$$

It can be seen immediately that all efficient coalitions are of size 2. All games for n even have cores. Furthermore

$$\lim_{s\to\infty}\frac{f(s)}{s}=\frac{3}{4}\left(\frac{s-1}{s}\right)+\frac{1}{2s}\to\frac{3}{4}\qquad(s\text{ odd});\qquad\qquad(13.33)$$

hence if we start with an economy with an even number of agents, g, and replicate (or alternatively "fractionate" the agents), then for any economy with gt agents ($t=1,2,\ldots$) the associated game (gt,f) will have a core, and in the limit the core may be interpreted in terms of a price system. For gt odd, only an ε-core exists, although in the limit the same price system emerges.

13.3.3 Near-market games
Market games can be modified to provide an overall way of considering a variety of economic structures that involve nonconvexities, coalition production, and local public goods. The necessary results concern the limit properties of ε-cores.

Shubik and Wooders (1982) discussed the concepts of near-market games and near-market economies. Informally, a sequence of replicated games is a sequence of near-market games if each game is superadditive and if all increasing returns to coalition size are eventually exhausted. The latter condition is expressed by saying that the sequence is "per-capita bounded." Large replicated economies are near-market economies if the derived games are near-market games. We note that sequences of near-market games satisfy a certain asymptotic total-balancedness property.

In the remainder of this section we develop only enough notation to specify two game-theoretic results formally. We use these with a variety of models to study economies with complexities beyond exchange and constant-returns-to-scale production. With economies involving joint ownership and public goods the difficulties encountered in the formulation of appropriate models are both mathematical and conceptual; this topic is pursued further in the discussion of stockholder-owned firms and public goods in chapters 19 and 20.

Given the economic data for each coalition S of agents, we define $V(S)$ as a set of utility vectors in $\mathbf{R}^n$ where n is the total number of agents in the economy. A member of $V(S)$, say $u=(u^1,u^2,\ldots,u^n)$, must have the property that there is a feasible state of the economy restricted to the members of S that yields each agent $i\in S$ the utility u^i (coordinates of u not associated with members of S are unrestricted). Let A denote the set of agents in the economy. Then the ordered pair (A,V) is the game derived from the economy. From a sequence of economies we can generate a sequence of games.

We consider sequences $(A_r,V_r)_{r=1}^\infty$, where A_r is the set of players of the rth game, consisting of r players of each of T types, and V_r is a correspondence of subsets of A_r to $\mathbf{R}^{rT}$. We assume that $A_r \subset A_{r+1}$ for all r. The sequence is then said to be a sequence of replicated games if (a) all players of the same type are substitutes for each other, and (b) $V_r(S)$ does not "decrease" as r increases; in formal terms, if $S \subset A_r$ and $S \subset A_{r'}$ where $r \leq r'$, then the projection of $V_r(S)$ on the subspace associated with the member of S is contained in that of $V_{r'}(S)$.

For our main theorem we require two assumptions on the sequence of replicated games. First, the games must be superadditive, so that for any r and any two disjoint subsets of A_r, say S and S', we have $V_r(S) \cap V_r(S') \subset V_r(S \cup S')$. Informally, the superadditivity property is that a larger coalition $S \cup S'$ can do "at least as well" by all its members as the two coalitions S and S' can do independently. The second condition is that equal-treatment utility vectors in $V_r(A)$ be bounded independently of r, so that there is a constant real number K, independent of r, such that if $u \in V_r(A_r)$, where $u^i = u^j$ for all players i and j of the same type, then $u^i \leq K$ for all $i \in A_r$.

Given a game (A, V) and $\varepsilon \geq 0$, a payoff x is in the ε-core of (A, V) if x is feasible and if, for all nonempty subsets S of A, there exists no $x' \in V(S)$ such that $x' \gg x + \varepsilon \mathbf{1}$ where $\mathbf{1} = (1, 1, \ldots, 1) \in \mathbf{R}^A$.

Let $(A_r, V_r)_{r=1}^{\infty}$ be a sequence of replicated games. We say that the sequence has a nonempty *strong asymptotic core* if given any $\varepsilon > 0$ there is a sufficiently large r^* such that for all $r \geq r^*$ the ε-core of (A_r, V_r) is nonempty. The sequence has a nonempty *weak asymptotic core* if given any $\varepsilon > 0$ and any $\lambda > 0$ there is an r^* such that for all $r \geq r^*$ and for some $x \in \mathbf{R}^{A_r}$ and some $\tilde{x} \in V_r(A_r)$, we have

(a) $\left| \{(t, q) \in A_r : x^{tq} \neq \tilde{x}^{tq} \} \right| < \lambda |A_r|$;

(b) $\tilde{x}$ cannot be ε-improved upon by any coalition S; that is, there does not exist an $S \subset A_r$ and an $\tilde{x}' \in V_r(S)$ such that $x' \gg \tilde{x} + \varepsilon \mathbf{1}$.

THEOREM 13.5.   *Let $(A_r, V_r)_{r=1}^{\infty}$ be a sequence of superadditive, per-capita bounded replicated games. Then the weak asymptotic core is nonempty.*

THEOREM 13.6.   *Let $(A_r, V_r)_{r=1}^{\infty}$ be a sequence of superadditive, per-capita bounded replica games in which $V_r(A_r)$ is convex for all r. Then the strong asymptotic core is nonempty.*

13.4 Entry

The problems involved in modeling entry, exit, and merger were introduced in section 7.4.2. As noted there, the subject requires an approach involving at least comparative statics if not dynamics. The problems are related to but different from the problems of nonconvexity or, more generally, nonbalancedness caused by set-up costs, indivisibilities, and other factors. With the latter, nonconvexity is the key factor; with the former, capital, time, information, and flexibility are central.

Models 1 and 2 above and the papers of Novshek (1980a, b) and Novshek and Sonnenschein (1978) provide reasonably adequate models of set-up costs but do not catch the fundamental nonsymmetry between a firm in existence and a "firm-in-being" or potential entrant.

At a minimum the following elements appear to be of central relevance to entry and exit: entry costs, exit costs, overhead costs, minimum efficient plant size, and timing problems. We sketch here the construction of a characteristic function using these elements that bypasses the extensive form.

General-equilibrium theory has been presented as closed in both space and time, but because everyone has to be somewhere, the essential features of exit and entry are avoided. As a crude approximation we introduce a money that is separable and linear in the utility function, which may be regarded as a proxy for the aggregate worth of capital stock not included in the model. The many reasons for introducing a money into economic models were discussed in chapter 1. Our purpose here is to clarify in an elementary way the distinction between set-up costs and overhead on the one hand and entry and exit costs on the other. A transparent way to show this is to modify model 2 of section 13.3.2.

Let the utility function of the representative individual be of the form

$$U = \min[x, y] + z. \tag{13.34}$$

The initial endowment of each agent is $(2, 0, m)$. There are n agents in all, divided into two classes: n_1 (those who own existing firms) and n_2 (those who could enter into competition by paying an entry cost, which in this simple example consists of money).

We distinguish three types of payment and also make a simplifying assumption concerning capacity. We assume that all firms and firms-in-being have the same capacity (or potential capacity) k. A firm in existence pays an overhead cost a, regardless of production level (including zero). If it wishes to avoid paying the overhead cost, it can exit from competition by paying an exit cost e. If it produces, it utilizes c units of input per unit of production as a variable cost. A firm-in-being pays nothing if it stays out. It pays a cost b to enter and an overhead cost d once it has entered.

Here b and e are on the capital account, while a and cx are on the current account, x being the level of production. Even in the crudest of estimates the first two items represent some sort of discounting or amortization of income or expenditure streams.

Because prices have not been introduced, the cost of production of the second commodity is given here in terms of quantities of the first, not in money.

We consider a game (N, f), where the set of players $N = N_1 \cup N_2$ consists of n_1 firms in existence and n_2 firms-in-being. The production function is

$$y = \max[0, cx - \text{overhead}].$$

Because there are two types of agents, we denote the characteristic function by $f(s_1, s_2)$, where $s_i = |S_i|$ and $S_i \subset N_i$ $(i = 1, 2)$.

Model 3 stresses the nonsymmetry between firms and firms-in-being. We set $a = c = d = 1$ and leave e and b as general parameters. We consider k very large and k small.

Model 3

$$f(s_1, 0) = \max[(s_1 - (s_1 - 1)e - 1), 0],$$
$$f(0, s_2) = \max[0, (s_2 - b) - 1],$$
$$f(s_1, s_2) = \max[((s_1 + s_2) - (s_1 - 1)e - 1), 0].$$

Suppose that exit costs are low and entry costs are high, say $e = 0$ and $b = 2$. Then

$$f(s_1, 0) = s_1 - 1,$$
$$f(0, s_2) = \max[0, s_2 - 3],$$
$$f(s_1, s_2) = s_1 + s_2 - 1.$$

Under replication the core will converge to a symmetric imputation. This is no paradox but occurs because unlimited capacity implies that only one firm is needed to produce for society as a whole.

When k is small, it is straightforward to construct games without cores, but the characteristic function will be parametrically sensitive to entry and exit costs and capacity.

It would be possible to develop a cooperative-game approach not only to exit and entry, but to merger as well, along the lines suggested above. No further development is given here, however, because it is my belief that for the study of oligopolistic competition, where numbers are clearly small, the cooperative form of the game, not derived from a strategic form, is inadequate. It ignores institutional structure but offers no justification for doing so. This theme is developed further in section 13.6.

13.5 The Core of a Market Game with Exogenous Uncertainty

13.5.1 Exchange under uncertainty with symmetric information
The existence of a competitive equilibrium in an exchange economy with exogenous uncertainty can easily be established by introducing contingent commodities. If there are m commodities and k states of nature, we consider trade in $m \cdot k$ contingent goods and define preferences over $m \cdot k$ goods (Debreu, 1959).

The enlarged exchange economy clearly gives rise to a market game. But although the existence of a core poses no problems, the demonstration of the shrinking of the core under replication or the existence of an equivalence theorem for the core and the competitive equilibrium poses problems as the commodity set becomes infinite if uncertainty is not correlated among types of traders (see Roberts, 1976).

The relation between the core and the competitive equilibrium was discussed by Shubik (1973b, 1975c), and the proof of core limit properties for an exchange economy with exogenous uncertainty was given by Caspi (1975, 1978).

Consider a trading economy E^r with r traders, one good, and s states of nature. Preferences are defined in R_+^s, and a consumption set for i is denoted by $y_i = [y_i(s)]$. Von Neumann–Morgenstern utility functions are assumed:

$$\sum_{i \in S} \pi(s)u_i[y_i(s)] = Eu[y_i].$$

All traders are considered to have the same utility functions, and $\pi(s)$ is the probability of event s.

THEOREM 13.7.   *Let $[y_1^r(s), y_2^r(s), \ldots, y_r^r(s)]$ be an allocation in the core of E^r. Then for every $\varepsilon > 0$ and $0 < \alpha < 1$ there exists an R such that for all $r > R$ the proportion of traders in E^r such that*

$$|Eu(y_i^r) - u(Ex)| < \varepsilon$$

is greater than $1 - \alpha$, where

$$Ex = \sum_{s \in S} \pi(s)x_i(s)$$

is the expected initial endowment.

THEOREM 13.8.   *Given the allocation in theorem 13.7, then for every $\varepsilon > 0$, $0 < \alpha < 1$, $0 < \beta < 1$, there exists an R such that for all $r > R$ the proportion of traders in E^r for which*

$$\text{prob}(|y_i^r - Ex| < \varepsilon) > 1 - \beta$$

is greater than $1 - \alpha$.

If risk is correlated completely for traders of the same type, then—since the commodity space remains constant—the core convergence and equivalence results follow immediately.

13.5.2 The core with nonsymmetric information

Core analysis is based on the assumption that an adequate description of the game in coalitional form exists. This means that there must be a straightforward way to calculate the feasible set for each coalition. Wilson (1978) suggested two ways to handle nonsymmetric information in an exchange economy. He defined a coarse core where agents acting in concert can condition their actions only upon information known to each member individually. His second definition for the fine core allowed them to pool all information. Wilson established the proposition that the coarse core is nonempty but provided an example of a game with an empty fine core.

Once more we must raise questions concerning the appropriateness of the modeling. To display distinctions in information clearly we need the extensive form of the game, since the coalitional form obliterates details concerning process. It is undoubtedly worthwhile to ask whether the characteristic-function or other cooperative form can be defined directly without having first to construct an extensive form that reflects differences in information and methods of communication. Even if this could be done, one must ask further whether the core is the appropriate solution concept for investigating problems involving differentials in information and communication. In spite of Wilson's innovative approach, the extension of core theory to these types of problems does not appear to be promising.

13.6 Oligopolistic Competition

13.6.1 Market games and the core

The prime uses of the core in economic analysis have been in a preinstitutional setting where the modeling can proceed naturally from the basic economic data directly to a coalitional form. The market games in chapters

10 and 11 provide examples. The most striking results have shown the shrinking of the core in large games and the coincidence of the core and competitive equilibria in market games with a continuum of agents.

A natural question to ask is whether core theory applied to market games yields real insight into oligopolistic markets. The answer suggested here is that it does not. At first glance it presents a highly attractive possibility that is not available with general-equilibrium analysis, namely the opportunity to study a mixed model in which oligopolists or other "large players" are represented by atoms with finite measure and small firms and consumers are represented by an ocean of players of insignificant size. Such a model would allow us to deduce the role of the individual in an economy with masses of consumers but few major firms.

The hope that core analysis of market games might yield insight into mixed oligopolistic and mass markets is not illusory but misplaced. The problem is not so much with the solution concept as it is with the model to which the core is applied. Market-game models like the general-equilibrium model are preinstitutional. They avoid the detail needed to describe actual markets. In fact the strategic form of the market game is never specified. The modeling goes from the economic data directly to the cooperative form. Yet the very essence of oligopolistic competition is in the strategic power of firms. The models of Cournot, Edgeworth, Bertrand, and others working with markets modeled as games in strategic form all specify the necessary detail to describe price formation. In general, given the strategic form, the noncooperative-equilibrium solution is studied. It is possible, however, to utilize the strategic form of the game to derive a new and institutionally biased cooperative form that can be used to study cartel behavior. This was done in chapter 7.

A searching analysis of a market game with a continuum of traders and several large traders or "atoms" was presented by Shitovitz (1973). Starting from the result of Aumann (1964) that for markets with a continuum of small traders the core and set of competitive allocations are equivalent, Shitovitz extended the analysis to situations with some large traders. Modeling an exchange economy, he established several theorems, two of which we shall note here.

THEOREM 13.9.   *Let x be an allocation in the core. Then there exists a price vector p such that (i) (p, x) is an efficiency equilibrium; and (ii) $p \cdot i(t) \geq p \cdot x(t)$ for almost all traders in the atomless part T_0 of the set of traders T. Here $i(t)$ and $x(t)$ stand for the initial and final holdings density profile of t, respectively.*

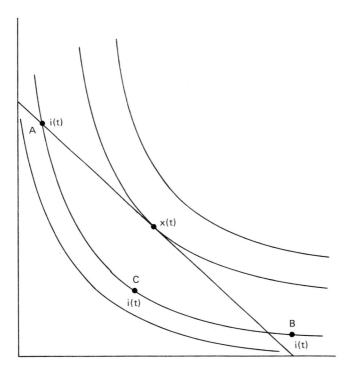

Figure 13.9
Illustrating an efficiency equilibrium.

THEOREM 13.10.   *Given at least two large traders and the fact that all large traders are of the same type, the core coincides with the set of competitive allocations.*

Two traders s and t are of the same type if $i(t) = i(s)$ and, for all x and y, $x \succ_t y$ if and only $x \succ_s y$. They are of the same kind if they are of the same type and have the same measure.

An efficiency equilibrium is not a competitive equilibrium but a point on the Pareto-optimal surface such that no trader can improve by exchanging his final allocation x at prices p for any other allocation. In figure 13.9 point A is a competitive equilibrium, with the values of the initial and final endowments equal; at point B the initial endowment is worth more, and at C it is worth less than the final endowment. A competitive equilibrium is a special type of efficiency equilibrium.

We can interpret the two theorems as follows. Theorem 13.9 says that small traders will almost always find that at the "price" that can be assigned to any point in the core the total "value" of their initial endowments will be larger than the total value of their final endowments. Because neither formal markets nor money exist in this model, the economic interpretation of the result must be given with extreme caution. In particular we cannot deduce that small traders are worse off than they would be at the competitive equilibrium.

The second theorem shows a coincidence between the core and competitive equilibrium if there are two or more large traders of the same type facing a continuum of small traders. At first glance this result appears to be problematic in that it takes no account of the fact that the sizes of the large players can be considerably different; for example, the introduction of even one extra trader with a finite measure appears to destroy the power of a monopolist who may be many times its size. This would seem to be an artifact of the modeling rather than a basic insight into oligopolistic competition. Shitovitz (1973, p. 495) suggested that the result is related to the Bertrand model of competition, but the relationship between the core and the noncooperative-equilibrium model is not evident. A simple example shows this. Consider a market where all preferences are representable by $\sqrt{x_1 x_2}$. There is a continuum of traders of type 1 with total measure $[0, 1]$ and initial holding density profile $(0, 1)$. There are two traders of type 2 with measures 0.9 and 0.1, respectively, and initial holding density profiles of $(1, 0)$ each. In figure 13.10 the core would stretch from E to C if there were only one large trader with measure 1, and it would consist of the single point E for two large traders (interpreting the allocation split $9:1$ for the large players). If this is modeled as a price-strategy Bertrand game (see Shubik, 1959b), there may be no pure-strategy perfect noncooperative equilibrium. If the strategic game is modeled as a price-quantity game as suggested by Dubey and Shubik (1980b), then the mechanism forces all trading at a single price, and a Pareto-optimal noncooperative equilibrium exists and coincides with the competitive equilibrium for two or more large players. If the noncooperative game is modeled with quantity strategies in the style of Cournot, pure-strategy equilibria exist but are not Pareto-optimal.

This point was developed in detail by Okuno, Postlewaite, and Roberts (1980), who studied noncooperative oligopoly with atoms and a continuum of traders utilizing a variant of the closed oligopoly model of Shubik (1973a).

Gabszewicz (1977) showed that the results of the Shitovitz paper do not

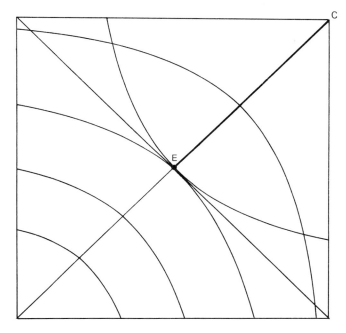

Figure 13.10
The core with monopoly and duopoly.

really depend on the assumption that the small traders are represented by a continuum. He also proved the asymptotic analogues of these propositions (see also Khan, 1976).

Shitovitz raised a question concerning the case of a single large trader and a continuum of small traders. Is the large trader necessarily at least as well off at every other point in the core as he is at the competitive equilibrium? Aumann (1973) answered this in the negative. This result is not particularly surprising when we consider the relationship between exchange economies and market games and between the set of competitive equilibria and the core. A specific exchange economy is associated with a specific market game; but if we start with the market game as our basic datum, there will be a set of exchange economies with which it can be associated. In particular, it is possible to select any point in the core of the market game and construct an exchange economy having that point as a competitive equilibrium (Shapley and Shubik, 1976). In one example Aumann selected the point in the core that yields the most to a monopolist and made that the competitive equilibrium of an exchange economy.

In general, with or without side payments, the cooperative form of the market game throws away economic detail portrayed in the exchange economy. Thus the mapping from market games to exchange economies is one-to-many, and the competitive equilibria of the exchange economies related to a particular market game cover its core.

The most disadvantageous Aumann monopoly is as follows. The initial bundle density of trader t is

$$i(t) = \begin{cases} (0,1) & \text{for the nonatomic traders,} \\ (1,0) & \text{for the monopolist.} \end{cases}$$

If we let (x, y) stand for an endowment of the two goods being traded, the utility functions are

$\min[5(2x + y), 4(x + 2y)]$ for the monopolist,

$\min[2(2x + y), x + 2y + 3/2]$ for small traders of type 1,

$2x + y$ for small traders of type 2.

The unique competitive equilibrium yields $(1/2, 1)$ to the monopolist, but the core goes from $(1/2, 1)$ for the monopolist to $(5/16, 5/8)$.

Greenberg and Shitovitz (1977) established that, in economies with one atom and one type of small trader, for each core allocation x there is a competitive allocation y whose utility to the atom is not greater than x whenever x is an equal-treatment core allocation or whenever the small traders have the same homogeneous preferences.

All of the cooperative-game studies of oligopoly noted above utilized exchange economies that are easily modeled as c-games. But, although the effect of few large buyers and sellers in exchange is of some interest, many of the more important questions concerning oligopolistic competition involve production. Shitovitz (1982) extended his earlier investigation to include two types of production economies. The first is a private production economy in which a production set is associated with each individual trader (as in Hildenbrand, 1968). The second has a single technology set available to all coalitions. Unfortunately all of the problems noted in section 13.3 concerning the modeling of production remain and are further compounded by the presence of oligopolistic elements.

13.6.2 Syndicates

Gabszewicz and Dreze (1971) considered syndicates of traders, where a *syndicate* is a set of agents who are required to act as a single entity. The idea of syndication provides a natural sensitivity analysis for game-theoretic solutions. We can take an n-person game, aggregate players into syndicates, and examine changes in the core with variations in syndication. Postlewaite and Rosenthal (1974) provided a simple five-person example of a side-payment game in which syndication is disadvantageous.

Let set M consist of players 1 and 2 and set N of players 3, 4, and 5. The characteristic function is

$$v(S) = \min[|S \cap M|, |S \cap N|/2].$$

There is a one-point core at $(0, 0, 1/2, 1/2, 1/2)$. If 3, 4, and 5 form a syndicate, a new three-person game can be defined with

$$v^*(s) = \begin{cases} 0 & \text{for } N \notin S, \\ 1 & \text{for } S = \{1, N\} \text{ or } \{2, N\}, \\ 3/2 & \text{for } S = \{1, 2, N\}. \end{cases}$$

This has as a core the convex hull of $(0, 0, 3/2)$, $(1/2, 0, 1)$, $(0, 1/2, 1)$, and $(1/2, 1/2, 1/2)$; hence the most the syndicate can get is $3/2$, but elsewhere in the core it gets less.

A simple three-agent example in which the reverse is true is the glove market. The set M consists of trader 1, and set N of traders 2 and 3; the characteristic function is

$$v(s) = \min[S \cap M, S \cap N].$$

There is a one-point core at $(1, 0, 0)$. If 2 and 3 form a syndicate, the resultant two-person game has a core going from $(0, 1)$ to $(1, 0)$.

13.6.3 Other solutions
The cooperative solutions utilize the assumption of Pareto optimality. This in and of itself is a strongly normative assumption. Even if we are willing to accept Pareto optimality as reasonable, we must, as we have already stressed, describe the power of all subgroups in an economy. This requires an adequate description of threats. One approach of a normative bent is that of the Harsanyi value (see chapter 6); Harsanyi offers a plausible way to evaluate threats in the calculation of his value solution.

The limitations of the von Neumann–Morgenstern stable-set solution were noted in *GTSS*, chapter 6, but Hart (1974) has provided an interesting application of stable-set theory to a nonatomic pure-exchange market with a finite number k of different types each owning disjoint sets of goods. He showed that if all traders of each type form a cartel that behaves like a single atomic player, then all solutions of the k-player finite game are obtained as the only solutions to the nonatomic game. This indicates that the stable-set solution endogenously lead to cartel organization.

In summary, we suggest that although work on mixed markets is clearly needed for developing our understanding of economies with oligopolistic and more closely competitive sectors (see also Shubik, 1959a; Gabszewicz and Mertens, 1971; Dreze et al., 1972; Shitovitz, 1974; and Dreze, Gabszewicz, and Postlewaite, 1977), the insights to be gained from the examination of market-game cores are limited. Other cooperative solutions may produce more insights, but little work has been done with them (for a start on the value see Gardner, 1977).

The study of syndicates is of considerable interest for analyzing the sensitivity of the core to certain types of aggregation. The relationship between cores of market games and the competitive equilibria of related exchange economies is also of interest; but when the cores are not sets of points, the relationship with the competitive equilibria does not appear to be particularly close.

13.7 Market Games: An Assessment

13.7.1 Uses and limitations

The market game has provided a valuable tool for the game-theoretic analysis of exchange economies. For both side-payment and no-side-payment games it is known that exchange economies map into totally balanced games. For side-payment games it is known that they map into exchange economies, and it is conjectured, but not yet proved or counter-exampled for no-side-payment games that every totally balanced game is representable by an exchange economy. Clearly the mappings are not one-to-one in both directions, and the market game contains far less information than does the exchange economy.

The intimate relationship between exchange economies and totally balanced games gives no indication of the relationship of the competitive equilibria as limit points of the core. To study this property we need to be able to define a sequence of exchange economies and a related sequence of totally balanced games. The fact that we can define a replicated series of exchange economies and associate with it a series of totally balanced games for which the core converges to the competitive equilibria in an economic result arising from the utilization of economic data to construct the sequence of totally balanced games.

A natural question is whether other economic phenomena give rise to market games or "near-market games" from which one can construct a sequence that may or may not show core convergence. In section 13.3.3

extensions of applications for near-market games were indicated. Unfortunately, once we depart from exchange economies or economies with constant returns to scale, a host of new modeling problems appear, and several other properties of economic significance may be present along with the market-game property. The c-game property provides a check on the acceptibility of the model, and the construction of a sequence of related games permits us to examine for large numbers the behavior of solutions based on the characteristic function. After considering joint ownership, public goods, and voting in chapters 19 and 20, we shall be able to summarize the possibilities for using near-market games in economic analysis.

Cooperative-game analysis based on the market game appears to be of limited value in studying problems involving information, oligopolistic competition, money, or virtually any phenomenon that stresses structure and process. For these the extensive or strategic forms are needed.

13.7.2 Open problems

Mathematical economics is, or should be, an applied mathematics. We must therefore ponder the economic interest of the questions being asked. In developing any set of analytical tools one can encounter deep and interesting problems in mathematics, but the basic reference point in any applied mathematics must be the topic to which the application is being made.

The characteristic-function form of a game, and the market game and simple game in particular, have proved to be of considerable value for studying classical problems in economics and political science, yielding new results and casting new light on old results. As already noted, though, there are many problems to which the cooperative form does not appear to be particularly well suited. Are there interesting problems in political economy that are amenable to cooperative analysis but have not been dealt with? There are probably many, and a few will be suggested here.

Minority rights and the core Simple games without dictators or veto players have no core. The simple-majority game, for instance, is characterized by winner-take-all. Chapter 20 offers an example to show how minority shareholder protection on dividend payments can put a core back into a voting game without a core. Can we find such rules for public-goods economies using voting mechanisms? The use of the veto appears to be intimately related to the protection of minority rights.

Corelessness and voting Figure 13.11 shows three games: the simple-majority game has a characteristic function indicated by $OACD$, the

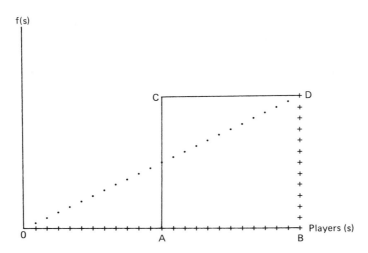

Figure 13.11
Three symmetric games.

inessential game by OD, and the unanimity game by $OABD$. If we use the
size of the ε needed for the existence of a strong ε-core as a criterion, then
the simple-majority game has $\varepsilon = 1/2$ and is the "most coreless" game
there is. At the other extreme the unanimity game (n-vote players) is a
voting game that is also a market game.

In some sense a market game with total balance seems to be at an
opposite extreme from the simple-majority game, which appears to be as
"unbalanced" as is possible for a game with superadditivity among coalitions. A closer examination indicates that one can construct even more
unbalanced games. If we consider an n-person symmetric superadditive
game, S. Weber has shown that the maximum number of coreless games of
size $k \geq n$ (counting only one game for each size) is $n - [\log_2 n] - 1$,
where $[g]$ stands for the integral part of g.[6]

A characteristic function for a 13-person game in which eight of the
subgame sizes do not have cores is

$f(1) = 0,$

$f(s) = \varepsilon \quad$ for $s = 2, 3$, where $0 < \varepsilon < 1/15,$

$f(s) = 4 \quad$ for $s = 4, 5,$

$f(6) = 4 + \varepsilon,$

$f(s) = 13 \quad$ for $s \geq 7.$

The simple-majority game has only six subgame sizes without cores.

Is the presence of a small core stabilizing? Should the designers of rules of the game for politicoeconomic decision systems try to create cores as a way to help protect minority claims? Is the degree of balance or total balance relevant in constructing a useful index to contrast games arising from exchange or voting?

Variations on side-payment possibilities   A game $\Gamma(v, N)$ is a side-payment game if $v(S)$ is a superadditive set function. But it is possible that the sub-Pareto-optimal surface is flat for some coalitions and not for others.

The following definition suggests itself. We could call Γ a side-payment game if $v(N)$ is a hyperplane and a totally side-payment game if all $v(S)$ are hyperplanes.

The current literature contrasts side-payment and no-side-payment games, but no thought seems to have been given to the possibility of limited side payments. It may be that in the development of welfare theory, the existence of side-payment possibilities among some groups is a reasonable assumption.

Splitting the core   Consider the class of n-trader exchange economies characterized by fixed preferences and the distribution of all resources. For each distribution a specific exchange economy is defined, and it has a given number of competitive equilibria associated with it. For each such economy we can define a replication sequence and associate with each member of the sequence a market game. For each replication sequence in which the exchange economy has more than one competitive equilibrium, there will be a replication number at which the core has split into as many parts as there are competitive equilibria. Do these splitting numbers have any economic significance? In particular, does the size of the splitting numbers tell us anything about "thickness" of markets?

Solutions to games in characteristic-function form   The core, value, nucleolus, kernel, and bargaining set have all been proposed as single-imputation solutions to games in characteristic-function form, that is, as solutions in the form of a single imputation satisfying certain conditions. The solution can be considered a prescription for selecting imputations obeying certain properties. The value, for example, has been described by axioms.

Can we construct any further solution concepts for games in characteristic-function form that have the interest and explanatory power of the core and value? Or have we more or less exhausted the possibilities for plausible cooperative solutions? My guess is that we shall not find a new solution concept as powerful as the core or value.

Cooperative solutions to strategic market games   In chapters 14 and 15 the relationship between market games and strategic market games will be noted. Strategic market games have been analyzed utilizing the non-cooperative-equilibrium solution. It appears to be worthwhile to derive the cooperative form from the strategic form and then to study the core and other cooperative solutions. This contrasts with the approach in section 13.6.

Enlargement of the characteristic function   A game (N, v) described by a set of players N and a characteristic function v is merely a shorthand or aggregate description of some form of physical reality. Enlarging the description allows us to model phenomena more closely but might also complicate the analysis. One enlargement that appears to be of interest is to introduce a vector of weights on the players, $\omega = (w_1, w_2, \ldots, w_n)$, where w_i is the weight attached to i and $\sum_{j \in N} w_j = 1$. The weights might represent some scale of relative importance of the players. The game is now described by (N, v, ω). Shapley (1981) and Shubik and Weber (1984) consider applications in which nonsymmetric weights appear to be useful. In each instance the value solution is employed. Can we usefully modify the core (maybe along the lines of Selten's equal-treatment core; see Selten, 1972) and other solutions for application to this richer description of the coalitional form?

Notes to chapter 13

1. Hence questions regarding the credibility and proper evaluation of threats do not arise in this case, though they play an important role in the general theory of cooperative games.

2. The use of $m + 1$ spanning points is sufficient to "concavify" any linear bounded function on E^m. Use of a larger number in (13.11) would not affect the definition of C.

3. Regardless of equal tastes, it is a simple matter to find the competitive solutions(s) of an exchange economy with money when utilities are concave.

4. *Proof:* If the coalition allots in integer units, U might as well be the lower step function in the figure (dotted lines). If fractional shares are used, the result can be no better than discarding one unit and then using the upper step function. In either case the value (13.22) is the best possible. ∎

5. LEMMA. *Let L^* be a support to C at x^*. Let there be a convex representation $x^* = \sum \lambda_h y^h$ such that $\sum \lambda_h U(y^h) = C(x^*)$. Assume that U possesses a radial derivative at each y^h. Let s be a fixed integer and k a variable integer. Then there exist convex representations $x^* = \sum \mu_h z^h$, depending on k, such that for each h, $ks\mu_h$ is an integer and*

$$ks|U(z^h) - L^*(z^h)| \to 0 \quad as \ k \to \infty. \tag{$*$}$$

Proof. Assume first that all λ_h are positive. For any k we can find nonnegative integers l_h with sum ks such that $|ks\lambda_h - l_h| \geq 1$. Now define $\mu_h \equiv l_h/ks$, $z^h \equiv (\lambda_h/\mu_h)y^h$. For k sufficiently large the λ_h will be positive and all the statements in the lemma are obviously satisfied, except for $(*)$. To verify the latter note that L^* is tangent to U at each y^h and that z^h approaches y^h along the ray Oy^h. (If $y^h = 0$ and there is no ray, then $(*)$ is trivial.) Since the derivative of U at y^h exists along that ray, we have

$$\frac{|L^*(z^h) - U(z^h)|}{\|z^h - y^h\|} \to 0 \quad as \ k \to \infty.$$

(We are concerned, of course, only with values of k for which $z^h \neq y^h$.) But for large k

$$\|z^h - y^h\| = \left|\frac{\lambda_h - \mu_h}{\mu_h}\right| \cdot \|y^h\| \leq \frac{1/ks}{\lambda_h - 1/ks}\|y^h\|.$$

Hence $ks\|z^h - y^h\|$ goes to zero, and $(*)$ follows.

If some of the λ_h are zero, we can set the corresponding $\mu_h = 0$ and $z^h = y^h$ and proceed as above, with h restricted to the indices for which λ_h is positive.

6. S. Weber, private discussions and communication. He has also provided a bound for the maximum number of coreless games counting all 2^n subgames separately.

IV Strategic Models of Closed Economic Systems

14 Trade Using a Commodity Money

14.1 Transaction Technologies and Strategic Market Games

Part II investigated open models of oligopolistic competition. The standard features of partial-equilibrium microeconomic analysis were all displayed. In particular, the firms were explicitly assumed to have an institutional existence, as were markets and trade in money. The strategic freedom of the firms was constrained by the existence of a dominant structure of trade. Although no discussion of the monetary mechanism per se was given, costs were measured in money, firms were considered as maximizing a monetary profit, and transactions involved the exchange of products for the money or monetary commodity.

In contrast to this approach, which has as its historical basis the work of Cournot and the underlying concept of the game in strategic form and its noncooperative-equilibrium solution, the approach in part III had as its basis the two-sided market model of Edgeworth and to some extent that of Böhm-Bawerk. The underlying concept, especially in the work of Edgeworth, is that of the game in cooperative form and the core solution.

Edgeworth and Böhm-Bawerk incorporated trade in money into their labor and horse markets. But this money can best be regarded as merely another commodity that may have distinguishing properties in the technology of exchange.[1] This contrasts with the u-money discussed in chapter 1 and used when we consider games in cooperative form with side payments.

In both parts games were analyzed under the assumption of the existence of a u-money. The cooperative solution is much simplified by this assumption, and in terms of economic reality it may be justified as a good first-order approximation in the region of interest to the analyst. Thus, for example, in cartel payments money may be regarded as approximately equivalent to a transferable utility with constant marginal worth. Lump-sum taxes and subsidies, if not too large, can be considered in the same way.

In chapter 7, where the closing of the models of oligopolistic competition was considered, it became clear that the important property of "moneyness" lies in its role as a strategic decoupling device and not in its role as u-money or in its transferability property. The natural way to embed the noncooperative-game models of oligopolistic competition into a closed economic model is to specify a market technology and invent money as a strategic decoupling device. Thus the modeling required to place the Cournot analysis in a general-equilibrium context represents a major step toward recasting the general-equilibrium system in an institutional, implicitly dynamic, and monetary format. This happens because the game must be described in strategic form; hence, without even considering the equilibrium of the system, we get a complete process description that specifies all the states the system can reach.

The way to reconcile general-equilibrium theory with macroeconomics is through oligopoly theory and a microeconomic theory of money. The monetary and credit mechanism supplies the extra strategic freedom that enables the system to function with ease in disequilibrium as well as equilibrium. Given the existence of money as an artifact of society and government, it in turn may be manipulated and controlled by government for purposes totally different from its use as an efficient device with which to operate a competitive system given a trading technology.

The three chapters composing part IV offer the essentials of the market and monetary mechanism as a device for reconciling strategic and cooperative models of the price system. We set up the basic apparatus that will enable us to consider public goods, taxation, and subsidies in part V; the detailed investigation of financial instruments and institutions required to understand the control implications of the existence of money and financial institutions is deferred to a further projected publication (for further discussion see Shubik, 1978b).

This chapter, remaining at the level of exposition consistent with the utilization of modifications of the Edgeworth box, presents the construction of a Cournot model of oligopolistic competition in a closed economy. The model is highly specific, and the sensitive economist will immediately be concerned about its lack of generality. In chapter 15, however, we shall note a large class of mechanisms that display the same equilibrium properties when competition involves many traders.

14.2 The Cournot Strategic Market Game

In order to describe a well-defined game of exchange in which a specific commodity is used as a means of payment, we must spell out how the prices are formed. The classic general-equilibrium model is used to establish the existence of prices (often not unique) *at equilibrium*. For a proper game model, however, rules that determine the prices for positions of disequilibrium are needed as well. With every player free to make an independent decision, the model must yield a well-defined output for every set of inputs.

Several price-formation mechanisms might be considered, each placing different restrictions on the strategic possibilities. In particular, the traders might control only the quantities offered or demanded, or they might name reservation prices or price ranges or even complete demand curves for their individual transactions. Multistage bargaining might be introduced, or a centralized procedure that converts a set of unilateral price declarations into a unique, marketwide price for each good.[2] Here, since we are interested in general, anonymous exchange, with marketwide prices but with a minimum of ad hoc institutional detail, we adopt a generalization of Cournot's original approach. The strategic variables are *quantities*, not prices, but they include quantities of the special good that serves as "cash" or "trading money." Indeed, in our simplest version, only that good will be subject to strategic choice.

Formally, in the prototype model, we assume that there are n traders trading in $m + 1$ goods, where the $(m + 1)$st good has a special operational role, in addition to its possible utility in consumption. We attribute to each trader an initial bundle of goods

$$a^i = (a_1^i, a_2^i, \ldots, a_m^i, a_{m+1}^i)$$

and a concave utility function

$$u^i(x_1^i, x_2^i, \ldots, x_m^i, x_{m+1}^i).$$

Superscripts denote traders, and we shall denote summation over traders by an overbar; thus $\bar{a}_j \equiv \sum_{i=1}^n a_j^i$. We emphasize that u^i need not actually depend on x_{m+1}^i; the possibility of a fiat money is not excluded.

The general procedure is for the traders to put up quantities of the first m goods to be sold and, simultaneously, quantities of the $(m + 1)$st good to buy them, all at prices determined by the marketwide supply and demand for each good. For expository purposes our prototype version requires traders to offer for sale all of their holdings of the first m goods, though they need not spend all of their $(m + 1)$st good. Traders may (and usually will) buy some of their own goods back, but they must go through the market. In other words, in this version of the model traders do not own their initial bundle outright; they merely own a claim on the proceeds when the bundle is sold.[3]

Let us imagine m separate "trading posts," one for each of the first m commodities, where the total supplies $(\bar{a}_1, \bar{a}_2, \ldots, \bar{a}_m)$ have been deposited for sale "on consignment" (figure 14.1). Each trader i makes bids by

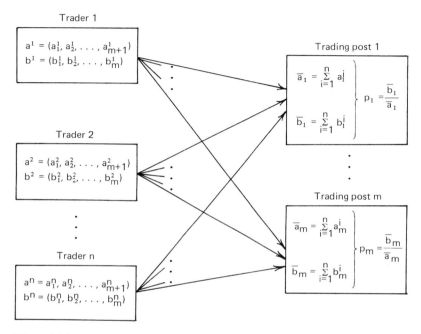

Figure 14.1
Traders and trading posts.

allocating amounts b_j^i of his $(m + 1)$st commodity among the m trading posts $(j = 1, 2, \ldots, m)$. We shall denote his strategy, in the game-theoretic sense, by the vector $b^i = (b_1^i, b_2^i, \ldots, b_m^i)$. There are a number of possible rules for governing the permitted range of bids. In the simplest case, with no credit of any kind, the limits on b^i are given by

$$\sum_{j=1}^{m} b_j^i \le a_{m+1}^i \quad \text{and} \quad b_j^i \ge 0 \quad (j = 1, 2, \ldots, m).$$

The interpretation of this spending limit is that the traders are required to pay cash in advance. More generally, we might allow them to defer payment, either in anticipation of receipts or under some other credit arrangement that would have to be made explicit in the model.[4]

14.2.1 Price formation
The prices now emerge in a natural way, as a result of the simultaneous bids of all buyers. We define

$p_j \equiv \bar{b}_j / \bar{a}_j \qquad (j = 1, 2, \ldots, m)$.

Thus bids precede prices. Traders allocate their budgets *fiscally*, committing quantities of their means of payment to the purchase of each good without definite knowledge of what the per-unit price will be. At an equilibrium this will not matter, since prices will be what the traders expect them to be. In a multiperiod, multitrader context, moreover, the traders will know the previous prices and may expect that fluctuations in individual behavior in a mass market will not change prices by much. Any deviation from expectations will result in a change in the quantity of goods received, rather than in the quantity of cash spent. In practice, if one allocates a portion of one's budget for the purchase of a certain good in a mass market, this will be different—but not too different—from a decision to buy a specific amount at an unspecified price. It is a matter of letting one's stomach rather than one's purse absorb the surprises.

The prices in our model are so determined that they will exactly balance the books at each trading post. The amount of the jth good that the ith trader receives in return for his bid b_j^i is

$$x_j^i = \begin{cases} b_j^i / p_j & \text{if } p_j > 0, \\ 0 & \text{if } p_j = 0. \end{cases}$$

(Note that $p_j = 0$ implies $b_j^i = 0$: A trader receives nothing if and only if he bids nothing.) His final amount of the $(m + 1)$st good, taking account of his sales as well as his purchases, is

$$x_{m+1}^i = a_{m+1}^i - \sum_{j=1}^{m} b_j^i + \sum_{j=1}^{m} a_j^i p_j.$$

His *payoff*, in the game-theoretic sense, must be expressed as a function of all the traders' strategies; accordingly we write

$$\Pi^i(b^1, b^2, \ldots, b^i, \ldots, b^n) = u^i(x_1^i, x_2^i, \ldots, x_{m+1}^i),$$

where the xs depend on the bs according to the three preceding displayed equations. It is noteworthy that Π^i is a concave function of b^i for each i; this is important for the existence proof.

Because of the mechanism for price formation and the anonymous allocation of sales, all traders pay the same price for the same good. However, the operation of the market system gives rise to what have been called *pecuniary externalities*, in the sense that the prices paid by any one trader are dependent on the monetary actions of the others (see, e.g., Viner, 1931, or Shubik, 1971c). In the classic barter market this is not

true; trading pairs or groups can form and exchange goods unaffected by
the actions of others.

14.2.2 The noncooperative solution

A noncooperative or "best-response" equilibrium has been defined in
game theory as a set of strategy choices by the players with the property
that no player, given that the choices of the others are fixed, can gain by
changing his own choice.[5] Specialized to the present model, this solution
concept will be recognized by economists as a close relative of the classic
Cournot oligopoly solution (for a modern treatment see Manas, 1972).
It will consist of an n-tuple of strategies,

$$\hat{b} = (\hat{b}^1, \hat{b}^2, \ldots, \hat{b}^n),$$

such that for each i the function $\Pi^i(\hat{b}^1, \hat{b}^2, \ldots, \hat{b}^i, \ldots, \hat{b}^n)$, considered as
a function of b^i alone, is maximized at $b^i = \hat{b}^i$.

The following existence theorem for the noncooperative equilibrium
(NE) may be proved by an application of the Kakutani fixed-point
theorem to the best-response adjustment process or transformation $b \to b'$,
where each b'^i is a best response by player i to the choices $\{b^j : j \neq i\}$
of the other players. The details of the original unpublished proof by
Shapley are not given here. A related proof by Dubey for a somewhat
more general model is given elsewhere (Dubey and Shubik, 1978a).

THEOREM 14.1.   *For each trader $i = 1, 2, \ldots, n$, let u^i be continuous,
concave, and nondecreasing. For each good $j = 1, 2, \ldots, m$, let there be
at least two traders with positive initial endowments of good $m + 1$ whose
utility for good j is strictly increasing. Then a noncooperative equilibrium
exists.*

Note that there is no assumption that good $m + 1$ has intrinsic value
to anyone. It must merely be available to enough people so that markets
for the other goods can be formed.

14.3 The Edgeworth Box

The case $m = 1$, $n = 2$ lends itself to simple two-dimensional descriptive
analysis based on the Edgeworth box. To avoid the confusion of too
many lines and curves in one place, we construct a sequence of diagrams,
using the same labels as far as possible. As we shall see, much of this
geometry will apply also to the general case, with many goods and traders,
because of the way in which the operation of the system "decouples"
both the traders and the trading posts.

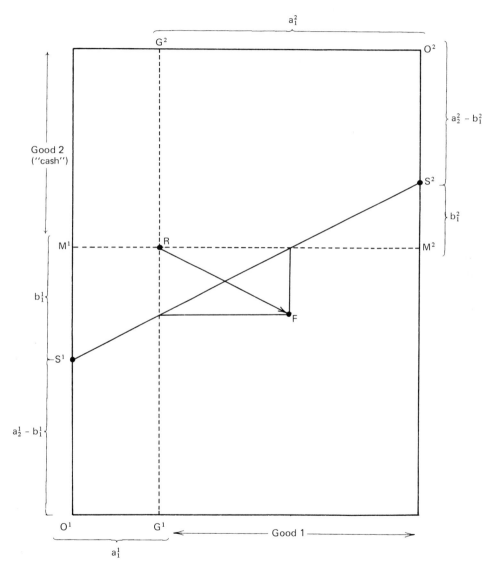

Figure 14.2
Price formation.

In figure 14.2 the first trader's holdings are measured up and to the right of the point O^1, while the second's are measured down and to the left of O^2. The dimensions of the box are $\bar{a}_2$ high by $\bar{a}_1$ wide. The point R represents a typical initial allocation; thus we have $a_1^1 = |M^1R|$, $a_2^1 = |G^1R|$, and so on, where $|M^1R|$ is the length of M^1R. The points S^1 and S^2 represent typical strategy choices; thus $b_1^1 = |M^1S^1|$ and $b_1^2 = |M^2S^2|$. They are restricted to lie along the edges M^1O^1 and M^2O^2, respectively, since we are requiring all of good 1 to be sent to market. (If we did not make this restriction, the strategies would lie arbitrarily in the rectangles $RM^1O^1G^1$ and $RM^2O^2G^2$, respectively.)

Now consider the line joining S^1 and S^2. Its slope is $(b_1^1 + b_1^2)/(a_1^1 + a_1^2)$, which is just the price p_1. Moreover, it divides the line M^1M^2 into two segments that are equal in length to the amounts x_1^1 and x_1^2 of good 1 purchased by traders 1 and 2, respectively. Similarly it divides the line G^1G^2 into segments equal to their final holdings x_2^1 and x_2^2 of the monetary commodity or "cash." Therefore the final allocation is represented by the point F. The vector RF represents the transaction that actually takes place; its slope, naturally, is equal (in absolute value) to the price p_1.

It is essential that the reader understand the nomogram demonstrated in figure 14.2, because it is the key to all the diagrams that follow.

Figure 14.3 shows the effect of holding S^2 fixed while varying S^1. As S^1 moves over the interval from M^1 to O^1, the point F traces out the curve A^1RB^1. This curve is a portion of a hyperbola whose asymptotes are the horizontal and vertical lines through S^2. If we reverse the process and move S^2, holding S^1 fixed, we trace out the curve A^2B^2, which is part of a similar rectangular hyperbola centered at S^1. Endpoints A^1 and A^2 correspond to zero bids, while endpoints B^1 and B^2 reflect the upper limit on the amount a trader can bid. It happens in this case that we did not allow trader 2 enough cash to be able to buy back his original holding when trader 1 plays S^1, so the curve A^2B^2 stops short of R.

These traces are comparable to the price rays or "budget sets" that confront a trader in the classical Walrasian model with its fixed prices. The difference is that in the present case the price is not constant but reacts to variations in a trader's own decisions, so that we get a curve instead of a line. The curve is concave, as one would expect: if a trader increases his purchase, he drives the price up; if he bids less, the price falls. The connection between the two approaches may be illustrated in figure 14.3 by supposing the second trader's holdings and bid to be very large, pushing points O^2 and S^2 far off the page. The first trader's hyperbolic "budget set" would then approximate a straight line-

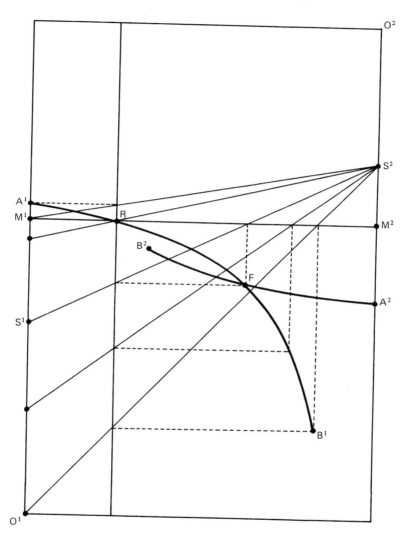

Figure 14.3
Budget sets.

through R and F, reflecting the fact that he now has little influence on the price.

14.3.1 Two kinds of equilibrium

So far we have discussed only the mechanics of the rules of exchange. We are now ready to add the traders' preferences to the picture, by super-imposing the contours of the utility functions u^1 and u^2. As shown in figure 14.4, S^1 happens to be the best response to S^2, since A^1B^1 is tangent at F to the contour of u^1. (Note that the curvature of A^1B^1 is such that there is always a unique point of tangency.) Similarly, S^2 is the best response to S^1, since A^2B^2 is tangent at F to one of the contours of u^2. Thus figure 14.4 illustrates a noncooperative or "Nash" equilibrium for the market. Neither trader, knowing the strategy of the other, would wish to change.

A striking feature of this kind of equilbrium is its nonoptimality. Since curves A^1B^1 and A^2B^2 are not generally tangent to each other, the point F cannot be expected to be Pareto-optimal or "efficient."[6] In effect, the traders are working with unequal marginal prices, represented by the unequal slopes of A^1B^1 and A^2B^2 at F. Any outcome in the shaded region would be preferred by both traders to the NE allocation at F. In particular, they would both profit from increased trade at the average price p_1 represented by the slope of RF.

The reader familiar with the Edgeworth diagram will recognize in figure 14.4 the contract curve $C^1EP^2C^2$, which is a subset of the more extensive Pareto set $O^1P^1C^1EP^2C^2O^2$. The competitive equilibrium (CE) is represented by the competitive price ray RE, which is tangent to both indifference curves at the competitive allocation E. The situation illustrated seems to be typical: There is less volume of trade at the NE than at the CE. But the reverse is also possible. In fact, by a somewhat contorted but perfectly legitimate arrangement of the indifference contours, we could make any point outside the dotted lines in figure 14.4 the location of a unique CE, while keeping a unique NE at F.

Although we have not illustrated it, it is also not difficult to construct utility functions for which several distinct strategy pairs (S_1, S_2) are in noncooperative equilibrium. This may or may not be accompanied by a corresponding multiplicity of CEs; the two kinds of solution are not directly interlinked. But their general mathematical properties are quite similar. For example, we would expect that even for general m and n, if the utility functions are smooth and the initial allocation is chosen according to a nonatomic probability distribution, then with probability 1 there will be a finite, odd number of NEs (cf. Debreu, 1970).

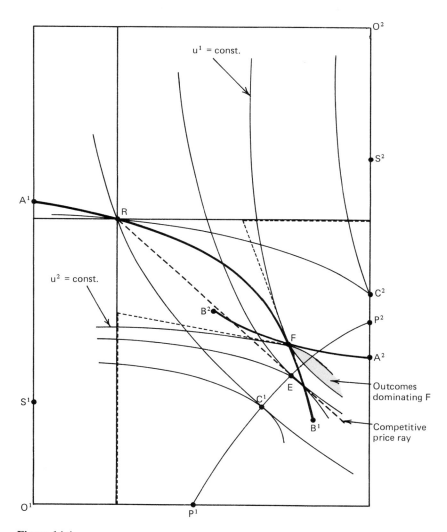

Figure 14.4
Noncooperative (F) and competitive (E) equilibria.

14.3.2 The feasible set and credit

The set of feasible outcomes can be determined by holding one trader's bid at its upper extreme O^i or lower extreme M^i and sweeping through the strategies of the other trader. The feasible set is shown in figure 14.5 (solid shading); for example, outcome L results if both traders bid their upper limit.[7] This feasible set has nothing to do with rationality or motivation; it merely describes those outcomes that the mechanism can be made to produce. It necessarily contains all NE allocations, but we know a priori that the CE allocations, lie in the quadrants of the Edgeworth box "northwest" or "southeast" of the point R. It may well be that some or all of the CE allocations fall outside the feasible set under our present trading rules.

By introducing credit we can enlarge the feasible set, permitting the traders to bid more of the "means of payment" commodity than they possess as cash on hand. In diagrammatic terms the first trader might be allowed the segment $C^1 M^1$ instead of $O^1 M^1$ in figure 14.5. The length $|O^1 C^1|$ has a simple interpretation in terms of banking: It is the largest amount of good 2 that could be loaned to trader 1 with the certainty that he will be able to repay. To see this, consider that the worst case is $S^1 = C^1$, $S^2 = M^2$, with trader 1 bidding the limit and trader 2 bidding nothing. This leads to the outcome Q^2, at which trader 1 is just barely solvent. A "conservative" credit limit C^2 for trader 2 can be determined in the same way.[8]

If we alter the rules of the game to enable both traders to use this conservative banking credit, the feasible set is extended as indicated by the stripes in figure 14.5. For example, the point L' results if both traders bid up to their new limits. The new feasible set still does not fill the two basic quadrants, however, and so we still cannot be sure that any competitive outcomes will be attainable.

With more liberal credit the feasible set would cover a larger part of the two basic rectangles, and eventually all of them, but it would also include areas above and below the Edgeworth box, representing situations in which one or the other trader is "caught short." If we regard credit as the issue of a financial instrument, the interpretation of a point outside the box is simple and familiar—it amounts to stating that after trade an individual ends up with none of the monetary commodity in hand and with outstanding claims he cannot meet. In order to complete the model we must either describe the utility to any player at such an outcome or add further moves to the game corresponding to bankruptcy proceedings.

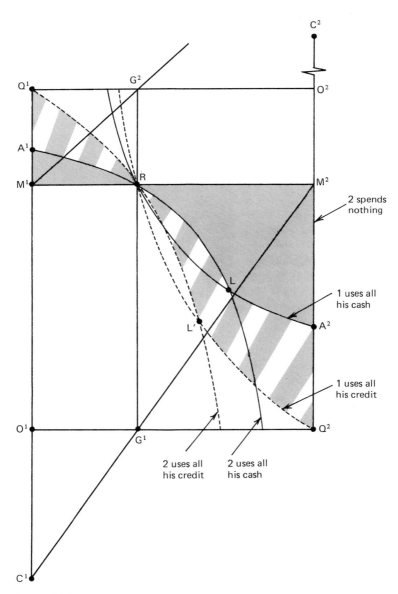

Figure 14.5
The feasible set with and without credit.

14.3.3 Individual rationality

In the present version of our model we are requiring that all of the initial endowments, except for the "payment" commodity, be put up for sale. (This requirement is removed in chapter 15.) Consequently the concept of ownership is somewhat different from that usually assumed in micro-economics; it is in fact closer to that in law. All goods are monetized, and trade is virtually anonymous. The economy is an accountant's dream, but by forcing goods to pass through the market we weaken ownership rights. In particular, it may not be possible for a person to recover his original bundle or to obtain an equivalent bundle. This contrasts with the classical Edgeworth and modern core models, in which a trader can always defend his initial holdings is he so desires.

The defensive possibilities are easily illustrated. In figure 14.6 the first trader is fortunate, since he has relatively little of good 1 that must go to market and relatively much of good 2 that he can use at his discretion. He cannot, of course, protect his actual initial holding, since this would mean being able to enforce the point R regardless of the other's choice of S^2. But he can force the outcome to have as much utility for him as R. In fact, by playing S^1 as shown, he restricts the possible outcomes to the set A^2B^2, which lies entirely on the "high" side of the indifference curve $u^1 = c^1$, as drawn. This is in fact the best he can do defensively: S^1 is his "maxmin" strategy, and c^1 his "maxmin" payoff. Moving S^1 either up or down would move B^2 into a region of lower payoff, either toward R or toward L.

The second trader, on the other hand, has a relatively poor defensive position. The highest u^2 indifference curve that completely contains one of the A^1B^1 sets is the curve $u^2 = c^2$, which is distinctly inferior to R for him. There are two critical points: the endpoint A^1 and the tangency point near B^1. As S^2 moves, the A^1B^1 curve rotates on R. Raising S^2 would make A^1 worse, while lowering S^2 would make the critical point near B^1 worse; S^2 is thus his "maxmin" strategy.

The shaded area in figure 14.6, bounded by the curves $u^1 = c^1$ and $u^2 = c^2$, represents the so-called individually rational allocations. The *feasible* individually rational allocations are just the ones that lie beneath the line RM^2, and it is a theorem that every NE solution will lie in that region. In contrast, the Walras–Edgeworth individually rational zone, which contains every CE solution, is defined by the two indifference curves through R (not shown). It is easy to see that this region could be entirely disjoint from the other. This is not too surprising, since the two regions arise from games with the same economic data but different rules of trade.

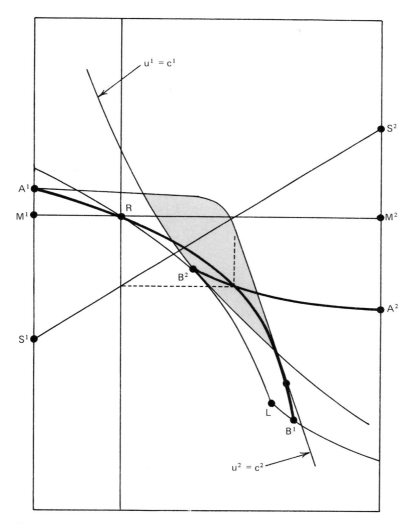

Figure 14.6
Maxmin strategies and the individual rationality zone.

14.3.4 Many traders

The same diagrams can be used, one-sidedly, when there are more than two traders. This is because our model has the "aggregation property," with both strategies and outcomes being additive over traders. Viewed by the other traders, a set or coalition of traders acting together is hardly distinguishable from a single, larger trader. In the diagrams, we may regard the point S^2 as not a single bid but the vector sum of bids by traders 2 through n, using R as the "origin" from which the vectors are defined. The first trader may notice a quantitative but not a qualitative difference from the two-person case: since the other traders combined may have far more resources than he does alone, the distance of S^2 from R and S^1 may make the slope of S^1S^2 (the price) almost insensitive to his choice.

It might appear at first glance that the feasible set, when there are many traders, would continue to be a sizable fraction of the set of outcomes that are feasible under unrestricted, Edgeworthian barter. But this is not the case. Let us count dimensions. The unrestricted allocation space has dimension $(m + 1)(n - 1)$.[9] Even if $m = 1$, there are $2n - 2$ dimensions of possible outcomes if trade is not required to pass through our "trading post" mechanism, compared with the at most n dimensions that can arise when n traders bid by each selecting a point on a line as his strategy. Thus, starting at $n = 3$, the feasible set is only a lower-dimensional surface or manifold in the set of outcomes that would be possible under restricted trading.

14.3.5 Many commodities

Since the trading posts operate independently of each other, it is possible to continue using these diagrams when there are more than two commodities (i.e., more than one trading post). But the markets remain uncoupled in two ways: (1) through the spending limits, which apply to all bids combined, so that a trader's upper bound at each trading post will depend on what he spends at the others, and (2) through the utility functions, which in general reflect complementarities, substitution effects, and so forth, among the different goods, so that the utility maps we superimpose on each Edgeworth box will depend on what is happening in the others. The second effect (as in the classical model) can only be visualized with hyperdimensional eyesight, but the first is still within reach of our diagrams.

Figure 14.7 illustrates a three-commodity situation. The two "boxes" are erected at right angles to each other, in the back of the three-

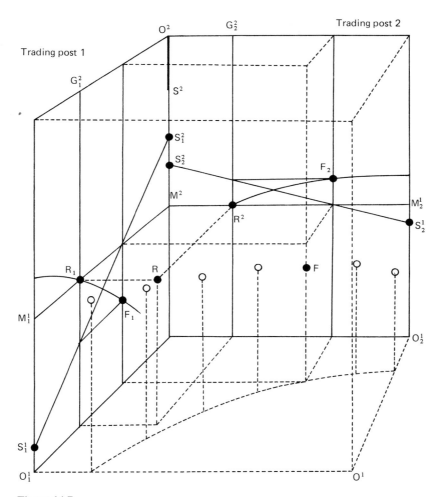

Figure 14.7
Two trading posts.

dimensional figure (solid lines). The initial point R projects to R_1 in the first box and R_2 in the second (the subscripts here referring to the two trading posts). We may conveniently regard R as the vector sum of $M^2 R_1$ and $M^2 R_2$. Trader 2's pair of bids b_1^2 and b_2^2 are shown at S_1^2 and S_2^2, and their sum at S^2. Thus $|M^2 S^2| = |M^2 S_1^2| + |M^2 S_2^2|$. The unspent balance is represented by the vertical bar $O^2 S^2$.

Trader 1's bids are shown at S_1^1 and S_2^1. As S_1^1 varies over the permitted range $O_1^1 M_1^1$, the outcome in the first marketplace sweeps out the curve through R_1 and F_1 in the usual way. Similarly the curve through R_2 and F_2 describes his possibilities in the second marketplace. But his joint choice of S_1^1 and S_2^1 is restricted by the spending limit

$$|M_1^1 S_1^1| + |M_2^1 S_2^1| \le |M_1^1 O_1^1| = |M_2^1 O_2^1|.$$

The case actually illustrated has him spending most of his cash on good 1 and the rest on good 2. (Had he held some back, we would have shown it by a vertical bar at O^1.) The resulting final allocation is found by taking the vector sum of $M^2 F_1$ and $M^2 F_2$; this yields the point F.

Now suppose that trader 1 changes his allocation of cash between goods 1 and 2, causing the points S_1^1 and S_2^1 to move in opposite directions. The point F will then trace out a curve in space, which we have tried to suggest by the open dots perched above the curve's projection on the base. This projection shows the tradeoff between goods 1 and 2 when a fixed amount of cash is bid by trader 1; note that it is concave to his origin O^1. If trader 1 bids less than the maximum allowed (strict inequality above), a curved triangular surface is generated, extending out from F and the open dots toward the viewer and rising to an apex directly above O^1. This locus, not shown, indicates ways in which trader 1 can obtain more of good 3 at the expense of goods 1 and 2; it is concave to the origin O^1, and its projection is the large, roughly triangular region in the base of the diagram. The first trader's best response to the other trader's given strategy (S_1^2, S_2^2) is determined by the relationship of this surface to the indifference surfaces of u^1 in the three-dimensional commodity space with origin at O^1.

14.4 Replication

Inquiries into the behavior of economic models with large numbers of participants often make sweeping assumptions of symmetry in the hope of keeping the models mathematically tractable and easy to visualize while capturing at least some of the characteristic effects of large numbers. We shall utilize the technique of replication introduced in chapter 12. Imagine a basic economic system juxtaposed to a large number of identical replicas of itself; then take away all barriers and form a "common market." Equivalently, assume that all traders in the full model are drawn from a small number of types, with an equal number of individuals of each type. Traders of the same type have identical endowments and identical tastes, but they are not constrained to act alike. That is, they are not members of a bloc or cartel but remain independent decision makers.[10]

The number of members of a type—the "replication number"—provides the modeler with a simple size parameter that he can vary without calling for additional data. Of course, we do not intend to treat replication as though it were some kind of actual expansion process, like growth by homogeneous population increase or by accretions of similar countries to a common market. Replication should be considered only as a technical device of comparative statics. As such, however, it has repeatedly proved its worth in explorations of the size effect (e.g., Edgeworth, 1881; Shubik, 1959a, 1968: Debreu and Scarf, 1963; Shapley and Shubik, 1966, 1969b; Debreu 1975; Owen, 1975; Shapley, 1975).

14.4.1 A simple case
The effect of replication on our model is illustrated in figure 14.8. Here $m = 1$ and $n = 2k$, where k is the replication number. The point S^1 represents the average of the bids of the k traders of type 1; similarly S^2 for type 2.[11] The point F therefore indicates the average final bundles for the two types.

Let us focus on a typical member of type 1. His own bid might lie, say, at $\tilde{S}^1$. To discover his personal final bundle $\tilde{F}$, we must draw the line through $\tilde{S}^1$ that is parallel to S^1S^2; we then locate the point F in the usual way. Of course, $\tilde{F}$ necessarily falls on the straight line through R and F since all transactions take place at the same price.

Now suppose our trader changes his bid from $\tilde{S}^1$ to M^1. That is, he decides to buy nothing. This depresses the average bid for type 1, moving it from S^1 to T^1, where $|S^1T^1|/|\tilde{S}^1M^1| = 1/k$. The new price is the slope of T^1S^2, so our trader's new final bundle is $\tilde{A}^1$, determined by the line through M^1 parallel to T^1S^2. Similarly, at the other extreme, if he decides to bid the limit, the result is $\tilde{B}^1$, determined by the line through O^1 parallel to U^1S^2, where $|U^1S^1|/|\tilde{S}^1O^1| = 1/k$. We should

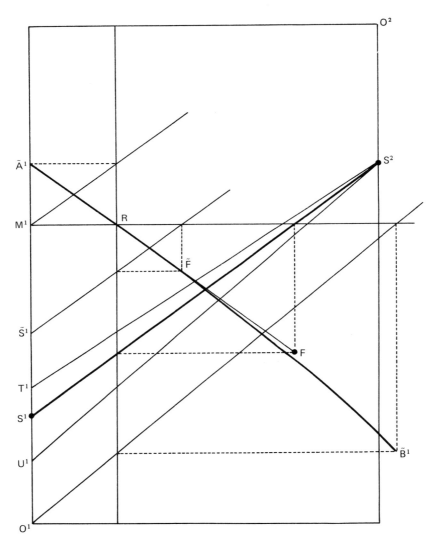

Figure 14.8
Price formation in a replicated market.

not be surprised to see $\tilde{B}^1$ fall outside the box. This means merely that our trader happens to have enough "cash" to buy more than the combined initial bundles of one trader of each type.

The locus of possible final bundles for our variable trader is the curve $\tilde{A}^1 R \tilde{F} \tilde{B}^1$, shown in figure 14.8 for the case $k = 4$. The flattening of the curve, as compared with the curve $A^1 R F B^1$ in figure 14.3 (which is the case $k = 1$), clearly shows the diminished influence of a single individual on price after replication. Indeed the price variation in the present case is encompassed by the thin pencil of sloping lines within the angle $U^1 S^2 T^1$. In the limit as $k \to \infty$, the curve becomes the fixed-price "budget set" of the classical CE model, but with one important difference: It is truncated at the $\tilde{B}^1$ endpoint instead of extending to the horizontal axis through O^1, in recognition of the limited quantity of the payment commodity available.[12]

14.4.2 The general case
For the replicated form of the general model presented in section 14.2, we consider a market with T types of traders and k of each type; thus $n = kT$. The initial holding of good j by trader s of type t will be denoted a_j^{ts}, which we can shorten to a_j^t since it does not depend on s. The total amount of good j (summed over both t and s) will be denoted $\bar{a}_j$ as before. A typical strategy will be denoted $b^{ts} = (b_1^{ts}, b_2^{ts}, \ldots, b_m^{ts})$. The defining equations of section 14.2 then become

$$p_j = \bar{b}_j / \bar{a}_j \quad (j = 1, 2, \ldots, m),$$

$$x_j^{ts} = \begin{cases} b_j^{ts}/p_j & \text{for } p_j \neq 0 \ (j = 1, 2, \ldots, m), \\ 0 & \text{for } p_j = 0 \ (j = 1, 2, \ldots, m), \end{cases}$$

$$x_{m+1}^{ts} = a_{m+1}^{ts} - \sum_{j=1}^{m} b_j^{ts} + \sum_{j=1}^{m} a_j^{ts} p_j,$$

$$\Pi^{ts}(b^{11}, b^{12}, \ldots, b^{1k}, b^{21}, b^{22}, \ldots, b^{2k}, \ldots, b^{nk}) = u^t(x_1^{ts}, x_2^{ts}, \ldots, x_{m+1}^{ts}),$$

where $u^t(x) \equiv u^{ts}(x)$ is the common utility function for members of type t.

Suppose that an NE has been found in which all traders of the same type make the same bids: $\hat{b}^{ts} = \hat{b}^t \ (s = 1, 2, \ldots, k)$.[13] It is instructive to look at the equilibrium conditions for the "interior" case, where all $\hat{b}_j^t$ are positive and

$$\sum_{j=1}^{m} \hat{b}_j^t < a_{m+1}^t \quad (t = 1, 2, \ldots, T).$$

Assuming that the concave functions $u^t(x)$ are differentiable, let $u_j^t(x)$ denote their partial derivatives with respect to x_j. Then setting $du^t/db_j^{ts} = 0$ gives us

$$u_j^t(x^{ts})\left(\frac{1}{p_j} - \frac{b_j^{ts}}{(p_j)^2\bar{a}_j}\right) = u_{m+1}^t(x^{ts})\left(\frac{a_j^{ts}}{\bar{a}_j}\right),$$

which must hold at $b = \hat{b}$. Since prices are in terms of good $m + 1$ as *numéraire*, we can introduce $p_{m+1} \equiv 1$ and rewrite the condition for a symmetric, interior NE as follows:

$$\frac{u_j^t(\hat{x}^t)}{\hat{p}_j}\left(1 - \frac{\hat{b}_j^t}{\hat{b}_j}\right) = \frac{u_{m+1}^t(\hat{x}^t)}{\hat{p}_{m+1}}\left(1 - \frac{a_j^t}{\bar{a}_j}\right) \qquad (j = 1, 2, \ldots, m),$$

where $\hat{p}$ and $\hat{x}$ are the prices and allocation corresponding to $\hat{b}$.

The expressions in parentheses reveal the effect of oligopoly, but note that they all lie between 1 and $1 - 1/k$. In the limit, therefore, these conditions for the NE reduce to the conditions for a CE, with the prices of the goods proportional to the marginal utilities of every trader. Thus we may formulate a convergence theorem, as follows:

THEOREM 14.2.   *Assume that for infinitely many values of k the market has a symmetric, interior NE, and let $\hat{p}^{(k)}$ be the corresponding m-vector of prices. Let $\tilde{p}$ be any limit point of the $\hat{p}^{(k)}$, and define $\tilde{p}_{m+1} = 1$. Then the $m + 1$ prices $\tilde{p}_1, \tilde{p}_2, \ldots, \tilde{p}_m, \tilde{p}_{m+1}$ will be competitive for the market (for any value of k); that is, an allocation $\tilde{x}$ will exist such that $\tilde{\tilde{x}} = \bar{a}$ and, for each s and t, $\tilde{x}^{ts}$ maximizes $u^t(x^{ts})$ subject to $x^{ts} \geq 0$ and*

$$\sum_{j=1}^{m+1} \tilde{p}_j(x_j^{ts} - a_j^{ts}) = 0.$$

It should be noted that the NE approaches the CE "from below," through outcomes that are not in general Pareto-optimal. This contrasts with the convergence of cooperative solutions such as the core and the value, which are by definition Pareto-optimal all the way (see, e.g., Debreu and Scarf, 1963; Shapley and Shubik, 1969b; Debreu, 1975; Owen, 1975; Shapley, 1975).

The type of convergence revealed in theorem 14.2 depends crucially on having interior solutions, with no trader up against his spending limit. All must have enough cash (or credit, in an extended model), where the meaning of "enough" depends on the payment commodity's marginal utility relative to that of the other goods. Of course, there can never be "enough" fiat money in this sense (in a one-period model), for the

NE will always have everyone spending the limit and wishing he could spend more. If the CE is considered socially desirable (as one road to the Pareto optimum, if for no other reason), then a society whose trading system resembles our replicated model should make sure that the means of payment is something that is both widely available and generally desirable, either as a consumption item or as a means of payment in future periods.

Notes to chapter 14

1. As is noted in chapter 15, when there are only two commodities being exchanged, either can be regarded as the means of exchange. A difference appears for three or more commodities.

2. Levitan and Shubik (1971a,b, 1972) have given examples of different strategy spaces and Pareto surfaces that are possible in oligopolistic models.

3. This simplifying condition, which is not essential to our general approach, is by no means as unreasonable as it might appear at first glance. In a multiperiod context it would amount to requiring that all goods in the economy be "monetized" in every trading period. Some other possibilities will be discussed in chapter 15.

4. The simplest way to model credit is to remove the spending limit entirely, while extending the domain of the utility function to include negative amounts of the $(m + 1)$st commodity so as to provide a suitable *disutility* for being caught short of cash when the sales and purchases are all added up. To close the model we would have to postulate an outside source of cash to cover the payments due the other traders when one trader defaults. In a dynamic multiperiod context we can conceive of durable goods, other than the "payment" commodity, as being carried forward and used as security for the granting of credit for commercial loans.

5. See Nash (1951). The term "best-response equilibrium" is due to Robert Wilson. Nash included the possibility of "mixed strategies"—strategies chosen by randomizing devices that the players construct. These have no plausible interpretation in our present model.

6. Indeed Pareto optimality in an NE can only occur at corners of the indifference curves or in special cases such as $F = R$ or $F = B^2$. See Dubey (1980) for a general discussion of the inefficiency of NEs.

7. Most boundary points are attainable, but those on the line M^1M^2 are not, except for R itself. There is, however, an exceptional "null" outcome, not in the Edgeworth box, in which trader 1 bids and gets M^1 and trader 2 bids and gets M^2. Our rule is that if a trader bids nothing he gets nothing, even if the price is zero. So if both traders bid nothing, the entire stock of good 1 is lost. (We may imagine that it goes to an otherwise unnoticed "scavenger," who sends infinitesimal bids to each trading post in the hope of making a killing.) This exceptional outcome is manifestly undesirable

and unstable, and it has no real effect on the solutions of the game, though it causes technical difficulties in the existence proof.

8. It will become clear (sections 14.3.4 and 14.4.1) that when there are many traders, the amount of conservative credit is likely to be negligible, since it depends on the amount of a trader's own money that will surely come back to him from his own bids. In this respect our two-trader diagrams may be misleading. We may also remark that conservative credit does not require the aid of a central clearing house for the traders' promissory notes.

9. The "+1" here is for the monetary good, while the "−1" is for the condition that the sum of the holdings is constant.

10. This distinction can be very important in the game-theoretic approach but is less important in a behavioristic theory. For example, as we shall see, replication changes the NE but not the CE.

11. More generally, if there were many types, then the analogue of S^2 would not be the average but $1/k$ times the sum of all bids from traders not of type 1.

12. It may be observed that the conservative line of credit for an individual shrinks to zero as $k \to \infty$. A simple calculation shows, in fact, that in the present case the amount of such credit is equal to $a_1^1 a_2^1 / [k(a_1^1 + a_1^2) - a_1^1]$.

13. The conditions given in theorem 14.1 are sufficient to guarantee the existence of such a symmetric NE. It is quite possible also to have nonsymmetric NEs.

15 Strategic Market Games

15.1 Strategic Market Games and Market Mechanisms

In chapter 11 we explored the concept of a market game at a reasonably high level of abstraction. An intimate relationship exists between exchange economies and market games, in which the economic features of untrammeled exchange are manifested in a highly special structure on the power of coalitions.

The market game is a powerful tool for investigating possibilities for economic cooperation that minimize considerations of institutional context. In the general-equilibrium analysis of the price system, markets are implicitly assumed to exist and prices are explicitly assumed; in the market game neither of these assumptions is made.

In chapter 14 the degree of abstraction in the strategic model of trade appeared to be considerably less. Because the game was specified in strategic form, all the rules had to be made explicit. Thus, although the analysis was able to establish a relationship between the noncooperative equilibria and the competitive equilibria, this result might have been an artifact of special rules and therefore of little generality. Fortunately this is not so. Dubey and Shubik (1978a), Dubey (1982), and Shubik (1981a) have investigated alternative models, one of which is given in detail in section 15.2, and have obtained a relationship between the noncooperative equilibria and competitive equilibria in models with different strategic structures.

At a broad level of generality Dubey, Mas-Colell, and Shubik (1980) have shown that for games with a continuum of players and for a certain class of market mechanisms the noncooperative and the competitive equilibria coincide.[1] Thus, as long as certain basic properties of market structure are satisfied, there are many institutional forms compatible with the competitive equilibrium. This result indicates that the concept of a *strategic market game* might be as important for economic analysis as that of the market game, the difference being that the strategic market game will be used for investigating the noncooperative solution whereas the market game is used for cooperative solutions. More important, the strategic market game will provide the detailed specification of structure that is called for in any attempt to construct a theory of economic dynamics.

The existence of the general relationship between the noncooperative and competitive equilibria for strategic market games shows that the presence of many traders removes the importance of much institutional detail in the study of equilibrium. Unfortunately this is no longer true when any of the traders is large with respect to the overall size of the market. The example in section 15.2.2 shows a difference in noncooperative equilibria between the "all-for-sale" model and the "offer-for-sale" model.

We have not studied the dynamics of the various games with different price-formulation mechanisms. But the fact that in the limit their noncooperative equilibria approach the same competitive equilibria is no guarantee that their dynamics will be the same for large numbers of traders. Even the static results are delicately influenced by information conditions. This will be even more relevant when we consider dynamics. An example of the sensitivity of noncooperative equilibria to information is given in section 15.4.

15.1.1 Strategic market games and efficiency axioms

A strategic market game based on an exchange economy is specified by a set of players, a strategy space, and an outcome rule that details the assignment of goods to all traders for each set of strategies selected. The strategies may be regarded as messages sent to the markets.

Given a strategic market game, we wish to identify the conditions or axioms that we need to impose on trade if the noncooperative equilibria of the strategic market game for a continuum of traders are to coincide with the competitive equilibria of the exchange economy. The required conditions are as follows:

Convexity: Each trader has available a convex set of strategies.

Anonymity: From the point of view of the market, only the message sent by the trader matters. The name of the trader is irrelevant to how the message is treated.

Continuity: The outcomes must be continuous with respect to the strategies.

Aggregation: The trading possibilities of any player are influenced by the messages of the other players only through the mean of those messages.

Nondegeneracy: Individual players must be able to influence to a substantial extent their trading possibilities in the market.

The proof that these axioms are sufficient to establish the efficiency of the noncooperative equilibria is given by Dubey, Mas-Colell, and Shubik (1980).

15.1.2 Market mechanisms and money

Among the economic structures that satisfy the foregoing conditions are mass-market trading economies using a money. Consider an economy trading in m commodities. We define a *simple market* as one in which a specific commodity i trades for another commodity j. The economy as a whole can be regarded as a market structure consisting of a collection of simple markets. We say that a market structure contains a money if there is one commodity that can be exchanged directly for every other commodity, that is, one commodity for which there exists complete simple markets. Figure 15.1 illustrates market structures with one, two, and four monies. Given m goods we may have $1, 2, \ldots, m-2$, or m monies (but not $m-1$).[2]

Each line in figure 15.1 is a simple market and as such is a device that accepts messages in some form and uses them to arrange trades. The strategic market game illustrated in chapter 14 and the games investigated in section 15.2 all utilize one commodity as a money. The treatment of the Walrasian system by Arrow and Debreu is consistent with an interpretation of the existence of complete simple markets, in that they treat all commodities (and services) as monies (see Rogawski and Shubik, 1983).

When an economy uses only one commodity as a money, it is possible that efficient trade can be prevented by a shortage of that commodity. Cash-flow constraints appear. This point is discussed in detail in chapter 16. When all commodities are monies in exchange, then because all the assets of every individual are completely liquid, directly exchangeable into anything else, the distinction between an individual's budget constraint and cash-flow constraint disappears. One's total net worth is completely liquid and hence available for trade.

15.2 The "Offer-for-Sale" Model

In chapter 14 a simple model of exchange using a single commodity as a money was considered. The rules of the strategic market game required that all traders offer all (nonmonetary) goods for sale. This condition was imposed for simplicity in exposition and because it is an accountant's dream in the sense that all nonmonetary wealth is actively evaluated by the markets.

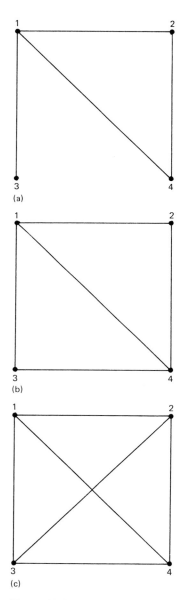

Figure 15.1
Simple markets and monies.

It may be argued that in many markets, and certainly in markets involving production and the carrying of inventory, forcing an individual to offer all his goods for sale is unreasonable. This restriction is relaxed here. Instead we assume that a trader will enter each market as a seller or buyer or both or neither.

Let there be n individuals, each with an endowment of $m + 1$ commodities. Thus individual i has a vector of resources $(a_1^i, a_2^i, \ldots, a_{m+1}^i)$ and a set of preferences represented by a continuous concave utility function $u_i(x_1^i, x_2^i, \ldots, x_{m+1}^i)$.

A strategy for trader i is a pair of vectors (q^i, b^i) such that

$$b_j^i \geq 0, \quad 0 \leq q_j^i \leq a_j^i \quad (j = 1, 2, \ldots, m), \tag{15.1}$$

$$\sum_{j=1}^{m} b_j^i \leq a_{m+1}^i, \tag{15.2}$$

where the amount of commodity j in the final possession of trader i is

$$x_j^i = \begin{cases} a_j^i - q_j^i + b_j^i \bar{q}_j / \bar{b}_j & \text{if } \bar{b}_j > 0, \\ a_j^i - q_j^i & \text{if } \bar{b}_j = 0, \end{cases} \tag{15.3}$$

for $j = 1, 2, \ldots, m$, and

$$x_{m+1}^i = a_{m+1}^i - \sum_{j=1}^{m} b_j^i + \sum_{j=1}^{m} q_j^i p_j, \tag{15.4}$$

where

$$p_j = \begin{cases} \bar{b}_j / \bar{q}_j & \text{if } \bar{q}_j > 0, \\ 0 & \text{if } \bar{q}_j = 0. \end{cases}$$

15.2.1 The strategy set

In order to give some insight into the nature of an individual's strategy sets and their relationship to final outcomes we consider a market with one commodity being bought or sold in trade with a commodity money.

In figure 15.2 the point labeled (A, M) represents the individual's initial endowment, with $A = a_1^i$ and $M = a_2^i$. (For simplicity in describing an individual's strategies we drop the superscript i since the meaning is clear.) His strategy set is a rectangle given by $0 \leq q \leq A$, $0 \leq b \leq M$. Any point in this rectangle is a strategy. Consider, for example, (q, b); we wish to study how it transforms the initial point (A, M). Suppose that all other traders have offered Q units of the good and a total of B units of money. Then a bid of (q, b) takes the initial holding of (A, M)

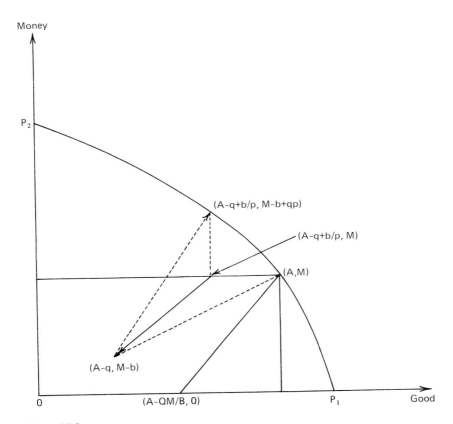

Figure 15.2
The "offer-for-sale" strategy set.

to a final holding of $(A - q + b/p, M - b + qp)$, where

$$p = \frac{B + b}{Q + q} \quad (Q > 0). \tag{15.5}$$

Had the individual bid been $(q - b/p, 0)$, this, too, would map (A, M) onto $(A - q + b/p, M - b + qp)$. The bids that map (A, M) onto itself are given by $A = A - q + b/p$ and $M = M - b + qp$ or

$$b = q \left(\frac{B + b}{Q + q} \right) \quad \text{or} \quad Qb = Bq. \tag{15.6}$$

All bids on the line connecting $(A - QM/B, 0)$ to (A, M) map (A, M) onto itself. Any strategy to the right of this line maps AM onto a point on the curve $P_1 P_2$ to the right.

All points on the curve $P_1 P_2$ can be obtained by bids on the L-shaped boundary of the strategy set, that is, bids of the form $(q, 0)$ or $(0, b)$, where $0 \le q \le A$ and $0 \le b \le M$. If (x, m) is a point on the curve $P_1 P_2$, it can be shown that the equation for this concave curve is

$$m = M + \frac{(A - x)B}{Q + A - x}. \tag{15.7}$$

We can generalize these observations for m commodities and a money. Let the initial holdings of individual i be given by $(a_1^i, a_2^i, \ldots, a_{m+1}^i)$. All others together have offered $(Q_1, Q_2, \ldots, Q_m)$ for sale and bid $(B_1, B_2, \ldots, B_m)$. A strategy by individual i is a point in a $2m$-dimensional rectangular set of the form $(q_1^i, q_2^i, \ldots, q_m^i, b_1^i, b_2^i, \ldots, b_m^i)$, which transforms the initial holdings into final holdings of

$$\left(a_1^i - q_1^i + b_1^i/p_1, a_2^i - q_2^i + b_2^i/p_2, \ldots, a_m^i - q_m^i + b_m^i/p_m; \right.$$
$$\left. a_{m+1}^i - \sum_{j=1}^{m} b_j^i + \sum_{j=1}^{m} q_j^i p_j \right). \tag{15.8}$$

We can derive the equation for the set of final holdings that can be reached by all bids. Let $(x_1^i, x_2^i, \ldots, x_{m+1}^i)$ be a point on the set of final holdings. Then the equation of this surface is given by

$$x_{m+1}^i = a_{m+1}^i + \sum_{j=1}^{m} \frac{B_j(a_j^i - x_j^i)}{Q_j + a_j^i - x_j^i}. \tag{15.9}$$

This is concave. Whereas in the example with one good any final outcome could be achieved by a line of strategies (as shown in figure 15.2), here any outcome can be achieved by the set of strategies formed by the product of m lines.[3]

To check that (15.9) is the surface of final allocations produced by the use of any strategy we can consider an arbitrary strategy (b_j^i, q_j^i) and show that it produces a final allocation satisfying (15.9). The final allocation produced by (b_j^i, q_j^i) is given in (15.8); substituting these values for x_j^i and x_{m+1}^i into (15.9) yields

$$\sum_{j=1}^{m}(q_j^i p_j - b_j^i) = \sum_{j=1}^{m} \frac{\dfrac{B_j}{p_j}(q_j^i p_j - b_j^i)}{Q_j + q_j^i - \dfrac{b_j^i}{p_j}}$$

$$= \sum_{j=1}^{m} \frac{\dfrac{B_j}{p_j}(q_j^i p_j - b_j^i)}{\dfrac{(Q_j + q_j^i)(b_j^i + B_j) - b_j^i(Q_j + q_j^i)}{b_j^i + B_j}}$$

$$= \sum_{j=1}^{m} \frac{\dfrac{B_j}{p_j}(q_j^i p_j - b_j^i)}{\dfrac{B_j}{p_j}} = \sum_{j=1}^{m}(q_j^i p_j - b_j^i). \tag{15.10}$$

15.2.2 A simple example

A simple example with two types of traders will help contrast the offer-for-sale model with the previously analyzed all-for-sale model. It will be important to maintain a clear distinction among the several features that together define the game:

1. The *bids* describe the moves.

2. The *market* transforms moves to outcomes.

3. The *information conditions* influence the domain of the strategies.

Here we assume that the individual can both bid and offer in the same market. The reader might wonder if this is a reasonable condition. We would like to prove rather than assume that if an individual wishes to buy a commodity, he will not simultaneously have to sell it.

Consider two sets of traders who differ only in their endowments. They all have utility functions of the form

$$u^i = \log x_1^i + \log x_2^i. \tag{15.11}$$

A trader of type 1 has a resource endowment of $(10, 30)$, and a trader of type 2 has an endowment of $(30, 10)$. We might expect that a trader of

Table 15.1
Thin-market equilibria

n	$\dfrac{n-1}{n}$	b	q	Trader of type 1	
				x	m
1	0	—	—	10	30
2	1/2	10/3	10/3	13.33	26.67
3	2/3	6	6	16	24
4	3/4	50/7	50/7	17.14	22.86
5	4/5	70/9	70/9	17.78	22.22
⋮	⋮	⋮	⋮	⋮	⋮
∞	1	10	10	20	20

type 1 will try to maximize by bidding for the good, whereas a trader of type 2 will offer it for sale. Final allocations will be given by

$$u^1 = \log\left(10 + \frac{b_i}{b}q\right) + \log(30 - b_i), \tag{15.12}$$

$$u^2 = \log(30 - q_j) + \log\left(10 + \frac{q_j}{q}b\right). \tag{15.13}$$

The first-order conditions for optimization call for

$$\frac{1}{10 + b_i q/b}\left[q\left(\frac{b - b_i}{b^2}\right)\right] = \frac{1}{30 - b_i}, \tag{15.14}$$

$$\frac{1}{30 - q_j} = \frac{1}{10 + q_j b/q}\left[b\left(\frac{q - q_j}{q^2}\right)\right]. \tag{15.15}$$

From these two equations we derive

$$q_i = b_j = \frac{10(2n - 3)}{(2n - 1)}. \tag{15.16}$$

Thus the equilibrium bids and offers can be portrayed as in table 15.1.

Figure 15.3 shows the Edgeworth box and the noncooperative equilibria on the main diagonal. The limiting NE is the competitive equilibrium shown in the center of the box. At the point E the price line is tangent to the indifference contours of both traders; furthermore their final allocation sets, which are curved as shown in figure 15.2, both flatten out and approach the main diagonal as $n \to \infty$.

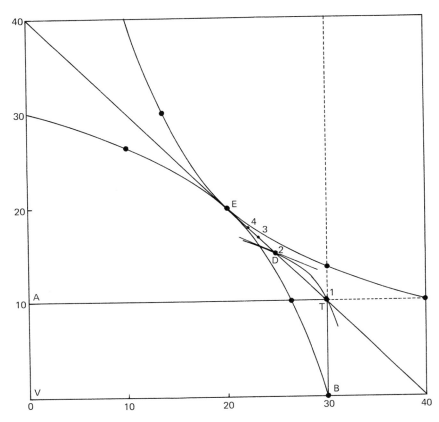

Figure 15.3
Noncooperative equilibria for $n = 1, 2, 3, \ldots$

At the NE for $n = 2$ the final allocation sets for traders of each type pass through the initial allocation point T and the equilibrium point D; thus the allocation at D is attainable by all simultaneously. At this equilibrium the final allocation set of trader 1 is tangent to his indifference contour, and similarly for trader 2. This Edgeworth box is drawn to illustrate symmetric strategies by traders of all types with a possible deviation by one trader. The diagram should be more properly viewed as being in $2n$ dimensions.

The equilibria shown in table 15.1 are equilibria arising in both the offer-for-sale model and the all-for-sale model analyzed in chapter 14. The offer-for-sale model, however, has other noncooperative equilibria.

Suppose that instead of restricting themselves to either bids or offers (this is equivalent to staying on the L-shaped boundary ATB of the rectangle $VATB$), traders made both bids and offers, thereby creating "wash sales" in which they sell and buy back the same commodity and thus create gross trade that is more voluminous than the net trade.

We could write the payoffs to the traders as follows:

$$u^1 = \log\left(10 + b_i\frac{q}{b} - q_i\right) + \log\left(30 - b_i + q_i\frac{b}{q}\right), \tag{15.17}$$

$$u^2 = \log\left(30 + b_j\frac{q}{b} - q_j\right) + \log\left(10 - b_j + q_j\frac{b}{q}\right). \tag{15.18}$$

From (15.17) we obtain

$$\frac{1}{10 + (b_iq/b) - q_i}\left(\frac{q(b - b_i)}{b^2}\right) = \frac{1 - \frac{q_i}{q}}{30 - b_i + q_ib/q}, \tag{15.19}$$

$$\frac{1 - \frac{b_i}{b}}{10 + (b_iq/q) - q_i} = \left(\frac{b(q - q_i)}{q^2}\right)\frac{1}{30 - b_i + q_ib/q}, \tag{15.20}$$

but we see that multiplying (15.19) by b/q yields (15.20).

Similarly from (15.18) we obtain

$$\frac{1 - \frac{b_j}{b}}{30 + (b_jq/b) - q_j} = \frac{1}{10 - b_j + q_jb/q}\left(\frac{b(q - q_j)}{q^2}\right). \tag{15.21}$$

If (15.20) and (15.21) had a solution other than the one previously obtained with $b_j = q_i = 0$, we would have an equilibrium with wash sales playing a role.

ASSERTION. *For a finite n there exists a symmetric equilibrium point to this game, with active wash sales. This equilibrium point will have a higher level of actual net trade than the equilibrium without wash sales.*

This assertion can be shown to be true by a simple example. Consider the equilibrium for $n = 3$. We had $b_i = q_j = 6$ and $b_j = q_i = 0$. Consider new strategies as follows:

$$b_i = q_j = 10, \qquad b_j = q_i = 4 - f. \tag{15.22}$$

From (15.20) and (15.22) we obtain

$$\frac{1 - \dfrac{10}{42 - 3f}}{10 + 10 - (4 - f)} = \frac{\dfrac{(42 - 3f) - (4 - f)}{42 - 3f}}{30 - 10 + (4 - f)}, \tag{15.23}$$

where $b = q = 42 - 3f$. This yields

$$\frac{32 - 3f}{16 + f} = \frac{38 - 2f}{24 - f}$$

or

$$5f^2 - 110f + 160 = 0. \tag{15.24}$$

Thus there is an equilibrium with strategies $(10, 2.434)$ and $(2.434, 10)$, where each finally trades 7.566 units. The payoffs from the equilibrium strategies without wash sales are $\log 16 + \log 24 = 2.584$ to each; and with wash sales, $\log 17.566 + \log 22.434 = 2.596$ to each.

We have shown that wash sales can create "thicker markets" and hence lower the impact of change by a single individual. Here, paradoxically, the market with heavy wash sales is best for all traders. For the model with a continuum of traders it appears that the effect of wash sales is attenuated; thus there will be a set of noncooperative equilibria, formed by the Cartesian product of strategies with wash sales, that are all equivalent to the competitive equilibrium.

If we imposed a "cash-flow minimization" condition, this indeterminacy would be removed. However, for a market with atomic traders an equilibrium point with wash sales may be better for all than one without wash sales. This implies that even with positive transaction costs there may be noncooperative equilibria with wash sales that are better for all than an equilibrium with gross trade equal to net trade.

Dubey and Shubik (1978a) gave a proof of the existence of noncooperative equilibria for the offer-for-sale model together with an exploration of the limit properties of the noncooperative equilibria.

15.3 Production and Ownership

When the type of strategic analysis called for by the strategic market game is applied to an economy with both production and exchange, there appear new difficulties over and above those encountered in modeling exchange as a game in strategic form. In particular, the strategic and extensive forms of a strategic market game involving only exchange are essentially the same. A strategy and a move are equivalent, as can be seen by considering the all-for-sale and offer-for-sale models previously described.

Once we decide to take account of production and exchange before constructing the game in strategic form, we must consider the extensive form in order to specify the sequencing of the procurement of resources, production, and exchange.

Furthermore, if firms are to be considered as strategic players, the nature of their control and ownership must be specified. The goals of those who control their decisions must be given. If the firms are owned jointly—for example, by means of common stock—the strategic aspects of the voting of stock must be taken into account. (We consider voting in chapter 20.)

Dubey and Shubik (1978b) analyzed a multistage strategic market game with both exchange and production. They showed that under appropriate conditions there exists a class of noncooperative equilibria that converge to the competitive equilibria. However, the complexity of the strategies involved and the possible existence of other equilibrium points depend delicately on the sequencing of moves and the information conditions assumed.

In particular, it is assumed in the model they analyzed that all goods are initially held by individuals. Money is held initially by both firms and individuals. Firms have nonvoting shares and are run by managers assumed to be profit-maximizing fiduciaries. The sequencing of moves is assumed to be as follows. First, there is a market in which all consumers and firms trade. After the first market, the firms produce. After they have produced, they offer all of their product for sale in a second market where the consumers buy and sell.

The noncooperative equilibria that converge to the competitive equilibria are consistent with the lowest levels of information and hence are robust against changes in information. This may be regarded as being consistent with economic intuition. However, the possible proliferation of noncooperative equilibria as information increases contains a strong warning for those who wish to develop an economic dynamics. Once information and communication conditions become even moderately abundant, many behavioral models of economic dynamics become consistent with the concept of noncooperative equilibria for a game in extensive form.

The strategic market game also offers a natural context for studying the goals of the managers and owners of firms. The simple assumption of profit-maximizing managers may in some circumstances serve as an adequate first approximation of what firms do; for many purposes of economic analysis, however, this assumption is inadequate. The main reasons are as follows:

Utility maximization: It is not an axiomatic truth that profit maximization by a sole owner and utility maximization are equivalent. If the manager or strategic player is a fiduciary, his personal utility maximization may not be in the best interests of stockholders.

Voting stock: If the firm is held by a group of stockholders with voting stock, control is in general of economic value. This is not reflected in most theorizing to date.

Taxes and profits: The economic and tax definitions of profits differ. Profit maximization by a corporate manager for stockholders requires careful interpretation of these differences, especially given the different tax positions of various stockholders, the manager, and the firm.

Profit maximization and risk profiles: When the economy is viewed strategically, there is always uncertainty present. Even leaving aside exogenous uncertainty, there will be endogenous uncertainty due to the strategic behavior of the individuals. Thus profit maximization must be modified to take into account the risk preferences of the manager of the firm and the stockholders. (There is a literature in finance on this topic.)

Profit maximization and the infinite horizon: If the horizon is unbounded and there is a positive probability for the death of individuals and the bankruptcy of firms, the definition and relevance of profit maximization require some qualification.

It can be shown that utility-maximizing managers will maximize profit for their firms regardless of their own shareholdings provided all markets are thick, existing corporate law is adequate to enforce equal treatment of all stockholders, and a combination of accounting and managerial controls makes self-dealing impossible (Dubey and Shubik, 1981). These conditions seldom prevail (Whitman and Shubik, 1979).

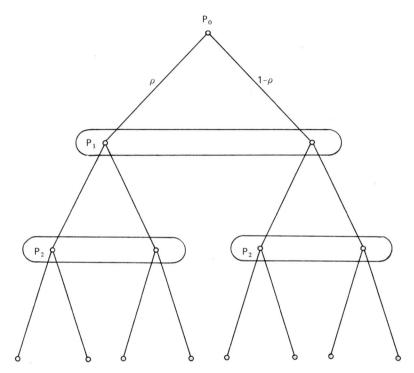

Figure 15.4
Extensive form with nonsymmetric information.

15.4   Uncertainty and Prices

15.4.1   Strategic market games with nonsymmetric information

Suppose that there is exogenous uncertainty present in a market and that different traders have different levels of information concerning Nature's moves. An example of this situation in the extensive form is shown in figure 15.4. First trader 1 moves without knowing the outcome of Nature's move; then trader 2 moves knowing Nature's move but not knowing the move of trader 1.

We can think of such nonsymmetric situations in terms of "black boxes," with some of the traders equipped with special glasses that enable them to see part or all of the contents of the boxes. Such a box might contain, for example, A oranges with probability ρ; otherwise it is empty.

A *pure future* is a single black box that pays out for some particular contingency. If the contingency does not arise, then all bids on that box are lost—they have turned out to be worthless. Arrow and Debreu modeled uncertainty in an equivalent way: Their traders treat contingent commodities as a new form of commodity to be traded, that is, as a future.[4]

The Arrow–Debreu analysis runs into difficulties when all traders no longer perceive the same number of contingent commodities. Radner (1968) showed that with nonsymmetric information conditions there may not be a competitive-equilibrium price system. In the strategic market game with markets and trade using a money there may nevertheless be a price system. It can be shown that a noncooperative equilibrium always exists even with nonsymmetric information (Dubey and Shubik, 1977a). The general proof is not given here, but we shall calculate a simple example to show the behavior of the noncooperative equilibrium under different conditions. What we find is that the more information an individual has concerning the possible states of nature, the more complicated his contingent planning may become.

Our simple two-person example will illustrate the possibilities opened up by changes in information. In particular, we shall show that the expected payoffs to the traders under symmetric incomplete information can be higher than under complete information, but that if one individual is informed and the other is not, the former gains and the latter loses.

We shall in fact consider three different two-person models. Each example consists of a modified version of the all-for-sale model described in chapter 14, in which individuals must offer all commodities except money for sale. (We could have modified the offer-for-sale model described in section 15.2, but the all-for-sale models provide the simplest example to illustrate the effect of changes of information on the noncooperative equilibrium.)

Suppose that there are two traders trading in one commodity using a commodity money. There are two states of the universe: "rain" or "shine." Under the first state the first individual has 4 units of the good and the second has 12. Under the second state ownership is reversed. Each individual has 100 units of money under all circumstances. The expected utility function of individual i is

$$U^i = \rho \log(q_1^i) + (1 - \rho)\log(q_2^i) + M - m^i \qquad (i = 1, \ 2),$$

where q_j^i is the amount of the consumer good in state j consumed by trader i and m^i is i's expected net change in money after trade.

Let x_1 and x_2 (y_1 and y_2) be the amounts of money spent by trader 1 (trader 2) in states 1 and 2. If the first trader cannot distinguish between states 1 and 2 (incomplete information), his decision variable will become x rather than x_1 and x_2. For simplicity we set $\rho = 1 - \rho = 1/2$.

Symmetric incomplete information: Here the payoff for trader 1 is

$$\Pi_1 = \rho \log\left(\frac{16x}{x+y}\right) + (1-\rho)\log\left(\frac{16x}{x+y}\right) - x + 100 + \frac{1}{2}(x+y),$$

and similarly for trader 2. It is easy to check that $x = y = 1$ and that the final expected payoff for each is $3\log 2 + 100 = 100.90309$.

Symmetric complete information: Here the payoff for trader 1 is

$$\Pi_1 = \rho \log\left(\frac{16x_1}{x_1+y_1}\right) + (1-\rho)\log\left(\frac{16x_2}{x_2+y_2}\right) - \rho x_1 - (1-\rho)x_2 + 100$$

$$+ \frac{\rho}{4}(x_1+y_1) + \frac{3}{4}(1-\rho)(x_2+y_2),$$

and similarly for trader 2. Hence $x_1 = 4/(1+\sqrt{3}) = y_2$. The final payoff for each is 100.8869, and $x_2 = 4/\sqrt{3}(1+\sqrt{3}) = y_1$. This is less than was obtained with incomplete information! Joint ignorance may be bliss.

Nonsymmetric incomplete-complete information: Here the payoff for trader 1 is

$$\Pi_1 = \rho \log\left(\frac{16x}{x+y_1}\right) + (1-\rho)\log\left(\frac{16x}{x+y_2}\right) - x + 100 + \frac{\rho}{4}(x+y_1)$$

$$+ \frac{3}{4}(1-\rho)(x+y_2)$$

and that for trader 2 is

$$\Pi_2 = \rho \log\left(\frac{16y_1}{x+y_1}\right) + (1-\rho)\log\left(\frac{16y_2}{x+y_2}\right) - \rho y_1 - (1-\rho)y_2 + 100$$

$$+ \frac{3}{4}\rho(x+y_1) + \frac{1}{4}(1-\rho)(x+y_2).$$

The maximization conditions give us

$$\frac{y_1}{x(x+y_1)} + \frac{y_2}{x(x+y_2)} = 1,$$

$$\frac{x}{y_1(x+y_1)} = \frac{1}{4} \quad \text{and} \quad \frac{x}{y_2(x+y_2)} = \frac{3}{4},$$

which have a solution $x \approx 1.032$, $y_1 = 1.580$, and $y_2 = 0.7655$, with payoffs $\Pi_1 = 100.8505$ and $\Pi_2 = 100.9410$.

A change from incomplete information to information for one trader benefits the recipient and hurts the other trader. A further increase to complete information may leave both worse off than with symmetric incomplete information.

The noncooperative equilibrium with nonsymmetric information even for many traders will not converge to the Arrow–Debreu competitive equilibrium. We argue, however, that in the context of the game with limited information, the feasible set is constrained, and hence the Pareto-optimal surface may be changed. Thus it is necessary to define efficiency with respect to the constrained feasible set of outcomes rather than the outcomes attainable if both had a two-dimensional strategy set. Even in this context the limit equilibria may not be efficient.

15.4.2 On markets for information
There is a literature in economic theory and finance that deals with the efficiency of a competitive market in reflecting differences in information in prices. This issue is broadly referred to as "rational expectations" (see, e.g., Radner, 1968, 1979), although a far better name would be "consistent expectations."

The game-theoretic model of trade with nonsymmetric information shows how individuals can benefit from special knowledge. It can be shown that with many traders trading repeatedly, prices will almost always reveal the special information of the traders after one round of trade. This indicates that in mass markets opportunities for arbitrage must be acted upon rapidly.

Because the strategic market game is process-oriented, it can illuminate several features that are obscured or ignored by the rational-expectations literature. In particular, it has been shown by Dubey, Geanakoplos, and Shubik (1982) that although under reasonable circumstances information will be generically revealed after one round of trade, those with information may still benefit. Furthermore if the numbers in the market are few, there is no reason to expect revelation. If information can be bought directly, it is easy to construct examples in which the pure-strategy price equilibrium is destroyed.

The market mechanism in which prices reveal information is only one of the ways in which information is revealed. In any financial and entre-preneurial community there are those who have raw information, those who interpret the meaning or worth of the information, and those who act. The data gatherers, the experts, the consultants and analysts, and the entrepreneurs are by no means the same individuals. Special data, interpretation of data, knowledge, and advice are bought and sold. There are markets for knowledge and information as well as markets that reflect differences in knowledge and information via the price system. (For a discussion of the modeling of the sale of information see Shubik, 1976.)

Modeling the characteristics of an expert belongs more to the domain of psychology than to that of economics. The assumption of *external symmetry* (see *GTSS*, chapter 2) so frequently made in game-theoretic models does not hold for experts. Despite the difficulty in characterizing experts, though, the economist may still be concerned with how information is appropriated, how experts' services are bought and sold, and what characterizes the rules for the direct markets for information.

The appropriation problem connects the study of information and communication with that of public goods. Copyright and patent laws are examples of extra legal rules of the game designed to protect ownership rights. Yet in many economic problems it is not what the numbers are, but what they mean that counts. Raw information may be plentiful, but without interpretation it is useless.

In making a decision about a major investment or about major surgery, an individual will normally elicit more than one expert opinion. Thus degree of belief in the expert consulted becomes a key factor.

These difficult problems in the modeling of economic reality are noted here not because we wish to propose a solution to them but as a caveat. Although it is easy to handle nonsymmetric information by means of strategic market games or so-called rational-expectations models, we must warn that they both avoid the basic economic fact that special knowledge, information interpretation, and expertise are directly bought and sold.

Furthermore, although the assumption of the existence of a continuum of economic agents may be adequate to portray a day of trading in General Electric shares, frequently it is not a relevant assumption. With regard to major investment decisions the market for information and expertise is at best oligopolistic. The old Wall Street saying, "There are always more deals than dealers," illustrates this point.

15.5 The Characteristic Function and Cooperative Solutions of a Strategic Market Game

The problem faced in defining the characteristic function for a strategic market game illustrates in a striking manner the conceptual differences between modeling from the economic data directly into the cooperative form and going from the data first into the strategic form and then into a cooperative form. The strategic market game requires process detail (in particular a description of price formation) that is not required of the market game. We may take the strategic market game as a datum and construct a game in coalitional form based on it. Because all individuals must trade through the same set of markets regardless of their coalition membership, the strategic market game is not a c-game. This contrasts with the market game, where as soon as the coalition S is formed it is completely independent of $\bar{S}$. In a strategic market game threats must be accounted for and will depend on features such as relative efficiency in production and capacities.

A useful way to account for threats is by evaluating a damage exchange rate in order to determine a zero point from which to measure cooperative bargains. The Harsanyi function h noted in section 7.3.2 can also account for threats. The following equations and indicate the calculations required to determine the side-payment Harsanyi function for the offer-for-sale strategic market game:

$$h(S) + h(\bar{S}) = v(N),$$
$$h(S) - h(\bar{S}) =$$

$$\text{maxmin}\left[\sum_{i \in S} \phi_i \left(a_1^i - q_1^i + b_1^i/p_j; \dots; a_{m+1}^i + \sum_{j=1}^m q_j^i p_j - \sum_{j=1}^m b_j^i\right)\right.$$
$$\left. - \sum_{k \in \bar{S}} \phi_k \left(a_1^k - q_1^k + b_1^k/p_1; \dots; a_{m+1}^k + \sum_{j=1}^m q_j^k p_j - \sum_{j=1}^m b_j^k\right)\right],$$

where

$$p_j = \sum_{i=1}^n b_j^i / \sum_{i=1}^n q_j^i \quad (j = 1, 2, \dots, m) \quad \text{and} \quad p_{m+1} = 1.$$

These equations are written as though there were a transferable utility available to all. The no-side-payment calculations are somewhat more complicated.

An example of a Harsanyi function for an open Cournot oligopoly model is given in figure 5.9. When the model is closed, as it is here, for large markets, the Harsanyi function of a strategic market game and the characteristic function of the associated market game will have core and value solutions that approach the same limits.

For large markets with many small traders, the coalitions of almost everyone will be approximately as powerful as they are in an exchange c-game. A handful of small mavericks cannot do much harm. By the law of large numbers, the profiles of coalitions of middling size and their complements will be the same; hence their threat possibilities will be attenuated. We may thus expect the core and value of any strategic market game satisfying the Dubey–Mas-Colell–Shubik axioms to coincide with the set of CEs for a continuum of traders and to converge to the CEs for a replication of the market with a finite number of types of traders, where each type has a finite number of traders. This will hold even though for few traders the core, value, and feasible set differ when exchange is constrained to take place through markets (as contrasted with completely unconstrained exchange).

The distinction between the characteristic function of a market game and the cooperative form of a strategic market game illustrates and enables us to resolve the paradox of "pecuniary externalities" posed by Viner (1931; see Shubik, 1971c).

Notes to chapter 15

1. Limit results are also obtained for a large number of small traders.

2. Perhaps an unwieldly but more accurate phrase than "money" would be "a commodity with the exchange property of a money." There are other properties such as *numéraire* or store of wealth that are attached to the usual meaning of money. These require extra specification beyond the transaction features.

3. Implicit in our discussion is that credit is available: Either money is sufficiently plentiful so that credit to finance the bids is not needed, or credit is costlessly granted and repaid at the end of the period. See chapter 16 for further discussion.

4. Common usage in the futures markets plays down the uncertainty description given above. A futures contract for delivery of 5000 bushels of wheat at a given price in September of next year involves a good that does not exist now. Spot prices may move due to uncertainty in the quantity to be produced for the market as a whole, but unless a *force majeure* occurs delivery will be expected.

16 Finance and Political Economy

"Let us suppose a whole generation of men to be born on the same day, to attain mature age on the same day, and to die on the same day, leaving a succeeding generation in the moment of attaining their mature age, all together. Let the ripe age be supposed of twenty-one years, and their period of life thirty-four years more, that being the average term given by the bills of mortality to persons of twenty-one years of age. Each successive generation would, in this way, come and go off the stage at a fixed moment, as individuals do now. Then I say, the earth belongs to each of these generations during its course, fully and in its own right. The second generation receives it clear of the debts and incumbrances of the first, the third of the second, and so on. For if the first could charge it with a debt, then the earth would belong to the dead and not to the living generation. Then, no generation can contract debts greater than may be paid during the course of its own existence."

Letter of Thomas Jefferson to James Madison, Paris, September 6, 1789

16.1 A Preliminary to Dynamics

The financial institutions of a modern society are its neural network. Most of the signals transmitted to control and direct investment, production, and the direct redistribution of wealth go directly through the financial network. It is through this system that government acting as the fiduciary for society taxes, subsidizes, and spends. It not only operates through the financial system but also controls its basic parameters and structure; thus interest rates are set, and a host of regulations limit the actions of financial intermediaries.

The government is the sociopolitical decision-making device that aggregates the social will and produces a socioeconomic policy based on individual and group decisions in a game of strategy. The rules of the game for the immediate operation of the economy are given by the existing laws, customs, and institutions of society. Voting mechanisms and the financial structure provide the politicoeconomic control system of society on government and vice versa.

Questions concerning equity, fairness, efficiency, and optimality, at least from the viewpoint of the political economist, are asked best at two levels. The first is directed at the model of the game and the underlying axioms behind the selection of the rules. The second concerns the properties of the outcomes that arise from playing the game as it is.

In this part it is suggested that the financial system appears naturally in the explanation of oligopolistic competition in a closed economy. The assumption of the existence of markets, money, and credit is natural to the specification of strategic market games. But as Bagehot (1873) noted, a financial instrument invented or useful for a single purpose may assume a totally different role in an economy. Money, markets, and credit were natural devices to facilitate trade, but they also put into place the web for governmental influence and control.

The embedding of a model of oligopolistic competition in a closed economic system, which can be achieved by strategic market games, does far more than reconcile oligopoly theory and general-equilibrium theory. It also naturally connects the new models with the structure of a monetary mechanism and hence opens the models to a much needed enlargement of scope.

It has been suggested that a successful reconciliation of microeconomic theory requires that four major features of the political economy be jointly modeled and analyzed at the same level of rigor as the general-equilibrium system or at a higher level. These are:

1. Production and distribution;

2. Money and financial institutions;

3. Government, voting, taxation, and public goods;

4. A multigenerational population.

This part offers a brief sketch of the strategic market game approach to money and financial institutions together with a discussion of how to model an economy with a multigenerational population. Part V will consider voting, taxation, and public goods.

For all of the topics noted above, it is on occasion worthwhile to consider the cooperative form of a game, as was done in part III, but for the most part we shall concentrate on building models in strategic form or in extensive form. This type of modeling forces the specification of all the rules of the game and hence describes basic institutions at a high level of abstraction. The modeling is implicitly dynamic even though the concentration of analysis on the noncooperative equilibrium emphasizes statics.

Before we can develop an economic dynamics, we must describe the carriers of process. The institutions that constrain and channel behavior must appear as part of the description of the game.

16.2 An Approach to Financial Institutions and Instruments

16.2.1 Mathematical institutional economics
The theme of mathematical institutional economics is used to suggest that the need to portray institutions may emerge from the application of game-theoretic modeling methods to basic economic problems.

Chapters 14 and 15 have already described strategic market games. The contrast between the efficient price system approached as a limit of noncooperative equilibria for games in strategic form and approached directly via general-equilibrium theory, illustrates the remarks above. Because the general-equilibrium approach is nonstrategic, no description of the details of individual strategic behavior or of the price-formation and market-clearance mechanisms is needed. In contrast, the strategic market game requires all of this detail.

Suppose trade takes place among $m + 1$ commodities. We have seen in chapter 15 that we could select as few as one and as many as $m + 1$ of them to serve as a means of exchange, or a money. If all of them are selected, we need $m(m + 1)/2$ markets; if only one is selected, then only m markets are needed.

When all goods are selected as money, everything exchanges directly for everything else. No liquidity problem exists, but there are many markets. For a modern economy the assumption of one money is a better approximation to the truth. With only one money there is a considerable saving in the number of markets. But the ability of the traders using the money to achieve efficiency without repeated trading may be impaired by a cash-flow constraint that appears when fewer than all commodities can be used in direct exchange.

Confining our considerations to a single commodity as a means of payment, we can easily see that if all trade must involve its exchange, an individual without any of the commodity will be unable to purchase anything. Society has solved this illiquidity problem by introducing various forms of credit: the personal extension of credit between two individuals, the issuance of bank money, and the issuance of fiat money by governments. Each brings with it a host of financial and legal problems in defining the rules of the game, and all three require that conditions for the handling of insolvency and bankruptcy be specified. These conditions are discussed in some detail in section 16.2.2.

When everyone uses a commodity money—that is, pays cash—no trust is required, and trade can remain completely anonymous. No clearinghouses are needed, and auditing and accounting are not necessary. When credit is granted, depending on the nature of the arrangements, documents must be drawn up, methods of verification must be agreed on, and clearance and enforcing agencies must be set up to terminate credit.

To fully define a game in which a private banking system is permitted to issue its own notes or checks, the rules concerning bank failure must be given. Bankruptcy and bank failure conditions at first glance appear to be peculiarly institutional; but just as the properties of mass markets could be axiomatized in chapter 15, so can the essential aspects of these rules be described. They are needed to discourage the unbounded issuance of debt. To do this the penalty for default must be made sufficiently severe that the expected gain from any strategic repudiation of debt is offset by the penalty.

Sometimes, as is well known, differences in size lead to qualitative differences. Thus the debt relationships between two private individuals, between an individual and a banker or moneylender, and between an individual and a central government are all qualitatively different. In particular, there may be laws against bank failure that protect individuals, but there are no similar laws that protect the public against the financial failure of a central government.

16.2.2 Credit, fiat money, and bankruptcy

This section sketches two models of strategic market games, the first with the immediate granting of individual credit and the second with the issuance of a specific quantity of fiat money by the referee or central government (see Shubik and Wilson, 1977; Dubey and Shubik, 1979; Postlewaite and Schmeidler, 1978; Dubey and Shapley, 1977). In both cases the treatment of the bankruptcy condition is the same.

Let each individual i have a continuous concave utility function defined on $m + 1$ commodities. Thus $u_i(x_1^i, x_2^i, \ldots, x_{m+1}^i)$ is defined on R_+^{m+1}, the nonnegative orthant of an $(m + 1)$-dimensional Euclidean space. Suppose that the $(m + 1)$st commodity is used as a money and that it serves both as means of exchange and as *numéraire*. Credit is granted in terms of the $(m + 1)$st commodity. The bankruptcy penalty is reflected by extending the domain of definition of u_i from R_+^{m+1} to $R_+^m \times R^1$; that is, we include in the evaluation by the utility function final bundles of resources involving money debts that have not been repaid.

Figure 16.1 shows two examples of indifference curves drawn between

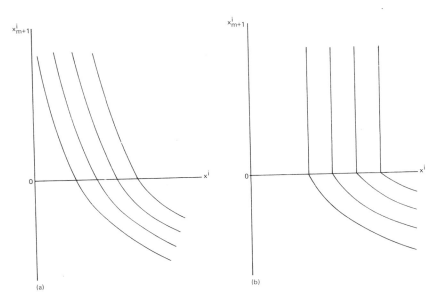

Figure 16.1
Money and debt.

money, the $(m + 1)$st commodity, and an aggregate of all other commodities denoted by x^i. In figure 16.1a we assume that the monetary commodity has intrinsic worth. In figure 16.1b a positive stock of the $(m + 1)$st commodity after trade has no value to the trader. This is shown by the vertical indifference curves. Yet whether the money is a commodity of intrinsic worth out of trade (as in part a) or pure fiat (as in part b), being in debt at the end of trade, that is, possessing negative amounts of money, carries a penalty. If the penalties can be made sufficiently harsh, all players will avoid incurring them, and the noncooperative game will have a solution in the positive orthant, without any bankruptcies. To attain a competitive equilibrium as a noncooperative equilibrium in a game with many traders, at equilibrium the marginal utility of an extra unit of income must be offset or more than offset by the bankruptcy penalty.

Unlimited credit   Mathematically the difference between the all-for-sale model studied in chapter 14 where there is no credit and the all-for-sale model with unlimited credit is as follows: For the all-for-sale model without credit the utility function of a trader i is defined as $u_i(x^i_1, x^i_2, \ldots, x^i_{m+1})$ on R^{m+1}_+; for the model with credit it is defined on $R^m_+ \times R^1$. A strategy in the model without credit is a vector of bids $(b_1^i, b_2^i, \ldots, b_m^i)$ subject to the constraint that

$$\sum_{j=1}^{m} b_j^i \leq a_{m+1}^i.$$

A strategy in the model with credit does not have this constraint. It is as though each trader i had an unconstrained line of credit that permitted him to write checks of any size.

If we postulate the existence of a central bank, then clearing and balancing the books is relatively simple. If there are many banks, both the specification of the clearing mechanism and the rules of default become more complicated.

In a model with unlimited credit or bank money it can be shown that any positive bankruptcy penalty will suffice to ensure a competitive equilibrium as a noncooperative equilibrium in the game with a continuum of traders (Dubey and Shapley, 1977). Intuitively the reason is straightforward. No matter how lenient the penalty selected, because credit is unbounded the players will always inflate the price system by borrowing up to the point at which the penalty for default is sufficient to deter further borrowing.

The overall amount of credit thus inflates so that any positive penalty for default becomes strong enough, but it should also be noted that in this model no interest is paid on credit. The players are required only to repay what they have borrowed. A little reflection indicates that this conclusion is reasonable. Time plays no essential role in the preferences of the traders; there is no capital investment. The only purpose of the credit is to finance circulating capital, or the float required by trade in money with all trade occurring simultaneously through anonymous markets.

A small credit charge is required to pay the expenses of issuance, of accounting, and of running the needed clearinghouses, but leaving that aside the monetary and credit system can be regarded as an external economy that can be supplied at little cost by a strong government if it is trusted and has powers of enforcement.

Fiat money   We do not suggest that the strategic model we shall propose contains a realistic description of how fiat money enters any economy. It does, however, provide a simple model of a game in which the government or referee, by controlling the quantity of paper money issued and the default penalty, can structure the game so that for appropriate values of

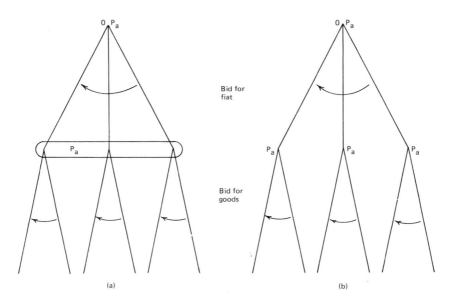

Figure 16.2
Extremes in information.

these parameters the competitive equilibria will be noncooperative equilibria. A detailed example and general proofs are given elsewhere (Shubik and Wilson, 1977; Dubey and Shubik, 1979).

The conditions on preferences are exactly the same as in the model with unlimited credit, but the monetary mechanism and the strategies of the traders are different. The game now becomes a two-stage rather than a one-stage game, and hence there will be variations depending on the information conditions assumed between stages. Figures 16.2a and 16.2b show two extremes in information. Figure 16.2a shows the case in which, first, all traders bid for part of a supply of fiat money and then, after all have bid, and in total ignorance of what has transpired, they all bid again for the m goods for sale. The symbol P_a indicates that all players bid simultaneously. Figure 16.2b shows the case in which, after all have bid for the supply of fiat, each trader is informed of what has transpired.

The game is as follows. The referee announces an amount M of legal tender up for auction. An individual i may bid any nonnegative amount y^i of his own personal IOU notes in order to obtain a share of M. If we denote the sum of all notes bid by

$$y = \sum_{j=1}^{n} y^i,$$

the amount of fiat money obtained by trader i is

$$s^i = y^i M / y. \tag{16.1}$$

Thus evidence of individual indebtedness is being exchanged for government debt. The visibility, trust, and power of the government enables it, by issuing its own paper, to monetize individual credit.

We note that the amount y/M can be rewritten as

$$y/M = 1 + \rho, \tag{16.2}$$

where ρ can be interpreted as a rate of interest that provides a risk reserve for the bank. The public as a whole offers to pay back y units in return for the M units they will get. If $y > M$, clearly there will be a positive rate of interest for fiat money. If $\rho > 0$, simple considerations of conservation indicate that someone must go bankrupt.

If we assume that decisions are made in complete ignorance, then the strategy for a player i can be described by $(y^i_j, b^i_1, b^i_2, \ldots, b^i_m)$, where

$$\sum_{j=1}^{m} b^i_j \le 1$$

and the b^i_j can be interpreted as the percentage of i's fiat money bid for commodity j.

If complete information is assumed, then a strategy consists of a number y^i and set of m functions b^i_j ($j = 1, 2, \ldots, m$) constrained so that

$$\sum_{j=1}^{m} b^i_j \le s^i.$$

Because the amount of fiat money M is fixed, there is an upper bound on the price system; hence, if the default penalties are made too low, there is no way the price system can rise sufficiently to cheapen the worth of fiat money to the point where the marginal disutility of default discourages strategic default.

16.2.3 Risk, insurance, and futures contracts
One method for handling both time periods and uncertainty is to expand the space of commodities being traded (Debreu, 1959). Consider $m + 1$ commodities, each of which can be in one of k states during any time period, and assume that there are T time periods. We may consider this

as a total of $(m + 1)kT$ commodities of the form "day-old bread if it is raining at time $t = 3$." If any of these compound commodities can be exchanged for any other directly, we require $(m + 1)kT[(m + 1)kT - 1]/2$ markets. An economy with 1000 goods trading 10 years into the future with 10 contingencies will require around 5×10^9 markets. If trade is confined to goods that are known to exist and to one-period futures in exchange for money, however, there will be at most 2000 active markets per period.

When time and chance are involved, the saving in the number of markets needed to operate an efficient economy by means of money and credit is even more important than when we consider one-period trade.

In the real world future risk is dealt with primarily by obtaining insurance from a private or public source, by self-insuring, or by buying futures contracts. The protection of supplies and protection against changes in commodity prices are usually dealt with through futures contracts, whereas protection of life, health, and property is done through insurance. Futures contracts tend to be standardized and have secondary markets; insurance contracts may be more complex and have no secondary market. Beyond these differentiations the basic properties that characterize the market mechanisms selected to deal with various types of risk are still unclear.

Apart from the work of Borch (1974), applications of game theory to risk, futures, and insurance have scarcely been developed. It appears to be feasible but not easy to construct strategic market games that take these features into account.

The difficulties caused by uncertainty are exemplified by an attempt to define an optimum bankruptcy law in the face of exogenous uncertainty. Without such uncertainty the optimum law is one that is just harsh enough to prevent strategic bankruptcy. If it is made harsher, it will not influence the physical outcome. Given exogenous uncertainty, however, an individual may be bankrupted by chance, which makes the definition and fine tuning of a bankruptcy law more difficult and more delicate. The meaning of an efficient or optimal penalty must be linked to a group or societal norm on the harshness or leniency of the law.

16.2.4 On financial instruments and institutions

How large and complex does a society have to be for it to give up barter and resort to organized markets and a commodity money? What are the essential preconditions for the appearance of fiat money, private banks, central banks, common stocks, bonds, public debt, organized stock and bond markets, futures contracts, insurance contracts, and other financial instruments and institutions? These are some of the questions that need to be asked in the context of strategic microeconomic models of economic behavior in attempting to reconcile micro- and macroeconomics.

Any student of taxation or finance will have noted that new financial instruments come and go with rapidity. A minor change in a tax law or in communication or transportation technology can wipe out one instrument and replace it by another. These instruments appear to be peculiarly institutional and therefore change with institutional changes. Is there, then, any underlying constancy in the basic characteristics of the economic goods, services, and paper used to run a modern economy?

We shall suggest that there are no more than eight basically different elements that need to be taken into account in the description of a modern economy (Shubik, 1975e). Two are goods and services, two are one-party paper, and four are contracts or essentially two-party paper. They are: goods; services; fiat money; ownership paper; futures contracts; service contracts; debt contracts; and puts, calls, and options. Most are self-explanatory. Ownership paper includes deeds and titles as well as stock in joint enterprises. Puts, calls, and options are contracts on ownership paper.

The essential question concerning the invention of a specific financial instrument is what strategic need can be fulfilled with this new instrument that was not as efficiently attainable within the old rules of the game.

16.3 Competition, Motivation, and the Infinite Horizon

16.3.1 General-equilibrium dynamics and macroeconomics
Much of the analysis in general-equilibrium theory has been done with models defined for a finite time horizon (Debreu, 1959; for good summaries see Arrow and Hahn, 1971; Arrow and Intrilligator, 1981). Although, as has already been noted, the general-equilibrium analysis is not strategic, the modeling used is related to the strategic form of a game. The analysis is static: Although time periods and exogenous uncertainty can be modeled by enlarging the space of commodities, all plans are essentially strategies for all time.

There has been some success in extending the analysis to the infinite horizon and to sequences of economies (for a survey see Grandmont, 1982). But it is important to distinguish between the successful extension of mathematical techniques from a model of finite horizon to one of infinite horizon and a drastic reorganization of the basic elements of the model. We must recognize that the extension of the domain of definition of an economic analysis from a few years to decades, generations, or centuries can fundamentally change the relevance and qualitative validity of the model being analyzed. An economic problem of two or three years' duration may well become primarily a political problem over a span of five to ten years and a social problem over the generations. The problem of where to locate a textile mill, for example, may be well solved for two or three years through operations research analysis. A ten-year solution must involve the political economy of votes on zoning, changes in taxation, and the local economic infrastructure. A solution for several generations must encompass the socioeconomic aspects of the traditions of textile workers. The verbal descriptions of Adam Smith (1776) and of Marshall (1922) clearly contained these points, but the mathematical structure of general-equilibrium theory does not reflect them.

The failure of general-equilibrium theory to reflect institutions, to encompass strategic analysis, and to be easily consistent with the political and social economy of the long run is noted not as a critique of the theory itself but as a caveat against misinterpreting its domain of application. The mathematical apparatus was not designed to handle mixed models with oligopolistic components, government, public goods, and a varying population. Macroeconomic theorizing deals with these problems, for better or for worse, as a matter of course.

The reconciliation of micro- and macroeconomic theory starting from microeconomics will not come from general-equilibrium theory because the basic model was designed to answer only relatively specific economic questions concerning prices, efficient production, and distribution. The results sketched in chapters 14 and 15 indicate that general-equilibrium theorizing can be regarded as a special limiting case of a class of strategic market games solved for their noncooperative equilibria.

The noncooperative-equilibrium solution is far more general than the competitive-equilibrium solution. It is defined on a far broader class of games, and this generality enables the modeler to extend the domain of definition of a strategic market game to include not only oligopolistic elements but nonsymmetric information, government and financial institutions as players, multigenerational models, voting bodies, public goods, and taxation in models for which a noncooperative equilibrium can be defined even though a competitive equilibrium has no meaning.[1]

The Debreu mathematization of general equilibrium produced a model that, while excellent in showing conditions for the existence of an efficient price system in equilibrium, has several basic weaknesses:

1. For finite numbers the results are uninfluenced by replication of the economic agents.

2. When there is exogenous uncertainty present and agents have different information concerning the uncertainty, no competitive equilibrium may exist.

3. The finite horizon, while an adequate approximation for some problems of short duration, is a poor approximation in a model designed to portray politicoeconomic dynamics.

4. Demographic variables are abstracted away. All individuals exist as economic agents at the start, and all disappear together at the end. There are no birth or death processes.

5. Money and financial institutions play no apparent role. The existence of complete markets and hence of total liquidity is implicit.

6. Joint ownership of the means of production is achieved by the ownership of stock; but it is nonvoting stock, and no consideration is given to voting and control.

7. The model is not designed to handle government, public goods, or other externalities.

Can the general-equilibrium model be modified to handle these factors? The immediate answer is, to a point, yes, but not completely. A better question is, Is there an alternative model that can accommodate all of these factors and also yield the valuable results obtained from the general-equilibrium analysis when constrained to a more limited domain? The answer to this question is yes. The strategic market game with a continuum of traders gives the key results of general-equilibrium analysis. Furthermore this type of model of the economy as a game in strategic form can be modified in a relatively straightforward manner to accommodate the other factors noted.

Oligopolistic competition   When analysis is constrained to markets with finite numbers of economic agents, the noncooperative equilibria of the various strategic market games are in general different from the competitive equilibria.[2] They change with replication and reflect the institutional differences of the different mechanisms (see section 15.3 for a comparison of two models).

Nonsymmetric information   Differences in information are modeled with ease in strategic market games by the appropriate modification of the strategy sets of the players (Dubey and Shubik, 1977a, b, 1981). An example is given in section 15.4.

Finite horizon   A natural modification to the strategic market game is the technique used in dynamic programming of introducing a salvage value to measure the worth of stock left over at the end of time. Under favorable circumstances the limit solution to a sequence of strategic market games with a continuum of traders as the length of time is increased will approach a solution to the infinite-horizon economy.

Demographic variables and population   At the sociopolitical and even at the macroeconomic level, the dynamics of population size and quality are too important to be subsumed implicitly in the shape of the utility functions of individuals with indefinite life. The way resources are transmitted between generations appears to depend on a mixture of instinct, culture, and societal, political, and economic factors. Several ways to "glue the generations together" are considered in section 16.4.

Money and financial institutions   We argue here that the very act of casting the economics of exchange and production as a game in strategic form creates the institutions in the rules of the game and that financial mechanisms emerge naturally as a response to efficiency requirements in a transaction technology and as a means of governmental control.

Voting and control   Because the general-equilibrium model is essentially nonstrategic, it has no place in its structure for voting stock. There are modeling difficulties in both cooperative and strategic game formulations for an economy with voting stock.

Government, public goods, and other externalities   Many of the features associated with public goods and externalities destroy the possibility of an efficient price system. The general-equilibrium analysis was not designed to answer questions concerning these features of a political economy. Both cooperative and noncooperative game-theoretic solutions hold out some promise for analysis of these factors. Results from cooperative theory are already known, but the modeling problems faced in the construction of satisfactory strategic forms are considerable.

In summary, there are three approaches to the study of an efficient price system: (1) general-equilibrium analysis; (2) analysis of cooperative solutions to market games; and (3) analysis of noncooperative solutions to strategic market games. If the questions to be answered directly concern the specifics of prices and efficient allocations, and if all the conditions for the competitive-equilibrium solution exist, then in all likelihood the direct methods of general-equilibrium analysis will be optimal. The simplicity of these methods is bought at the price of extreme parsimony in modeling when the detailed structure of the economy can be avoided by ruling out strategic behavior.

If, however, we wish to incorporate additional features of a political economy, remaining in touch with the considerable contributions of general-equilibrium analysis but going beyond them, then the methods of games in both cooperative and strategic form (but especially the latter) offer an appropriate extension of generality.

16.3.2 A capital-stock-constrained competitive equilibrium: Inside and outside money

The family and society must provide the motivations and mechanisms for the individual to leave over capital stock for future generations. Family motivations alone may not guarantee survival.

At the end of the last period in a general-equilibrium model, the value of leftover stock is zero. At the start of a general-equilibrium model, individuals with privately owned goods appear *ex machina*.

A more satisfactory way to study a time slice of an economy is to postulate initial conditions that reflect the prehistory, such as the existence of a national debt. A finite ending requires that boundary conditions be specified to indicate how span of the economy being studied connects with the future.

The model of the economically nonaltruistic individual with a utility function defined on tradeable economic goods and services does not explain initial capital stocks or provide the motivation for the leaving over of capital stock. This point will be considered in further detail when we address the general question of how to glue the generations together. Here, without fully specifying a formal model, we suggest that the introduction of outside money and a rate of interest together with inter-generational trade is sufficient to coax a sequence of perfectly selfish finite-lived individuals into leaving over capital stock.[3]

The general-equilibrium model gives traders their initial assets at the start and asks for nothing back at the end. We can set up a game in which individuals are given some assets (inheritance) and can borrow money to buy other assets. At the end of the game, though, they are required to pay back the amount they owe including any interest. In this way the economy becomes "cash-consuming." At time T the books cannot balance because if the government has issued M units of money, it is owed $M(1 + \rho)^T$. If there is a salvage price for leftover capital stock, then it is possible to design a game such that

$$M[(1 + \rho)^T - 1] = \pi K, \tag{16.3}$$

where K is the ending capital stock, π its price, and M the amount spent to buy initial endowments not given to the players.

The money rate of interest essentially creates a tax whose size can be set equal to the value of the extra capital stock required for the growth of the economy. Individuals leave over capital stock in payment of their indebtedness. An outside or government money, the interest rate, and taxes provide control instruments on distribution and capital stock. Variation of the money supply for the optimal needs of trade can be achieved in the context of a strategic market game by introducing an inside money and a commercial banking system. Given a privately owned banking system, the profits earned by the system will be paid out to its owners; hence, regardless of the size of issue or the rate of interest charged, the books will always balance.[4]

16.4 On Gluing the Generations Together

It could be argued, much in the same way as supporters of the Ptolemaic system added epicycles to account for planetary motions, that the multi-generational model is implicit in an infinite-horizon formulation of the general-equilibrium system. After all, we could shape the utility functions of the economic actors to show a periodicity after every seventy years, thus reflecting a change in generations. But such a formulation does not capture the desire of one generation to have children or the concern of individuals or of society as a whole for the young and the old.

We argue here that the glue that binds the generations is not given in any strictly economic model. Samuelson's (1958) perceptive essay on the pure consumption loan characterized money as a social contrivance, but the significance of this model for economists, political scientists, and others has not yet been fully exploited.

The problems we face in describing the essentials of a multigenerational model are empirical as well as methodological. What controls family size? Why do some societies look after the old better than other societies?

These are questions that cannot be easily answered by an appeal to economic analysis alone, yet they are critical in forging the links between generations. And if we are even to contemplate infinite-horizon models of the economy, the connections between generations must be described explicitly.

The full development of a theory of multistage variable-player games has yet to be carried out. In this section we shall explore variations on a model in which individuals live 3 time periods, to illustrate some of the ways in which the generations may be joined.

16.4.1 Multistage variable-player games
Consider a game with individuals who each live 3 periods. Each individual is strategically active only during his second period. Births occur at the start of period 2. The birth process is an exogenously given population replacement.

When an individual of generation g is called upon to move at time $t + 1$, he is presented with 1 unit of "manna" (which cannot be stored); a move is thus a distribution of resources. The move of generation g can be described as a distribution x_g^1, x_g, x_g^{-1}, where

$$x_g^1 + x_g + x_g^{-1} = 1. \tag{16.4}$$

The subsistence level D, below which the individual dies, is set at some number considerably less than 1.

Figure 16.3 illustrates the game for periods $t = 1, 2, 3$. This encompasses the full life of generation 1, whose parent's strategy (in generation 0) may have been contingent on *his* parent's move (in generation -1) in period -1. If we assume that the formulation of an individual's strategy is most dependent on the actions and income of his parent, we need go back only 2 periods before $t = 1$. Initial conditions require that the move of generation -1 and part of the move of generation -2 be specified in advance.

We also require conditions to be specified for $t = 4$ and 5, but the terminal conditions may be somewhat more complicated than the initial conditions because the strategy of generation g at equilibrium may be contingent on the strategies of generations $g + 1$ and $g + 2$. Thus for terminal conditions we need the strategies of generations 3 and 4 as data.

Given the moves of generations -1 and -2 and the full strategies of generations 3 and 4, the test for a stationary state is whether there will exist a noncooperative equilibrium in the three-person game played by

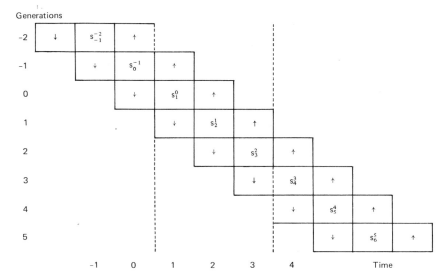

Figure 16.3
Links between the generations. Here s_{t+1}^t is the strategy of generation t at period $t+1$.

generations 0, 1, and 2 that has the same strategies as those assigned to generations 3 and 4 and produces the same moves as those assigned to generations -1 and -2.

The consumption of generation g at age i is $_gc_i$, where in this simple example

$$_gc_1 = x_{g-1}^1, \qquad _gc_2 = x_g, \qquad _gc_3 = x_{g+1}^{-1}. \qquad (16.5)$$

16.4.2 Utility functions
The utility function of an individual of generation g is concave,

$$U(_gc_1, _gc_2, _gc_3), \qquad (16.6)$$

if he is modeled as being purely self-centered.

We might argue for some index of love, altruism, or concern between the generations. The simplest would be a coefficient of intergenerational concern or sympathy. This type of link was suggested by Edgeworth (1881). We must, however, face several problems in modeling:

1. How many generations should be linked?

2. Should the linkage go in one direction, down the generational tree, or should it go both ways?

3. Should the linkage be measured in terms of the direct transfer of resources, or in terms of the donor's perception of the satisfaction or welfare of the recipient?

Even causal empiricism indicates that personal concern for "generations unborn," while a splendid political phrase, has little if any operational content beyond possibly a desire for grandchildren. Most of our concern is for those who exist. Humans appear to be the only species that have the concept of grandchild, and although there may in some cases be five or even six generations alive at the same time, direct interaction is at most considerable only between parent and child; even in the extended family it is far less between grandparent and child, and beyond that hardly of significance. The approximation suggested here is that only proximate generations need to be linked. For a finer relationship we might wish to include the concern of grandparents for grandchildren.

The linkage of concern appears to go heavily in one direction, as considerations for the survival of the species would indicate. The support of elderly and weak parents or grandparents requires resources that could be used to sustain the young and vigorous.

"Eat your spinach because it is good for you" and "My happiness is in seeing you happy" present two different views of interpersonal concern. The first expresses concern with what the young get, not particularly with how they like it. The second expresses concern with the preferences of others.

We now sketch some forms for the utility functions reflecting these conditions of proximate-generation concern. The individual's utility function contains the consumption of young offspring and elderly parent as arguments:

$$U(_{g-1}c_3, _gc_1, _gc_2, _gc_3, _{g+1}c_1). \tag{16.7a}$$

We might wish to modify this structure by introducing coefficients of concern or sympathy, so that

$$U(_gc_1, _gc_2, _gc_3) + \eta_{g-1}c_3 + \theta_{g+1}c_1, \tag{16.7b}$$

where $\eta(\theta)$ is a coefficient of concern of offspring for parent (parent for offspring).

Forms (16.7a) and (16.7b) portray the "eat your spinach" or "make sure they are fed" type of concern. Utility functions expressing preferences for the preferences of others are difficult to operationalize and can give rise to infinite regressions. One way to define such a function using the separability suggested in (16.7b) is as follows:

$$\phi_g = U_g(_gc_1, {}_gc_2, {}_gc_3) + \eta \hat{U}_{g-1}(_{g-1}\bar{c}_1, {}_{g-1}\bar{c}_2, {}_{g-1}c_3)$$
$$+ \theta \hat{U}_{g+1}(_{g+1}c_1, {}_{g+1}\hat{c}_2, {}_{g+2}\hat{c}_3). \tag{16.7c}$$

Here the utility function of g is broken into three separable parts. The first depends only on his lifetime consumption. The second depends on his perception of his parent's preference for his lifetime's consumption (here the first two arguments are data). The third component is his perception of his offspring's preference for his lifetime consumption. The last two components have to be estimates since they will be evaluated after the decision of generation g.

If all generations have the same preferences and perceptions, then $\phi_g = \phi$; if, furthermore, $\eta = \theta = 1$, then

$$\phi = U(_gc_1, {}_gc_2, {}_gc_3) + U(_{g-1}\bar{c}_1, {}_{g-1}\bar{c}_2, {}_{g-1}c_3) + U(_{g+1}c_1, {}_{g+1}\hat{c}_2, {}_{g+1}\hat{c}_3), \tag{16.7d}$$

and the successive generations act as if they were a single individual.

16.4.3 Extensive form and strategies
In order to draw a full game tree for illustration we limit the moves of each generation to the three alternatives $(0, 1, 0)$, $(1/2, 1/2, 0)$, and $(1/3, 1/3, 1/3)$ rather than the continuum. We call these 1, 2, and 3, respectively. We assume $D < 1/3$.

In figure 16.4 no information sets are indicated, implying that this is a game with perfect information; that is, at each stage all previous history is known to all. Thus in this simple example, viewed as a finite three-stage three-player game, g_0 has 3 strategies, g_1 has $3^2 = 9$ strategies, and g_2 has $3^4 = 81$ strategies (g_2 can recognize 4 positions at which he has 3 choices and hence has 3^4 strategies).

If we are to capture the effect of continuing generations, the strategic interlinkage must look the same from any generation. Thus we need at least the moves of generations -1 and -2 as data if generation 0 is to have a strategy set of 81 elements.

Similarly, in order to calculate the full payoffs to generations 1 and 2 we must be given the strategies for generations 3 and 4 as data. The example calculated in section 16.5.1 will fully specify why and how this extra information is used in calculating the payoffs that are not indicated at the bottom of the game tree in figure 16.4.

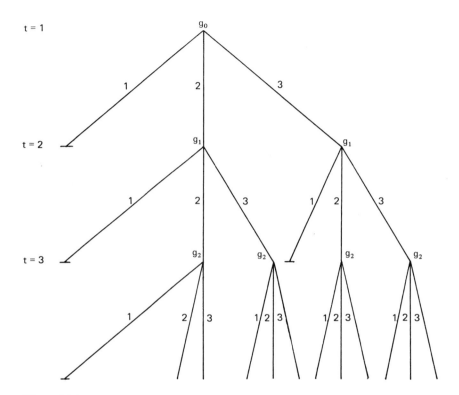

Figure 16.4
A generational game tree.

16.5 Solutions to Multistage Games with Three-Period Lives

16.5.1 Selfish individuals and threat strategies (model 1)
In this section an example is specified and solved to show the possibility of a stationary state existing via threat. This will complete the discussion of figure 16.4.

We consider that an individual of generation g has an individualistic utility function of the type indicated in (16.6). The conditions for positive marginal utility for each period's consumption are assumed, together with decreasing marginal utility for additional consumption. We add the condition that a subsistence level $D < 1/3$ is highly undesirable.[5] The only further conditions imposed are that

$$U(1,1,0) < \max U(c_1, c_2, c_3),\tag{16.8}$$

where $c_1 + c_2 + c_3 = 1$, and that the maximum on the right-hand side of (16.8) is achieved at three numbers c_1^*, c_2^*, c_3^* all greater than or equal to D.

A strategy by an individual of generation g is a function of the information he has on the moves of the two previous generations. We shall display a specific strategy, interpret it, and show that if all individuals adopt this strategy, the resultant set of strategies form an equilibrium. The strategy is:

$$\text{Set } x_g^1 = c_1^*, \quad x_g = c_2^*, \quad x_g^{-1} = c_3^* \quad \text{if} \quad x_{g-1}^1 \geq c_1^* \quad \text{and} \quad x_{g-1}^{-1} \geq c_3^*.$$
$$\text{Set } x_g^1 = c_1^*, \quad x_g = c_2^* + c_3^*, \quad x_g^{-1} = 0 \quad \text{if} \quad x_{g-1}^1 < c_1^* \quad \text{or} \quad x_{g-1}^{-1} < c_3^*.\tag{16.9}$$

In words, g will feed his parent and offspring in the manner noted on the right side of equation (16.8) if his parent did the same for him and his grandparent. If his parent failed to do so, he lets the parent starve.

We are given the following initial conditions in this game, as shown in figure 16.3 and 16.4:

$$x_{-2}^1 = c_1^*, \quad x_{-1}^1 = c_1^*, \quad x_{-1}^{-1} = c_3^*.$$

We are also given the fact that generations 3 and 4 both employ the strategy set forth in (16.9). Without this information it would not be possible for generations 1 and 2, who are active players in this game, to calculate their payoffs.

If we denote a strategy employed by an individual of generation g by s_g, we can write the payoffs in this particular game with three strategic players as follows:

$$\Pi_0(s_0, s_1) = U(_0c_1, _0c_2, _0c_3),$$
$$\Pi_1(s_0, s_1, s_2) = U(_1c_1, _1c_2, _1c_3),\tag{16.10}$$
$$\Pi_2(s_1, s_2) = U(_2c_1, _2c_2, _2c_3).$$

We can now check to see that if all use the strategy given by (16.9), the system is in equilibrium. Generation 0 has already been sustained in childhood by -1 at a level $_0c_1 = c_1^*$. He faces a strategy of the type (16.9) played by generation 1. If he fails to conform in setting $x \geq c_1^*$ and $x \geq c_3^*$, the most he can obtain is $(c_1^*, 1, 0)$; but

$$U(c_1^*, 1, 0) < U(c_1^*, c_2^*, c_3^*),$$

so he is in equilbrium if he sticks to the strategy in (16.9). We can apply the same argument to generations 1 and 2. An extension to any arbitrary number of generations is straightforward.

A comment on sensitivity analysis Not only is the existence of an equilibrium that is enforceable by threats robust with respect to variations over period payoffs and classes of threat strategies, it is too robust. There is a folk theorem in game theory to the effect that in an infinitely repeated game with disclosure, after each move *any* (appropriately averaged over time) payoff that is individually rational for all can be achieved as an equilibrium.

Furthermore, this example does not depend on the representative-individual feature of the simple model used above. It does not even require a constant population. This assertion can easily be illustrated by a verbal description of strategies that provide such an equilibrium. Let there be n_g individuals in generation g (a variable birth rate must be exogenously given). Individual i of generation g adopts the following strategy:

"I shall feed my parents and offspring in the manner noted on the right-hand side of (16.8) if my parents fed me and my grandparents that way and at least 90 percent of their cohort did the same. Otherwise let them starve."

It is a tedious but straightforward exercise to develop the notation needed and to specify details such as how resources vary with population size in order to mathematize strategies such as the one above and to demonstrate stability more formally. Our example characterized a combination of family or individual threat with social threat. It must be stressed that as soon as one lets in history and social pressures, the combinations tending to stability are enormous. In particular, one can introduce a random variable on both features, such as the individual's knowledge of population size and resources available and his information concerning the behavior of the previous generation. This may lead to equilibria or to contingent equilibria (equilibria that will persist as long as certain factors stay within given bounds). Without building the formal model we can give a verbal example of a strategy that might lead to an equilibrium or contingent equilibrium in which there is randomness with respect to numbers, resources, and level of information:

"I shall feed my parents and offspring in the manner noted on the right-hand side of (16.8) subject to the availability of food. If there is not enough for joint survival, I shall let my parents starve, then starve myself. This policy is contingent on my observation that my parents distributed their resources to within around 10 percent of the way I would have distributed them. This policy is further contingent on my expectation that my resultant behavior was manifested as a norm by at least 80 percent of the population of the last generation."

16.5.2 Selfish individuals and simplistic strategies: Not enough glue (model 2)

The simplest strategies are ones that ignore all information, so that they become equivalent to moves. A strategy by generation g is then a triad of numbers (x_g^1, x_g, x_g^{-1}) with

$$x_g^1 + x_g + x_g^{-1} = 1.$$

The only information needed from the past to initialize any game in which these types of strategies are employed is that $x_{-1}^1 \geq D$, that is, generation 0 survived childhood, so that it is alive and strategically active at $t = 1$. Suppose that $x_{-1}^1 = k_1 \geq D$, that is, above the subsistence level; then it is simple to show that no stationary equilibrium exists. We need only check generation 0. Consider a stationary equilibrium that requires $x_1^{-1} = k_2 \geq D = x_0^{-1}$ if the old are to survive. This cannot be because

$$U(k_1, 1 - k_1, k_2) > U(k_1, 1 - k_1 - k_2, k_2). \tag{16.11}$$

In words, if generation 0 has been raised by -1 and knows that if it raises generation 1 it will obtain k_2 regardless of its strategy, it can gain by not supporting its parent, as shown in (16.11). Thus if a stationary strategy did exist, it would not include support of the old. Suppose $x_1^{-1} = x_0^{-1} = 0$. If generation 0 is selfish and knows that generation 1 does not intend to provide support in its old age, then its optimal strategy will be to set $x_0^1 = 0$ since

$$U(k_1, 1, 0) > U(k_1, 1 - k_1, 0). \tag{16.12}$$

This means that generation 1 will not survive childhood and the species will die out if noncontingent strategies are employed.

16.5.3 Linkage by coding or instinctive behavior (model 3)

When there is enough food around, most animals instinctively feed their young. This can be modeled here by removing the selection of x_g^1 as part of the strategy set and setting it to some number $k_1 \geq D$. If we do this, it is simple to check that there will be a stationary noncooperative equilibrium with $x_g = 1 - k_1$ and $x_g^{-1} = 0$, at which each individual will obtain

$$U(k_1, 1 - k_1, 0) < U(c_1^*, c_2^*, c_3^*). \tag{16.13}$$

This is clearly not Pareto-optimal. Thus an instinct to support the young does not necessarily help the survival of the old.

16.5.4 Linkage by love: The altruism finesse (model 4)

Suppose an individual has a utility function of the shape indicated in (16.7d); that is, generation g's concern for its parent and offspring is as for itself. Equations (16.10) now become

$$\Pi_0(s_0, s_1) = U(_{-1}c_1, _{-1}c_2, _{-1}c_3) + U(_0c_1, _0c_2, _0c_3)$$
$$+ U(_1c_1, _1c_2, _1c_3),$$
$$\Pi_1(s_0, s_1, s_2) = U(_0c_1, _0c_2, _0c_3) + U(_1c_1, _1c_2, _1c_3)$$
$$+ U(_2c_1, _2c_2, _2c_3), \tag{16.14}$$
$$\Pi_2(s_1, s_2) = U(_1c_1, _1c_2, _1c_3) + U(_2c_1, _2c_2, _2c_3)$$
$$+ U(_3c_1, _3c_2, _3c_3).$$

Because of the overlap in the arguments of the utility functions, it is easy to show that there will be a Pareto-optimal stationary noncooperative equilibrium with simplistic strategies. We check by assuming that all employ $x_g^1 = c_1^*, x_g = c_2^*, x_g^{-1} = c_3^*$.

Consider generation 0. Given that $x_{-2}^1 = c_1^*, x_{-1} = c_2^*, x_{-1}^1 = c_1^*$, then

$$\Pi_0(s_0, s_1^*) = U(c_1^*, c_2^*, x_0^{-1}) + U(c_1^*, x_0, c_3^*) + U(x_0^1, c_2^*, c_3^*). \tag{16.15}$$

An optimal strategy for generation 0, given information concerning what -1 has done and knowing the strategy s_1^* of generation 1, is one that maximizes $\Pi_0(s_0, s_1^*)$. A strategy here is to select three numbers (x_g^1, x_g, x_g^{-1}) subject to

$$x_g^1 + x_g + x_g^{-1} = 1.$$

From the fact that U is concave and has a maximum at (c_1^*, c_2^*, c_3^*) when consumption is constrained to sum to 1, it follows that $\Pi_0(s_0, s_1^*)$ has a maximum at

$$x_g^1 = c_1^*, \quad x_g = c_2^*, \quad x_g^{-1} = c_3^*.$$

We can now consider $\Pi_1(s_0^*, s_1, s_2^*)$, showing that $s_1 = s_1^*$ is in equilibrium, and then $\Pi_2(s_1^*, s_2)$.

It should be noted that the assumption of enough love turns a "game" into a "team." Furthermore, if love were only of parent for child, this would be enough to achieve a stationary state but not one with the Pareto-optimal survival of the old enforced by simplistic strategies. More complex strategies of the variety employed in model 1 will do.

It is suggested here that the coefficients of concern or sympathy are not symmetric. The prime concern of parents is for their children; the secondary concern is for parents and grandchildren in a Western society with its stress on the nuclear family. To what extent this concern is biologically, sociologically, or economically determined appears to be an open question; great variety is seen among different nations, tribes, and other social groupings.

Institutions and the game within the game   An important reason why the "love or altruism" model is attractive to economists with a noninstitutional viewpoint is that enough love minimizes the need for institutions, laws, rules, or any social or political paraphernalia. The need for a system design of any complexity to produce optimal behavior from individuals motivated by self-interest and with different goals vanishes if each cares for the other as himself.

Much of the value of considering the noncooperative-equilibrium solution is that it requires little explicit cooperation yet can be mutually beneficial (even Pareto-optimal) if the rules of the game are appropriately specified. A way of looking at institutions is that they are part of the rules of the game called for in the design of self-policing systems.

How institutions change, how fast they change, and what factors cause their change, are open questions. A Marxist, a Manchester liberal, and a Chicago conservative would agree that institutions are heavily influenced by economic pressures. A laissez-faire view would further have us believe that the appropriate institutions will be molded quickly and correctly by economic forces. The possibility that institutions and customs take time to form suggests a need to formalize "the game within the game" (see, e.g., Schotter, 1981). Individuals not only operate in the short term within the rules, but they also devote part of their activity to influencing and changing the rules and institutions in the longer run.

16.5.5 Pure consumption loan models

A hundred and fifty years ago it might have been argued that in many parts of Europe and the United States children were economic goods; in other words, parents could use them on the farm, sell them, or hire them out to the mine or mill in such a manner that income from the child, net of cost of raising, was positive. In many societies children have been put to work by parents who took the proceeds. Child labor laws, compulsory schooling, and changes in social custom have wiped out the "cash crop" view of child maintenance in most of the Western world, although economic considerations still play an important role in education and other aspects of upbringing (see G. S. Becker, 1975).

In Paul Samuelson's pure consumption loan model instinct accounted for child support and economics for old age support via the social contrivance of money. Two game-theoretic variants of Samuelson's model are given by Shubik (1981a). It is suggested here that hidden in the pure consumption loan model is a noncooperative-game interpretation in which the fiat money symbolizes ownership of an unspecified capital stock and is needed to produce a stationary-state economy that must be left at the end if the process is to continue.

Even more important than the observation that the interlinking of generations can be accomplished through the introduction of a money is the parsimonious way in which the consumption loan model calls attention to the *strategic openness* of the economic model. It provides an elementary format for embedding an exclusively economic model into a larger context involving strategic moves by the actors pertaining to politics, society, and demographic factors.

There is a fast-growing literature on multigenerational models in economic theory. We shall not survey it because it is complementary with rather than central to the theme of strategic choice that is stressed here.

16.6 Concluding Remarks

16.6.1 Money and threats
We can blend the threat model of section 16.5.1 together with the consumption loan model. It is straightforward to achieve blended equilibria in which the threat-imposed transfers range from zero to full support of the old by their children. This mixture of market and individual threat can be interpreted as an mixture of social custom and markets.

16.6.2 Endogenous population and nonstationary solutions
This chapter has sketched more models and stated more problems than it has solved. Because the models have been, for the most part, extremely simple, one might be concerned that they are artifacts of the stationary state and of endogenous population assumptions. Neither appears to be the case. A few comments, however, are in order.

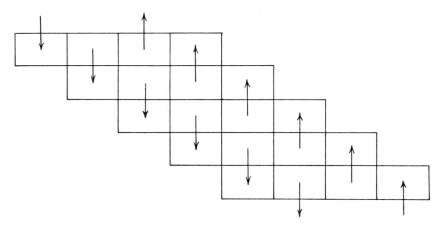

Figure 16.5
Four-period lives with support of children and the aged.

Devising a formal multigenerational game including endogenous marriage, birth, and up to a point death, together with markets, at least one reproducible capital good, land, labor, one consumer good, and even a public good and a rudimentary political structure is a difficult, somewhat tedious, but feasible and worthwhile task. Handtailored models with a judicious mixture of demographic, economic, and other features should cast light on topics such as the burden of social security considered by Samuelson (1975) and Arthur and McNicoll (1978).

If population is to be made endogenous, however, even though the conceptual task of constructing a variable-player multistage game is relatively clear, the empirical problem of deciding the causal components of family size is not clear. Furthermore, if population is made endogenous and individuals have a preference for a certain number of offspring, some relatively subtle problems appear in the specification of Pareto optimality.

16.6.3 Politics, voting, economics, and demography
Some simple multigenerational models with individual actions aggregated into two or three time periods have been suggested. If we consider four periods, an interesting possibility appears for modeling a rudimentary political structure. Figure 16.5 illustrates a society with four age ranges. We may consider the young to be supported by the young middle-aged and by education subsidies, and the old to be supported by the older middle-aged and by social security. The young are neither economically

nor politically strategic players. The middle-aged are both; and the old may not be economically strategic players, but they may still be politically active. The direct burden of the young falls primarily on the younger middle-aged, and the direct burden of the old falls on the older middle-aged. But all three—younger and older middle-aged and the old—have voting coalition possibilities, with the older middle-aged wishing to cut down on the burden of the old, the younger middle-aged wishing to cut down on the burden of the young, and the old having considerable voting power. As the age profile of the population varies, one would expect to see large swings in political programs.

16.6.4 Is economics one or all of the social sciences?

The noncooperative equilibrium is by no means a completely satisfactory solution concept in the study of economics, but it is useful and also contains the competitive equilibrium as a somewhat restricted special case.

The economizing process appears to be common as a means for investigating all of the social sciences. But the fact that a psychiatrist wishes to explain an individual's actions as trying to minimize "tension" does not imply that we can stick tension into a utility function and call psychiatry economics.

Economic behavior takes place in a societal, legal, political, biological, and psychological context. This is painfully evident in work on development economics. It should be clear in any attempt at theory construction involving the interlinking of generations that there are more forces in the world than economics. The domain of definition for the noncooperative equilibrium is far broader than that of the general-equilibrium model, and we may thus define and solve mixed economic-social, economic-political, or other models and obtain price systems and nonmarket transfers that are compatible.

Table 16.1 suggests that at least six different considerations should be taken into account in the study of intergenerational models. Suggested levels of importance for the United States are given. Even casual empiricism suggests that the elements of importance for the support of the young and old differ considerably.

It may be that some basic elements of genetic coding and love are needed for the survival of the young and even for the old. A totally loveless society might well lead to more and earlier suicides, and even items such as bodily contact between parents and offspring appear important to the survival of the young. Earlier generations may not have

Table 16.1
Ways of gluing the generations together

	Necessary?	Sufficient alone?	Suggested importance	
			Young	Old
1. Genetic coding	?	yes	very high	small or 0
2. Love, altruism	?	yes (if enough)	moderate	moderate
3. Economics	no	yes (sometimes)	very small	moderate
4. Money, law, existing institutions	no	yes (if well designed)	very small	moderate
5. Social pressure, threat, tradition	no	yes (sometimes)	very small	moderate
6. Politics	no	?	very small	moderate

survived in high luxury without economics and politics, but they did survive. Many mixes of custom, tradition, laws, politics, and markets appear able to sustain the generations.

The general-equilibrium theory was a masterful first step toward seeing the economic problem clearly in a noninstitutional of preinstitutional, nonbiological, static context. The noncooperative solution provides a means for the analysis of richer and more relevant models for political economy and other social sciences.

Notes to chapter 16

1. In the past few years there has been considerable work devoted to directly modifying the general-equilibrium model to account for many of these features (see the articles by Grandmont and Radner in Arrow and Intrilligator, 1982). Much of this work is consistent with a game-theoretical approach with a continuum of traders. Nevertheless it is suggested here that the strategic form with its express concern for process offers a methodologically better way to proceed than competitive equilibrium theory.

2. For a broad discussion of the noncooperative-solution approach to the competitive price system see Mas-Colell (1980).

3. Examples of simple formal models of the economy with capital stock and a money rate of interest are given in Shubik (1980).

4. We conjecture that it is not possible to design an efficient, competitive banking system without central bank control in each period of either the rate of interest or the quantity of money. Furthermore, if there is exogenous uncertainty in the economy, it is not possible to design a neutral commerical banking system, that is,

a system in which the commercial banks do not have a strategic role in allocating funds, unless the central bank totally takes over control of variations in the money supply.

5. We need the condition $D \geq 1/3$ for our result because otherwise $3D \geq 1$ would imply that society could not survive keeping the old. This condition amounts to stating that a longer life is preferable to a shorter one with higher per-period consumption; furthermore, it is no fun to starve at any time.

V   Externalities and Public Goods

17 Ownership and Production

17.1 Introduction

An extremely simple view of private property is implicit in all of the foregoing analysis. All items have been treated as chattel with no encumbrances whatsoever; that is, they have been items such as oranges or apples over which the owner has total and unrestricted control; he can transport them, trade them, give them away, throw them away, or destroy them at will. His decision to maintain them or bequest them is his alone and is not limited by society.

This simple concept of property implicit in many classical models of a competitive economy is, we suggest, an insufficiently basic representation of the phenomenon of ownership. More fundamental is the view that an individual has operational or strategic control over certain goods or processes but is subject to laws (natural and man-made) that define his rights and powers. As long as there is no possibility of public interaction caused by private use, the simple "chattel" view of ownership may suffice; but in more complex economic situations, such as when the rate of production of A influences (perhaps through a waste product) the costs of B, an adequate solution of the competitive model may be impossible unless constraints are imposed on the individual's strategies, over and above the physical limitations of technology. The nature of the solution will depend crucially on the nature of these constraints.

This thesis will be elaborated through a series of simple, highly symmetric models based on the same technological facts but incorporating different institutional constraints. Several solution concepts will be invoked to illuminate different aspects of the situation, and the characteristic function will play a central role. Our object is not an exhaustive analysis of any of the models but an exploration in sufficient depth to highlight the features that differentiate each from the others.

The models in this chapter serve as an introduction to the broader problems of externalities and public goods considered in chapters 18–21. They provide a context for economic analysis, though we shall not venture into the domain of legal philosophy, which would require us to supply a justification for the basic sociolegal underpinnings of property rights.

(For a discussion of the philosophical foundations of property rights see L. C. Becker, 1977.)

17.2 Mathematical-Institutional Economics and Agrarian Reform

Although the scope of this chapter does not permit the detailed applications that would be needed to explain the considerable differences in land policies and practices in various parts of the world, we shall offer a sketch of the connection between our mathematical approach and institutional investigations.

The distribution and tenure of land involve an intermix of economic, political, and social factors. Our approach stresses the strategic role of the individual, a role determined not only by strictly economic considerations but by political and social factors as well. We have selected a few suggestive forms of ownership to analyze, omitting slave and forced-labor systems such as were in fact used to develop the large plantations and mines of Latin America (see, e.g., Lewin, 1963). The principles of the various land tenure systems are basically the same and have been summed up by Barraclough and Domike (1965, p. 7): "Income from land, however, cannot be realized without labor. Rights to land have therefore been accompanied by law and custom which assure the landowners of a continuing and compliant labor supply. These land tenure institutions are a product of the power structure. Plainly speaking, ownership or control of land is power in the sense of real or potential ability to make another person do one's will."

In our discussion we shall neglect several important economic factors, such as the quality of the land, that go a long way toward explaining the low intensity of use of regions such as Patagonia or parts of the Altiplano. Relative productivity of land and differing transportation costs constitute only partial data for the explanation of land prices, agricultural wage rates, and tenure systems. What other factors might be relevant to structural phenomena such as the million-acre size of sheep farms or *estancias*?[1] Factors such as a monopoly on the local water supply or on transportation, combined with a high probability that a large landowner's family will also supply the judges and politicians of a region, help to delineate the power and threat structure our theory will attempt to utilize.

The extremes to which the social aspects of the economic power structure may extend are indicated in the following observation by Barraclough and Domike (1965, p. 11): "In some cases, the administration's consent is required even to receive visitors from outside or to make visits off the property. Even corporal punishment is still occasionally encountered on some of the most traditional plantations and *haciendas*. Tenants and workers depend on the *patrón* for credit, for marketing their products and even for medical aid in emergencies.... With the abolition of compulsory servitude during the last century, *peones* and tenants now have the right to leave, but with few alternative job opportunities, little education, and because they are usually in debt, this possibility often appears to be as much of a threat as an opportunity for improving his lot."

The evaluation of the price of land in traditional economic theory is based at the least on the existence of a fair-sized market. When most of the land supply is locked up in the hands of a very few owners, who are able to maintain this position through a combination of political, social, and economic power, the economic concept of the price of land becomes hard to define without including institutional costs as well as economic alternative costs. An interesting illustration of the role of institutional factors is the very different costs of beach property of similar quality in various islands of the Caribbean, depending on which government controls the island.

When, as in the case of Hawaii in 1965, one ranch owns 262,000 acres out of a total farmland area of about 2.5 million acres, any question of land prices and taxation levels, not to mention land reform, must realistically assess potential changes in ways of life rather than simply considerations of market prices and economic use within a fixed institutional framework.

In figure 17.1 the Lorentz curves for Peru, Chile, the United States, and Argentina are drawn. The Gini indices of concentration (the area between the curve and the diagonal, as compared to the total area under the diagonal) are approximately 0.71 for Argentina, somewhat higher for the United States, and around 0.87 for Chile and 0.95 for Peru.

Although this chapter is not concerned with policy, we must stress that the existence, as in Latin America, of a more or less stable system of large *latifundia* controlling much of the land and great numbers of *minifundia* (holdings too small to employ a single family at a socially acceptable minimum income) points to problems of policy that are far more involved with institutional change and the specification of welfare and educational goals, political power, and so forth, than with the classical problem of resource optimization within a given system.

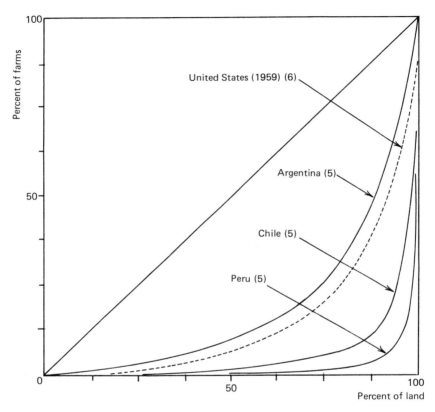

Figure 17.1
Typical land-distribution curves. Sources: Barraclough and Domike (1965, p. 5),
based on Interamerican Committee for Agricultural Development studies, and
Statistical Abstract of the United States (1963, p. 613).

17.3 A Simple Production Function

A simple example of a production process, which has been used to illustrate increasing, constant, and then decreasing marginal returns from an input, is that of several farm laborers working a single field (see, e.g., Ricardo, 1817, chapter 2, esp. p. 45). As the number of laborers is increased, there is an increasing rise in the amount of food they produce per man, until at some point they begin to run short of land to work. Then, even with the best of organizations, the added product due to added labor begins to drop off. Conceivably, the added product might even become negative, as when "too many cooks spoil the broth."

Figure 17.2 illustrates such a situation, where s is the number of laborers and $f(s)$ is the output of food from a fixed area of land L. When we want to consider the amount of land as variable, we instead write $\phi(s, l)$, where l is the amount of land, and $\phi(s, L) \equiv f(s)$. Thus the technological possibilities, though not the strategic possibilities, are completely determined by the functions f or ϕ. In this chapter we usually assume that f is S-shaped, that is, convex over an initial interval and concave thereafter. It may be bounded or unbounded. Its maximum value, if any, will be denoted by f_{max}, and the first s at which $f(s) = f_{max}$ by m^*, as in figure 17.2. If there is no maximum, we formally set $m^* = \infty$. It will be convenient to introduce the auxiliary function f^*, defined by $f^*(s) = \max f(t)$, $t \le s$, which is of course necessarily monotonic. The existence of first and even second derivatives for f and f^* will sometimes also be needed. For the assumptions on ϕ see section 17.6.

Taking this simple example, with the limited resource *land*, the variable resource *labor*, and the output *food*, we construct several game-theoretic models reflecting different social conditions for the ownership and working of land. Land, food, and labor (but not people!) are assumed to be homogeneous and infinitely divisible. We also assume for simplicity that all laborers have the same linear utility for food. Whether they actually consume the food they acquire or sell it in an outside market is immaterial for our purposes. These simplifying assumptions make little or no conceptual difference to the examples we discuss.

Because our examples are studied as cooperative games, we use a characteristic function $v(S)$ that specifies the amount of food any coalition S of individuals is able to obtain for its members under the technical, social, and legal conditions of the model, regardless of the actions of those outside the coalition. This amount will depend on the ownership and use conditions for the land and the freedom of action allowed individ-

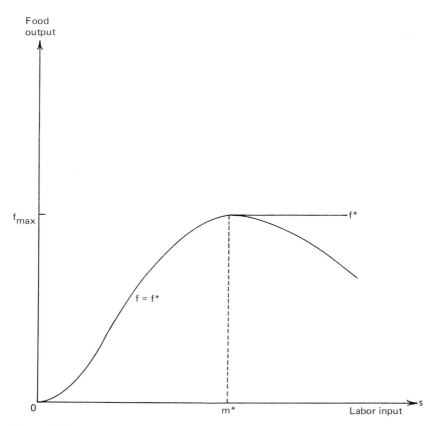

Figure 17.2
Production function for one unit of land.

ual participants. In contrast with the characteristic function, the production function specifies only a technical optimum and has no ownership or strategic implications whatsoever.

Before proceeding we must consider the meaning of a *negative marginal value* of labor. This possibility cannot be dismissed unless we assume that there is a costless method of disposing of any unwanted surplus of labor—that the master engineer in charge of production can keep unwanted labor off the field at no cost. In a closed economy with fixed technology and fixed nonhuman resources, this assumption would permit an extreme case of the Malthusian view, according to which the productivity of added labor would in the end not only drop below subsistence wage but actually diminish total produce. In our models we permit negative marginal productivity but do not insist on it.

17.4 The Feudal System

Consider an economy consisting of $n + 1$ individuals, of whom n are landless peasants with nothing to contribute but their labor and one is the lord owning the land. We must distinguish several cases.

In a strict feudal relationship there is no true characteristic function because there are no coalition possibilities available to either the lord or his serfs. Nor do they have strategic choices; rather, they have duties toward each other, which will define the division of the total product. Production might be improved if some of the serfs could be removed from the domain, but this may not be feasible. Hence, if the marginal product of the serfs fails to cover their subsistence needs, as might happen under crowded conditions, then an increase in numbers would result in a loss in the amount of product accruing to the feudal lord.

This strictly feudal model is trivial from the game-theoretic viewpoint, since everyone's behavior is prescribed. In subsequent models the rules of the game will always leave some scope for individual or collective initiative, and we shall have to turn to the solutions of the game, which embody various principles of individual or societal rationality, to obtain predictions of behavior. The basic purpose of the theory of games, after all, is to provide systematic techniques for resolving the indeterminacies inherent in multilateral decision processes.

17.5 The Capitalist and Landless Peasants

The relationship between the landlord and landless peasants of a capitalist society gives rise to a true characteristic function with the superadditivity property; that is, if coalitions S and T have no members in common and U is their union, then $v(U) \geq v(S) + v(T)$. Let us call the landlord player 1 and the peasants players 2, 3, ..., $n + 1$. Then, for a coalition S, we have

$$v(S) = \begin{cases} 0 & \text{if 1 is not in } S, \\ f(s - 1) & \text{if 1 is in } S \text{ and } s - 1 < m^*, \\ f_{\max} & \text{if 1 is in } S \text{ and } s - 1 \geq m^*, \end{cases}$$

where s denotes the number of individuals in S. (We assume that the landlord does not work.) If the number of laborers is greater than m^*, it is assumed that the landlord has no responsibility for them and can keep them off the land.

In this description of the characteristic function, we have not specified the subsistence-level requirements of the individuals as an input or cost to be met. Thus we ascribe a value of $v(S) = 0$ to every coalition of peasants alone. This implies that (at least in the short run) they are not able to obtain alternative employment to cover subsistence. If alternative employment were available that just covered the subsistence requirement k, we might instead assume $v(S) = ks$, where $1 \notin S$. In a chronically overpopulated area the original assumption might be reasonable, but in a model that introduced dynamic aspects into the relationship between the workers and landowners the zero value (below subsistence) for some coalitions would more accurately depict the "threat" potentials in the game.[2]

Viewing the model as an open market, we find that as the number of laborers becomes large, the marginal productivity of labor declines, as does its price. The rewards to the landlord therefore rise if we add returns to satisfy the conditions of competitive equilibrium. If $f(s)$ is a bounded function, then both the wage rate and the total wages paid approach zero, and in the limit the landlord reaps all of the gain from the economic activity. When m^* is finite, he attains this position as soon as n exceeds m^*.

The game-theoretic solutions supplement this economic solution. Consider first the core. We note first that the imputation that gives all to the landlord is always in the core, since he is absolutely essential to any production. Next we note that if the coalition $\{1, 3, 4, \ldots, n + 1\}$ is to be satisfied, then x_2 cannot exceed $f^*(n) - f^*(n - 1)$. The same applies to $x_3, x_4, \ldots, x_{n+1}$. In particular, if $f(s)$ is bounded, each peasant's maximum share in the core tends to zero as n increases; indeed the total share to the peasants tends to zero (see figure 17.3a). Thus the core of the game in this case shrinks down upon the competitive solution, a phenomenon that has already been encountered in part III.

If the production function is not bounded, the laborers may retain a positive fraction of the total output even in the limit. For example, if we take $f(s) = 2\sqrt{s}$, it can be shown that the imputation $(\sqrt{n}, 1/\sqrt{n}, \ldots, 1/\sqrt{n})$, which gives exactly half to the landlord and half to the peasants, satisfies all coalitions and is therefore in the core. (This imputation is also the competitive-equilibrium solution.) Of course, the core also includes imputations more favorable to the landlord, such as $(2\sqrt{n}, 0, \ldots, 0)$ as previously noted, but it includes nothing appreciably more favorable to the peasants if n is large.

The other game-theoretic solution we shall consider is the value. It is easily determined that the value to the landlord is given by

$$\Phi_1 = \frac{1}{n+1} \sum_{s=0}^{n} f^*(s) \approx \frac{1}{n} \int_0^n f^*(s)\,ds,$$

since when he enters the randomly forming coalition, it may already contain anywhere from 0 to n members with equal probability. Since the sum of all values must be $f^*(n)$, the total value to the peasants is $f^*(n) - \Phi_1$. This is depicted in figure 17.3b; the values are in the same ratio as the two areas.

When $f(s)$ is bounded above, the value apportionment converges to the other solutions: The landlord gets everything in the limit. But if m^* is finite, the peasants' share does not drop to zero as soon as $n > m^*$, as in the other solutions; they still receive some small credit for their ability to thwart the owner of the land by forming a large enough coalition.

In our unbounded example, $f(s) = 2\sqrt{s}$, we note that the value solution awards 2/3 of the total produce to the landlord in the limit, as compared with 1/2 in the competitive solution and anywhere between 1/2 and 1 in the core.

17.6 A Small-Landowner Capitalist Society

Consider a symmetric equalitarian society in which each individual owns $1/n$ of the land as his share, as well as his own labor. Before the characteristic function can be constructed, some further technological assumptions are needed concerning the cultivation of smaller plots of land. That is, a production function $\phi(s, l)$ must be specified for $0 \le l \le L$, where L is the total amount of land and $\phi(s, L) \equiv f(s)$.

One way to do this is to make ϕ homogeneous in the first degree: $\phi(ks, kl) = k\phi(s, l)$. This implies

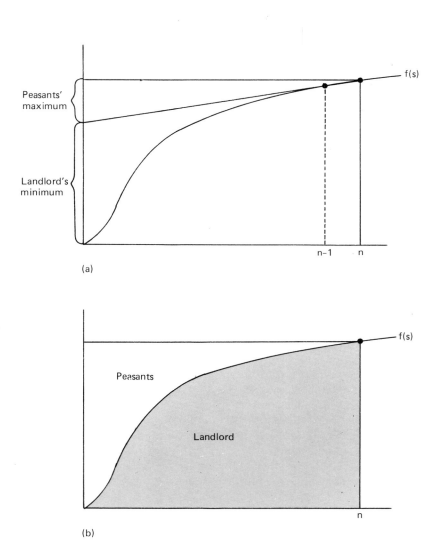

Figure 17.3
Landless peasants. (a) Apportionment of the core (and competitive equilibrium).
(b) Apportionment of the value (approximate).

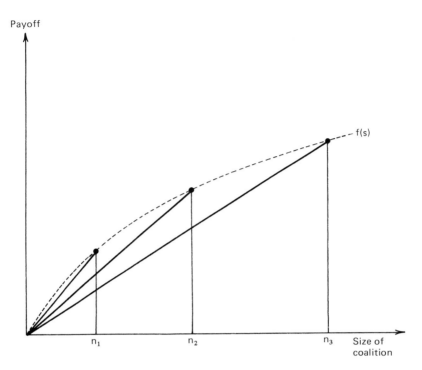

Figure 17.4
Small-landowner model with homogeneous production. Typical characteristic functions.

$$\phi(s,l) = \frac{l}{L} f\left(\frac{Ls}{l}\right).$$

Such a function makes sense only if f is concave throughout, rather than S-shaped, since otherwise some labor forces would be able to produce more on a small plot of land than on a large one. Accordingly, for this example only, we shall have to assume that f is concave, as in figure 17.4.

The characteristic function is

$$v(S) = \phi^*(s, Ls/n) = \frac{s}{n} f^*(n),$$

where $\phi^*(s,l)$ is defined in analogy with f^* as the maximum of $\phi(t,l)$ for $0 \leq t \leq s$. (In a symmetric game the function on sets S is replaced by a function on integers s, since all coalitions of the same size are equivalent.)

Figure 17.4 shows some typical characteristic functions for games of this kind. The important thing to observe is that each function is additive; hence each game is "inessential," and all significant solution concepts coincide. The payoff to each player is just $1/n$ of the total output $f^*(n)$, and he can always achieve this payoff, unaided if need be, by cultivating his own plot of land. There is no gain in collusion.

We note that with f concave, per-capita income is always a decreasing function of population size.

A more interesting variant is obtained if we retain the S-shape and drop homogeneity. Instead of the production process being infinitely divisible, we assume that there is a decrease in efficiency, for some reason, when plots of land smaller than L are cultivated. To keep things simple we use the form

$$\phi(s, l) = \frac{l}{L} f(s) \quad \text{for } 0 \leq l \leq L.$$

It is easily verified that this function satisfies $\sum \phi(s_i, l_i) \leq \phi(s, l)$ for $\sum l_i = l \leq L$ and $\sum s_i = s \leq m^*$; that is, it is not possible for subplots of land to be worked at different intensities with a gain in total output. Thus there is no longer any inconsistency in an S-shaped production curve.

The characteristic function is

$$v(S) = \phi^* \left(s, \frac{Ls}{n} \right) = \frac{s}{n} f^*(s),$$

as illustrated in figure 17.5. This is not additive but is superadditive, and the n-person game is therefore "essential." A core exists, since no subcoalition of s members can produce more per capita than the society as a whole.[3] Indeed, if $n \leq m^*$, all subcoalitions will be distinctly less efficient, and the core will contain many asymmetric imputations in addition to the "equal-split" payoff. But if $n > m^*$, as at n_2, coalitions of size $s \geq m^*$ will be able to block all imputations other than the equal split, and a one-point core results. This may be translated: If the marginal productivity of labor is greater than zero, there will exist asymmetric distributions of product that cannot be successfully challenged by any disaffected coalition. But if the marginal productivity is zero (or negative), only the unique symmetric distribution is coalitionally stable.

The value solution also gives the equal split, as might be expected from the symmetry of the model. If we suppose that the landholdings are

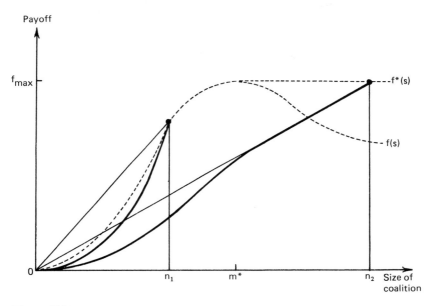

Figure 17.5
Small-landowner model with increasing returns to scale.

unequal in size, however, the result is more interesting. By a computation that we shall not detail, we find that the fraction of the total product that an individual receives in the value imputation (which purports to represent a "fair division") lies between his fraction of the total land and his fraction of the total labor. The influence of the landholdings in the solution depends on the shape of the production curve—specifically on the ratio of the area beneath it to the area to the left. (Compare figure 17.3b.) A small area to the left, for example, means that labor is unlikely to be in short supply, so that an individual's value to a coalition depends chiefly on how much land he brings in. Conversely, a small area under the curve means that labor is generally the critical input, and the value solution gives little weight to any differences in landholdings.[4]

Finally, we remark that the present, nonhomogeneous model has no competitive solution unless $n \geq m^*$, whereupon labor gets a zero wage and land rents for $f^*(n)/L$. Indeed, if $n < m^*$, the marginal return on labor is positive and we have increasing returns to scale:

$$\phi(\lambda n, \lambda L) = \lambda f(\lambda n) > \lambda f(n) = \lambda \phi(n, L),$$

for λ slightly greater than 1 (assuming $\partial \phi / \partial l$ continuous at $l = L$). Hence no prices for land and labor can ever lead to the required production level.

17.7 The Village Commune

Rather than being held individually, land may be held jointly as in a primitive village or a kibbutz, with the use of the land controlled by majority vote. To define such a situation fully we must specify the obligations of the majority and the rights of the minority.

For a first, extreme case we assume that the majority exercises absolute control, and that once they have made a decision, the minority is in no position to obstruct, either by abstaining from ordered work or by carrying out other threats against the society. The characteristic function for this game is then

$$v(S) = \begin{cases} 0 & \text{if } s \le n/2, \\ f^*(n) & \text{if } s > n/2. \end{cases}$$

Figure 17.6 shows some characteristic functions for different n. Games of this type are called *simple-majority games* (see *GTSS*, chapter 7). Any winning coalition takes all, where "all" is defined by the adjusted production function f^*.

In a situation of this kind the imputation of wealth becomes more a sociopolitical than an economic problem. The political mechanism of the vote is used to decide the disposition of jointly produced goods, in contrast to having the economic mechanism of the market determine the disposition of individually owned resources. This prompts the observation that political processes in general may be interpreted economically as choice mechanisms for jointly deciding the individual allocation of products obtained from a jointly owned resource.

When we apply our three solution concepts to this game, we find, first, that the competitive equilibrium is not defined. Even if we permit the sale of votes, no equilibrating price schedule exists. Second, the core of this game is empty. There is no imputation upon which some group of more than half of the players would not be able to improve by exploiting the rest. Finally, the value of the game, by symmetry, must award exactly $f^*(n)/n$ to each player. This is not a particularly informative result. However, if we imagine a nonsymmetric version of this game, as when the players are family units with unequal numbers of votes or unequal

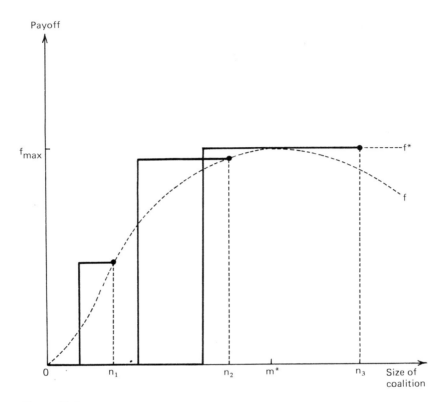

Figure 17.6
A village commune.

supplies of labor, the value profile gives an interesting measure of the
relative "political power" of the players and provides a plausible, though
hardy enforceable, formula for translating "voting strength" into
economic terms (see *GTSS*, chapter 7; Shapley, 1953; Shapley and
Shubik, 1954).

The absence of a core implies that there is no distribution of output
that is free from social pressure. Some coalition will always be able to
obstruct any proposal. The imputation of proceeds actually observed in
a situation like this can therefore best be explained in sociological terms.
The von Neumann–Morgenstern stable-set solutions (see *GTSS*, chapter
6), which can be regarded as sociologically oriented, might well be
appropriate here.

17.8 Corporate Ownership

We next assume that the land is jointly owned under majority rule but
that the power of the majority is not absolute. For example, it might
be agreed that a majority vote controls how the land is to be utilized
and that the minority must abide by the decision and not hamper the
work in any manner, yet each individual is guaranteed by law an equal
share in the total proceeds. (In the nonsymmetric case both votes and
dividends would be proportional to the individual's share of ownership.)
The (symmetric) characteristic function is

$$v(S) = \begin{cases} 0 & \text{if } s \le n/2, \\ \dfrac{s}{n}f^*(n) & \text{if } s > n/2. \end{cases}$$

Figure 17.7 shows typical characteristic functions for different n. As
before, the adjusted production function f^* yields the locus of the
$v(\{1, 2, \ldots, n\})$ (heavy black dots). These characteristic functions represent a sort of compromise between those of figures 17.4 and 17.6.

For $n \ge 3$ the core consists of a single imputation. This is because a
coalition of $n - 1$ players can always prevent the other player from getting
more than $f^*(n)/n$, his symmetric portion of the total product. By symmetry, the value coincides with the core, although this is not necessarily
the case with one-point cores in nonsymmetric games.

In order to consider the competitive equilibrium, which is not a purely
game-theoretic concept, we must introduce the possibility of selling votes.
If we permit this, then a competitive price for votes can be established,
and it will in this case yield the same symmetric imputation as the value
and the core.

While these solutions resemble those obtained for the inessential model
of section 17.6, there are some significant underlying differences. Technically, we note that the present characteristic function does not depend
on the homogeneity of the extended production function $\phi(s, l)$, whereas
in the small-landowner model homogeneity was crucial. Strategically, it
is apparent that individuals and small groups are powerless under the
"corporate-ownership" assumptions and must rely for their share of the
output on the rationality of the controlling majority's behavior; the
opposite is true for the small landowners. Sociologically, there is an
incentive toward formation of large coalitions (such as political parties)
to govern the corporation; this tendency is not present in the small-
landowner society. The stable-set and bargaining-set solutions might shed
more light on these differences.

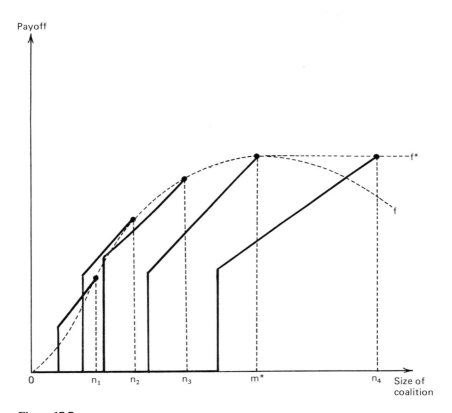

Figure 17.7
Characteristic functions for the first corporate model.

Extremely simple forms of strategic control have been chosen in order to provide a group of contrasting, easily analyzed models. We must not, however, lose sight of the fact that much more complicated patterns of control are generally found in practice, when many "owners" have a hand in the same productive process. Even when the rules are unambiguous and can be stated in a few words, the logical ramifications of the rules are likely to be so intricate that an extended mathematical analysis may be required to calculate the characteristic function.

To illustrate this point we shall present four variants of the corporate model, derived from the present case by modifying in various ways the rights and responsibilities of the participants. Questions of wage and hiring policy, and the managerial function, can then be introduced naturally, without expanding the technological side of the model. Mathematical details aside, it will be clear from a glance at figures 17.8–17.10 and 17.12 that the characteristic function responds quite sensitively to nuances in the control and decision structure.

Our four additional models are related more to corporate management than to land tenure as such, but they serve to show how more intricate considerations of ownership and strategic control can be handled in game-theoretic analysis. The mathematical derivations omitted here are given by Shapley and Shubik (1967b).

One possible elaboration of the corporate-ownership model would be to separate control of the land from control over labor. We may suppose that the majority controls use of the land but by law must pay a uniform wage to all labor employed. Furthermore, individuals are free to accept or reject the offer for work at the wages named. After wages have been paid, the group in control must prorate any remaining "profits" equally to all owners, whether or not they belong to the controlling group, and whether or not they have worked.

To complete the model we must specify how the production decision is reached. If all applicants at the proferred wage are employed, the corporation may not be able to meet its payroll. (We are assuming that both wages and dividends are paid in kind; there is no money or credit, and no stored inventory to draw on.) Accordingly we shall constrain the corporation not to operate at a loss and give it the option of hiring only some of the applicants, or even none at all. We can still distinguish two cases: (1) the controlling majority is free to hire its own members first, and (2) the controlling majority chooses only the number to be hired (the production level).

The logical structure underlying the two characteristic functions can be expressed as follows, always assuming that $s > n/2$:

$$v(S) = \max_{w} \text{max-min}_{s' \quad s''} \max_{h} \left(\frac{s}{n}(f(h) - wh) + w\min(s', h) \right), \quad (17.1)$$

$$v(S) = \max_{w} \text{max-min}_{s' \quad s''} \max_{h} \left(\frac{s}{n}(f(h) - wh) + \frac{ws'h}{s' + s''} \right). \quad (17.2)$$

Here w denotes the wage rate, s' the number of members of S who apply for work, s'' the number of nonmembers of S who apply for work, and h the number actually hired. These variables are constrained by $w \geq 0$,

$0 \leq s' \leq s$, $0 \leq s'' \leq n - s$, $0 \leq h \leq s' + s''$. The hyphenated "max-min" indicates that s' and s'' are to be chosen simultaneously, although, as it will turn out, the order of choice makes no difference. In both cases the first term represents the dividends received by the members of S, the second term the wages.

17.8.1 Model 1: Direct control, discriminatory hiring

The indicated computations in (17.1) are easily carried out. On the one hand, it is clear that a majority coalition can always arrange to hire just its own members and collect the entire output in the form of wages, with no corporate "profit" to distribute. On the other hand, since they cannot force the others to apply for work, it is clear that they can do no better. Hence (17.1) reduces to

$$v(S) = \begin{cases} f^*(s) & \text{if } s > n/2, \\ 0 & \text{if } s \leq n/2. \end{cases} \tag{17.3}$$

(See figure 17.8.)

This game has a core for small values of n; it is generally not unique (see note 3). As n increases, the core disappears when the marginal productivity of the nth laborer drops below the average productivity (when $n > m_1$ in the figure). For large values of n, if $f(s)$ is bounded, the game grows to resemble the "village-commune" model with its "winners-take-all" feature (figure 17.6). This is because the protection accorded the minority stockholders has been circumvented by discriminatory hiring, and their last remaining recourse—refusal to work—has less and less effect as the production function levels off and a surplus of labor appears.

17.8.2 Model 2: Direct control, nondiscriminatory hiring

The simplification of (17.2) is slightly less straightforward in this case. The most effective strategy for a majority coalition S turns out to be: (a) set the wage at $w = \min(f^*(s)/s, f^*(n)/n)$; (b) apply for work *en masse*: $s' = s$; and (c) maximize total output: $h = \min(m^*, s + s'')$. The characteristic function turns out to be

$$v(S) = \begin{cases} \min\left(f^*(s), \dfrac{s}{n} f^*(n)\right) & \text{if } s > n/2, \\ 0 & \text{if } s \leq n/2. \end{cases} \tag{17.4}$$

We omit the details

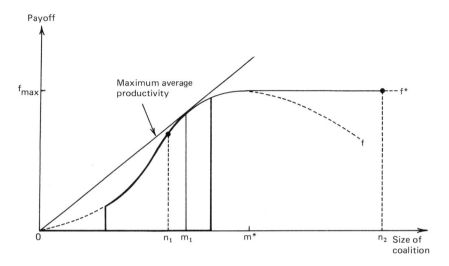

Figure 17.8
Corporate ownership with discriminatory hiring. The core exists only for $n \le m_1$.

This characteristic function, shown in figure 17.9, is a sort of hybrid of the two previous corporate-ownership models (figures 17.7 and 17.8). The antidiscrimination rule restores the core for large n, and with it the possibility of a socially stable outcome, while the option of refusing employment destroys the uniqueness of the core for small n.

17.8.3 Model 3: Indirect control, discriminatory hiring
As a further variation on the theme of corporate ownership, we introduce a production manager whose fixed objective is to maximize the profits of the corporation. The manager is merely a mechanism, not a player or potential coalition member. He chooses the production level, but the owners still set the wage rate by majority vote.

We consider first the discriminatory case, in which the members of a majority coalition can demand priority in being hired. The logical structure of the model is given by

$$v(S) = \max_{w} \max_{s'} \text{-} \min_{s''} \left(\frac{s}{n} \max_{h}(f(h) - wh) + w \min(s', h(w)) \right), \qquad (17.5)$$

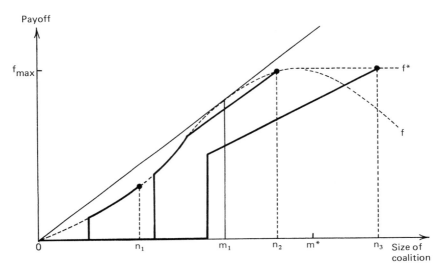

Figure 17.9
Corporate ownership with nondiscriminatory hiring. The core always exists.
There is a one-point core only if $n > m_1$.

for coalitions S with $s > n/2$. (Compare (17.1) and (17.2) above.) Here
$h(w)$ maximizes $f(h) - wh$ subject to $0 \le h \le s' + s''$, and the other
variables are as before.[5] This expression differs from (17.1) only in the
scope of the innermost "max."

The reduction of (17.5) begins with the observation that the max-min
is attained by $s' = s$, $s'' = 0$, and proceeds through a rather lengthy
argument to the following characteristic function:

$$
v(S) = \begin{cases}
\max\limits_{m_1 \le h \le s} \left(\dfrac{s}{n} f(h) + \dfrac{n-s}{n} h f'(h) \right) & \text{for } s > m_1, s > n/2, \\
f(s) & \text{for } s \le m_1, s > n/2, \qquad (17.5a) \\
0 & \text{for } s \le n/2,
\end{cases}
$$

where m_1, as before, is the point of maximum average productivity of
labor. In the top line (largest coalitions), the strategic wage rate is given
by the marginal productivity relation $w = f'(h(w))$; in the second line
the wage is simply $f(s)/s$, permitting the ruling coalition S to take the

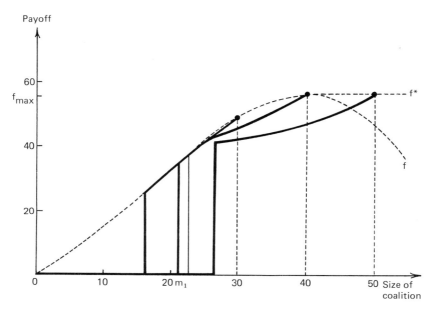

Figure 17.10
Corporation with manager (discriminatory). Characteristic functions for $n = 30$,
40, 50. There is no core if $n > m_1 + 1$.

entire output in wages. The transition between the two cases (at $s = m_1$)
is continuous.

This characteristic function is illustrated in figure 17.10 for $n = 30$,
40, 50, under the assumption that f is given by the following cubic:

$$f(s) = 1.2s + 0.045s^2 - 0.001s^3.$$

This has $m_1 = 22.5$, $m^* = 40$, and there is a point of inflection at $s = 15$.

For $n \leq m_1$, the case of ever-increasing average productivity, model 3
has the same characteristic function as model 2, and a core always exists.
For larger n there is almost never a core; in fact there is no chance for
one unless $f(s)$ is linear in the interval $\max(m_1, n/2) \leq s \leq n$, and even
this very special condition is only necessary, not sufficient, for a core.

17.8.4 Model 4: Indirect control, nondiscriminatory hiring
Finally, we consider the nondiscriminatory-hiring version of the managerial game. We have

$$v(S) = \max_{w} \max_{s'}\text{-}\min_{s''} \left(\frac{s}{n} \max_{h}(f(h) - wh) + \frac{ws'h(w)}{s' + s''} \right) \quad \text{for } s < n/2,$$

(17.6)

with $h(w)$ as in (17.3). Again this can be simplified considerably; the result is

$$v(S) = \begin{cases} \dfrac{s}{n}f(h) = \dfrac{s}{n}f^*(s) + \dfrac{n-s}{n}sf'(h) & \text{for } s > s_0, s > n/2, \\ f(s) & \text{for } s \le s_0, s > n/2, \\ 0 & \text{for } s \le n/2. \end{cases}$$

(17.6a)

Here h is defined by $(n - s)f'(h) = f(h) - f^*(s)$, and s_0 by $f(s_0)/s_0 = f(h_0)/n = f'(h_0)$. Figure 17.11 may be helpful in visualizing these relationships. The strategic wage rate is indicated by the slope of the lines labeled w.

Figure 17.12 is based on the same cubic production function as figure 17.10. For $n = 24$, s_0 is about 16; for larger n, $s_0 < n/2$ and hence is inoperative as a case discriminator. The curve for $n = 40$ is at first barely convex, then barely concave, with an inflection point at about $s = 30$; the curve for $n = 50$ is slightly convex up to $s = 40$, then linear.

To verify that the game always has a core it suffices to note, from (17.6a), that $v(S) \le (s/n)f^*(n)$. In words: no coalition can ever get on its own more than its proportionate share of the total optimal product.

17.8.5 Conclusion
Both with and without a manager, an open market for labor leads to a stable economy in which there is no particular advantage to a controlling coalition of less than all the participants (figures 17.9 and 17.12). The possibility of preferential hiring practices destroys this stability (figures 17.8 and 17.10) if the economy is in the region of decreasing average productivity ($n > m_1$), even though the production decisions themselves are made for the good of society as a whole.

17.9 Threats and Joint Product

We have now seen many examples with the same technical economic background but different legal and sociopolitical structures of ownership. One important feature is the threat potential of the individual or the minority group as it is explicitly or implicitly included in the legal structure. We could construct many other variants by allowing minority groups to

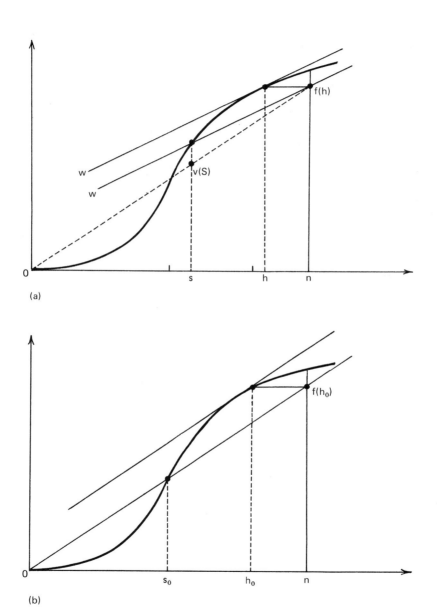

Figure 17.11
Graphical derivation of the characteristic function.

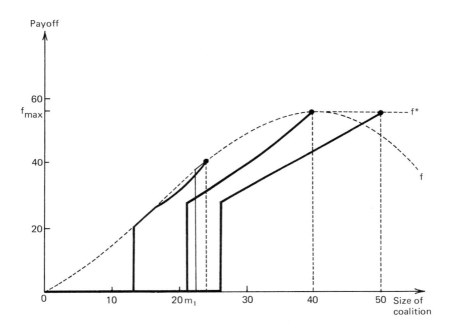

Figure 17.12
Corporation with manager (nondiscriminatory). Characteristic functions for
$n = 24, 40, 50$.

obstruct the production plans in different ways, such as refusing to work
or voting against all production decisions. Because the characteristic
function does not take account of the cost to the threateners of carrying
out their threats, however, a game-theoretic analysis of such variants
would not be fruitful without additional apparatus.

Notes to chapter 17

1. The holdings of the Compania Explotadora de Tierra del Fuego in 1965 were
approximately 2.5 million acres.

2. The lack of alternative employment for laborers has been suggested as an
important factor in the stability of the *hacienda*-dominated agricultural economy
(Mintz and Wolfe, 1957).

3. The existence of a core, in symmetric games of this kind, depends on whether
the payoff point for the all-player coalition (heavy black dot) is "visible" from the

origin. If the core exists, it always contains the symmetric imputation $(f^*(n)/n,$ $f^*(n)/n, \ldots, f^*(n)/n)$, which is also the value of the game. If the all-player point is "clearly visible," as at n_1 in figure 17.5, then the core will contain other imputations as well.

4. A good approximation to the value, when all of the plots are small, is

$$\Phi_i = \left(A \frac{l_i}{L} + (1 - A)\frac{1}{n} \right) f^*(n),$$

where l_i is the size of the ith plot and $A = \int_0^n f^*(s)ds/nf^*(n)$, the relative area under the production curve.

5. We take the largest maximizing h if there is a choice. Thus we assume that the manager will choose to operate at zero profit rather than shut down.

18 On Public Goods and Other Externalities

"Moreover, propositions stated in universal terms are rarely assumed by men of common sense to imply universality in practice; to the frequent dismay of logicians, a common tendency of mankind—and not the least of Americans—is to qualify universals in application while leaving them intact in rhetoric."

18.1 General Considerations

The initial focus of this chapter will be on situations that arise from society's need and desire to control the use of goods or services that are not allocated efficiently by the price mechanism alone. These situations involve an intermix of political, economic, and social conditions. The goods and services are ones that cause nuisance or harm to others, that must be jointly constructed through taxation of privately appropriated resources, that are unique natural resources such as beauty spots, that are held in common (*res communes*) such as air and light, and so forth (see, e.g., Maine, 1861).

The special structural features of communal goods are set in a game-theoretic framework. Here the competitive market and voting systems may appear as aspects of a general set of games whose most important properties depend on the nature of the threats exercised by individuals, groups of individuals, and society as a whole.

The appeal of an efficient price system in the context of a game-theoretic analysis is considerable. Given all the conditions concerning preferences and structure necessary for the existence of such a system, we can carry out three different sets of analyses. These view the competitive equilibrium as:

1. a nonstrategic description of behavior in a price-decentralized market;

2. a limit outcome in a noncooperative game with markets or institutionally defined price-generating mechanisms; or

3. a limit imputation in a game in cooperative form, where there is no specified institutional structure on exchange or production (the efficient

price system emerges in the interpretation of the limit imputation; no price formation mechanism is specified in the model).

Work devoted to the mathematization of the Walrasian system (Walras, 1954) provides an existence proof for a set of prices that, if known to all economic actors, enables them independently to maximize profits or utility in such a manner that all supplies and demands are balanced and the outcome is Pareto-optimal (see, e.g., Debreu, 1959; Arrow and Hahn, 1971).

The model provides no description of price formation. Only existence is considered; the institutional structure needed to describe process is not supplied. Scarf (1973) provides an algorithm that can be used to calculate an efficient price system. A natural way to institutionalize Scarf's method would be to introduce a central agency, with considerable information about the preference and technology of the society, that calculates and announces prices.

The two explicitly game-theoretic approaches differ in their treatment or avoidance of institutional detail. The formulation of the economy as a *strategic market game*, as in part IV, requires the direct modeling of a price-formation mechanism. The formulation of the economy as a *market game*, as in part III, not only does not require a price-formation mechanism but does not even require assumptions concerning the existence of prices; rather, prices are deduced from certain solutions.

The strategic market game formulation provides a large class of models of an economy, each differing from the others in institutional details related to the method of price formation. Because the games are cast in strategic form, the noncooperative-equilibrium solution can be applied to them. If it is assumed that economic agents are individually of negligible influence in the market, then for a variety of institutional forms it can be shown that the competitive and noncooperative equilibria lead to the same outcome (see Dubey, Mas-Colell, and Shubik, 1980; Dubey and Shapley, 1977; Dubey and Shubik, 1978a). It is also possible to construct a strategic market game in which the government plays a central role in controlling prices, and then the efficient prices and noncooperative equilibria lead to the same outcomes (Shubik, 1977). Such a model is consistent with the original mathematical model suggested by Arrow and Debreu (1954) for a competitive economy.

If we are only interested in a static, noninstitutional analysis of an efficient price system, the price equilibria we obtain are consistent with both a competitive decentralized economy and a managed economy in which prices are calculated and announced by a central agency. The distinction between these two highly different forms of economic organization does not appear until we examine disequilibrium behavior. To make this distinction we must construct the model of the economy at the strategic level. At this point the rules of the game must be fully formulated, and the rudimentary institutional structure of the economy then appears.

When we formulate an exchange economy directly as a game in cooperative form, as in part III, we obtain a market game that has the property of being a c-game. This is not true if we postulate that all individuals are required to trade via a market mechanism. As noted in chapter 14, "pecuniary externalities" are real, even if weak.

We can summarize the results of the analysis for mass economies with private ownership and the appropriate conditions on preferences and technology as follows. The imputations giving rise to the efficient price system have the following solution properties:

1. They are efficient and can arise from decentralized individual optimization given prices (the *competitive-equilibrium property*).

2. They are the outcomes from equilibrium strategies in strategic market games in which institutional forms of trade are given (the *noncooperative-game property*).

3. They are stable against the economic power of all coalitions, so that no coalition can obtain more than it obtains at the efficient price system imputation by unilateral behavior (the *core property*).

4. They are fair and equitable in the sense of the Shapley axioms (the *value property*).

The coincidence of the various solutions provides considerable support for the price system as the way to handle a mass individual-ownership economy.[1] Because the nucleolus is within the core, the coincidence holds true for the nucleolus as well. Some limited results lead us to observe that there is also a relationship between the bargaining set and the efficient price system (see chapter 12).

Unfortunately, this coming together of diverse solution concepts, which obliterates the importance of institutional structure, appears to be the exception rather than the rule. It fails for situations in which there are economic agents of any significant size, and in many markets there are agents of at least one type who are few in number. It also fails when externalities and other complications in preference and production structures are present, and this is almost always the case with public goods.

In this chapter three approaches to the study of social welfare are noted and contrasted: (1) the classical search for a social-welfare function and the study of societal optimization; (2) the construction of games in coalitional form without specifying strategic form; and (3) the modeling of constraints on process into the actual rules of the game, thereby defining a strategic form (depending on the solution concept to be considered, the strategic form may then be used to derive a coalitional form, or it may be used directly to investigate noncooperative equilibria).

The third approach supplements rather than contrasts with the second approach. It stresses and operationalizes the proposition that historical, demographic, social, legal, and political considerations, all of which operate on time scales longer than that of most market forces, modify and constrain the rules of the game. This can affect individuals' strategy sets and thus greatly influence the existence and location of various solutions.

A grand theory of political economy might try to explain institutional types and the dynamics of sociopolitical change as part of the game. No attempt is made to do so here. Instead we acknowledge the sociopolitical environment as given and concentrate on its economic and game-theoretic features, acknowledging that this provides only a medium-term approximation to the dynamics of society's handling of social welfare.

Figure 18.1 illustrates the three levels of modeling and the types of analyses associated with them. The listing is in order of increasing specification of assumptions, not historical development. Thus the Arrow approach to social welfare comes before that of Bergson because it has weaker assumptions.

We shall not attempt a comprehensive survey of the development of welfare economics. Mishan (1960) and Chipman and Moore (1978) cover the period from 1939 to 1974 in detail. Much of that work examines optimality conditions, given a social-welfare function and the existence of competitive sectors, monopoly sectors, tariffs, compensation tests, and lump-sum transfers; consumer surplus in its many variants; and "second-best" criteria (Lancaster and Lipsey, 1959).

Leaving aside questions of logic and solution concepts, a major contrast between the non-game-theoretic and game-theoretic approaches to welfare economics comes in the explicitness of the modeling. The game-theoretic approaches to welfare economics, public goods, and externalities only started in the 1960s. A survey including some of this work is given by Milleron (1972).

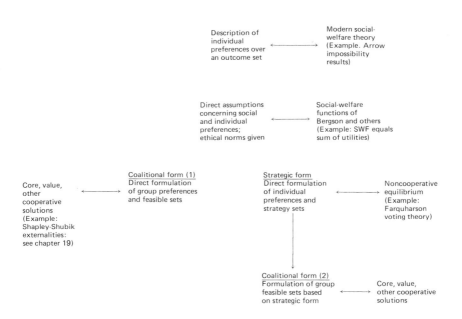

Figure 18.1
Types of models and analyses.

18.2 Modeling Economies with Public Goods and Other Externalities

The discussion concerning public goods and externalities takes place at many levels of generality and implicitly involves considerably different time spans. The span of welfare-economic problems stretches from how to tax for the building of a bridge to global socioeconomic questions that will determine the heritage of generations unborn. The basic assumptions differ considerably with the type of question being asked.

18.2.1 The players
Who are the strategic players, and whose preferences count? The answers to these questions are not necessarily the same. Institutions may be regarded as strategic players without direct preferences, and children, the old, or the sick may have preferences without strategic power. We shall discuss five categories of players:

1. (a) the living, (b) the unborn, (c) the dead;

2. (a) national residents, (b) national nonresidents, (c) foreign residents, (d) foreign nonresidents;

3. (a) the family, (b) the individual, (c) the adult, (d) the child;

4. (a) the institutionalized individual, (b) the noninstitutionalized individual;

5. (a) government institutions, (b) not-for-profit corporations, (c) corporations, (d) formal clubs and groups, (e) informal groups.

Most discussions of public goods assume that the preferences and strategic power of the living are what count. Honoring the dead and providing for generations unborn have meaning in intergenerational quid pro quo and interlinked preferences.

Most questions concerning public goods are constrained to national or local jurisdictions and tend to concern residents, possibly with some distinction being made between nationals and foreigners both strategically and with regard to the importance of their preferences.

The strategic unit is frequently the individual adult, although for welfare purposes families may be considered as units. Children are generally not considered as strategic players, and their preferences are subsumed in those of their parents or others.

In many countries the serving of lengthy prison terms or being declared mentally incompetent may partially or fully disenfranchise an individual. Thus a considerable part of the institutional population of a country may be excluded as strategic players; either their preferences are not considered, or they are only considered by trustees or fiduciaries.

Much theorizing in welfare economics has been carried on at a high level of abstraction or vagueness. Furthermore, much of it has been institution-free or decision-system-free. Thus we are restricted to three primitive concepts: (1) individuals; (2) a set of prospects, outcomes, or states of the world; and (3) individual preferences defined over this set. Optimality, efficiency, or social welfare can then be explored axiomatically or by means of "thought experiments" in which we assume that all know and correctly reveal their preferences.

At a lesser level of generality we may be concerned with mechanisms of choice and hence with institutions. In every country, government and other institutions are strategic players in the determination of social welfare and the production and distribution of goods and services. Central,

state, and local governments and other governmental institutions, corporations, not-for-profit corporations, and formal clubs and groups
generally pay powerful roles in the determination of social welfare. On
occasion informal groups and the husbanding of public opinion may have
force.

Although it is relatively easy to model institutions as strategic players,
basic problems are encountered in describing institutional goals and preferences. Are they pure fiduciaries for individuals, or do they have a life
of their own? Are institutions fully determined by grand economic forces,
or do culture, society, politics, and other noneconomic forces help determine their structures. The view adopted here is that a Grand Economics
that attempts to explain the evolution of societies, classes, wars, and so
forth in primarily economic terms, vastly overestimates the importance of
economics in human affairs. Furthermore, even if economic forces were
the prime determinants of institutional evolution, the process at best is
slow. Hence for the study of much of social welfare on the time scale of
10–20 years or less it is reasonable to take most institutions as given.

18.2.2 The roles of time and space
Time and space enter the modeling of economic activity in two basically
different but equally important ways. They are factors in defining the
openness or closure of the model and also in mediating the role of information and causality.

An economic model may be open or closed to the past and the future
depending on how initial and ending conditions are specified. As noted in
chapter 1, the use of money and a credit system in which the books are not
required to balance provides a means for opening a model in time. The
stating of initial conditions going back several periods before the starting
period of the model provides a way to incorporate history (see chapter 16,
for example).

We stress here once more that if we consider as part of social-welfare
theory broad questions concerning intergenerational equity, then we must
make some basic demographic assumptions together with assumptions
concerning the "rights" and preferences of those unborn.

Another way to keep an economic model open is to postulate an outside
world or a foreign sector. The foreign sector may even be considered as a
strategic player whose welfare is not taken directly into account in measuring social welfare.

In the type of equilibrium analysis represented by general-equilibrium theory or core theory the roles of both space and time are essentially suppressed. In the mechanics of social distribution the timing and costs of distribution may need to be considered directly.

18.2.3 Preferences, utility, and values

The assumption that any individual has a well-defined preference ordering over all prospects is at best highly simplistic and of relevance only to a few economic problems in which the set of prospects is restricted. Frequently the assumption involves a blatant ignoring of elementary observations on life. Current interest in the application of behavioral theory to economic analysis attests to a recognition of the limitations of human perception and cognition and the importance of these limitations in social and economic choice.

The study of welfare economics in general, and the social and political control of public goods and externalities in particular, requires assumptions concerning complex individual and group evaluations of public goods, services, and policies. The average consumer may have reasonably well-defined preferences over a usually purchased set of goods and services, but when we consider personal, private, and public investment, preferences and the meaning of preferences become vaguer.

How are values to be distinguished from preferences? Where do beliefs, ideologies, instincts, and moral codes fit into the individual's decision-making process? We shall not answer these questions here; to do so would require a volume with a more philosophical bent than this one. We raise the questions, however, to stress the dange of spurious generalization in the study of social welfare. The economist's concept of preference does not easily cover the concepts of values, ideology, beliefs, or moral codes, yet many of the problems concerning social welfare do. Pigou (1932) restricted his remarks to those phenomena to which the measuring rod of money could be applied. While an economist can measure expenditures on justice, however, this does not tell us about the quality or even give much operationally useful meaning to the quantity of justice being delivered.

When we worry about community swimming pools, sewage systems, or postal services, we are on easier and narrower grounds than when our concern is justice, defence, or programs for the poor. For the development of good theory and useful application, the problems of welfare economics and public goods must be separated and given specific structure.

Given the assumption of some form of individual preference structure, it must still be decided whether the preference structures of the family, of groups, and of institutions are assumed as primitive concepts or are built up from individual preferences.

Given a decision on the units of preference, the nature of the preference structure must still be specified. In chapters 4 and 5 of *GTSS* the possibilities for both individual and group preferences were described in some detail. Here we shall briefly summarize some of the assumptions. The most elemental approach is to consider a *choice function*, which is nothing more than a rule that selects a single element from any set of elements confronting the individual. Otherwise we might consider, for example, a partial ordering of preferences, a lexicographic ordering, or a complete ordering. We might go a step further and assume that a utility function exists and can be defined up to a linear transformation.

Beyond the simple existence of utility functions, we might wish to consider the possibility of transferable and comparable utility. Clearly if there existed in profusion some magic u-money or transferable utility, then many public goods and social-welfare problems could be solved easily. The Pareto-optimal surface could be reasonably approximated by a hyperplane whose slope would provide an intrinsic measure of comparability of utility. The social-welfare problem would then amount to a joint maximization with equity considerations accounted for by means of side payments.

For many small partial-equilibrium problems, the assumption that money is a reasonable approximation to a transferable utility of constant marginal worth to all may be empirically justified when income effects are low. This will not hold true in general, however, for major changes in social policy.

Pareto was critically concerned with the development of economics as an applied and experimental science that would take into account the interaction with political and sociological phenomena. In the formal development of the preinstitutional properties of production and exchange the simplification attained by omitting all institutional detail was justified by the results and insights made available by an in-depth analysis that would have been difficult, if not impossible, to execute with more complex models.

When our attention turns to public goods, the very nature of the subject makes it impossible to generalize without recognizing the political, sociological, and legal constraints on the economic problems. At this stage in the development of economic theory there appear to be three contrasting alternatives: (1) to proceed with preinstitutional models, ignoring the sociopolitical environment as much as possible; (2) to model institutions, laws, and other sociopolitical factors as explicit constraints or boundary conditions on the economic models; or (3) to build explicit models in which economic, political, and sociological factors are all considered parts of a single reactive system.

The first alternative is typified by the preliminary steps of Samuelson (1954) in defining and studying an economy with "pure public goods." As he showed, one can carry out some useful analysis concerning prices and production with virtually no institutional assumptions, but the scope of the analysis is necessarily limited.

The third alternative is to model the global unified sociopolitical economic system and then develop a dynamics that explains—possibly in economic terms—the rise and fall of political and sociological as well as economic institutions. This procedure may eventually prove successful, although I suspect that political and sociological dynamics will not be subsumed as special cases of an economic dynamics. At this point in the development of microeconomic theory, however, emphasis on this type of modeling would appear to be premature.

We are now being forced to proceed from preinstitutional statics or equilibrium models to models in which mechanisms are specified. Even at the most abstract level, the rules of the game describe these mechanisms, which can be regarded as elemental descriptions of the institutions of a society. The institutions are the carriers of process. Before we can fruitfully develop an economic dynamics, a politicoeconomic dynamics, or a sociopolitical economic dynamics, we must model the structure of the relevant institutions. These extra features are needed to avoid spurious and vacuous generality.

The research strategy suggested here has three stages: (1) preinstitutional statics; (2) institutional statics and comparative dynamics; (3) institutional dynamics. The preinstitutional development of microeconomic theory has prepared the way for the second stage. In taking this step the methods of game theory can be used to model situations that include economic, political, and even bureaucratic and sociological features. This is not new to economic theorizing, but in certain instances unfortunate phrasing such as "the theory of the second best" has been used, as if to apologize to the economist for having suggested that political, administrative, or sociological realities can influence the best of all

Table 18.1
U.S. governmental institutions (1978)

	Number of institutions	Budget revenues	Expenditures (in $ billions)	Debt
Federal government	1	430	400	780
States	50	172	137	103
Local governments	79,913[a]	131	209	178
Total	—	732	745	1061

a. 1977.

Table 18.2
Tax revenues (billions of $)

	Federal	State	Local	Total
Individual income	181.0	29.1	4.1	214.2
Corporate income	60.0	10.7	—	70.7
Sales and gross receipts	25.4	58.3	9.3	93.0
Property	—	2.4	64.0	66.4
Other	8.1	12.8	2.9	23.8
Total	274.5	113.2	80.4	468.1

possible pure economic solutions in a world unsullied by administrative or political processes and costs.

The third stage, building and analyzing satisfactory dynamic systems, is in my opinion currently fruitful only where specific institutional structure serves to delimit the dynamics. The development of the second stage will make the development of the third stage easier.

18.2.4 A few figures relevant to modeling

How important are public goods? A glance at the *Statistical Abstract of the United States* provides some useful insights.

Table 18.1 indicates the governmental structure at various regional levels in 1978. The local governments included 3042 countries, 18,862 municipalities, 16,822 townships and towns, 15,174 school districts, and 25,962 special districts.

Per-capita revenues at the federal level in 1978 were $1970 and at state and local levels $1385. Expenditures were $1835 and $1584, respectively.

Table 18.3
Nontax revenues (billions of $)

	Federal	State	Local	Total
Charges and miscellaneous revenues[a]	44.7	22.4	30.3	97.4
Utility revenue	—	1.0	16.3	17.3
Liquor stores	—	2.4	0.4	2.8
Insurance trusts	110.5	32.6	3.0	146.1
Total	155.2	58.4	50.0	263.6

a. Includes postal service earnings, school lunch sales, hospitals, natural resources, parks
and recreation, air and water transport terminals.

Table 18.4
General expenditures (billions of $)

	Federal	State and local	Total
National defense, international relations	114.8	—	114.8
Postal service	15.3	—	15.3
Education	19.6	110.8	130.4
Highways	6.5	24.6	31.1
Public welfare	36.6	39.1	75.7
Health and hospitals	10.6	24.9	35.5
Natural resources	23.7	4.2	27.9
Housing and urban renewal	5.3	3.7	9.0
Space research	4.0	—	4.0
Air transportation	2.9	1.6	4.5
Social insurance administration	3.7	1.8	5.5
Interest on general debt	39.3	12.0	51.3
Other	65.7	74.2	139.9
Total	348.0	297.0	645.0

Gross National Product in 1978 was $2127.6 billion; thus expenditures
were 37.3 percent of GNP.

To instill an appreciation of the magnitude of public finance, we offer a
breakdown of the $732 billion of revenue and $745 billion of expenditure.
Total tax revenues in 1978 were $468 billion. Table 18.2 indicates the
breakdown of major taxes for various levels of government. The income
tax dominates for the federal government, sales taxes for the states, and
property taxes for local governments. International comparisons show
considerable institutional variability in this aspect of public control over
the raising of funds.

Taxes account for only $468.1 out of $731.7 billion. We must also consider governmental economic activities that generate revenues. These are shown in table 18.3.

In the category of miscellaneous general revenues the federal government is large in postal and natural-resource income; the states in higher-education income; and local governments in lower-education, hospital, sewage, and sanitation income.

Table 18.4 indicates the considerable difference in the rendering of national and more local services. In particular, the federal government has the sole or dominant role in national defense, postal services, natural resources, and space research. The state and local governments are dominant in education, highways, and health and hospitals.

A glance back at tables 3.3 and 3.4 provides information on the work-force used to deliver governmental services.

In summary, in terms of both finance and employment the federal, state, and local governments are major economic forces in the economy. They are neither individual utility maximizers nor profit maximizers. They are complex institutions run by elected and appointed fiduciaries with goals of their own constrained by economic, legal, political, and social forces.

18.3 A Taxonomy of Public Goods and Institutional Forms

The strategic powers of individuals, groups, and societies vary considerably as a function of technology and institutional arrangements. An adequate analysis by means of games in either strategic or cooperative form requires an understanding of the basic properties of public goods. An analysis using the strategic form also requires a specification of institutional arrangements.

18.3.1 Some problem areas

Federal, state, and local government expenditures amount to around 35 percent of gross national product in the United States and even more in countries such as Sweden. Corporations, trusts, and other institutions swell the amount of economic activities performed by collectivities and fiduciaries. The wide variety of goods and services dealt with by groups within society, and by society as a whole, pose a number of different problems of control.[2]

Among these varied public goods are: museums, public societies supporting the arts, bridges and roads, armed forces, police, courts, jails, government, parks, harbors, dams, monuments, weather stations, and public health services. An increasingly important category of goods and services with communal properties involves communication and information processing: telephone and telegraph systems, postal services, educational institutions, radio, television, communication satellites, transportation networks, libraries, oversight of access to the electromagnetic spectrum, data banks, books, computer programs, inventions, trade secrets, and many other knowledge-related items. Finally, among the more important "public diseconomies" are: smoke, nuclear waste, noise, sewage, general pollution, crowding, billboards, blocking of light, and other invasions of privacy.

All of these public goods have the property that the gain or harm in production or use goes beyond any single individual. Every society creates elaborate political, social, and legal systems to define and delimit property and ownership rules for these inherently social or antisocial goods.

It should be noted that some public goods are not produced from private goods, but are inherited by society as a unit. In these instances the problem becomes one of arranging for individual use of the communal good. The high seas and the electromagnetic spectrum fall into this category.

The prime factors in the construction, enjoyment, and use of public goods can be characterized in terms of the powers, rights, and threats of individuals and groups. These can be portrayed in game-theoretic terms somewhat institutionally through the strategic form, and less institutionally through the characteristic function. These procedures reflect the intermix of the political and economic powers of various groups.

18.3.2 Factors that delineate the game
In this section we provide a listing of institutional considerations that go into the construction of models of an economy with public goods and externalities. In the next section we shall count the variants to get a sense of the scope of possibilities.

Production conditions

1. The item is privately produced: office supplies used by the government, official automobiles, many weapons.

2. The item is produced or controlled in some or all countries by a government-owned industry: services such as justice, the post office,

telephones, police, administration, and foreign affairs, and goods such as tobacco or liquor.

3. The item is exogenously supplied: air, weather, other natural resources.

4. The item is virtually costlessly reproducible: raw information and some knowledge.

Measurability and divisibility

1. The item is divisible and measurable: sugar, gasoline.

2. The item is divisible, but there are problems in grading the quality of the product: labor.

3. The item is essentially indivisible from the viewpoint of a consumer, but is clearly measurable: most consumer durables.

4. The item is indivisible, and there is a problem in defining quantity and quality: a hydroelectric plant.

5. There is no simple natural measure for the service being delivered: justice, quality of government, safety, and virtually all information services.

Appropriation conditions

1. The item can be privately and individually owned: chattels, houses, some land.

2. The item can be privately and jointly owned: corporations, private parks, buildings, and other large items.

3. Law and tradition require that the item be publicly owned: the armed forces, the justice system.

4. The item cannot even be easily owned by the nation-state: the high seas, outer space.

Externalities, excludability, directability, and avoidability

1. The item or activity can be (i) a diseconomy to all, (ii) an economy, or (iii) a mixed economy/diseconomy: various types of pollution can typify all three; the level of literacy and general educational level may be regarded as generating an external economy to individuals; the playing of a specific type of music in a public place may be regarded as an external economy by those who enjoy it and as a diseconomy by those who do not. The fourth possibility is that of a good with no externalities.

2. Exclusion from use in practically impossible: it may not be possible to jam the broadcast of a program to individuals within transmission range.

3. Exclusion from use is possible: one can put barriers on roads, at park or museum entrances, and exclude or extract a fee from users.

4. The externality can be directed or targeted: a neighbor may have the choice of directing his noise-making activities in a particular direction; a town can select where to locate its garbage dump.

5. The externality may be diffuse or only randomly contractable: a rabid dog may go in any direction; smoke or radioactive fallout will go with the prevailing winds.

6. An individual can at little cost avoid being the recipient of an externality: one can wear ear plugs to avoid minor noise, and it may sometimes be possible to move outside the range of a disturbance (for example, if there are several more or less equally convenient routes through an area, the ones with bad smog or traffic can be avoided).

7. An individual cannot, except at great cost, avoid being the recipient of an externality: if the local water system is treated with fluorine, it may be too expensive to switch to a private water supply in order to avoid it; even if one disapproves of governmental behavior or the social climate, one may have little chance to avoid the consequences, short of emigration.

Trade conditions

1. Trade for most private goods is assumed to be through a market system using money; barter is not significant in most modern societies except for tax-avoidance purposes.

2. Public goods are bought by government from private industry via the market, bidding, or contracts or are directly manufactured by the government.

Actors   At a minimum we require economic agents, and frequently we need an actor representing government. Depending on the questions to be answered and the depth of our analysis, we may wish to model political players and bureaucrats explicitly. A discussion of behavioral types was given in *GTSS*, chapter 2. Here, if a government is modeled, we must be concerned with its control and motivation, and hence must consider goals with strategic fiduciary players.

Goals and preference conditions   Although it seems reasonable to adopt a view that independent individual preferences exist for many if not all private goods, both preferences and choice mechanisms for the quality and quantity of social security or justice appear to be fundamentally different from the preferences and choice mechanisms for ordinary consumer products.

Setting aside the question of concern for the welfare of others, we must still specify preferences for three types of actors in any model involving public goods or governmental control of externalities. These are the consumer/voter, the producers, and the "government" or the politicians. And even if we assume that an individual consumer/voter has a complete preference ordering over all outcomes, we must still make assumptions about the other actors. At the risk of gross oversimplification, we might assume that the producers try to maximize an appropriately defined profit. In actuality the intermix of bureaucratic structure, fiduciary rules, tax considerations, and pliable accounting frequently make this assumption inadequate (Whitman and Shubik, 1979). As noted in chapter 13, we can handle the corporate-goal problem by assuming coalition production; otherwise, for simplicity, we can adopt the profit-maximizing assumption.

What remains is the specification of preferences for either an aggregate entity called "government" or a group of individuals called politicians. Even in the simplest economic model with public goods, we must make a choice between modeling government directly as an aggregate player with a set of preferences of its own or considering politicians as striving for power by offering the electorate a program. This problem will be taken up in chapter 20; it is also close to the treatment of political competition by Downs (1957), Young (1978b), and others (see *GTSS*, chapter 12). When government is considered directly as an aggregate player, we must specify its preference system exogenously. If it is considered not as a player but as a mechanism to transmit the will of the electorate via the politicians, then the politicians' goals and strategy sets must be specified.

The voting mechanism   In most modern societies the vote and taxation are intimately related to the delivery of public goods and the control of externalities. Here we consider some of the constraints on voting.

1. Does the decision depend on a vote? Is the vote direct as in a referendum for a bond issue, or is it indirect as in the case of the military budget (where people who have been elected vote as trustees of the electorate)?

2. What constitutes a winning vote? An act of union may well require unanimity; an impeachment may call for 75 percent; a veto for 2/3 majority; and ordinary business for a simple majority. When more than one item is being voted on, as in the election of directors to a corporate board, votes may be cumulative. There are several different cumulative vote mechanisms.

3. Are votes for sale? In the case of corporations votes may be purchased legally in the open market. In theory, votes are not for sale in most political bodies, though political payoffs and logrolling are well-known phenomena.

4. Can a winning coalition legally and successfully impose its taxation scheme on others? Individuals may oppose military expenditures, but they are nevertheless forced to pay their taxes. In the case of a public monument, a vote may be taken on whether to build, though the actual erection will depend on the private financing of a particular interested group.

5. To specify the politicoeconomic mechanism for the implementation of policies concerning public goods or the control of diseconomies, we must explicitly introduce a governmental body and a voting mechanism. In our search for the Philosopher's Stone we would like to keep our models as "institution-free" and as uncluttered with details as possible. Unfortunately, even a model for a competitive economy, despite its aesthetic appeal and apparent freedom from institutional features, carries implicit assumptions that make it far less general and institution-free than it might at first appear to be.

We begin by restricting ourselves to a rudimentary institution we shall call "the government" and to a description of the voting process and its interaction with the market process. We consider some type of voting system to be specified. The government performs the following tasks: (i) it administers the vote; (ii) it collects taxes and disburses subsidies; and (iii) it arranges for the production, supervision, and distribution of public goods in coordination with the competitive sector of the economy.

Each of these points brings up a host of problems. Even though the administration of the vote appears to be a straightforward task, we must immediately ask how the item to be voted on comes into being. There are always many alternative possibilities for the routing of a superhighway. How is a particular proposal selected for the vote? Voting is often time-consuming and expensive. How many different alternatives can be considered by means of a voting mechanism? Who selects the agenda?

We could start with heroic assumption concerning zero costs of data processing and zero expense to voting. We could then assume a board of experts that studies and prepares the motions. The generation of alternatives to vote on causes no problem when we consider solution concepts such as the Pareto-optimal set, the core, the value, or other approaches to equity. If we wish to consider the noncooperative equilibrium, however, then the extensive or strategic form is called for and the mechanism for agenda selection must be specified.

The second role of the government is to collect taxes and disburse subsidies. We discuss below the importance of distinguishing between money and commodity taxes and subsidies. All possible variations have been and still are encountered in human affairs. Taxes have been gathered in money, salt, hours of labor, and so forth, and subsidies, even in the United States today, may be paid in food stamps.

As already noted, tax collection and concepts of equity cannot be easily treated as separate items. "Unpopular taxes" may be hard and costly to collect. The law of administrative inconvenience says that if a tax is easy to collect and the group against whom it is levied is not in a position to cause too much trouble, one can more or less forget abstract problems of equity and continue the tax.

Following the policy of abstracting out extra difficulties whenever we can, we assume that at this level of the discussion there are no problems concerning the levying or collection of taxes, provided the individuals have the amounts demanded from them.

Neither in economic theory nor in game theory to date has the concept of an institution been adequately reflected. A coalition is not necessarily an ongoing organization. Yet in practical politics there are organizations and party faithfuls who "can deliver the vote." The existence of a "city machine" can remove much of the guesswork from deciding what civic expenditures should be approved and what contractors and suppliers should be used.

Closely interlinked with the direct power involved in the control and influence of voting systems and the administrative control of government procurement is "insider's knowledge." Examples include the leak to a friend of information on where a new state highway will go and the discreet use of information by members of a board of directors, their families, and friends about a change in the price of sulphur or a new uranium strike. To reflect insider's information the model must include time lags between when a vote is passed and when various groups are informed of the results. This is different from the other important problem caused by uncertainty, namely, the estimation of a vote whose outcome is not a foregone conclusion.[3]

Means of taxation and payment   The importance of the difference between taxation and the government's purchase of resources using actual commodities or an institutionally accepted money only arises when the distribution of public goods and public control are considered from a strategic viewpoint.

The basic difference between asking simple questions concerning the existence of distributions satisfying conditions of optimality and equity and viewing processes as parts of a strategic game is that certain legitimate strategies may in fact violate Walras's law. Bankruptcy conditions and penalties for failure to comply must be specified. A government may find that it is unable to construct the park it promised with the funds voted for it.

There is an important difference between a mandate to spend $10 million on a public good and a mandate to complete the building of a public good of a certain specification while spending no more than $10 million. There is also an important difference between situations in which eminent domain and the printing of money are or are not feasible moves.

If there is a chance that the government will not be able to carry out a mandate within a stated budget, then a simple utility formula such as "minimize the cost of a project" is not sufficient to describe its goals. We need to know how to evaluate a weapons system or an opera house that is 90 percent completed.

There are a host of institutional variations of tax methods. Among the better-known types are (i) income tax, (ii) property tax, (iii) poll tax, (iv) sales tax, (v) estate tax, and (vi) usage tax or toll. Various states in the United States use combinations of income, property, and sales taxes as their major source of revenue; failure to pay taxes can lead to legal action, prison terms, and the impounding of property.

A poll tax takes the form of a single equal levy on all. Those who do not pay are barred from enjoying a right such as voting. Sales taxes are a surcharge collected on the purchase of the taxed commodity. Usage taxes or tolls are related to sales taxes in the sense that they vary directly with the amount utilized by the individual. They are often applied to special highways, bridges, ports, national parks, and beaches. The individual usually has the choice of not paying and not obtaining the services, regardless of the fact that he may already be subsidizing them. Estate taxes are especially interesting inasmuch as they raise several fundamental questions concerning our views of economic and social man and our attitude toward intergenerational transfer and death.

Considerations of equity or power can limit the ways in which taxation is applied. Equity questions frequently arise in debates about whether an income tax rate should be progressive, constant, or regressive and about the relationship between tax size and property or estate size. Historically, all possibilities have existed. Considerations of equity and power are virtually always intermixed. To cite an extreme example, a society may impose special taxes on certain politically powerless groups. Following the Arab conquest of North Africa very different tax rates were levied against the unbelievers; and throughout history Jews, merchants, and other minority groups have had special tax burdens levied against them.

Equity and conveniences are also intermixed. For example, the price of an admission ticket to a public park is the same for all (except perhaps for schoolchildren and a few other special groups). It is likely that the proposition that individuals should pay different prices for their use of a park would be strongly opposed both for reasons of equity and because of the difficulty in trying to specify and administer such a tax scheme.[4]

Equity is in some countries interpreted as requiring "one adult, one vote." A poll tax or property requirement may be regarded as an extension of this principle to "equal vote, equal financial stake."

In summary, we must stress that a necessary modeling point is the decision on whether "conditions on taxation" are to be considered as part of the "rules of the game" or as part of the goals.

18.3.3 On the number of strategically different economies with externalities and public goods

Utilizing the factors and distinctions made in section 18.3.2, we can make a crude estimate of the number of different game models that arise from combinations of physical properties of goods, production, trade, voting, and taxation procedures.[5]

The first grouping of factors concerns the physical properties of goods or services. The number in parentheses is the number of alternatives possible.

Physical properties

1. Measurability and divisibility (5)
2. Appropriation conditions (4)
3. Externalities (4)
4. Excludability (2)

5. Directability (2)

6. Avoidability (2)

Each of these items has already been discussed in some detail. Here we indicate how the number of cases is estimated. Consider the measurability and divisibility conditions. Five possibilities were suggested in section 18.3.2; at least one of these must hold in an economy, and any set of them could hold for the various combinations of goods and services present in any economy. Hence there are $2^5 - 1$ modeling cases that must be considered. The other possibilities are estimated in a similar manner.

The upper bound on the number of goods or services distinguishable by the various combinations of physical attributes noted above is $5 \times 4^2 \times 2^3 = 640$. This is somewhat higher than the number of actual cases because some choices in one category limit alternatives in another. For example, if the goods and services are measurable and divisible, and neither external economies nor diseconomies are associated with them, then questions concerning exclusion, directability of the externality, and avoidability do not arise.

Production conditions (4)

Four possibilities have been noted, at least one of which must be present for any good.

Trade conditions (4)

As a reasonable first-order approximation in a modern economy, goods and services are distributed via markets, bidding, contract, or gift. We omit force, fraud, deceit, and chance (for further discussion see Shubik, 1970).

Actors and goals (3)

Even at the most abstract level, at least two actors are needed to describe any politicoeconomic model involving public goods. Apart from the consumer (and the producer treated as a profit-maximizing automaton), we need either government as a player or politicians as players with government as a mechanism. The two combinations are (i) consumers and government or (ii) consumers and politicians. As a first approximation, consumers are assumed to maximize utility. We can model government either as a given mechanism or aggregating device with neither strategies nor preferences, or as a strategic player with an exogenously given welfare function that it attempts to maximize. If instead of government we model politicians as players, then a simple motivation for these players might be that they wish to stay in power.

Combining the two models of actors with different models of goals gives three cases: (i) consumers with government as an automaton; (ii) consumers with government maximizing a welfare function; (iii) consumers with politicians maximizing their power.

The voting mechanism

1. Election type (2: direct or indirect)

2. Percentage needed to win (we count the 5 most common: 100%, 75%, $66\frac{2}{3}$%, 50%, or dictatorship)

3. Veto conditions (2: yes or no)

4. Cumulative voting (2: yes or no)

5. Votes for sale (2: yes or no)

6. Power to tax (3: a winning coalition can tax everyone, themselves only, or no one)

7. Proposal or agenda selection (?)

In an economy as a whole where many goods and services are supplied in parallel by ongoing processes, each with a different time horizon and event schedule, many different types of votes, direct and indirect, are employed simultaneously for different aspects of politicoeconomic decision making. Thus for society as a whole there is no need to choose between direct and indirect voting; some processes may employ one, some the other. In particular, a modern economy, in the running of both private corporations and public bureaus, depends heavily on fiduciary decision makers whose posts are at best controlled indirectly by stockholders or the electorate through elections for membership to directorates or political posts.

Five of the most common types of winning conditions are noted as item 2. There are a host of others. In many states, for example, bicameral arrangements require majorities in more than one house before a bill is passed. The relationship among the Senate, the House, and the president might be investigated through a model of voting in a tricameral system.

Items 3–6 are self-explanatory. Item 7, which is of considerable importance in the characterization of the decision process, is noted here but cannot be dealt with adequately without explicit study of political and administrative process.

Considering a single vote on a single item, then, and leaving out agenda selection, the number of possible variants is $5 \times 3 \times 2^4 = 240$.

Taxation

1. Types of feasible taxes (8)

2. Conditions on taxation (4)

3. Taxation or subsidies in money or in kind (2)

4. Eminent domain (2)

Many different taxes have been invented, but here we count only eight, including subsidy and inflation (see section 18.3.2). Conditions on taxation include progressive, constant, regressive, or individually designated taxes.

Can a society take away a specific asset from an individual? The possibility of eminent domain is operationally a form of taxation.

We included variations in the power to tax in our discussion of voting. This was done to stress the intimate relationship between voting and taxation, and to avoid double counting we do not list it again here.

The four conditions noted above give rise to $8 \times 4 \times 2^2 = 128$ possibilities, many of which are not generally relevant because once a specific type of tax is given, the other conditions are more or less limited by that choice. Possibly no more than around 30 of these cases are of importance.

18.4 Toward a General Theory of Public Goods and Other Externalities

18.4.1 Building the game
A game in strategic form must take account of all the factors noted in section 18.3.3. If we model directly in cooperative form, we can avoid some of the strategic-form detail. In subsequent chapters we shall model both ways.

Given the number of conditions of varying relevance to the construction of a game in strategic form, we can quickly do a "big number" calculation:

Physical properties (640 variations)

Production conditions (4)

Trade conditions (4)

Actors and goals (2)

Voting (240)

Taxation (30)

For a political economy with one type of good, production, trade, voting, and taxation, there are thus 147,456,000 possible cases.

Many of the distinctions are important, but it should not be assumed that just because there are vast numbers of cases no general theory can emerge. We must search for classes of games that are of socioeconomic or politicoeconomic importance and that can be analyzed for "nice" core, value, or noncooperative-equilibrium properties.

Modern welfare economics and voting theory—replete with the Condorcet paradox, impossibility theorems, and problems in the revelation of true preferences—teach an important lesson that is easy to misinterpret. They teach that there is no Philosopher's Stone that can be used to find a unique, satisfactory static aggregation of individual preferences into an overall social-welfare function under all circumstances.

The trend in social-welfare theory in the work of Bergson (1938), Samuelson (1948), Arrow (1951), and many others (Rothenberg, 1961; Little, 1957; Sen, 1963) has been to make as few restrictive assumptions as possible concerning the nature of preferences, institutional limits on choice mechanisms, or the special properties of goods and economic or sociopolitical services.

Now that economists understand that there is no unique general solution to the problems posed by social welfare and public finance,[6] their approach appears to be changing, as evinced by the concern they show for the study of specific mechanisms. A judicious addition of physical facts is called for, combined with an exploration of the meaning of the constraints imposed by custom and by social, legal, and political mechanisms.

18.4.2 A mathematical institutional approach

We suggest here that for many, but not all, economic questions of interest it is difficult if not impossible to build completely institution-free models.

If we are willing to limit our concern to statics or to equilibrium conditions, then, at least up to a point, we may be able to avoid a detailed discussion of process. Because institutions are the essential carriers of process, we can minimize the amount of institutional detail. A natural and appropriate model of economies with public goods and other socio-economic complications at the highest level of abstraction, minimizing institutional detail, is a game in cooperative form using the characteristic function (see *GTSS*, chapter 7). Examples of this approach are provided in the work on external economies and public goods in chapter 19 (see also Shapley and Shubik, 1969c; Foley, 1970b). If modeling is done at the level of abstraction of the game in cooperative form, we can even avoid making assumptions concerning the existence of a price system.

As a preliminary step to a theory of economic dynamics, the construction of models of the economy as games in strategic form requires considerable specification of the institutions given implicitly by the rules of the games. Given the formulation of economic problems as games in strategic or cooperative form, the next step in this approach is to examine classes of games for the properties of their Pareto sets, cores, values, bargaining sets, and noncooperative equilibria.

Notes to chapter 18

1. When exogenous uncertainty and nonsymmetric information conditions are considered, several new difficulties in strategic modeling appear. We shall not deal with these here.

2. A useful elementary survey of current theory and practice of public finance is provided by Musgrave and Musgrave (1973).

3. Recent work by Shapley (1981) has been devoted to the use of the weighted value to study voting with biases. See also *GTSS*, chapter 7.

4. This example poses some difficult problems in truth revelation. How does a central government find out about the true preferences of its citizens when it may pay them to lie or otherwise conceal those preferences? There is a fast-growing literature on truth-revelation mechanisms and incentive systems in strategic games.

5. We quote from the *Jubilé du Professeur V. Pareto* (1917; reprinted 1975 by Geneve Librairie Droz):

Arrivé à un certain point de mes recherches d'économie politique, je me trouvai en une impasse. Je voyais la réalité expérimentale et ne pouvais l'atteindre. Plusieurs obstacles m'arrêtaient: entre autres la mutuelle dépendance des phénomènes sociaux; laquelle ne permet pas d'isoler entièrement les études des différents genres de ces phénomènes, et qui s'oppose à ce que l'une d'elles puisse progresser indéfiniment si elle demeure privée de l'aide des autres. C'est ainsi, par exemple, que, de nos jours, les progrès des théories de la chimie se sont trouvés liés à ceux des théories de l'électricité, et vice-versa.

Il est hors de doute que fort souvent les conclusions des théories économiques ne sont pas vérifiées par l'expérience; et nous nous trouvons embarrassés pour les y faire correspondre. Comment lever cette difficulté?

Trois moyens se présentent: (1) On peut rejeter entièrement la science économique, lui dénier toute existence, et c'est ce qu'ont fait les adeptes d'une école assez nombreuse. Si, en des circonstances analogues, les savants qui ont créé l'astronomie, la physique, la chimie et d'autres sciences de ce genre, s'étaient arrêtés a un semblable parti, ces sciences séraient encore dans le néant. (2) On peut se résigner à ce defaut de correspondance, et dire que nous cherchons non ce qui est, mais ce qui devrait être. Nous sortons ainsi du domaine de la science expérimentale, et nous nous acheminons vers les régions de l'utopie. (3) Enfin, instruits par les exemples que nous fournissent les sciences naturelles, nous pouvons rechercher si le défaut de correspondance ne provient pas de ce que certains effets, étudiés séparément, se trouvent modifiés par d'autres effets que nous avons négligé de considérer.

6. Modifications and alternatives to the cooperative and strategic forms and the solutions stressed here have been considered elsewhere. See *GTSS*, chapters 3, 10, and 11, and Harsanyi (1982).

19 Externalities and Public Goods: The Cooperative Form

"A person may make use of his own property or ... conduct his own affairs at the expense of some harm to his neighbours. He may operate a factory whose noise and smoke cause some discomfort to others, so long as he keeps within a reasonable bound. It is only when his conduct is unreasonable, in the light of its utility and the harm which results, that it becomes a nuisance.... As it was said in an ancient case in regard to candlemaking in a town, 'Le utility del chose excusera le noisomeness del stink.'"

Prosser on Torts (1964)

19.1 Introduction

Without attempting to lay out a systematic approach to externalities and public goods in general, we used cooperative-game models in chapter 17 to consider variations in rights regarding the ownership of land. This topic is of considerable interest from the viewpoint of both economics and law (see Schlatter, 1951; L. C. Becker, 1977). Many of the distinctions between levels of ownership come from an intermix of the physical properties of the items involved and societal actions and rules.

Chapter 18 broadly sketched a taxonomy of the physical, political, and administrative factors involved in analysis of public goods and externalities. This chapter and the next will attempt to systematize the application of game-theoretic analysis to the study of public goods and other externalities. Our approach to modeling is illustrated in figure 19.1. Our first concern is with the selection of basic politicoeconomic and other assumptions. This involves an ad hoc decision based on empirical knowledge of the phenomenon to be examined.

Given the basic assumptions, the form of the game model must be selected. For a more or less static analysis the choice is between the strategic and the coalitional form, although the coalitional form can also be derived from a game that is first specified in strategic form. The latter method is used if institutional arrangements are important, and possibly also if the investigator wishes to contrast the application of a cooperative solution to the game in coalitional form with the application of a non-cooperative solution to the game in strategic form.

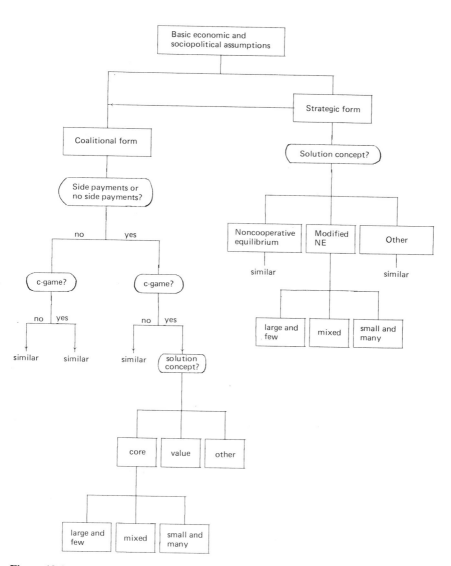

Figure 19.1
A guide to modeling.

19.1.1 The strategic form

When the strategic form is used, a full specification of a playable game must be given. A good test of a model in strategic form is whether it could actually be played as an experimental game.

It must be stressed that the specification of a game in strategic form states nothing whatsoever about equilibrium. The game merely describes all feasible outcomes—how they can be attained and the payoffs associated with them. Until a solution concept is specified, there is no way to distinguish outcomes that are in equilibrium or disequilibrium.

Once the phenomenon has been fully modeled as a game in strategic form, a solution concept must be selected. Several solution concepts have been suggested (see *GTSS*, chapters 8, 9, and 10), the most utilized of which is the noncooperative equilibrium. But for games of any complexity, especially those with sequential moves and the possibility of threats, there are frequently large classes of noncooperative equilibria that have considerably different payoffs associated with them. Then the economist may wish to add extra conditions in order to select among the equilibria. Ideally it might be desirable to have enough conditions so that we can select out a single equilibrium point or at least some small finite subset.

Among the ways one selects subclasses of equilibrium points is to consider extra properties such as Pareto optimality or perfectness (see *GTSS*, chapter 9).

In most applications there are three basic cases that merit investigation:

1. The numbers of players are few, and most or all of them have significant strategic influence on the outcomes of the game.

2. The players are many, and each is so small that he has no measurable influence when acting by himself. This is the basic condition required for the study of mass economies, polities, and societies. Much of the successful work in the applications of game theory to economics has involved the study of mass competitive markets. We suggest that political and sociological phenomena might also show regularities when mass behavior is considered.

3. The best approximation for many of the economic problems of a modern society might well be a model with a mass of participants and a few large strategic players. The large strategic players could be institutions such as firms, government agencies, or financial institutions. They tend to be not merely large but differentiated from the ordinary players who are usually individuals, families, or small economic enterprises. The institutions are really pseudoplayers with no will of their own; their

moves are the outcome of subgames played by fiduciaries and employees who operate them.

19.1.2 The coalitional form

Modeling in the coalitional form can be done directly from economic, political, or other information or indirectly on the basis of an already specified strategic form. These alternatives make a difference even in the modeling of an exchange economy. We can begin with the basic economic information consisting of players, preferences, and endowments and construct a *market game* (see chapter 11), or we can first construct a *strategic market game* (see chapter 14) and then utilize that game to construct a game in coalitional form that we call a *strategy-constrained market game*. The characteristic function of this game will not be the same as that of the other. In the former, trade through markets is not postulated; in the latter, it is.

Given that we have decided to use the coalitional form, we must decide whether or not to assume the presence of a side-payment mechanism. Several factors govern this decision. In general, when the problem is one clearly involving partial-equilibrium analysis, such as the construction of a bridge or the pollution control of a river, the use of money as a transferable commodity with constant marginal utility to all appears to be reasonable. When the economy is being studied as a whole, for the effects of social security payments, subsidies, or taxes, the side-payment assumption may be unreasonable. On occasion it may be desirable to define conditions of quasitransferability under which a specific commodity that does not have constant marginal utility is used as a money and means of side payment.

Another question that is independent of the side-payment assumption is whether or not the coalitional form adequately reflects the threat structure intrinsic to the underlying politicoeconomic situation. The game shown in strategic form in table 19.1 with the side-payment characteristic

Table 19.1
A game with nonsymmetric threat structure

		Player 2			
		1	2		
Player 1	1	0, -100	10, 2	$v(1) = 0,$	$v(2) = 0$
	2	2, 0	0, 0	$v(12) = 12$	

function next to it is not a c-game. Vital information has been thrown away. The threat structure is not symmetric, for it would cost player 2 $100 to hold player 1 to 0.

Having ensured the adequacy of the coalitional representation of the game, we must choose a solution concept to apply. The two strongest candidates are the core and the value, although there are other cooperative solution concepts such as the bargaining set, stable set, kernel, and nucleolus. One of the attractive features of the value is that it always exists and, at least for games with side payments, is unique.

Our comments on the sensitivity of noncooperative equilibria of games in strategic form to variations in the number and sizes of players also apply to games in coalitional form solved for the core, value, or other cooperative solutions.

19.2 External Economies and Diseconomies

The major distinction between externalities and public goods is that the former can be caused by any number of individuals or groups usually engaged in economic activity, while the latter involve politically sponsored joint production by a major institution of society. We may not need to make this distinction unless we are studying mechanisms; otherwise we shall refer to externalities and public goods more or less interchangeably.

The distinctive property of an external, as opposed to a normal, economic good, is that of *appropriability*. Externalities are not owned in the ordinary sense. An externality in production usually comes in the form of a joint product, or by-product, that is not appropriated by the producer but is transmitted by noneconomic means to other individuals. The smoke from the factory is not kept, or even counted in its output statistics, but is carried by the winds to the shirts and lungs of passers-by or the walls and furnishings of nearby homes. The orchardist does not appropriate and sell the nectar, nor the apiarist the pollination service.

We shall limit our immediate discussion to externalities in production, because they are easier to define and quantify than those arising on the consumption side. Our results could perhaps be made to apply, at least at the formal level, to both cases, but consumption externalities entail interlinked consumer preferences and involve sociopsychological motivations such as envy, status, conformity, and even pity.

19.2.1 External economies[1]
It is well known that if a productive socioeconomic system generates external economies or diseconomies, the existence of prices that will

maintain an efficient or Pareto-optimal distribution of goods and services is not generally assured (Bator, 1958). Hence a social incentive may exist for other methods of allocation. In this chapter we are concerned especially with the social stability of agreements that imput the costs of benefits associated with such externalities according to the core of an n-person cooperative game. We shall also make some remarks on the possibility of taxation or subsidization schemes to restore optimality to the competitive market.

We begin by assuming an economy in which the production and consumption (utility) functions meet suitable conditions that would, *except for the presence of externalities of production*, assure the existence of a Pareto-optimal (PO) competitive equilibrium.[2] Does a core nevertheless exist? The answer is yes if there are only external economies, but no (or rather, not necessarily) if external diseconomies are present.

We first consider the case in which the external factors have only beneficial effects. To demonstrate the existence of a core is quite straightforward—so much so that most of the formal trappings can be dispensed with.

Let us note in advance that the proof does not depend on the existence of a characteristic-function representation, which would entail the availability of u-money or something closely akin to it.[3] Indeed group rationality (GR) is basically an *ordinal* condition—like Pareto optimality and individual rationality (IR), which it generalizes—and requires neither measurability nor transferability of the individual utilities.[4]

The proof is as follows. Let Γ denote a productive economic system having k external economies and no diseconomies. Let n denote the total number of individuals (households or firms). We construct an associated, artificial system Γ' without externalities, as follows: Every external product in Γ is replaced by n separately tradable "labeled" products in Γ', each one "addressed" to a particular individual. These new commodities (there are nk of them), though freely transferable, have value only to their addressees; in fact, each one enters its addressee's utility or production function in Γ' in exactly the same way as its original counterpart did in Γ.[5] Similarly the new commodities are produced in Γ' exactly as their counterparts were in Γ. That is, where in Γ one unit of an external good would be produced, in Γ' one unit of each of the n associated labeled goods is forthcoming from the same inputs. But in the latter case the producer appropriates all of his outputs and trades them as normal commodities.

How are the cores of Γ and Γ' related? How effective are the potential "blocking" coalitions in the two models? Let X denote a distribution that is attainable in Γ' by a subeconomy if it breaks off and ignores the possibilities of trade with the rest. If X is efficient, that is, PO with respect to the capabilities of the subeconomy, then we might as well assume that all labeled goods are handed over to their addressees whenever possible, since they have no value to anyone else. But then it follows that X can also be attained by the corresponding subeconomy of the original system Γ, since in that model the corresponding external factors are delivered automatically to their beneficiaries. If production activity outside the subeconomy bestows further involuntary benefits, so much the better. We conclude that the original system Γ is *at least as favorable* to any coalition as the associated system Γ'.[6]

On the other hand, a disaffected coalition cannot rely on receiving outside benefits even in the Γ model, in assessing the prospects of a separatist subeconomy. The only external economies it can count on are those that can be internalized, that is, produced within the coalition. But these benefits can be obtained in the Γ' model as well, via ordinary trading within the coalition. Thus, insofar as determining the core is concerned, Γ is no more favorable than Γ' to any coalition. Thus the two models are equivalent for the purpose of our proof, and their cores are the same.[7]

Our starting assumption was that, except for the externalities, the production and utility functions satisfy sufficient conditions for the existence of an efficient competitive equilibrium. In passing from Γ to Γ' we have not changed this; hence Γ', which by definition is free from externalities, has a PO competitive equilibrium. It follows from the basic theorem mentioned near the beginning of section 19.1 that Γ' has a core. Hence Γ also has a core, as was to be demonstrated.

In this section we have modeled an economy with k external economies as a no-side-payment game in coalitional form and have suggested that it can, at least pessimistically, be treated as a c-game. The "threats" of players outside any coalition can only improve the payoff for any coalition S.

Considering the checklist presented in chapter 18, and as long as only external economies are considered, we can model directional, diffuse, randomly spread economies as variants of the game described above with the same results.

We must still consider the possibility and meaning of convergence conditions for this model as players become many and small, and also the possibility of constructing a taxation system that will enable an otherwise decentralized pricing system to function.

19.2.2 External diseconomies

Our results regarding external diseconomies are on the negative side and are best displayed by means of examples, which can be most easily constructed with side-payment games.

THE GARBAGE GAME (Shapley and Shubik, 1969c). *Each player has a bag of garbage to be dumped in someone's yard. The utility of having b bags dumped in one's yard is $-b$. There is no free disposal outside of the players' yards.*

The diseconomy here is "directed" rather than "diffuse"; but we can eliminate the problem of directed threats by assuming that a coalition can "take care of its own," shifting the burden either by money side payments or by redistributing garbage within the coalition. It therefore makes sense to use a characteristic function, and we have

$$v(S) = \begin{cases} -(n-s) & \text{if } s < n, \\ -n & \text{if } s = n, \end{cases}$$

where n is the number of players and S is any subset of players of size s. The all-player set is in a special position, since it alone cannot avoid "fouling its own nest."

To see whether there is a core, we proceed as in the last section. Let α be any GR payoff vector (distribution of utility). For S of size $s = n - 1$ we have

$$\sum_{i \in S} \alpha_i \geq v(S) = -1.$$

There are n such inequalities, and adding them yields

$$(n-1) \sum_{i=1}^{n} \alpha_i \geq -n.$$

Feasibility requires that

$$\sum_{i=1}^{n} \alpha_i = v(\text{all-player set}) = -n.$$

Eliminating α, we obtain

$$(n-1)(-n) \geq -n,$$

that is, $n^2 \leq 2n$ or $n \leq 2$. We conclude that if there are more than two players, there is no core. No agreement on garbage disposal can satisfy every group of players to the point where they cannot, by violating it, be sure of doing better.

We shall see presently that the directability of the diseconomy in this example was not solely responsible for the lack of a core. First, however, we illustrate a common type of nondirected diseconomy, which happens to give rise to a very large core.

THE LAKE.   *There are n factories around a lake. It costs an amount B for a factory to treat its wastes before discharging them into the lake. It costs an amount uC for a factory to purify its own water supply, where u is the number of factories that do not treat their wastes. We assume that C < B < nC.*

Here IR sets an upper bound of nC on what a single factory should consent to spend, while Pareto optimality says that all factories together should pay no more than nB. The potential social gain from cooperative action is therefore $n(nC - B)$, which may be a substantial amount.

Assuming that u-money is available for side payments, we have

$$v(S) = \begin{cases} -snC & \text{if } s \le B/C, \\ -snC + s(sC - B) & \text{if } s > B/C, \end{cases}$$

where s again denotes the size of S. For small sets $v(S)$ is merely an additive function, so there is no incentive to form coalitions. For large sets $v(S)$ exhibits increasing returns to scale; in fact, each new adherent to a coalition brings in more than the last, and cooperation becomes increasingly profitable. Two effects combine to produce this condition: (1) a larger coalition can control at the source a more significant fraction of the pollution, and (2) a larger coalition includes more of the beneficiaries of such control. In short, it can afford to internalize the diseconomy.

Technically we have here a *convex game* (Shapley, 1965, Maschler, Peleg, and Shapley, 1979).[8] There is a core, but it is so large that it tells us little about how to assign the costs of pollution control. In fact, there are among the outcomes in the core some that assess several factories the maximum cost permitted by IR, while the other factories enjoy all the benefits. Although such a control arrangement is patently "unfair," the victims' threat to secede does not suffice to block it.[9]

It should not be inferred from this example that large cores are the rule in this type of application. For example, if we change the self-purification cost from uC to $\max((u - 1)C, 0)$, then the core collapses to a single point, representing the control arrangement that has everyone pay just for treating his own effluent.

Our third example again has a diffuse diseconomy.

THE SMELTING GAME. *One "load" of ore plus one "load" of coke make one "load" of iron plus one "cloud" of smoke. At the start, n_1 players have loads of ore and n_2 have loads of coke. At the end, each player's payoff is the amount of iron he has, reduced by K (a small constant) times the amount of smoke in the air.*

There is enough symmetry in this game so that all that matters is the profile of a coalition, that is, its composition by player types. In fact, if S contains s_1 and s_2 of the "ore" and "coke" types, respectively, then we have

$$v(S) = \begin{cases} \min(s_1, s_2) - Ks[\min(s_1, s_2) + \min(n_1 - s_1, n_2 - s_2)] & \\ & \text{if } s \leq 1/K, \\ -Ks\min(n_1 - s_1, n_2 - s_2) & \text{if } s \geq 1/K, \end{cases}$$

where $s = s_1 + s_2$. Again there are two cases. The larger coalitions are disinclined to go into production, while the smaller coalitions, with less to lose from the smoke, are not so inhibited.

Although the diseconomy is diffuse, as in the last example, this game is not convex, and whether or not a core exists depends in a rather complicated way on the values of the three parameters n_1, n_2, and K.

To illustrate we set $n_1 = n_2 = n/2$ and $K = 1/10$. Table 19.2 shows v as a function of s_1 and s_2 for small n; for convenience all entries have been multiplied by 10.[10]

The four-person game has a core; indeed any payoff distribution of the form $(a, a; 6 - a, 6 - a)$ with $1 \leq a \leq 5$ is unblockable. The first (last) two entries are payoffs to players of type 1 (type 2). The only operative constraints are that profile $(1, 1)$ must get at least 6 points, and profiles $(1, 2)$ and $(2, 1)$ at least 7. Thus the core is a line segment.

The six-person game also has a core, but it contains only the single distribution $(2, 2, 2; 2, 2, 2)$. Any other feasible distribution would give some five-person set less than the 10 points it can claim under GR. The eight-person game has no core at all, because every seven-person set can demand 9, whereas an average of only 1 per capita is available in the game as a whole. Note that all of the games thus far are so small that full production is still socially desirable, despite the smoke.

If we continue the series, we find that the core remains in eclipse for $n = 10, 12, 14,$ and 16. Although production is no longer socially desirable, some subeconomies can still attain a positive payoff on their own and will therefore block any agreement that shuts them down. At $n = 18$ and

Table 19.2
A pollution game

	$n = 4$		
$s_2 = 0$	1	2
$s_1 = 0$	0	-1	0
1	-1	6	7
2	0	7	12

	$n = 6$			
$s_2 = 0$	1	2	3
$s_1 = 0$	0	-2	-2	0
1	-2	4	4	6
2	-2	4	8	10
3	0	6	10	12

	$n = 8$				
$s_2 = 0$	1	2	3	4
$s_1 = 0$	0	-3	-4	-3	0
1	-3	2	1	2	5
2	-4	1	4	5	8
3	-3	2	5	6	9
4	0	5	8	9	8

beyond this is no longer true and the core reappears; but it consists only of the zero vector, representing a general agreement to stop all production.

When $n_1 \neq n_2$, it can be shown that the zero vector is the only possible core; the smaller games, in which production is socially desirable, are all coreless.

19.2.3 Taxes and subsidies
We return briefly to the discussion of external economies. In section 19.2.1 we proved the existence of the core with the aid of an artificial associated model Γ' in which the external products were neatly packaged, addressed, and transmitted to their beneficiaries through normal channels of trade. This artificial model always has a competitive equilibrium, however, and it is interesting to attempt an interpretation for it in terms of the original model Γ.

Fixing on a particular set of competitive prices for Γ' (in case the equilibrium is not unique), we let each normal good in Γ be assigned the same price as in Γ'. Let each person in Γ who benefits from an external good be *taxed*—that is, made to pay for it—at the price of the corresponding labeled good in Γ'. Finally, let each producer of an external economy in Γ be *subsidized*—that is, paid for the product—at a rate equal to the sum of the prices of its n labeled counterparts in Γ'. These taxes and subsidies are of course stated in terms of the same valueless accounting money used in the sale and purchase of normal goods in Γ, and each individual is required to take his tax and subsidy payments into account in balancing his budget.

Because of the direct relationship between Γ and Γ', the above prescription of prices, taxes, and subsidies constitutes a kind of generalized competitive equilibrium for Γ. Among its virtues is that it is in the core, so that no faction will be tempted to split off and "go it alone," even though they can thereby escape the taxes. Among its drawbacks (both administrative and philosophical) is the fact that each beneficiary of an external economy would in general have to be taxed differently, not only for a different amount but at a different rate, depending on how much enjoyment he personally derives from the benefits thrust upon him.

This description of taxation is institution-free and even vote-free. The explicit assumption that the cooperative solution must be Pareto-optimal is a way of stating that the final outcome is realized by general agreement of society as a whole. No methods are indicated or costs attributed to calculating or collecting the taxes or subsidies.

This taxation scheme was first suggested by Lindahl (1919) for public goods. The models presented thus far, however, contain few of the administrative, legal, and other institutional details that can be used to distinguish public goods from privately generated externalities. The key common factor in the study of public goods and externalities is the dependence of the payoffs of any group S on the actions of its complement $\bar{S}$.

19.3 Public Goods: Cooperative and Noncooperative Approaches

We adopt the same general approach to the analysis of public goods and externalities as we used to study exchange economies. We shall employ three different types of models and four solutions. First we consider what, if any, models of economies with public goods or externalities might have efficient price systems that play a role similar to or the same as that of a price system in an exchange economy. Then we examine how to represent the economy in coalitional form in order to examine the behavior of the core and value solutions. In contrast with the cooperative-game approach, especially if mechanisms and details of the market or administrative structure of interest, it becomes desirable to model in the strategic form and to consider the noncooperative-equilibrium solution.

19.3.1 The Foley model

Cooperative games were used in the last section to consider externalities and the core. Foley (1970b) provides a treatment of an economy without side payments and with pure public goods in the sense of Samuelson (1954). He presents two models, one a non-game-theoretic extension of the price system including taxation and subsidies and another based on an n-person game in coalitional form.

Samuelson's "pure public good" is a good that may be produced publicly or privately but upon being produced is available to all individuals in its totality. The consumption by individual i does not diminish the amount available for individual j. A radio broadcast is a frequently used example of a pure public good. The listening in by one does not diminish the listening in by another. Samuelson himself notes that the pure public good is an extreme case and that in fact many public goods are subject to crowding and other factors that limit their availability to all on equal terms. Nevertheless it is useful to analyze and contrast this extreme case with the pure private goods economy.

We consider an economy with m pure public goods and k private goods. There are n consumers. Each consumer i owns an initial endowment of private goods w^i and has a complete and transitive preference ordering over all bundles of private and public goods. Such a bundle is denoted by

$$(x;y^i) = (x_1, x_2, \ldots, x_m; y_1^i, y_2^i, \ldots, y_k^i),$$

where the first m components are the public goods and the next k components are the private goods.

Foley assumes that the production set Y for the economy is represented by a closed convex cone containing the origin. There is always a way to produce the public goods, and public goods are not needed as inputs to production.

An *allocation* is a vector of public goods and a set of n vectors of private goods each lying in one of the consumption sets. A *feasible allocation* $(x; y^1, y^2, \ldots, y^n)$ is one such that

$$\left(x; \sum_{i=1}^{n} (y^i - w^i) \right) \in Y;$$

that is, one that can be produced from the initial resources.

A feasible allocation $(x; y^1, y^2, \ldots, y^n)$ is Pareto-optimal if there is no other feasible allocation $(\bar{x}; \bar{y}^1, \bar{y}^2, \ldots, \bar{y}^n)$ preferred by all consumers.

A *public competitive equilibrium* consists of a feasible allocation $(x; y^1, y^2, \ldots, y^n)$, a price system $p = (p_x; p_y)$, and a tax bill $(t^1, t^2, \ldots, t^n)$ with

$$p_x \cdot x = \sum_{i=1}^{n} t^i,$$

such that

1. $p \cdot \left(x; \sum_{i=1}^{n} (y^i - w^i) \right) \geq p \cdot (\bar{x}; \bar{z})$ for all $(\bar{x}; \bar{z}) \in Y$;

2. $p_y \cdot y^i = p_y \cdot w^i - t^i$, and if $(x; \bar{y}^i)$ is preferred by i to (x, y^i), then $p_y \cdot \bar{y}^i > p_y \cdot y^i$;

3. there is no array of public goods and taxes $(\bar{x}; \bar{t}^1, \bar{t}^2, \ldots, \bar{t}^n)$ with $p_x \cdot \bar{x} = \sum_{i=1}^{n} t^i$ such that there exists a $\bar{y}^i$ for all i with $(\bar{x}; \bar{y}^i)$ preferred to $(x; y^i)$ and $p_y \cdot \bar{y}^i \leq p_y \cdot w^i - \bar{t}^i$.

A public competitive equilibrium has profit maximization by the producers and preference maximization by consumers subject to an after-tax budget constraint, together with the condition that there is no other combination of public goods and taxes that could leave all better off.

Foley establishes the existence of a public competitive equilibrium. In general there will be many because lump-sum taxes are unconstrained and enable initial endowments to be redistributed in any way. As Milleron (1972, p. 432) has aptly noted, the public competitive equilibrium is nothing more than an interpretation of Pareto optimality.

A much more constrained equilibrium would be one in which the taxes levied against any individual are precisely equal to the value of the public goods he purchases. Foley defines a *Lindahl equilibrium* with respect to a given set of endowments $w = (w^1, w^2, \ldots, w^n)$ to be a feasible allocation $(x; y^1, y^2, \ldots, y^n)$ and a price system $(p_x^1, p_x^2, \ldots, p_x^n, p_y)$ with all $p \geq 0$ such that

1. $\left(\sum_{i=1}^{n} p_x^i; p_y \right) \cdot \left(x; \sum_{i=1}^{n} (y^i - w^i) \right) \geq \left(\sum_{i=1}^{n} p_x^i; p_y \right) \cdot (\bar{x}, \bar{y})$ for all $(\bar{x}, \bar{y}) \in Y$;

2. if $(\bar{x}^i; \bar{y}^i) > (x; y^i)$, then $p_x^i \cdot \bar{x}^i + p_y \cdot \bar{y}^i > p_x^i \cdot x + p_y \cdot y^i = p_y \cdot w^i$.

He proves that such an equilibrium exists and that it is in the core of a no-side-payment game that he defines. This equilibrium, originally suggested by Lindahl (1919), at first glance seems to be an attractive generalization of the competitive equilibrium. On closer examination, unfortunately, this does not appear to be the case.

One way of proving the existence of the equilibrium amounts to reinterpreting the public and private goods economy as a pure private goods economy with $k + nm$ private goods and then using Debreu's existence proof (Debreu, 1959).

Foley (1970, p. 71) makes a connection between the Lindahl equilibrium and the core of an economy with exchange, production, and public goods in his definition of the power of coalitions in a cooperative game. The production technology is assumed to be available to all. Thus any subset and its complement can use it simultaneously. A coalition S may use its own resources in any way it chooses. An imputation (allocation) $(x; y^1, y^2, \ldots, y^n)$ is dominated by an imputation $(\bar{x}; \bar{y}^1, \bar{y}^2, \ldots, \bar{y}^n)$ via S as an effective set if $(\bar{x}, \bar{y}) \succ_i (x, y)$ for all $i \in S$ and $(\bar{x}; \sum_{i \in S} (\bar{y}^i - w^i)) \in Y$.

Given this definition of domination (Foley uses the term "blocking"), a simple pricing argument establishes that the Lindahl equilibrium is undominated and hence in the core.

Suppose S could rule out $(x; y^1, y^2, \ldots, y^n)$ by demanding $(\bar{x}; \bar{y}^1, \bar{y}^2, \ldots, \bar{y}^n)$. Since $(\bar{x}, \bar{y}^i) \succ_i (x, y^i)$ for all $i \in S$, we have

$$\sum_{i \in S} p_x^i \cdot \bar{x} + p_y \cdot \sum_{i \in S} \bar{y}^i > \sum_{i \in S} p_x^i \cdot x + p_y \cdot \sum_{i \in S} y^i = p_y \cdot \sum_{i \in S} w^i.$$

Since $p_x^i \geq 0$ for all i,

$$\sum_{i=1}^n p_x^i \geq \sum_{i \in S} p_x^i.$$

Since $\bar{x} \geq 0$, this implies

$$\sum_{i=1}^n p_x^i \cdot \bar{x} + p_y \cdot \sum_{i \in S} (\bar{y}^i - w^i) > 0.$$

But the profit-maximization condition at the Lindahl equilibrium requires that

$$\sum_{i=1}^n p_x^i \cdot \bar{x} + p_y \cdot \bar{z} \leq 0 \quad \text{for all } (\bar{x}; \bar{z}) \in Y.$$

This is a contradiction; hence $(x; y^1, y^2, \ldots, y^n)$ is in the core.

Milleron (1972) presents a more general model than Foley, including the possibility that public goods are used in production; he also explicitly stresses the importance of a free disposal assumption and considers a production possibility set that is convex rather than a cone. He cites the related model of Fabre-Sender (1969), which has a finite set of firms, public good inputs, and convex production sets.

19.3.2 Ownership and the characteristic function

In the private goods exchange economy there is an intuitively satisfactory and natural way to model the domain of effectiveness of any coalition. Each is assumed able to operate independently with its own resources, and the actions of one group are assumed to have no effect on the payoffs of others. For virtually any solution concept, then, the characteristic function is an adequate representation of the underlying economic reality.

The concurrent use of the characteristic-function representation of an exchange economy, the limit theorems for the core and value of games with a finite number of traders, and the equivalence theorems for the core, value, and competitive equilibria for exchange economies modeled as games with a continuum of traders provides a striking example of the power of intersolutional analysis (Shubik, 1959a; Debreu and Scarf, 1963; Shapley and Shubik, 1969a; Aumann, 1964; Aumann and Shapley, 1974). Moreover, the intimate relationships among the competitive equilibria, core, and value of large exchange economies allow an important sensitivity analysis of the robustness of the price system as an efficient allocation mechanism for economic exchange.

As indicated in chapters 7, 14, and 15, the intersolutional analysis can be extended to include both limit and equivalence theorems for the relationship between the outcomes from the noncooperative-equilibrium solution and the competitive-equilibrium solution to exchange economies.

Our sensitivity analysis of the price system includes both cooperative and strategic representations of an exchange economy and four major solution concepts. The competitive equilibrium stresses efficiency and decentralization; the noncooperative equilibrium stresses individual strategic power; the core characterizes combinatoric stability or countervailing power; and the value reflects axioms of fair division.

The coincidence of outcomes arising from fundamentally different considerations of trade provides considerable economic justification of the price system in an exchange economy. Unfortunately, when we generalize beyond exchange economies, a host of new difficulties appear, and applying a variety of solution concepts no longer yields reinforcing confirmations.

Before we can explore the solutions in any depth, we must examine the problems that arise in defining the coalitional form or characteristic function of the economic system, many of which are due to inadequate assumptions concerning ownership and property rights.[11] Implicit in models of exchange is a concept of ownership that allows unlimited control over utilization, employment, or disposition of a commodity or service. A more game-theoretic and legal view of ownership defines a domain of feasible acts that can be taken by an individual with respect to a good or service; this view reflects the nuances of the many different forms of ownership. An individual's usage rights are delimited by legal, political, and societal conditions and form part of the given rules of the game for the economic analyst. The nature of these rules is particularly critical for describing threat structures, which must be considered when a game in cooperative form is not a c-game.

Starrett (1973), in a well-directed critique of the Shapley–Shubik Garbage Game, argues that one must distinguish between a *common rule* and a *possession rule* in describing the rules associated with the generation of different externalities. Under the common rule citizens in many countries are required to keep their own garbage until its disposal can be arranged through a public or private service. Under the possession rule the individual may pollute or congest as he chooses. In the law there is a continuous shading between these rules, as can be seen in the cases cited by Coase (1960).

Rosenthal (1971) argues against the Shapley–Shubik construction of the characteristic function; he suggests that economies with externalities are not adequately modeled by characteristic functions describing games with cores. He is concerned with what constitutes "reasonable actions" by individuals in the coalition complementary to S when one is trying to evaluate $v(S)$. A three-person example indicates his approach. Consider three individuals each endowed with one unit of an all-purpose input good. An individual i can convert his endowment on a $1:1$ basis into a private good x_i. Each private good generates an externality y_i that benefits a neighbor. The three individuals have the following utility functions:

$$u^1(x_0, x_1, x_2, x_3, y_1, y_2, y_3) = x_1 + 5y_2,$$
$$u^2(x_0, x_1, x_2, x_3, y_1, y_2, y_3) = x_2 + 5y_3,$$
$$u^3(x_0, x_1, x_2, x_3, y_1, y_2, y_3) = x_3 + 5y_1,$$

where x_0 is the amount of the input commodity and x_i and y_i are, respectively, the private good and the externality created by the individual i.

If each individual converts his input to a private good, all can obtain $(6, 6, 6)$. This is in the core as defined by Shapley and Shubik. Rosenthal notes, however, that if 2 and 3 form a coalition to produce only the private good 3 and its externality, which benefits 2, the Shapley–Shubik way of calculating the characteristic function would assign payoffs of $(1, 2, 10)$, that is, the amounts that 1, 2, and 3 can guarantee for themselves. Rosenthal suggests that in this circumstance it is rational for 1 to produce a single unit of his own good, creating payoffs of $(1, 7, 10)$; because this imputation dominates $(6, 6, 6)$ via the coalition of 2 and 3, under this definition of domination the game has no core. In considering the core solution for external economies, I would suggest, however, that the Shapley–Shubik calculation gives a good pessimistic lower bound on what a group can obtain, even though it rules out the possibility that they might obtain more if those excluded from their coalition acted "reasonably."

Protection against soot, noise, or smoke, or against losing a view or being shaded by a neighbor's building, is provided by law and custom in most societies. A means of obtaining compensation for generating a positive externality such as a garden others can see or music others want to listen to is not in general provided by the law or the polity; at best, societal norms or social pressures may allow for some form of quid pro quo.

Public goods are supplied for the most part by a political process, and minority rights are protected by a mixture of legal, economic, and political considerations. Thus, although it is not a logical necessity, when we contemplate the domination (or blocking) power of groups in deciding on public goods, it is reasonable to be explicit in modeling the rules of the relevant voting system (see chapter 20).

19.3.3 The strategic form

There are several strong reasons associated with satisfactory modeling that make it difficult to produce adequate models of a closed economy with public goods. These concern the need to model government, production, voting, taxation, and consumption all as moves in an extensive form that can be reduced to a strategic form suitable for fruitful analysis. The differences in time scales and information conditions among economic, administrative, and political processes are sufficient to raise difficult problems in portraying a useful and believable extensive form that reduces to a strategic form.

In short, although it will eventually be both desirable and feasible to model closed economies with public goods and externalities as games in extensive and strategic form and to solve them for noncooperative equilibria whose politicoeconomic interpretations are of interest, this has not been done yet. At this time the exploration of games in coalitional form appears to be easier and more fruitful. The extension of this work should also make the eventual building of models in extensive and strategic form easier.

There is one clear exception to these caveats. It is possible to employ the strategic form in a relatively simple way to study partial-equilibrium problems when externalities are present. The relatively simple (usually two-party) examples of externalities noted by Meade (1952), Bator (1958), Coase (1960), and Baumol (1972) can be viewed as simple forms of games in strategic form being analyzed for their noncooperative equilibria. This has been noted by Davis and Whinston (1962, 1966).

19.3.4 A partial-equilibrium analysis of production externalities

Using a simple two-firm model in which each firm produces a production externality for the other, Davis and Whinston (1962) argue that two types of externality must be considered—"separable" and "nonseparable"— and that taxes and subsidies will be effective for separable but generally not for nonseparable externalities.

The assumption that both firms are in a competitive industry not only allows us to dispense with worrying about price adjustments in final and factor markets, but also enables us to consider profit as a surrogate for a linear separable utility. In a small region, maximization of joint profit becomes the Pigou (1932) criterion of maximizing "national dividend," with money treated as a measurable transferable utility. In a general-equilibrium context this may well be false, but for two small firms next to each other the approximation may be adequate.[12]

Let the price of the industry's output be p and the cost functions of the two firms be $c_1(q_1, q_2)$ and $c_2(q_1, q_2)$, respectively, where q_1 and q_2 are the output levels of firms 1 and 2, respectively, and c_1 and c_2 are twice differentiable.

If each firm i independently attempts to maximize its profit π_i, then

$$\frac{\partial \pi_i}{\partial q_i} = \frac{\partial}{\partial q_i}(pq_i - c_i) = 0 \quad (i = 1, 2) \tag{19.1}$$

or

$$p = \frac{\partial c_i}{\partial q_i} \quad (i = 1, 2), \tag{19.2}$$

where social benefit is given by $p(q_1 + q_2)$ and social costs by $c_1(q_1, q_2) + c_2(q_1, q_2)$. Thus to maximize welfare the firms should maximize their joint profit

$$\pi = \pi_1 + \pi_2 = p(q_1 + q_2) - c_1(q_1, q_2) - c_2(q_1, q_2),$$ (19.3)

for which the first-order conditions are

$$\frac{\partial \pi}{\partial q_i} = p - \frac{\partial c_1}{\partial q_i} - \frac{\partial c_2}{\partial q_i} = 0 \quad (i = 1, 2)$$ (19.4)

and the second-order conditions are

$$\begin{vmatrix} \dfrac{\partial^2 \pi}{\partial q_1^2} & \dfrac{\partial^2 \pi}{\partial q_1 \partial q_2} \\[2ex] \dfrac{\partial^2 \pi}{\partial q_2 \partial q_1} & \dfrac{\partial^2 \pi}{\partial q_2^2} \end{vmatrix} > 0 \quad \text{and} \quad \frac{\partial^2 \pi}{\partial q_1^2} < 0, \quad \frac{\partial^2 \pi}{\partial q_2^2} < 0.$$ (19.5)

If either or both of $\partial c_1 / \partial q_2$ and $\partial c_2 / \partial q_1$ are not equal to zero, then (19.2) and (19.4) do not coincide. Then independent maximization will not lead to a social optimum, and another mode of operation must be considered. The Marshall–Pigou–Meade solution calls for taxes and subsidies. Another alternative would be to have the firms internalize their individual externalities by merger. One may argue, as Williamson (1975) and others have done, that optimum firm size is considerably influenced by considerations of internalizable externalities and costs of administration and hierarchical operation (in contrast with subcontracting or other uses of markets).

Ruling out merger possibilities at this time, it is easy to stress the game-theoretic structure of this market with externalities by observing that each firm has a payoff function that depends on the strategic variables of both:

$$\pi_i(q_1, q_2) = pq_i - c_i(q_1, q_2) \quad (i = 1, 2).$$ (19.6)

A function $f(x, y)$ is said to be *separable* if it can be written in the form $f(x, y) = f_1(x) + f_2(y)$. If the cost functions of the firms are separable, then (19.6) can be rewritten as

$$\pi_i(q_1, q_2) = pq_i - D_i(q_i) - E_j(q_j) \quad (i = 1, 2; j = 2, 1)$$ (19.7)

for some functions D_i and E_j, and the first-order optimization conditions are

$$\frac{\partial \pi_i}{\partial q_i} = p - \frac{dD_i}{dq_i} = 0 \quad \text{or} \quad p = \frac{dD_i}{dq_i},$$ (19.8)

Table 19.3
Externalities with and without equilibria

	a Player 2			b Player 2	
	1	2		1	2
Player 1 1	1, 1	−10, 30	Player 1 1	1, 5	2, 3
2	30, −10	5, 5	2	2, 3	1, 5

that is, individual marginal cost equals price. The externality can be regarded as a lump-sum tax or subsidy. Joint maximization, however, requires a recognition of the harm or assistance the firms render each other; thus it involves

$$\pi = \pi_1 + \pi_2 = p(q_1 + q_2) - D_1(q_1) - D_2(q_1) - E_1(q_1) - E_2(q_2), \quad (19.9)$$

and the first-order optimization conditions are

$$p = \frac{dD_i}{dq_i} + \frac{dE_i}{dq_i} \quad (i = 1, 2). \tag{19.10}$$

Setting the unit tax or subsidy for firm i to $t_i = dE_i/dq_i$, the individual optimization could be guided to the social maximum. For an agency to calculate these would be hard but possibly manageable.

The above remarks hold only if joint profits are positive and are maximized with both firms active. Otherwise we must consider solutions with one or both firms exiting from competition.

If the cost functions $c_i(q_1, q_2)$ are not separable, then the resulting noncooperative game will not have the strong row and column domination relationship of the matrix in table 19.3a, which guarantees the existence of a pure-strategy equilibrium. It could have a form such as that shown in table 19.3b, where no pure strategy exists. The examples are given as simple matrix games, but continuous versions can be constructed.

Baumol (1972, p. 307) challenges the assumptions but not the argument of Davis and Whinston. He claims that their difficulties come because of the oligopolistic aspects of their model and not because of the externalities. This critique calls attention to a fundamental empirical and modeling problem: the relationship between numbers and the nature of externalities. The results depend delicately upon how one envisions the externality changing with increasing numbers of firms. If we assume a continuum of firms of both types, with members of each type identical and with each firm receiving the externality caused by the average production of all firms of the other type, then (19.1) and (19.2) can be reinterpreted as representating a pair of extremely small firms of different types. If we denote by i and j representative members of types 1 and 2, respectively, their payoffs are

$$\pi_1 = pq_{i1} - c_1(q_{i1}, \bar{q}_2),$$
$$\pi_2 = pq_{j2} - c_2(\bar{q}_1, q_{j2}). \tag{19.11}$$

The externality problems remain the same.

19.3.5 A simple example contrasting cooperative, noncooperative, and other approaches

Constraining ourselves to a partial-equilibrium model with two firms, one of which generates an external diseconomy to the other, we shall illustrate the noncooperative game, the characteristic function, the core, the value, and the Pigou tax and discuss the alternatives of merger or preventing the diseconomy.

Let the outputs of firms 1 and 2 be denoted by x and y, respectively. Let the market price of their final product be $p = 10$ per unit. Let their profit functions be

$$\pi_1 = 10x - x^2,$$
$$\pi_2 = \begin{cases} 10y - xy^2 & \text{for } x \geq 1, \\ 10y - y^2 & \text{for } x < 1, \end{cases} \tag{19.12}$$

where $x = 1$ is a threshold at which pollution starts to do damage.

The noncooperative game   From (19.12), first-order conditions yield

$$10 - 2x = 0 \quad \text{and} \quad 10 - 2xy = 0. \tag{19.13}$$

Hence $x = 5$, $y = 1$, and the payoffs are $\pi_1 = 25$ and $\pi_2 = 5$.

The characteristic function   The joint profit is

$$\pi = \pi_1 + \pi_2 = \begin{cases} 10x + 10y - x^2 - xy^2 & \text{for } x \geq 1, \\ 10x + 10y - x^2 - y^2 & \text{for } x < 1. \end{cases} \tag{19.14}$$

It is easy to check that there is a boundary maximum with $x = 1$, $y = 5$. Hence

$$v(\overline{12}) = \pi = 34. \tag{19.15}$$

Before we can fully describe the characteristic function, we must specify the worth of the one-person coalitions. But this depends delicately on the threat structure, and the threat structure in turn depends on the basic legal concepts of property rights used by a society. Individual property rights, individual and group incentives, and overall efficiency and optimality all reflect legal, administrative, and economic considerations. The evaluation of the Pareto set for society as a whole is independent of subgroup (including individual) property rights, but the distribution of decentralized production utilizing prices, taxes, and subsidies depends directly on the specification of property rights. The distribution of resources determined by cooperative solutions such as the core or value also depends directly on property rights. We consider three cases:

1. Unrestricted pollution. If firm 1 is legally entitled to pollute without redress, it can guarantee itself 25 but firm 2 cannot guarantee for itself more than

$$\max_{y} \min_{x} (10y - xy^2). \tag{19.16}$$

If x is regarded as unbounded, this can approach 0. In general, though, it will be reasonable to assume some bound X for x. Then $y = 5/X$, and the firm obtains $25/X$. Hence

$$v(1) = 25 \quad \text{and} \quad v(2) = 25/X. \tag{19.17}$$

2. Pollution internalized. If firm 1 can prevent its own pollution at a cost of $K(x)$ for $x > 1$, then its payoff becomes

$$\pi_1 = \begin{cases} 10x - x^2 & \text{if it does not control its pollution,} \\ 10x - x^2 - K(x) & \text{if it controls its pollution,} \end{cases} \tag{19.18}$$

and the payoff for firm 2 becomes

$$\pi_2 = 10y - y^2.$$

3. Pollution forbidden. With pollution forbidden, and if there is no technological fix or threshold below which it does not matter, firm 1 will have to close. If the pollution threshold is at $x = 1$, it can produce to that point.

For purposes of illustration consider (i) $K(x) = x$, (ii) $K(x) = 28x^3$. We are now in a position to define four characteristic functions:

1. Unrestricted: $v(\overline{1}) = 25, \quad v(\overline{2}) = 25/X, \quad v(\overline{12}) = 34.$

2. Internalized (i): $v(\overline{1}) = 20.25, \quad v(\overline{2}) = 25, \quad v(\overline{12}) = 45.25.$

3. Internalized (ii): $v(\bar{1}) = 9, \quad v(\bar{2}) = 25, \quad v(\overline{12}) = 34.$

4. Forbidden: $v(\bar{1}) = 9, \quad v(\bar{2}) = 25, \quad v(\overline{12}) = 34.$

The core and value can be calculated trivially in all examples as shown in table 19.2. We observe that in this example, depending on the costs of internalizing the external diseconomy, the economy as a whole may benefit more or less than by any tax scheme. In general, forbidding the diseconomy outright may make matters worse. In this example we have assumed that the polluting firm is required to pay for its clean-up completely. This is to a great extent a matter of law, administration, and public policy. Distribution (but not efficiency) will be influenced by a different arrangement.

The Shapley and Harsanyi values: Unrestricted pollution Suppose $X = 10$ is the upper bound on the productive capacity of firm 1. It might be deemed unreasonable to assume that, even in an economic war, firm 1 would produce that amount, given the cost of carrying out such a threat. If it did, however, the characteristic function would be

$$v(\bar{1}) = 25, \quad v(\bar{2}) = 2.5, \quad v(\overline{12}) = 34.$$

The Shapley value would be $\varphi_1 = 28.25$, $\varphi_2 = 5.25$. For the Harsanyi value we must solve

$$\pi_1 + \pi_2 = 34,$$

$$\pi_1 - \pi_2 = \max_x \min_y (10x - 10y - x^2 + xy^2) = 20.21, \tag{19.19}$$

where $x = 5.425$, $y = 0.9217$. Solving equations (19.19), we obtain $\pi_1 = 27.105$ and $\pi_2 = 6.895$.

The Pigou tax Only firm 1 should be taxed at a unit rate

$$t = \frac{\partial c_2(x, y)}{\partial x} = y^2 \quad \text{evaluated at } y = 5 \text{ for any production level if } x \geq 1;$$

thus $t = 25$, $\pi_1 = 9$, and $\pi_2 = 25$. (The tax is 0 if $x < 1$.)

The following policy conclusions are suggested by examining table 19.4. The first natural question is whether there is a socially optimal technological fix that internalizes the diseconomy. This depends on technological feasibility and costs. Two examples are given in table 19.4; the first is more efficient and the second less efficient than living with the diseconomy.

Table 19.4
A comparison of solutions

Case	Social product	Core		Value		Noncooperative equilibrium		Pigou tax/price
		min π_1	max π_1	π_1	π_2	π_1	π_2	
1. Internalized (i)	45.25	20.25[a]		20.25	25	20.25	25	—
2. Unrestricted	34	25	31.5	$\left\{\begin{array}{l}28.25 \\ 27.105\end{array}\right.$ $\left.\begin{array}{l}5.75 \\ 6.897\end{array}\right\}$		25 (not Pareto-optimal)	5	$\begin{cases} t = 25,\ \text{tax} = 0\ \text{for}\ x < 1, \\ \pi_1 = 5,\ \pi_2 = 25 \end{cases}$
3. Internalized (ii)	34	9[a]		9	25	9	25	—
4. Forbidden	34	9[a]		9	25	9	25	—
5. Choose from all	45.25	25	42.75	33.875	11.375	not defined		—

a. One-point core.

It is a politicoeconomic problem to motivate or force selection of the best solution. If, for example, the firms had the strategic choice of which solutions to select for themselves individually or as a group, we would obtain a fifth characteristic function:

$$v(\overline{1}) = 25, \quad v(\overline{2}) = 2.5, \quad v(\overline{12}) = 45.25.$$

We assume here that if the polluting firm has the legal right to generate its externality, it is not going to adopt at its own expense a clean-up technology that lowers its profits; but if society is willing to pick up some of the costs, so that the firm is no worse off financially, then it will be willing to change. Thus $v(\overline{1}) = 25$ shows the minimum the firm needs to accept, and $v(\overline{12}) = 45.25$ indicates the best solution for society.

Cases 1, 3, and 4 have a flat characteristic function in which the externality is removed. This leads trivially to a one-point core that coincides with the value and the noncooperative equilibrium. This is not so for cases 2 and 5. When the generation of the externality is uncontrolled, as is well known, the noncooperative equilibrium is not Pareto-optimal. This is the only case dealt with by the Pigou tax, which is used to restore Pareto optimality and is not as a method of fair division.

It is reasonable to ask about the relationship between the Pigou tax scheme and the Lindahl equilibrium. We suggest that they are conceptually the same. In both cases the government invents some "shadow-private goods" and prices them. With the Lindahl equilibria taxes and subsidies must add to zero, but with the Pigou tax this is not the case. The government collects the tax but need not pay it to the other firm. The tax presumably goes somewhere, but since in the partial-equilibrium model all prices are assumed to be fixed, as a first-order approximation the tax can be treated as a transferable commodity with constant marginal utility to all and can be redistributed in a lump sum without influencing production.

Examining the Shapley values for cases 1, 2, and 5, we note that the polluting firm does better when it has more strategic freedom. This is because its individually rational obtainable level is improved. Comparing cases 2 and 3, we note that a tax scheme that can restore Pareto optimality does not necessarily encourage a firm to internalize its nuisance, even though doing so would change the feasible set of outcomes and lead to a new Pareto set that would dominate the other.

Cases 1 and 3 assume a "technological fix" for the externality. In many instances this may not be available. Case 2 gives the needed background to decide on taxation or merger. Case 4 is in general a bad, simplistic solution. Case 5 contains all of the above mechanisms but gives more control to the firm producing the externalities than is provided by cases 1, 3, and 4.

19.3.6 Questions concerning numbers

Before investigating models with large numbers, we must deal with two questions: How important or relevant is it to study public goods and externalities within a general-equilibrium rather than a partial-equilibrium framework? How important is the study of large numbers with public goods and externalities, and what are good representations of large numbers?

For many applied problems such as municipal services, airports, zoning, or local pollution control, partial-equilibrium analysis appears to be relevant and sufficient. However, when we consider national policy on space exploration, military spending, or health and education programs, we require a general-equilibrium approach in order to estimate first-order effects. Furthermore, as we have shown in previous sections, the results of the analysis are surprisingly robust for different solutions when the numbers are large. We therefore have a motivation for seeing if this robustness carries over to economies with public goods and externalities. It appears that in general it does not.

Mathematically, in nonstrategic models of the political economy the distinction between public goods and externalities is simple. A pure public good will enter into the arguments of all agents' utility functions in the same quantities; an externality can be modeled as entering some of the utility functions in the same or different quantities. Both an externality and a public good can be of positive or negative worth to some: A pacifist may oppose public expenditures on defense; a fisherman may oppose private pollution of a stream.

As long as we have clear measures of inputs and outputs and the convexity of choice and production sets is preserved, a nonstrategic theory such as the Lindahl equilibrium can be modified to treat externalities as well as public goods. This is exemplified by Bergstrom's (1970) proof of the existence of Lindahl equilibria for an exchange economy. If there are m commodities and n individuals and everyone is positively concerned with the welfare of others, we may consider that everything is a public good. The utility function of consumer i is

$$u_i = u_i(x^i_{11}, x^i_{12}, \ldots, x^i_{mn}),$$ (19.20)

where x^i_{jk} is the final amount of good j held by k as valued by i, or in a less unreasonable but more special form, as used by Bergstrom,

$$u_i = u_i(v_1(x_{11}, x_{21}, \ldots, x_{m1}), v_2(x_{12}, x_{22}, \ldots, x_{m2}), \ldots,$$
$$v_n(x_{1n}, x_{2n}, \ldots, x_{mn})).$$

To use (19.20) we must have the condition that all public goods of the same type are consumed in the same amount; thus

$$x_{jk}^i = x_{jk}^g \quad (g = 1, 2, \ldots, n; j = 1, 2, \ldots, m).$$

When we consider the strategic aspects of public goods and externalities, an important distinction appears. In general, public goods are supplied by processes that aggregate individual decisions politically (a direct vote for school bonds or to build an opera house) or by administrative groups controlled in theory, if not in practice, by political parties that presumably act as fiduciaries for the public as a whole. External economies and diseconomies are usually under the strategic control of individuals or sets of individuals who can act directly. The first line of defense against external diseconomies is usually legal or social, and the second line is political. Public pressure and the law are frequently used as a first resort against those who block views, replace vineyards with shopping centers, or destroy old buildings and markets to build condominiums. If these means fail, then political means are brought to bear to make the laws more effective.

The implication of the above remarks for solutions such as the core, value, or noncooperative equilibrium is that until the political and other constraints on feasible actions have been specified, the game is not sufficiently well defined for analysis. In general, we must at least have some description of the strategic power of voting blocks.

The study of most externalities, in contrast with public goods, frequently does not require specification of voting or other aspects of the political mechanism, but it does require specification of the legal and societal constraints on property and the strategic limits on usage rights.

Many externalities such as industrial pollution may be caused by a few large firms operating in an environment with many small firms and consumers. Some externalities are produced by mass behavior influencing mass consumption. Phenomena involving crowding provide the prime examples. When our concern turns to public goods, we have several choices with regard to modeling style. We may take the governmental, administrative, and political presence as a mechanism, so that the only strategic agents are the consumers (and possibly firms) modeled as economic agents and voters. Or we may introduce government, administration, and political parties as large active players. Either way it appears to be desirable to consider mass markets and polities. The question of whether the electorate should be represented by a large but finite n or by a continuum can only be answered on an ad hoc basis.

19.4 Economies with Few and Many Agents

19.4.1 Pure public goods and externalities

Samuelson (1954), Foley (1970b), Milleron (1972), and others have shown the existence of Lindahl equilibria for economies with pure public goods. The analysis is, for the most part, nonstrategic and independent of the number of economic agents.

A conceptual problem is encountered if the Samuelson model of an economy with public goods is replicated. In particular, because the pure public goods enter into everyone's utility functions, we have invented the "Widow's cruse." The cost of supplying any level of a public good approaches zero per capita as the numbers increase.

It is desirable from the point of view of even casual empiricism and also from that of mathematical tractability to limit or bound the level of utilization of any public good. Crowding limits the use of parks, beaches, and theaters, and even radio and television transmission costs depend on location and audience size.

Both the general-equilibrium price system analysis and the extended or pseudoprice system analysis associated with the Lindahl equilibria have been contrasted with the cooperative-game models of the same economic phenomena. It is at this point that several more conceptual problems appear when we try to model an economy with public goods as a cooperative game. The three basic problems are:

1. the replication process or other mass-market modeling;

2. the loss of the c-game property;

3. the modeling of the vote or social decision mechanism.

The first item has already been discussed, and we suggest that for any physical item the notion of a pure public good does not stand scrutiny when population is increased.

The other two problems are intertwined but should be discussed separately because of their importance for understanding what economic, political, or social phenomena we claim to be modeling. The c-game property has been a critical factor in giving plausibility to both the core and the value analysis of an exchange economy. Unfortunately, in an economy with public goods or externalities, not only is the c-game property lost because of technological features of the goods involved, but the structure of the characteristic function is influenced by the social or political decision rule used to determine the supply of the public goods or the control of the externalities. To put matters simply, when public goods or externalities are present, the characteristic function used as a basis for the analysis of the core must be justified in an ad hoc manner, and reasons must be given for why that characteristic function is a good enough representation of the situation to merit further calculation.[13]

In this section we once more consider market games and arrive at the following conclusions. Economies for which Lindahl equilibria exist can be modeled as market games, but for more or less pure public goods there is no guarantee whatsoever that we can find a natural sequence of market games which are a good representation of the economy and for which the sequence of cores converge to the Lindahl equilibria. With plausible conditions on "crowding," local public goods economies may be associated with sequences of ε-cores and may show regular properties.

Economies with positive externalities will have cores under at least one pessimistic definition of the characteristic function (see Shapley and Shubik, 1969c), but they may fail to have cores under a different definition (see Rosenthal, 1971). Even if cores exist, there is no guarantee that a sequence of market games with shrinking cores can be constructed. With external diseconomies, under any reasonable definition of the characteristic function there is no guarantee that the core will exist.

Muench (1972) provides a simple example with one private and one public good, a constant-proportions technology for producing the public from the private good, and a continuum of identical consumers. The example demonstrates that even with a continuum of traders, the core may be larger than the set of Lindahl equilibria. Milleron (1972) provides another example adopting an asymptotic approach rather than assuming a continuum of traders; he, too, obtains a core larger than the Lindahl equilibria.

Rather than reproduce these particular counterexamples, we return to the modeling problems that signal why they should be there. But even before that, we must ask several questions: Why are the Lindahl equilibria interesting as an economic phenomenon? Why is the core an interesting solution concept for public goods problems, and is it in any way related to the Lindahl equilibria?

It is an interesting and perceptive observation that one can find combinations of private and public goods prices and individual taxes that produce a Pareto-optimal outcome. The immediate analogy with the competitive equilibrium is clear. Yet upon closer inspection the Lindahl equilibria are not as attractive as the competitive equilibria. In particular, in this tax structure different individuals are charged different "prices" for the same goods; hence there is a natural incentive to conceal true preferences in order to avoid taxation. This system would be feasible if there were an all-powerful, omniscient central government that knew everyone's preferences and could enforce individually differentiated taxes. There is a growing literature relevant to the design of incentive schemes, truth-revealing mechanisms, and allocation procedures (see, e.g., Hurwicz, 1973; Groves and Ledyard, 1977; Holmstrom, 1982).

At a somewhat more technical level than most of this discussion, Champsaur (1976) has shown that Lindahl equilibria are not even necessarily symmetric; that is, it is possible to construct an example in which agents with identical characteristics are treated differently.

In my opinion, the Lindahl equilibrium is of limited value and interest to those concerned with public goods policy. The problems with implementation of individual taxation alone are enough to doom it. And the failure of symmetry and the lack of any strong relationship with either the core or the value reconfirm this opinion.

The striking relationship between the core and the competitive equilibria of an exchange economy reinforces our interest in the price system. It is fairly natural to ask if this relationship can be extended to economies with public goods. The answer is basically no. But the real answer is that there are modeling problems that must be considered prior to calculating the core. To make this clear we consider a simple economy with n individuals each having an endowment $\omega^i = (1, 0)$, one unit of a private good and 0 of a public good. The public good is manufactured from the sum of the inputs of the private good. For specificity we suppose that the preferences of individual i can be represented by

$$u^i = f(s, n)(x^i y)^\alpha, \quad 0 < \alpha < 1, \tag{19.21}$$

where x^i is his final amount of the private good, y is the amount of the public good, and $f(s, n)$ represents the influence of the overall size n of the society and the size s of his coalition on his preferences. Let the commonly owned production function be

$$y = \sum_{j=1}^{n} z^j. \tag{19.22}$$

We have now given data sufficient to calculate the characteristic function and hence the core. This example is used to illustrate possible relationships among the Lindahl equilibrium, the core, and the ε-core. Because it is essentially symmetric (except for government), any value solution will be uninteresting in that it will merely reflect the symmetry. But it can be used to illustrate many of the modeling problems concerning pure public goods, local public goods, c-games, exclusion, taxation, and voting. In this section we limit ourselves to a pure public good with no voting. In the next section we consider local public goods, and in chapter 20 we consider voting.

First we must specify what is meant by the "commonly owned production function." Do individuals have ownership shares? Is a vote needed for control? How is usage for any group less than the whole to be determined?

If we want to avoid voting and politics as much as possible and to produce a model close to that of the exchange economy, we will try to limit any subset S to the use of its own resources. But does a commonly owned production function belong to S's resources? Can $\bar{S}$ use the same production function simultaneously? If there are constant returns to scale, this poses no problem (as is the case in this simple example). But if there are decreasing returns, we must specify how the decreasing productivity is split.

Regardless of who gets to use the production sets, we must also specify whether $\bar{S}$ obtains its share of the public good produced by S.

If there is literally a publicly owned production facility, unless levels are set by a dictator or outside bureaucrats, some form of voting mechanism appears to be required. Three (among many) rules can be immediately suggested: (1) unanimity; (2) simple majority with unlimited right to tax; (3) simple majority with minority protection. The first rule gives a fat nonconverging core; the second no core at all; and the existence of the core for the third depends on the form of minority protection. Whether the core shrinks or not (given that it exists) will depend on the assumptions we make concerning $f(s, n)$.

It is my belief that the interesting question is not "Do the Lindahl equilibria and core coincide for many players?" but "What is a reasonable description of the characteristic function of an economy modeled as a cooperative game, for the purposes of calculating a core?" Furthermore, I suggest that the conditions noted in chapter 18, such as excludability and enforced use, require the construction of many different characteristic functions.[14]

No matter how one models, economies with externalities or public goods do not generally become c-games. The very nature of their interconnectedness rules this out. When we calculate the power of a coalition S, we must therefore take account of the threats of $\bar{S}$. A way of doing this when calculating the value solution has been suggested by Harsanyi (1959) and used here in chapter 6. There appears to be no connection between the Lindahl equilibria and the value of a game with many players and public goods. An example showing that the Lindahl solution, the Shapley value, and the Harsanyi–Selten value differ significantly in an economy with two types of traders, one private good, one public good, and money has been provided by Rosenthal (1976). Aumann, Gardner, and Rosenthal (1977) offer an example without voting, with two types of agents, one private good, and one public good where the value is not in the core.

We can calculate the characteristic function for our simple example. For a pure public good we must assume $f(s, n) = 1$. Thus the amount obtainable by a coalition of size s is

$$v(s) = \max \sum_{i=1}^{s} \left(x^i \cdot \sum_{j=1}^{s} (1 - x^j) \right)^\alpha = s \left(\frac{s}{1+s} \right)^{2\alpha}, \text{ where } x^i = \frac{s}{1+s}.$$

(19.23)

As $n \to \infty$, $x^i \to 1$, and the public good is provided for nothing. In this example superadditivity is lost for $\alpha < 1/2$, and the core does not converge for $\alpha > 1/2$.

The characteristic function (19.23) is based on the pessimistic assumption that all members of $\bar{S}$ refrain from any public good production of their own. Thus, even though positive spillover is virtually certain to occur because it is in the self-interest of every group, no one is given any credit for it because no group can guarantee it.

19.4.2 Local public goods

In a stimulating and suggestive article Tiebout (1956) conjectured that in contrast to the demand for national public goods, where the citizen is trapped unless he emigrates, for local public goods "the consumer-voter may be viewed as picking that community which best satisfies his preference pattern for public goods." He then suggested that the larger the number of communities and the larger the variance among them, the closer the consumer will come to realizing his preferences and for that matter revealing them to the local jurisdiction.

Some years later Buchanan (1965) offered an economic theory of clubs. A club consists of a homogeneous group of members who equally share and pay for a local public good. It can costlessly bar all nonmembers from use of the good. Furthermore, the enjoyment of the good eventually diminishes due to crowding. Thus it is easy to formulate fairly realistic conditions under which there is an optimum club size. There is a large literature on clubs that has been extensively surveyed by Sandler and Tschirhart (1980); we shall not discuss the subject here except for the following general remarks.

Local public goods pose many different operational problems at the level of partial-equilibrium analysis. The provision of a club swimming pool, town dump, bus system, or special school system all pose ad hoc problems to the applied economist saddled with the job of producing a tax, toll, or levy. In particular, the literature is virtually devoid of discussion of the frequently important oligopolistic aspects of clubs, jurisdictions, and municipalities. The voting aspects of the allocation of local public goods are hardly touched upon, and the time dimension in general is not accounted for, even to the extent of providing a static approximation by attributing high costs to certain actions.

To some extent a club can be viewed as a device for internalizing or quasiprivatizing an externality or possible public good. This is not unlike a firm with stockholders. As long as the optimum size of the club is small relative to the economy as a whole and there is an appropriate sort of bound on the heterogeneity of the population, we have a sporting chance of finding cores, or at least ε-cores.

Pauly (1967, 1970) has provided examples of clubs with homogeneous and (in a limited sense) heterogeneous membership with optimum club sizes with and without cores. Wooders (1980) establishes the existence of ε-cores supporting the Tiebout hypothesis for an economy with m types of consumer, one private and one public good, and endogenous jurisdiction structures (i.e., all partitions of all consumers are considered). All members of the same jurisdiction consume the same quantity of local public goods. Wooders obtains existence and convergence results on approximate equilibria whose imputations are in the approximate core. Based on further game-theoretic results concerning ε-cores (Wooders, 1984), Shubik and Wooders (1984a,b) suggest that the class of games with approximate cores fits into a broad class of local public good models. This is demonstrated in Shubik and Wooders (1982).

The papers cited offer a number of examples (see also the critical survey by Bewely, 1981), but here we shall simply continue developing models based on (19.23) and (19.24) in order to stress that a basic sensitivity analysis of the model building should be enough to stop us from searching for a Philosopher's Stone. Sorting out the many cases involving different public goods and externalities is arduous but feasible. After a while we become more interested in special possibility results (providing the special conditions are plausible) than in general impossibility results.

Referring to (19.22), if we set $\alpha = 1/2$ with $f(s, n) = 1$, we obtain a game

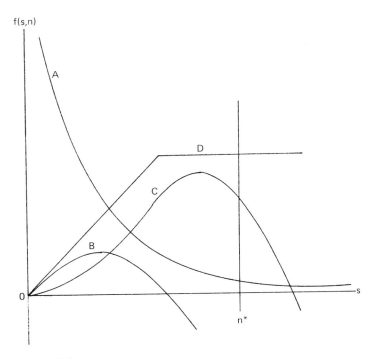

Figure 19.2
The population effect.

whose core converges. For local public goods, however, much of the meat is specifically in the functional form of $f(s, n)$. It will control increasing as well as decreasing returns to scale.[15]

In a game-theoretic analysis of a specific game, n is a parameter while s is a variable. When we compare sequences of games, both s and n are variables.

Figure 19.2 suggests various plausible shapes for $f(s, n)$ for a fixed $n = n^*$. Curve A represents a situation in which the crowding effect enters immediately:

$$f(s, n) = 1/s \quad \text{for} \quad 1 \le s \le n^*.$$

Here, if they can split into separate jurisdictions,

$$v(s) = \max_{t} \left\{ \frac{1}{t} \left[\frac{s}{t} \right] \max \left(x^i \sum_{j=1}^{t} (1 - x^j) \right)^{\alpha} + \max \frac{1}{g} \left(x^i \sum_{j=1}^{g} (1 - x^j) \right)^{\alpha} \right\},$$

$$(19.24)$$

where $g = s - [s/t]t$, t is the number of members of set T, and $[s/t]$ is the largest integer in s/t. When $\alpha = 1/2$, (19.24) can be written as

$$v(s) = \max_{t} \left\{ \frac{1}{t} \left[\frac{s}{t} \right] \left(\frac{t}{t+1} \right) + \frac{1}{g} \left(\frac{g}{g+1} \right) \right\} \tag{19.25}$$
$$= s/2.$$

The game is inessential; each individual prefers isolation to building a society.

Curve B shows a slowing of increasing returns to population size followed by a range of decreasing returns that can lead to negative productivity well before the upper bound of population n^*. Curve C shows a region of increasing returns followed by a slowing of returns and then decreasing returns. Curve D shows increasing returns up to a plateau.

If $f(s, n) = s$ for any n, then a little calculation gives

$$v(s) = \frac{s^3}{1+s} \quad (s = 1, 2, \ldots, n). \tag{19.26}$$

This is a convex game, has a large core, and leads to one jurisdiction with the Lindahl equilibrium of the no-side-payment game at the symmetric imputation.

The local public goods problem is not one but many problems. The key problem in applying core theory involves the appropriate specification of threats in the description of the characteristic function. Much of the threat structure is accounted for by facts of life involving specific considerations of set-up costs and the relative lengths of decision and survival times for individuals, corporations, government bureaus, and other institutions that can threaten each other. Every good lawyer or politician knows that one of the first calculations one must make is what a fight is going to cost all sides. This is then used in attempts to obtain a settlement.

The fact that the Lindahl equilibrium is in the core is an artifact of modeling. The core's existence depends on the characteristic function; the Lindahl equilibrium does not.[16]

Even when it exists, the Lindahl equilibrium is not a particularly interesting or practical solution. For example, living near one's friends or playing in the weekly poker game are "local public goods" that to a good first-order approximation use few if any joint economic resources, are often important, and defy even the Lindahl tax collector. (One might, of course, postulate a "perfect" world in which all degrees of friendship are measured and taxed accordingly!)

Governments, municipalities, and even golf clubs are considerably larger than individuals. This fact alone makes it imperative that we build strategic models of general and local public good production and of allocation procedures.

If we wish to construct a model that is as institution and detail-free as possible, yet overcome some of the difficulties with the threat structure in a parsimonious manner, then the value solution, modified if necessary by Harsanyi's calculation for variable threats, appears to offer far more promise than the core.

The joint-cost allocation and overhead problem in corporate accounting is closely related to the problem of public goods. A reasoned case can be made that the value solution also offers some help there (see Shubik, 1962; Littlechild, 1970; Moriarity, 1981).

As a matter of modeling technique one can directly impose on the characteristic function rules such as specific tax structures. This adds an extra set of constraints without involving process and institutional detail.

It is my belief that we shall eventually be able to build models in strategic or extensive form rather than in coalitional form. However, the empirical, modeling, and mathematical difficulties are formidable. It is difficult to provide details of process without becoming trapped in ephemeral institutional trivia.

Notes to chapter 19

1. This section is based on Shapley and Shubik (1969c).

2. By "externalities of production" we mean external factors that arise out of the production processes. Their impact may be felt either in other production processes or directly in the utility functions.

3. This term "u-money," introduced in chapters 1 and 2, denotes an idealized money that is freely transferable, is present in sufficient supply, and enters each utility function as a separable, linear term. It is useful in economic game theory in much the way that an "ideal gas" is useful in thermodynamics.

4. See *GTSS*, chapter 7. A distinction is made between two kinds of core ("alpha" and "beta"). This makes no difference in the case of external economies, but the distinction can be significant in the case of a "directed" external diseconomy without money.

5. Some of these new goods may be completely valueless, since we do not assume that everyone actually benefits from every externality.

6. In characteristic-function terms we would have $v(S) > v'(S)$ for all S. In the next paragraph the reverse inequality is established.

7. In other respects the two models, though usefully related, are not equivalent; see section 19.2.3.

8. A formal definition of convexity is that

$$v(S) - v(S - i) \leq v(T) - v(T - i)$$

where $i \in S \subset T$.

9. Other game-theoretic solution principles, notably the value and the nucleolus, could be invoked to provide more determinate guidelines, but we shall not discuss them here. Of course, this example is so symmetrical that it is obviously "fair" that each factory take care of its own effluent. But we could easily desymmetrize the model, for example, by introducing unequal cost coefficients (B_i, C_i) for the different factories, or unequal outputs of waste matter. The game would still be convex, and the core excessively large, but the "proper" or "fair" imputation of cost would no longer be so obvious.

10. For example, when $n = 8$ (four players of each type), a coalition with profile $(2, 0)$ is worth only -4 points, since it can produce no iron yet must breathe the others' smoke. Nevertheless, out of coalition they would be even worse off, since the IR limit is -3 per capita. Including people of the other type would rapidly strengthen the coalition: Reading across the table we see that the first would add 5 points, the second 3, the third 1, and the fourth 3.

Note that the data in the table all come from the top line of the formula for $v(S)$; that is, we are still only considering "small" coalitions, with $s \leq 1/K$.

11. For a discussion of the importance of ownership conditions see Coase (1960).

12. Marshall (1922) introduced GNP under the name "national dividend," and Pigou (1932) considered economic welfare limited to those aspects of the economy, both public and private, that could be examined using the measuring rod of money. Pigou's concern was with finding out when changes in national dividend could be related to changes in welfare. Could it serve as an index of economic welfare? Chipman and Moore (1976) provide a simple counterexample with yet another versatile use of the Edgeworth box.

13. Rosenthal (1972) has suggested a modification, which he calls "cooperative games in effectiveness form."

14. See also Richter (1974), Roberts (1974, 1976), Champsaur, Roberts, and Rosenthal (1975), Champsaur (1975).

15. See Roberts (1974) for a discussion of increasing returns to group size.

16. This statement appears to ignore the fact that the competitive equilibrium is independent of the characteristic function, yet coincides with the core for a continuum of traders. The difference is that for an exchange economy the characteristic function is uniquely defined. This is not so for the Lindahl equilibrium and public goods: There are several plausible ways to specify the characteristic function, each leading to a different core.

20 Voting

20.1 Introducing a Political Perspective

20.1.1 The characteristic function, politics, and sociology

The value solutions developed by Nash, Shapley, Harsanyi, Selten, and others were all aimed at axiomatizing fair division or the "just outcome" from a bargain; yet the first application of the value to a political problem involved the development of the Shapley–Shubik "power" index. This was not accidental. We suggest here that there is a fundamental difference between an intrinsic measure of fair division or equity taking the game as given and one that raises questions about the structure of the game to be played. If the game to be played is recognized as a legitimate representation of individual and group entitlements given any form of nonsymmetry in the original entitlements, then the axioms of fairness and efficiency operating on this datum will produce a nonsymmetric outcome reflecting the nonsymmetry in legitimate claims.

A simple resort to an original position argument will restore full symmetry to the structure of the game and hence to the outcome selected by the value. Suppose that we have a game described by a characteristic function (with or without side payments). In general, the characteristic function will reflect the different talents, wealth, social positions, and other differentiating features of the players. If we subscribe to the proposition that all individuals are to be treated precisely as though they were equal, we can homogenize the population and create a new and completely symmetric characteristic function by requiring that they play the game under a "veil of ignorance." Each player has an equal probability of having been born as any other. Who he is will only be revealed after the outcome has been agreed upon.

Although this game is undoubtedly somewhat exotic to contemplate in the real world, it has the merit that it can be used for experiment. The following example has been used:

$$v(\overline{1}) = v(\overline{2}) = v(\overline{3}) = 0,$$
$$v(\overline{12}) = 1, \quad v(\overline{13}) = 2, \quad v(\overline{23}) = 3,$$
$$v(\overline{123}) = 4.$$

The value of this game is (5/6, 8/6, 11/6), and the core is large. When individuals are given this game and told that they must act as judge for three workers who have decided to cooperate and earn $4 but who cannot decide how to split the $4 among themselves, the overwhelming tendency is to select a point in the core (Shubik, 1975b, 1978a), although some egalitarians may opt for (4/3, 4/3, 4/3). If, however, people are told that players A, B, and C have agreed to cooperate, but that the identities of players 1, 2, and 3 will be determined only later by a lottery with equal probabilities, then the judgment switches heavily to (4/3, 4/3, 4/3), which is the value for the symmetric game and is in the center of its core.

Although the full symmetry arguments have great appeal,[1] most economic arguments take as given some nonsymmetric initial position, even if it is limited to recognizing different native talents in a state without other forms of private property.

Individuals are born into a society which by the time they enter into its political and economic life has provided the rules to define their individual domain of strategic choice and their freedom of action.[2] This includes the various societal forms of ownership of goods, one's own talents, and oneself. The economist applying the methods of cooperative game theory to economic problems would expect that the biological, sociological, legal, and political constraints and restrictions placed on individual and group powers and rights are already reflected implicitly in the modeling required to justify the characteristic function or other form as an adequate representation of the problem to be studied.

20.1.2 The game within the game

Even if the analysis proposed is primarily static, or at best involves dynamics implicitly as comparative statics, it is important to recognize that many of the questions concerning human behavior asked in the different behavioral sciences involve different time scales.

Biological changes may require millennia; sociological changes may involve several generations. Political changes are on a shorter time scale and can take place in a few years. The time scale of much of economic life varies from a few days to a few months. It is only when we consider major capital investments that the time horizons of individuals and firms are extended to several years. When we consider public goods and services, the economic and political processes become entwined and involve horizons longer than in other parts of economic activity.

An approach to building unified models that specifically recognize noneconomic factors is to consider games within games, where a game played at the political level, for example, might determine the conditions or set the environment for a shorter-term game to be played at the level of economics. We might consider a vote to determine tax and subsidy rates prior to examining the economy with these rates as given.

This chapter takes a first step toward the game within the game by introducing voting, taxation, and then a government as a player. In chapters 21 and 22, this interlinkage of games with different time scales is extended by considering political parties and bureaucracies explicitly.

Eventually an economic theory that purports to be adequate for the long run, say 20 or 30 years, must take into account political, sociological, and other feedbacks. A development theory without such features is doomed to failure. Here, because our scope is relatively restricted, we limit ourselves to political behavior, with no attempt to account for political or sociological changes.

Although the models in this volume have tended to stress an individual's conscious, rational, goal-oriented behavior, it appears that on an extremely short time scale behavior is instinctive, and on a long time scale it is more conditioned by habit and sociological factors than by the type of conscious problem formulation and analysis most favored in models of *Homo oeconomicus*. A fully successful blend of learning and adaptation theories with game theory has not yet been achieved. Such a blend would require insights into and a development of dynamics that have not yet been attained.

20.2 Voting, the Core, and the Law

The surprising feature of the relationship between the price system and market games with many economic agents is that the market game is essentially mechanism-free but the limit of various cooperative solutions can be interpreted as tantamount to the existence of a price system. Unfortunately, as soon as any of a variety of socioeconomic and politico-economic realities is introduced, the essential structure of the market game may be destroyed.

For example, the apparently innocent assumption of joint ownership of the firm by means of shares in the corporation, which enables the Debreu (1959) model of market equilibrium to include one more realistic feature, poses problems in modeling the economy cooperatively or strategically. In particular, if stock is meant to be voting stock, the core of the game may be destroyed, so that no efficient price system will exist.

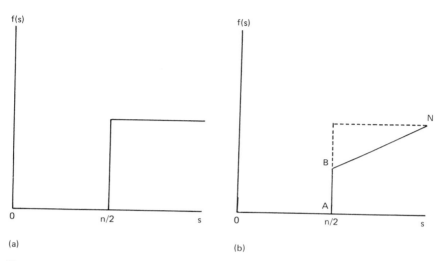

Figure 20.1
Protection of minority stockholders.

20.2.1 A simple example

Both in fact and in theory the price system in an enterprise economy with corporations owned by shareholders with voting stock can be preserved by laws protecting the rights of the minority stockholders. A simple example will illustrate this for the side-payment game.

Figure 20.1 shows the characteristic functions for the symmetric simple-majority voting game without and with minority stockholder protection. In the first instance

$$f(s) = \begin{cases} 0 & \text{for } s \le n/2, \\ 1 & \text{for } s > n/2. \end{cases} \tag{20.1}$$

Any group less than or equal to $n/2$ cannot guarantee itself anything. Any group larger than $n/2$ can take everything.

In the second instance

$$f(s) = \begin{cases} 0 & \text{for } s \le n/2, \\ s/n & \text{for } s > n/2. \end{cases} \tag{20.2}$$

As before, a group less than or equal to $n/2$ cannot guarantee itself anything. However, any group greater than $n/2$, even though it can gain control, must when it pays out its gain pay all individuals, including those out of the coalition, in proportion to their stockholdings. It is easy to check that this game has a single-point core, whereas the simple-majority game with no stockholder protection has no core (see *GTSS*, chapter 7).

Given minority protection by the prorating rule, the value will coincide with the core for the symmetric game but not necessarily otherwise. Another simple example shows this.

Consider a firm with 4 stockholders with votes of 2, 1, 1, and 1. Suppose a simple majority is needed for control. The core and the value are calculated for two cases: a simple-majority game with no protection of minorities, and a simple-majority corporate or stockholder game. In the first case the core, as we have already noted, is empty. The value is given by the imputation

$$(\tfrac{1}{2}, \tfrac{1}{6}, \tfrac{1}{6}, \tfrac{1}{6}).$$

In the second case the core is given by the solitary imputation

$$(\tfrac{2}{5}, \tfrac{1}{5}, \tfrac{1}{5}, \tfrac{1}{5}),$$

and the value is given by the imputation

$$(\tfrac{9}{20}, \tfrac{11}{60}, \tfrac{11}{60}, \tfrac{11}{60}).$$

In the second case the higher return to the man with 2 votes in the value as opposed to the core reflects his relative importance for the formation of winning coalitions. The value is somewhat less than in the first case for the 2-vote individual; this decrement is caused by the introduction of minority stockholder protection.

20.2.2 The core and value of a corporate economy with voting

In chapter 13 we discussed the core of a market game with production and exchange. The firm is essentially a special form of local public good. This is reflected in our various ways of modeling coalition production. Although one can in a pro forma way introduce shares and call them ownership fractions of the firms, as was done by Arrow and Debreu (1954), the cooperative-game and general-equilibrium treatments provide no insight into three important economic aspects of corporate-share ownership: that individuals trade shares; that shares have votes, which can be used to gain control of the corporation and force a change in management; and that corporate policy is usually set by a group of individuals acting as fiduciaries for most of the stockholders. The rules of the game for political voting systems normally forbid the sale of votes; rather, votes are used to control the various levels of government, and the agencies of government act as fiduciaries for the voters in setting policy and controlling taxation, subsidies, and the disbursement of public goods and services.

An adequate theory explicit enough to account for the trading of shares and the selection of corporate policy requires the construction of models of the economy in strategic form.

The stockholder minority protection scheme suggested in figure 20.1b has its natural counterpart in corporate law, where it is recognized that the firm's profits are declared in money.[3] This gives the one-dimensional measure usually provided by a price system.

If we take preferences and ownership claims as given and wish to construct a game and study its core properties, we do not have a price system available to define a stockholder protection rule a priori. We must resort to defining it in terms of goods.

Consider a trading and production economy with a continuum of n types of individual economic agents. Let there be a set G of g production technologies, utilizing as inputs and outputs m commodities. The initial density of endowment of any agent i of type i consists of a set of goods (a) and shares (b) in the production technologies (or corporations):

$$(a^i, b^i) = (a_1^i, a_2^i, \ldots, a_m^i; b_1^i, b_2^i, \ldots, b_g^i).$$

We define the feasible set of outcomes achievable by a coalition S of positive measure as any production and exchange among the members of S, where the imputs are limited to their own initial resources of commodities, the production technologies are only those for which members of S hold a majority of the shares, and the output from any production technology employed is a fraction of the vector of outputs selected by S, scaled back in proportion to the percentage of shares held by the members of S.

The last condition provides a somewhat contorted but liberal means of protecting minority shareholders. It is liberal because the minority participates in the output in proportion to its shares. It is liberal enough to preserve the market-game property of the overall game even though control of a majority of shares is required before a coalition S can use a production set. The game with this rule is closely related to the game illustrated in figure 20.1b. If we had failed to provide minority protection, it would be closer to the game in figure 20.1a, and the market-game property would be lost. If we tried to protect the minority stockholders by giving them veto power, the market-game property would be preserved but the core would remain large even with a continuum of traders.

20.3 Public Goods, Direct Voting, and Taxation

20.3.1 Politics precedes economics

The simple examples provided in the last section and in the discussion of externalities in chapter 19 indicate how legal considerations and taxation can be used to modify the individual control structure when complex forms of economic interaction are encountered.

Much of economic theory, whether interpreted from a conservative or a socialist viewpoint, has been concerned with the uses of a price system in determining an efficient allocation of resources. (There is, of course, a great difference between the emergence of efficient prices through the forces of mass competition and the creation of centrally controlled and calculated prices that result in efficient trade.) In contrast, the vote is featured more centrally in democratic political and administrative organizations than in other forms of government.

Organized political life appears to have preceded the development of the economy. The infrastructure of institutions that provide protection, communication, law, and order formed the environment in which trade and commerce could develop. Likewise, formal taxation probably preceded the organization of formal markets. In the early empires there is no evidence of the popular vote being used to determine tax levels. The original tax authorities were the nobles. It was not until the late seventeenth century that the king's privy purse was distinguished from the national assets and income of any society. (In Saudi Arabia this distinction was not made until well after World War II.)

Even in the time of Egypt, Babylon, and Rome, public buildings, palaces, temples, tombs, and wars had to be financed, an infrastructure of communication created, justice and some form of protection supplied to individuals. The economic engine of society was and still is heavily guided by the political powers of the state.

It is suggested that political powers and needs lead to a formalized tax system and the construction of public (or the emperor's) goods even without a market economy or a voting system. Considerations of efficiency in economic production and equity in political power eventually create roles for both prices and votes in the determination of taxes and public goods.

20.3.2 A digression on direct voting

In the course of human history, markets, auctions, lotteries, bargains, covenants, contracts, and votes have all come into existence, evolved, and survived in various forms as means for dealing more efficiently (by some appropriate measure) with sociopolitical and politicoeconomic distribution.[4] Hierarchies and bureaucracies involving state and private not-for-profit and for-profit firms have evolved to provide production and services.

At the level of theorizing presented here, auctions and lotteries do not appear to be central to the major problems involving public goods and services.[5] Distribution by bargain and contract is undoubtedly of central importance. The various value solutions reflect this method at a high level of abstraction and in a static manner; to go further would involve the development of a dynamics encompassing psychological characteristics and institutional, legal, and other details beyond the scope of this inquiry. Thus our venture beyond markets is largely constrained to the vote.

In modern mass societies voting is used mainly to elect fiduciaries who are given the task of acting for others. Thus for the most part people do not vote directly for individual or even sets of public goods and services, but rather vote for other people who promise to support generally phrased programs. At virtually all levels of political life legislators and other officials are elected from "below." Thus, in the United States the president is elected by all voters in the country. Governors, mayors, state legislators, judges, dogcatchers, and others are chosen by more limited electorates. In economic life corporation directors are elected by stockholders who, in theory, give them a mandate to supervise the running of the firm. Union officials are elected by union members as trustees.

In universities, the church, learned societies, many clubs, and most social and professional organizations the elections are from "above." Promotion to bishop or full professor or membership of the Drones is determined by a vote of those who already have that status.

The direct vote is also used for referenda at various levels of government, primarily for special taxes and programs such as bond issues or tax assessments for school districts or public buildings. The direct vote is used in Switzerland to cover many more items. In clubs, special projects and assessments are frequently voted upon.

Recent work in economic theory aimed at the inclusion of voting along with the functioning of markets has largely been concerned with direct voting for a set of prospects that can be variously interpreted as public goods, political candidates, projects, or states of the world. Yet political institutions tend to distinguish direct and indirect voting, and indirect voting appears to provide society with an especially important aggregating device. But when we try to move forward from general-equilibrium theory, we find that the direct vote, taxation, pure and local public goods, and some externalities that are quantifiable in a reasonably straightforward manner are the easiest features to add on to the theory without going into institutional detail. Government can be formulated exogenously as a set of constraints or endogenously as a (probably powerful) player with its own goals. By considering models of this variety, we avoid the need to provide a link between the populace and the government and we finesse the problems of bureaucracy. The government proposes and the people vote.

The properties of direct voting systems in which everyone reveals his true preferences, or in which individuals play as though involved in a cooperative or noncooperative game, are a subject for lengthy study in and of themselves. No attempt is made here to cover the large body of literature. (For an excellent survey see Moulin, 1981.)

20.3.3 Prices and taxation in general equilibrium with public goods

"Tax me not in mournful numbers
Come and make a total haul
For the residue that slumbers
Is no good to me at all."
    Samuel Hoffenstein

Prior to introducing voting or other explicitly game-theoretic concepts, a natural question to ask is, Under how general a set of conditions can we establish the existence of a tax structure and competitive price system that is optimal from a social point of view when a government supplies the public goods? The Lindahl equilibrium requires lump-sum taxes in an economy where it is likely that the government knows neither the endowments of the consumers nor the plans of the producers.

In chapter 18 we listed the major sources of tax revenues in the United States. A cursory glance should be enough to remind us of the importance of sales, property, individual, and corporate income taxes.

Until the late 1960s most of the literature on taxation was devoted to partial-equilibrium analysis. One of the more important results was the development of the theory of excess burden (Walker, 1955; Musgrave, 1959), where it was shown that a lump-sum tax will always be a better (or no worse) way of raising a specific amount of tax revenue than a sales tax. The papers of Fourgeaud (1969) and Diamond and Mirrlees (1971) were among the earliest to ask and answer this type of question in the context of a general-equilibrium system. The models and results of two later articles are discussed here to illustrate the new questions and their modeling problems.

Mantel (1975, p. 189) noted that even in the most centralized of economic systems, the state is not generally in a position to expropriate totally the endowment of all individuals. For example, if we include labor skills and knowledge among the personal endowments of the citizenry, even the most coercive of states may find itself stymied: it can kill its citizens, but it cannot demand the use of all their skills.

Given public goods, private goods, and government, our question of interest, broadly stated, is, Utilizing a general array of taxes, can a government arrange its policy so that there will be the appropriate generalized equilibrium together with a production of public goods such that a social optimum is achieved?

In order to make this question more precise one must specify how government is to be modeled, what is meant by social optimality (as contrasted, for example, with Pareto optimality), and what conditions are placed on individual preferences, firm behavior, and government finance.

Mantel's main assumptions are as follows. There are m consumers, n producers, and e commodities. Each consumer i has a consumption set x_i that is a closed convex subset of R^e, the commodity space. Preferences may depend on the consumption of others, including that of the government.[6] For each firm j the production set Y_j is a closed convex subset of Y, the set bounding production; and $-\Omega \subset Y_j$, where $\Omega = R_+^e$. For each firm j there is a profit function b_j that depends on prices, j's production, and the tax scheme. This profit function is continuous and, for fixed prices and taxes, is quasiconcave and increasing with a value of 0 at zero output.

The government is explicitly modeled as both a special consumer and a producer (indexed by $i = j = 0$). There are k goods ($k \leq e$) that are either public goods or are consumed by the government. Consumption by the public sector is representable by a closed convex subset of R^e, bounded from below.

The government is exogenously given a *social-preference correspondence*. Furthermore social preferences are *acyclic*; every finite collection of elements will have an undominated element.[7]

The tax structure is assumed to be such that the government's budget is nonempty whenever consumers balance their budgets and producers obtain the profits on which the consumer-owners base their budgets.

The government obtains its revenue from its own production, its shares in private industry, and taxes on consumers and producers.

Mantel established (1) the existence of a competitive equilibrium for a given tax structure and (2) the existence of a socially optimal tax structure. He noted that in general the equilibrium will not be Pareto-optimal (one could get Pareto optimality by restricting oneself to lump-sum taxes and considering the usual independent consumer preferences; that is, the Foley–Lindahl model may be regarded as a special case).

Greenberg (1975) contrasted lump-sum and sales taxes in a general-equilibrium context and sought a public competitive equilibrium. He began with the observation, taken from the earlier work of Foley and Milleron, that all public goods have prices and are produced to maximize profit. Unless markets for public goods really exist, the prices can be interpreted as efficiency or shadow prices. If we assume that the government has no production technology of its own and buys all public goods from firms in competitive markets, there is a justification for prices. Examples might include contractors who clean both government and private buildings or landlords who rent to both the private and the public sector. When we consider the courts, police, the military, public parks, foreign affairs, and its many other functions, however, it is clear that government in fact has its own technology and produces many public goods and services.

Greenberg suggested that government production is motivated by its desire to maximize a social-welfare function rather than profits.

In his model there are n consumers and one "aggregate" private firm that produces all of the e private goods. There are q public goods produced by the government from inputs purchased from the private sector.

Each consumer i has an initial endowment w^i of private goods and a preference ordering on his consumption set, which is defined over the $q + e$ commodities. The preference ordering is assumed to be convex, continuous, and strongly monotonic. The private production technology is a closed convex set containing zero and having free disposal. Private goods are manufactured from private goods.

The only condition imposed on the welfare function is that it be monotonic with respect to unanimous preference.

Greenberg defined a "public competitive equilibrium: lump sum" (PCEL). Its basic parameters are the output x of public goods, the input z of private goods to the government, the allocation y^i of private goods to the ith consumer, a price system p for private goods ($p \geq 0$), and taxes t^i such that $p \cdot z = \sum_{i=1}^{n} t^i$. The PCEL is a feasible allocation such that profits are maximized in the private firm and (x, y^i) is optimal on the budget set of each consumer i. Furthermore, the allocation must be such that at the existing prices there is no way to finance the production of a vector of public goods $\bar{x}$ that would enable individual i to buy a stock of goods $\bar{y}^i$ that together with $\bar{x}$ is preferred to the PCEL allocation of (x, y^i). This fulfills the weak condition on the social-welfare function.

In a variation of his model Greenberg modified both production and tax conditions so that the firm utilized public goods in production (free disposal is assumed) and was taxed. He proved that in both models every PCEL is Pareto-optimal.

He then defined a "public competitive equilibrium: sales tax" (PCES), where the tax was assumed to apply per unit of sales: If the selling price is p, the buyer pays $p + t$. He distinguished two cases, one with two classes of goods—"primary goods," which are not taxed, and "final goods," which are taxed—and another with no distinction among goods. For the latter case he proved the existence of a PCES and showed that in general it does not yield a Pareto-optimal outcome. For the former case, assuming that each individual owns only primary goods, that the firm uses only these goods to produce its output of final goods, and that the utility of each individual depends only on the bundle of final private and public goods, Greenberg was able to prove the existence of a PCES whose allocation is Pareto-optimal.

The papers of Mantel and Greenberg represent an important step toward the study of political economy in a general yet rigorous framework. The assumptions of Mantel are more general than those of Greenberg. Yet both have the drawback that in each instance a new player, government, is introduced basically ex machina. This player is clearly large with respect to the economy and other institutions, yet it is a price taker. From the point of view of parsimony and mathematical tractability the introduction of government as an extra player with goals of its own is a natural first step, but it is only a first step. If we are to develop a coherent theory that includes the production and distribution of public goods, we must specify how the government forms its social-welfare function, if it does in fact do so. If it does not have such a function or a set of preferences, what motivates it to act? We shall return to this problem in the next two chapters.

Greenberg assumed the existence of Samuelson pure public goods, whereas Mantel's assumptions about consumer preferences even include a concern for the welfare of others.[8]

From the game-theoretic point of view, both of these models suggest the possibility of reformulating the economy as a strategic market game with a continuum of consumers and firms and with government as an atomic player. Efficient or Pareto-optimal noncooperative equilibria are in general the exception, and I conjecture that the same results can be obtained for models of the economy in strategic form.

Greenberg himself appears to indicate that his model, in which goods are strictly divided into primary goods and final goods, is not satisfactory even from the viewpoint of casual empiricism. Many items, such as labor-leisure and energy fuels, are clearly both final goods and primary goods. Even so, tax policies in many countries treat commodities primarily used by firms differently from those used by voters. Hence, at a slightly more detailed level of modeling it appears to be worth considering the degree to which an item is purchased for final consumption or as a factor of production.

A natural step toward a game-theoretic treatment of taxes is to introduce tax-rate restrictions directly into the definition of the characteristic function. Guesnerie and Oddou (1979, 1981) did so by considering an economy with one public and one private good in which all individuals pay the same percentage of their initial private endowment. Greenberg and Weber (1982) have been able to extend this work to prove that the proportional-tax game is balanced if it is "binary superadditive" relative to N.[9]

20.3.4 The core of economic voting games

The great strength of the price system as a solution to the problem of exchange among many traders, each individually small with respect to the whole market, is that it is not one solution but many. The price system, core, value, and noncooperative equilibrium all coincide. The Lindahl equilibrium, despite its impracticality, at first glance offered some hope that similar results might be found, but the listing of counterexamples in chapter 19 shows that this was a false hope. The examples there did not, however, take into account political or voting aspects of public-goods decision making.

Taking the pure-public-good, increasing-returns-to-scale model with characteristic function

$$v(s) = \frac{s^3}{1 + s} \quad (s = 1, 2, \ldots, n), \tag{20.3}$$

which was derived in section 19.4.2, we offer three voting-game modifications:

1. The simple-majority game:

$$v(s) = \begin{cases} \dfrac{n^3}{1 + s} & \text{for } s > n/2, \\ 0 & \text{for } s \leq n/2. \end{cases} \tag{20.4}$$

The second part of this characteristic function has a value of zero if a minority can be taxed by the majority at a level of confiscation. There is no core.

2. The unanimity game:

$$v(s) = \begin{cases} \dfrac{n^3}{1+n} & \text{for } s = n, \\ 0 & \text{for } s \neq n. \end{cases}$$

(20.5)

Every individual has a veto, but no subgroup is permitted to produce a public good without approval of the whole. The core is the whole of the imputation set.

3. The minority-protection rule:

$$v(s) = \begin{cases} \dfrac{s}{n}\left(\dfrac{n^3}{1+n}\right) = \dfrac{sn^2}{1+n} & \text{for } s > n/2, \\ 0 & \text{for } s \leq n/2. \end{cases}$$

(20.6)

The core is a single point for $n \geq 3$.

Some simple examples showing how the presence or absence of voting to control an external diseconomy can affect the core have been constructed by Rosenthal (1973). The voters may tax or ban the diseconomy.[10] Clearly we could graft onto the public-goods problem any voting scheme in which, for example, foreigners, felons, minors, slaves, or others are denied the vote. In each instance the characteristic function would change.

Foley proved that when the production set is a cone, the Lindahl equilibria belong to the core of the cooperative game defined without voting and with any set of players being in a position to use the production process. However, this result does not necessarily hold when production sets are not cones. When there are decreasing returns, the producer obtains a profit, and the location of the Lindahl equilibrium in relation to the core depends on the distribution of these profits. A simple example illustrates this. Consider three traders, one public good, and one private good, with shares available in a private firm that produces the public good. Let the utility functions be $u_i(x^i, y) = x^i + y$ $(i = 1, 2)$ and $u_3(x^3, y) = x^3$, where x^i is i's amount of the private good and y is the public good. The production function is

$$y = \sqrt{\sum_{j=1}^{3} z^j},$$

where $z^j = 1 - x^j$. The initial endowment for i is $(1, 0, s_i)$, where s_i is the percentage of shares he holds in the firm.

The problem in modeling is what we take as the characteristic function in order to calculate the core. We note three cases, but first we calculate the Lindahl equilibrium, giving the profits to the government to distribute as it sees fit. By inspection, $p_1 = p_2 = \sqrt{2}$ and $p_3 = 0$, given that the price of the input private good is set at $p = 1$. Because trader 3 has no value for the public good, he will not be taxed at the Lindahl equilibrium.

Trader 1 will maximize $x^1 + y$ subject to $1 - x^1 - p_1 y + t_1 = 0$, and trader 2 will maximize $x^2 + y$ subject to $1 - x^2 - p_2 y + t_2 = 0$, where t_1 and t_2 are subsidies. The firm maximizes

$$\pi = (p_1 + p_2)y - (1 - x^1) - (1 - x^2), \quad \text{where} \quad y = \sqrt{2 - x^1 - x^2}.$$

We have $x^1 = x^2 = 0$, $y = \sqrt{2}$, $\pi = 0.828$, and $t_1 = t_2 = 0.414$. The Lindahl equilibrium payoff is $(1.414, 1.414, 1)$, where corporate profits are split as a subsidy to the first two traders. But suppose ownership of the shares fixed the disposal of the profits, with $s_1 = s_2 = 1/2$ and $s_3 = 0$ giving the desired result. What would happen if we had $s_1 = s_2 = 0$ and $s_3 = 1$? What characteristic function should be used for the core?

Case 1: We ignore both corporate and political control and assume that any coalition can use the production function with its own resources. Shares and votes do not matter, and corporate profits are not defined.

A one-person coalition can obtain 1. The coalition $(1, 2)$ can obtain divisions on the set bounded by $(2, 0, -)$ on one side, $(0, 2, -)$ on the other, and $(1.414, 1.414, -)$ in the middle. Coalitions $(1, 3)$ and $(2, 3)$ can split 2 between them. The coalition $(1, 2, 3)$ can give any individual 3. The best symmetric split is $(5/4, 5/4, 5/4)$.

Case 2: We ignore political control but include corporate ownership and control. Consider $s_1 = s_2 = 0$ and $s_3 = 1$. The one- and three-person coalitions are as before, as are $(1, 3)$ and $(2, 3)$. The coalition $(1, 2)$ is now flat because they cannot produce the public good; in this instance, if the Lindahl scheme were used with $y = \sqrt{2}$, the books would not balance because there would be no way to pay the needed subsidy of 0.828, which would now go to the third trader.

Case 3: If we include both political and corporate control, then a simple majority is required for taxation. If their power is unlimited, then a 100 percent corporate-profits tax voted by 1 and 2 could set up the condition for a Lindahl equilibrium. The one- and three-person coalitions are as before, but the two-person coalitions now become all-powerful, and this game has no core if taxation is unlimited and not symmetric.

In two papers Kaneko (1977a, b) applied the concept of ratio equilibrium and introduced voting into a public-goods economy.[11] He considered m public goods and one private good, with a public bureau producing and supplying the public goods and setting tax ratios specifying how public-goods production costs are to be imposed on each individual; hence the name "ratio equilibrium." This device takes care of the division of profits. He then introduced a voting game in which the level of public goods to be produced is decided by majority vote. In his first voting game, $G(N, W, r)$, the ratios r are given in advance, N is the set of all players, and W is the set of winning coalitions. He proved that there exists a ratio equilibrium r and that an allocation x belongs to the core if and only if (r, x) is a ratio equilibrium. He also established that the core of $G(N, W, r)$ is nonempty if and only if r is an equilibrium ratio.

In his second paper Kaneko presented a new voting game, $G(N, W)$, with the ratio r selected endogenously. To make this feasible, a bargaining rule is specified in the voting game such that if a winning coalition S wishes to propose a new configuration y to replace the currently proposed x, then it must bear a share of the cost of y equal to or greater than its share of the cost of x.[12]

A coalition S can improve upon configuration x with y if $S \in W$, if at y it pays at as high a proportion of taxes as at x, and if $u^i(y^i) > u^i(x^i)$ for all $i \in S$. The core of $G(N, W)$ is the set of all configurations x that cannot be improved upon and that satisfy $u^i(x^i) \geq u^2(0)$, where $u^i(0)$ is i's initial endowment.[13] Kaneko proved that the core of $G(N, W)$ coincides with the ratio equilibria.

Kaneko's assumption that there are many public goods but only one consumer good is not really as restrictive as it might appear at first glance, for we can interpret the consumer good as a nonlinear money that serves as proxy for income exclusive of the share of public goods. The assumptions of Mantel (1975) nevertheless appear to be broader than those of Kaneko, and it would be interesting to know whether the concept of ratio equilibrium, which is clearly related to minority rights protection, can be fruitfully extended to Mantel's model reformulated as a cooperative game with voting.

20.3.5 The value, power, and taxes
A series of articles by Aumann and Kurz (1977a, b), Osborne (1981), and Aumann, Kurz, and Neyman (1980) has investigated voting and taxation

under several assumptions concerning private and public goods and the
threat structure of the voting majority and minority. In each instance the
solution employed is the no-side-payment or λ-transfer value.

In their first two papers Aumann and Kurz (1977a, b) considered a
one-commodity "wealth" economy and a many-commodity economy,
respectively; in each instance a voting majority can impose arbitrary
taxes upon the minority. The minority has the choice of paying its taxes
or destroying its goods. Osborne (1980) considered two types of privately
held goods, "labor and land"; members of a minority can destroy (with-
hold) their labor rather than pay taxes but cannot destroy their land. All
three of these papers deal with a pure distribution problem in which the
politicoeconomic definition of private ownership differs considerably
from the pure economic definition. The game-theoretic distinction is clear.
In an exchange economy with individual ownership, if $(w_1^i, w_2^i, \ldots, w_m^i)$
describes individual i's initial endowment of m commodities and $\varphi_i(x_1^i,
x_2^i, \ldots, x_m^i)$ is his utility function, the worth of the one-person coalition
$\{i\}$ is $\varphi_i(w_1^i, w_2^i, \ldots, w_m^i)$. If taxation is permitted, however, the worth
of the one-person coalition will be some amount greater than or equal
to $\varphi_i(0, 0, \ldots, 0)$ and less than $\varphi_i(w_1^i, w_2^i, \ldots, w_m^i)$.

The no-side-payment or λ-transfer value is the solution concept applied
(see *GTSS*, chapter 7). In their first paper Aumann and Kurz began
by assuming a game with small agents, each of whom has an initial
endowment and the strategic opportunity to destroy some or all of
that endowment; a societal redistribution decision is made by majority
vote.

The formal model is as follows. The set of agents T is assumed to be continuous. An agent is denoted by t (standing for a point in the subset dt).
A nonnegative measure μ on the coalitions is defined such that $\mu(T) = 1$
is the measure of the population. For each $t \in T$, $e(t)$ (nonnegative)
denotes t's endowment and u_t his utility function. Thus the endowment
of a coalition S is $\int_S e(t)\mu(dt)$, which we abbreviate to $\int_S e$.

The further assumptions made are that μ is nonatomic (all agents
individually are of negligible size); total endowments are positive and
bounded; and the u_t are all increasing, concave, continuously differentiable for positive values, continuous at 0, and uniformly bounded with
$u_t(1)$ uniformly positive and $u_t(0) = 0$.

An allocation is a nonnegative function x on T such that $\int x = \int e$.
The central result of the paper is that the income redistribution game has
a unique value allocation x such that

$$\frac{u_t(x(t))}{u_t^1(x(t))} + x(t) = c + e(t) \quad \text{for all } t, \tag{20.7}$$

where c is a positive constant and u_t^1 is the first derivative of u_t.

The level of individual t's tax is $e(t) - x(t)$; by differentiating this with respect to e, we obtain the marginal tax, using (20.7) for the implicit definition of x as a function of e:

$$M(t) = 1 - \frac{1}{2 + (-u_t^{11} u_t / u_t^{12})} \quad \text{evaluated at } x(t). \tag{20.8}$$

Hence $1/2 \leq M(t) < 1$.

If all agents have linear utility functions, the marginal tax rate is 50 percent. This result can be understood by observing that the Harsanyi function for any S and $\bar{S}$, where S is winning, will have

$$h(S) + h(\bar{S}) = e,$$

$$h(S) - h(\bar{S}) = e - \int_{\bar{S}} e,$$

hence

$$h(S) = e - \frac{1}{2} \int_{\bar{S}} e. \tag{20.9}$$

This is illustrated in figure 20.2, which shows the threat point P and the split-the-difference resolution point at H on the joint-maximum line.

In their second paper, in place of considering the redistribution of a single commodity, "wealth" or money, Aumann and Kurz (1977b) considered a full exchange model with m commodities in which a majority can tax the minority however it pleases but the minority can destroy any part of its goods. If there is a tie, each side uses its own goods but cannot tax the other side. Two further results are proved. First, every nontrivial bounded market has a commodity-tax allocation and a money-tax allocation. (A market is trivial if there are just two agents and one or both of them have no initial endowment.) Second, in a nonatomic bounded market the commodity- and money-tax allocations coincide.

This coincidence does not hold if there are finitely many agents. The basic reason why the two forms of tax allocation differ is that, while the Pareto-optimal or agreement payoffs are the same, the disagreement payoffs differ; hence the values differ.

Osborne (1981) introduced a somewhat more satisfactory view of the abilities of a majority to tax a minority. In particular, he allowed the

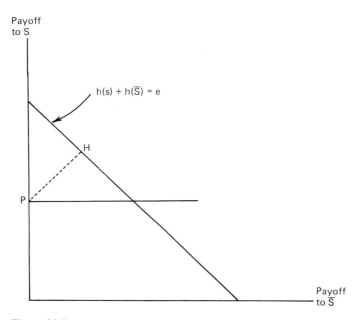

Figure 20.2
Threat and taxation.

influence of individual agents to vary by introducing a voting measure on the space of agents. A "majority" coalition is defined as one with a measure greater than some number $\alpha > 1/2$. The heuristic argument given is that if a voting group is to have enough force to change anything, it may need more than a slim majority.

In the first case investigated by Osborne the minority cannot destroy its resources. Thus the optimal threat of any majority is total expropriation. The Harsanyi function is easy to calculate; for a winning coalition S it is a division of all resources among its members, and for a losing coalition it is zero. Osborne considered a finite number of agent types, where agents are of the same type if they have the same utility functions and the same endowments (the Aumann–Shapley definition required only the same utility functions; see Aumann and Shapley, 1974).

Suppose that all individuals are equally risk-averse. Each has a utility function homogeneous of degree β with $0 < \beta < 1$. The tax rate depends on the individual's risk aversion, the worth of his initial bundle (at after-tax equilibrium prices), and his relative voting weight.

If everyone has the same voting weight and a majority is 50 percent ($\alpha = 1/2$), then, as is to be expected, the final distribution of resources is at the equal-income competitive allocation. The taxes are lump-sum leveling taxes.

Osborne explored the relationship between α, the size of the majority, and β, where $1 - \beta$ can be regarded as a measure of relative risk aversion of individuals with respect to wealth. He found that, for a given α, a lower β means a higher tax rate; that is, at a lower β the wealthy are more concerned about threats. For a fixed β, the higher α the lower the tax rate.[14]

Osborne's next case appears to me to be a considerable step forward in relevant modeling. A world with two commodity types is considered, with individuals owning land and labor. In the face of a majority the individual can destroy his labor but not his land. More generally, if there are k goods, we suppose that n of them can be destroyed but $m = k - n$ cannot.

In terms of labor, the word "destroyed" is possibly an unfortunate choice. A better phrasing might be "withheld" or "concealed." This also applies to family heirlooms and other personal possessions that can be kept from the tax collector's eye and, were it not for the level of taxation, might be sold.

Osborne's qualitative result is that the marginal tax rate on goods that cannot be concealed or destroyed is higher than the rate on goods that can be concealed.

A rudimentary principle in taxation is that it is not desirable from the viewpoint of society as a whole that the tax rate be so rapacious or the law so arbitrary that the tax base is destroyed by the diminution of productivity and trade, or by the exit or destruction of the population.[15]

In fourth paper on voting and taxation, Aumann, Kurz, and Neyman (1980) analyzed a public-goods economy without exclusion (any public good produced is available to all). They considered a set of agents, public goods, and nonconsumable resources. A technology was given that enables the public goods to be produced from the resources. Each agent has a utility function for public goods, a voting weight, and an initial endowment. There are no private consumption goods in the model.

In the voting game any coalition with a majority can produce public goods using its resources only, but all then benefit. In the nonvoting game any coalition can produce using its own resources.

The driving mechanism behind this tax analysis is the threat structure. The application of the value appears to be eminently reasonable. What must be questioned is the intuitive acceptability of the threat description, that is, of who can tax what and who can destroy what. In a modern society, apart from concealing small valuables and withholding personal services, it is more difficult to destroy one's personal possessions than one might think. An occasional citizen demolishes his house rather than pay taxes, but such destruction is costly and cumbersome and may in some instances even be criminal. Furthermore, in a rich society many assets are financial paper or ownership claims; because these are abstractions with only symbolic physical representations, they are hard to destroy—burning a stock certificate may afford some psychic pleasure, but it does not extinguish one's ownership claim. In the United States charity has provided a way to beat the tax collector.

20.3.6 Committees and assemblies
In this chapter considerable emphasis has been given to the direct vote. The citizenry may vote in a referendum to change a constitution or limit a tax. But the type of mass, more or less anonymous, individualistic voting implicitly described here is used for the most part in the election of individuals to political or administrative posts or to directorates and trusteeships—in short, to posts where they decide for others, plan and formulate policy for others, or vote for others.

Two institutional arrangements where direct voting is important are committees and legislative assemblies. Furthermore, the generation of programs and alternatives appears to take place mostly in subcommittees and in bureaucratic organizations, often with the chairman playing a special role.

Quantitative differences frequently serve as indicators of qualitative differences. We suggest that the study of voting could well merit a division into at least five categories, as indicated in table 20.1. The second column indicates (very approximately) the range of players involved. One-member committees are included to cover the case where a single individual is in a position to make decisions alone. The numbers for committees are based on the sizes of congressional committees, corporate directorates, state and university committees. Legislative assemblies range in size from that of India to the Icelandic Stortung. The upper bound on the mass vote is suggested by the Indian electorate.

The number of alternatives suggested is more symbolic of an order of magnitude and psychological and sociopsychological factors than a number to be taken seriously. It is "the magic number 7 ± 2" suggested by Miller (1956). The question is, How many serious items of business can an assembly handle in a meeting? An agenda may list 15 or 20 items,

Table 20.1
Five voting mechanisms

	Number of players	Alternatives	Communication; knowledge[a]	Substance of vote	Role of players	Appropriate game type[b]
Committee	1–15	up to 7 ± 2	face to face; high	policy (people)	fiduciary	coop
Legislature	20–800	up to 7 ± 2	aggregate; moderately high	policy	fiduciary	coop/noncoop
Town meeting (direct democracy)	up to a few hundred	up to 7 ± 2	between face to face and aggregate; moderately high	policy	act for self	coop/noncoop
Mass vote	few hundred to half a billion	up to 7 ± 2	mass and anonymous; low	people	act for self	noncoop behavioral
Referenda	few hundred to half a billion	up to 7 ± 2	mass and anonymous; low	policy	act for self	noncoop behavioral

a. Form of communication among voters; level of individual knowledge.
b. coop = cooperative; noncoop = noncooperative.

but when it does, frequently most of them are pro forma items for which the formal approval by vote is a foregone conclusion. In a meeting that lasts even ten hours, it is unlikely that more than a handful of items can be dealt with. In both committees and legislative assemblies most of the work of data gathering, planning, bargaining, and negotiation is done outside the formal meeting.

The fourth column contains a brief description of communication and knowledge conditions. In most committees, whether political, bureaucratic, or business, members tend to know each other quite well. They talk to each other directly both in and out of meetings, and they usually know each others' preferences and positions on most items. In legislative assemblies size soon mitigates against deep personal contact and general individual knowledge. At best, groups form who know each other well. Otherwise knowledge and communication must be judged on an aggregate basis. In town meetings, as their size increases, more or less the same conditions apply. Mass voting for political candidates or in referenda involves little direct communication between individuals in significant numbers. Communication methods are mass and anonymous. Circulars are addressed "to the householder" (even if modern computerized addressing can personalize the anonymity by adding a name and imitating the handwriting of a candidate).

The fifth column (no pun intended!) notes that committees for the most part vote on policy or recommend policy to another body. On occasion they vote to elect new members. Legislative assemblies deal for the most part in policy but also elect committees. Town meetings deal with policy. With the exception of policy referenda most mass voting is for the election of fiduciaries.

The sixth column indicates that committees and legislative assemblies are almost always composed of fiduciaries acting on the behalf of others. Town meetings, mass votes, and referenda have principals as voters. The last column indicates the type of game (or other) model that seems most reasonable for the given voting situation.

20.4 The Role of Government

The models discussed above mark an important step toward enlarging the scope of microeconomic theorizing by directly accounting for voting and taxes within a general-equilibrium description of the economy. This first step is extremely parsimonious. No new actors enter except for a shadow government introduced more or less at the same level of modeling as the profit-maximizing firm. A glance at any nation-state suggests that legal persons and institutions such as governments, political parties, and bureaucracies play central roles in the politicoeconomic process. Taxation, subsidies, and public goods and services are determined or supplied by governments and their bureaus. The power of the voter is at best indirect.

The next step in the modeling requires the explicit introduction of government, political parties, and bureaucracy either as players or at least as clearly specified constraints on the game. Here we shall confine our attention to the explicit introduction of government.

20.4.1 The government as the only strategic player
"Quis custodiet ipsos custodes?"

We begin with a radically centralist, utopian, and paternalistic government. Let us suppose that it knows everyone's preferences, can plan and compute whatever is necessary, and has only the best interests of the populace in mind. For an economy with production and exchange but no public goods, a central planning board simply calculates, fixes, and announces all prices. This is essentially an interpretation of the original Arrow–Debreu (1954) proof of the existence of an efficient price system when government is introduced as a player or at least as an explicit device announcing prices and minimizing a loss function.

We can extend the scope of government to include lump-sum transfers. Samuelson's early work showed that if there are no restrictions on governmental powers to tax, subsidize, or expropriate, then any point on the Pareto-optimal surface of the feasible set can be attained by the use of taxes and prices. Mantel (1975) and Greenberg (1975), as noted above, introduced an outside government to tax and provide public goods.

20.4.2 The government as a strategic player or a mechanism
Foley (1967, 1970b) used a government that offers a tax and subsidy bill together with a proposed package of public goods. The citizens then vote on this package, with the understanding that it will be rejected if a Pareto-improving set of taxes, subsidies, and public-goods production can be found at the given prices. Otherwise it is accepted.

It is not clear from the context if the government is considered an active player whose goals are the welfare of the citizens or whether it is a mechanism or part of the rules of the game. In particular, no indication is given as to how the government selects the proposal presented to the

Table 20.2
An agenda problem

Voter	Proposal		
	1	2	3
A	30	20	10
B	10	30	20
C*	20	10	30

*Chairman.
Entries are preference weightings.

public. We would suggest that the genesis of programs, the agenda problem, and the presentation of plans can frequently be key sources of technical difficulty and political power.[16]

20.4.3 The selection of programs and the agenda problem

Part of the work of a politician, administrator, committee chairman, or anyone else in a position of responsibility is to formulate and propose programs. Key committees frequently wield a power far greater than their formal position would indicate. A chairman with only a tie-breaking vote may appear to be no more powerful (at best) than a committee member with a vote. Yet the reverse is usually true. The selection of the agenda and the order in which business is taken up appears to be of considerable import.

A simple illustration is provided by a three-person committee considering three proposals only one of which can be accepted. Suppose that they must be considered one at a time and accepted or rejected. The preferences of A, B, and C for proposals 1, 2, and 3 are shown in table 20.2. We consider the game played noncooperatively in extensive form. The chairman selects the order of vote as 3, 1, 2. Figure 20.3 shows the extensive form, with P_{123} indicating that all three act on the proposal at hand.

Each branch in figure 20.3 combines the four possible ways in which a proposal can be voted in or out. By backward induction, if the third stage were reached, proposal 2 would be chosen, and at stage 2 proposal 1 would be chosen. Hence at stage 1 proposal 3 would be chosen over 1, and this gives rise to a perfect equilibrium.

The study of agenda selection is of both theoretical and experimental interest (see Plott and Levine, 1978) but will be pursued no further here.

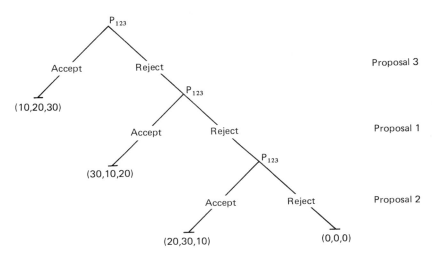

Figure 20.3
The Condorcet agenda.

20.5 On Logrolling or Vote Trading

20.5.1 Prices for votes

The literature of political science and economics contains a large number of discussions of *logrolling*, which is defined by Arrow (1963, p. 108) as "the possibility of trading votes on different issues" (see, e.g., Bentley, 1908; Bernholz, 1974; Black, 1958; Buchanan and Tullock, 1962; Coleman, 1966; Farquharson, 1969; Koehler, 1975; Riker and Brams, 1973; Tullock, 1970; Wilson, 1969a). We refer the reader to Ferejohn (1974) for a critical survey of this area.

Tullock (1070) illustrates the concept of logrolling with the classical example of harbor dredging. Representatives A, B, and C each want their harbor dredged at the expense of the general taxpayer, but they have much feebler feelings about seeing taxpayers' money diverted to the dredging of someone else's harbor. If the voting rule in this three-person committee is simple-majority voting and each representative votes for his preferences, there will be two votes against each proposal and all will fail. If for some reason representatives A and B feel strongly against the dredging of representative C's harbor, an agreement between them is rational (they prefer the agreement to the situation without agreement);

then representative C's harbor will not being dredged, while he (or his district) pays taxes to dredge the other two.

We may thus think of logrolling as the purchase by an individual of other people's votes on his favored issue, using as a money his own vote on different issues. *Equilibrium prices* are ones that clear this market in votes.

The way we address the question of the existence of an equilibrium price system for the trading in votes is to examine the possibility of formalizing the resultant game in cooperative form as a market game. To motivate the analysis we formalize a class of budget-allocation games. Starting with a description of the voting mechanism, we compute the characteristic function of the game it generates. We then show that, unless all voters have identical preferences, the game in characteristic form is not totally balanced. We conclude that budget-allocation games are not generally market games; thus we cannot find an exchange economy that gives rise to the characteristic function of a budget-allocation game. In other words, this class of games does not contain an underlying structure describable in terms of economic trade.

Two caveats are in order before we start the formal analysis and proof of the claims. The negative conclusion reached here allows us to omit the discussion of two items. First, even if we were able to interpret the votes as the commodities of a trading economy, they still remain *indivisible* (one cannot sell 3/4 of a vote on a bill), which makes the quest for a price system arduous. Second, even if a budget allocation in characteristic form turned out to be totally balanced, it is far from obvious what the price mechanism would be.

20.5.2 Budget-allocation games

For purposes of exposition we begin with a simple version of the side-payment game. Consider n individuals with distinct utility functions and m bills or items of appropriation to be voted on. We assume that individual i places a value u_j^i on item j and that his values are additive if several bills are accepted by the committee. Item j has a total cost c_j, and we also assume that there is an upper limit to spending: Not more than some bound B can be spent on all appropriations.

Let W be the set of successful bills. Then

$$\sum_{j \in W} c_j \leq B. \tag{20.10}$$

In the side-payment games considered here we may assume that the costs are measured in a money that can be treated as a linear utility. Thus the net worth to i of having bill j pass is given by the number u^i_j.

We assume that all bills are to be voted on in sequence until the upper bound on appropriations is reached. All individuals are completely informed, and the game can be played cooperatively.

An arbitrary voting rule is required to pass any bill. The voters are not required to spend all appropriations. If they wished, they could spend nothing.

The mechanism described above is sufficient to generate the characteristic functions of this set of games. It is easy to see that the simple-majority games form a special subset of these games. In general, the calculation of the characteristic function for a game of any size will be a large, tedious combinatoric problem. Here, however, we consider the properties of the core of this whole class of games without necessarily calculating the characteristic functions explicitly. This examination will enable us to consider when an economic market for votes exists and when it does not.

20.5.3 Simple budget-allocation games

At this point we need a more formal and general definition of the class of games under study. We define a *simple budget-allocation game* as a triple $(N, \mathcal{W}, U)$, where $(N, \mathcal{W})$ is a *proper simple game* and where the *utility matrix* U gives the preferences of the players (or voters) of N over a finite set of outcomes.

Following Shapley (1962), we define a simple game as a pair $(N, \mathcal{W})$, where $\mathcal{W}$ is a set of subsets of N called the set of "winning" coalitions. We can define the set of "losing" coalitions $\mathcal{L}$ by

$$\mathcal{L} = N - \mathcal{W}. \tag{20.11}$$

A simple game is proper if the complement in N of every winning coalition is losing. *Blocking coalitions* are the losing coalitions whose complement in N is also losing.[17] Defining $\mathcal{W}^+$ as the set of supersets of the elements of $\mathcal{W}$, the collection $\mathcal{W}$ satisfies

$$\mathcal{W} = \mathcal{W}^+, \tag{20.12}$$

$$\mathcal{W} \neq \varnothing, N. \tag{20.13}$$

Condition (20.12) asserts that any superset of a winning coalition is winning, while (20.13) eliminates the trivial cases in which all coalitions are winning or none is. We assume further that all coalitions of size $n-1$ are winning, or more formally that

$N - \{i\} \in \mathcal{W}$ for all $i \in N$.   (20.14)

A player i violating this assumption is called a *veto player*.

The players are presented with a finite set $P = \{1, 2, \ldots, p\}$ of *projects* (or outcomes), out of which a single one must be selected.[18] A project is selected as soon as there is a winning coalition in favor of it. To define the game completely we specify that if no winning coalition is formed, project 1 is selected. This is really a "dummy" project needed to reveal the voters' preferences for the status quo in which none of the "real" projects, labeled 2–p, is selected. The preferences of the players are, as already mentioned, given by the utility matrix $U = \{u_j^i : i \in N, j \in P\}$, where u_j^i is a real number representing the utility of player i for project j.

The question we want to answer is, When does there exist an underlying economic market in which voters trade votes at equilibrium prices? Given the work of Shapley and Shubik (1969a, 1976) for the side-payment case and of Billera (1974) and Billera and Bixby (1973, 1974) for the no-side-payment case, this question can be reformulated as, When are our simple budget-allocation games totally balanced?

20.5.4 The side-payment game
The characteristic function v of a simple budget-allocation game $(N, \mathcal{W}, U)$ can be defined in the following way:

$$v(S) = \begin{cases} \max\limits_{j \in P} u_j(S) & \text{for } S \in \mathcal{W}, \\ u_1(S) & \text{for } S \in \mathcal{L}, \ N - S \in \mathcal{L}, \\ \min\limits_{j \in P} u_j(S) & \text{for } S \in \mathcal{L}, \ N - S \in \mathcal{W}. \end{cases}$$ (20.15)

Here $u_j(S) = \sum_{i \in S} u_j^i$. This definition indicates that a winning coalition seeks to maximize its joint value, while a blocking coalition can impose the status quo. Losing coalitions that are not blocking can ensure themselves only the worst outcome.

We first establish that in the absence of veto players, any payoff vector in the core must coincide with an outcome. We then derive a necessary condition for the game to have a core.

THEOREM 20.1.   *A simple budget-allocation game without veto players has at most a one-point core coinciding with one of the outcomes.*

Proof.   If the payoff vector x belongs to the core, then $x(N) = u_k(N)$ for some project k. If x is not identical to some project in P, we can find two players i and h with $x^i > u_k^i$ and $x^h < u_k^h$. Hence it follows, since $N - \{i\} \in \mathcal{W}$, that

$$x(N - \{i\}) < u_k(N - \{i\}) \le v(N - \{i\}), \tag{20.16}$$

contradicting the assumption that x belongs to the core. ∎

Assume now that the one-point core is given by outcome k. If a winning coalition S strictly prefers an outcome j different from k, we have

$$u_k(S) < u_j(S) \le v(S), \tag{20.17}$$

contradicting the assertion that the payoff vector $u_k = \{u_k^i : i \in N\}$ is in the core. Similarly, if a blocking coalition S can do better for itself by imposing the status quo, then the core must also be empty. We summarize both facts in the following theorem.

THEOREM 20.2.   *For a simple budget-allocation game* $(N, \mathcal{W}, U)$ *with blocking coalitions* $\mathcal{B}$, *the existence of a core requires the existence of a project* k *such that*

$$u_k(S) = \max_{j \in P} u_j(S) \quad \text{for all } S \in \mathcal{W}, \tag{20.18}$$

$$u_k(S) \ge u_1(S) \quad \text{for all } S \in \mathcal{B}. \tag{20.19}$$

If there is a project k satisfying conditions (20.18) and (20.19), one can immediately write that $v(T) = u_k(T)$ if $T \in \mathcal{W}$ and $v(T) \le u_1(T)$ otherwise. Hence, if R is a winning coalition,

$$v(R) = u_k(R) \tag{20.20}$$

and

$$v(T) \le u_k(T) \quad \text{for all } T \subset R. \tag{20.21}$$

If R is a blocking coalition, any subset T of R is either blocking or losing, so that (20.20) and (20.21) hold with k replaced by 1. If R is losing without being blocking, then by the definition of $v(R)$, $v(R) = u_j(R)$ for some $j \in P$, and any subset T of R satisfies $v(T) \le u_j(T)$. So we have shown that in this case, too, (20.20) and (20.21) are satisfied with j instead of k.

The above discussion has shown that, given any subgame (R, v), there is a project k satisfying (20.20) and (20.21). Considering any nonnegative vector of weights $f \in \Gamma$ associated with a balanced collection τ of subsets of R, we are now in a position to establish that

$$\sum_{T \in \tau} f_T v(T) \le \sum_{T \in \tau} f_T u_k(T) = \sum_{i \in R} u_k^i \left(\sum_{T \in \tau_i} f_T \right) = u_k(R) = v(R). \tag{20.22}$$

Hence any subgame (R, v) is balanced, and our simple budget-allocation game is totally balanced.

THEOREM 20.3. *A simple budget-allocation game without veto players is totally balanced if and only if there is a project preferred by all winning coalitions and preferred over the status quo by all blocking coalitions.*[19]

The analysis of budget-allocation games with side payments may be extended to games without side payments. The results are substantially the same (see Shubik and Van der Heyden, 1978).

We assumed here (as did Wilson, 1969a) that preferences over the bills are additive. More generally, we could have introduced valuations over every combination of goods. This essentially negative result would still hold.

20.5.5 Logrolling as an ongoing process
A glance at the actual political process in any legislature is enough to persuade most individuals that vote trading is a normal part of the political quid pro quo. But vote trading does not imply a market price for votes in the same sense as there is a price for goods in a mass-market economy.

It is possible that the exchange rates for votes are characterized by a solution concept other than the core—for example, the value or the Aumann–Maschler bargaining set (Aumann and Maschler, 1964; see also Schofield, 1980). It is also possible that the intuitive idea of vote trading can be analyzed adequately only by a model in extensive form, directed toward the analysis of process, rather than by one cast in an essentially static strategic form.

Our major purpose here is to examine in a rather literal manner the possibility of a connection between static economic markets and a market for votes. Our essentially negative conclusion is that the highly attractive analogy between economic markets and the trading of votes in a legislature almost never holds true, at least not in a direct, simple, static form. The phenomenon of vote trading is real, but trade, especially among indivisible objects, can rarely be achieved with much generality by a price system.

The political system in its smooth functioning usually implies a continuity in time and the possibility of a future settling of accounts. None of these measures is picked up by the precise but limited model presented here.

20.5.6 On budgets and ballots
The breezy popular analogies between voting and markets much extolled in simple expositions ("your budget is your economic ballot") are grossly misleading. The simple comparison between "spending" one's vote and one's money does not survive scrutiny. Not only do primarily economic

processes differ from political processes in the structure of the relevant preferences and values, but in general the knowledge and information conditions also differ substantially. Furthermore, the analogy between representative government and the corporation wears thin. The economic mechanisms appear to be designed to promote efficient satisfaction of reasonably well-defined preferences, whereas the political processes appear in general not only not to be truth-revealing but, if anything, to be truth-evolving—they are designed to be run by fiduciaries who seek to interpret and evolve a viable consensus.

Notes to chapter 20

1. Even at this level of abstraction with no-side-payment games, a symmetric game may have several nonsymmetric solutions. Hence, as noted by Harsanyi, a further argument must be given in order to select a unique outcome. Furthermore, for full symmetry with a veil of ignorance, the uninformed players must have the same risk aversion.

2. Where these rules come from and how laws are formed are basic questions in political science and philosophy.

3. As a matter of fact, a control group can still discriminate against a minority by hiding profits and removing a disproportionate share of the gain through inflated salaries, expenses, and perquisites. There is a special section of the Tax Code to cover nonmonetary dividends.

4. For further discussion of this point see Williamson (1975), Lindblom (1977), and Shubik (1970c).

5. In Roman times war booty was sold by auction (Talamanca, 1954); in the United States conscription calls have been done by lottery.

6. "The only property required of the preference relation is that it be a subset of some irreflexive relation with convex upper contour sets" (Mantel, 1975, p. 189).

7. For a discussion of acyclicity see *GTSS*, appendix A.

8. Richter (1975) and, somewhat more generally, Greenberg (1977) considered local public goods. Assuming K exogenous jurisdictions, Greenberg developed conditions that enabled him to prove the existence of a Pareto-optimal public competitive equilibrium for a broad class of tax schemes.

9. The game V is binary superadditive relative to N if for any two disjoint coalitions (S_1, S_2), two tax rates (t_1, t_2), and two individuals $(i \in S_1, j \in S_2)$, there is a tax rate t such that

$$\varphi^i(t_1, S_1) \leq \varphi^i(t_1, N) \quad \text{and} \quad \varphi^i(t_2, S_2) \leq \varphi^i(t_1, N),$$

where if $u^i(x_1, y)$ is the original utility function of i and $y = f(x)$ is the production function for the public good, then

$$\varphi^i(t,S) = u^i\left((1-t)w^i, f\left(t\sum_{j\in S} w^j\right)\right).$$

10. Related work by Klevorick and Kramer (1973) on voting and the control of pollution contains an interesting discussion of the *Genossenschaften* of the Ruhr district of West Germany. Given a region with households and firms requiring different levels of water purity, how should one control pollution along a river basin? The *Genossenschaften* have the power to set water-quality standards and effluent charges. Their general assemblies have representatives from firms, local communities, and the waterworks. The votes are proportional to the members' "contributions," that is, their charges or taxes.

11. Ito and Kaneko (1981) observe that if we use the liability rule suggested by Coase (1960), under which a polluting firm must obtain a license and pay compensation if it pollutes above a certain level and those wishing still lower levels of pollution must compensate the firm, we can treat the externality as a public good and apply Kaneko's ratio-equilibria analysis.

12. In the first paper x was defined as an allocation; in the second it was a configuration with a slightly different definition.

13. This assumption suggests that an individual's entitlement will not be reduced below his pretax initial endowment; that is, confiscation is not possible. It should be further noted that Kaneko employed the effectiveness form of Rosenthal (1972) in which the effective sets of coalitions are specified for each current proposal.

14. A limited study of taxes with different risk-aversion levels is made for a one-good economy (the more risk-averse the individual is, the higher his taxes) and the possibility of a positive relation between wealth and votes. The wealthier an individual, the more political "clout" he may have. This gives the expected results for one good.

15. For a discussion of taxation from an earlier (fourteenth-century) perspective see Ibn Khaldun (1958, chapter III.36). The burden of taxation for war was noted around 500 B.C. by Sun Tzu (1944).

16. Although much of its argument is dangerously simplistic in praising the virtues of a mystical market and profit-oriented system, the small book on bureaucracy by von Mises (1944) presents a useful, if extreme, characterization of the dangers of statism and the belief that in human affairs the great government and bureaucracy in the sky will somehow take care of all mortals.

17. Sometimes blocking coalitions are defined as the coalitions whose complements in N are also losing.

18. This formulation includes the one given earlier. A project is then any affordable set of bills, with the empty set defining project 1.

19. We use the word "prefer" in its weakest sense: Someone is said to prefer project j over project k if he strictly prefers j over k or if he is indifferent between j and k.

21 Welfare and the Sociopolitical Control of the Economy

"The working of self-interest is generally beneficent, not because of some natural coincidence between the self-interest of each and the good of all, but because human institutions are arranged so as to compel self-interest to work in directions in which it will be beneficent."
Edward Cannan (1913)

21.1 Sociopolitical and Economic Public Decisions

21.1.1 Economics and the social sciences

Economics is at best a supporting actor on the stage of human life. Painters paint, generals fight, politicians scheme for power, and even economic theorists write, not to maximize some relatively bloodless set of economic efficiency criteria, but because of the many other imperatives that motivate human existence.

It is the basic theme of these volumes that part of developing an economic science involves separating out phenomena and understanding the limits as well as the possibilities of economic analysis. The economic analyst has a responsibility to question the assumptions, axioms, and models that are being taken as given in the analysis. Yet even the most hypercritical must stop at some point and accept some structure as a point of departure for his analysis.

When the economics of pure exchange is studied, we start with the axiom that individuals are, to a first-order approximation, rational, sufficiently intelligent, and perceptive, with well-defined preferences and socially accepted ownership claims; the description and analysis of exchange as an economic problem follows.

Given a description of a society specifying the strategic players, their rights to use resources, and their preferences, economic analysis can be used to investigate the problems of efficient (in the context given) production, allocation, and distribution of economic resources.

When is a resource an economic resource? There is a continuum of shadings, and the answer must therefore be taxonomic, pragmatic, and to some extent ad hoc, depending on the question at hand. Fungible chattels such as oranges, pencils, or bars of gold are easily labeled economic goods. Love, faith, scholarship, honor, or patriotism are not usually considered economic goods, although there are occasions when faith is sold for a mess of pottage or scholarship is applied for a price.

There are serious economic aspects to having children, just as there are considerable economic consequences to theft, murder, and other criminal activities. This suggests that economic analysis can be applied to some aspects of family formation and some aspects of criminal activity. But in multivariate systems one investigator's data are another's variables. If in certain contexts the explanatory power of a partial analysis linking family size to income appears to be good, this does not imply that economics alone provides the key to understanding family formation.

Given a society's sociopolitical rules, and the assumption that these rules change more slowly than does its economic activity, the economist can carry out investigations and even make limited predictions within the sociopolitical context. The first-order approximations will not provide for full feedback through time, which would require inclusion of changes in institutional structures caused by the intermix of social, political, economic, and other factors. But it should include as part of the description of the game, at the same level of abstraction as the economic sector, political parties, government, and bureaucracies.

Our first attempts at a parsimonious microdescription of these features may yield naive and somewhat unsatisfactory models. Yet I suspect that such a start will indicate the way to sort out basic phenomena and that this will facilitate collaboration and division of labor in the construction of a much-needed mathematical, institutional sociopolitical economy.

The progression in human wants, needs, desires, and aspirations is subtle and cannot be encompassed in economic theorizing alone. For most purposes a bar of chocolate is a clearly defined private good; a national gallery of art and national archives are physical public goods to which the measuring stick of money can be more or less usefully applied up to a point. When we start to consider public services such as justice or national defense, however, our measures become vague. It has been suggested that in a democratic society at least four freedoms are striven for:

1. Social freedom: There should be no superiors by fiat.

2. Psychological freedom: Desires should coincide with actions.

3. Political freedom: There should be no feeling of manipulation.

4. Economic freedom: There should be no great feeling of economic need.

These are not economic goods; nor are ideology, patriotism, and friendship. In society and in politics quid pro quo is invariably the rule, yet the bribing of a concentration-camp guard or the buying of friendship are only marginally economic acts. The existence of organized efficient markets implies exchange, but the existence of exchange tells us little about markets, the existence of prices, or the coin, be it gold, blood, power, or faith, in which accounts are settled.

It is my belief that the utilitarian or neoutilitarian basis that has provided much of the underpinnings for the development of political economy in the last two hundred years has created a surprisingly robust basis for both constructing and modifying useful theory and for helping us to understand the limits to a political economy based primarily upon a model of individual rational man.

The theory of games provides a natural next step in the explanation of how far one can go with the model of a political economy built up from the unit of the approximately rational individual. There are, of course, many grand sociological theories or historical vistas in which the theorist presents the state, the people, the civilization, or the philosopher-king as an entity apart from the individuals who compose the society. Such an approach is eschewed here.

Although I firmly believe that there is a need for distinct disciplines such as economics, political science, and sociology, I also believe that it may be of considerable value to explore the interfaces among them, especially in terms of (1) the perception and formulation of preference and values, (2) the nature of decision making, (3) the time scales involved, and (4) the relevance of numbers.

Starting, as we have here, with a more or less classical microeconomic view of preference, knowledge, and decision making, when we enlarge our scope of enquiry beyond private goods and mass markets, we are forced to do more than merely consider changes in certain physical properties of goods in a previously given context, such as the change from private to pure public goods. We must face up to the new conceptual problems posed by the nature of preference and value formation, the limits on information, knowledge, and perception, and the basic differences in decision-making mechanisms brought about by a complex inter-mix of transaction costs and social arrangements that are not necessarily of economic origin. In short, an institution-free theory must be modified or abandoned.

In table 21.1 a crude classification has been made of the items the individual buys, votes for, or has thrust upon him. Depending on the

Table 21.1
The substance of economic decisions

Program, product, or service	Preference or value formation	Decision making	Frequency of decision	Numbers and institutions
Frequently bought basic consumer goods	reasonably well defined	individual, utilitarian, modified by habit and custom	frequent (days, weeks, months)	consumer competition, producer competition, oligopoly, or state control
Consumer durables	moderately well defined with areas of ignorance	individual, utilitarian, modified by high information search and valuation costs	anywhere from annual to once every 10–15 years or longer	consumer competition, producer competition, oligopoly, or state control
Local public goods: tangibles	moderately well defined, modified face-to-face	town meeting	weekly, monthly, annual	small or middle-sized polity, cliques, and cronies
	poor to well defined, formed by pressure groups	referendum	annual, biennial	small to large polity, bureaucracy, and representatives
		delegated to elected representative	biennial	small to large polity, bureaucracy, and representatives
		delegated to appointed official	?	control by officials or by higher agency

Table 21.1 (continued)

Program, product, or service	Preference or value formation	Decision making	Frequency of decision	Numbers and institutions
Local public goods: intangibles (ordinances, rules of conduct, quality of services)	moderately well defined	incorporation proceedings, town meeting	weekly, monthly, annual	small or middle-sized polity
	poor to well defined, formed by pressure groups	initiative, petition, referendum	annual, biennial	any size polity
		delegated to elected representative	biennial	any size polity
		delegated to appointed official	?	any size polity
Externalities	injury poorly to well perceived, influenced by pressure groups, costs rarely understood except by experts	referendum, delegated to elected representative, legal process	annual, biennial, ongoing	any size polity, organized industrial or other opposition, bureaucracy
National public goods (health, education, justice, foreign policy)	habit, ideology, heavily noneconomic in some dimensions, socioeconomic in others, political parties, other pressure groups	delegated to elected representative	two, four, or six years	mass polity, national legistature, or dictator; pressure groups include bureaucracy, lawyers, armed forces, churches, business, technocrats, press, labor, intellectuals

complexity and frequency of an item and his familiarity with it, the
individual has more or less well-formed preferences and values. For
example, microwave radiation is an externality scarcely understood by a
majority of the individuals affected by it. The decision making for
frequently bought basic consumer goods may be somewhat influenced
by habit and advertising, but much of it can be explained by a utilitarian
model.

Under the heading "numbers and institutions" we indicate the number
and types of actors engaged in the decision making. The heading "program, product, or service" indicates the item being ultimately supplied.
This method of decision making may be direct or representative. Thus,
for example, the control of externalities may take place by referendum,
by the actions of elected representative, or by law suits.

For items such as local public goods there is a sufficient variety in the
decision-making mechanism that four are noted separately.

21.1.2 On parsimonious modeling

"What is the answer?"
You can do better than that Gertrude.
"Well, then, what is the question?"
    Probably apocryphal attribution of Gertrude Stein's last words

These last two chapters are both a summary and an introduction. Section
22.5 offers a summary of results on a sequence of progressively more
complicated problems in political economy. In the earlier parts of this
chapter an attempt is made to break out of the mold that characterizes
much of the work in microeconomic theory. In this attempt it is important
to decide early on the number of new phenomena and the level of detail
we wish to add. There is a voluminous literature on planning, the delivery
of social services, specific public goods, contracting, incentive systems,
city government, accounting, auditing, and many other topics of direct
importance to any effort to answer questions about specific problems or
programs. Some references are made here to these studies. But because
the basic question we deal with is different, we shall not describe or
develop this work, except where it is necessary for the construction of
politicoeconomic models in a parsimoniously described institutional
setting.

Our question is, How can we construct at a high level of abstraction
a model that blends economic, political, and bureaucratic process in such
a way that we can compare and contrast the relative importance of the

economic, bureaucratic, and political features in the delivery of public goods?

Realism in modeling is a chimera. The abstraction is related to the question to be answered. It is my contention, argued in these two volumes, that the methods of the theory of games provide a flexible means for modeling that can simultaneously produce more institutionally oriented and mathematically precise models than most of current political economy.

The extension of mathematical methods in the behavioral sciences depends on a blend of substantive understanding and the use of an adequate methodology. The addition of political, sociological, administrative, and bureaucratic factors calls for insight and skills beyond those of the economist alone. In these remaining chapters we construct a highly oversimplified model whose purpose is to suggest that even a small admixture to an economic structure is of use in asking and answering basic questions concerning the representative political systems and fiduciary-controlled economic systems that dominate modern mass societies.

21.1.3 Perception, perference mechanisms, and social choice

It has been suggested that one should never blame the excesses of members of a religion on its founder. And it is with this in mind that we consider the important contribution of Arrow to the study of social choice before constructing a mixed politicoeconomic model of modern society.

The modeling conditions underlying the Arrow theorem on the impossibility of finding a social-welfare function (SWF) that satisfies a certain set of axioms are as follows. There is a finite, fixed set of individuals and a given finite set of outcomes, alternatives, or social states of the system or prospects. As Black (1969) has noted, one interpretation is that the community as a whole acts as a single committee voting directly.

Making only a few weak assumptions about preferences and choice, Arrow showed that the aggregation of individual preferences into a social preference cannot be solved in the sense that all five of the conditions noted below are satisfied. This is an important proposition in logic whose relevance to political economy depends on the validity and relevance of the assumptions made.

Before questioning the Arrow model, because it has been of such importance in the recent literature of social choice, we review the assumptions and proof, following the clear and concise exposition of Vickrey (1960), whose version differs slightly from that of Arrow. The five assumptions are:

1. Unanimity: If an individual's preference is unopposed by any contrary preference of any other individual, this preference must be preserved in the resulting social ordering.

2. Nondictatorship: No individual can hold a position such that whenever he expresses a preference between any two alternative and all other individuals express the opposite preference, his preference is always preferred in the social ordering.

3. Transitivity: The social ranking given by the SWF is in each case a consistent ordering of all feasible alternatives.

4. Range: There is some "universal" alternative u such that, for every pair of other alternatives x and y and for every individual, each of the six possible strict orderings of u, x, and y is contained in some ranking of all alternatives that is admissible for the individual.

5. Independence: The social choice between any two alternatives is not affected by the removal or addition of other alternatives to the field of feasible alternatives under consideration.

Proof. A set of individuals D is defined to be *decisive* for x against y in the context of a given SWF if, when all in D prefer x over y and all in $\bar{D}$ prefer y over x, the SWF yields a social preference of x over y.

   Let D be decisive for x against y. Then by assumption 4 there exists some ranking in which x, y, and u are ranked $xPyPu$ and likewise another admissible ranking in which $yPuPx$. The SWF must be defined in such a way that all of D have a preference ranking $xPyPu$ and all of $\bar{D}$ have $yPuPx$. But because D is decisive for x against y, the SWF yields a social ranking with x preferred to y. By unanimity y is preferred to u; hence by transitivity x is preferred to u. But only members of D have xPu; for $\bar{D}$, uPx. By assumption 5 the preference of x over u must persist regardless of changes in the ranking of y; thus D is decisive for x against u.

   A repetition of the argument with D in support of $zPxPu$ and $\bar{D}$ in support of $uPzPx$ shows that D is decisive for z against u. Furthermore, D in support of $zPuPw$ and $\bar{D}$ in support of $uPwPz$ shows that D is decisive for z against w.

   Let D contain two or more individuals and let A be a proper subset of D. Define $B = D - A$. Some decisive set D must exist by assumption 1. Suppose members of A have a preference ranking $xPyPu$, B have $yPuPx$, and $\bar{D}$ have $uPxPy$. Because A and B have yPu and together are decisive, while $\bar{D}$ has uPy, the SWF must put y above u. If it also selects y above x, then B must be decisive. If, however, x is not below y, then by transitivity x must be above u and A must be decisive for x against u. In either instance the decisive set D can be split in two. A repetition of this argument must lead to requiring a one-person decisive set, or a dictator. ∎

In *GTSS*, chapter 5, it was noted that the Arrow theorem may be sensitive to parametric variations. Here the commentary is of a somewhat different form. How reasonable is the Arrow model, and how relevant are the results to the problems of political economy?

Among the explicit or implicit assumptions made in the various formulations of the Arrow model of social choice are the following:

1. The set of social states is finite and well defined.

2. The set of social states is known, perceived, and comprehended by all.

3. Each individual has a complete preference ordering on all states.

4. Information conditions are implicitly symmetric, and strategic choice is not relevant.[1]

5. The mechanism of choice is cost-free.[2]

6. The aggregation of choice is direct.

7. The set of individuals is finite and fixed.

8. Probability mixes over social states are not considered.

9. Initial conditions or prior claims are implicitly taken into account in the social states.

10. All choice making is implicitly error-free.

11. Abstention from the vote is irrational or impossible.

If all of these conditions are met, then unanimity, nondictatorship, transitivity, and range appear to me to be reasonable normative properties. Independence is regarded by some as being reasonable, but not by all.

What little evidence there is from psychology indicates that virtually every one of these assumptions is counterfactual. It could be argued, however, that some are reasonable approximations to the way individuals perceive and behave, whereas others are not. The reader is encouraged to consider the plausibility of each assumption and to contemplate the possibility that there may be other important implicit assumptions not included in this list. We shall not attempt an exhaustive exegesis of each assumption, but we shall offer some observations concerning choice making and the objects of choice. Much of consumer choice involves selection among known, comprehended items. Although it may be reasonable to consider selection among collections of goods without uncertainty, the limitations on our perceptions and knowledge convert the purchase of an item as prosaic as an automobile or a basket of strawberries into a lottery in which the car may be a lemon and the berries overripe.

When we consider political choice, however, the very essence of the choices is a selection from a limited set of broadly defined lotteries. One votes mainly for promises and people, not for products. The candidate of one's choice is not the equivalent of a guaranteed vector of well-defined public goods, taxes, and subsidies. He is a fiduciary with a track record, a reputation, and a personal and party program that he presents as his promise to the electorate. The promise is not a guarantee. The voter knows that at best, in the course of time, features that were unclear in the program may be resolved in a way that he finds satisfactory.

The voter's political choice is not a search among hundreds of consumer items, but a selection involving at most three or four perceived programs and candidates, a memory of three or four previously offered programs and candidates, and a handful of broadly defined ideals.

The current concern in the social sciences with the formation of subjective probabilities is well placed. The key question is, How do we arrive at an overall assessment of trust in the honesty and competence of a representative? How do we assess the plausibility of a political promise? If we accept the observation that political choice is essentially choice among lotteries and that choice making is smooth with respect to changes in such subjective probabilities, then we may accept the existence of a utility function and avoid the Arrow paradox.

In terms of an approximation to human political choice and perception, the proposition that individuals have a complete preference ordering over an arbitrarily large set of social outcomes is less plausible than the proposition that they are capable of evaluating the worth of a few lotteries over a small set of fuzzily defined programs.

The Arrow result was a brilliant application of a new and rigorous methodology to political science. It has virtually founded a modern approach to certain problems in group choice theory. Yet in my opinion its very power has drawn attention away from the characteristics of sociopolitical choice and its context. Representative government with the election of fiduciaries is a major feature of political choice. Voting for president is a form of social choice different from deciding to murder one's neighbor, yet there is scarcely enough structure on the set of social states to distinguish sociopolitical choice from a general theory of choice.

The sensitivity of results with formal models to slight changes in the specification of assumptions demands an appreciation of modeling and context, not logic alone.

21.2 Information and the Cost of Decisions

"The owl was the wisest of animals. A centipede with 99 sore feet came to him seeking advice. 'Walk for two weeks one inch above the ground; the air under your feet and the lack of pressure will cure you,' said the owl. 'How am I to do that?' asked the centipede. 'I have solved your conceptual problem, do not bother me with trivia concerning implementation,' replied the owl."

This and the next two sections are devoted to a few comments on the possible basis for joining together a preinstitutional microeconomics and political science. We are a long way from developing a satisfactory dynamics. The link between statics and dynamics and between preinstitutional and an abstract but nevertheless institutional description is the strategic or extensive form of a game. Both of these forms require a full and careful specification of the rules of the game. But the rules themselves may be viewed as an institutional description.

Without attempting to offer a grand dynamics of economic, political, or social behavior, we shall argue here that even a casual empiricism concerning the accuracy of measurement, the cost of information, administration, and control, and the problems of auditing provides enough structure to suggest important qualifications to any form of utopian theorizing.

21.2.1 Accounting, auditing, and control
Commissar: "How much is two plus two?"
Accountant (cautiously): "How much do you need them to be?"
    Old Soviet story

Accounting, auditing, and control are simultaneously the stepchildren of economic theory and the administrative recording instruments that determine the nature of the biases in the economic reporting system.

The general biases recorded in documents such as *Generally Accepted Accounting Principles* reflect a conservative and risk-averse attitude sensitive to modification by both custom and law. They also provide an outline of rules for an important institutional and bureaucratic set of games. These involve tax avoidance, quota compliance, norm fulfillment, stategic bankruptcy, merger and reorganization, loan rescheduling, and a host of other intricate maneuvers that employ the highest of talent among businessmen, commissars, other bureaucrats, lawyers, accountants, and legislators.

The ability to pad expense accounts, charge off investments, manipulate profits reports, and move around the allocation of overheads provides strategic freedom in a complex sociopoliticoeconomic environment. The complexity of the legal and accounting system enables politicians, bureaucrats, businessmen, and other members of the elite simultaneously to pay lip service to simplistic populism, to pass blanket laws, and to take care of their own.

The frequent gaps of up to several hundred percent in one direction or the other between stock-market valuations and declared asset values indicate the magnitude of the leeway in the economic accounting system and the stickiness of institutional adjustment.

I suggest neither a devil theory nor a Panglossian view of tax laws and accounting. The imputation problems are intrinsically hard, but with the difficulties come opportunities. Side payments can be made, and accommodations can be reached which would not be feasible or politic in a simpler structure. If one postulates a sometimes less than rational public, the complexity may provide a damping mechanism in what would otherwise be a system susceptible to great instability.

21.2.2 On public finance

Another stepchild of modern economic theory is public finance, which brings together a peculiar blend of ordinary microeconomic theory, administration, bureaucracy, welfare economics, and a theory of the state. Excellent summaries of both the topic and its historical roots have been provided by Musgrave and Peacock (1958), Musgrave (1959), and Musgrave and Musgrave (1973).

From the viewpoint of both economics and political science, public finance, with much of its roots in the German *Staatswirtschaft*, is an unsatisfactory topic. The easy way to give it high intellectual status and to make it teachable to the budding *staatsbeamte*, *apparachnik*, functionary, and other-people's budgeteer is to invent an all-wise state that knows what is good for its populace and is run by selfless, self-effacing public servants whose only goal is to promote the exogenously given social-welfare function.

If one chooses not to invent the utopian state and its civil servants, one must consider politics and mechanisms for the expression of societal goals. A brief summary of budget determination through voting is given in chapter 6 of Musgrave (1959), and Musgrave and Musgrave (1973) include a chapter on "fiscal politics" wherein several pages are devoted to noting that there are problems in reconciling public finance with representative government. Reference is made to Downs (1957) and Schumpeter (1950), but beyond a comment on vote maximization, no theoretical constructions or practical observations are supplied. (Chapter 22 of the present work is directly addressed to this problem.)

Musgrave suggests three objectives for the public household. He considers (1) allocations of resources for production; (2) adjustments in the distribution of income and wealth for social policy; and (3) economic stabilization for social policy. The concept of *merit wants* including items such as subsidized low-cost housing and free education is introduced in an essentially ad hoc way. No source for these wants is offered. A stabilization policy with full employment and price-level stability is specified as a desideratum.

Given governmental goals, public finance involves the search for efficient implementation. The array of subproblems includes public production and procurement and the choice between two approaches to the satisfaction of public wants. In the *benefit approach* the relation between the taxpayer and government is one of quid pro quo, with the emphasis on exchange; this leads naturally to ideas such as the Lindahl equilibrium noted in chapter 19. The *ability-to-pay approach* separates contributions from benefits received. Strategically there also is a third approach, related to the second, which we could call the *ability-to-avoid-payment approach*. This last approach recognizes the political, social, bureaucratic, and economic forces available to all groups in their efforts to enforce a tax structure favoring themselves. It also recognizes the safe havens—created by measurement difficulties, structural complexity, and enforcement costs—that enable tax or task avoidance to be achieved by many of the target groups.

The ability-to-pay approach to taxation cannot be justified by economic individualism alone. However, as soon as we recognize that joint goods are chosen by political or social means, even though taxation might be viewed as the price paid for services rendered by the state, voting without minority protection tends to yield an ability-to-pay outcome.

Questions concerning the concept of equal sacrifice and other measures of equality, definitions of income, wealth, and the tax-paying unit, and arguments concerning the relative merits of different types of taxes all belong to the domain of public finance. So do classical economic problems concerning subsidies for decreasing-cost industries, neutrality of taxation, and avoidance of excess burden (the principle that taxes should place no more burden on the group taxed than is necessary to raise the required amount). A final domain of concern for public finance is the public debt. The question of debt versus tax financing may both influence the proportions of public and private investment and raise questions concerning intergenerational equity.

21.2.3 Administration and bureaucracy
"When one wants something done by a bureaucracy, present it in such a way that it is more inconvenient for them not to do it than to do it."
The Law of Administrative Inconvenience

The stress on individual utility, economic choice, and voting draws attention away from the institutional, fiduciary, and strategic structure of most decision making in a modern society. In the groups, firms, bureaus, and other multiperson institutional structures that shape and carry the processes of society, the problems of executive decision making involve not merely direct choice to one's own account among perceived fixed alternatives but (1) goal selection for the organization, (2) environment setting and delegation of responsibilities to subordinates, (3) responsibility taking for activities resulting from delegation, and (4) accountability to those for whom the executive acts as fiduciary.

In government, industry, and other institutions the distances between perceived desire and decision, between decision and implementation, and between outcome and intended outcome are often great. The economist attempting to sketch a general theory of economic behavior may be tempted to simplify away institutions, administration, and bureaucracy under a general catchall of transactions costs. For some purposes this may be reasonable, but for others the key to the understanding of the strategic realities of political economy lies in portraying the rules of the game and the costs imposed by process.

In considering public administrators, Kaufman (1968) suggested that their directive to implement policy decisions can be usefully divided into three roles: administrative legislation, administrative adjudication, and administrators as interest groups. As legislators they hold hearings, much in the way a legislative body does; as adjudicators they rule on appeals and complaints concerning administrative action; and as interest groups they draft, propose, and promote legislation deemed valuable to their agency. The tenure of senior administrators is generally longer than that of the politicians; and whether they be Chinese administrators for Kublai Khan, the *Kuprili* of the Ottomans, civil servants of the British Raj in Victorian India, the *staatsbeamter* of Prussian Germany, or federal employees of the New Deal, they all have professionalism and a large body of specialized knowledge in common. This knowledge includes "know-who" as well as know-how.

Kaufman noted three approaches to the study of administration, broadly described as engineering (I suggest engineering-economic), political analysis, and sociological. The first is basically concerned with the efficiency of the team. The second is more congenial to a game-theoretic view that recognizes the explicit strategic role of administrators in the control of the execution of policy. The sociological approach is more concerned with the description of organizational behavior. The approach initiated by Simon (1947) in his work on administrative behavior has led to an intermix of mathematical methods and simulation techniques portraying limited rationality.

Max Weber (1947) offered as the first formal definition of bureaucracy a system of administration organized hierarchically and staffed by full-time paid professionals with formalized positions, procedures, and promotions. He noted the following aspects of the individual officials:

1. They are personally free and subject to authority only with respect to their impersonal official obligations.

2. They are organized in a clearly defined hierarchy of offices.

3. Each office has a clearly defined sphere of competence in the legal sense.

4. The office is filled by a free contractual relationship. Thus, in principle there is free selection.

5. Candidates are selected on the basis of technical qualifications. In the most rational case this is tested by examination or guaranteed by diplomas certifying technical training or both. They are *appointed*, not elected.

6. They are remunerated by fixed salaries in money, for the most part with a right to pensions. Only under certain circumstances does the employing authority, especially in private organizations, have a right to terminate the appointment, but the official is always free to resign. The salary scale is primarily graded according to rank in the hierarchy; but in addition to this criterion the responsibility of the position and the

requirements of the position and of the incumbent's social status may be taken into account.

7. The office is treated as the incumbent's sole, or at least primary, occupation.

8. The office constitutes a career. There is a system of "promotion" according to seniority or to achievement or both. Promotion is dependent on the judgment of superiors.

9. The official works entirely separated from ownership of the means of administration and without appropriation of his position.

10. He is subject to strict and systematic discipline and control in the conduct of the office.

Weber noted that "this type of organization is in principle applicable with equal facility to a wide variety of different fields. It may be applied in profit-making business or in charitable organizations, or in any number of other types of private enterprises serving ideal or material ends."

A valuable historical discussion of bureaucracy together with a chronology from the sixteenth century to the present is given by Aylmer (1979).

What, if anything, does the modern bureau or corporation or not-for-profit institution maximize? An even more pertinent question is, What are the goals pursued by the fiduciaries who run these organizations? Is the only coin economic? Can we always translate power, pomp, and prestige to pennies? Baumol (1959), Marris (1964, 1979), Shubik (1961), and others have offered observations on sales maximization and a host of other artifacts that arise when the goals of the managers of a corporation are translated into manifest behavior.

21.2.4 The process of program formulation and implementation
The Arrow social-welfare choosers or the Foley voters for public goods are blessed with the twin abstractions of the direct vote and a bureaucracy that prepares all proposals and selflessly and costlessly informs the public of the choices available.

It has already been observed that the public usually votes for programs or candidates, not for products. What are these programs and who prepares them? Tinbergen (1968) notes Kirschen's (1964) list of policy goals for the mixed economies of Western Europe and the United States. These include:

1. full employment,

2. price stability,

3. improvement in the balance of payments,

4. expansion of production,

5. promotion of internal competition,

6. promotion of coordination,

7. increase in the mobility of labor,

8. increase in the mobility of capital,

9. international division of labor,

10. satisfaction of collective needs,

11. improvement in the distribution of income and wealth,

12. protection and priorities to regions or industries,

13. improvement in the pattern of private consumption,

14. security of supply,

15. improvement in the size or structure of population,

16. reduction in working hours.

Who proposes, who plans, and who presents the programs to the public or their representatives? Modern man lives in a world of magic. Checks are cashed by magic, letters are delivered by magic. Airline reservations, telephone calls, the stocking of supermarkets, are all taken care of by nameless trolls who become visible only during strikes or breakdowns in service. Political oratory, modern microeconomics, and decision theory help to provide an intellectual justification for the magic. The smooth functioning of the market will cause the flow of resources from one program to another. The implementation systems are a mere institutional shadow on the sands of time.

Whether the goal is delivering social-welfare programs or designing a new washing machine, there is a lengthy intra- and interorganizational process to be performed. For social welfare Gilbert and Specht (1974) suggest that the process consists of (1) identification of the problem, (2) analysis, (3) informing the public, (4) development of policy goals, (5) building public support and legitimation, (6) program design, (7) implementation, and (8) evaluation and assessment.

A cursory glance at the list of policy goals and the list of steps in program formulation should be sufficient to suggest that even the most parsimonious, black-box model of program formulation and planning requires some aggregate measures of what is asked for and what is obtained.[3]

21.2.5 An aside on the role of labor

One of the important next steps in reconciling micro- and macroeconomics involves recognizing the special properties associated with labor as an input to the economic process. Although in chapter 22 these extra properties are not utilized, some of them are noted here to indicate the direction in which further development might go.

The first observation is that "labor units" are inseparable from people; even in concentration camps people are the players in the game, not inanimate factors of production.

Furthermore, it has been customary to treat an individual's time as a single continuous commodity, "labor–leisure." There are several reasons why this is not an adequate representation for the study of many economic situations, let alone socio- or politicoeconomic situations. From the viewpoint of individual decision making, although the individual's time may be assumed to be continuous, jobs are in general discrete. From the viewpoint of the mass employer or planning economist, many job positions can be treated as continuous, but especially among the elite there can only be so many senators, governors, generals, ambassadors, corporate presidents and vice presidents, heads of bureaus, university presidents, chair professors, judges, bishops, commissars, party secretaries and top administrators, legislators, and even advisors. Thus it is precisely at the level of describing the controlling positions of the polity and economy that microeconomics has little to say. But without a specific description of the job market for control positions, no reconciliation between micro- and macroeconomics can be made.

The decision problem for the ordinary worker seeking a job appears for the most part to be one of discrete and sometimes haphazard search (Parnes, 1968), and for many purposes a continuous probabilistic or deterministic model can be used. The decision problem for a member of an elite is far different and involves a move in a finite structure of special positions where professional and acquaintance networks, tenure, and the age structure of occupants play critical roles.

When we wish to model sociopolitical as well as economic factors, the division of time into labor and leisure is not adequate. A better division is into (1) constructive work, (2) maintenance or chores, and (3) leisure. This is illustrated in a distinction in the British Royal Navy between leave days and days without formal duties for "make and mend." Expressions such as spring-cleaning time indicate the split of time among general work, maintenance, and leisure.[4]

Even if we do not model at a level of economic detail fine enough to require a distinction between maintenance and leisure, the consideration of social and political actions requires another distinction. This is the amount of time (and money) one must spend in political and societal activities actively advocating or defending one's position even if one is neither a professional politician nor a social advocate. The French phrase *"on se defend"* sums up the common awareness that even the status quo does not continue without conscious effort.

21.3 On Constitutional Change

A constitution, whether written or unwritten, provides the basic laws or rules of the game for the functioning of government. These rules represent a blending of custom and law.

Any constitution is subject to interpretation and modification. In the United States the executive, legislative, and judiciary branches of the government all play a role in interpreting the constitution, with the Supreme Court given the major role. Changes in all constitutions are generally more difficult to achieve by amendment than by reinterpretation. In democracies amendment is usually a lengthy and difficult task.

The creation and interpretation of a constitution may be viewed as the way in which society designs and controls the rules of the game to provide bounds on the environment and strategies available to the polity. Political activities and daily legislation, in turn, mold the environment and activities of the economy. Undoubtedly there are feedbacks among the economy, government policy, and society; in this complex multivariate stochastic system there is no neat structure of causality. A key factor that does emerge, though, is the time scale of an activity and its product. People outlast loaves of bread; the lifespan of a Dupont Corporation or Hudson Bay Company may be longer than that of any individual, but the reverse is generally true for the corner candy store. Despite a Thousand Year Reich that lasted for twelve years or the multiplicity of French republics, short of major revolutions and wars, the spirit if not the form of a constitution tends to outlast the individual, as do tribes, states, and nations.

In the fullness of time captains and kings depart, institutions change, empires decay, coastlines crumble, headlands rise, deserts bloom, and fertile valleys become arid. Floods and earthquakes wipe out the citizens of Atlantis. Species vanish, new ice caps appear, and even planets are destroyed. But much of this has little to do with the price of a cup of tea, or even with the price of liberty.

As a necessary first-order approximation to enable individuals to act, many longer-run processes are regarded as fixed. But some of these processes are controlled by man himself. In particular, man is not merely a tool-making but also a rule-making animal. Rule making involves guiding fiduciary behavior at many levels, including the intergenerational links. The successful planting of a *Sequoia semper virens* for the generations to come is a complex multiperson undertaking. Each generation in its turn acts as fiduciary for the old and young. Yet all that is needed is a two- or three-generation link among the living to provide a continuity of fiduciary relationships among the living, the dead, and the unborn.

Despite political oratory, which often suggests that the present generation can have great concern for or power over that of a hundred years from now, the transmission of influence is by direct act (the planting of the tree) and by changing the rules of the game for the next set of players. Furthering the analogy here, this generation, with much more effort than is required to plant a tree, may legislate a national park system together with a heavy penalty for those who cut sequoias. They may also try to institutionalize an educational program in support of national parks. In short, although in another quarter century the immediate operational decisions will not be in the hands of this generation, it will not only have supplied the tree to the next generation but will have tried to make it administratively more inconvenient and volitionally less desirable to cut it down.

Even at the level of the family unit, nature requires that parents act for their young. In societies consisting even of a few dozen individuals, the time limits on communication and the advantages of more complex social organization bring forth arrangements in which some individuals act on behalf of others. When a polity involves more than several hundred people, the need for stewardship is unavoidable.

Without implying any pejorative connotation in the use of the word "elite," all societies produce their charismatic, traditional, or professional leaders who staff the positions of control. The legitimacy and accountability of these elites form a central problem in the design of political institutions.

Creating a constitution to provide checks and balances among competing elites is tantamount to selecting rules of the game in the construction of a self-policing system. The search is for a circular stability. From a strategic or game-theoretic point of view, at the very least a noncooperative equilibrium with desirable properties is sought.

21.4 Political Voting Models

21.4.1 The economic analogy and constant-sum models of two-party competition

Downs (1957) introduced political parties explicitly into a model with a mass of sincere voters who vote their preferences by "buying" the program of one of the two political parties competing for their votes. This development followed directly from a reinterpretation of Hotelling's (1929) duopoly model of spatial competition. As in Hotelling's model, Downs postulated a continuous one-dimensional space of alternatives. This line can be interpreted as the breadth of the political spectrum, and the spatial competition of Hotelling's firms is translated into the choices of the political parties in locating themselves on the political spectrum in order to attract voters. For example, voters might be assumed to have single peaked preferences, the natural example being an overall ideological measure that goes from extreme left to extreme right. The presumption is that parties further to the left or right are progressively less preferred than the party best representing one's position on the political spectrum.

The analogy with monopolistic competition can be taken even further. One may consider the different party programs as being explicit manifestations of "product differentiation." Parties in a two-party system who are trying to maximize votes and who would prefer to be elected rather than stick to an ideology may be driven by competition toward presenting the same program. Such a conclusion will depend explicitly, however, on the assumptions concerning the one-dimensional representation of voter preferences and such items as whether a voter prefers to abstain rather than vote for parties that are too distant ideologically (see Downs, 1957, pp. 118–119).

Downs suggested that with a government that maximizes votes, a democratic society will rarely reach a Pareto-optimal outcome. Shubik (1970c), at a somewhat more formal and narrow level, asked whether optimality might be achieved in a society that uses the vote rather than a price system to distribute private goods. The political system is modeled at its simplest. We assume the existence of two players called "political parties." The goal of each player is to win an election by as large a vote as possible. A strategy for each player is to name a policy that it will carry out if elected. A policy is any point in the set of feasible distributions of final products. It follows immediately that, although any policy may be considered as a strategy, non-Pareto-optimal policies are dominated by any policy that is optimal. It is assumed that the voters are passive,

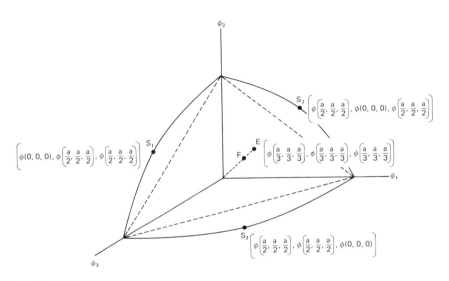

Figure 21.1
Majority vote and distribution.

simplistic, and honest; that is, they do not form groups but merely vote individually, selecting optimally between the two policies offered.

Consider a three-person symmetric market. The three traders have initial endowments $(a, 0, 0)$, $(0, a, 0)$, and $(0, 0, a)$. Each has the same differentiable utility function $\phi_1 = \phi_2 = \phi_3 = \phi(x, y, z)$. It is easy to show that in this case the unique price system will be $(1, 1, 1)$ and the final imputation to each will be $(a/3, a/3, a/3)$. The worth of this imputation is the point E in figure 21.1.

Suppose that instead of using a price system a society decided to adopt a simple-majority voting procedure for the distribution of all goods. We would need a condition for the protection of minority property rights. For simplicity we could assume either that any taxation up to confiscation of all possessions is sanctioned, or that any redistribution must satisfy conditions of individual rationality as defined by the preferences and distribution that exist before the vote. For this example we shall assume that any taxation is possible, so that an individual can end up with nothing. The result will be shown not to depend on this assumption.

In figure 21.1 S_1, S_2, or S_3 could be obtained by a majority. They are not preferred to each other, yet one of them is preferred to any other policy that can be named. For example, suppose the parties limited themselves to seven programs consisting of the three policies noted and the following four others: E, $((e,f,g), (g,e,f), (f,g,e))$, $((f,g,e), (e,f,g), (g,e,f))$, and $((g,e,f), (f,g,e), (e,f,g))$, where $e + f + g = a$. Suppose that $e > f > g > 0$ and $f > a/3$. The resulting 7×7 matrix game is

Party 2

		1	2	3	4	5	6	7
	1	0	0	0	-1	-1	1	1
	2	0	0	0	-1	1	-1	1
	3	0	0	0	1	-1	-1	1
Party 1	4	1	1	-1	0	1	-1	1
	5	1	-1	1	-1	0	1	1
	6	-1	1	1	1	-1	0	1
	7	-1	-1	-1	-1	-1	-1	0

Here 1 indicates a win by one vote, 0 a tie, and -1 a loss by one vote.[5] This game has a mixed strategy solution of $(0,0,0,1/3,1/3,1/3,0)$ for each party. As is to be expected, each names the same (mixed) strategy and each stands the same chance of winning the election.

A possible interpretation of the mixed strategy is that majority rule emphasizes the diversity of interests: Any majority wants to benefit by taxing the minority. Because this situation is symmetric, parties wish to appear to be all things to all men at the same time; hence they mix their strategies over different nonsymmetric outcomes favoring different interest groups.[6]

The individual consumer obtains $(\phi(e,f,g) + \phi(g,e,f) + \phi(f,g,e))/3$ from this policy. However, if he is risk-neutral or risk-averse, then from the assumption that he has a convex set of preferences,

$$\phi(a/3, a/3, a/3) \geq (\phi(e,f,g) + \phi(g,e,f) + \phi(f,g,e))/3.$$

This is shown at the point F in figure 21.1. If his preference set is strictly convex, the midpoint solution that is the outcome of the competitive market is strictly preferred to the outcome obtained through the voting procedure.

Had there been a limitation on taxation, the same result would hold,

with the modification that some of the more extreme policies that discriminate against minorities would be limited.

The result does not depend on our selecting a finite number of policies
for the two parties to offer. If all points on the optimal surface are available, then the strategic problem becomes equivalent to that of a continuous
Blotto game, which was solved by Gross and Wagner (1950). All of the
solutions place a zero probability density on the center.

It might be thought that the result would depend strictly on the symmetry of voter preferences, but this is not the case. If voters are risk-
neutral or risk-averse, then whenever the "political noncooperative game"
has no pure-strategy solution, the result will not be Pareto-optimal.
Depending on the degree of symmetry and the level of risk aversion, the
competitive-equilibrium point may lie above the expected value of the
vote in a zone of the Pareto-optimal surface such that everyone is better off
at the competitive equilibrium.

A possible interpretation of the general result is that if in some sense the
original distribution of resources is regarded by the voters as more or less
equitable or symmetric, the economic process keeps this property, whereas
the political process introduces the possibility of considerable asymmetry
as the majority takes from the minority. Without special laws to protect
the minority, and since anyone could be in the minority, all participants
evaluate the expected worth of the mix of outcomes offered by the voting
process as worse than the economic outcome.

In the continuous case the policies not used are the ones that give a
single individual more than two-thirds of the gain. A coalition of the
remaining two players can always be effective against such an extreme
division. The midpoint or even split is also ruled out because any two
players can improve their lot by taking from the third.

This model is obviously highly unrealistic and restrictive. Nevertheless
the result is instructive and has a useful interpretation. An outcome is
Pareto-optimal, but the expected outcome is not. The loss of efficiency
appears to be related to the power struggle and the inherent favoring of
a nonsymmetric solution by the majority in a political situation. The
economic mechanism, given the initial distribution of resources, is
anonymous and egalitarian.

It must be stressed that the usual reasons for using a voting system are
dissatisfaction with the price system or the absence of a price system. This
is almost always the case when we deal with the production of public
goods.

Two points should be noted. First, in the analysis of exchange implicit in any of the economic models, there is an assumption of well-defined private ownership and no taxation. Here private ownership is merely a whim of the state; the party in power can "nationalize" and redistribute as it sees fit. The second point is that the parties have been modeled symmetrically, with a simple utility for power and with no historical structure and essentially no institutional form. This is an extremely crude approximation, representing not merely a noninstitutional but even a nonideological view of the political party. Furthermore, the symmetry obliterates the difference in strategic opportunity between the party that forms the current government and the challenger.

21.4.2 Buying votes: Cooperative and noncooperative versions
Logrolling or vote trading and vote buying pose different problems. The questions we ask concerning the former involve the exchange of votes for votes. Vote buying involves a payment for votes using a different coin.

Riker (1962), utilizing a simple game model, argued in his theory of political coalitions for the importance of minimal winning coalitions. Spoils or payoffs should be split among as few individuals as are necessary for the achievement of the political goal.

Young (1978a) approached the purchase of votes by considering a simple game with n players and a lobbyist with unlimited funds who wishes to buy a minimal winning coalition at least cost. The votes are assumed to be for sale: Players are all willing to sell their allegiance. Young's voting game is described by a set N of players and a collection of winning coalitions $\mathcal{W}$ (see *GTSS*, chapter 7). Let $p_i \geq 0$ be the price of player $i \in N$. Then $p(s) = \sum_{i \in s} p_i$ is the total cost of buying the subset S. Young considered a process in which voters each signal their price and the lobbyist then buys a least-cost winning coalition S. There are no veto players. A payment schedule for the lobbyist is a function f that yields a set $f(p) = s \in \mathcal{W}$ satisfying $p(s) \leq p(s')$ for all $s' \in \mathcal{W}$ for any price vector p.

Given f, Young considered an n-person game defined on N in which each player i quotes a price p_i and obtains a payoff p_i if $i \in f(p)$ and zero otherwise. He proved that for this *political-favors game* there exists a strong noncooperative equilibrium, that is, an equilibrium point at which no set of players can improve by deviating from the equilibrium.

Shubik and Weber (1981, 1984) consider a somewhat different method of influencing voters (see *GTSS*, section 10.2.3). A general characteristic function $v(S)$ is regarded as a "production function" indicating the value of a coalition S. Two party managers or "superplayers" with resources a and b must each decide how to spend their money in the n districts being contested. The probability that the candidate of the first party will win is $p_i(a_i, b_i)$, where $\sum_{i=1}^{n} a_i \leq a$ and $\sum_{i=1}^{n} b_i \leq b$. As with Young, a game in characteristic-function form, rather than being analyzed cooperatively, is converted into a game in strategic form and solved for noncooperative equilibria.

The Shapley–Shubik power index based on the Shapley value can in a sense be regarded as a cooperative evaluation of the Hobbesian price of a voter; it defines an imputation based upon the power structure. Both the Young and the Shubik–Weber games yield evaluations different from the Shapley value.

All of the models and measures in this section concentrate on the power or worth of an individual legislator in a 0–1 struggle outside of an institutional or temporal context. This suppresses the element of quid pro quo and the ongoing bargaining that characterize much of political life.

21.4.3 Political process as a game
Kramer (1977, 1978) proposed a dynamic model. He examined a political process driven by competition for votes in a series of elections of indefinite length. The parties advocate policies in each period in competing for votes. The winning party takes office and attempts to implement its policy. Kramer's analysis was concerned with the trajectories of policies. He showed that (under appropriately defined conditions) an equilibrium is reached at what he described as "a small proper subset of the Pareto set." The parties are assumed to try to maximize vote share. Each voter i has a preference ordering over all points in a k-dimensional space R^k such that he is saturated at s^i and $x \succsim_i y$ if and only if $\|x - s^i\| \leq \|y - s^i\|$, where

$$\|z\| = \left(\sum_{i=1}^{k} z_i^2 \right)^{1/2}.$$

Kramer's analysis generalized that of Downs to multiple-issue elections, with the size of the set of equilibrium outcomes providing a crude measure of the degree of consensus in a society. The model is myopic, however, in that each party concentrates on the next election with little regard for anything else.

In his second paper Kramer established the existence of mixed-strategy equilibria in elections with a policy space of many dimensions. The previous work of Shubik (1970), Ordeshook (1971), and McKelvey and

Ordeshook (1976), although they used mixed strategies, did not provide general proofs for their existence.

The model sketched in chapter 22, although influenced by the foregoing work, is designed to illustrate a different point than the one made in those papers. In particular, we shall argue that politicoeconomic competition can be explicitly embedded in a sociobureaucratic context and that it is possible to describe the presence of considerable economic indeterminacy in the system, much of which can be removed with the specification of processual details involving political, sociological, and other factors. In the work noted above the parties are treated as players, and the fiduciary role of politicians and others who hold top posts in the institutions of society are not differentiated from that of the party itself. The approach adopted here is to bring out the fiduciary role explicitly.

Table 21.2 sketches the different types of fiduciaries present in most societies together with an indication of their claims to legitimacy and accountability. The last two columns indicate the regular and emergency methods of replacement for the occupants of the posts.

The general thesis advanced here is that people, not institutions, are the players. But the time spans and the dynamics are such that in the short run institutions provide fixed rules for all subgames, though in the longer run the rules themselves can be modified as part of a broader-scale multiperson interaction.

21.4.4 A comment on many parties
Little formal analysis has been done of multiparty competition (see, however, Owen, 1971). Kramer (1977) noted that competition among three or more parties seems to be inherently unstable. Although chapter 22 focuses its attention on two-party competition, we suggest here that once our view becomes concentrated more on candidates than on parties, the introduction of more than two parties is neither as important nor as complicated as might be feared.

21.5 Players, Utility, and Goals Revisited

Several political voting models have been suggested, but no real differentiation of agents has been made beyond suggesting that political parties or politicians try to maximize votes. Why should one set of individuals try to maximize votes, another wealth, a third virtuosity in playing the violin, and so forth? The question appears to belong more to the domain of psychology and sociology than to that of political economy. Indoc-

Table 21.2
Accountability and control of fiduciaries

	Source of legitimacy	Control	Expected method of succession	Emergency removal
King, emperor, pope	God, apostolic succession	the barons and cardinals	inheritance, elite election	abdication, revolution
Dictator	the state, the people in abstract	the party, police, and armed forces	appointment by incumbent, power struggle	coup, revolution
Elected representatives	electorate	next level of representation, courts, public opinion	election	impeachment, recall
Supreme-court justices	constitution	legislature and executive, criticism in major law journals	appointment by executive (with elite support)	impeachment, packing
Politically appointed public officers	ruler, elite support	ruler, top bureaucracy, public opinion	return to public sector, resignation with change in government	dismissal, forced retirement
Bureaucratically appointed public officers	top bureaucracy, peer group	ruler	internal control of promotion	dismissal, forced retirement

Table 21.2 (continued)

	Source of legitimacy	Control	Expected method of succession	Emergency removal
Military officers	ruler	ruler, top bureaucracy, peer group	control of promotion	dismissal, forced retirement, revolution
Elected private business officials	directors, stockholders	directors, peer group, outside analysts	annual vote	dismissal by directors, takeover, raid
Bureaucratically appointed business officials	company officers	higher bureaucracy	control of promotion (some competition)	dismissal
Church officials	higher bureaucracy, tradition or covenant	higher bureaucracy	control of promotion	excommunication, dismissal by congregation
Educators, other institutionalized professionals	higher bureaucracy	professional association, higher bureaucracy	control of promotion and tenure (some competition)	forced resignation or retirement

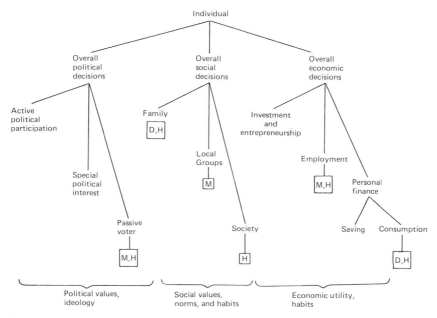

Figure 21.2
The individual as a set of agents.

trination and recruitment processes are acknowledged here rather than
explained. They do, however, suggest a basis for a model with many
different agents that will be proposed in chapter 22.

21.5.1 The individual as a set of agents

Without venturing too deeply into the terra incognita of psychology and
information processing, we choose to regard the individual as a collection
of cooperative agents each used for a different type of decision and each
operating on a different configuration or aggregation of information.
Thus figure 21.2, without pretending to particular rigor, suggests a
structure in which a single rational player is represented in agent form
(Selten, 1975; Harsanyi, 1976), where the agents may be required to act
on aggregated or limited information concerning the overall set of decision
problems faced by the individual.

The interpretation of the figure is as follows. The individual operates
in at least economic, political, and social modes. Different types of individuals lay different emphasis on different routines. The symbol *D* stands

for the presence of many detailed subroutines; M indicates the presence of a middling number of subroutines; and H indicates the presence of a set of subroutines many of which may be wholly or heavily dependent on habit and other forms of socialization.

21.5.2 Economic agents

Economic decisions may be divided into those concerning investment and entrepreneurship, employment, and personal finance. As was observed by Keynes (1936) and others, investment and saving are not the same activities. Most individuals are neither entrepreneurs nor investors; their resources that become involved in investment activities do so for the most part via financial instruments that are used for saving. Those individuals in society distinguished as investors or entrepreneurs, however, do have highly developed subroutines for such activities. These are not indicated here.

Of central concern to many individuals, and occupying much of an adult's available time, is the question of employment. The concern with job permanency, tenure, seniority, mobility, promotion prospects, pensions, and unemployment appears to vary with both personal and societal attitudes and mores. We suggest that most individuals have at least some conscious and habitual subroutines dealing directly with their employment.

Personal finance includes both saving and consumption. It may be that for many individuals saving is a residual category: Whatever is not spent is saved. But some people do seem to make a conscious effort at some form of budgeting. Beyond the earning of income, possibly the area where most of an individual's economic choices have to be made is in personal finance. Here, especially in consumption, the individual appears to have detailed sets of consciously followed and habitual routines.[7] Shopping for bargains, being an expert on automobiles, knowing where the best stores are, and recognizing different gradations in quality are all manifestations of these routines.

21.5.3 Political agents

Dahl's (1961) perceptive work on political activity suggested that we should at least distinguish politically active individuals and professionals from more or less passive voters and pressure groups or lobbyists. At one extreme we have the dedicated professional politician whose life and employment are politics. All working hours are directed to politics, and it may be that politics are dreamed as well. At the other extreme is the individual who scarcely even bothers to vote, let alone invest time in obtaining the information needed for rational decision making.

Here three divisions are suggested. First, the professional politicians will in general include office holders, office seekers, and active party workers. They will have many politically oriented subroutines, and sociopolitical concerns such as power, position, prestige, and ideology may figure highly in their preference structures. Second, the ordinary voter may have a poorly developed or even a well-developed preference structure over configurations of policies but nevertheless may not manifest much political activity beyond voting, the occasional petition, and a certain amount of conscious and habitual data gathering, processing, and evaluation. Finally, an individual with no other particular interests in the political process or its control may nevertheless develop a deep interest in some aspect of the political process that affects him and that calls for actions within his strategic scope such as lobbying, making political donations, or formally or informally joining an organized special-interest group. Thus gun lobbies, pro- or antiabortion groups, environmental lobbies, and other special-interest organizations may be designed to enlarge the strategic possibilities for individuals whose political interests and other political activities are otherwise minimal.

21.5.4 Social agents
Little detailed consideration is given here to the more sociological aspects of an individual's conscious and habitual behavior. Much of the activity at this level involves longer-term factors than we are dealing with. Changes in customs, modifications of institutions, evolution of norms and of social structures occur for the most part on a time scale far longer than two or even three elections. Figure 21.2 suggests a relatively crude division of the social individual's activities into parts that involve his immediate family, local groups with whom interaction is frequent, and society as a whole; social values and mores may be inchoate and dimly perceived, but they are nevertheless important.

21.5.5 The central controller
The model sketched in figure 21.2 is at best a crude static approximation to a behavioral (and essentially dynamic) approach that acknowledges the extremely large differences in specialized perceptions, routines, and abilities among individuals.

Among the missing features in this model is a description of how the individual might recognize changes in the environment that will affect his immediate self-interest. Furthermore, how does he create new agents and routines to deal with those features of the changed environment that need to be considered in detail?

A second item left out is the apparent proclivity of some, if not all, individuals to act on occasion against what is apparently their own self-interest. Both of these features require more dynamics and more psychological knowledge than can be offered here. Yet at the risk of presenting casual analogy, we suggest that the concept of inhibition and of high communication costs among different agents at different levels in the hierarchy offers some insight. The individual who has instructed himself carefully on the necessity of undertaking a strict diet but then two hours later eats half a cream cake can be considered as "not listening to himself." When confronted with the immediate temptation, the agent who takes care of gourmandise acts alone. It is as if the cost of getting him to pay attention to the higher decision to abandon or severely limit his activities is too high.

The analogy between bureaucracies and individuals suggests that when we have developed specialized agents and systems to attend to and act for special aspects of our everyday life or special events, those agents will neither give up their domain of discretion nor coordinate their communication with others except at great bureaucratic cost.

Even when the behavior of one's agents is not obviously dysfunctional, the costs of centralizing decisions may still be too high. When political action is required, for example, the organizational and informational costs of invoking the needed economic and other information may limit behavior.

It must be stressed, however, that the parable of sets of agents and subagents does not imply that in their suboptimizing the individual agents have totally different preference systems and ignore all the information possessed by other agents. On the contrary, it is as though each had a different representation of the whole. Thus, when one thinks about politics, consumer concerns are present in a highly aggregated representation such as a general concept of "wealth" or "economic well being"; strategic detail concerning consumption is not necessary and hence not represented.

21.6 An Aside on Status, Wealth, and Equality

The explanatory value of economic analysis for the supply and demand for groceries rests on a firmer basis than that for theft, murder, marriage, friendship, or family size. The problem is not with the methodology but with our understanding and our basic description of the phenomena.

Joy, grief, envy, concern, respect, honor, trust, faith, and other basic human motivations do not fit easily into the utility function or even a preference ordering. Yet they play important roles in shaping the controls of a society. Power, status, glory, prestige, and influence may be intangible systemic factors of societies and polities, but they have provided more motivation for kings, chiefs, generals, ministers, senators, courtiers, and functionaries than any economic drives.

The challenge to the social scientist is to describe, measure, and analyze the implications of these motivating factors. The high-ranking English civil servant waiting to be knighted, the old senator running one more time, the politician, painter, poet, and scholar are not counting box-office receipts, even though most of them will prefer more money to less and a high standard of living to a low one. The essential reason for the failure of economic dynamics to develop except in sociopolitical essay form (see Marx, 1932; Schumpeter, 1950; or Keynes, 1936) is that a noninstitutional analogue of an equilibrium theory *cannot* be constructed. A dynamics requires specification of the laws of motion and the medium in which the motion takes place. The context of the economy is the polity, that of the polity is the society, and the driving forces of the politicians and societal elites control the shaping and modification of the structure in which economic activity takes place.

Status or position is often more important in a society or in socio-political and socioeconomic situations than wealth or other physical goods. In an affluent society many individuals can be rich. Barring ties, however, there can only be one richest person. The potlatch and the pecking order, obtaining more power over people, keeping up with the Joneses or exceeding them, saving face or gaining face, are all manifestations of human or animal social behavior.

In experimental gaming and in many parlor games, examinations, competitions, and social situations where the payoffs are apparently relatively well defined and measurable, the behavior of individuals does not always support the hypothesis that the point score of the game, the grade on the examination, or the performance criterion in competition is being maximized. Nor do observed patterns of behavior even support the hypothesis that a utility function positively correlated with the score is maximizea.

Experimental work on two-person non-zero-sum games has shown that in some instances individuals play to maximize the difference between their scores. Thus, if we denote the strategy set of the ith player by S_i and the payoff (measured in whatever points, money, grades, or numbers are used in the game) by $p_i(s_1, s_2)$, then in the two-person game the players act as though they were playing a strictly competitive game with a payoff of $p_1(s_1, s_2) - p_2(s_1, s_2)$ to the first player and the negative of this to the second. In this instance the non-zero-sum game has been converted into a straightforward zero-sum game. When status is at stake, this is further reduced to a game with only three outcomes or, at most, only three important sets of outcomes: win, draw, or lose, where win is defined as doing better than one's competitor in the sense of making more points.

Two variants of this type of game in the two-person case merit distinction. The first can be called a *game of pure status* and the second a *game of status and welfare* (Shubik, 1971b). In the first game the point score obtained by both players is only of interest to them in determining who has been able to win or do better. In the second game status is the most important aspect of the individual's utility, but as long as further actions will not influence his status, he places a positive value on increasing joint welfare in terms of the distribution of wealth or services obtainable from the game. A player's valuation may be lexicographic in two dimensions in a game of status and welfare. The philosopher-king, dictator, politician, corporate president, or dean may easily have the welfare of all others as his secondary concern, provided that this welfare does not challenge his position as "number one," in whatever system of precedence he calculates his rank.

Notes to chapter 21

1. Wilson (1972) has reconsidered Arrow's possibility theorem in terms of a cooperative game in which the aggregation of choice is reflected in the domination structure of the coalitions.

2. The introduction of costs to voting and other aspects of the political process might be sufficient to provide the continuity needed to define utility functions for all individuals.

3. A cursory glance at an elementary text such as that of Berkeley (1975) serves to remind the theorist of the cost, complexity, and drudgery involved in implementation.

4. It is also of interest to note the three-way split of the gods in the Hindu religion into Creators, Destroyers, and Preservers. Maintenance and the bureaucracy have their recognized role!

5. Two models can be considered, one in which a party's goal is to win by as large a vote as possible, and one in which its goal is just to win. In this example the latter assumption appears to be the more reasonable.

6. Kenneth Arrow has pointed out that one must distinguish between the case in which the parties announce their (mixed) strategies to the public and one in which the parties randomize first and then announce their results to the public. If we adopt the first interpretation, we may view the mixed strategy as being a "degree of belief" in the mind of the voter. He perceives some of the contradictions in the statements of the parties; hence he has only a tentative view of what their actions will be. In the second instance we assume that the parties polarize the issues for the voters. In the first case we must assume a cardinal utility scale for voters who must evaluate uncertain outcomes.

7. For a discussion of some of the problems in developing a satisfactory theory of consumer choice see Thaler (1980).

22 A Two-Party System with Government, Bureaucracy, and Mass Voting

22.1 On Institutions and Fiduciary Control

This volume has been devoted to the diverse aspects of microeconomic and politicoeconomic theory that must be brought together if we are to start answering basic questions about the state and the economy in a reasonably objective manner.

The merits or failings of a price system are not artifacts of ideology but somewhat special properties of a configuration of tastes and technology. A mass society with many public goods and services and a complex blend of evolving, poorly perceived tastes, desires, and goals cannot rely solely upon a simplistic faith in an invisible hand or a Lenin-like father-figure presiding over the withering away of the state.

Much of political economy is dull. But unfortunately it is precisely the dull detail consisting of an intermix of physical and social facts and political and legal rules of the game which provides the structure needed to examine process.

Complexity for the sake of complexity is something that the good model builder should try to avoid. A frequent sign of a lack of appreciation of the power and importance of abstraction is a tendency to add extra variables and parameters to a model prematurely in the name of "realism."

At the other extreme, simplification beyond a certain level may remove the possibility of studying phenomena that do not appear before an appropriate level of complexity in the relationship among parts has been attained. A tradeoff between the complexity of the model and our ability to analyze it must be made. Given the questions to be answered, we seek the most parsimonious description.

Neither the general-equilibrium system nor the work on direct voting and social choice provides a sufficient explanation of how who gets what. The level of abstraction of much of price theory, social-welfare theory, and political philosophy is such that the models are not specified sufficiently to describe process. Yet to a great extent the answers to how who gets what lie in the understanding of the process and of who controls it.

The first part of this chapter sketches the outlines of a game. It is presented verbally and diagrammatically, although it would be feasible to present a complete mathematical structure if we were willing to limit ourselves to some fairly simple and somewhat ad hoc functional forms. The model is designed to encompass economic factors, political structure, and bureaucracy. Furthermore, it is explicitly game-theoretic, involving a sequence of games with different actors. It is based more or less (but not closely) on the political structure of the United States, but it should be regarded more as representative of a class of models than as a statement of the specific importance of a single structure.

22.1.1 Actors and institutions

The individual actors considered are (1) the citizen–voter–consumer–worker; (2) active political party members, political office holders, and candidates; (3) the business elite; (4) the elite other than politicians and businessmen; (5) politically appointed controllers and other members of the bureaucratic elite; and (6) nonelite members of the governmental bureaucracy. A more ambitious model would include (7) elites in other not-for-profit institutions (including organized pressure groups, unions, universities, the church); (8) members of these institutions; (9) other members of corporate bureaucracies; (10) entrepreneurs; (11) the financial elite; and (12) other members of the financial bureaucracies.

Just as a coral may appear to the casual observer to be a single entity, so may an institution such as a political party or government or an organization such as a corporation appear as a single purposeful entity even though it is an agglomeration of many individuals. The approach adopted here is that institutions in the short run (say up to four or five years) may be taken as given and more or less unchanging (clearly there are exceptions, especially in times of great social, political, or economic stress). The institutions may be described, then, as part of the rules of the game. The behavior of an institution is to be explained as the output of the joint strategies of the members of the institution; in other words, it is the result of the playing of a subgame. The system as a whole functions by virtue of the interactions of real players manifesting their activities in the strategies of the institutional players. These institutional players provide the context for the subgames that are played.

The institutions considered directly in the model are (1) political parties; (2) government; and (3) government bureaucracies. Among the institutions left out are (4) corporations; (5) unions; (6) the armed forces; (7) religious institutions; (8) financial institutions; and (9) formally organized pressure groups. The first three are adequate for a model sufficiently complex to characterize much of the overall behavior that would be manifested even with further complications.

22.1.2 The individual and the state: A false dichotomy

When we attempt to model the politicoeconomic process as a game of strategy, the formal requirement of rule specification forces us to question the operational meaning of the theory that presents the state as a supreme entity with goals of its own, to which all individuals are subservient, as well as the contrasting individualistic theory that builds upon the individual actor abstracted from a societal context.

The state is a construct whose existence depends on the existence of individuals, but not vice versa. Because the rule makers are individuals or groupings of individuals, any attempt to present the state as an independent player is a crude approximation, based on shaky logical foundations, that can at best be justified by an ad hoc argument.[1]

Individuals are born into an existing society and are in one form or another socialized before they become independent actors. Thus even the most libertarian of scenarios requires, for logical completeness and consistency, the specification of rules describing the institutional setting and the constraints that socialization imposes on individual behavior.

When we move to the arena of grand theorizing on the broad sweep of sociopolitical dynamics, the evolutionary aspects of society, the polity, and the economy cannot be ignored. In even the most individualistic of societies groups of individuals must play according to the rules that constrain near-term behavior and then modify the rules that will control the next round of play. In the most dictatorial, centralized, or traditional of states the magnitude of change may be constrained, but whether it is the high priests, the commissars of the people, the barons of the realm, or the defenders of the faith who are the agents of change, they are people. Any attempt to operationalize a model of society as a game reduces the concept of the state, as an entity unto itself, to an ill-conceived idea whose only support is rhetoric.

22.2 The Games within the Game

22.2.1 The elements of the game

The utility function used in the exposition of microeconomic theory has, in general, a finite number of arguments usually interpreted as specific quantities of goods or services. Large firms often sell to each other and to government not products or services but whole systems or programs. Governments are usually concerned with programs, not products or even individual services.

It is suggested here that the number of items needed to provide a good macrosocioeconomic picture of government programs is around fifteen to thirty. As a first cut, most of the headings in the *Statistical Abstract of the United States* or other national statistics handbooks will do. A sample list might include:

defense,

justice and safety,

international relations,

population,

immigration,

health,

education,

welfare,

housing,

social security,

employment, working conditions,

science and technology,

communications and transportation,

cultural activities,

agriculture,

basic resources,

manufacturing,

environment,

finance,

taxation.

Each one of these items calls for a relatively high-level declaration of policy, and none appears to enter directly into the type of utility function set forth in conventional consumer choice theory.

Behind each policy choice there must be an implementation plan and a budget. The budget will contain a listing of line items such as the number of police cars, revolvers, two-way communication systems, and so forth required to carry out a law-enforcement program. The list of physical inputs alone does not, of course, describe the quantity or quality of the outputs. Both government and voters propose and vote on policies and programs, not lists of products.

Where, then, are the public goods? Most of them appear as part of the program packages. On occasion a specific item will be of direct concern to individuals who are in a position to take direct action such as voting on a bond issue, but this is the exception and not the rule at the federal level and covers only a fraction of state and city expenditures.

The Bergson–Samuelson social-welfare function was described with little explicit discussion of such "fussy mathematical details" as linear structure, continuity, or convexity which might seem to be of only secondary importance for the development of an abstract description of preference but which are in fact often critical.

Arrow (1951), in contrast with Bergson and Samuelson, was explicitly structure-free in his discussion of social choice and individual values. He considered a finite set of general social states or general prospects with no structure whatsoever and with no probability mixes among states.

In contrast with the generality of these approaches, a large literature has sprung up in political science and public choice theory in which individuals have preferences over a domain of m policies, which may be assumed to vary continuously over an m-dimensional Euclidean space. Figure 22.1 presents a typical example of R_2^+. Here two types of programs are considered. We assume that somehow we can define "more" of each program. An easy way to do so would be to assume that a larger money value proposed for a program implies more of the program. A total saturation point is noted at S for the combination of the two programs.

The attitude adopted here is that the standard utility function offers a fruitful description for the consumption of private goods and for saving. The voter confronted by an election involving overall sociopolitical and economic issues collapses the dimensionality of his economic activity into one or, in special-interest situations, at most two or three dimensions. These are money, his job, and his business activity. The money—without specifying details on income and exposed or hidden wealth—provides a one-dimensional measure for general economic well-being.

When the ordinary voter votes in an election, he more or less consciously takes into account the candidates, their promised programs, and his perception of their previous performance in delivering what they promised. He has a choice function that enables him to select among the collection of candidates and promised programs. To put it simply, we assume that the voter considers how good the candidate is personally and how attractive his promised program is.

The evaluation of how good the candidate is includes assessments of honesty, trustworthiness, and other perceived personal attributes. These

Program 2
"National defense"

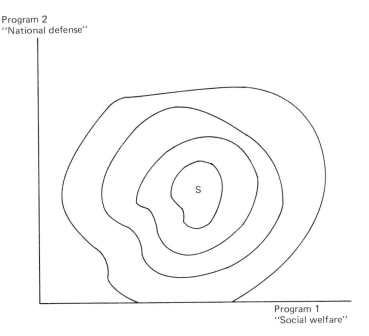

Program 1
"Social welfare"

Figure 22.1
Guns and butter.

features may be influenced by the actions of the candidate. In particular, in many democracies candidates must make themselves known to the electorate through public relations, news coverage, and other such activities.

There is a tradeoff between a good candidate and a bad cause. "Can he do the job he promises?" may be the first question. But "Do I want that job done?" must also be asked. How is the promised program perceived?

Not only do individuals usually vote for candidates rather than for vectors of public goods; the promised programs of the candidates are not neat packages of public goods, budgets, and taxes, but word-pictures of approaches to be adopted. Even if we considered policy as a menu of public goods, we would have to add the list of programs mentioned above together with one dimension for how the individual's overall wealth is affected and, in some instances, an extra dimension if his particular job or other economic activity is under direct attack. More appropriately, his choice must be based not merely on what he has now in the way of services delivered but also on what he is being promised by the parties. This involves an appropriate description of how the expectations that are used to discount promised programs are formed.

How does the voter evaluate public goods? Many local public goods and services are close enough to being well-defined physical goods that the voters can evaluate and compare them with other hypothetical alternatives. However, public programs involving justice, equity, freedom, and other general virtues or social desiderata cannot be measured with such ease.

Many aspects of political platforms are broad statements loosely or not at all connected to physical specifics and to cost–benefit analysis. The costs are at most loose constraints. I suggest that an individual voter confronted with two or three programs generally makes a comparison among the programs proposed without considering a large set of alternative programs. At most the voter and even most politicians conceptualize no more than five to ten *qualitatively* different programs. These are primarily the programs being offered, the previously proposed and enacted programs, and one or two other programs that have been sufficiently conceptualized that they can be considered as operational alternatives or normative benchmarks.

The aspects of political purpose and public programs that deal with qualitative features of policy are not fruitfully dealt with by the same type of intellectual apparatus as serves for externalities such as toll highways. Furthermore, the concept of the Pareto-optimal surface is not the most fruitful construct for describing the strivings of the vote seekers or the choices of the voters. Politicians and voters know that even if their feelings are strong, they are not all philosophers, and their ability to formalize their concepts of freedom or justice or other qualitatively critical concepts is limited.

Most individuals can distinguish which of several programs has the most appeal for them. This perceptual exercise utilizes all the help or hindrance obtainable from philosophers, news commentators, poets, and politicians. For some, the conceptual filters depend heavily on sausages and circuses; for others, on Socrates, Adam Smith, or the Federalist papers.

Rather than describe in a vacuum abstract Pareto-optimal surfaces, we suggest that formalization be directed toward process. Thus our concern must be with those who select policies and programs and with the individuals who vote on the appointment of the politicians who facilitate the execution of the programs.

One way of representing voter behavior is to assume that each individual has a set of five to ten programs conceptualized, namely, what he perceives he is being offered by the candidates, what he was offered previously, what he perceives he obtained previously, and one or two ideals. Call the total set S, and let X_i be the set of all possible programs that i might promise. Let x_i be a particular promised program ($x_i \in X_i$), and let $\hat{x}_i \in \hat{X}_i$ be his previously promised program. Voter j has a *choice rule* $C_j(S; x, \hat{x})$, where $x = \{x_1, x_2, \dots, x_s\}$ and $s = |S|$, which enables him to decide to vote for one of the candidates or to abstain.

It is the task of the political scientist, sociologist, and moral philosopher to specify the mechanisms of program generation, the special properties of the domain of choice (such as its mathematical structure), and the nature of the individual's choice rules. By default, the economist often takes an easy way out. For example, we might assume that all programs can be mapped onto a single dimension, "wealth"—that all individuals have a preference ordering over wealth that can be represented by a continuous utility function and that the choice operator is maximization of utility. Such a representation manifests a poverty of sociopolitical understanding but, like a Hun attacking well-kept city walls, has a certain straightforward vigor to recommend it.

In sketching a model of process, I shall make many simplifications, not because I believe in them but to indicate how the parts of an overall scheme can be made to fit together in a manner useful for analysis.

22.2.2 The four parts of a model of representative elections

An adequate model of representative elections should cover at least four topics: (1) the primarily economic concerns of individuals as consumers, producers, and voters on economic matters; (2) the role of bureaucratic behavior in the execution of policy; (3) the short-term political concerns of voters reflected in the election of representatives according to given rules of the game; and (4) the longer-term sociopolitical factors reflected in rule making, interpretation, and amendment, which modify the rules that apply to further play.

An evolutionary theory of constitutional change is well beyond our present goals. Such a theory calls for an understanding of sociopolitical dynamics. Yet even casual empiricism concerning voting and the structure of legislatures indicates an elaborate evolutionary process that goes far beyond the simplicity of the voting games and power indices we have considered (see *GTSS*, chapter 7). Simple-majority voting is frequently used for the election of political officers and the passing of ordinary bills, but a

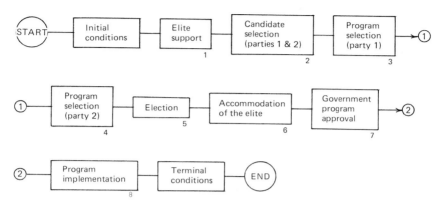

Figure 22.2
The electoral process.

majority of two-thirds or more may be required for changes in procedures or constitutional amendments. Vetos are used to protect minorities; and as Bagehot (1867) noted, an institution such as the House of Lords, which to the simplistic model builder seems to be irrelevant, has a use both as a time delay and a symbol of dignity and continuity to the voter.

Voting is part of an evolutionary mechanism to control those who govern and to facilitate democratic consensus and compromise; it is not merely a fixed device for direct and unchanging social choice.

22.2.3 A sketch of a model

The political process will be modeled as a set of linked games with individually distinguished players consisting of politically active people, the various elites considered in aggregate, bureaucrats, and citizen–voters.

We shall describe a cycle that begins before the selection of political candidates to run in an election and ends before the selection for the next election. Figure 22.2 shows a flow diagram of the process. It can be viewed as a set of six to eight "local-interest games," each played by the subgroup of players (or agents) directly concerned.

Initial conditions include the populations of players: the voter–consumer–workers are assumed to constitute a very large population; the politically active number a few thousand; the elite a few thousand; and the lower and middle bureaucracy is assumed to be large. The data also include the current office holders, the program promised on its election by the party in power, the program actually delivered by the incumbent party, and the position of the electorate prior to the last election. The latter includes not only its private endowments but the public program delivered before the previous selection of candidates.

To build a full local-interest game at this level, we would have to present a relatively detailed model of candidate competition. In the next step of the process interested members of the elites (including corporate presidents, lawyers, union leaders, clerics, and professors) make their bargains and place their bets. The coin they pay in may be money, time, talent, propaganda, or perhaps promises of future positions such as affiliations "of council" to large law firms or special advisory roles in investment houses. The coin they will be paid in if their ship comes in will be appropriate positions in the high administrative level of government and other forms of influence on policy.

All candidates require a local and a party platform, which we represent by a set of social and taxation programs. Each candidate's probability for being elected depends on the voters in the district and thus will vary with both local and overall policy.

As a function of how well he and his party do, a politician gains or loses both indirect and direct influence, including control over a set of positions in the top bureaucracy that he can fill from the nonelected elite. In practice, many top businessmen, professors, generals, lawyers, and others are available, and they will have indicated their availability by services already rendered. At a later point quid pro quo in the form of government contracts, ideological constraints, or modified programs may appear.

If there are k_1 candidates for party 1 and k_2 for party 2, the selection of a program for each may be viewed as a k_1- or k_2-person cooperative game. Figure 22.2 is drawn on the assumption that party 1, the current incumbent, must declare its policy first.

After the policies have been declared, the election takes place. We may view the election as a two-person constant-sum game that we can evaluate using a probabilistic value (see Shubik and Weber, 1981, 1984) or a game to be solved using the weighted value (Shapley, 1981).

When the election is over, the winners have an opportunity to remove some of the previous top staff and replace them with their own people. (We are not attempting to describe at this level of generality the many different rules for bureaucratic tenure and the variations in quid pro quo that exist between politicians and those whom they are in a position to appoint.) This step may be regarded as a payoff for support rather than a new game.

In contrast with Downs, Kramer, and others, given the disaggregation to individual elected members of an assembly, we may treat the actions of the government as a whole as the outcome of a multiperson game in which the vote is not necessarily decided along party lines.

In its simplest form, the government as a whole must approve of the program to be implemented by the bureaucracy. At the extreme of simplicity, this amounts to jointly approving a single set of programs which might easily differ from both of their original platforms.

Given that a program has been chosen by some type of bargaining characterized as the value or as a point in the core of the cooperative game, then the problem of implementation must be resolved.

We shall model implementation as a bargaining game between the politically appointed and the permanent upper bureaucracy, with the latter intending to outlast the former. From country to country and culture to culture, the size and attitudes of the bureaucracy vary considerably and pure economic theorizing can at best explain a not very large fraction of these variations. A simple model of bureaucratic motivation might assume that bureaucrats maximize budgets and size;[2] or that the permanent bureaucracy is characterized by individuals who place a high value on job security and on relatively low variability in their environment. Security, size, and a quiet life are certainly high among goals to be sought. This does not imply unthinking opposition to change, but opposition may be generated if the costs the bureaucrats are asked to bear in the name of flexibility and adjustment to change are not accompanied by some offsetting compensation.

A key element in understanding the role of bureaucracy in the public or the private sector is an appreciation of the costs and limits on any decision process. All but the most elementary of organisms or organizations are complex information-aggregating and disaggregating devices. As the focus of attention changes, one set of details disappears and is replaced by another. Williamson (1975), Nelson and Winter (1982), and many others have stressed the underlying rationale that in many instances calls for hierarchies and bureaucracies where the conditions for the operation of a market as an efficient alternative are not present. Indivisibilities, fewness in numbers, a need for highly specialized nonmarketable information, and a need for highly differentiated routines depending on location and environment are but a handful of the factors that engender structured organizations to do what the market does badly or cannot do at all.

In the process outlined here, the input to the final game is the agreed upon program, and the output is the program as implemented. The cycle is complete, and the public now has the data to update its expectations for the next set of nominations and elections.

There is, of course, no need for budgets to balance or for expected costs, promised costs, and actual costs to be the same. But if we endow the public with a reasonable amount of skepticism, then the larger the gap between what is promised and what is delivered (assuming it is unfavorable), the greater will be the inclination to change votes.

22.2.4 A playable game

At this point we are confronted with three choices: We could attempt to specify the game together with all local-interest games in full formal generality. We could, with relative ease, specify simple functional forms that would allow the game to be played. Or we could continue our qualitative discussion.

It is premature to attempt a general model, but the second approach has several merits. First, it keeps accessibility high for readers who are not fluent in mathematics, while indicating that despite the broad coverage and complexity of the model, it is within the range of both formal specification and analysis. Second, by submitting to the discipline of fully formulating a specific game, we can infer the nature of the structure of the general mathematical model. Furthermore, both empirical and logical difficulties are illustrated in any attempt to be specific about the "rules of the game."

What we gain by being specific is that we can pose certain questions in an operational form. Many of the rules suggested for deciding the selection of programs or describing the behavior of a bureaucracy may seem simplistic to the point of caricature. No apology is made. A sociologist with a deep understanding of bureaucracy may well believe that a considerably different model of motivation should apply. That could be true: A casual assumption from the viewpoint of one social science is often a central program for another.

Our assertion here is that the game-theoretic modeling approach provides a conceptual framework within which economics, political science, and sociology all fit together naturally. The trend in much of both economic and sociological theory has been toward separation almost to the point of isolation.

One of the dangers in specifying a complete but simplistic mathematical model is that both the model and any results may be interpreted as displaying political or social bias. Thus, for example, extremely simple models may seem to reflect utopian or democratic or communist ideals, and facile assumptions about how business elites and politicians take care of each other could easily produce what seems to be a neomarxist scenario. Needless to say, no such interpretations are intended.

The problems we must face in modeling involve purpose, mathematics, and empiricism. If our purpose is persuasion, it is not difficult to select a few intuitively appealing assertions as to "how the system works." Thus a whole theory of bureaucracy might be based on an assumption of size or budget maximization, even though this assumption might be a proxy for a deeper motivation that happens to correlate with the simpler one for certain institutional structures. A different theory could be based on an assumption of extreme risk avoidance by the types of individuals who become bureaucrats. Or we could include both factors.

Standing in favor of the mathematical model are precision, logical consistency, and the potential for analysis. Against it are the dangers caused by premature simplification and specious precision. There are also subtle biases caused by omission which can be missed by the unwary, partially because they confuse the use of mathematical methodology with scientific method and empirical research.

I am a proponent not only of the uses of the theory of games but also of research, operational, and educational gaming (see Shubik, 1975a,b; Brewer and Shubik, 1979). The exercise of constructing a playable game provides a way to organize data, to structure and challenge casual empiricism, and to create a way station between verbal description and formal analytical structures. Although a simple formal model playable as a game is projected, we shall continue here with a qualitative discussion rather than a fully mathematized model.

22.3 The Game

22.3.1 The structure as a whole and limited rationality

An overall description of the process sketched above is given in figure 22.3. The local-interest games are described and related to this figure.

Local-interest game 1: Elite Support

Players: Candidates and the elite.

Game form: Cooperative resource bargaining.

Resources: Expected positions, skills of the elite, own money, "other people's money" (or OPIUM; see Whitman and Shubik, 1979), programs, expected contracts.

Solution: The core.

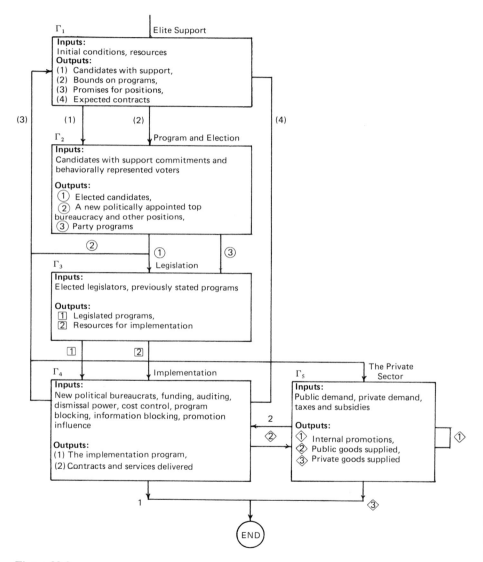

Figure 22.3
The games within the game.

Outputs: (1) Candidates with support; (2) bounds on programs; (3) commitments or promises for positions; (4) expected contracts.

In all societies various elites whose positions are owed to skill or other forms of recruitment (Pareto, 1935) make their accommodations with each other.[3] In a democracy one element of the elite, the politicians, are directly exposed to the public; hence they must make their accommodation with the others taking into account the reaction of a mass constituency.

The political elite in the United States consists of the president, 100 senators, 435 representatives, 50 state governors, 1929 state senators, and 5481 state representatives. There are somewhere between 5000 and 7000 executives who hold most of the power in the top 500 corporations, which account in turn for a considerable fraction of total manufacturing. Considering the top 50 banks, insurance companies, retailers, financiers, law firms, and universities, the 36 religious bodies with more than 50,000 members, the top accounting firms, entrepreneurs, generals, judges, ambassadors, civil servants, independent professionals such as writers, actors, doctors, or scientists—in short, a major sampling of *Who's Who*—one arrives at a number between 20,000 and 50,000. If we considered merely millionaires (in assets), there would probably be between half a million and a million, most of whom do not appear in *Who's Who* and would not consider themselves part of an elite.

Without pretending to more than back-of-the-envelope rigor, we may consider a pool of 15,000–25,000 for the political elite, with 100,000 ± 50,000 to account for other elites. Most of these people have solved their basic economic problems, and their energies are directed to other goals. There are clear exceptions, of course, but even for individuals such as a Getty, a Hughes, or a Rothschild the pursuit of the first hundred million or the first billion dollars is not qualitatively covered by parables describing the maximization of neoclassical Benthamite utility functions.

For the elite I would suggest that "the game" is best considered as a game of position, power, and status. At the top of formal hierarchies, professions, and looser structures there are a few handfuls of positions with a distinctly finite group of contestants.

Without attempting to impose too much structure too quickly, we may say that the most attractive representations of the control, mobility, and preference structures for positions appear to be partial orderings and lattices. Admirals, senators, corporate presidents, senior partners, ambassadors, top bureaucrats, and governors may from one point of

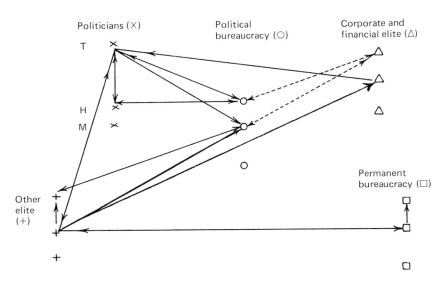

Figure 22.4
A game of position. Three levels are shown for each elite: top (*T*), high (*H*), and
middle (*M*). Arrows indicate whether the moves are one- or two-way. Possible
moves are shown for top politicians, top corporate and financial elite, and middle
other elite.

view be considered equivalent. Furthermore, they may play musical
chairs according to complex rules, but they are not fungible, and their
chains of command and authority, their patterns of mobility, and their
preferences for positions vary considerably.

The process of recruitment for and retirement from high positions in
a government with a political "spoils" system may be two-way from some
parts of the elite but not from other parts. Thus the probability that a
secretary of state will be recruited from a professorship and then, after
his term of office, wait for the next "tide to be taken on the flood" as
a special advisor to an investment bank is much higher than the probability
the he will be recruited from an investment bank and returned to a chair
professorship.

Leaving aside any attempt to characterize the details of positional
control structures (this level of detail does not appear to be absolutely
necessary for the model), figure 22.4 suggests the positional mobility of
politicians, bureaucrats, and other elites. It shows where they can go if
they lose tenure or choose to give up their position.

Three sets of moves have been depicted. The politician who loses an election can accept or choose a lesser political position. Without loss of face, an ex-president can sit as a senator. He could, but it is unlikely that he would, take a job as cabinet secretary or ambassador; it is more likely that a purposely undefined title such as "advisor" would be invented (this and titles such as "of counsel" in corporations and law firms carry the appropriate rank without disturbing the internal hierarchy).

A corporate president may take a secretaryship or an ambassador's post or an undersecretaryship. But in the corporate structure it is harder to move down or back to a lower position without loss of face and probably effectiveness.

A member of another elite, such as a partner in a law firm or a professor, is the third individual portrayed. He could move more or less at the equivalent level into specialized parts of the political or permanent bureaucracy and the corporate elite. He could also move up in the permanent bureaucracy or in his own elite.

In general, the professional politician has too much of himself and his expertise invested in politics to be interested in freely choosing another occupation. His concern with possible mobility is for insurance, and the nature of the quid pro quo in the elites certainly does offer such opportunities. Corporate presidents, lawyers, and professors, in contrast, may view the interlude close to the top of political power as a prelude to a return to an improved position in their own hierarchies. The crudeness of the three-position ordering presented here does not show this in sufficient detail.

Especially for corporate officials, lawyers, and consultants, the financial aspects of having made all of the right connections cannot be ignored. The "financial sacrifices" often broadcast with great piety by those who take up temporary high government service may frequently be seen as bread cast carefully upon the waters. The returns may be manyfold.

It appears that for many members of the elite, preferences range over a mix of positions and money. The politician in his commerce with the elites buys resources to support his political campaigns and as insurance against his departure from the political scene.[4] The elites in return buy two types of informal future contracts contingent on the politician's career: direct contracts, which involve joining the top bureaucracy, and indirect contracts, which involve higher probabilities of contacts, contracts, and influence on program selection.

The essence of any large modern society is that there are many elites, because there are many differentiated high fiduciary and advisory positions to be filled. In a pluralistic society virtually all of them have their own powers. Thus while the religious elite may have little influence on corporate antitrust policy, it may have a central role in discussions of social issues such as abortion, education, or old age policy. The church fathers do not appear to calculate the marginal utility of a little more effort on an antiabortion campaign, although church accountants may worry about limits on spending. Yet the description of the motivation of the members of the church hierarchy who determine overall policy appears to belong more to the realm of sociology than to casual economic utilitarian modeling.

In like manner, although Bagehot (1867, p. 153) suggests that "the newspapers only repeat the side their purchasers like," the press as a whole in a country such as Great Britain, France, or the United States is not a monolithic entity whose writers, commentators, and owners speak with one voice in an unconstrained attempt to maximize circulation.

Undoubtedly doctors, lawyers, accountants, professors, generals, and bishops devote much of their time to taking care of themselves. If each group controls recruitment to its ranks, if each achieves considerable differentiation from the others, and if each has a power base of its own, then the sociopolitical accommodation among politicians and other elites can be modeled as a 10–15-person game.[5] But with such diversity a form of noncooperative solution is to be expected. If we wish to push the economic analogy further, the control structure in a democratic two-party state can be described as a duopoly–oligopoly in which each elite is differentiated from the others by the nature of its powers and by its purpose.

Given the view of elites suggested here, much of the distinction between pluralistic and monolithic societies depends on the relative strengths of the various groups.

Local-interest game 2: Program Selection and Elections

Players: The candidates and the electorate modeled as a behavioral mechanism (or several mechanisms to reflect blocks such as the bureaucracies or unions).

Game form: Extensive form with the incumbent party naming its program first, followed by the opposition, after which the voters vote. The selection of the party programs can be regarded as cooperative subgames by the party candidates.

Resources: Candidates with support and commitments, programs, and votes.

Solution: The noncooperative equilibrium.

Outputs: (1) Elected candidates; (2) a new politically appointed top bureaucracy and other position changes; (3) party programs.

In most instances voters can be represented by a nonatomic game or a behavioral mechanism. If we elect a game-theoretic model for voting, then we face logical problems in describing the length of the future to be taken into account.

Downs (1957) suggested a vote-maximization model for party behavior, and Riker (1962) suggested minimal winning coalitions. But when we consider a slightly more disaggregated system, the individual politician must consider what happens to him both when he wins and when he loses. Furthermore, the power of a party appears to be a highly nonlinear function of its vote majority. The Downs model does not reflect the risk evaluation of majorities of various sizes, the price of losing, or the cost of insurance.

Local-interest game 3: Legislation

Players: The elected representatives and outside pressure groups.

Game form: Cooperative form.

Resources: Votes and other.

Solution: The core (the value might also be considered).

Outputs: (1) Programs; (2) resources conveyed to the bureaucracy for implementation.

Although an election appears to be close to a game of opposition, this is definitely not so for the legislative process. As a first approximation, the goal of the individual legislator is to improve both his "upside" and his "downside" position in a future election.

Local-interest game 4: Implementation

Players: The newly appointed political bureaucrats, the permanent bureaucratic elite, and the mass members of the bureaucracy.

Game form: Cooperative form (alternatively, as a simple example, the strategic form; in either instance the mass bureaucracy is modeled as a resource for the permanent elite rather than as a mass of active players).

Resources: Lower bureaucracy, cost and information control, funding, promotions, ability to dismiss, audit, blocking power.

Table 22.1
Government receipts and outlays, 1979 (billions of $)

Gross National Product	2414
Personal consumption	1511
Private investment (gross)	416
Total federal government purchases	474
Total federal government outlays[a]	493.6
Total federal government receipts	465.9
Total government payrolls (all levels)	53.6
State and local receipts	351.2
State and local expenditures	324.4
State and local payrolls	13.3

a. "Uncontrollable" outlays amounted to $366.1 billion. The
remainder were "relatively uncontrollable."

Source: *Statistical Abstract of the United States*, 1981, pp. 247, 266,
285, 306, 421.

Solution: The core (alternatively a noncooperative equilibrium).

Outputs: (1) The implemented program; (2) promised contracts or services delivered.

The public sees and feels the effects of taxes and some public goods, but it is less aware of the process whereby programs are planned, budgets allocated, and the details of taxation worked out. The control over a black or grey box that takes in large sums of other people's money and uses it directly or disburses it to implement programs whose costs the controllers have helped to estimate gives the controllers strategic power.

As a first crude approximation the money sums spent internally and externally may be regarded as "value added" in the manufacture of the delivered package of programs. In the United States the value added by government bureaus appears to be somewhere around 10–20 percent (see Weidenbaum, 1969, chapter 6).

Depending on the program, the country, and the accounting conventions, government income as a percent of GNP may range from 20 or 30 up to 50 percent for the democracies (with Sweden at the upper end). In the United States in 1979 the items displayed in table 22.1 are relevant. In particular, approximately 73 percent of government outlays are classified as uncontrollable.

There has recently been a resurgence of interest by political scientists and economists in the study of bureaucracy. Examples include Downs (1966), Niskanen (1971), Breton (1974), Miller (1977), Fiorina and Noll (1978), and Fiorina (1983). Weber (1946) offered a classic definition of the properties of a bureaucracy, and von Mises (1944) provided a fine caricature of all that can go astray in the running of a bureaucracy.

A Weberian ideal bureaucracy is supposed to hire and promote employees according to performance measured by professional standards; it should have well-defined job descriptions, maintain formal records of its activities, and provide an optimal hierarchical structure. Given that the forces of market competition are not directly at play in this formal structure, what are the motivations of its managers, and how does its structure influence behavior?

Niskanen (1971) suggested that the power and perquisites of a top bureaucrat are positively correlated with the size of the organization, which in turn is correlated with its budget size. Reasons why a program sponsor might pay a bureau an apparently high price to produce a program include ignorance of true costs, expense in auditing or investigating, fear of program sabotage or slowdowns, and a host of quid pro quo arrangements.

Although large corporations may still compete in the market, Williamson (1975) noted that they, too, may have bureaucracies that are not completely subject to market forces.

A satisfactory model of the political-administrative functioning of a modern society requires an explicit recognition of industrial, commerical, financial, and other bureaucracies beyond the political-administrative structures. In the United States in 1979, for example, the top 500 manufacturing corporations employed 16,195,000 individuals, while the federal government employed 2,897,000 (excluding the military) and state and local governments 13,102,000 out of a labor force of 102,908,000. This indicates around 15 percent of the work force in governmental civil bureaucracy and another 15 percent in large oligopolistic firms.

The economist's view that much of bureaucratic behavior can be explained by some form of a simple maximization model is attractive. But the empirical problem is twofold. What does the bureaucrat maximize? And given that we know what is being maximized, how important is the structure of the game in determining whether we can study simple bureaucratic maximization or whether we must study a non-constant-sum game of strategy?

In studying government bureaucracy, the twilight zone of economics, we must take political science and sociology into account. The idea of the bureaucrat maximizing budget size may be reasonable for some situations, but the British civil servant working for the honors list or the French official aiming at membership in the Legion d'Honneur might be an equally or more valid model for other situations. There is an informal consensus that power, perquisites, prestige, and pelf all form part of the goal structure of the senior official, whereas tenure and the quiet life may be of more concern to the lower and middle members of the bureaucracy. The easiest of these to model and mathematize is money in either salary or revenue size. Unfortunately, mathematical ease and empirical plausibility do not necessarily coincide.

Although it has been possible to create virtually institution-free theories of production and consumption, such a development is impossible for any viable theory of oligopoly or bureaucracy. Both must be process-oriented and take into account less-than-perfect competition. The institutions appear in the rules of the game, and manifest behavior (such as bargaining over budget size or market share) must be considered in terms of competition among the few.

In any modern society there is a considerable diversity in the size, structure, function, professional requirements, political exposure, tenure conditions, and measurability of output of the various bureaucracies required at different governmental levels. A glance at the perceptive study by Sayre and Kaufman (1960) of New York City provides a broad vista of line agencies with diverse products, services, and overhead or staff agencies with equally diverse and even more nebulous products.

In some agencies the maximization of budget size may be a useful proxy goal for a complex of motivations. But where direct delivery of services is involved, as in social work, the maximization of direct employment might serve as well if not better. In other agencies whose role is primarily disbursement or procurement, the growth in employment size may be far less significant than the control over patronage that comes with the ability to select or influence the selection of contractors. In still other agencies power may be reflected in the size of the internal payroll or the number of external employees being supported on service contracts.

The ability to influence or control the definition of the criteria of worth or efficiency in the measurement of public goods and services is another key source of bureaucratic power. For example, how does society or its fiduciaries evaluate the worth and the efficiency of the production of a newly designed nuclear aircraft carrier?

The amount of money available to an agency may be a poor proxy for power if it has all been earmarked for historical commitments. Maximizing one's budget and maximizing discretionary budget may be considerably different goals.

Where a bureau is a monopsonist or near-monopsonist (as is the case for many weapons procurement agencies), should we expect or desire to find monopsonistic behavior? Are there societal and bureaucratic reasons to expect that something will be left on the table for the other parties?

The mobility of top bureaucrats varies among bureaus and societies. For example, in the United States the lower echelons of admirals and generals tend to retire relatively early on pension and then take up another career (often as consultants or corporate employees).

The ability to dismiss a top regular civil servant varies from not easy to virtually impossible. Individuals are moved laterally or sent into various forms of exile. The weapon of tenure is of considerable importance in enabling bureaucrats to outlast the politician or political appointee in a hurry.

In the United States the pay of the upper federal bureaucracy is tied by law to that of the executive and legislators. This complicates the design of incentives for the bureaucrats.[6] In 1977 the president's salary was $200,000; the vice president, speaker of the house, and chief justice earned $75,000; senators and representatives, $57,000.[7]

In the federal government there are around 2500 politically appointed senior staff. Because an appointee of this type is in a real sense a transient, he is concerned with actions leading to visible, relatively short-term results that will improve his position when he moves on. A key element to him is his "report card" as seen by others.

At best the political appointee is faced with a cooperative bargaining game with the permanent bureaucracy. Producing technical studies and special reports, arranging for subcontracting, auditing, meeting specifications, and haggling over standards are all part of the domain of the permanent bureaucracy. The political appointees can create "guidelines" and suggest unpleasant consequences if these are not met; but they may then have to face "working-to-rule," harassment over fine points, and sly use of the operators' considerably greater knowledge of process and the productive capabilities of the system.

No attempt is made here to provide a specific description of the interfacing task of the high political appointee with managerial responsibilities. His goals are neither the same as nor opposed to those of the 30,000-odd senior bureaucrats in the upper levels of the permanent civil service. The relationship is sufficiently direct and bilateral, and reflects a sufficient

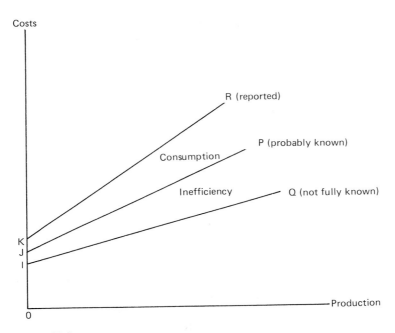

Figure 22.5
Organizational slack.

community of interest, that there is generally room for accommodation. In a detailed model the subgame between the political appointees and the permanent bureaucrats would have a large core under almost all circumstances.

Local-interest game 5: The Private Industrial Sector   The natural description of the private sector is as a strategic market game with oligopolistic sectors. If these sectors are ignored, we can use the approximation of a general-equilibrium system in which taxes and orders for public goods are exogenously determined.

There is a grey area of slack in real business bureaucracy (Selten, 1982) because, as indicated in figure 22.5 and in expense accounts and the daily running of large and small businesses, living well off the firm is recognized in virtually all environments. In the figure *OK* and *KR* are the reported fixed and variable costs; *OJ* and *JP* are the costs more or less known to management, which leave a little something off the top for everyone;

and OI and IQ are fixed and variable costs known only to God, the all-seeing statistician, or the utopian commissar.

Another degree of freedom in the system also appears in the costing of new public goods. Consider two government contracts. The first is for a space shuttle and the second for army flashlights. The first will call for original research and development; the budget will be broken down into hundreds of thousands of line items with overheads tucked in everywhere and with many of the items from a sole source supplier to a sole sink demand. In contrast, the order for flashlights could be filled by many different firms, so that (given that mechanisms such as the GAO audit exist) a price differential can be maintained only by appeals to special qualities such as durability that can be defended as forms of product variation sufficient to justify a price spread from ordinary private-sector flashlights (see Gansler, 1980).

Finally, reported profits may play an important role in the internal promotion system of the private sector. Thus, even though the correlation between some form of expected profit maximization and the career pattern of a member of the industrial elite will be less than 1, it may nevertheless be high.

The book by Downs (1966) is filled with dozens of insights and hypotheses concerning conservatism, imperfect control, free goods, bureaucratic imperialism, and so forth. Niskanen (1971) offered a far more parsimonious and economic view, and those who work on administrative behavior offer other views. In order to build a politicoeconomic system that reconciles the public and private sectors we must clearly describe the bureaucratic subgame. The nature of a parsimonious yet useful representation is still an open empirical question. However, a reflection on how goods and services, public or private, are really delivered is enough to suggest that even at a high level of abstraction an economic dynamics cannot exists without a description of the bureaucratic delivery system. As a first approximation, especially when studying statics, we can ignore process times, structure, and costs. But any attempt at reconciliation between microeconomic theory and macroeconomics calls for a specification of delivery systems. At the least these involve a description of the bureaucracy and of the politicoeconomic decision structure.

22.3.2 Subsolutions and the system as a whole

The games described above are played more or less sequentially, with the outputs from one serving as inputs to others. To separate the strategic behavior of many of the agents we need some dei ex machina in the form of estimates of how the expected results from future games might feed back on the local game about to be played. Clearly, in some instances the forecasts must be about future games whose outcome that forecast will have changed. Those more comfortable with equilibrium analysis might look for self-fulfilling prophecies, "rational expectations," and steady states. But our view is that sociopolitical choice takes place in a system where problems of moral philosophy are posed and refined, and that the implementation of programs and the clarification of values are in constant interaction. Thus it is more natural to conceive of the normal state of the system as being in disequilibrium: "The grail is in the seeking not the cup." Paradoxically, perhaps, the approach suggested is via a sequence of subgames each played and analyzable in terms of some form of statics and limited rationality, but all linked dynamically by hope or expectations.

Although the local-interest games and the system as a whole have not been formalized to a level at which strict game-theoretic analysis can be applied, we can nevertheless make some comments about the parts and the system as a whole with varying degrees of formality.

Without particularly restrictive conditions, the local-interest election game may have a unique (up to inessential degeneracy) equilibrium point for any set of expectations and any random, after-the-fact events. Under some circumstances all the other local-interest games will have cores. It is conjectured that under reasonable circumstances there will be a considerable indeterminacy in the system, which can be demonstrated by showing that a strategy with a point in the core of the first local-interest game generates a noncooperative equilibrium in the second; the set of all noncooperative equilibria so generated leads to a class of local-interest games at the next stage, many of which will have cores. Any point in any of these cores may be considered as feeding into the last stage, and many of these last games will also have cores.

The meaning of this conjecture is that the system is considerably underdetermined even though its economic aspects are fully described— unless one adopts the view that the missing political, sociological, and psychological detail can be entirely explained by economics.

It must also be stressed that in this formulation the individuals, not the institutions, are the players. They have free will and they play strategically on a limited stage.

The higher the level of activity of the individuals, the more likely it is that their strategies consist of "environment setting" for others. A move of one player may amount to limiting the domain of moves of another.

In sketching the model we have included legislation, and legislation may take the form of modifying the local-interest games by changing the institutions and organizations. At a longer-run and more profound level we would also wish to contemplate constitutional change and changes in overall societal mores (see Ostrom, 1982). But it is precisely as we move to the higher-order features of society such as the evolution of the concept of freedom and the institutions that operationalize the concept that the limitations of the simpler variables and techniques of the economist become clearer.

All of the analysis in this argument has been based directly on individual optimization. But goal-seeking strategic behavior is far more than economic optimization. An attempt to explain freedom or war as a manifestation of economic determinism is to ignore history and to replace a multivariate evolving system with only its simplest and most quantifiable local-interest game.

22.4 Summary Remarks

22.4.1 The role of Pareto optimality

A sketch has been given of a closed system with local maximization achieved through a limited scope of strategic activity, where the institutions appear as special rules of the game. No claim is made for the empirical accuracy of the particular model. Nor are casual political conclusions to be drawn. On the contrary, it appears that the performance of the system will depend considerably on the specifics of the power of the elites and the bureaucracy.

In models of human behavior with no costs or limits to decision making, the institutional arrangements do not matter because we can assume that rules are costlessly created and can be changed at will. The simplifying assumptions made by von Neumann and Morgenstern (1944) to describe the cooperative stable-set solution exemplify this approach. All coalition formation and communication costs are left out of the game and do not affect the set of optimal outcomes. Choice theory and general-equilibrium theory are similarly process-free. Hence, in all of these theories the Pareto-optimal set is fixed in advance and is independent of institutional arrangements, bargaining costs, and implementation systems.

If, however, we adopt the view that at any point in time institutions and other rules of the game are given and that changing the rules is costly and takes some time, then the feasible set of outcomes will be constrained by the resources utilized in resource allocation. Thus Pareto optimality must be defined as depending on the allocation mechanism, which imposes a limit on the feasible set of final outcomes. This limitation would not exist if all alternative allocation mechanisms were free. The Pareto set thus becomes the optimal surface of the constrained feasible set. Given that we must always start from some initial conditions, the feasible set will depend on the extant institutional arrangements. Thus the relative efficiency of two institutional arrangements may hinge on the initial conditions.

The above observations are based on an acceptance of the validity of the Pareto-optimal surface as a useful concept in political economy. Although I support the use of and reasoning behind the Pareto-optimal surface for the study of a limited set of problems in microeconomics, such as the simple exchange economy, it is not clear how valid a concept it is in either positive or normative social-welfare theory. Even a normative theory that begins with "people should" must provide a reasoned argument that it is physically feasible for people to do what they should be doing. Thus to require that individuals dispassionately review all alternatives and calculate an overall Pareto-optimal surface may entail not only norms about how people should behave but counterfactual normative assumptions about how people should be designed in order to make them capable of computation and perception at levels unknown to the current species.

22.4.2 Communism, democracy, and limited rationality
"Under capitalism man exploits man; under communism it is the reverse."
    East European saying

Comparisons of democratic and primarily market-oriented societies with communist societies can be considered in the context of the variants of game-theoretic analysis.[8]

Viewed in their most favorable light, both democratic market-oriented theories of human sociopolitical welfare and communist theories are concerned with the welfare of all individuals. However, taking the emergence of a people's democracy and the final withering away of the state as a serious operational problem, we find that implicit in this view is a philosophical position (shared with utopian utilitarians) on the perfectibility of the human being. In contrast, democratic models tend to be based on a view that not merely stresses individual motivation but also implicitly or explicitly assumes limitations on individual capabilities.

We may adopt at least three models of human governance:

1. Humans are and will in all probability remain limited in their perceptual, conceptual, and coordinating capabilities and will persist in maintaining individual differences in abilities, values, and preferences.

2. Humans may maintain individual differences in abilities, values, and preferences, but they can be considered to be striving toward perfect individual rationality.

3. In the perfect state, education, indoctrination, and individual realization of social identity will yield rule-free, institution-free rational cooperation.

The first model not only is closest to much of the spirit of political theorizing on representative government but is also allied with much of market-economy theorizing from Adam Smith onward. Even more recently the trend in economic thought has been toward formalizing the concept of limited rationality. This includes limitations on perceptions of choice and of preference formation, on computation, and on the selection of search routines.

Most work on game theory, except for some attempts to devise behavioral or myopic solutions for dynamic games, has been based on fully rational models of man. One of the most difficult open problems is how to reconcile behavioral theories with game theory. A potentially satisfactory way to achieve a theory with an intermix of behavioral and strategic components is to postulate that organization, information, communication, and evaluation costs are all sufficiently high that it is optimal to delegate short-run decisions to agents who perform local or parochial optimizations.

The game-theoretic approach based on the individualistic rational actor gives rise to two distinct points of view on the social system and on solution theory. A major thrust of the work of Harsanyi has been the search for a single equilibrium point that can be calculated as the appropriate outcome to any given strategic situation. In contrast with this resolutely philosophical approach is the pluralistic willingness to entertain many different solution concepts, as manifested in the work of Aumann, Maschler, Selten, Shapley, and others. In part, the pluralistic view comes from a pragmatic orientation toward the uses of game theory in application to special models built for a variety of purposes. Both the model and the solution concept to be used may vary with the nature of the questions to be answered.

A justification of the eclectic approach is that our models are invariably simplifications and aggregations of the phenomena we wish to study.

Thus, for example, the crudeness of a solution concept such as the core may indicate that the model cannot be expected to yield a more determinate solution without the addition of further detail concerning psychological, social, political, or other factors.

A third game-theoretic approach suggested here is to try to blend limited rationality with strategic individualism.

A priori the methodology of game theory provides no rules or axioms for correlating individual preferences or values. Team theory does provide such rules, as does the rhetoric of Lenin in which all individuals are agents serving a higher purpose. Costs and difficulties in communication make the problem of coordination and joint optimization difficult, but goal orientation or social cohesion are supplied by axiom. Thus it appears that in game-theoretic terms a perfect communist or other utopian state requires both unlimited rationality and a sense of "brotherhood" or correlation of individual concerns. When communication is costly and rationality is limited, identity of interests can offer only a limited utopia in which the state does not wither away because organizations and institutions are still needed to supply guidance in the form of rules of the game for the socially cooperative but less than perfectly rational members of society.

22.4.3 Economics, politics, and sociology
The problems involved in the social and political control of public programs do not stand in opposition to price systems in either controlled economies or competitive markets.

The progressive refinements of microeconomic theory have produced at a high level of abstraction and with minimal institutional description an economic theory of markets and prices. The increasing precision in the specification of prices, goods, services, and markets has been achieved at the cost of a virtually complete separation of economics from political economy. The results have, however, proven highly beneficial for exploring technical conditions for the existence of systems that can be efficiently decentralized by prices.

The very power of the general-equilibrium analysis suggests that the time is ripe to take two steps beyond it in terms of the scope of the questions being asked and the problems being investigated. The first step, initiated in the last few years, is to consider the effects of taxation, subsidies, and the supply of public goods on the general-equilibrium system, ignoring the genesis of societal demand. The second step is to describe and analyze the control mechanism that places public requirements and constraints on the economy.

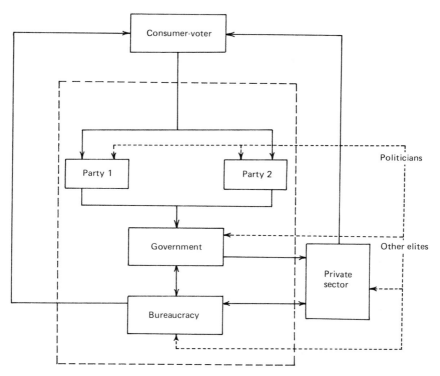

Figure 22.6
The engine and control mechanism.

Explanations of the mechanisms for the formation and delivery of public programs involve our understanding of the structure and motivations of those fiduciaries who act for others in the proposal, formulation, legislation, and implementation of public programs. A sociopolitico-economic control system has been connected here with the economic engine. It is suggested that such an interconnection opens the way to an analysis of mixed sociopolitical and economic systems that simultaneously separates out considerations of economics, politics, administration, bureaucratic structure, and the power of elites (to mention a few items) and formalizes a specification of their interconnections and feedbacks.

Figure 22.6 outlines the politicoeconomic engine and its control mechanism in a society with a two-party representative government. The solid lines indicate the engine and the dashed lines the control mechanism. If we regard the elites as small in number in relation to society as a whole, and as playing their own game, we can represent their influence by replacing the party–government–bureaucracy mechanisms by a black box or special player whose behavior is given exogenously. The black box is indicated by the long dashed lines.[9]

22.5 On Game Theory in the Social Sciences

22.5.1 A note on optimization

Maximizing functions, selecting optimal subsets of elements from given sets, and solving competitive games are not the central tasks of the economist. It is not only in mathematical manipulations that economists show their virtues, but in constructing models to be analyzed and in establishing the relevance and realism of the questions that are asked.

The power of economic theory lies not in the optimization process alone, but in the structure imposed on utility functions defined on commodity sets, given properties such as the existence of quantitative measures on commodities and the continuity of preferences. The economics is in the description and the questions, not in the mathematics.

The political scientist who wishes to describe election behavior can borrow from the mathematician the same techniques already borrowed by the economist. But the problem of describing choice sets, preferences, and values lies in the domain of politics, not in that of economics. More than a relabeling of axes is needed to go from economic analysis to political analysis.

Turning to sociology for another example, the controlling positions in any society belong to a group of elites who appear to pursue ends involving position, power, professionalism, self-esteem, fame, popularity, and many other goals beyond wealth and worldly goods. A good sociological theory of elite behavior must be based on an appropriate description of the choice set and a selection process. Sociologically motivated goals and powers may then become one part of the process that endows institutions with long-run structure though they are composed of individuals who for the most part display short-term behavior.

The argument here is that when we enlarge the model of a politico-economic process to include program and candidate selection, party elections, and a bureaucracy, we introduce new degrees of freedom that are not explained adequately by either the economics or the politics alone. We must then fit these different features together as a conceptual whole to provide a framework for interdisciplinary research toward a unified understanding of sociopolitical processes.

22.5.2 Toward a mathematical political economy

"The economic world in much of its working is somewhat nonconvex and operates with limitations on information. Hidden in each nonconvexity or pool of special information is a group of millionaires or fat commissars."

Utilizing the methodology of game theory, we have constructed a series of progressively more complex economic and politicoeconomic models. Those phenomena least dependent on institutional structure are modeled directly from economic or politicoeconomic data into a coalitional or a characteristic-function form. Other phenomena require modeling in strategic or even extensive form.

Table 22.2 lists economic structures that can be modeled as games in coalitional form. Exchange economies with or without indivisibilities and production and exchange economies with constant returns to scale are easily modeled in this form, but nothing else is. By appropriately defining coalition production, we can model economies with decreasing returns as though the coalitional description were adequate, but unlike the case of an economy with constant returns, the distinction between individually owned or publicly available production technology becomes critical.

In the production and exchange economy with decreasing returns to scale, the general-equilibrium model has both consumers and firms as economic agents, nonvoting shares, and distributed profits.

Large indivisibilities, joint production, and public goods all provide technical conditions that lead to sociopolitical arrangements involving joint ownership and voting. The joint stock corporation is essentially a form of local public good. We can extend any of the last five models noted in table 22.2 to include voting. Table 22.3 shows three voting rules applied to pure public goods. In each instance the voting is direct.

When unanimity is required, all imputations are in the core. With simple-majority voting and unlimited taxation there is no core. If minorities are forbidden to destroy resources to avoid taxation, the simple model in which a majority takes everything and a minority is given nothing is a c-game. If the minority can destroy its resources, then we need to take this threat into account (see chapter 13).

It has been noted in chapters 19 and 20 that minority protection and the existence of a core seem to be related. In chapter 20 we noted Kaneko's construction of a taxation game with minority protection through ratio taxation. In actual legal codes the protection of minority stockholders and taxpayers is specified in terms of payments of dividends or taxes in money; thus a price system is implicitly assumed to exist. This situation

Table 22.2
Near-market games: A summary

	Conceptual modeling problems	c-Game	Core	CE or LE	Equivalence of game with continuum of agents to CE or LE	
					Core	Value
Exchange economy	no	yes	yes	yes	yes	yes
Exchange economy, nonconvex preferences	no	yes	ε-core	yes[a]	yes	NYI
Exchange economy with one indivisible good desired by any trader	no	yes	yes	yes	yes with money, no without	NYI
Exchange economy with general indivisible goods	no	yes	no[b]	no[b]	no	no
Production and exchange, constant returns	no	yes	yes	yes	yes	yes
Production and exchange, decreasing returns	yes	yes and no	yes	yes	NYI	NYI
Production and exchange with set-up and capacities	yes	yes and no	ε-core	yes[a]	NYI	NYI
Local public goods	yes	no	ε-core	yes[a] (LE)	NYI	NYI
Pure public goods	yes	no	yes and no	LE	no	no
Externalities and mixed public goods	yes	no	no[b]	no[b]	no	no

NYI = not yet investigated; CE = competitive equilibrium; LE = Lindahl equilibrium.
a. An appropriately defined ε-price system is needed. b. In general. c. See table 22.3.

Table 22.3
Near-market games with voting: Pure public goods

Voting rule	Conceptual modeling problems	c-Game	Core	LE	Equivalence of game with continuum of agents to LE Core	Value
Unanimity	no	yes	yes	yes	no	no
Simple majority	no	yes and no	no	yes	no	no
Ratio taxation	yes	yes and no	yes	yes	yes[a]	NYI

NYI = not yet investigated; LE = Lindahl equilibrium.
a. An appropriately defined ε-price system is needed.

can be treated formally by first modeling the economy as a strategic market game and then considering the core of that game.

The Kaneko model is somewhat special, and he is able to obtain a coincidence between the core and the Lindahl equilibrium. Explorations of the relationship between the Lindahl equilibrium and the core, however, indicate that the former does not depend on the characteristic function, whereas the latter does. As can be seen from table 22.3, some voting rules lead to empty cores. Thus any hope for a theorem on the equivalence of the core and the Lindahl equilibrium must rest on our being able to select a model with an appropriate rule for minority rights protection.

Before we consider the representation of economic or politicoeconomic structures by games in strategic form, we must add a few further general comments on modeling and analysis using the coalitional form. In this book much use has been made of games with side payments, but for many economic problems the no-side-payment formulation appears to provide a more faithful model. Qualitatively many of the results are the same for both classes of games. The key distinction appears to be that with side payments the competitive equilibrium and value of a market game are unique and the core is a convex set. All these properties are lost in games without side payments. Furthermore, although it is known that with side payments all totally balanced games are market games, this has not yet been shown for totally balanced no-side-payment games using the ordinal balance definition of Scarf (see *GTSS*, chapter 6).

The coalitional form and core theory do not appear to be particularly suited to the study of situations involving uncertainty and nonsymmetric information (see chapter 13), although some results with contingent commodities can be obtained. Uncertainty in coalition formation can be reflected by the use of the weighted value of "fuzzy" coalitions (see *GTSS*, section 7.7.3).

Table 22.4 displays strategic-market-game versions of two of the economic structures in table 22.2. The exchange economy (as noted in chapters 14 and 15) can be modeled in several different ways as a strategic market game. If trade is through markets, then at least for the small individual in a large market with noncooperative trade, the need to trade through a price-formation mechanism creates a weak externality. Even for the game played cooperatively, a large coalition is scarcely influenced by the buying or selling power of a small coalition. As suggested in chapter 7, the Harsanyi modification for calculating the characteristic function can be used to reflect the importance of threats. Dubey and Shubik (1978a,b, 1981) considered the three strategic market games noted in table 22.4. Although no one has yet formally investigated the core and value properties of the cooperative games derived from these three games, it is conjectured that in all instances the core–competitive equilibrium equivalence can be obtained. Even when nonvoting shares are introduced, though, it is unlikely that a value–competitive equilibrium equivalence will be obtained (see section 20.2.2).

When voting or economic action involves control by fiduciaries, a host of new problems appear. In particular, as suggested in these last two chapters, it seems reasonable to model a variety of types of players and institutions. As indicated in table 22.3, a certain amount of direct voting can be modeled immediately in coalitional form. In general, however, the extension of our models to take into account the elemental features of production and distribution as a costly politicoeconomic process forces us to the strategic and even the extensive form.

The building blocks for the mechanisms are institutions. We need to acknowledge at least firms, political parties, government, financial institutions, and bureaucracies. For some purposes they may be modeled as mechanisms or as aggregate players. They may also be modeled as subgames or as part of the rules of a game in which (by constitutional change, for instance) the rules governing subgames can be changed over time. Among the players who merit differentiation are consumer–voters, politicians, entrepreneurs, financiers, administrator–bureaucrats, and possibly some other elites. The sociological, legal, and political bounds on the politicoeconomic process appear more or less naturally as we try to specify even the most abstract of rules reflecting the presence of institutions as the carriers of process.

Table 22.4
Strategic market games: A summary

Economic structure	Strategic market game	Coalitional form	c-Game	NE	CE	Equivalence of game with continuum of agents to CE		
						NE	Core	Value
Exchange economy	many models	h-function	almost	yes	yes	yes	yes?	yes?
Production and exchange, profit-maximizing firms	many models	h-function	almost	yes	yes	yes	yes?	yes?
Production and exchange, utility-maximizing managers	many models	h-function	almost	yes	yes	yes	yes?	yes?

CE = competitive equilibrium; NE = noncooperative equilibrium.

The general-equilibrium theory was an important preinstitutional contribution to economic understanding. The methods of cooperative game theory provided a means to consider many more features of the economy while still minimizing institutional content. Yet the needs of political economy and the reconciliation of micro- and macroeconomics require models of process. Moreover, our need to understand the evolution of stable politicoeconomic structures makes the investigation of noncooperative solutions in the construction of self-policing systems a natural next step.

Once we start to model politicoeconomic systems of any complexity in strategic or extensive form, we immediately recognize the importance of limitations to information, knowledge, communication, and data processing. The reconciliation of the strategic models of game theory with models of limited rationality appears to be of considerable importance not only to the development of political economy but to the reconsideration of both welfare theory and basic political philosophy.

Notes to chapter 22

1. The study of a brief time slice of society to consider the impact of taxes, all other things being equal, provides a situation in which one might argue that modeling the state as an extra and powerful player is legitimate for the limited purpose at hand. (See chapter 20.)

2. This reflects an approach adopted by Niskanen (1971).

3. See Burch (1980) for a description of the background, recruitment, and connections of members of United States governments.

4. In 1975–76 reported campaign finances were divided as follows (in millions of dollars):

	Democratic	Republican	Other	Total
President	61.7	50.2	2.0	114
Senate	18.8	18.5	0.8	38.1
House	32.4	28.1	0.5	60.9

This breaks down to approximately $56,000,000, $186,500, and $69,500 per major presidential, senatorial, and house of representatives candidate.

5. By "person" I really mean a grouping of specialized individuals into a profession or institution such as medicine or the church.

6. See the collection of essays edited by Hartman and Weber (1980).

7. These numbers can be contrasted with those of the highest-paid executives.

In 1977 the salaries of executives in the *Fortune* top 50 ranged from around $300,000 to over $800,000 per annum.

8. For a recent non-game-theoretic discussion see Lindblom (1977).

9. The elite in a society with one vote per voter may be approximated by a set of measure zero as voters. They may or may not hold a measurable amount of economic resources. For example, in the United States a 1972 estimate gives 20.7 percent of personal wealth to the top 1 percent of wealth holders (*Statistical Abstract of the United States*, 1981, p. 453).

Appendix A
Definition of the Inner Core

An interesting link between side-payment and no-side-payment games comes in the study of the inner core, defined as follows.

Let N be a finite set with n members, and let E^N be the n-dimensional Euclidean space of vectors α with coordinates α^i indexed by $i \in N$. For each $S \subseteq N$, let E^S denote the subspace of E^N defined by $\alpha^i = 0$, $i \in N \backslash S$, let E^S_+ denote the nonnegative orthant of E^S, and let e^S denote the vector in E^S defined by $e^S_i = 1$ for $i \in S$ and 0 for $i \in N \backslash S$. We shall use $\cdot$ for the ordinary inner product and $\times$ for componentwise multiplication of vectors; thus $\alpha \cdot e^S$ denotes $\sum_{i \in S} \alpha^i$, while $\alpha \times e^S$ denotes the projection of α on E^S. A subset X of E^S will be called S-comprehensive if $X = X - E^S_+$ (algebraic subtraction).

A *game* $\mathscr{G}$ is a pair (N, V), where V, called the *characteristic function* of $\mathscr{G}$, is a function from subsets of N to subsets of E^N such that, for each $S \subseteq N$, $V(S)$ is a closed, nonempty, S-comprehensive subset of E^S. Intuitively the elements of $V(S)$ represent payoff vectors that the members of S, acting in concert, can achieve for themselves (or improve upon). Sometimes we shall specify a game by a pair (N, F), where the sets $F(S)$ are not necessarily S-comprehensive; in that case it will be understood that the actual characteristic function is defined by $V(S) = F(S) - E^S_+$. A game $\mathscr{G}$ is said to be *compact* (or *convex*) if it can be represented as (N, F) with all the $F(S)$ compact (or convex).

Let $\mathscr{G}$ be a compact game, and let $\lambda \in E^N_+$. Define the real-valued set function v_λ by

$$v_\lambda(S) = \max\{\lambda \cdot \alpha : \alpha \in V(S)\},$$

and define the new game $\mathscr{G}_\lambda = (N, V_\lambda)$ by

$$V_\lambda(S) = \{\alpha \in E^S : \lambda \cdot \alpha \leq v_\lambda(S)\}.$$

This will be called the *λ-transfer game of $\mathscr{G}$*; this term may be explained by defining *λ-side-payment spaces*,

$$H^S_\lambda = \{\alpha \in E^S : \lambda \cdot \alpha = 0\} \quad \text{for } S \subseteq N,$$

and noting that $V_\lambda(S) = V(S) + H^S_\lambda$. It is clear that $\mathscr{G}_\lambda$ is convex but not compact; note that it depends only on the ratios of the λ^i.

The *core* of any game $\mathscr{G} = (N, V)$ is defined as the set of vectors $\alpha \in V(N)$ such that for each nonempty $S \subseteq N$, $\alpha \times e^S$ is in the closure of $E^S \backslash V(S)$. The *inner core* of a compact game $\mathscr{G}$ is defined as the set of vectors $\alpha \in V(N)$ such that for some $\lambda \in E_+^N$, α is in the core of $\mathscr{G}_\lambda$. Intuitively a vector in the core represents a feasible outcome of the game that cannot be improved upon by any coalition. A vector in the inner core cannot be improved upon even if λ-side-payments are allowed, for at least one λ.

Appendix B
Convergence of the Bargaining Set for Differentiable Market Games

This appendix contains the proof by Shapley that the bargaining set $\mathcal{B}$ (which contains the bargaining set $\mathcal{M}_1^{(i)}$) shrinks down to the core $\mathcal{C}$ for certain sequences of monetary economies in which the trader types are held fixed while the number of traders of each type increases without limit. An essential condition is the differentiability of the characteristic function in profile form, a condition that also ensures the shrinkage of the core itself to a single point, namely, the payoff vector generated by the unique (in this case) competitive price vector. The same differentiability condition has been shown to ensure convergence of the Shapley value to the same point; thus four different kinds of solution come together in the limit.

Let $N = \{1, 2, \ldots, n\}$ be the set of player types, and let there be k players of each type; in the following, n will be fixed, but not k. A particular player will be denoted by $\langle t, h \rangle$, where $t \in N$ and $1 \leq h \leq k$. If S is a coalition, its *profile* is the vector of integers $\sigma = (\sigma_1, \sigma_2, \ldots, \sigma_n)$, where σ_t is the number of players in S of type t. The all-player set is denoted by kN.

Let $k\Gamma$ denote the nk-person game $(kN; v)$ with characteristic function

$$v(S) = \phi(\sigma/k). \tag{B.1}$$

Here ϕ is a function that is defined on the closed positive orthant E_+^n. It is assumed to be concave, positively homogeneous of degree 1, and continuously differentiable. By the latter we mean that for each $t \in N$ a continuous function ϕ_i can be defined on $E_+^n - \{0\}$ that agrees with the partial derivative $\partial \phi / \partial x_t$ when $x_t > 0$ and with the one-sided partial derivative $\partial \varphi / \partial x_t^+$ when $x_t = 0$. It follows that ϕ, being concave, has a continuous gradient throughout the interior of E_+^n. Since the functions φ_t are homogeneous of degree 0 (that is, constant on rays out of the origin), it is clear that we must except the origin from any continuity statement.

It is possible to think of ϕ as a production function, with each player type providing a different input and all players having linear utility for the output. More generally, ϕ would be derived through an optimization procedure from the utility and production functions and the initial endowment of the underlying economic model. The differentiability of ϕ can be assured by imposing suitable differentiability and boundary conditions on the underlying model.

Let $\|x\| = \max_t x_t$ for $x \in E^n$. (The range of the index t is always N.) Let $Q = \{x \in E_+^n : \|x\| \leq 1\}$ and $\bar{Q} = \{x \in E_+^n : \|x\| = 1\}$. Thus Q is the cube of points with all coordinates between 0 and 1, and $\bar{Q}$ is its "outer" boundary. The partial derivatives ϕ_t are continuous on the compact set $\bar{Q}$ and hence are bounded and uniformly continuous there. Consequently we can define

$$M = \max_{x, y \in \bar{Q}} \max_t |\phi_t(x) - \phi_t(y)| \tag{B.2}$$

and find a positive, increasing function h on $(0, \infty)$ such that for any $\varepsilon > 0$ and any $x, y \in \bar{Q}$,

$$\|x - y\| < h(\varepsilon) \Rightarrow \max_t |\phi_t(x) - \phi_t(y)| < \varepsilon. \tag{B.3}$$

Let us represent a payoff vector in the game $k\Gamma$ by a doubly indexed array, thus:

$$a = \{a_{th} : t \in N, h = 1, 2, \ldots, k\}. \tag{B.4}$$

We denote by $a(S)$ the sum of the payoffs in a to the members of a coalition $S \subseteq kN$. The *excess* of S at a is defined as $v(S) - a(S)$. For any imputation (that is, efficient, individually rational payoff vector) of k we have a total payoff of

$$a(kN) = v(kN) = \phi(1, 1, \ldots, 1). \tag{B.5}$$

The fact that this is independent of k emphasizes that we are working with a "fractured" rather than a "replicated" model. Of course, the latter can be obtained from our present treatment by inserting factors of k at the proper places. However, note that the strong ε-core of the fractured model corresponds to the strong $k\varepsilon$-core of the replicated model, which is in a certain sense "weaker" than the weak ε-core of that model.

THEOREM B.1.   *For any $\varepsilon > 0$, the bargaining set $\mathcal{B}$ of $k\Gamma$ is contained in the strong ε-core $\mathcal{C}_\varepsilon$ for all sufficiently large k. Specifically, it suffices that*

$$k \geq \frac{M}{\varepsilon' h(\varepsilon')}, \tag{B.6}$$

where $\varepsilon' = 2\varepsilon/n^2$ and M and h are given by (B.2) and (B.3).

Proof. Let a be an imputation of $k\Gamma$ outside $\mathcal{C}_\varepsilon$, so that the maximum excess at a, over all coalitions, is greater than ε. Our eventual goal is to show that there is a justified objection to a. Without loss of generality we may assume that

$$a_{t1} \le a_{t2} \le \cdots \le a_{tk} \quad \text{for all } t \in N. \tag{B.7}$$

Then, for the excess of any S at a we have

$$v(S) - a(S) \le \phi(\sigma/k) - \sum_t \sum_{h=1}^{s_t} a_{th}. \tag{B.8}$$

Intuitively (B.7) makes the coalitions whose members are the lowest-numbered members of their respective types the most "effective" at a.

Now we introduce a sort of "ideal maximum excess" at a; it is the excess that could be attained if coalitions with fractional players could be formed. Define the functions

$$\alpha_t(u) = ka_{t,[ku]+1} \quad \text{for } t \in N, \tag{B.9}$$

where the brackets denote "greatest integer in"; then we have

$$a_{th} = \int_{(h-1)/k}^{h/k} \alpha_t(u)\,du. \tag{B.10}$$

These functions present the payoff vector a in the form of a "bar graph" (see figure B.1). Next we define the excess of $x \in Q$ at a by

$$e(x) = \phi(x) - \sum \int_{t_0}^{x_t} \alpha_t(u)\,du. \tag{B.11}$$

This is a continuous concave function of x, since ϕ is continuous and concave and the integral of an increasing function is continuous and convex. We see that if kx is integer-valued and if S is a coalition consisting of the first kx_t players of each type t, then $e(x) = v(S) - a(S)$. In view of (B.8) and the fact that $a \notin \mathscr{C}_\varepsilon$ we have

$$E^* = \max_{x \in Q} e(x) > \varepsilon. \tag{B.12}$$

Let x^* be a maximal element of the (closed, convex) set of elements of Q that achieve this maximum; then for all $x \in Q - \{x^*\}$,

$$x \ge x^* \Rightarrow e(x) < E^*. \tag{B.13}$$

Note that

$$\|x^*\| \ge 1/k, \tag{B.14}$$

since otherwise we could increase x^* by multiplying by $1/(k\|x^*\|)$ and

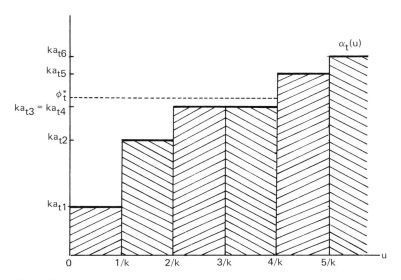

Figure B.1
Coalition excess.

increase the excess in proportion. The "ideal coalition" x^* will play a central role in the proof.

Denote $\phi_t(x^*)$ by ϕ_t^*. By Euler's theorem,

$$\phi(x^*) = \sum_t x_t^* \phi_t^*. \tag{B.15}$$

Hence for any $x \in Q$ we have

$$\phi(x) \le \phi(x^*) + \sum_t (x_t - x_t^*)\phi_t^* = \sum_t x_t \phi_t^*, \tag{B.16}$$

since ϕ is concave. In other words, the linear function $\sum_t x_t \phi_t^*$ is tangent to the homogeneous concave function along the entire ray from 0 through x^*.

The following payoff vector will help us in constructing the objection to a. Let b be given by

$$b_{th} = \max(\phi_t^*/k, a_{th}). \tag{B.17}$$

We first observe that for any $S \subseteq kN$,

$$b(S) \ge \sum_t \sigma_t \phi_t^*/k \ge \phi(\sigma/k) = v(S), \tag{B.18}$$

using (B.16) with $x = \sigma/k$. This means that b can be feasible for a coalition S only if equality holds at both places in (B.18). But if S is sufficiently near to the "ideal" coalition represented by x^*, the "deficit" $b(S) - v(S)$ will not be too great.

To make this precise, set ϕ_t^* equal to the nearest integer to kx_t^* (rounded up at the halves, say), so that

$$kx_t^* - \tfrac{1}{2} < \sigma_t^* \leq kx_t^* + \tfrac{1}{2} \quad \text{for all } t \in N. \tag{B.19}$$

Let S^* be the coalition consisting of the first σ_t^* players of each type t. This is the coalition we shall use for the objection; by (B.14) it is not empty. Moreover, we have:

LEMMA B.1. *If* $\langle t, h \rangle \in S^*$, *then* $b_{th} = \phi_t^*/k$; *and if* $\langle t, h \rangle \notin S^*$, *then* $b_{th} = a_{th}$.

Proof. The maximization of (B.12) entails [see (B.11)] that for each $t \in N$ one of the following holds:

$$\begin{aligned}
&\phi_t^* = \alpha_t(x_t^*), \\
&\phi_t^* < \alpha_t(x_t^*) \quad \text{and} \quad x_t^* = 0, \\
&\phi_t^* > \alpha_t(x_t^*) \quad \text{and} \quad x_t^* = 1.
\end{aligned} \tag{B.20}$$

If $\langle t, h \rangle \in S^*$, then $1 \leq h \leq \sigma_t^*$, and so $0 < h - 1/2 \leq kx_t^*$ by (B.19), whence

$$x_t^* \neq 0 \quad \text{and} \quad \alpha_t(x_t^*) \geq \alpha_t\left(\frac{h - 1/2}{k}\right) = ka_{th}. \tag{B.21}$$

Similarly, if $\langle t, h \rangle \notin S^*$, then $\sigma_t^* + 1 \leq h \leq k$, and so $kx_t^* < h - 1/2 < k$, whence

$$x_t^* \neq 1 \quad \text{and} \quad \alpha_t(x_t^*) \leq \alpha_t\left(\frac{h - 1/2}{k}\right) = ka_{th}. \tag{B.22}$$

The result now follows from (B.20)–(B.22) and (B.17). ∎

One consequence of this lemma is that the first equality in (B.18) holds for $S = S^*$, so that we have

$$b(S^*) = \phi(x^*) = \sum_t (\sigma_t^*/k - x_t^*)\phi_t^*, \tag{B.23}$$

with the aid of (B.15). On the other hand, the differentiability of ϕ and the mean-value theorem imply that

$$v(S^*) - \phi(x^*) = \sum_t (\sigma_t^*/k - x_t^*)\phi_t(z) \tag{B.24}$$

holds for some $z \in Q$ that lies on the line segment between σ^*/k and x^*. Note that $z \neq 0$, by (B.14). Combining (B.23) and (B.24) yields

$$b(S^*) - v(S^*) = \sum_t (\sigma_t^*/k - x_t^*)[\phi_t^* - \phi_t(z)], \tag{B.25}$$

which will be used presently to estimate the "deficit" of S^* at b.

We now elect the "leader" of the objection. Let $\langle t_0, h_0 \rangle$ be any player for whom the difference between b and a is maximized, and let

$$\Delta = b_{t_0 h_0} - a_{t_0 h_0}. \tag{B.26}$$

We must show that Δ is big enough to cover the "deficit." First we have the simple inequality

$$nk\Delta\|x^*\| \geq E^*. \tag{B.27}$$

This can be seen by noting that E^* is the area between $\alpha_t(x_t)$ and the constant function ϕ_t^*, for $0 \leq x_t \leq x_t^*$, summed over $t \in N$ (see figure B.1). The heights of these n regions are bounded by k, and their width by $\|x^*\|$. Since $E^* > \varepsilon$, and $x^* \in Q$, we have

$$nk\Delta > \frac{\varepsilon}{\|x^*\|} \geq \varepsilon. \tag{B.28}$$

We are ready now to make use of the hypothesis (B.6) on the size of k.

LEMMA B.2. *We have either*

$$\frac{2k\Delta}{n} > M \tag{B.29}$$

or

$$h\left(\frac{2k\Delta}{n}\right) > \frac{1}{k\|x^*\|}. \tag{B.30}$$

Proof. Suppose (B.29) fails. Then we have

$$h\left(\frac{2k}{n}\right) \geq h\left(\frac{2\varepsilon}{n^2}\right) \geq \frac{n^2 M}{2\varepsilon k} \geq \frac{m}{\varepsilon} > \frac{1}{k\|x^*\|},$$

using in succession (B.28) and the monotonicity of h, (B.6), the denial of (B.29), and (B.28) again. This proves the lemma. ∎

LEMMA B.3. *We have*

$$b(S^*) - v(S^*) < \Delta. \tag{B.31}$$

Proof. By (B.25), (B.19), and the homogeneity of ϕ, we have

$$b(S^*) - v(S^*) \le \frac{n}{2k} \max_t |\phi_t(x^*) - \phi_t(z)|$$

$$= \frac{n}{2k} \max_t \left| \phi_t \left(\frac{x^*}{\|x^*\|} \right) - \phi_t \left(\frac{z}{\|z\|} \right) \right|. \tag{B.32}$$

If the first alternative of lemma B.2 holds, (B.31) follows immediately from (B.2), the definition of M. Therefore assume (B.30). We wish to apply (B.3), the definition of h, but first we must establish a property of the norm $\|\cdot\|$ under projections from $Q - \{0\}$ to Q. We have (see figure B.2)

$$\left\| \frac{x^*}{\|x^*\|} - \frac{z}{\|z\|} \right\| = \frac{\| \|z\|(x^* - z) + (\|z\| - \|x^*\|)z \|}{\|x^*\| \cdot \|z\|}$$

$$\le \frac{\|z\| \cdot \|x^* - z\| + |\|z\| - \|x^*\|| \cdot \|z\|}{\|x^*\| \cdot \|z\|}$$

$$= \frac{\|x^* - z\|}{\|x^*\|} + \frac{|\|z\| - \|x^*\||}{\|x^*\|} \tag{B.33}$$

$$\le \frac{2}{\|x^*\|} \|x^* - z\|.$$

If we recall that z lies between s^*/k and x^*, we see that $\|x^* - z\| \le 1/(2k)$. Hence

$$\left\| \frac{x^*}{\|x^*\|} - \frac{z}{\|z\|} \right\| \le \frac{1}{k\|x^*\|} < h\left(\frac{2k\Delta}{n} \right) \tag{B.34}$$

using (B.30). Now applying (B.3), we obtain

$$\max_t \left| \phi_t \left(\frac{x^*}{\|x^*\|} \right) - \phi_t \left(\frac{z}{\|z\|} \right) \right| < \frac{2k\Delta}{n}, \tag{B.35}$$

and (B.31) follows at once from this and (B.32), proving the lemma. ∎

Lemma B.3 means that player $\langle t_0, h_0 \rangle$, were he to accept just $a_{t_0 h_0}$ instead of $b_{t_0 h_0}$, would release enough payoff to achieve b. Accordingly, we set $\delta = \Delta - (b(S^*) - v(S^*)) > 0$ and define a new payoff vector c by

$$c_{t_0 h_0} = a_{t_0 h_0} + \delta/s^*,$$
$$c_{th} = b_{th} + \delta/s^* \quad \text{for} \quad \langle t, h \rangle \in S^* - \{\langle t_0, h_0 \rangle\}, \tag{B.36}$$
$$c_{th} = b_{th} = a_{th} \quad \text{for} \quad \langle t, h \rangle \in N^k - S^*,$$

where s^* denotes the number of elements of S^*. Then by construction c

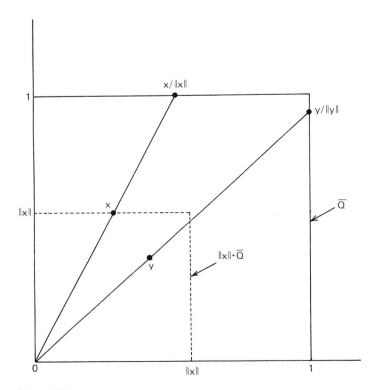

Figure B.2
Constructing an objection.

is exactly feasible for S^* and is strictly greater than a on S^*. Hence $(\langle t_0, h_0 \rangle, S^*, c)$ constitutes a bona fide objection.

It remains to show that there is no counterobjection. In order to mount a counterobjection, a nonempty coalition T^* would have to exist that has a nonnegative excess at c. If T^* included player $\langle t_0, h_0 \rangle$, it would have to have a nonnegative excess at b as well (see (B.36)) and, indeed, a positive excess if $T^* \cap S^* \neq \varnothing$, because of the term δ/s^*. But a positive excess at b is impossible, by (B.18), and so the only remaining hope for a counterobjection lies in a T^* for which the excess at b is zero and for which $T^* \cap S^* = \varnothing$. The former implies, by (B.18), that

$$b_{th} = \phi_t^*/k \quad \text{for all } \langle t, h \rangle \in T^* \tag{B.37}$$

and

$$\sum_t \tau_t^* \phi_t^*/k = \phi(\tau^*/k). \tag{B.38}$$

The latter implies that

$$\sigma_t^* + \tau_t^* \leq k \quad \text{for all } t \in N \tag{B.39}$$

and, by lemma B.1,

$$a_{th} = b_{th} \quad \text{for all } \langle t, h \rangle \in T^*. \tag{B.40}$$

These are all necessary conditions on any T^* that might be used in a counterobjection.

Let $0 < \zeta \leq 1/(2k)$, and define $z^* = x^* + \zeta \tau^*$. Then we have, for each $t \in N$ with $\tau_t^* \neq 0$,

$$kz_t^* \leq kx_t^* + \frac{1}{2}\tau_t^* \leq \left(kx_t^* - \frac{1}{2}\right) + \frac{1}{2}\left(\tau_t^* + 1\right) \leq \sigma_t^* + \tau_t^*. \tag{B.41}$$

With (B.39), this shows that $z^* \in Q$. Since T^* cannot be empty, we have $z^* \geq x^*$ and $z^* \neq x^*$. By condition (B.13), expressing the maximality of x^* among maximizers of $e(x)$ in Q, this means that $e(z^*)$ must be strictly less than E^*. If, on the other hand, we can establish that $e(z^*) \geq E^*$, then this final contradiction will show the impossibility of a counterobjection and complete the proof of the theorem. To do this we need one more simple fact.

LEMMA B.4.   For each $t \in N$, if $\tau_t^* > 0$, then $\alpha_t(u) \leq \phi_t^*$ for all $u \leq z_t^*$.

Proof. Let $\tau_t^* > 0$ and $u \leq z_t^*$. Then $ku \leq \sigma_t^* + \tau_t^*$ by (B.41), and so $ku \leq h$ for some h such that $\langle t, h \rangle \in T^*$, by the disjointedness of S^* and T^* and the fact that S^* has the lowest-numbered members of each type. Hence we have, for this h,

$$\alpha_t(u) \le \alpha_t(h/k) = ka_{th} = kb_{th} = \phi_t^*, \tag{B.42}$$

by (B.9), (B.40), and (B.37). This proves the lemma. ∎

Now, finally, using (B.11), lemma B.4, the concave homogeneity of ϕ, and (B.38), in that order, we have

$$
\begin{aligned}
e(z^*) - e(x^*) &= \varphi(x^* + \zeta\tau^*) - \varphi(x^*) - \sum_t \int_{x_t^*}^{z_t^*} \alpha_t(u)\, du \\
&\ge \varphi(x^* + \zeta\tau^*) - \varphi(x^*) - \sum_t \int_{x_t^*}^{z_t^*} \phi_t^*\, du \\
&\ge \varphi(\zeta\tau^*) - \sum_t (z_t^* - x_t^*)\varphi_t^* \\
&= k\zeta\varphi(\tau^*/k) - \sum_t \zeta\tau_t^* \varphi_t^* \\
&= 0.
\end{aligned}
$$

This is the desired contradiction. ∎

Appendix C
Determination of Cores in the Example of Section 13.2.1

Generalizing (13.4), let the utility function be given by

$$U(x) = \max[\min[ax_1, x_2], \min[x_1, ax_2]], \tag{C.1}$$

where $a > 1$. Set $A = 2a/(1 + a)$, and note that $a > A > 1$.

Suppose first that money side payments are permitted. Then it is easily verified that any set of s players, with $2 \le s \le n$, can achieve a combined payoff of sA and no more. Thus the payoff vector P that assigns A to each player is undominated and lies in the core. Any other payoff vector will assign less than $(n - 1)A$ to the $n - 1$ least-favored players; hence, if $n \ge 3$, that set of players can block it. Thus the core consists of the single point P. When $n = 2$, however, blocking only occurs if one player is assigned less than 1, or if the two together get less than $2A$. Thus the core is the line segment joining the points $(1, 2A - 1)$ and $(2A - 1, 1)$ (Q' and R' in figure 13.2).

Next, let side payments be prohibited, and let $\alpha = (\alpha_1, \alpha_2, \ldots, \alpha_n)$ be an undominated payoff vector. We may assume that

$$\alpha_1 \le \alpha_2 \le \cdots \le \alpha_n. \tag{C.2}$$

Now, the coalition $\{1, 2\}$ can divide its assets by giving $(t, t/a)$ to 1 and $(2 - t, 2 - t/a)$ to 2, thereby achieving payoffs $\beta_1 = t$ and $\beta_2 = 2 - t/a$ for any t between 0 and A (i.e., any point on the line from S to P in figure 13.2). To avoid domination of α by such β, we must have

$$\alpha_1 \ge 2a - a\alpha_2. \tag{C.3}$$

Combined with (C.2), this entails

$$\alpha_2 \ge \frac{2a}{a + 1} = A. \tag{C.4}$$

We also have, of course,

$$\alpha_1 \ge 1. \tag{C.5}$$

Let $\{(x_1^i, x_2^i)\}$ be an allocation that yields α. Let p be the number of indices $i > 1$ such that $x_1^i \le x_2^i$, and let $q = n - 1 - p$. We note from (C.1) that $x_1^i \le x_2^i$ implies that $\alpha_i = \min[ax_1^i, x_2^i]$, and that $x_1^i > x_2^i$ implies that

$\alpha_i = \min[x_1^i, ax_2^i]$. Hence, by (C.2),

$$p\alpha_2/a + q\alpha_2 \le \sum_{i=2}^{n} x_1^i = n - x_1^1,$$

and thus

$$x_1^1 \le n - (p/a + q)\alpha_2 = B_1.$$

Similarly

$$x_2^1 \le n - (p + q/a)\alpha_2 = B_2.$$

Without loss of generality, we can assume that $p \ge q$. Then $B_1 \ge B_2$, and we have

$$\alpha_1 \le \min[B_1, aB_2]. \tag{C.6}$$

Case 1: Suppose $p = q$. Then $n = 2p + 1$, and

$$1 \le \alpha_1 \le B_1 = (2p + 1) - p\left(\frac{1}{a} + 1\right)\alpha_2 \quad \text{(by (C.5) and (C.6))}$$

$$\le 2p + 1 - p\frac{a + 1}{a}A \qquad \text{(by (C.4))} \tag{C.7}$$

$$= 1.$$

Thus equality holds throughout (C.7), and $\alpha_1 = 1$, $\alpha_2 = A$. But this violates (C.3); hence we cannot have $p = q$.

Case 2: Suppose $p \ge q + 2$. Then

$$
\begin{aligned}
1 \le \alpha_1 \le aB_2 &= (p + q + 1)a - (pa + q)\alpha_2 \quad \text{(by (C.5) and (C.6))} \\
&\le a + p(a - aA) + q(a - A) \quad \text{(by (C.4))} \\
&\le a + p(a - aA) + (p - 2)(a - A) = 2A - a \\
&= 1 - \frac{(a - 1)^2}{a + 1} < 1.
\end{aligned}
$$

Hence we cannot have $p \ge q + 2$.

Case 3: Suppose $p = q + 1$. Then $n = 2p$, and

$$2a - a\alpha_2 \le \alpha_1 \le aB_2 = 2pa - (pa + p - 1)\alpha_2,$$

from (C.3) and (C.6). Hence

$$(p - 1)(a + 1)\alpha_2 \le 2(p - 1)a. \tag{C.8}$$

If $p > 1$, this gives $\alpha_2 \leq A$; hence, by (C.4), $\alpha_2 = A$, and we have equality in (C.8). But in deriving (C.7) we made essential use of (C.3) and most of (C.2); therefore equality must prevail there as well, and we find that all the α_i are equal to A. In other words, the only possible candidate for the core (if $p > 1$) is the vector $\alpha = (A, A, \ldots, A)$. It is easily verified that this vector is in fact a feasible payoff and is undominated; hence we have a one-point core as claimed. Note that n in this case is even; for n odd there is no core.

If $p = 1$ (i.e., if $n = 2$), then (C.8) is no restriction, and it is easy to show that the core consists of the bent line from $(1, 2 - 1/a)$ to (A, A) to $(2 - 1/a, 1)$ (QPR in figure 13.2).

Bibliography

Alchian, A. A., 1953. The meaning of utility measurement. *American Economic Review* 42:26–50.

Allais, M., 1953. Le comportement de l'homme rationnel devant le risque: Critique des postulats et axioms de l'école Américaine. *Econometrica* 21:503–546.

Allen, R. G. D., and A. L. Bowley, 1935. *Family Expenditure*. London: King & Son.

Anderson, B. F., D. H. Deane, K. R. Hammond, G. H. McClelland, and J. C. Shanteau, 1981. *Concepts in Judgement and Decision Research*. New York: Praeger.

Anderson, R. M., 1978. An elementary core equivalence theorem. *Econometrica* 46:1483–1487.

Arrow, K. J., 1951. *Social Choice and Individual Values*, 1st ed. New York: John Wiley (2nd ed., 1963).

Arrow, K. J., 1953. Le rôle des valeurs Boursières pour la repartition la meilleure des risques. *Econometrie*. Paris: Centre National de la Recherche Scientifique, 41–48.

Arrow, K. J., 1982. Risk perception in psychology and economics. *Economic Enquiry* 20:1–9.

Arrow, K. J., and G. Debreu, 1954. Existence of an equilibrium for a competitive economy. *Econometrica* 22:265–290.

Arrow, K. J., and F. H. Hahn, 1971. *General Competitive Analysis*. San Francisco, CA: Holden-Day, chapter 7.

Arrow, K. J., and M. D. Intrilligator, eds., 1981. *Handbook of Mathematical Economics*, vol. I. Amsterdam: North-Holland.

Arthur, W. B., and G. McNicoll, 1978. Samuelson, population and intergenerational transfers. *International Economic Review* 19:241–246.

Aumann, R. J., 1964. Markets with a continuum of traders. *Econometrica* 32:39–50.

Aumann, R. J., 1966. Existence of competitive equilibria in markets with a continuum of traders. *Econometrica* 34:1–17.

Aumann, R. J., 1973. Disadvantageous monopolies. *Journal of Economic Theory* 6:1–11.

Aumann, R. J., 1975. Values of markets with a continuum of traders. *Econometrica* 43:611–646.

Aumann, R. J., 1977. On the rate of convergence of the core. Technical Report No. 246, Institute for Mathematical Studies in the Social Sciences, Stanford University.

Aumann, R. J., R. J. Gardner, and R. W. Rosenthal, 1977. Core and value for a public goods economy: An example. *Journal of Economic Theory* 15:363–365.

Aumann, R. J., and M. Kurz, 1977a. Power and taxes in a multicommodity economy. *Israel Journal of Mathematics* 27:185–234.

Aumann, R. J., and M. Kurz, 1977b. Power and taxes. *Econometrica* 45:1137–1161.

Aumann, R. J., M. Kurz, and A. Neyman, 1980. Public goods and power. Technical Report No. 273 (revised), Institute for Mathematical Studies in the Social Sciences, Stanford University.

Aumann, R. J., and M. Maschler, 1964. The bargaining set for cooperative games. In *Advances in Game Theory*, eds. M. Dresher, L. S. Shapley, and A. W. Tucker. Princeton, NJ: Princeton University Press, pp. 443–447.

Aumann, R. J., and L. S. Shapley, 1974. *Values on Non-Atomic Games*. Princeton, NJ: Princeton University Press.

Aylmer, G. E., 1979. Bureaucracy. In *New Cambridge Modern History*, vol. XIII, ed. Peter Burke. New York: Cambridge University Press, pp. 164–200.

Bagehot, W. 1867. *The English Constitution*. London: Fortena Library (1963).

Bagehot, W., 1873. *Lombard Street*. New York: R. O. Irwin (reprinted from London: Scribner Armstrong & Co.).

Bain, J. S., 1956. *Barriers to New Competition, Their Character and Consequences in Manufacturing Industries*. Cambridge, MA: Harvard University Press.

Barraclough, S. L., and A. L. Domike, 1965. *Evolution and Reform of Agrarian Structure in Latin America*. Santiago: Instituto de Capacitacion e Investigacion en Reforma Agraria.

Bator, F. M., 1958. The anatomy of market failure. *Quarterly Journal of Economics* 72:351–379.

Baumol, W. J., 1959. *Business Behavior, Value, and Growth*. New York: Macmillan.

Baumol, W. J., 1972. On taxation and the control of externalities. *American Economic Review* 62:307–321.

Baumol, W. J., J. C. Panzer, and R. D. Willig, 1982. *Contestable Markets and the Theory of Industry Structure*. San Diego, CA: Harcourt Brace Jovanovich.

Becker, G. S,, 1975. *Human Capital*. New York: National Bureau of Economic Research (distributed by Columbia University Press).

Becker, L. C., 1977. *Property Rights: Philosophic Foundations*. Boston, MA: Routledge and Kegan Paul.

Bentley, A. F., 1908. *The Process of Government*. Chicago, IL: University of Chicago Press.

Berge, C., 1963. *Topological Spaces*. New York: Macmillan.

Bergson, A., 1938. A reformulation of certain aspects of welfare economics. *Quarterly Journal of Economics* 52:310–334.

Bergstrom, T. C., 1970. *Collective Choice and the Lindahl Allocation Method* (mimeographed), Washington University, St. Louis, MO.

Berkeley, G. E., 1975. *The Craft of Public Administration*. Boston, MA: Allyn and Bacon (3rd ed., 1981).

Berle, A. A., and G. C. Means, 1932. *The Modern Corporation and Private Property*. New York: Macmillan.

Bernholz, P., 1974. Logrolling, Arrow-paradox and decision rules: A generalization. *Kyklos* 27:49–62.

Bernoulli, D., 1954. Exposition of a new theory on the measurement of risk. *Econometrica* 22:23–26 (translated from Latin by Louise Sommer; original, 1738).

Bertrand, J., 1883. Théorie mathématique de la richesse sociale (review). *Journal des Savants* (Paris) 68:499–508.

Bewley, T., 1972. Existence of equilibria in economies with infinitely many commodities. *Journal of Economic Theory* 4:514–540.

Bewley, T., 1981. A critique of Tiebout's theory of local public expenditures. *Econometrica* 49:713–740.

Billera, L. J., 1974. On games without side payments arising from a general class of markets. *Journal of Mathematical Economics* 1:129–139.

Billera, L. J., and R. E. Bixby, 1973. A characterization of polyhedral market games. *International Journal of Game Theory* 2:253–261.

Billera, L. J., and R. E. Bixby, 1974. Market representations of *n*-person games. *Bulletin of the American Mathematical Society* 80:522–526.

Billera, L. J., and R. E. Bixby, 1976. Pareto surfaces of complexity 1. *SIAM Journal of Applied Mathematics* 30:81–89.

Billera, L. J., and R. J. Weber, 1979. Dense families of low-complexity attainable sets of markets. *Journal of Mathematical Economics* 6:67–73.

Bishop, R. L., 1952. Elasticities and market relationships. *American Economic Review* 42:779–803.

Black, D., 1958. *The Theory of Committees and Elections*. Cambridge, England: Cambridge University Press.

Black, D., 1969. On Arrow's impossibility theorem. *Journal of Law and Economics* 12:227–248.

Boehm, V., 1974a. The limit of the core of an economy with production. *International Economic Review* 15:143–148.

Boehm, V., 1974b. The core of an economy with production. *Review of Economic Studies* 41:429–436.

Böhm-Bawerk, E. von, 1923. *Positive Theory of Capital* (translated from German; original, 1891). New York: G. E. Stechert and Co.

Bondareva, O. N., 1963. Nekotorye primeneiia metodor linejnogo programmirovaniia k teorii kooperativnkkh igr [Some applications of linear programming methods to the theory of cooperative games]. *Problemy Kibernetiki* 10:119–139.

Bonini, C. P., 1963. *Simulation of Information and Decision Systems in the Firm*. Englewood Cliffs, NJ: Prentice-Hall.

Borch, K., 1974. *The Mathematical Theory of Insurance*. Lexington, MA: Lexington Books.

Brams, S. J., 1975. *Game Theory and Politics*. New York: Free Press.

Brems, H., 1951. *Product Equilibrium Under Monopolistic Competition*. Cambridge: MA: Harvard University Press.

Breton, A., 1974. *The Economic Theory of Representative Government*. Chicago, IL: Aldine-Atherton, Inc.

Brewer, G., and M. Shubik, 1979. *The War Game*. Cambridge, MA: Harvard University Press.

Brito, D. L., 1975. Becker's theory of the allocation of time and the St. Petersburg paradox. *Journal of Economic Theory* 10:123–126.

Broome, J., 1972. Approximate equilibrium in economies with indivisible commodities. *Journal of Economic Theory* 5:224–249.

Buchanan, J. M., 1965. An economic theory of clubs. *Economica* 32:1–14.

Buchanan, J. M., and G. Tullock, 1962. *The Calculus of Consent*. Ann Arbor, MI:University of Michigan Press.

Burch, P. H., 1980. *Elites in American History*, vol. III. New York: Holmes & Meier.

Caspi, Y. M., 1975. A limit theorem on competitive equilibrium of an economy under uncertainty. *International Economic Review* 16:336–344.

Caspi, Y. M., 1978. A limit theorem on the core of an economy with individual risks. *Economic Studies* 45:267–271.

Chamberlin, E. H., 1933. *The Theory of Monopolistic Competition: A Re-Orientation of the Theory of Values*. Cambridge: MA: Harvard University Press.

Chamberlin, E. H., 1948. An experimental imperfect market. *Journal of Political Economy* 56:95–108.

Champsaur, P., 1974. Note sur le noyau d'une économie avec production. *Econometrica* 42:933–945.

Champsaur, P., 1975. How to share the cost of a public good? *International Journal of Game Theory* 4:113–129.

Champsaur, P., 1976. Symmetry and continuity properties of Lindahl equilibria. *Journal of Mathematical Economics* 3:19–36.

Champsaur, P., J. P. Roberts, and R. W. Rosenthal, 1975. On cores in economies with public goods. *International Economic Review* 16:751–764.

Charnes, A., and K. O. Kortanek, 1967. On balanced sets, cores, and linear programming. *Cahiers du Centre d'Etudes de Recherche Opérationnelle* (Brussels) 9:32–43.

Chipman, J. S., 1965. A survey of the theory of international trade: Part 2, the neoclassical theory. *Econometrica* 33:685–760.

Chipman, J. S., and J. C. Moore, 1976. Why an increase in GNP need not imply an improvement in potential welfare. *Kyklos* 29:391–418.

Chipman, J. S., and J. C. Moore, 1978. The new welfare economics 1939–1974. *International Economic Review* 19:547–584.

Clarkson, G. P. C., 1962. *Portfolio Selection: A Simulation of Trust Investment.* Englewood Cliffs, NJ: Prentice-Hall.

Clower, R., ed., 1969. *Monetary Theory: Selected Readings.* Harmondsworth, England: Penguin.

Coase, R. H., 1960. The problem of social cost. *Journal of Law and Economics* 3:1–44.

Cohen, K. J., 1960. *Computer Models of the Shoe, Leather, Hide Sequence.* Englewood, Cliffs, NJ: Prentice-Hall.

Coleman, J. S., 1966. The possibility of a social welfare function. *American Economic Review* 56:1105–1122.

Cournot, A. A., 1897. *Researches into the Mathematical Principles of the Theory of Wealth* (translated from French; original, 1838). New York: Macmillan.

Crawford, V. P., and E. M. Knoer, 1981. Job matching with heterogeneous firms and workers. *Econometrica* 49:437–450.

Cyert, R. M., and J. G. March, 1963. *A Behavioral Theory of the Firm.* Englewood Cliffs, NJ: Prentice-Hall.

Dahl, R. A., 1961. *Who Governs? Democracy and Power in an American City.* New Haven, CT: Yale University Press.

Dantzig, G. 1963. *Linear Programming and Extensions.* Princeton, NJ: Princeton University Press.

Davis, O. A., and A. B. Whinston, 1962. Externalities, welfare and the theory of games. *Journal of Political Economy* 70:241–262.

Davis, O. A., and A. B. Whinston, 1966. On externalities, information and the government assisted invisible hand. *Economica* 33:303–318.

Debreu, G., 1951. The coefficient of resource utilization. *Econometrica* 19:273–292.

Debreu, G., 1954. Representation of a preference ordering by a numerical function. In *Decision Processes*, eds. R. M. Thrall, C. H. Coombs, and R. L. Davis. New York: John Wiley, pp. 159–165.

Debreu, G., 1959. *Theory of Value.* New York: John Wiley.

Debreu, G., 1964. Continuity properties of Paretian utility. *International Economic Review* 5:285–293.

Debreu, G., 1970. Economies with a finite set of equilibria. *Econometrica* 38:387–392.

Debreu, G., 1975. The rate of convergence of the core of an economy. *Journal of Mathematical Economics* 2:1–7.

Debreu, G., 1976a. Regular differentiable economies. *American Economic Review* 66:280–287.

Debreu, G., 1976b. Least concave utility functions. *Journal of Mathematical Economics* 3:121–129.

Debreu, G., and H. E. Scarf, 1963. A limit theorem on the core of an economy. *International Economic Review* 4:235–246.

de Finetti, B., 1949. Sulle stratificazioni convesse. *Annali di Matematica Pura ed Applicata* 4, 30:173–183.

Demange, G., 1982. Strategyproofness in the assignment market games. Working Paper, Laboratoire d'Econometrie de l'Ecole Polytechnique (Paris).

Diamond, P. A., 1967. The role of a stock market in a general equilibrium model with technological uncertainty. *American Economic Review* 57:759–776.

Diamond, P. A., and J. Mirrlees, 1971. Optimal taxation and public production. *American Economic Review* 61:8–27.

Dierker, E., 1971. Equilibrium analysis of exchange economies with indivisible commodities. *Econometrica* 39:997–1008.

Diewert, W. E., 1969. Functional forms for utility and expenditure functions. Report 6932, University of Chicago, Center for Mathematical Studies in Business and Economics.

Downs, A., 1957. *An Economic Theory of Democracy*. New York: Harper & Row.

Downs, A., 1966. *Inside Bureaucracy*. Boston, MA: Little Brown.

Dreze, J. H., J. Gabszewicz, and A. Postlewaite, 1977. Disadvantageous monopolies and disadvantageous endowments. *Journal of Economic Theory* 16:116–121.

Dreze, J., J. Gabszewicz, D. Schmeidler, and K. Vind, 1972. Cores and prices in an exchange economy with an atomless sector. *Econometrica* 40:1091–1108.

Dubey, P., 1978. Finiteness and inefficiency of Nash equilibria. Discussion Paper 508, Cowles Foundation, Yale University.

Dubey, P., 1980. Nash equilibria of market games: Finiteness and inefficiency. *Journal of Economic Theory* 22:363–376.

Dubey, P., 1982. Price-quantity strategic market games. *Econometrica* 50:111–126.

Dubey, P., J. Geanakoplos, and M. Shubik, 1982. Revelation of information in strategic market games: A critique of rational expectations. Discussion Paper 643, Cowles Foundation, Yale University.

Dubey, P., A. Mas-Colell, and M. Shubik, 1980. Efficiency properties of strategic market games: An axiomatic approach. *Journal of Economic Theory* 22:339–362.

Dubey, P., and A. Neyman, 1984. Payoffs in non-atomic economies: An axiomatic approach. *Econometrica* (forthcoming).

Dubey, P., and J. D. Rogawski, 1982. Inefficiency of Nash equilibria in a private goods economy. Discussion Paper 631, Cowles Foundation, Yale University.

Dubey, P., and L. S. Shapley, 1977. Noncooperative exchange with a continuum of traders. Discussion Paper 447, Cowles Foundation, Yale University.

Dubey, P., and M. Shubik, 1977a. Trade and prices in a closed economy with exogenous uncertainty and different levels of information. *Econometrica* 45:1657–1680.

Dubey, P., and M. Shubik, 1977b. A closed economy with exogenous uncertainty, different levels of information, money, futures and spot markets. *International Journal of Game Theory* 6:231–248.

Dubey, P., and M. Shubik, 1978a. The noncooperative equilibria of a closed trading economy with market supply and bidding strategies. *Journal of Economic Theory* 7:1–20.

Dubey, P., and M. Shubik, 1978b. A closed economic system with production and exchange modelled as a game of strategy. *Journal of Mathematical Economics* 4:253–287.

Dubey, P., and M. Shubik, 1979. Bankruptcy and optimality in a closed trading mass economy modelled as a noncooperative game. *Journal of Mathematical Economics* 6:115–134.

Dubey, P., and M. Shubik, 1980a. The profit maximizing firm: Managers and stockholders. *Economies et Sociétés* (Cahiers de l'Institut de sciences mathématiques et économiques appliquées, Série EM No. 6, Laboratoire associé au CNRS) 14:1369–1388.

Dubey, P., and M. Shubik, 1980b. A strategic market game with price and quantity strategies. *Zeitschrift für Nationalökonomie* 40:1–2, 25–34.

Dubey, P., and M. Shubik, 1981. Information conditions, communication and general equilibrium. *Mathematics of Operations Research* 6:186–189.

Dubins, L. E. and D. A. Freedman, 1981. Machiavelli and the Gale-Shapley algorithm. *American Mathematics Monthly* 88:485–494.

Edgeworth, F. Y., 1881. *Mathematical Psychics: An Essay on the Application of Mathematics to the Moral Sciences*. London: C. Kegan Paul.

Edgeworth, F. Y., 1925. *Papers Relating to Political Economy*, vol. 1, New York: B. Franklin.

Edwards, H. R., 1955. Price formation in manufacturing industry and excess capacity. *Oxford Economic Papers* 7:94–118.

Einzig, P., 1948. *Primitive Money*. London: Eyre & Spottiswoode (reprinted 1951).

Ekern, S., and R. Wilson, 1974. On the theory of the firm in an economy with incomplete markets. *Bell Journal of Economics and Management Science* 5:171–180.

Fabre-Sender, F., 1969. Biens collectifs et biens à qualité variable. Paris: CEPREMAP.

Farquharson, R., 1969. *Theory of Voting*. New Haven, CT: Yale University Press.

Farrell, M. J., 1959. The convexity assumption in the theory of competitive markets. *Journal of Political Economy* 67:377–391.

Fellner, W., 1949. *Competition Among the Few*. New York: Knopf.

Ferejohn, J. A., 1974. Sour notes on the theory of vote trading. Working Paper No. 41, California Institute of Technology, Pasadena, CA.

Fiorina, M. P., 1983. Flagellating the Federal Bureaucracy. *Society* 20:66–73.

Fiorina, M. P., and R. G. Noll, 1978. Voters, bureaucrats and legislators. *Journal of Public Economics* 9:239–254.

Fleming, J. S., 1969. The utility of wealth and the utility of windfalls. *Review of Economic Studies* 36:55–66.

Foley, D. K., 1967. Resource allocation and the public sector. *Yale Economic Essays* 7:45–98.

Foley, D. K., 1970a. Economic equilibrium with costly marketing. *Journal of Economic Theory* 2:276–281.

Foley, D. K., 1970b. Lindahl's solution and the core of an economy with public goods. *Econometrica* 38:66–72.

Fourgeaud, C., 1969. Contribution à l'étude du rôle des administrations dans la théorie mathématique de l'équilibre et de l'optimum. *Econometrica* 37:307–323.

Friedman, J. W., 1967. An experimental study of cooperative duopoly. *Econometrica*, 35:379–397.

Friedman, J. W., 1977a. *Oligopoly and the Theory of Games*. Amsterdam: North-Holland.

Friedman, J. W., 1977b. Non-cooperative equilibrium for exit supergames. Discussion Paper 77-1, Department of Economics, University of Rochester.

Friedman, J. W., 1982. Oligopoly theory. In *Handbook of Mathematical Economics*, eds. K. J. Arrow and M. D. Intrilligator. Amsterdam: North-Holland, pp. 491–534.

Friedman, M., and L. J. Savage, 1948. The utility analysis of choices involving risk. *Journal of Political Economy* 56:279–304.

Fry, T. C., 1928. *Probability and Its Engineering Uses*. New York: Van Nostrand.

Gabszewicz, J. J., 1977. Asymmetric duopoly and the core. *Journal of Economic Theory* 14:172–179.

Gabszewicz, J. J., and J. H. Dreze, 1971. Syndicates of traders in an exchange economy. In *Differential Games and Related Topics*, eds. H. W. Kuhn and G. P. Szegö. Amsterdam: North-Holland, pp. 399–414.

Gabszewicz, J. J., and J. F. Mertens, 1971. An equivalence theorem for the core of an economy whose atoms are not 'too' big. *Econometrica* 39:713–721.

Gabszewicz, J. J., and J. P. Vial, 1972. Oligopoly "à la Cournot" in a general equilibrium analysis. *Journal of Economic Theory* 4:381–400.

Gale, D., 1963. A note on global instability of competitive equilibrium. *Naval Research Logistics Quarterly* 10:81–87.

Gale, D., and L. S. Shapley, 1962. College admission and the stability of marriage. *American Mathematics Monthly* 69:9–15.

Gansler, J. S., 1980. *The Defense Industry*. Cambridge, MA: MIT Press.

Gardner, R., 1977. Shapley value and disadvantageous monopolies. *Journal of Economic Theory* 16:513–517.

Gaskins, D. W., Jr., 1971. Dynamic limit pricing, optimal pricing under threat of entry. *Journal of Economic Theory* 3:306–322.

Gilbert, N., and H. Specht, 1974. *Dimensions of Social Welfare Policy*. Englewood Cliffs, NJ: Prentice-Hall.

Gillies, D. B., 1953. Some theorems on n-person games. Ph.D. dissertation, Department of Mathematics, Princeton University.

Gillies, D. B., 1959. Solutions to general non-zero-sum games. *Annals of Mathematics Studies* 40:47–85.

Goodman, J. C., 1980. A note on existence and uniqueness of equilibrium points for concave n-person games. *Econometrica* 48:251.

Grandmont, J. M., 1982. Temporary general equilibrium theory. In *Handbook of Mathematical Economics*, vol. 2, eds. K. J. Arrow and M. D. Intrilligator. Amsterdam: North-Holland.

Greenberg, J., 1975. Efficiency of tax systems financing public goods in general equilibrium analysis. *Journal of Economic Theory* 11:168–195.

Greenberg, J., 1977. Existence of an equilibrium with arbitrary tax schemes for financing local public goods. *Journal of Economic Theory* 16:137–150.

Greenberg, J., and B. Shitovitz, 1977. Advantageous monopolies. *Journal of Economic Theory* 16:394–402.

Greenberg, J., and S. Weber, 1982. The equivalence of superadditivity and balancedness in the proportional tax game. *Economics Letters* 9:113–117.

Grodal, B., 1975. The rate of convergence of the core for a purely competitive sequence of economies. *Journal of Mathematical Economics* 2:171–186.

Gross, O., and R. Wagner, 1950. A continuous Blotto game. RAND Publication RM-408, Santa Monica, CA.

Grossman, S. J., and O. D. Hart, 1979. A theory of competitive equilibrum in stock market economies. *Econometrica* 47:293–329.

Groves, T., and J. Ledyard, 1977. Optimal allocation of public goods: A solution to the "free rider" problem. *Econometrica* 45:783–809.

Guesnerie, R., and C. Oddou, 1979. On economic games which are not necessarily superadditive. *Economics Letters* 3:301–306.

Guesnerie, R., and C. Oddou, 1981. Second best taxation as a game. *Journal of Economic Theory* 25:67–91.

Hahn, F. H. 1955. Excess capacity and imperfect competition. *Oxford Economics Papers* 7:229–240.

Hahn, F. H., 1971. Equilibrium with transactions cost. *Econometrica* 39:417–439.

Hakansson, N. H., 1970. Friedman–Savage utility functions consistent with risk aversion. *Quarterly Journal of Economics* 84:472–487.

Harberger, A. C., 1963. The dynamics of inflation in Chile. In *Measurement in Economics: Studies in Mathematical Economics and Econometrics in Memory of Yehuda Gruenfeld*. Stanford, CA: Stanford University Press, pp. 220–250.

Harrod, R. F., 1952. Theory of imperfect competition revised. In *Economic Essays*. London: Macmillan, pp. 139–187.

Harsanyi, J. C., 1956. Approaches to the bargaining problem before and after the theory of games. *Econometrica* 24:144–157.

Harsanyi, J. C., 1959. A bargaining model for the cooperative *n*-person game. In *Contributions to the Theory of Games*, vol. 4, eds. A. W. Tucker and R. D. Luce. Princeton, NJ: Princeton University Press, pp. 324–356.

Harsanyi, J. C., 1963. A simplified bargaining model for the *n*-person cooperative game. *International Economic Review* 4:194–220.

Harsanyi, J. C., 1965. Bargaining and the conflict situation in the light of a new approach to game theory. *American Economic Review* 55:447–457.

Harsanyi, J. C., 1967. Games with incomplete information played by "Bayesian" players, I: The basic model. *Management Science* 14:159–182.

Harsanyi, J. C., 1968a. Games with incomplete information played by "Bayesian" players, II: Bayesian equilibrium points. *Management Science* 14:320–334.

Harsanyi, J. C., 1968b. Games with incomplete information played by "Bayesian" players, III: The basic distribution of the games. *Management Science* 14:486–502.

Harsanyi, J. C., 1982. Solutions for some bargaining games under the Harsanyi–Selten solution theory, I: Theoretical preliminaries; II: Analysis of specific bargaining games. *Mathematical Social Sciences* 3:179–191.

Hart, O. D., 1982. Imperfect competition in general equilibrium: An overview of recent work. Discussion Paper, Workshop in Theoretical Economics at the International Centre for Economics and Related Disciplines (ICERD), London School of Economics.

Hart, S., 1974. Formation of cartels in large markets. *Journal of Economic Theory* 7:453–466.

Hart, S., 1977. Values of non-differentiable markets with a continuum of traders. *Journal of Mathematical Economics* 4:103–116.

Hart, S., 1982. The number of commodities required to represent a market game. *Journal of Economic Theory* 27:163–169.

Hartman, R. W., and A. R. Weber, 1980. *The Rewards of Public Service*. Washington, DC: The Brookings Institution.

Hellwig, M. F., 1977. A model of borrowing and lending with bankruptcy. *Econometrica* 45:1879–1906.

Hellwig, M. F., 1981. Bankruptcy, limited liability and the Modigliani–Miller theorem. *American Economic Review* 71:150–170.

Henry, C., 1972. Market games with indivisible commodities and nonconvex preferences. *Review of Economic Studies* 39:73–76.

Hicks, J. R., 1939. *Value and Capital: An Inquiry into Some Fundamental Principles of Economic Theory*. London: Oxford University Press, pp. 36–37.

Hicks, J. R., 1954. The process of imperfect competition. *Oxford Economic Papers*, New Series, 41–54.

Hicks, J. R., and R. D. G. Allen, 1934. A reconsideration of the theory of value. *Economica* 1: 52–76, 196–219.

Hildenbrand, W., 1968. On the core of an economy with a measure space of economic agents. *Review of Econometric Studies* 35:443–452.

Hildenbrand, W., 1970. Existence of equilibria for economies with production and a measure space of consumers. *Econometrica* 38:608–623.

Hildenbrand, W., 1974. *Cores and Equilibria of a Large Economy*. Princeton, NJ: Princeton University Press.

Hildenbrand, W., 1982. Core of an economy. In *Handbook of Mathematical Economics*, eds. K. J. Arrow and M. D. Intrilligator. Amsterdam: North-Holland, chapter 18.

Hirshleifer, J., 1966. Investment decision under uncertainty: Applications of the state-preference approach. *Quarterly Journal of Economics* 80:252–277.

Hoggatt, A. C., 1959. An experimental business game. *Behavioral Science* 4:192–203.

Holmstrom, B., 1982. Design of incentive schemes and the new Soviet incentive model. *European Economic Review* 17:127–148.

Hotelling, H., 1929. Stability in competition. *Economic Journal* 39:41–57.

Hurwicz, L., 1973. The design of mechanisms for resource allocation. *American Economic Review* 63:1–30.

Huxley, A., 1932. *Brave New World*. London: Chatto and Windus.

Ibn Khaldun, 1958. *The Muquaddimah* (translated from Arabic; original, fifteenth century). New Haven, CT: Yale University Press.

Ichiishi, T., 1977. Coalition structure in a labor managed market economy. *Econometrica* 45:341–360.

Ito, Y., and M. Kaneko, 1981. Ratio equilibrium in an economy with externalities. *Zeitschrift für Nationalökonomie* 41:279–294.

Joseph, M. W., 1933. A discontinuous cost curve and the tendency to increasing returns. *Economic Journal* 43:390–398.

Kadane, J. B., and P. D. Larkey, 1982. Subjective probability and the theory of games. *Management Science* 28:113–120.

Kamien, M. I., and N. L. Schwartz, 1971. Limit pricing and uncertain entry. *Econometrica* 39:441–454.

Kaneko, M., 1976. On the core and competitive equilibria of a market with indivisible goods. *Naval Research Logistics Quarterly* 23:321–337.

Kaneko, M., 1977a. The ratio equilibrium and a voting game in a public goods economy. *Journal of Economic Theory* 16:123–136.

Kaneko, M., 1977b. The ratio equilibria and the core of the voting game $G(N, W)$ in a public goods economy. *Econometrica* 45:1589–1594.

Kaneko, M., 1982. The central assignment game and the assignment markets. *Journal of Mathematical Economics* 10:205–232.

Kaneko, M., and M. Wooders, 1982. Cores of partitioning games. *Mathematical Social Sciences* 3:313–327.

Kaufman, H., 1968. The administrative function. In *International Encyclopedia of the Social Sciences*, vol. 1, ed. D. L. Sills. New York: Macmillan and Free Press, pp. 61–67.

Kemeny, J. G., and G. L. Thompson, 1957. The effect of psychological attitudes on the outcomes of games. *Annals of Mathematics Studies* 39:273–298.

Keynes, J. M., 1921. *A Treatise on Probability*. London: Macmillan.

Keynes, J. M., 1936. *The General Theory of Employment, Interest and Money*. London: Macmillan.

Khan, M. A., 1976. Oligopoly in markets with a continuum of traders: An asymptotic interpretation. *Journal of Economic Theory* 12:273–297.

Khan, M. A., and A. Yamazaki, 1981. On the cores of economies with indivisible commodities and a continuum of traders. *Journal of Economic Theory* 24:218–225.

Kim, Y. C., 1973. Choice in the lottery-insurance situation: Augmented-income approach. *Quarterly Journal of Economics* 87:148–156.

Kirschen, E. S., et al., 1964. *Economic Policy in Our Time*. Amsterdam: North-Holland.

Klevorick, A. K., and G. H. Kramer, 1973. Social choice on pollution management: The *Genossenschaften*. *Journal of Public Economics* 2:101–146.

Koehler, D. H., 1975. Vote trading and the voting paradox: A proof of logical equivalence. *American Political Science Review* 69:954–960.

Kotler, P., 1980. *Marketing Management Analysis, Planning and Control*, 4th ed. Englewood Cliffs, NJ: Prentice-Hall.

Kramer, G. H., 1977. A dynamical model of political equilibrium. *Journal of Economic Theory* 16:310–334.

Kramer, G. H., 1978. Existence of electoral equilibrium. In *Game Theory and Political Science*, ed. P. C. Ordeshook. New York: New York University Press, pp. 375–391.

Kramer, G. H., and A. K. Klevorick, 1974. Existence of a "local" cooperative equilibrium in a class of voting games. *Review of Economic Studies* 41:539–547.

Krelle, W., 1961. *Preistheorie*. Tübingen: Mohr.

Kreps, D. M., and R. Wilson, 1982a. Reputation and imperfect information. *Journal of Economic Theory* 27:253–279.

Kreps, D. M., and R. Wilson, 1982b. Sequential equilibria. *Econometrica* 50:863–894.

Krooss, H. E., and M. R. Blyn, 1971. *A History of Financial Intermediaries*. New York: Random House.

Lancaster, K., and R. G. Lipsey, 1959. McManus on second best. *Review of Economic Studies* 26:225–226.

Larner, R. J., 1966. Ownership and control in the 200 largest nonfinancial corporations 1929 and 1963. *American Economic Review* 56:777–787.

Leland, H. E., 1974. Production theory and the stock market. *Bell Journal of Economics and Management Science* 5:125–244.

Lemke, C. E., and J. T. Howson, Jr., 1964. Equilibrium points of bimatrix games. *SIAM of Applied Mathematics Journal* 12:413–423.

Lesourne, J., 1975. Individual choice in a probabilistic environment. Paris: Con. Nat. des Arts et Métiers.

Levitan, R. E., 1966. Demand in an oligopolistic market and the theory of rationing. Publication RC-1545, IBM Thomas J. Watson Research Center, Yorktown Heights, NY.

Levitan, R. E., and M. Shubik, 1971a. Noncooperative equilibria and strategy spaces in an oligopolistic market. In *Differential Games and Related Topics*, eds. H. Kuhn and G. Szegö. Amsterdam: North-Holland.

Levitan R. E., and M. Shubik, 1971b. Price variation duopoly with differentiated products and random demand. *Journal of Economic Theory* 3:23–29.

Levitan, R. E., and M. Shubik, 1972. Price duopoly and capacity constraints. *International Economic Review* 13:111–122.

Lewin, B., 1963. *La Insurreccion de Tupac Amaru.* Buenos Aires: Editorial Universitaria de Buenos Aires.

Lindahl, E., 1919. Just taxation: A positive solution. Reprinted in part in *Classics in the Theory of Public Finance*, eds. R. Musgrave and A. Peacock. London, Macmillan (1958).

Lindblom, C. E., 1977. *Politics and Markets: The World's Political-Economic Systems.* New York: Basic Books.

Lippman, S. A., 1980. Optimal pricing to retard entry. *Review of Economic Studies* 47:723–731.

Little, I. M. D., 1957. *A Critique of Welfare Economics*, 2nd ed. London: Oxford University Press.

Littlechild, S. C., 1970. A game theoretic approach to public utility pricing. *Western Economic Journal* 8:162–166.

Lucas, W. F., 1967a. Solutions for a class of *n*-person games in partition function form. *Naval Research Logistics Quarterly* 14:15–21.

Lucas, W. F., 1967b. A counterexample in game theory. *Management Science* 13:766–767.

Lucas, W. F., 1968. A game in partition function form with no solution. *SIAM Journal of Applied Mathematics* 16:582–585.

Luce, R. D., and H. Raiffa, 1957. *Games and Decisions.* New York: John Wiley.

Maine, H. J. S., 1861. *Ancient Law.* London: J. M. Dent.

Majumdar, M., 1972. Some general theorems of efficiency prices with infinite dimensional commodity space. *Journal of Economic Theory* 5:1–13.

Manas, M., 1972. A linear oligopoly game. *Econometrica* 40:917–922.

Mantel, R. R., 1975. General equilibrium and optimal taxes. *Journal of Mathematical Economics* 2:187–200.

March, J. G., and H. A. Simon, 1958. *Organizations.* New York: John Wiley.

Markowitz, H., 1952. The utility of wealth. *Journal of Political Economy* 60:151–159.

Marris, R., 1964. *Economic Theory of Managerial Capitalism*. New York: Free Press of Glencoe.

Marris, R., 1979. *Theory and Future of the Corporate Economy and Society*. Amsterdam: North-Holland.

Marris, R., and D. C. Mueller, 1980. The corporation and competition. *Journal of Economic Literature* 18:32–63.

Marshall, A., 1922. *Principles of Economics*, 8th ed. London: Macmillan.

Marx, K., 1932. *Capital* (translated from German; original, 1867). New York: Random House (Modern Library edition).

Maschler, M., 1976. An advantage of the bargaining set over the core. *Journal of Economic Theory* 13:184–194.

Maschler, M., B. Peleg, and L. S. Shapley, 1979. Geometric properties of the kernel, nucleolus and related solution concepts. *Mathematics of Operations Research* 4:303–338.

Mas-Colell, A., 1975a. A further result on the representation of games by markets. *Journal of Economic Theory* 10:117–122.

Mas-Colell, A., 1975b. A model of equilibrium with differentiated commodities. *Journal of Mathematical Economy* 2:263–295.

Mas-Colell, A., 1977a. Indivisible commodities and general equilibrium theory. *Journal of Economic Theory* 16:443–445.

Mas-Colell, A., 1977b. Regular non-convex economies. *Econometrica* 45:1387–1407.

Mas-Colell, A., 1977c. Competitive and value allocations of large exchange economies. *Journal of Economic Theory* 14:419–438.

Mas-Colell, A., 1979. A refinement of the core equivalence theorem. *Economics Letters* 3:307–310.

Mas-Colell, A., 1980. Non-cooperative approaches to the theory of perfect competition: Presentation. *Journal of Economic Theory* 22:121–135.

Mas-Colell, A., 1981. Walrasian equilibria as limits of mixed strategy noncooperative equilibria. Working Paper in Economic Theory and Econometrics, University of California, Berkeley.

Mayberry, J. P., J. F. Nash, Jr., and M. Shubik, 1953. A comparison of treatments of a duopoly situation. *Econometrica* 21:141–155.

McDonald, J., 1975. *The Game of Business*. New York: Doubleday.

McKelvey, R. D., and P. C. Ordeshook, 1976. Symmetric spatial games without majority rule equilibria. *American Political Science Review* 70:1172–1184.

Meade, J. E., 1952. External economies and diseconomies in a competitive situation. *The Economic Journal* 62:54–67.

Menger, K., 1934. The role of uncertainty in economics. In *Essays in Mathematical Economics in Honor of Oskar Morgenstern*, ed. M. Shubik. Princeton, NJ: Princeton University Press (1967), pp. 211–231.

Milgrom, P., and R. J. Weber, 1982. A theory of auctions and competitive bidding. *Econometrica* 50:1089–1122.

Miller, G. A., 1956. The magic number seven plus or minus two: Some limits in our capacity for processing information. *The Psychological Review* 63:81–97.

Miller, G. J., 1977. Bureaucratic compliance as a game on the unit square. *Public Choice* 29:37–51.

Milleron, J. C., 1972. Theory of value with public goods: A survey article. *Journal of Economic Theory* 5:419–477.

Milnor, J. W., 1952. Reasonable outcomes for *n*-person games. RAND Publication RM-916.

Mintz, S. W., and E. R. Wolfe, 1957. Haciendas and plantations in Middle America and the Caribbean. *Social and Economic Studies* 6:380–412.

Mishan, E. J., 1960. A survey of welfare economics 1939–59. *The Economic Journal* 70:197–265.

Miyasawa, K., 1962. An economic survival game. *Journal of the Operations Research Society of Japan* 2:95–113.

Modigliani, F., 1959. New Developments on the oligopoly front. *Journal of Political Economy* 67:215–232.

Moriarity, S., ed., 1981. *Joint Cost Allocations*. Norman, OK: Center for Economic and Management Research.

Moulin, H., 1981. *The Strategy of Social Choice*. Paris: Laboratoire d'Econométrie de l'Ecole Polytechnique et CEREMADE, Université Paris IX–Dauphine, No. A229.

Muench, T., 1972. The core and the Lindahl equilibrium of an economy with a public good: An example. *Journal of Economic Theory* 4:241–255.

Musgrave, R. A., 1959. *The Theory of Public Finance*. New York: McGraw-Hill.

Musgrave, R. A., and P. B. Musgrave, 1973. *Public Finance in Theory and Practice*. New York: McGraw-Hill.

Musgrave, R. A., and A. T. Peacock, eds., 1958. *Classics in the Theory of Public Finance*. London, Macmillan.

Nash, J. F., Jr., 1950. The bargaining problem. *Econometrica* 18:155–162.

Nash, J. F., Jr., 1951. Noncooperative games. *Annals of Mathematics* 54:286–295.

Nash, J. F., Jr., 1953. Two-person cooperative games. *Econometrica* 21:128–140.

Negishi, T., 1962. The stability of a competitive economy: A survey article. *Econometrica* 30:635–669.

Nelson, R., and S. Winter. 1982. *An Evolutionary Theory of Economic Capabilities and Behavior*. Cambridge, MA: Harvard University Press.

Niskanen, W., 1971. *Bureaucracy and Representative Government.* Chicago, IL: Aldine-Atherton, Inc.

Novshek, W., 1980a. Cournot equilibrium with free entry. *Review of Economic Studies* 47: 473–486.

Novshek, W., 1980b. Small efficient scale as a foundation for Walrasian equilibrium. *Journal of Economic Theory* 22: 243–255.

Novshek, W., and H. Sonnenschein, 1978. Cournot and Walras equilibria. *Journal of Economic Theory* 19: 223–266.

Nti, K. O., and M. Shubik, 1981a. Noncooperative oligopoly with entry. *Journal of Economic Theory* 24: 187–204.

Nti, K. O., and M. Shubik, 1981b. Duopoly with differentiated products and entry barriers. *Southern Economic Journal* 48: 179–186.

Oddou, C., 1982. The core of a coalition production economy. *Journal of Mathematical Economics* 9: 1–21.

Okuno, M., A. Postlewaite, and J. Roberts, 1980. Oligopoly and competition in large markets. *American Economic Review* 70: 22–31.

Ordeshook, P. C., 1971. Pareto optimality and electoral competition. *American Political Science Review* 65: 1141–1145.

Osborne, M. J., 1980. An analysis of power in exchange economies. Technical Report No. 291, Institute for Mathematical Studies in the Social Sciences, Stanford University.

Osborne, M. J., 1981. On explaining the tax system: Why do some goods bear higher taxes than others? Discussion Paper Series, No. 100, Columbia University.

Ostrom, V., 1982. A forgotten tradition: The Constitutional level of analysis. In *Missing Elements in Political Inquiry*, eds. J. A. Gillespie and D. A. Zinnes. Beverly Hills, CA: Sage Publications.

Ostroy, J. M., and R. M. Starr, 1974. Money and the decentralization of exchange. *Econometrica* 42: 1093–1113.

Owen, G., 1971. Political games. *Naval Research Logistics Quarterly* 18: 345–355.

Owen, G., 1975. On the core of linear production games. *Mathematical Programming* 9: 358–370.

Packer, H. L., 1963. *The State of Research in Antitrust Law.* New Haven: Meyer Research Institute of Law.

Pareto, V., 1935. *The Mind and Society* (translated from Italian; original, 1916). New York: Harcourt Brace and Co.

Parnes, H. S., 1968. Labor force: Markets and mobility. In *International Encyclopedia of the Social Sciences*, vol. 8, ed. D. L. Sills. New York: Macmillan and Free Press, pp. 481–486.

Pashigian, B. P., 1968. Limit price and the market share of the leading firm. *Journal of Industrial Economics* 16: 165–177.

Paul, M. E., 1954. Notes on excess capacity. *Oxford Economic Papers* 6:33–40.

Pauly, M. V., 1967. Clubs, commonality, and the core: An integration of game theory and the theory of public goods. *Economica* 34:314–324.

Pauly, M. V., 1970. Cores and clubs. *Public Choice* 9:53–65.

Payne, P. L., 1978. The early Scottish limited companies, 1856–1895: An historical and analytical survey. Social Science Working Paper 222, California Institute of Technology, Pasadena.

Peleg, B., and M. Yaari, 1970. Efficiency prices in an infinite dimensional commodity space. *Journal of Economic Theory* 2:41–85.

Pigou, A. C., 1932. *The Economics of Welfare*, 4th ed. London: Macmillan.

Plott, C. R., and M. E. Levine, 1978. A model of agenda influence on committee decisions. *American Economic Review* 68:146–160.

Posner, R. A., 1972. *Economic Analysis of Law*. Boston, MA: Little Brown.

Posner, R. A., 1976. *Antitrust Law*. Chicago, IL: University of Chicago Press.

Postlewaite, A., and R. W. Rosenthal, 1974. Disadvantageous syndicates. *Journal of Economic Theory* 9:324–326.

Postlewaite, A., and D. Schmeidler, 1978. Approximate efficiency of non-Walrasian Nash equilibria. *Econometrica* 46:127–135.

Quinzii, M., 1982a. Core and competitive equilibria with indivisibilities. Discussion Paper 644, Cowles Foundation, Yale University.

Quinzii, M., 1982b. An existence theorem for the core of a productive economy with increasing returns. *Journal of Economic Theory* 28:32–50.

Rader, T., 1963. The existence of a utility function to represent preferences. *Review of Economic Studies* 31:229–232.

Rader, T., 1966. Quasi-transferable preferences: A new concept for welfare economics. Working Paper, Department of Economics, Washington University, St. Louis, MO.

Rader, T., 1972. *Theory of Microeconomics*. New York: Academic Press.

Radner, R., 1968. Competitive equilibrium under uncertainty. *Econometrica* 36:31–58.

Radner, R., 1979. Rational expectations equilibrium: Generic existence and the information revealed by prices. *Econometrica* 47:655–678.

Raiffa, H., 1968. *Decision Analysis: Introductory Lectures on Choices Under Uncertainty*. Reading, MA: Addison-Wesley.

Raiffa, H., 1982. *The Art and Science of Negotiation*. Cambridge, MA: Harvard University Press.

Rawlinson, G., 1910. *The History of Herodotus*. New York: E. P. Dutton, vol. I, p. 100.

Reid, G., 1981. *The Kinked Demand Curve Analysis of Oligopoly*. Edinburgh: Edinburgh University Press.

Ricardo, D., 1817. *The Principles of Political Economy and Taxation*. London (Everyman edition, 1923).

Richter, D. K., 1974. The core of a public goods economy. *International Economic Review* 15:131–142.

Richter, D. K., 1975. Existence of general equilibrium in multiregional economies with public goods. *International Economic Review* 16:201–221.

Riker, W. H., 1962. *The Theory of Political Coalitions*. New Haven, CT: Yale University Press.

Riker, W. H., and S. Brams, 1973. The paradox of vote trading. *American Political Science Review* 67:1235–1247.

Roberts, D. J., 1974. The Lindahl solution for economies with public goods. *Journal of Public Economics* 3:23–42.

Roberts, D. J., 1976. A note on the core with increasing numbers of consumers and commodities. *International Economic Review* 17:503–505.

Roberts, D. J., and H. Sonnenschein, 1977. On the foundations of the theory of monopolistic competition. *Econometrica* 45:101–113.

Rockafeller, R. T., 1970. *Convex Analysis*. Princeton, NJ: Princeton University Press.

Rogawski, J., and M. Shubik, 1983. A strategic market game with transaction costs. Discussion Paper 661, Cowles Foundation, Yale University.

Rosen, J. B., 1965. Existence and equilibrium points for concave n-person games. *Econometrica* 33:520–534.

Rosenthal, R. W., 1971. External economies and cores. *Journal of Economic Theory* 3:182–188.

Rosenthal, R. W., 1972. Cooperative games in effectiveness form. *Journal of Economic Theory* 5:88–101.

Rosenthal, R. W., 1973. Taxation vs. prohibition of an external diseconomy by direct vote: A game theoretic approach. *International Economic Review* 14:414–420.

Rosenthal, R. W., 1976. Lindahl's solution and values for a public goods example. *Journal of Mathematical Economics* 3:1437–1441.

Rothenberg, J., 1961. *The Measurement of Social Welfare*. Englewood Cliffs, NJ: Prentice-Hall.

Samuelson, P. A., 1948. *Foundations of Economic Analysis*. Cambridge, MA: Harvard University Press.

Samuelson, P. A., 1954. The pure theory of public expenditure. *Review of Economics and Statistics* 36:387–389.

Samuelson, P. A., 1958. An exact consumption loan model of interest with or without the social contrivance of money. *Journal of Political Economy* 66:467–482.

Samuelson, P. A., 1975. The optimum growth rate for population. *International Economic Review* 16:531–538.

Samuelson, P. A., 1977. St. Petersburg paradoxes: Defanged, dissected, and historically described. *Journal of Economic Literature* 15:24–55.

Sandler, T., and J. T. Tschirhart, 1980. The economic theory of clubs: An evolution survey. *Journal of Economic Literature* 43:1481–1521.

Sauermann, H., ed., 1967, 1970, 1972, 1974, 1976, 1977, 1978. *Contributions to Experimental Economics*, vols. 1–7. Tübingen: Mohr.

Sayre, W. S., and H. Kaufman, 1960. *Governing New York City*. New York: W. W. Norton.

Scarf, H. E., 1960. Some examples of global instability of the competitive equilibrium. *International Economic Review* 1:157–172.

Scarf, H. E., 1967. The core of a *n*-person game. *Econometrica* 35:50–69.

Scarf, H. E., 1973. *The Computation of Economic Equilibrium*. New Haven, CT: Yale University Press.

Scherer, F. M., 1980. *Industrial Market Structure and Economic Performance*, 2nd ed. Chicago, IL: Rand McNally.

Schlatter, R., 1951. *Private Property: The History of an Idea*. New Brunswick, NJ: Rutgers University Press.

Schmeidler, D., 1969. The nucleolus of a characteristic function game. *SIAM Journal of Applied Mathematics* 17:1163–1170.

Schofield, N., 1980. The bargaining set in voting games. *Behavioral Science* 25:120–129.

Schotter, A., 1974. Auctioning Böhm-Bawerk's horses. Discussion Paper 74-11, Center for Applied Economics, New York University.

Schotter, A., 1981. *The Economic Theory of Social Institutions*. Cambridge, England: Cambridge University Press.

Schumpeter, J. A. 1934. *The Theory of Economic Development*. Cambridge, MA: Harvard University Press.

Schumpeter, J. A., 1950. *Capitalism, Socialism and Democracy*. New York: Harper & Row.

Schwödiauer, G., 1970. Die strukturelle monopolisierungsneigung oligopolistiker markete. *Jahrbuchern für Nationalökonomie und Statistik* 183 (6):465–486.

Scitovsky, T., 1976. *The Joyless Economy*. New York: Oxford University Press.

Selten, R., 1960. Bewertung Strategischer Speile. *Zeitschrift für die gesamte Staatswissenschaft* 116:221–282.

Selten, R., 1964. Valuation of *n*-person games. *Annals of Mathematics Studies* 52:577–626.

Selten, R., 1972. The equal-treatment core of characteristic function experimenting. In *Contributions to Experimental Economics*, vol. 2, ed. H. Sauermann. Tübingen: Mohr, pp. 130–165.

Selten, R., 1973. A simple model of imperfect competition where 4 are few and 6 are many. *International Journal of Game Theory* 2:141–201.

Selten, R., 1974. Chain-store paradox. Working Paper No. 18, Institute of Mathematical Economics, Universität Bielefeld.

Selten, R., 1975. Re-examination of the perfectness concept of equilibrium points in extensive games. *International Journal of Game Theory* 4:25–55.

Selten, R., 1982. Elementary theory of slack ridden imperfect competition. Working Paper No. 117, Institute of Mathematical Economics, Universität Bielefeld.

Sen, A., 1963. Distribution, transitivity and Little's welfare criteria. *Economic Journal* 73:771–778.

Shannon, H. A., 1932. The first five thousand limited companies and their duration. *Economic History* 2:396.

Shapiro, N. Z., and L. S. Shapley, 1960. Values of large games, I: A limit theorem. RAND Publication RM-2648, Santa Monica, CA.

Shapley, L. S., 1952. Notes on the *n*-person game, III: Some variants of the von Neumann–Morgenstern definition of solution. RAND Publication RM-817, Santa Monica, CA.

Shapley, L. S., 1953. A value for *n*-person games. In *Contributions to the Theory of Games*, vol. 2, eds. H. W. Kuhn and A. W. Tucker. Princeton, NJ: Princeton University Press.

Shapley, L. S., 1959a. A solution containing an arbitrary closed component. *Annuals of Mathematics Studies* 40:87–93.

Shapley, L. S., 1959b. The solutions of a symmetric market games. *Annals of Mathematics Studies* 40:145–162.

Shapley, L. S., 1962a. Complements and substitutes in the optimal assignment problem. *Naval Research Logistics Quarterly* 9:45–48.

Shapley, L. S., 1962b. On simple games: An outline of the descriptive theory. *Behavioral Science* 7:59–66.

Shapley, L. S., 1964a. Some topics in two person games. *Annals of Mathematics Studies* 52:1–28.

Shapley, L. S., 1964b. Values of large games, VII: A general exchange economy with money. RAND Publication RM-4248, Santa Monica, CA.

Shapley, L. S., 1967. On balanced sets and cores. *Naval Research Logistics Quarterly* 14:453–460.

Shapley, L. S., 1968. Notes on *n*-person games, VIII: A game with infinitely "flaky" solutions. RAND Publication RM-5481, Santa Monica, CA.

Shapley, L. S., 1972. The St. Petersburg paradox—A con game? RAND Publication P4940, Santa Monica, CA.

Shapley, L. S., 1975. An example of a slow converging core. *International Economic Review* 16:345–351.

Shapley, L. S., 1981. (Discussant's comments) Equity considerations in traditional full cost allocation practices: An axiomatic perspective. In *Joint Cost Allocations*, S. Moriarty, ed., Proceedings of the University of Oklahoma Conference on Cost Allocations, pp. 131–136.

Shapley, L. S., and H. E. Scarf, 1974. On cores and indivisibility. *Journal of Mathematical Economics* 1:23–27.

Shapley, L. S., and M. Shubik, 1954. A method for evaluating the distribution power in a committee system. *American Political Science Review* 48:787–792.

Shapley, L. S., and M. Shubik, 1966. Quasi-cores in a monetary economy with non-convex preferences. *Econometrica* 34:805–827.

Shapley, L. and M. Shubik, 1967a. Concepts and theories of pure competition. In *Essays in Mathematical Economics in Honor of Oskar Morgenstern*, ed. M. Shubik. Princeton, NJ: Princeton University Press, pp. 63–79.

Shapley, L. S., and M. Shubik, 1967b. Ownership and the production function. *Quarterly Journal of Economics* 81:88–111.

Shapley, L. S., and M. Shubik, 1969a. On market games. *Journal of Economic Theory* 1:9–25.

Shapley, L. S., and M. Shubik, 1969b. Pure competition, coalitional power, and fair division. *International Economic Review* 10:337–362.

Shapley, L. S., and M. Shubik, 1969c. On the core of an economic system with externalities. *American Economic Review* 59:678–684.

Shapley, L. S., and M. Shubik, 1969d. Price strategy oligopoly with product variation. *Kyklos* 22:30–44.

Shapley, L. S., and M. Shubik, 1971. The assignment game, I: The core. *International Journal of Game Theory* 1:111–130.

Shapley, L. S., and M. Shubik, 1972–74. Unpublished working notes on strategic market games.

Shapley, L. S., and M. Shubik, 1976. Competitive outcomes in the cores of market games. *International Journal of Game Theory* 4:229–237.

Shapley, L. S., and M. Shubik, 1977a. An example of a trading economy with three competitive equilibria. *Journal of Political Economy* 85:873–875.

Shapley, L. S., and M. Shubik, 1977b. Trade using one commodity as a means of payment. *Journal of Political Economy* 85:937–968.

Shaw, G. B., 1944. The vice of gambling and the virtue of insurance. In *Everybody's Political What's What*. London: Constable & Co.

Sherman, R., 1972. *Oligopoly*. Lexington, MA: Lexington Books.

Shitovitz, B., 1973. Oligopoly in markets with a continuum of traders. *Econometrica* 41:467–501.

Shitovitz, B., 1974. On some problems arising in markets with some large traders and a continuum of small traders. *Journal of Economic Theory* 8:458–470.

Shitovitz, B., 1982. Some notes on the core of a production economy with some large traders and a continuum of small traders. *Journal of Mathematical Economics* 9:99–105.

Shubik, M., 1955a. A comparison of treatments of a duopoly problem, 2. *Econometrica* 23:417–431.

Shubik, M., 1955b. Edgeworth market games. Mimeographed notes, Center for Advanced Study in the Behavioral Sciences, Palo Alto, CA.

Shubik, M., 1959a. Edgeworth market games. In *Contributions to the Theory of Games*, vol. 4, eds. R. D., Luce and A. W. Tucker. Princeton, NJ: Princeton University Press.

Shubik, M., 1959b. *Strategy and Market Structure*. New York: John Wiley.

Shubik, M., 1961. Objective functions and models of corporate optimization. *Quarterly Journal of Economics* 75 : 345–375.

Shubik, M., 1962. Incentives, decentralized control, the assignment of joint costs and internal pricing. *Management Science* 8 : 325–343.

Shubik, M., 1968. Extended Edgeworth bargaining games and competitive equilibrium. *Metroeconomica* 20 : 299–312.

Shubik, M., 1970a. A further comparison of some models of duopoly. *Western Economic Journal* 6 : 260–276.

Shubik, M., 1970b. On different methods for allocating resources. *Kyklos* 23 : 332–337.

Shubik, M., 1970c. Voting, or a price system in a competitive market structure. *American Political Science Review* 63 : 179–181.

Shubik, M., 1971a. The "Bridge Game" economy. *Journal of Political Economy* 79 : 909–912.

Shubik, M., 1971b. Games of status. *Behavioral Science* 16 : 117–129.

Shubik, M., 1971c. Pecuniary externalities: A game theoretic analysis. *American Economic Review* 61 : 713–718.

Shubik, M., 1973a. Commodity money, oligopoly, credit and bankruptcy in a general equilibrium model. *Western Economic Journal* 11 : 24–38.

Shubik, M., 1973b. Core of a market game with exogenous risk and insurance. *New Zealand Economic Papers* 7.

Shubik, M., 1975a. *Games for Society, Business and War*. Amsterdam: Elsevier.

Shubik, M., 1975b. *The Uses and Methods of Gaming*. New York: Elsevier.

Shubik, M., 1975c. Competitive equilibrium, the core, preferences for risk and insurance markets. *Economic Record* 51 : 73–83.

Shubik, M., 1975d. The general equilibrium model is incomplete and not adequate for the reconciliation of micro and macroeconomic theory. *Kyklos* 28 : 74–93.

Shubik, M., 1975e. On the eight basic units of a dynamic economy with spot and futures markets. *Review of Income and Wealth* 21 : 183–201.

Shubik, M., 1976. A theory of money and financial institutions, XXXIII: On the value of market information. Discussion Paper 439, Cowles Foundation, Yale University.

Shubik, M., 1977. Competitive and controlled price economies: The Arrow–Debreu model revisited. In *Equilibrium and Disequilibrium in Economic Theory*, ed. G. Schwodiauer. Dordrecht, Holland: Reidel, pp. 213–224.

Shubik, M., 1978a. Opinions on how one should play a three-person nonconstant sum game. *Games and Simulation* 9 : 302–308.

Shubik, M., 1978b. A theory of money and financial institutions. *Economie Appliquée* 31 : 61–84.

Shubik, M., 1979a. Cooperative game solutions: Australian, Indian and U.S. opinions. Discussion Paper 517, Cowles Foundation, Yale University.

Shubik, M., 1979b. On the number of types of markets with trade in money: Theory and possible experimentation. In *Research in Experimental Economics*, vol. 1, ed. V. L. Smith. Greenwich, CT: JAI Press.

Shubik, M., 1980. The capital stock modified competitive equilibrium. In *Models of Monetary Economies*, eds. J. H. Karaken and N. Wallace. Minneapolis MN: Federal Reserve Bank.

Shubik, M., 1981a. A price–quantity buy sell market with and without contingent bids. In *Studies in Economic Theory and Practice*, ed. J. Los et al. Amsterdam: North-Holland, pp. 117–124.

Shubik, M., 1981b. Society, land, love or money (A strategic model of how to glue the generations together). *Journal of Economic Behavior and Organization* 2 : 359–385.

Shubik, M., with R. E. Levitan, 1980. *Market Structure and Behavior*. Cambridge, MA: Harvard University Press.

Shubik, M., and M. Sobel, 1980. Stochastic games, oligopoly theory and competitive resource allocation. In *Dynamic Optimization and Mathematical Economics*, ed. P.-T. Liu. New York: Plenum, pp. 89–104.

Shubik, M., and G. L. Thompson, 1959. Games of economic survival. *Naval Logistics Research Quarterly* 6 : 111–123.

Shubik, M., and L. Van der Heyden, 1978. Logrolling and budget allocation games. *International Journal of Game Theory* 7 : 151–162.

Shubik, M., and R. Weber, 1981. Systems defense games: Colonel Blotto, command and control. *Naval Research Logistics Quarterly* 28 : 281–287.

Shubik, M., and R. Weber, 1984. Competitive valuation of cooperative games. *Mathematics of Operations Research* (forthcoming).

Shubik, M., and C. Wilson, 1977. The optimal bankruptcy rule in a trading economy using fiat money. *Zeitschrift für Nationalökonomie* 37 : 337–354.

Shubik, M., G. Wolf, and H. Eisenberg, 1972. Some experiences with an experimental oligopoly business game. *General Systems* 13 : 61–75.

Shubik, M., and M. Wooders, 1982. Near-market games. Discussion Paper 657, Cowles Foundation, Yale University.

Shubik, M., and M. Wooders, 1984a. Approximate cores of replica games and economies, I: Replica games, externalities, and approximate cores. *Mathematical Social Sciences* (forthcoming).

Shubik, M., and M. Wooders, 1984b. Approximate cores of replica games and economies, II:

Set-up costs and firm formation in coalition production economies. *Mathematical Social Sciences* (forthcoming).

Siegal, S., and L. Fouraker, 1960. *Bargaining and Group Decision Making: Experiments in Bilateral Monopoly*. New York: McGraw-Hill.

Simon, H., 1947. *Administrative Behavior*. New York: Macmillan.

Simon, L. K., 1981. Bertrand and Walras equilibrium. Ph.D. dissertation, Department of Economics, Princeton University.

Slutsky, E., 1915. Sulla teoria del bilancio del consumatore. *Giornale Degli Economisti* 51:1–26.

Smale, S., 1981. Global analysis in economics. In *Handbook of Mathematical Economics*, vol. 1, eds. K. J. Arrow and M. D. Intrilligator. Amsterdam: North-Holland.

Smith, A., 1776. *An Inquiry into the Nature and Causes of the Wealth of Nations*. London: W. Strahan.

Smith, V. L., 1962. Experimental studies of competitive market behavior. *Journal of political Economy* 70:111–137.

Smith, V. L., 1979. *Research in Experimental Economics*, vol. I. Greenwich, CT: JAI Press.

Sondermann, D., 1974. Economies of scale and equilibria in coalition production economies. *Journal of Economic Theory* 8:259–291.

Spence, A. M., 1977. Entry, capacity, investment, and oligopolistic pricing. *The Bell Journal of Economics* 8:534–544.

Stackelberg, H. von, 1952. *The Theory of the Market Economy* (translated from German; original, 1934). London: William Hodge.

Starr, R., 1969. Quasi-equilibria in markets with non-convex preferences. *Econometrica* 37:25–38.

Starrett, D. A., 1973. A note on externalities and the core. *Econometrica* 41:179–183.

Stigler, G. L., 1966. *The Theory of Price*. London: Macmillan.

Sun-Tzu, 1944. *The Art of War: The Oldest Military Treatise in the World* (translated from Chinese; original c. 500 B.C.). Harrisburg, PA: Military Services.

Sweezy, P. M., 1939. Demand under conditions of oligopoly. *Journal of Political Economy* 47:568–573.

Sylos-Labini, P., 1962. *Oligopoly and Technical Progress* (translated from Italian; original, 1956). Cambridge, MA: Harvard University Press.

Talamanca, M., 1954. Contributi allo studio delle vendite all'asta nel mondo classico. Serie VIII, vol. VI, fasc. 2, Accademia Nazionale dei Lincei, Roma.

Telser, L. G., 1972. *Competition, Collusion and Game Theory*. Chicago, IL: Aldine-Atherton.

Telser, L. G., 1978. *Economic Theory and the Core*. Chicago, IL: University of Chicago Press.

Thaler, R., 1980. Toward a positive theory of consumer choice. *Journal of Economic Behavior and Organization* 1:39–60.

Thompson, G. L., 1978. Computing the core of a market game. Mathematics and Statistics Research Report No. 411, Carnegie-Mellon University, Pittsburgh, PA.

Tiebout, C. M., 1956. A pure theory of local expenditures. *Journal of Political Economy* 64:416–424.

Tinbergen, J., 1968. Economic planning: Western Europe. In *International Encyclopedia of the Social Sciences*, vol. 12, ed. D. L. Sills. New York: Macmillan and Free Press, pp. 102–110.

Tobin, J., 1961. Money, capital and other stores of value. *American Economic Review* 51:26–37.

Triffin, R., 1940. *Monopolistic Competition and General Equilibrium Theory*. Cambridge, MA: Harvard University Press, chapter 3.

Tullock, G., 1970. A simple algebraic logrolling model. *American Economic Review* 60:419–426.

Tversky, A., and D. Kahneman, 1981. The framing of decisions and the psychology of choice. *Science* 211:453–458.

Veblen, T., 1899. *The Theory of the Leisure Class: An Economic Study of Institutions*. New York: Macmillan.

Vickrey, W., 1960. Utility, strategy and social decision rules. *Quarterly Journal of Economics* 74:507–535.

Viner, J., 1931. Cost curves and supply curves. *Zeitschrift für Nationalökonomie* 3:23–46.

von Mises, L., 1944. *Bureaucracy*. New Haven, CT: Yale University Press.

von Neumann, J., and O. Morgenstern, 1944. *The Theory of Games and Economic Behavior*. Princeton, NJ: Princeton University Press (2nd ed., 1947).

Wald, A., 1951. On some systems of equations of mathematical economics (translated; original, 1938). *Econometrica* 19:368–403.

Walker, D., 1955. The direct indirect tax problem: Fifteen years of controversy. *Public Finance* 10:153–176.

Walras, L., 1954. *Elements of Pure Economics* (translated from French; original, 1874). London: Allen and Unwin.

Weber, M., 1946. Bureaucracy. In *From Max Weber: Essays in Sociology*, eds. H. H. Gerth and C. Wright Mills. New York: Oxford University Press.

Weber, M., 1947. *The Theory of Social and Economic Organization* (translated from German; original, 1922). Glencoe, IL: Free Press, pp. 324–336.

Weber, R. J., 1977. Attainable sets of quasiconcave markets. *Proceedings of the American Mathematical Society* 64:104–111.

Weber, R. J., 1978. Attainable sets of quasiconcave markets, II: Convexifiable sets. *Mathematics of Operations Research* 3:257–264.

Weber, R. J., 1980. Attainable sets of markets: An overview. J. R. Kellogg Graduate School of Management, Northwestern University, Evanston, IL.

Weidenbaum, M., 1969. *The Modern Public Sector*. New York: Basic Books.

Whitman, M. J., and M. Shubik, 1979. *The Aggressive Conservative Investor*. New York: Random House.

Williamson, O. E., 1963. Selling expense as a barrier to entry. *Quarterly Journal of Economics* 77:112–128.

Williamson, O. E., 1975. *Markets and Hierarchies: Analysis and Antitrust Implications*. New York: Free Press.

Williamson, O. E., 1981. The modern corporation: Origins, evolution, attributes. *Journal of Economic Literature* 19:1537–1568.

Wilson, R., 1969a. An axiomatic model of logrolling. *American Economic Review* 3:331–341.

Wilson, R., 1969b. Computing equilibria of n-person games. Stanford University Working Paper No. 163.

Wilson, R., 1972. The game-theoretic structure of Arrow's general possibility theorem. *Journal of Economic Theory* 5:14–20.

Wilson, R., 1978. Information, efficiency, and the core of an economy. *Econometrica* 46:807–816.

Wooders, M., 1980. The Tiebout hypothesis; near optimality in local public good economies. *Econometrica* 48:1467–1485.

Wooders, M., 1984. Epsilon core of a large replica game. *Journal of Mathematical Economics* (forthcoming).

Yaari, M. E., 1965. Convexity in the theory of choice under risk. *Quarterly Journal of Economics* 79:278–290.

Young, H. P., 1978a. The allocation of funds in lobbying and campaigning. *Behavioral Science* 23:21–31.

Young, H. P., 1978b. Power, prices and incomes in voting systems *Mathematical Programming* 14:129–148.

Zeuthen, F., 1930. *Problems of Monopoly and Economic Warfare*. London: G. Routledge & Sons.

Index